MY HUMBOLDT DIARY:
A True Story of Betrayal of the Public Trust

*A Former Force Reconnaissance Marine and
Nuclear Control Technician Tells His Story . . .*

Bob Rowen

Former nuclear control technician, Bob Rowen, who was employed at Pacific Gas and Electric Company's Humboldt Bay Nuclear Power Plant from 1964 to 1970, wrote this book.

This book – *My Humboldt Diary: A True Story of Betrayal of the Public Trust* – is more than a telling of the story about PG&E's Humboldt Bay Nuclear Power Plant. It is Bob Rowen's account of what happened during his Humboldt Bay ordeal that turned him against nuclear power, caused him to become disenchanted with America's system of justice, and made him realize how powerful and sinister America's nuclear juggernaut truly is and why we must not allow even one more nuclear power plant to be built.

Cover Image: Courtesy of the Clark Museum, Eureka, California.
Cover Design by Theresa M. Wood.

Image #3 – "Humboldt Bay and Eureka aerial view" by Robert Campbell - U.S. Army Corps of Engineers Digital Visual Library Image page Image description page Digital Visual Library home page. Licensed under Creative Commons Attribution-Share Alike 3.0 .

Printed and bound in the United States of America and distributed by My Humboldt Diary, LLC.

First edition.

First printing: December 2014.

ISBN 978-0-9863694-1-4

To my family

They endured much beyond measure while I battled the Pacific Gas and Electric Company, the U. S. Atomic Commission, and others who endeavored to protect PG&E's failed and dangerous technology at Humboldt Bay;

And to Edith Krause Straus, her classmates, and the community of Humboldt Hill who, due to fault of their own, had the misfortune of being downwind from the Humboldt Bay Nuclear Power Plant.

In memory of

Forrest "Bud" Edsel Williams Jr.
December 27, 1933 – August 8, 2014

Forrest Williams was more than my co-worker at Humboldt Bay, he was more than a colleague at College of the Redwoods and Humboldt State University, he was more than a nuclear warrior who would not kowtow to PG&E's corporate America; he was above all my friend.

Forrest was honest, courageous, and he was not only concerned about employee and public safety, but was also willing to speak up and "do the right thing" about the horrendous abuses that occurred in our nuclear workplace.

Like everyone who knew Forrest well, I shall remember him for his high standards, his integrity, and for his well-thought-out stewardship of humanity that made him so uniquely special.

RIP my friend,

Bob Rowen

Contents

CONTENTS

Forward

How does one reconcile aspirations with disillusionment when it comes to the Humboldt Bay Nuclear Power Plant? When I was a young child, my father worked at the plant as a nuclear control technician. I vividly remember how his initial excitement about a career in the nuclear energy field with the Pacific Gas and Electric Company (PG&E), slowly became a nightmare with concerns about not only his own safety and the safety of his coworkers, but also about the safety of his family and community.

As early as I can remember, PG&E and the Atomic Energy Commission (AEC) always seemed to be a topic of discussion in our home. In the beginning, there were get-togethers in our home or the in home of my father's coworkers and friends, and things seemed "normal" from the perspective of a young child. Slowly however, that "normalcy" began to change, and I began to sense an uneasiness that became fear and uncertainty.

Not knowing the scope of my father's efforts to protect not only himself, but also the public in general, I can only speak to the affect this ordeal had on my family through the eyes of a child. I remember my father coming home from work, only to have to return immediately due to some problem at the atomic plant. I also remember the times he came home from work without wearing the clothes he left wearing to work that morning. Then there were the "adult" conversations about concerns regarding conditions at work, and my father's dilemma as to what to do about issues he could not ignore. You might ask what all of this would mean to a child. The answer is fear, uncertainty, and not knowing what tomorrow will bring.

After my father went public with his concerns and allegations regarding PG&E and the AEC, things really began to get "strange." There were the phone calls late at night with just breathing on the other end, and then there were those who made direct threats to the safety of our family. The police department continuously harassed us; I did not understand why at the time — but I do understand now! I vividly remember my mother being put at risk by the police department. My father's *Diary* explains the police involvement.

Then it seemed that all of a sudden, things like toys, vacation activities, even food, became scarce. People that used to come over and visit or call, no longer were heard from. Even my grandparents and great-grandparents, all of whom lived around the corner from us, were concerned about my father's decision to go public. From my perspective this could only be due to the incredible power and influence PG&E was bringing to bear in our small community.

I remember in the spring of 1972, my mother saying how hurt she was to have to move from the place she had called home her entire life. After being forced out of his job in 1970, my father finished his schooling and obtained his teaching credential from Humboldt State University. Given all of the political fallout from his ordeal with PG&E, my parents determined that seeking employment in the area was simply not an option. My father accepted a teaching position in Weaverville, California, packing up the family and moving from the only home we had ever known.

Looking back, I now understand how severely the PG&E experience affected my father as well as my whole family. My mother was forced from the community she was born and raised in, leaving her closest friends and family behind. My father carried bitterness and anger that a corporation that proclaimed to "care" about its employees and the public it serves, would go to such extreme lengths to destroy an employee.

From a falsified police report to death threats, from charges of conspiracy to commit industrial espionage to labeling my father a disgruntled former employee, PG&E destroyed my father's reputation and essentially blacklisted him from the nuclear industry. These are the issues my father has wrestled with for decades. After all, he was a proud former Marine whose character and ethics were publicly called into question by PG&E. For those who are concerned about corporate abuse, my father's *Diary* is a must read.

Several years following my father's employment at Humboldt Bay, my mother developed a rare form of brain cancer, passing away in 1987, just two months after the birth of my first child, her grandson. I have always wondered about the possibility that my mother's cancer was directly related to her handling of my father's laundry from the years he worked at the power plant. And although my father was always very cautious and extremely careful, there were still occasions when my father might have come home from work with the very real possibility of radioactive contamination on some of his clothing, and my mom was the one who did the laundry. My father's *Diary* explains how this could have happened in his treatment of the impact the nuclear unit had on the students at the South Bay Elementary School and the residents of the Humboldt Hill community.

This book offers in easy to understand laymen terms a unique insight into the technical aspects of the PG&E Humboldt Bay Nuclear Power Plant, the problems it presented, and PG&E's commitment to conceal those problems from the general public. It also gives the reader a personal insight into the tactics and unscrupulous behavior a giant corporation will bring to bear, stopping at nothing to protect its image, regardless of the consequences to employees and the general public. For those who are concerned about the environment, corporate responsibility and accountability, and the future wellbeing of their children and grandchildren, this book is a must read.

PG&E is the biggest electric and gas supplier in the west, and the company's history of abuses and corporate malfeasance is a concern to us all. From Hinkley to Humboldt, the true legacy of PG&E is countless betrayals of the public trust.

Rob Rowen

An important, special note from the author

My *Dairy* was self-published because the publishers I had contacted were fearful of possible repercussions from America's powerful nuclear establishment.

One senior publishing consultant said, "After reviewing your documentation, we would prevail in a libelous suit brought against us but *they* could tie us up in the courts for years."

My response: Nothing is libelous unless it's untrue! I would never claim something was said or done without supportive evidence, which I have provided throughout my *Diary*. Furthermore, I am entitled to express my personal and professional opinions, in which case I have provided the basis for every one of them. Therefore, after prolonged arguing with publishers that resulted in countless and needless delays, I decided to self-publish!

The critics of my *Diary* (and there undoubtably will be some) will likely argue that the plant no longer exists, so what's the big deal? The answer to that question is easily contained in a twofold response: First, *My Humboldt Diary* reveals the all too often intertwined nefarious behavior of corporate America and government and second, my *Diary* provides historical knowledge for understanding the inadequacies of our system of justice and the horrible legacy of the ill-fated Humboldt Bay Nuclear Power Plant that will live on forever.

Finally, *My Humboldt Diary* reads more like a *diary* and contains an ample amount of syntax errors (especially in the quoted documentation).The reader of my *Diary* will at times experience some redundancy because of the way it was written, that is, during many different sittings over a long period of time. In certtain cases I have purposefully repeated some things either for emphasis or required continuity. The reason I have included photos of my military experience in my *Diary* will become evident during the reading of chapters one, eleven, twelve, and especially chapter fourteen.

Preface

When President Obama made his announcement of loan guarantees to America's nuclear-industrial complex in February 2010, I decided once again to continue the writing of *My Humboldt Diary: A True Story of Betrayal of the Public Trust.* Quite honestly, I had started this task many times but each time became too stressed to continue with it.

Following my ordeal as a nuclear control technician at the Humboldt Bay Nuclear Power Plant, I entered into a *survival mode* after the Pacific Gas and Electric Company (PG&E) fired me. (I was planning to quit my job in the fall, but was not yet financially ready to loose my paycheck when PG&E terminated me).The needs of my family had to come first so consequently it was difficult to find the time and energy this writing project would require. But there was also another problem, a very real problem, which has kept me from finishing my *Diary* before now.

Many people had warned me about the dangerous situation I had created for myself. This weighed heavily on my mind for many years, and for very good reason! Fortunately a number of truly good people came forward with excellent suggestions and support that proved extremely helpful on how to protect my family and myself. At that time in my life there was little in my bundle of life-experiences that prepared me for dealing with what followed my life-changing decision to address the radiation safety problems at Humboldt Bay and the failed and dangerous technology that gave rise to them.

In the naivety of my youth I believed in an America that was based on the principles of fair play, honesty, and justice. What I learned, and I learned it the hard way, is that America does not guarantee justice; nor is America generally capable of responding to corporate lawlessness and corruption.

The system favors the special interests, and in this case, the pronuclear power brokers, what I have referred to as America's nuclear-industrial complex (to paraphrase President Eisenhower). My paraphrase of President Eisenhower also embodies his dire warning to the American people regarding the power and undue influence of America's military-industrial complex. My warning, however, addresses an even greater threat to the welfare of the American people; a threat posed by the nuclear power brokers that I shall call America's nuclear juggernaut (in honor of two renowned American atomic researchers, Drs. John Gofman and Arthur Tamplin, both of whom first used the phrase in their book *Poison Power: The Case Against Nuclear Power Plants*). Gofman and Tamplin also experienced the wrath of the powerfully ruthless people who make up America's nuclear juggernaut.

When *Pandora's Promise* aired on CNN, I decided it was time for me to pick up the pen and get back to writing *My Humboldt Diary — and this time finish it!* Let's be clear. *Pandora's Promise* is not a documentary on nuclear power as its producers purport it to be. It is pure pronuclear propaganda! I found this "documentary" totally disgusting and extraordinarily misleading. It was obviously produced by pronuclear people who have either never set foot inside a nuclear power plant, are oblivious to the dangers of radiation and nuclear power, or they have simply sold their souls to America's nuclear juggernaut!

I have lived for more than forty years in constant fear of the nuclear power brokers. I have learned from firsthand experience what these people are capable. They are powerful, they are ruthless, and they are capable of doing whatever is necessary to protect their interests! William W. "Bill" Coshow, a northern California attorney, once said to me, "I'm surprised you have not met with the same fate as Karen Silkwood." Mr. Coshow knew exactly what he was talking about and he clearly understood what I had been living with, as did Emmy Award winning NBC documentary news producer Don Widener (Chapter 15). I will always be eternally grateful for Mr. Coshow's willingness to help me (Chapter 14).

My Humboldt Diary: A True Story of Betrayal of the Public Trust provides more than just a peek into America's nuclear juggernaut. It reveals a rare inside view of the Machiavellian behavior of corporate America's steadfast commitment to protect a failed and dangerous technology. What happened during the sixties and early seventies at the Pacific Gas and Electric Company's Humboldt Bay Nuclear Power Plant needs to be told and I am truly in the best position to tell the whole incredible and appalling story. A PG&E public relations specialist referred to it all as "happening back in the Stone Age" and, therefore, "not worth talking about any more." Nothing could be further from the truth and my *Diary* explains why.

Since I am fully retired from a 40-year career in education and in the twilight years of my life, I am now turning my attention with absolute resolve to the Humboldt Bay Nuclear Power Plant and the telling of the full story of what happened there. Although parts of the story have been told by others, each time with a singular motivation or slant, I believe I can tell the whole story far better than anyone has and with much better results.

The Humboldt Bay story needs to be told for principally two reasons. First because the resurgence of nuclear power looms on the horizon, and second, because the attitudes and underlying philosophies that gave rise to it still pose a serious threat to those wonderful ideals we all cherish and hold most dear. We can't just give lip service and blind allegiance to the assumptions that make us who we think we are but rather we must be willing to examine our institutions in business and government and hold them accountable to our expectations of them.

After all these years I still have my records, company documents, transcripts and my personal diaries of PG&E's shenanigans and corporate misconduct. The company documents and transcripts, along with my diaries, have made it possible for me to write *My Humboldt Diary.*

Particularly useful, however, are the transcripts of my two hearings before the California Unemployment Insurance Appeals Board, for it was at these hearings that I was able to question PG&E plant management and certain other nuclear employees under oath. I was also able to subpoena certain documents that enabled me to present my case before the Appeals Board. Additionally, the transcription of the audio recording of my September 7, 1971 meeting with John J. Ward, Chief Investigator for the Atomic Energy Commission (AEC), serves as another invaluable resource.

Without these transcripts and documents, I would not have been able to clearly and unquestionably expose what actually took place at Humboldt Bay. The testimony of key personnel speaks for itself along with citations from confidential company memoranda. Once again, without these resources, *My Humboldt Diary* could never have been written.

There is still considerable interest in what happened at Humboldt Bay even though some, especially PG&E's public relations department, consider it "ancient history." The implications are clear, in light of the posturing by nuclear proponents now occurring, and the framing of their new argument: "Today's reactors are far cleaner and more economical than the dirty, atavistic behemoths of yore."[1]

This pending argument by the pronuclear folks begs the question of what happened at Humboldt Bay (1963-1976), not to mention Three Mile Island (1979), Chernobyl (1986), Millstone (1992), and Fukushima (2011) among others. When I hear people in Washington talking about nuclear energy as a viable source of energy to deal with our ever-increasing energy needs, it runs chills up and down my spine. After reading my *Diary,* the reasons why will become evident.

My account of what happened at Humboldt Bay reveals not only the need for much stricter regulation and oversight of the nuclear industry, notwithstanding the swapping of the AEC (Atomic Energy Commission) for the NRC (Nuclear Regulatory Commission), but also argues it may not be possible in America's free enterprise, democratic society that has the "best government" corporate money can buy.

My *Diary* exposes through a multitude of documented, real life examples of the blatant disregard for public safety, corruption in the nuclear community, and corporate power run amuck, which amongst others is not a bit unlike America's financial communities of Wall Street, the oil industry in the gulf, and the pharmaceutical industry, to name a few.

Using documented examples, my *Diary* unveils the dynamics and significance of corporate *workplace emulation* by addressing the greedy, mean-spirited and ego driven behavior of PG&E management at all levels, and the large number of employees aspiring to enter the ranks of management. Of course, America's corporate *workplace emulation* is not unique to the PG&E culture but my experience inside that culture provided a clear understanding of it.

Moreover, the Humboldt Bay story reveals a mindset that is grounded in self-serving interests, ignorance, and greed: *Self-serving interests* of individuals who are willing to do whatever it takes to move up the "ladder of success" in government or business; widespread *ignorance* in the general public that is victimized by multimillion dollar PR campaigns; and plain old-fashion corporate *greed* giving rise to unscrupulous conduct in pursuit of the bottom line.

My *Diary* is a well-documented explanation of why the general public cannot rely on the operators of nuclear power plants, as well as the regulators of them, to provide for the welfare and safety of the American public. The stakes are simply too high due to the unimaginable ramifications of the dangerous nuclear consequences – chronic exposure to low level ionizing radiation, in gestation of radioactive airborne and particulate matter, disposal of nuclear wastes, radioactive contamination of our soil and water, and the demonstrated willingness of the nuclear juggernaut to put the public and employees at risk for the sake of protecting the technology.

Also exposed in my *Diary* is PG&E's web of entanglements with all levels of government, the mass media, and the business community, as well as an incredible abuse of corporate and political power reeking of McCarthyism.

There promises to be a resurgence of interest in and commitment to advancing nuclear power once again in the wake of "global warming" and concern over the skyrocketing price of oil. The proponents of nuclear power enthusiastically claim nuclear power will become *out of necessity* a major source of energy in the 21st Century. My *Diary* will hopefully provide pause to the clamor for more nuclear power plants!

The pronuclear people behind *Pandora's Promise* cited the large number of deaths caused by the use of fossil fuels to generate electricity and then stated "there has not been a single death resulting from the use of nuclear power to produce electricity." Although my *Diary* is primarily concerned with what happened at Humboldt Bay, it also addresses this ludicrously, imprudent claim while addressing the real hazards of radiation expressed by the experts who have no financial or political connections to America's nuclear juggernaut. My *Diary* clearly demonstrates why the public cannot trust the claims of safety made by the nuclear industry.

PG&E's nuclear unit at Humboldt Bay was the first commercial boiling water reactor west of the Mississippi with AEC License No. 7. It was the very first totally private funded nuclear venture in the world! The Humboldt Nuke first went on-line in August 1963 and I showed up at the power station a few months later in early 1964. My initial position at the facility was that of apprentice instrument repairman but six months later I was selected for PG&E's nuclear control technician-training program. At the time I considered my selection for this program an opportunity of a lifetime. Little did I realize my decision to become a nuclear control technician would turn into a nightmare.

I have written *My Humboldt Diary: A True Story of Betrayal of the Public Trust* as a former nuclear control technician who blew the whistle on the Pacific Gas and Electric Company and the U.S. Atomic Energy Commission. No one that I'm aware of ever set out to become a whistleblower, leastwise me! But as I became entangled in an ever-expanding web of governmental and corporate corruption at Humboldt Bay, my contempt for PG&E as well as the AEC grew until it literally reached a boiling point at the now "legendary" May 20, 1970 PG&E company safety meeting at Humboldt Bay. I had witnessed time and again an incredibly blatant disregard for employee and public safety and numerous cover-ups of radiation safety problems (Chapters 2, 3, 4, 6, 7, 8, and 9).

It was at the May 20, 1970 PG&E company safety meeting that I asked some embarrassing questions and demanded answers to them! This resulted in an investigation by PG&E's Security Department spawned at corporate headquarters that included the Eureka Police Department and the Federal Bureau of Investigation (Chapters 10, 11, and 12). There was nothing in my background that prepared me for the developments that followed.

Very honestly, I did not know how to respond to the ruthless and unscrupulous means used by the Pacific Gas and Electric Company and the U. S. Atomic Energy Commission for dealing with those of us who refused to go along in order to get along in the nuclear workplace. At my own peril, I had routinely used company safety meetings in the past as a means to address safety issues that my supervisors had refused to act on, each time with some degree of success but always with warnings of dire consequences if I continued in this vein.

I had always used the PG&E's safety meetings "as a means of last resort" because minutes were kept and supposedly reviewed by the AEC during compliance inspections. As it turned out, a review of the minutes by the AEC wasn't really the problem. I eventually learned the AEC paid little attention to those minutes as was the case with entries into the "official" radiation control log kept by the nuclear control technicians. PG&E's real concern was over the possibility of public disclosure.

If the minutes of the company safety meetings containing deleterious information ever became public, they would prove to be problematic for PG&E for basically three reasons: (1) That the safety problem(s) existed in the first place, (2) the damaging effect they would have on PG&E's plan to "go nuclear," and (3) the very real possibility of legal consequences of the radiation protection safety problems that were never properly addressed by the company and intentionally concealed from the public by PG&E.

PG&E's "investigation of its dissident employees" produced an array of absurdly incredible charges including, amongst other things, that we were plotting to blow up the nuclear power plant (Chapters 11 and 12).

We were openly opposed to the company's view of radiation safety, openly opposed to the inept regulatory role of the AEC (Chapter 13), and openly opposed to any release of radiation from the plant in violation of Humboldt Bay's Radiation Control Standards; therefore, PG&E charged us with continued "acts tantamount to industrial sabotage" to bolster the company's claim we were plotting to blow up the nuclear facility (Chapter 11).

The company conspired with Chief Cedric Emahiser of the Eureka Police Department to produce a completely false "confidential and privileged" law enforcement document and then circulated it back to PG&E and to the Federal Bureau of Investigation (Chapter 12).

Although four of the seven nuclear control technicians at the plant were named in it, the primary purpose of this document was to make me a security risk so I would not be able to obtain employment ever again in the security-sensitive environment of the nuclear industry. This was clearly an act of "nuclear blacklisting."

We were never supposed to see this "privileged" document; its purpose was simply to keep any of us, and especially me, from getting security clearances in the future through the required background checks. My *Diary* reveals how I discovered the existence of this "privileged" document, how I eventually obtained a copy of it, how PG&E chose to respond to its discovery, and how PG&E then protected the company from its involvement in the commissioning of it.

There were a number of radiation safety issues that were brought up at the May 20, 1970 company safety meeting by two nuclear control technicians, Forrest Williams and Bob Rowen. Again, every one of these safety issues had been previously presented to plant management personnel to no avail.

The two issues that were the cause of plant management going completely berserk, and consequently the folks in PG&E's corporate headquarters at 245 Market Street in San Francisco, were the intentional setting of the high alarm limits on the hand-and-foot counter at the exit point of the nuclear unit's control room (Chapter 10) and the removal of the constant air sample monitor from the South Bay Elementary School (Chapters 9 and 10).

Plant management had told me prior to the safety meeting that I was once again overstepping my authority to demand an explanation of why the constant air sample monitor was removed from the school. So, consequently, I not only raised the question at the May 20th safety meeting but also emphatically and very publicly demanded an answer. The removal of the constant air sample monitor from the elementary school was clearly one of the most grievous actions taken by PG&E, and the company was then aided by the AEC in the cover up of it following my tenure at Humboldt Bay.

Because my credibility became a huge public issue brought on by PG&E's mudslinging tactics and false accusations, I have allocated a small amount of space in chapter one to provide some personal background and to describe the road I traveled to become a nuclear control technician at Humboldt Bay. By the time I reached the end of that road, I was immersed in controversy simply because I was asking questions I wasn't supposed to ask and making "statements" that I wasn't supposed to make.

I refused to compromise on my commitment to provide the safest radiation work environment possible and to protect the public from the company's violations of its own radiation control standards that was promised to the public. During my struggles with plant management, I developed a stalwart willingness to do what I considered to be the right thing; I absolutely refused to succumb to intimidation and coercion.

Chapter two provides the necessary backstory that explains how and why the original fuel cladding in the core of the reactor used by PG&E caused the Humboldt Bay nuke to become "the dirtiest atomic plant in the nation"[2] leaving PG&E with the challenge *for naught* of promoting and protecting a failed and dangerous technology in PG&E's first "go-nuclear" flagship: The now infamous Humboldt Bay Nuclear Power Plant.

Acknowledgements

I HAVE BEEN ENCOURAGED BY MANY throughout the years to tell the whole story about what actually happened at the Humboldt Bay Nuclear Power Plant. Now that I am fully retired from a second career in education, I have been able to turn my attention to writing *My Humboldt Diary*. It has not been easy for me to revisit that turbulent time in my life filled with so much frustration, anguish, and pain; however, because of the endearing support and heartfelt encouragement of several very special people, I have been able to accomplish the task of writing this book. I want to thank those, who each in their own way made *My Humboldt Diary: A True Story of Betrayal of the Public Trust* a reality.

First I want to give a special acknowledgment to my family Rob, Todd, and their mother, Shirley, who endured much beyond measure during my time at the Humboldt Bay Nuclear Plant and all the turmoil that followed. I also want to acknowledge Humboldt Bay nuclear control technicians Forrest Williams, Raymond Skidmore, and Howard Darington IV for whom I have a great deal of admiration and respect and with whom I spent countless hours discussing the radiation safety problems at Humboldt Bay.

I owe a debt of gratitude to four very special people at Humboldt State University (HSU): My economics professors Dr. Bob Kittleson, Dr. Jacqueline Kasun, and Dr. Bob Dickerson; all of whom in various ways advised and supported me in my struggles with PG&E. It was Dr. Kasun who first suggested, in fact, insisted I go public as quickly and in as many ways as possible, which she said was my best form of protection. Dr. Kasun also hired me as a regular guest speaker in the HSU Cluster Program, which provided me not only a modest and much needed income for my family but also an opportunity to address "societal issues" based on my personal experiences. And then there was Dr. James Householder in the Mathematics Department, who spent long hours sharing with me his delightful and therapeutic philosophy of life. It was Dr. Householder who gave me a position reading calculus papers in the math department, which also provided additional income for my family.

There was also another Humboldt State University professor for whom I owe a debt of gratitude, Dr. Fredrick Cranston, who served in the HSU Department of Physics and who had previously worked at Los Alamos. Dr. Cranston participated in a symposium on the feasibility of nuclear energy I had organized at my high school a few years after I had graduated from

Acknowledgements

HSU. He provided a unique understanding and moral support for my difficulties I had had with the Atomic Energy Commission and was continuing to have with the Pacific Gas and Electric Company.

While I was organizing my symposium on nuclear energy I became acquainted with Dr. Homer Ibser, who served in the Departments of Physics and Astronomy at Sacramento State University. Dr. Ibser is another one of those special people who made it possible for me to "survive" my lingering difficulties with the AEC and my continuing mayhem with PG&E.

I want to thank Professor Bill Rodgers at the University of Washington School of Law with whom I collaborated on his treatment of my problems at Humboldt Bay in his book entitled *Corporate Country*; Ray Tobis of California Citizens for Clean Energy who provided me much insight into the problems of dealing with the giant and powerful PG&E corporation; Roger Rapoport, author of the Great American Bomb Machine, with whom I became acquainted. It was Mr. Rapoport who first suggested I should "write my own book about what happened at Humboldt Bay." Mr. Rapoport introduced me to Stan Sesser, a staff reporter for the Wall Street Journal, who helped me realize the magnitude of the challenge of dealing with the nuclear juggernaut. Stan Sesser was amazing and for me, most inspirational.

My manuscript needed a lot of attention, which was provided by my brother and his wife, Fred and Virginia Rowen to whom I owe a debt of gratitude for not only making my *Diary* more readable but for their love and support during the process of bringing it to fruition.

And finally, I owe a debt of gratitude to Roger Hardison, who was instrumentally involved in helping me land a teaching job at Trinity High School in spite of PG&E's efforts to the contrary; to Weaverville attorney Al Wilkins and Redding attorney Bill Coshow, both of whom truly recognized what PG&E had done to me and to my family; to the members of the 1971 Humboldt County Grand Jury, who stood up to the AEC and PG&E; and above all to my loving and understanding wife, Moneca Darnel, who stood by me while I struggled with a wide range of emotional challenges during the final writing of my *Diary*.

List of Images

Img 1. Atoms for Peace U.S. Postage Stamp – (From the author's collection)

Img 2. PG&E's Nuclear Control Technician Job Description – (From the author's employment file)

Img 3. Aerial view of Humboldt Bay – (Courtesy of Robert Campbell – U.S. Army Corps of Engineers)

Img 4. Construction begins on the HBPP Nuclear Unit site for Unit 3 – (Courtesy of the Clarke Historical Museum)

Img 5. Early construction of HBPP Unit 3 showing reactor vessel and generator in upper left hand corner of photo and construction of railroad spur to refueling building yet to be built – (Courtesy of the Clarke Historical Museum)

Img 6. Site preparation for HBPP Unit 3 Reactor installation – (Courtesy of the Humboldt County Historical Society)

Img 7. Construction of the Suppression Chamber for Unit 3 Reactor – (Courtesy of the Clarke Historical Museum)

Img 8. Installing the Reactor Vessel in Unit 3 – (Courtesy of the Clarke Historical Museum)

Img 9. Units 1 & 2 with Nuclear Unit under construction (the radioactive gaseous waste discharge stack has not yet been installed) – (Courtesy of the Clarke Historical Museum)

Img 10. Nuclear Unit Construction with radioactive gaseous waste discharge stack in place – Bay view – (Courtesy of the Humboldt County Historical Society)

Img 11. Nuclear Unit Construction with radioactive gaseous waste discharge stack in place – U.S. 101 View – (Courtesy of the Clarke Historical Museum)

Img 12. Artist Rendering of PG&E's Humboldt Bay Nuclear Power Plant – (Courtesy of the Humboldt County Historical Society)

Img 13. Boiling Water Reactor System – Single Loop System – (From the author's employment file)

LIST OF IMAGES

Img 14. "GM" Beta-Gamma Detection Instrument – (From the author's employment file)

Img 15. "CP" Radiation Dose Rate Instrument – (From the author's employment file)

Img 16. Beta-Gamma Hand and Foot Counter – (From the author's employment file)

Img 17. Nilsen Company Feed Store – (Photo by author)

Img 18. Radiation Danger Sign – (From the author's file)

Img 19. Nuclear Fuel Transfer Cask over the reactor core – (From the author's file)

Img 20. Nuclear Fuel Transfer Cask on its way to the spent fuel – (From the author's file)

Img 21. WP Scotia Bluffs Trestle – (Courtesy of the Fortuna Depot Museum)

Img 22. NWP Railway Engine No. 184 Scotia Bluffs Salvage Project – 1953 – (Courtesy of the Fortuna Depot Museum)

Img 23. Ingomar Club (Photo by Fred & Virginia Rowen)

Img 24. Pellets of Uranium Dioxide Fuel – (From author's employment file)

List of Appendices

_I_

1. PG&E's First Nuclear Flagship

"And to a world that would be free the Humboldt Bay Nuclear Power Plant will be a shinning example of free enterprise in a free America."[3] [Senator John Pastore]

Pacific Gas and Electric Company's (PG&E's) Humboldt Bay Nuclear Power Plant operated from August 1963 to July 1976 on the coast of northern California, a short distance south of Eureka. Acclaimed as the power source of the future, nuclear power promised to be a safe, clean, reliable, and cheap source of electrical energy, and the Humboldt Bay nuclear facility was the spearhead of PG&E's grandiose plan to "go nuclear,"[4] thus providing a shinning example for the rest of the nation and perhaps the entire world.

PG&E's Humboldt Bay Nuke was considered the company's flagship for the hopeful birth of a "Twenty-first Century nuclear world."

The promise of nuclear power was enthusiastically embraced and promoted by government, academic institutions, labor unions, and corporate America.

The United States Atomic Energy Commission (AEC) handled the government's role in promoting what was viewed as the unquestioned godsend to America's emerging energy crisis. The jubilant unfolding of a new dawn that sprung from passing the Atomic Energy Act of 1946 began with the development of the atomic bomb, which was dropped on Hiroshima, Japan, on August 6, 1945.

Three days later, the United States dropped a second atomic bomb on Nagasaki, Japan. Six days following the dropping of the second bomb, the doggedly committed Japanese to their war effort against the United States announced their unconditional surrender. The long miserable war was finally over.

America, now in a state of euphoria, experienced a postwar transformation that included the immediate emergence of the nuclear

29

power brokers that eventually became America's powerful nuclear juggernaut. Congress swiftly responded with hearings on the future of the atom late in 1945 and early 1946.

The United States experienced a marvelous transformation from a long decade of Great Depression misery followed by the tremendous sacrifices made by the American people during a world at war to a time of postwar jubilation. Nylon hosiery returned to the American marketplace with a vengeance. Rock and roll blossomed, which influenced lifestyles, fashion, and attitudes. It was time to make up for lost-time and the American people wasted no time in doing it. Since America now had an obvious newfound hunger for energy, conditions were ripe for the emergence of America's nuclear juggernaut.

In less than a year following the end of World War II, the U.S. Congress put the bill authorizing the Atomic Energy Act of 1946 on President Truman's desk. The U.S. Senate had unanimously passed the bill by a voice vote, and the House of Representatives overwhelming passed it. The AEC was born with nuclear regulation as its initial prime responsibility.

Eight years later, after a new breed of American nuclear capitalists had laid the necessary groundwork, Dwight D. Eisenhower launched his "Atoms for Peace" program. President Eisenhower's program was to supply equipment and information to schools, hospitals, and research institutions to advance his "Atoms for Peace" program, and to ultimately gain public acceptance of the idea of building atomic power plants to produce electricity for the American consumer.

Image 1. Atoms For Peace U.S. Postage Stamp
(From the author's collection)

Congress then replaced the original Atomic Energy Act of 1946 with the Atomic Energy Act of 1954, which made the development of commercial nuclear power possible. The government began its promotion of the peaceful use of atomic energy with the issuance of the "Atoms For Peace" U.S. First-class postage stamp and the America's nuclear propaganda program was launched.

Interestingly enough, the U.S. "Atoms for Peace" First-class stamp, that every American viewed whenever a letter was mailed and received, read: "To Find The Way By Which The Inventiveness Of Man Shall Be Consecrated To His Life." This subliminal message surrounded the stamp's central message of "ATOMS FOR PEACE." (To "consecrate" is to sanctify, bless, make holy, make sacred, dedicate to God, anoint, ordain, etc.)

Like many others and I think probably most people during that time, I, too, came to believe nuclear power was America's energy source of the future. Because of this belief it became my endearing personal goal powered by an incredible amount of motivation, tenacity, and commitment to make a career for myself in the nuclear industry.

My aspiration of becoming a nuclear power plant worker eventually led me to pursue an emerging job classification that was completed by PG&E and the International Brotherhood of Electrical Workers (IBEW), Local 1245 on February 17, 1965: Nuclear Control Technician. PG&E's control technician-training program was extremely demanding.

245 Market Street
San Francisco, California 94106

Control Technician

An employee who, without direct supervision, is regularly assigned to and who maintains, calibrates and services the individual components and integrated systems of all conventional power plant instruments in the plant, all nuclear instruments, all radiation detection instruments, all counting equipment and accessories; performs contamination and radiation level surveys to assure nonhazardous conditions, maintains records of survey results, instructs shift personnel in proper radiation protection; assists and advises other employees in the decontamination of equipment and the handling, packaging and storing of solid radioactive waste; collects and analyzes samples both radioactive and non-radioactive in accordance with standard procedures and makes recommendation to the appropriate supervisor based on such analysis. May be required to assist an engineer in performing plant tests and evaluating data or to assist shift personnel in handling and operating chemical process equipment and waste disposal plants. His background of apprenticeship and experience must be such as to qualify him to perform these duties with skill and efficiency.

Image 2. Official PG&E "Nuclear" Control Technician Job Description-1965 (From the author's employment file)

I was blessed with the necessary skill set, ability, and discipline to make it all happen and my desire of becoming a nuclear power plant worker became a reality. Once realized, however, all that I had worked so hard to accomplish eventually turned into a quagmire of controversy. Consequently, I ultimately found myself living with controversy as a constant companion for many years.

My *Diary* chronicles my journey into the nuclear world and the events that led to my disillusionment with the promise of nuclear power, thanks to PG&E, the AEC, and the inability of the judicial system to adequately respond to the gross misconduct of the perpetrators of totally unacceptable wrongdoings by corporate America and the government.

Strangely enough, the 1954 Act had assigned to the AEC the functions of both promoting the use of nuclear power and regulating its safety.

It was an interesting and convoluted arrangement in that the AEC took its role of promoting nuclear power much more seriously than its responsibility of regulating it; my *Diary* will explain why this is true by a multitude of well-documented examples. On the regulatory side of the AEC's legislative mandate was the movement of private enterprise people into the AEC and then back to private industry. Many of the AEC compliance inspectors who visited the Humboldt Bay Plant came from private industry.

The AEC "regulators" who worked favorably with the operators of privately owned reactor facilities found lucrative offers of employment when they returned to private industry. When I pointed out the absurdity of this arrangement to AEC Investigator, J. J. Ward, his flimsy response was simply, "Where else are we going to get the expertise we need?"[5] This arrangement was analogous to "the fox guarding the hen house," which was cited many times by scores of people who were critical of the AEC's regulatory role.

With the arrival of the Atoms for Peace Program, there was a feeding frenzy at the public trough by private industry for federal research and development (R&D) funds and the desire to take advantage of the R&D the government had already done. It was a fantastic windfall for a large number of companies that included the American Machine and Foundry Company, Bechtel Corporation, Westinghouse, General Electric (GE), and PG&E to name a few.

PG&E was among the first primary benefactors of Eisenhower's Atoms for Peace Program. The company was in on the ground floor, having first joined with GE in 1957 to operate the Vallecitos Atomic Laboratory facility in Livermore, California. Vallecitos received the very first AEC license. PG&E's Vallecitos experience was then followed by the company's first sole nuclear venture known as Unit 3 in the Humboldt Bay Power Plant facility.

It is difficult to understand why PG&E selected the Eureka area for the siting of the Humboldt Bay reactor. Eureka is known for its frequent earthquakes. The exact location selected for the nuclear unit was on Buhne Point at King Salmon located about three miles south of downtown Eureka. Of course, its location was directly across the bay from the entrance to Humboldt Bay, which provided a convenient way to discharge radioactive liquids so long as those discharges were made on outgoing tides (see Image 3). However, in addition to "frequent earthquakes," there were a couple of other serious drawbacks to putting the nuclear unit at Humboldt Bay. The prevailing northwest winds put the plume of the radioactive gaseous waste directly over an elementary school that was located approximately 400 meters downwind from the plant.

Image 3. Aerial view of Humboldt Bay
(Courtesy of Robert Campbell, U.S. Army Corps of Engineers)

Referring to Image 3, notice the smoke plumes from the two pulp mills north of the Humboldt reactor. Those plumes are parallel to the invisible radioactive gaseous waste plume from the Humboldt Bay Nuclear Power Plant that is over the South Bay Elementary School.

The other drawback of putting the Humboldt reactor on Humboldt Bay was the need to transport nuclear spent fuel by rail across the Northwestern Pacific Railway trestle under the Scotia Bluff's approximately thirty miles south of Eureka. NWP workers referred to that section of rail as the Scotia Bluffs' "treacherous trestle" (see Chapter 6, pages 160-161).

How was it possible for the U. S. Atomic Energy Commission, the U. S. Department of Transportation, and the general public of Humboldt County to have approved putting the atomic plant on Humboldt Bay with all the problems the plant posed? The Humboldt Bay nuke with its flawed design, which will be fully explained later, was the first commercial boiling water reactor west of the Mississippi. It went into commercial operation in August 1963 under the authority of the Atomic Energy Commission's operating license number 7 (DPR 7).[6] Humboldt Bay was the world's first privately funded nuclear venture.

Image 4. Construction begins on the HBPP Nuclear Unit site for Unit 3
(Courtesy of the Clarke Historical Museum)

Image 5. Early construction of HBPP Unit 3 showing reactor vessel and generator
in upper left hand corner of photo and the construction of a railroad spur into the
refueling building yet to be built" (Courtesy of the Clarke Historical Museum)

Image 6. Site preparation for Humboldt Bay Unit 3 reactor
(Courtesy of the Humboldt County Historical Society)

Image 7. Early construction of HBPP Unit 3 showing progress on the installation
of the reactor suppression (Courtesy of the Clarke Historical Museum)

Image 8. Installing the reactor vessel in HBPP Unit 3
(Courtesy of the Clarke Historical Museum)

Image 9. Units 1 and 2 with Unit 3 under construction – the radioactive
gaseous waste discharge stack has not yet been installed
(Courtesy of the Clarke Historical Museum)

Image 10. HBPP Nuclear Unit under construction with radioactive gaseous waste discharge stack in place – bay view (Courtesy of the Clarke Historical Museum)

Image 11. Nuclear Unit under construction with radioactive gaseous waste discharge stack – U.S. 101 view (Courtesy of the Clarke Historical Museum)

While the nuclear unit was under construction, there was a mad rush to get everybody in PG&E's proposed nuclear plant management unit up to speed with just a minimal amount of skills and knowledge pertaining to the radiation safety of employees and the general public (see PG&E's "Nuclear Task Force" in Chapter 2). The people in PG&E's corporate headquarters, who virtually had no knowledge about the technology's radiation hazards, were developing strategic plans and making financial decisions with only one principal goal in mind: "Let's make this thing work!" The Unit 3 technical management staff accepted the mandate and complied with it.

The people in PG&E corporate headquarters had no idea about what the long-term ramifications would be from the failure of the initial nuclear fuel cladding, and those people refused to accept responsibility for the decision to use the cheaper stainless steel cladding when a far superior cladding was available.

PG&E management has never addressed its odious decision to place the nuclear reactor upwind a distance of merely the length of four football fields from an established elementary school. Nor has PG&E ever addressed the inadequacy of the facility's high-level radiation waste storage vault. Then there were the numerous violations of the company's own radiation control standards that PG&E, with the help of the AEC, covered up with blatant lies and deception.

PG&E chose to use unsavory PR tactics rather than to do the right thing and come clean on the mistakes that were made by company management at all levels.

To deal with the unfolding of the plant's nuclear difficulties and in concert with the rest of the emerging nuclear industry, PG&E assembled an army of public relations specialists in its San Francisco corporate offices. These public relations people wantonly used smear tactics and were willing to malign and defame anyone who gave PG&E management the heebie-jeebies because of their radiation safety concerns.

The marching orders of PG&E's public relations department were to use any and all means necessary to convince the public "nuclear power is safe, reliable, and economically feasible." This public relations message costing millions of dollars was repeated *repeatedly at every twist and turn* in America's nuclear juggernaut's campaign to win over public acceptance of nuclear energy.

PG&E's public relations department stooped so low as to promote the safety of the Humboldt Bay reactor during the sixties with a photo on the front of a PG&E public relations brochure showing children playing in the schoolyard of the South Bay Elementary School located a short distance downwind from the 250-foot radioactive gaseous waste discharge stack. (I wanted to use this particular photo on the cover of *My Humboldt Diary* but couldn't because PG&E prevented its use with a 2013 copyright)

The previously mentioned schoolyard photo reveals how ignorant PG&E's public relations people were and exposes the unscrupulous *decision making* at the highest levels of PG&E management, for all of these kinds of decisions were made in PG&E's San Francisco corporate office. It was important for PG&E to convince the public just how safe Humboldt Bay was, and what better way than to use children to do it.

Adding insult to injury, PG&E then staged an outdoor classroom complete with students sitting at their desks topped with textbooks and classroom materials. The students were sitting in front of a chalkboard with "A is for Atom" written on it. This temporary classroom provided PG&E not one but two photos for its public relations program promoting nuclear safety at Humboldt Bay. For me (besides the obvious), the most galling aspect of this charade is the ground upon which this "temporary classroom" was located, which was in the very location of where PG&E's infamous rabbit caper testing for radioactive iodine took place (Chapter 4).

All three of the aforementioned photos were included in a PG&E publication entitled "From Sawdust to Uranium" with a 2013 copyright and can be found on page 69 of that publication. All three of the photos (with the schoolyard photo flanked by the two outdoor classroom photos) are underscored with the following PG&E caption:[7]

> A teacher, complete with an apple on her desk, teaches students about the atom within the shadow of Humboldt Bay Power Plant Unit 3. In the background the chalkboard reads "A is for Atom" and nuclear fuel rod boxes are visible outside the refueling building. These photographs (left and right) were likely used to promote nuclear power safety. At center, boys and girls of South Bay Elementary School play during recess with Humboldt Bay Power Plant in the background.

I cannot state emphatically enough how disgusting this kind of PR garbage is to me; it was PG&E's *modus operandi* to engage in such conduct and my *Diary* provides many examples of it.

Private enterprise needed the protection of the Price-Anderson Act so Congress provided it in 1957 limiting the liability of a reactor accident to $560 million. "A major accident, it [was] estimated, could lead to 7 billion dollars worth of damage in terms of 1970 dollars. The public (stood) to recover a *maximum* of seven cents on each dollar in such an event. And the public (paid) 80% even of this inadequate protection."[8]

The limited liability provision of the Price-Anderson Act was absolutely necessary because without it the lack of financial security would have hindered, if not altogether prevented, the development of the private nuclear industry in America. One must ask: *How could the American people have ever accepted such an arrangement?*

PG&E then launched a massive advertising and public relations campaign with the company's startup of its first nuclear power plant at Humboldt Bay claiming repeatedly *ad nauseam* that "Nuclear power is safe, reliable, and economical." Woe betide any employee who dared question PG&E's claim of just how safe the Humboldt Nuclear Plant was and the necessity for having the shield of the Price-Anderson Act. My feelings at the time were based on the claims made by PG&E and the AEC that the plant was totally safe. *Why then did the nuclear industry need the protection of the Price-Anderson Act?*

There were several areas of concern for safety. One was the possibility of a maximum credible accident (reactor core meltdown) and the adequacy of the Emergency Core Cooling System (ECCS), which received a huge amount of public attention when all the early ECCS tests that were done at the AEC Testing Lab in Idaho failed. Other areas of concern included radiation releases from the plant as radioactive gaseous, solid, and liquid discharges; and the chronic exposure to ionizing radiation, which became a major concern of mine especially when employees were subjected to unnecessary and senseless exposures in order to save on operating costs.

Regarding the first mentioned safety concern, one only needs to look at the entire West Coast of the United States and ask, "Where on earth can a nuclear power plant be safely located?" The location would have to be free from serious threats of earthquakes and tsunamis. About six months after the Humboldt Nuke went on line, the Great Alaskan earthquake on March 27, 1964, with a magnitude of 9.2[9] sent a tsunami south causing approximately 15 million dollars damage (in terms of 1960 dollars) to Crescent City,[10] located in northwestern California 70 miles up the coast from Humboldt Bay. The Humboldt Bay Power Plant was placed on alert and operators were ready to shut the plant down because of three surges from the bay that went clear up to the top of the intake pumps.[11] *However lucky the Humboldt Nuke may have been, an active seismic fault was eventually discovered directly under its reactor vessel in 1976 resulting in the permanent shutdown of the reactor.*

There was much chatter among the nuclear plant employees about what an earthquake would do to the reactor vessel. The more I thought about it, the more I came to realize just how vulnerable the nuclear unit was. I remembered the frequent earthquakes as a youngster growing up in Eureka, and I particularly remember the Eureka Quake in December 1954.

I was 14-years old. My family lived on Albee Street in Eureka, which was about three to four miles from where the Humboldt Bay Nuclear Plant was eventually built. The earthquake hit as I was going up a flight of stairs carrying a box of canning jars for placement in the attic for storage. Everything started moving in the stairwell and I landed at the bottom of the stairs with broken glass all around me.

It was a horribly frightful experience and when I made it to the front porch the power lines were slapping together and sparking. We lost our brick chimney and experienced much damage to our home. We were not alone. When I shared my experience with the workers at the plant, most of them just pooh-poohed it saying the plant was designed to withstand an earthquake. It was a reoccurring argumentative discussion that never reached resolution.

Congress decided to abolish the AEC in 1974 due to the groundswell of adverse public opinion during the 1960s and early 1970s because the agency was "insufficiently rigorous in several important regulatory areas including radiation protection standards, reactor safety, and environmental protection."[12] My AEC experience as a nuclear control technician with the Pacific Gas and Electric Company relates to the same period of period - 1964 through 1973 (which included my wrangling with the AEC after I was fired from PG&E in June 1970). My *Diary* will provide a full accounting in Chapters 11 and 12 of how four of the seven nuclear control technicians at PG&E's Humboldt Bay Nuclear Power Plant during that time became the sacrificial lambs of a failed and dangerous technology, the misguided regulatory function of the AEC, and the Machiavellian philosophy of PG&E management.

When I went to work for PG&E, I was twenty-one years old and fresh out of the Marine Corps. I had served honorably for four years, winding up my hitch in the Marines as a pathfinder in a Marine force reconnaissance unit. I remember the return trip from overseas on a troopship where I spent most of our steaming time on the fantail watching the albatross glide back and forth above the wake of our ship thinking about my future. It was a long ride home.

Nearly three weeks earlier, we had boarded the old troop transport (referred to as an APA) that was destined for mothballs. The 18-day trip from Naha, Okinawa, was the highly decorated APA's final voyage across the Pacific. With her battle ribbons proudly displayed on the bridge, the APA maneuvered her way into San Diego Bay ending the final chapter of her glorious career transporting leathernecks to and from the Orient for more than a quarter century. She had done her duty. I felt very much like that old ship, for I too, had done my duty; but unlike the APA, I was eagerly looking forward to whatever my uncertain future had in store for me. I was confident that I could do whatever I set my mind to and do it well. My Marine Corps experience had instilled this high level of confidence in me.

The salt air, the Pacific winds, and the graceful movement of the large birds above the water was mesmerizing while I was focused on thinking about where I had been and what I wanted to do with the rest of my life. Staring me in the face was a major decision I had to make when we arrived in San Diego. Do I reenlist in the Marines, and if so, for how many years? Or do I leave my beloved Corps and go in another direction with my life? It was a tough decision for me because I loved the Corps, everything it stood for, and what it had done for me.

The ideals of honor, duty, hard work, esprit de corps, and Semper Fidelis had become deeply engrained in my character. I was unquestionably proud of who I was and what I had accomplished in the Corps. I was now fearlessly confidant and believed I could be tremendously successful whatever my decision. Fortunately I had nearly three weeks of reflective thinking on the fantail of the ship; if we had flown home, I would have most likely re-upped for six more years of service in the Corps. By the time we arrived in San Diego I had made my decision. I was going to leave the Marines and explore my options in civilian life, which were yet to be discovered.

When I entered the Marines, I was barely 17-years old with only an AWOL bag filled with a change of skivvies, socks, toiletries, a second pair of trousers, two shirts, a thin, well-worn jacket, and just under $10 to my name. I had no idea what lay ahead, but I knew there was no turning back when the Greyhound pulled out of the bus depot in my hometown.

A dysfunctional family life had made it necessary for me to drop out of school during the Christmas break of my junior year in high school. When my classmates returned to school in January 1958, I was in Marine boot camp. Upon graduating from boot camp at MCRD, San Diego, and later, advanced combat training at Camp Pendleton, I was assigned to a communications company in Headquarters Battalion of the First Marine Division where I spent the next 18 months of my military career. This duty was not what I had hoped for and I constantly made requests for transfer.

With commitment and determination, I forged ahead in my preparation for a better duty assignment. Reading the *Marine Corps Manual* nearly every night before taps, running the obstacle course and swimming in the base pool at every possible opportunity, and working out in the gym during my off-duty time became an obsession. In December 1959, I finally got the break I was hoping for when my orders arrived transferring me into the paramarine pathfinders of First Force Reconnaissance Company.

Force reconnaissance Marines were few in number and we received the best training in the world. I believed the paramarine pathfinders were the Marine Corps' elite. Force recon Marines were highly trained specialists in demolitions, escape and evasion, reconnaissance work behind enemy lines and along coastal areas, weaponry, guerrilla warfare tactics, communications, and combat intelligence.

We also received specialized training in atomic, biological, and chemical warfare. The pathfinder platoon of the First Force Reconnaissance Company also had a primary function unique to its basic combat mission: we were heavy equipment jumpers trained in setting up helicopter and fixed-wing landing zones in virgin enemy territory. We were among the Marines with the shortest life expectancies in combat zones because of the unique nature of our combat role. The training was tough and the standards were high.

This was a formidable period in my life, one that I would not have traded for anything in the world. I was proud to be a member of the finest unit in the American military; there were only 88 paramarine pathfinders in all the United States Marine Corps consisting in those days of nearly quarter-million active duty Marines.

I had accomplished much to be proud of during my four-year

enlistment, which would have served as a springboard to an extremely successful career in the Marine Corps. My accomplishments included graduating in the top 1 percent of my class in non-commissioned officers school on the "Rock," and by the standards of the time, rapid promotion to Corporal (E-4), which was the old buck-sergeant rating that had just been phased out of the Marine Corps' enlisted rank structure with the introduction of the new L.Cpl. (E-3) rating.

It would have never entered my mind under any conceivable circumstances, even in my worst nightmares, that someday all of this would be used against me, especially by those in government and corporate America for whom I had proudly served. I was young and naive, filled with convictions of loyalty and a sense of duty to America and all the things for which I believed my country stood.

When I left Camp Pendleton following my discharge with all my worldly belongings packed into a 1953 Chevy station wagon, I stopped by Lake Elsinore near Riverside, California, to make four free fall jumps on Christmas Eve with Marine Sgt. Roy Fryman (I was a member of the Okinawan Third Marine Division Sport Parachute Team during 1961).

Sgt. Fryman, who provided technical advice and assistance to the T.V. series "Ripcord" during the early sixties, was later killed in action in Vietnam.

My jumps with Sgt. Fryman represented a personal gift to myself, as I was leaving the Corps and heading home to Eureka, California, where I had enlisted four years earlier. At this point I did not have a detailed plan for my immediate future except to obtain a job of some kind, because a sizable portion of my modest savings had been spent on the purchase of the Chevy station wagon (which I needed to haul around my sport parachute equipment).

Following the Christmas holidays, I began my search for a civilian job. I came face to face with just how difficult it would be to find a good job without a high school diploma, even though I had passed my GED while in the service.

The Georgia-Pacific sawmill on Humboldt Bay hired me to pull green chain on the swing shift. I remember the first several weeks of pulling lumber on the resort chain. The resort chain had a crew of six and the job of resorting the overflow from the bonus chain by putting the dimensional lumber into designated pockets according to grade.

I found myself pulling not only the pockets assigned to me but also some of the pockets belonging to the other workers. I wanted to make a good impression with foreman Palmer Flowhog, so I continued to work hard even though I knew the other workers were taking advantage of me.

The game played by the other workers backfired on them when Flowhog promoted me, the worker with the least seniority, to the bonus chain a few weeks later when the next opening became available. This promotion meant a larger paycheck on payday!

During my free time away from the sawmill job, I completed two Marine Corps Institute (MCI) courses, offered through the independent studies department of Oklahoma State University. I had started these courses before going overseas. One course of study was a forest management course and the other was advanced algebra. Education was extremely important to me because I believed I could gain more control over my own destiny by acquiring additional knowledge and developing new skills. Much of my spare time in the service was devoted to various self-improvement activities. As I searched for a better job than that of pulling green chain, it became apparent I needed a high school diploma because my GED wasn't cutting it.

During the next few weeks I learned that PG&E was building a nuclear unit just south of Eureka on Buhne Point at King Salmon, which was located directly across from the entrance to Humboldt Bay. PG&E's nuclear facility was to become Unit 3 of the Humboldt Bay Power Plant facility, and it was expected to go on-line along aside of Units 1 and 2 in about 18 months. Units 1 and 2 were fossil fuel units burning oil and natural gas and were rated at 52 megawatts (MW) and 53 MW, respectively.

I looked into the possibility of getting a job at the Humboldt Bay Power Plant and concluded that I needed to first get a job with PG&E, any kind of job just to get my foot in the door. Since my hours at Georgia-Pacific were from 5:00 pm to 2:00 am, Monday through Friday, I was able to go to the PG&E personnel office during the morning hours one day in April without missing any work at Georgia-Pacific. I had learned PG&E gave a pre-employment test to all applicants so I brushed up on mostly my math skills. I definitely remember the day that I went to the PG&E personnel office.

The woman in the front office told me in a rather cold-hearted fashion that there were "no openings at this time." I asked to fill out an application anyway. When I finished completing the employment application, I asked if I could take the pre-employment test and have the results attached to my application. The office woman wasn't at all enthusiastic about my brazen persistence. Then, as it looked as though I was going to have to leave the office without taking the test, the personnel manager walked in.

The front-office woman told him that she had already told me there were no openings at this time but that I had insisted upon filling out an employment application, which she said I had done. Then she said that I was "now insisting on taking the pre-employment test." To my pleasant surprise, the personnel manager simply said, "Why not?" and he had me to follow him into his office where he first gave me the written test, which was followed by a timed manual dexterity test.

The manual dexterity test involved the mirror-transfer of an array of wrench-tight bolts, nuts, and washers from one side of a U-shaped wooden structure to the other with all bolts and nuts having to be wrench-tightened.

While I was waiting for the personnel manager to score my tests, I noticed an artist rendering of an atomic plant hanging on the wall that would someday become Unit 3 of the Humboldt Bay Power Plant facility.

I passed all tests successfully. My score on the written test was among the highest scores the personnel manager had ever seen.

The personnel manager cleared his throat, looked directly at me, and following a brief rather intense and somewhat puzzling stare, then asked, "Are you willing do anything?"

I was surprised by his question, and the manner in which he had asked it, but immediately responded with a resounding, "Yes, sir!"

Image 12. Artist Rendering of PG&E's Humboldt Bay Nuclear Power Plant (Courtesy of the Humboldt County Historical Society)

While I was sitting in my chair and staring up at the drawing of the nuclear plant on the wall, the personnel manager picked up the phone and called the PG&E Myrtle Street Service Center in Eureka, California. Moments later he said to the Service Center General Manager, "I know you don't have any openings right now, but can we create something? I've got someone in my office the company will want to keep a hold of."

What the personnel manager said made me feel really good, and after he hung up the phone, he asked me how soon I could start. I told him I needed to give Georgia-Pacific a two-week notice and would be available immediately thereafter. It was a done deal.

Three months after going to work at the sawmill I now had a new job as a laborer for the Pacific Gas and Electric Company. I spent the first few weeks working as a laborer with Labor Foreman Paul Grinsel carrying around a grunt-bucket picking up trash and cigarette butts in the loading dock areas of the service center. It was degrading work, especially when a lineman would throw his cigarette down in front of me, put it out by twisting the toe of his boot back and forth over it, then step back while looking me in the eye waiting for me to pick it up. I sucked it up and did what was expected of me because it was some kind of dumb tradition. I put up with this nonsense because I was not only on probation for the first six months of my employ, but also because I was looking ahead to better days with the company. I played the game and got glowing evaluations.

Paul Grinsel took me to Garberville, some 70 miles south of Eureka, for a couple of temporary jobs that lasted about three weeks each. While in Garberville I sized up the needs of the two line crews permanently stationed there. Eventually, I was promoted to grunt (a groundman on a line-crew) and assigned to Art Beckman's line-crew in Eureka. Within a couple of months I successfully bid a grunt job in Garberville, which also provided me an opportunity to learn the PG&E job of senior line truck driver.

After a few months in Garberville, my big opportunity, the one I had been waiting for, finally came in early in 1964. I successfully bid into the Humboldt Bay Power Plant as an apprentice instrument repairman, a three-year training program. I knew this job would from time to time put me into Unit 3, the nuclear unit, which had gone on-line in August 1963. I knew that working in Unit 3 would provide me the opportunity to show plant management what I could do. I had made a good impression with Green Chain Foreman Palmer Flowhog at Georgia-Pacific; PG&E Labor Foreman Paul Grinsel; and two PG&E Line-crew Foremen, Art Beckman in Eureka, and Paul Connolly in Garberville.

This new day-job at the power plant provided me an opportunity to attend evening classes, which enabled me to earn my high school diploma from Eureka Adult Evening High School and eventually my AA degree from College of the Redwoods. My first six months in the power plant as an apprentice instrument repairman went exceptionally well, receiving the highest possible marks on all my training cycles. At every juncture in my instrument repairman apprenticeship-training program, I received outstanding evaluations by my immediate supervisor, Mr. Bob Chaffey. I was a quick study with both pneumatic and electrical instrumentation in the fossil fuel units as well as in the nuclear unit, although the nuclear control technicians did most of that work.

Even though I was still an apprentice instrument repairman, there were times when I was provided opportunities to do work in the nuclear unit. I later learned that for much of that work, I was simply being used as a "radiation sponge."

It became my goal to spend as much time as possible with the nuclear control technicians, with Unit 3 control operators, and with other plant personnel (electricians, machinists, mechanics, and GC painters) who worked in Unit 3. I studied the nuclear facility's "cookbook" chemistry manuals, Unit 3's instrumentation manuals, and Unit 3's radiation protection standards and procedures.

The way I figured it, I had a real good chance of successfully bidding the next apprentice nuclear control technician opening and I wanted to be as prepared for it as possible. I was excited and extremely enthusiastic about my future prospects for getting into the small, elite nuclear control technician group at the Humboldt Bay nuclear facility. Up to this point I had very little direct involvement with plant management involved in Unit 3 operations.

After nearly six months in the instrument repairman-training program in Units 1 and 2, I got my chance to bid for a newly created opening in the nuclear control technician-training program in Unit 3. I was successful!

In a relatively short time I had worked my way up the employment ladder within the Pacific Gas and Electric Company from a laborer to a grunt on a line-crew, to temporary senior-line truck driver, to apprentice instrument repairman in a power generation facility, to apprentice nuclear control tech, and finally to a journeyman nuclear control technician.

It was about the same time I became a journeyman nuclear control tech that I started working toward my BA degree in economics by taking night classes at both College of the Redwoods and Humboldt State University.

My curricular studies included extensive coursework in economics, mathematics, psychology, sociology, cultural studies, philosophy, law, and political science. Edgar Weeks, PG&E's HBPP Plant Engineer, who was my second-line supervisor at the nuclear facility, criticized me for taking the majority of these classes, stating I should be focusing on coursework that directly related to my work as a nuclear control tech.[13] The criticism was of no concern to me for I had already become acutely aware of the general feeling of the technical staff, especially the engineers, that any coursework in the humanities was "a complete waste of time."

When I entered the nuclear control technician apprenticeship training program, it was apparent my schooling and hard work had paid off for I had achieved in civilian life what I had achieved in the Marines. My hard work in the Corps put me with the elite and now I had joined what I viewed as another elite group, this time in private industry.

The Pacific Gas and Electric Company had advanced me into the nuclear control tech field at The Humboldt Bay Nuclear Power Plant. I was excited to be on the ground floor of what sprung from Dwight D. Eisenhower's Atoms for Peace Program, launched by the government a few years earlier. It was clear to me at the time of my decision to go on-board at the nuclear facility that the promises incorporated in the radiation control standards and procedures of the plant's operating license were of paramount importance to both the government and to the Pacific Gas and Electric Company.

The concern for public safety and the safety of the employees working in the nuclear unit would dictate how the plant would operate; this was what I believed when I entered into the employment compact with my employer and with the U.S. Atomic Energy Commission. This belief was the foundation of my confidence that I had made the right decision to pursue a career in the nuclear field, one that I believed would provide boundless opportunities.

There was never any doubt in the early days of my tenure at the nuclear facility that the government would oversee everything we did at the plant to ensure public and employee safety.   Besides the AEC, there were a number of federal and state agencies including the U.S. Department of Transportation (DOT), and the California Department of Public Health with oversight responsibilities, as well, or so I thought.

I believed early on in my tenure at the plant that the unions would also insist on safe working conditions in the nuclear facility. There was the International Brotherhood of Electrical Workers, Local Union 1245, and the Oil, Chemical and Atomic Workers International Union that would work to ensure the safety of workers in a nuclear facility (I eventually learned, however, that the Oil, Chemical, and Atomic Workers Union had nothing to do with PG&E employees).

Nonetheless, I truly believed in the beginning of my employment that the safety of employees was of paramount importance and guaranteed by adequate government regulation. This was because I had heard repeatedly from PG&E that the nuclear industry was the most regulated industry in America. I learned later, much later, that PG&E was already working to consolidate regulatory control into the hands of the AEC, which worked hand-in-glove with PG&E to ensure the viability of nuclear power. During my California Unemployment Appeals Board Hearing, I was able to address this issue and expose PG&E's senior plant management's attitude about regulatory control over radiation safety at the plant.

Eventually my enthusiasm for my chosen vocation waned because I lost faith in my employer and the government to do the right thing. I entered into an ever-increasing struggle with PG&E management and the AEC because I was not willing to "play what was turning into a senseless game of maintaining the pretense of safety in the nuclear workplace." *My Humboldt Diary* chronicles this struggle and the issues creating it. It is usually difficult, if not impossible, for a whistleblower to tell his story effectively. This is particularly true with a company like PG&E. What PG&E did to four of its seven nuclear control technicians was villainous and unforgivable, as was the company's disregard for employee and public safety.

I am lucky to have been able to put PG&E management personnel under oath and then procure the transcripts of their testimonies. It was fortunate for me to have had the foresight to gather up certain documents and to have met some wonderful people who helped me through my prolonged dreadful PG&E experience. Many of them are mentioned in the acknowledgements section of *My Humboldt Diary*.

Regarding PG&E's desire to consolidate regulatory control, I was able to put under oath Edgar Weeks, supervisor in charge of all technical staff at the nuclear facility. Mr. Weeks was one of the four "nuclear engineers" who served on the original nuclear task force for the Humboldt Bay Nuclear Power Plant (Chapter 2). I was able to conduct a direct examination of Mr. Weeks at my California Unemployment Appeals Board Hearing. His testimony revealed PG&E's attitude toward the California Department of Public Health being involved in providing oversight of PG&E's radiation protection safety program.

PG&E wanted absolute control over all matters pertaining to its nuclear facility's radiation safety program to be in the exclusive jurisdiction of the AEC, with whom PG&E had a very cozy relationship (Chapter 13).

The following is Mr. Weeks' testimony, first with finishing up my cross-examination of him regarding his denial of my request to speak with an AEC compliance inspector (Chapter 10), followed by my questions concerning the jurisdiction of the California Department of Public Health regarding the Humboldt Bay Nuclear Power Plant's radiation monitoring program for employees:[14]

> **Mr. Rowen:** (Directed to Mr. Weeks . . .) Then, let me ask you this. Does this "inadvisable" statement that you made regarding my going to the AEC include off the job as well as on the job?
>
> **Mr. Weeks:** I thought I answered that. I said that.
>
> **Mr. Brown (PG&E Attorney):** Excuse me. He has already answered that question.
>
> **THE REFEREE:** Agreed. He has answered the question. He said that it applied to off the job.
>
> **Mr. Rowen:** Oh, I see. During the week preceding my suspension from work, did I ask to see a copy of the California Administrative Code, Title 17?
>
> **Mr. Weeks:** Would you repeat the question, please?
>
> **Mr. Rowen:** During the week preceding my suspension from work, did I ask to see a copy of the State of California Administrative Code, Title 17?
>
> **Mr. Weeks:** Yes, you did.
>
> **Mr. Rowen:** At the time of my original request, was there a copy in the plant?
>
> **Mr. Weeks:** There is a copy in the rad protection-chemical engineer's office, which happens to be in the trailer out the door just outside the plant, in an auxiliary office.
>
> **Mr. Rowen:** At the time of this request, were you under the impression the State of California, Department of Public Health, still had jurisdiction as stated in the 1966 copy of the regulations?

Mr. Weeks: I wasn't sure because the company, (PAUSE) -- I had been told that the law department (of PG&E) had taken steps to put all of this under the AEC, and I had understood that this had been done, but I wasn't sure of it, so I got a clarification on that and I found out that the letter was still in the mill. It was essential for all intensive purposes; the in-plant radiation-monitoring program was not under the State of California jurisdiction anymore but was under the federal jurisdiction and not the State of California. This has finally been completely resolved so that the state does not have jurisdiction on the in-plant monitoring program.

(Weeks' testimony given in October 1970 was pertaining to an event that took place during May of that year, while I was still employed at the plant)

Mr. Rowen: But at the time there was still a question?

Mr. Weeks: At the time, apparently, there was some question. Somebody got fouled up on the mailing or something of this sort.

This eventual discovery confirmed my ever-growing suspicions that PG&E wanted to consolidate regulatory control under the AEC and get it totally out from under the California Department of Public Health as well as all other agencies. I did not realize this early on in my tenure as a nuclear control technician but I eventually began to suspect that PG&E was moving in this direction.

Why did PG&E favor the AEC? What was so terribly wrong with having the California Department of Public Health overseeing the radiation protection safety program of the Humboldt Bay Nuclear Power Plant pertaining to its employees and to the general public? Why did PG&E oppose the involvement of local and state agencies in the oversight function of employee and public safety? Why did all other federal and state agencies (especially the U.S. DOT and the California Department of Public Health) yield to the AEC? Why did the IBEW, Local 1245 refuse to join with the Oil, Chemical, and Atomic Workers Union to petition rule changes to protect nuclear plant workers? My *Diary* will address all of these questions.

I truly believed early in my PG&E employment history that my dream of starting a promising career in the nuclear field had been realized. Little did I know I was about to experience the mother of all nightmares; there was nothing in my background, in my bundle of life-experiences, that prepared me for what was about to happen.

PG&E corporate headquarters accused me of being involved in "acts tantamount to industrial sabotage at the Humboldt Bay Nuclear Power Plant,"[15] of using my military training as a Marine pathfinder trained in demolitions "to carry out certain planned jobs at Humboldt and elsewhere,"[16] of "threatening the plant engineer with bodily harm,"[17] of being a "disciple of Gofman and Tamplin (authors of *Poison Power: The Case Against Nuclear Power Plants).*"[18]

PG&E nuclear power plant personnel accused me of engaging in a campaign that would have caused PG&E to "prevent all radiation from leaving the plant; force the company to eliminate all radiation from plant personnel, and that I would 'pick to pieces company radiation protection policy and AEC regulations." (Andrew Kennedy, Nuclear Instrumentation Engineer.)[19]

Other charges made by plant personnel included "both (referring to Rowen and Williams) have made unproven accusations about conditions as being unsafe, including the high level radiation waste storage vault and radioactive fallout near the school" (John Kamberg, Nuclear Instrumentation Foreman),[20] and they "intended a plain move [sic] to disrupt and cause dissension among the physical forces" (George Tully, Plant Electrical Foreman).[21] All of these accusations made by PG&E plant personnel served as red herrings for reasons that will be thoroughly explained in my *Diary.*

Law Professor Bill Rodgers wrote in his book *Corporate Country:*[22]

Another Rowen indiscretion was recorded in May 1970 when he attempted to raise safety questions at the company safety meeting, something about which he had been warned in the past (Chapter 10). He even went so far as to attempt to speak to an AEC inspector. 'I had the impression Bob was satisfied with the discussion we had on the subject,' Edgar Weeks wrote, 'and wouldn't try to see the AEC inspector on his own. I advised him that this was, in my opinion, inadvisable.' This man was to say with pride on another occasion: 'Our operation is a fishbowl.' Rowen's attempts to help others peep into the nuclear fishbowl at the Humboldt Bay plant offended corporate policy and maligned its nuclear technology. Disruption of corporate harmony must be eliminated, whether it be caused by unsatisfactory laws, hostile administrators or disloyal employees.

Professor Rodgers continued:

Rowen was fired. The company cited a history of misconduct. A referee of the California Unemployment Insurance Appeals Board decided the 'principal cause' of the discharge was Rowen's extreme safety consciousness: 'His efforts in this direction were to some extent a reproof of the more sanguinary attitude of certain of his supervisors. His attempts to bring this matter to the attention of the Atomic Energy Commission and to the attention of fellow employees were also greatly resented.' The company took other steps to rid itself of Rowen's memory: it inspired a police investigation of Rowen and his friends, alleged the existence of a conspiracy to stir up discontent about safety practices within the plant (Chapters 11 and 12), launched a public relations campaign to dispel community concerns, suppressed information about in-plant safety and wooed the Atomic Energy Commission into a slap-on-the-wrist response[23] (Chapter 13).

On December 23, 1971, the Humboldt County Grand Jury issued an interim report recommending the "Atomic Energy Commission increase surveillance of the Humboldt Bay Nuclear Plant" and "commending Bob Rowen for his continued and determined efforts in bringing this situation to the attention of the public"[24] (Chapter 13).

The design of what proved to be the failed and dangerous technology incorporated into the Humboldt Bay Nuclear Power Plant presented the South Bay Elementary School and the surrounding communities of Humboldt Hill and beyond with a *fait accompli*.

The deterioration of the original stainless steel fuel cladding proved disastrous to plant operation and resulted in ever-increasing levels of radiation. The increased levels of radiation at Humboldt Bay presented many problems that had an adverse impact on employee safety and the welfare of the general public. The mission of the Atomic Energy Commission was to promote the technology; PG&E's mission was to protect its investment, with both entities diligently and cooperatively working with each other to accomplish these two main goals while at the same time ignoring employee and public safety.

2. Reactor Water Samples & Radiation Sponges

Summer 1967

"The Pacific Gas and Electric Company and its reactor design partners decided on the cheaper fuel cladding, which proved to be a catastrophic mistake of epic proportions."[25] [Bob Rowen]

"We can state unequivocally, and without fear of contradiction, that no one has ever produced evidence that any specific amount of radiation will be without harm. Indeed, quite the opposite appears to be the case."[26] [Drs. Gofman & Tamplin]

The Humboldt Bay reactor was originally loaded with nuclear fuel housed in stainless steel fuel cladding. A far superior fuel cladding was available. The United States Navy had developed a zircaloy cladding during the late fifties for use in its nuclear powered vessels and it was available for commercial use in the early sixties but it was considerably more expensive than the stainless steel option.[27] Pacific Gas and Electric Company and its reactor design partners decided on the cheaper fuel cladding, which proved to be a catastrophic mistake of epic proportions.

The utilization of stainless steel cladding was one of the many fatal flaws in plant design. It totally discredited PG&E's "safe, reliable, and economical" nuclear claims so tenaciously hung on to and promoted by the company for more than a decade, even after this horrendous reactor design flaw had reared its ugly head.

This fundamental design flaw, coupled with the steam turbine being driven by highly radioactive steam and the poorly designed high-level radiation waste storage vault, led to a multitude of appalling radiation safety problems at PG&E's Humboldt Bay nuclear facility.

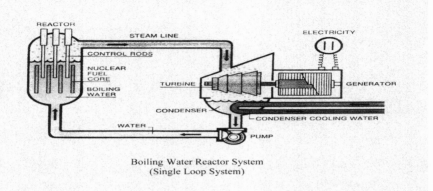

Boiling Water Reactor System
(Single Loop System)

Image 13. Boiling Water Reactor Design–Single Loop System
(From the author's employment file)

I showed up a few months after the original startup of the nuclear unit, and soon found myself asking questions, which ultimately proved to be unwelcome. In the early going I believe they were generally perceived as simple, nonthreatening, easy-to-answer questions. As time passed, however, my questions gradually transitioned from "nonthreatening" to "statements of concern" that were eventually viewed as "accusations," thus putting me on a collusion course with PG&E's management personnel. I never before experienced anything like what was beginning to unfold in my employee-employer relationship as I became more aware and knowledgeable of the changing conditions in the nuclear facility. I grew increasingly uncomfortable with plant management's willingness to ignore legitimate radiation protection safety concerns.

My questions and "statements of concern" were central to the problem of the increasing radiation dose rate levels along with the amount of radioactive contamination we were finding throughout the plant. It was everywhere! These problems were clearly not anticipated in the original design of the plant, and it was equally clear plant management was ill prepared to address these problems when they arose. At least that was my take on why plant management personnel started responding to my "tougher questions" and "statements of concern" the way they did.

I became frustrated with plant management and I began to question their qualifications to deal adequately with radiation safety matters. They just didn't care about the issue of employees receiving "unnecessary and senseless" amounts of radiation exposure. I considered my concern regarding unnecessary and senseless radiation exposure of paramount importance to the adequacy of the company's radiation protection safety program for employees. Plant management resented my questions and viewed them and the concerns I raised, as accusations against the company and my supervisors, rather than as a genuine concern for employee and public safety.

My discussions with plant management personnel regarding unnecessary and senseless radiation exposure always seemed to turn into an argumentative discussion, which resulted each time in my being chastised for "overstepping my authority," a phrase often used by management to address my concerns. In short, I was frequently "counseled" to quit being a troublemaker and constantly stirring the pot.

These "counseling sessions" were polarizing and I doggedly dug in my heels and stood toe to toe with my supervisors, especially Edgar Weeks. I remained adamant that employees should not be subjected to policies and practices resulting in unnecessary and senseless amounts of radiation exposure. This became a bedrock principle for me in my role as a nuclear control technician even though plant management remained at odds with it.

Management's argument was simply that whatever employees were required to do in whatever manner management specified was okay, as long as employees did not go over their quarterly and annual radiation exposure limits. Employees were limited to a maximum of 3 rems per quarter, and to a maximum of 5 rems per year (rem is a unit of radiation dose and is an abbreviation for "roentgen equivalent in man"). Plant management's position was contrary to PG&E's own Radiation Control Standards. I believed it was criminal for the company to expose employees to unnecessary and senseless amounts of radiation simply because it was more cost effective not to find ways to reduce the exposure. Management constantly made it clear that it was not my responsibility to be concerned about the amount of radiation employees were being exposed to except to make sure we were keeping track of the exposure through the proper use of pocket dosimeters and film badges.

It wasn't until after I left PG&E that I became familiar with the work of Drs. John W. Gofman and Arthur R. Tamplin, an important point that will be addressed later in my *Diary*. It is helpful to mention here, however, that what I eventually learned from them simply reinforced what I had already learned on my own early on in my tenure at Humboldt Bay from a variety of other credible sources. I found myself choosing to believe what a large number of experts in the field of radiation biology had to say about the dangers of chronic exposure to low-level amounts of ionizing radiation over the information PG&E was providing the atomic workers.

Since PG&E's plant management was unwilling or unable to address the conflicting information, I found myself questioning the motives and values underlying PG&E's claims. I came to the only conclusion that made any sense. On the PG&E side of the conflicting information rested the profit motive, the commitment to make Humboldt Bay a success so the company could "go nuclear," and the daily operational decision-making placed in the hands of engineers who had only the singular orientation of "let's-make-this-thing-work mentality." On the other side were experts void of these sorts of motivations, and who possessed solid research findings to support their claims relating to the dangers of chronic exposure to low-level ionizing radiation.

Gofman and Tamplin confidently wrote in their widely acclaimed book, *Poisoned Power,* "We can state unequivocally, and without fear of contradiction, that no one has ever produced evidence that any specific amount of radiation will be without harm. Indeed, quite the opposite appears to be the case."[28] (The reader needs only to consider what happens at the dentist – the use of lead aprons, etc., when dental x-rays are taken.)

We were receiving radiation exposures far exceeding many times the amount of exposure involved with the taking of dental x-rays. Gofman and Tamplin went on to say, "It came as a great shock to us, during our study of radiation hazards to man, that nuclear electricity generation has been developed under the false illusion that there exists some safe amount of radiation."[29]

Gofman and Tamplin concluded:

> What is more, the false illusion of a safe amount of radiation has pervaded all the highest circles concerned with the development and promotion of nuclear electric power. The Congress, the nuclear manufacturing industry, and the electric utility industry have all been led to believe that some safe amount of radiation does indeed exist. They were hoping to develop this industry with exposures below this limit – a limit we now know is anything but safe.[30]

(The impeccable qualifications of Drs. John Gofman and Arthur Tamplin are provided in Chapter 11 of my *Diary* entitled "PG&E's Conspiracy – May-June, 1970")

I remember my first experiences of asking questions that riled my supervisors. As I was beginning my formal training to become a nuclear control technician, I carefully read PG&E's *Radiation Protection Training Manual*, which was prepared by J. C. Carroll, PG&E's Nuclear Engineer at corporate headquarters; Edgar Weeks, Nuclear Engineer (later to be named Plant Engineer at Humboldt Bay in charge of all technical staff); Gail Allen, Radiation Protection Engineer at the Humboldt Bay nuclear facility; and Robert Patterson, Nuclear Engineer at Humboldt Bay.[31] These four PG&E management employees: Carroll, Weeks, Allen, and Patterson, were designated as the Nuclear Task Force for PG&E's General Office of the Steam Generation Department.[32]

PG&E's "Nuclear Task Force" is cited on the second page of the training manual as the manual's "principal contributors."[33] The Humboldt Bay Power Plant Radiation Protection Training Manual was used "as the primary textbook for the Radiation Protection Training Course given to all personnel assigned to the Humboldt Bay Power Plant whose work involved exposure to radiation."[34] I attempted without success to reconcile the discrepancies between the information contained in the company's radiation protection training manual with what I had learned in the ABC (Atomic, Biological, and Chemical) Warfare training I had received during my military service.

From almost the very beginning of my nuclear control technician-training program, I started to question the qualifications of PG&E's "Nuclear Task Force." This was largely because they always seemed to get defensive every time I asked "probing" questions regarding radiation protection safety. It became apparent they had limited knowledge on the subject matter and I, therefore, decided to look into their backgrounds.

My findings were as I suspected, which explained why they always responded as though their authority was being challenged and that they were being personally attacked every time I attempted to address my radiation safety issues and concerns with them (mostly Edgar Weeks and Gail Allen, and later Jerome Boots, who was not part of PG&E's original nuclear task force).

A summary of their qualifications relating to radiation safety clearly reveals they were not heavily invested in the science of radiation protection and the biological effects of chronic exposure to ionizing radiation over a long period of time (see Appendix I for the detailed information providing the "Title, Education, and Formal Nuclear Training" of each member of PG&E's "Nuclear Task Force" taken directly from "classified" PG&E documents dated January 1962).

Gail Allen, the Humboldt Bay Nuclear Facility's Radiation Protection Engineer, was the oldest member of the Nuclear Task Force. He had a B.S. Degree in Air Conditioning from California State Polytechnic College in June 1950. His first work experience following graduation from college was with York Chico Company designing and installing air conditioning and refrigeration equipment. All of Allen's formal nuclear training consisted of three 1-week courses, one 2-week course, and a one-semester extension course.

Allen did spend some time at the experimental Vallecitos nuclear power plant, although his tenure at Vallecitos consisted of being a supervisor in charge of turbine overhaul and general plant maintenance and it included three months of "operations training." Allen also spent three weeks in March 1961 and one week in September 1961 at the Dresden Nuclear Power Plant.[35]

Edgar Weeks, Nuclear Engineer, received a B.S. Degree in Electrical Engineering from University of California in February 1953. Weeks' "formal nuclear training courses" consisted of a one-six week APED technology course, May-June in 1957 (I was never able to determine what "APED" actually stood for); 1 60-hour radiation monitors course, 1958; a one-semester nuclear instrumentation extension course; a three week course covering radiological health; a one-semester reactor survey course covering instrumentation, core and fuel design, APED; Spring Semester 1961 (sections on instrumentation, core and fuel design); and a basic nuclear instrumentation one-semester course.[36]

Edgar Weeks was promoted from "Nuclear Engineer" to "Plant Engineer" in late 1964, after participating in the initial startup operations of the Humboldt Bay nuclear facility.[37] The Plant Engineer was in charge of all technical departments and personnel, which included the radiation protection safety program. Weeks was assigned to the experimental Vallecitos Atomic Laboratory on a part-time basis, splitting his time between the Moss Landing fossil fuel power generation facility and Vallecitos from October 1957 to March 1961.[38]

Weeks also spent two months at the Dresden nuclear facility in 1957 and three additional weeks at Dresden in 1961.[39] What is worth noting here among other observations is that Weeks was in charge of the Radiation Protection Engineer who had a degree in air conditioning, when Weeks, himself, only had a 60-hour "radiation monitor" course and a 3-week course in "radiological health."[40] This constituted his entire "formal training and education" in radiation protection and safety.

Mr. James C. Carroll, Nuclear Engineer/Senior Steam Generation Engineer in PG&E's corporate headquarters in San Francisco, had a B.S. Degree in Chemical Engineering. Carroll's "formal nuclear training" consisted of the same training that Weeks had and they participated in those trainings together. Other than the 60-hour "radiation monitors" course and the 3-week "radiological health" course (the same as that of Weeks), there is no mention of formal training and education in radiation protection and safety.[41]

Mr. Robert Patterson, Nuclear Engineer, had a B.S. Degree in Mechanical Engineering from Cooper Union School of Engineering. Patterson's "formal nuclear training" was somewhat more extensive consisting of the following: Introduction to Nuclear Physics, U. C. Extension, Fall Semester 1956; Nuclear Reactor Engineering, U. C. Extension, Spring Semester 1957; Radiological Health, USPH California Public Health Department, 3 weeks, spring 1958; Nuclear Physics, U. C. Extension, Fall Semester, 1958; Nuclear Radiation Detection, U. C. Extension, Spring Semester, 1959; Radiation Biology, U. C. Extension, Spring Semester, 1961; Reactor Survey Course, APED, Spring Semester 1961 (sections on instrumentation, core design, and operation).[42]

Patterson's "formal training and education" in matters of radiation protection and safety looked like the other members of PG&E's "Nuclear Task Force" with one exception. He had taken one Radiation Biology U. C. Extension course during the Spring Semester 1961.

Patterson didn't seem to be much of a player at Humboldt Bay; at least I don't remember him having much contact with the nuclear control technicians. For me, he just kind of unceremoniously faded away. When I asked Forrest Williams if he remembered whatever happened to Patterson, he said, "Bob Patterson was a pretty good guy but I don't know whatever happened to him. It was like he just disappeared from the plant, here one day and gone the next."[43]

The take away from this review of "formal nuclear training" of these men specifically relating to radiation protection and safety issues is simply that they didn't have much. They certainly were in no position to take issue with the experts in the field of radiation safety and the biological effects of radiation, which I had extensively researched. The more I learned and experienced dealing with these people, especially with Allen and Weeks, the greater my concerns for the adequacy of PG&E's Humboldt Bay nuclear unit's radiation protection safety program.

In the "Biological Damage - Repair and Recovery" section of the manual's Chapter IV, I came across several items that were in conflict with the ABC Warfare training I had received in the military. I decided to do some research of my own on the biological effects of exposure to radiation. During my research I eventually developed a particular interest in the biological effects of *chronic exposure to low levels of ionizing radiation.* PG&E's training manual stated: "A *chronic exposure* refers to receipt of very small doses of radiation over a long time."[44]

I naturally assumed this statement was meant to define the phrase "chronic exposure" as referring to just very small doses of radiation over time and not to higher radiation exposures, a distinction that became a serious point of contention later on. Then I came across a very troubling statement in PG&E's radiation protection training manual: "The body has the ability to recover and repair damaged parts. It is capable of replacing cells which are damaged by radiation in the same manner as those damaged by mechanical, heat, or chemical injuries."[45] I took special notice of the following statement in PG&E's training manual: "There is no evidence that shows that continuous low-level irradiation contributes any appreciable amount to life span shortening."[46]

I continued my research on my own totally outside of the PG&E radiation protection-training program. Most of my research was done in the research section of the Humboldt State University Library, which was available to any of the employees at the plant who wanted to avail themselves to the information. To the best of my knowledge, I was the only plant employee engaged in this effort.

The more I read, the more I questioned the claims made in the PG&E's radiation protection training manual and the company's radiation safety training program. I kept a diary of my discoveries made during my readings, and then I wrote an informal white paper based on my readings that got me into much hot water with PG&E's plant management when I made it available for other employees to read. The results of my research were in stark contrast to the information contained in PG&E's radiation protection training program materials.

Here are ten entries that were based on my readings, along with their sources of information (see endnotes), that were taken from my diary exactly as I wrote them back in the day:

Entry #1

"Fortunately the cells have a remarkable capacity for self-repair, but if they are subjected to injury for a long enough time they will finally die and cause cancer-producing cells. Small doses of radiation below the permissible levels produce a significant though small depression of the white-cell numbers.

This was shown, for example, at Los Alamos in 1948 by Dr. N. P. Knowlton, Jr., in a group of ten workers who received on the average 200 mr a week of gamma radiation for 77 weeks. But still smaller doses of irradiation will produce detectable abnormalities in the lymphocytes even when the white-cell count is unchanged, as was shown first at the University of Rochester by Dr. M. Ingraham II in 1952.

Although the very small changes in the blood-cell numbers do not seem to produce any immediate ill effects, they may be the forerunners of anemia, leukemia, and other serious and fatal blood diseases."[47] [Schubert & Lapp]

Entry #2

"With genetic damage: the numbers of mutations induced is simply proportional to the amount of the radiation administered, and there is no minimal or 'safe' dose of radiation below which no injury occurs (my emphasis was added)."[48] [Dobzhansky]

Entry #3

"Exposure to radiation over the total body shortens the life span. This is true whether the exposures to radiation are given over short or long periods of time (within limits, the effects seem independent of dose-rate level).

Life shortening is not restricted to the aftermath of total-body radiation; if only parts of the body are exposed, this effect can be elicited as well.

The life shortening effect is dependent on dose-rate as well as total dose."[49] [Pizzarello & Witcofski]

Entry #4

"It is known that chronic exposure to radiation dose levels two or three times the orders of magnitude higher than natural sources (amounting, on the average, to 125 mr per year) could result in any number of various categories of pathological injury, including leucopenia, anemia and leukemia or other forms of cancer."[50] [American Public Health Association]

Entry #5

"Each exposure to ionizing radiation adds to the body's burden of insults or stresses. Chronic effects of radiation are cumulative and irreversible. Avoid or prevent unnecessary exposure."[51] [American Public Health Association]

Entry #6

"Each person chronically exposed to small doses of radiation may develop grave physical disturbance years after the exposure."[52] [Wallace]

Entry #7

"For mankind any increase in mutation frequency remains highly undesirable"[53] [Aierbach]

Entry #8

"Certain technological inventions have inadvertently increased the mutability . . . ionizing radiations are mutagenic, that is, they increase the frequency of mutations in the progeny of exposed individuals."[54] [Dobzhansky]

Entry #9

"Genetic damage includes the mutations induced in the reproductive tissues and transmitted to the progeny. The physiological damage, no matter how grievous, is confined to the exposed generation; the injury dies with the injured persons. The genetic damage may inflict harm on the descendants of the exposed persons, and for many generations after the exposure."[55] [Dobzhansky]

Entry #10

"One of the strangest and most perplexing aspects of radiation is its ability to leave its imprint on tissue in such a way that injury may become manifest after a long period of time (known as the *latent period*).

One case has been recorded in which forty-nine years elapsed between irradiation and appearance of injury. Radiologists and dentists who have worked with radiation for many years without apparent injury have retired only to have delayed injuries — skin ulcers and cancer — show up many years afterwards.

The very fact that cause and effect are so widely separated

in time makes it difficult to enforce strict rules about radiation safety. Frequently men who *overexpose* themselves develop a cavalier 'I can take it' attitude, based upon the lack of immediate ill effects, only to learn years later that they were not immune to damage."[56] [Schubert & Lapp]

I wrote a "white paper" to which I referred earlier; the one that got me into a lot of hot water with PG&E plant management, and with the people at PG&E corporate headquarters. The casual reader of *My Humboldt Diary* may want to skip over this "white paper" because I wanted to keep my *Diary* nontechnical as possible for the widest range of the general public. If you do decide to read my "white paper," see Appendix II.

After voluminous reading and extensive note taking, I approached Humboldt Bay's Radiation Protection Engineer, Gail Allen, with an outline of my concerns, which included the ten foregoing statements. I wanted to discuss with Allen what I saw as major discrepancies between what PG&E had in its basic radiation protection training manual that was an essential part of the company's radiation protection training program and what I had discovered elsewhere. I also wanted to discuss my "white paper" with him.

Mr. Allen immediately referred me to Edgar Weeks, my second-line supervisor in charge of all technical staff at the nuclear facility. My meeting with Mr. Weeks turned out to be a very unpleasant experience. After reviewing my materials, Weeks said the information I had was absolutely and totally wrong and that he did not appreciate the accusations I was making against PG&E and its management personnel. I could not believe Weeks was responding to me in this way. Edgar Weeks made it clear I should just stay with company approved training materials; "That way," Weeks said, "You'd be much better off."

I became frustrated; Weeks' posturing with me was infuriating. I told Weeks that "I will always try to make sense out of things that didn't make any sense." There were claims in PG&E's radiation protection training materials that made absolutely no sense. PG&E's claims were contrary to the overwhelming amount of evidence I had acquired elsewhere. Our discussion intensified as Weeks vehemently disagreed with me and he refused to address any of my concerns. After further discussion of my research findings was taken completely off the table by Weeks, we started talking about some of my other concerns, which didn't fare any better.

Before things went totally south for us, however, I told Weeks "The company should always do what is reasonably necessary to minimize radiation exposure." What had started as a discussion became an argumentative exchange that turned into a name calling shouting match. It was an exchange that started with me saying I had often observed employees not making reasonable attempts to minimize their exposures because they simply wanted to do things the easiest and quickest way possible. I also told Weeks plant management personnel usually seemed to agree with employees cutting corners and that these practices should be considered unacceptable to him and to the company.

I reminded Weeks of the problems we had with the reactor water and off-gas sampling stations that I brought up at the December 12, 1967, company safety meeting (which is covered later in this chapter).

When I mentioned the reactor water and off-gas problems, Weeks became absolutely enraged and it wasn't pleasant. Nevertheless, I clearly stated the company should never make an exception to the principle of minimizing radiation exposure, adding that it was not okay for employees to take shortcuts that compromised good radiation safety practices.

My meeting with Weeks became a heated argument that blew up and accomplished nothing. Weeks did not like what I was telling him and said I was making trouble for myself. I was only expressing my observation of practices I considered unacceptable and worthy of review.

After all, I thought that what I was trying to talk to Weeks about was an important part of the nuclear control technician's job responsibilities.

Weeks just said that if I was looking for trouble, I was going to find it. My response to Weeks as I was leaving his office, "I do not respond well to bullying, not by you or by any one else in company management."[57]

Our meeting ended with my leaving his office with each of us extremely upset with the other, and that was about all that was accomplished. This exchange was more of the same in that I was again being chastised for asking questions and trying to carry on intelligent conversations about radiation safety to improve working conditions in the plant, something I thought a conscientious nuclear control technician should want to do.

On February 17, 1965, PG&E's corporate headquarters in San Francisco established a formal job description for the nuclear control technician at the Humboldt Bay nuclear facility already presented in Chapter 1 (page 31). The following is a summary of the formal job description using less technical jargon. The nuclear control technician job classification involved three areas of responsibilities: (1) Installing, servicing, maintaining, and conducting routine calibrations on nuclear instrumentation and monitoring equipment; (2) Collecting and analyzing in the radiochemistry lab radioactive liquid and gaseous samples taken from areas throughout the nuclear facility; and (3) Radiation monitoring of personnel and workplaces throughout the plant, which included establishing dose rates for employees (electricians, mechanics, welders, machinists, painters, etc.) assigned to perform necessary work throughout the nuclear facility.

In short, control techs routinely rotated between **Nuclear Instrumentation** (working in the nuclear instrument lab under the supervision of the Nuclear Instrument Engineer), **Radiochemistry** (working under the supervision of the Chemical Engineer), and **Radiation Protection** (working under the supervision of the Radiation Protection Engineer).

It was extremely challenging to have three different first-line supervisors, all of whom answered directly to the Plant Engineer who constantly gave dictatorial marching orders aimed at maintaining a rosy picture of the plant. Ensuring the plant looked good was of paramount importance to corporate headquarters in San Francisco. This task, however, became increasingly difficult and eventually all consuming as the radiation levels in the nuclear facility rose way beyond the original design specifications of the plant.

The Plant Engineer owed and freely gave his blind allegiance to the company's Nuclear Engineer in PG&E's corporate headquarters, Mr. Jay C. Carroll. Mr. Carroll was a longtime colleague and friend of Edgar Weeks; Carroll had one primary mission and they both knew and understood what that mission was: To make the Humboldt Bay Nuclear Power Plant a *success* whatever the cost so PG&E could "go nuclear."[58] (I use the phrase "go nuclear" throughout my *Diary* for emphasis because PG&E management used it often and it best illustrates PG&Es mindset during those years).

During my time at Humboldt, the nuclear unit's operating structure and the value system underlying it coupled with employee personal motivation, ego, and desire for advancement became increasingly clearer to me, and I found myself becoming increasingly at odds with it. Most of the employees in the personnel hierarchy within the nuclear facility were emulating their superiors in order to receive favorable ratings for advancement.

Employees emulating their superiors produced a peculiar state of affairs causing them to ignore the real dangers of radiation exposure thus playing into the established singular — "go nuclear" — frame of reference that was fostered by Edgar Weeks. In order to maintain what I shall call "this blissful state of ignorance," it was necessary for every employee to be cooperative and promote harmony, which required employees to not question or challenge anything.

For the most part, this arrangement worked well because most of the older employees providing leadership within the ranks were of the WW II generation; they never questioned anything. The vast majority just accepted whatever the company told them and the same was true of their view of the AEC.

In like fashion, the younger employees were caught up in the *emulation culture* and thus complied with whatever marching orders they were given. Working in harmony with the Plant Engineer was a necessary prerequisite for advancement, which required blind allegiance to the company. The nuclear employees believed there was no need to question PG&E or the AEC, and to criticize either was simply not in their frames of reference. In other words, the vast majority of employees in the plant trusted the AEC and PG&E simply because they had misguided blind faith in both.

The following is one example of the kinds of things that put me at odds with plant management and many of my coworkers. During one of the major refueling outages with the reactor shutdown and all systems opened up for overhaul and maintenance, PG&E had brought into the nuclear facility a large number of "radiation sponges." The "radiation sponges" were PG&E employees who worked and lived in areas throughout the PG&E system; they were not permanent Humboldt Bay Nuclear Power Plant employees.

These "radiation sponges" consisted of mechanics, machinists, electricians, welders, etc., who would be assigned to work in mostly "hot" areas of the plant (radioactively speaking), absorbing radiation doses so permanent plant employees could stay within their occupational limits thereby remaining available for work in the nuclear facility following the reactor shutdown. As previously stated, employees were limited to a maximum of 3 rems per quarter, not to exceed 5 rems of radiation exposure per year. If a permanent plant employee reached either maximum limit, he *(supposedly)* would not be able to go into the radiation controlled area of the plant for the balance of the exposure-limiting-period.

I remember having lunch one day in the cold instrument repair shop with some of the employees from next-door in the electrician's shop located in Unit 1. While we were eating lunch a number of topics were being discussed and somehow we started talking about cancer. I don't remember how that subject came up. What I do remember, however, was a statement by one of the "radiation sponges." He was an electrician, I believe from PG&E's Moro Bay Power Plant, and he stated he had been treated for cancer with radiation and chemotherapy and was now into his second year of remission. Upon hearing what the electrician had disclosed, I told him he should not be working in the radiation-controlled areas of the plant.

I asked him if anyone had talked to him about his cancer and he said, "No."

I asked if he had been screened before accepting the temporary assignment at Humboldt Bay. Again, he said, "No."

All he knew was the wonderful opportunity PG&E had offered him to temporarily work at Humboldt Bay. The offer was, "An opportunity too lucrative to pass up," he said.

I immediately reported the matter to the Radiation Protection Engineer and stated the electrician should not be allowed to go back across the step-off pad (re-enter into the radiation controlled area) after lunch that afternoon. I told Gail Allen, and Jerry Boots was part of the conversation, that PG&E should have discovered the electrician's situation before he was picked up to do temporary work at our plant. As it turned out the electrician did not re-enter the radiation controlled area that afternoon and he was sent home. Later that day I was called to the front office for a meeting with Edgar Weeks. On the way down to his office I thought I was going to get an attaboy from him for my discovery of the problem but I was absolutely dead wrong! Instead I was chastised for making trouble, embarrassing plant management, and for criticizing PG&E's lack of enforcement of the company's radiation safety policy. He lost his cool with me and in turn, quite honestly, I ended up losing mine with him. It turned ugly in a hurry!

I left his office in total disgust and later had some things to say in the CT area (control technician work area in the nuclear instrumentation lab) of Unit 3 after I arrived upstairs. I was then called back to the front office because someone reported to Mr. Weeks that I was "ranting and raving" about how I was treated downstairs and the ridiculous position Weeks had taken with me. I took a timeout and stayed in the CT area. A little while later, Weeks showed up and ordered me to go with him back to his office. Again, I had another unpleasant exchange in what the Plant Engineer called a "counseling session."

As previously stated at the beginning of this chapter of my *Diary*, it didn't take long after the original startup of the Humboldt reactor in 1963 for a huge problem to rear its ugly head. The original nuclear fuel cladding was made of stainless steel. The fuel claddings were long tubes, much like copper pipe used in plumbing around the home that contained the uranium dioxide fuel pellets. The stainless steel cladding started breaking down allowing the uranium fuel to "leak" into the reactor water where it became suspended particulate matter containing the byproducts of nuclear fission. This problem made the reactor water more radioactive than was originally expected in the plant's design; it also made the gaseous discharge more radioactive than was originally expected; and the plant was generating higher levels and larger quantities of radioactive solid waste than was originally expected.

The dirtier reactor water made the steam the reactor was producing increasingly more radioactive than was originally expected. All systems became highly radioactive with particulate matter settling in the depressions of plant plumbing, sampling stations, packing glands, and in the bottom of the reactor itself. The number one culprit for all these problems was the original design failure of the stainless steel cladding. Questioning PG&E's Jay Carroll on this very problem caused an Emmy Award winning producer of NBC news documentaries, Don Widener, to lose his job (Chapter 15).

Eventually a decision was made to use a new fuel cladding made of zircaloy; however, the damage caused by the failure of the old fuel elements relying on stainless steel cladding was already done. One might argue PG&E faced a Catch 22 with my suggestion of shutting down the reactor, removing all the failed fuel elements and starting over with a complete reloading of the core containing fuel elements with the zircaloy cladding. This proposition would have been extremely costly (perhaps prohibitively so) and it would have cast the Humboldt Bay Nuclear Plant in a very bad light as not being an economical source of electrical energy. Nevertheless, it could have leveled off the amount of radioactive contamination the plant was generating.

There was still another problem, however. The plant was already extremely contaminated throughout and there wasn't much that could be done about that short of permanently shutting down the plant and building another plant elsewhere. Of course this would still involve the whole process of decommissioning and dismantling the plant. All of these costs would have to be applied (one would think) against the actual amount of electricity produced by the facility.

PG&E's decision was to continue operating the plant even though high radiation levels continued to be a problem throughout the plant. For example, the radiation dose rate levels at the reactor water sampling station was initially 5-50 mr/hr in 1963 and it increased to more than one hundred-fifty times that by early 1967. The reactor water samples themselves went from 5-50 mr/hr in 1963 to more than 2 R/hr (and sometimes it reached 3R/hr) during the same period, an increase by more than a factor of forty (and at times by as much as a factor of 60). (To understand the difference between a reading of "1mr" and "1R" – 1,000mr equals 1R)

In another attempt to keep the nuclear unit's operating costs down, it was a common practice to charge the more expensive parts and materials to the two fossil fuel units, and the less expensive parts and materials to the nuclear unit. For example, a stainless steel fitting that would be used in the nuclear unit would be charged against one of the fossil fuel units and a similar item made of copper or brass to be used in one of the fossil fuel units would be charged against the nuclear unit. It was an accounting game played to make the nuclear unit, in comparison to the fossil fuel units, look more economical.

A series of events occurred that generated a personal concern for what PG&E management was doing, which resulted in an ever-growing constant state of turmoil between plant management and myself (Chapter 4). One of those concerns that were among the more serious regarding employee safety issues had to do with the daily sampling and analysis of reactor water.

I raised the issue often with the plant's radiation protection engineer, Gail Allen, and the plant's chemical engineer, Jerome Boots; both of these men were my first-line supervisors. I made it clear to Allen and Boots that the exposure the nuclear control techs were receiving while collecting the samples and transporting them to our radiochemistry lab was too high and the company needed to do something about it.

My concern for unnecessary and senseless radiation exposure was ignored! Nevertheless, I remained adamant and continued in my efforts to cause some change in working conditions. Eventually I was sent to Edgar Weeks because of my constant "criticizing and complaining." Mr. Weeks reminded me for the umpteenth time that I needed to be more cooperative with my supervisors and stop making accusations against the company. I responded to Weeks by demanding the company do something about the problem.

My "demands" continued to be ignored and the radiation exposure levels associated with the reactor water-sampling procedures continued to be a major unresolved radiation safety problem.

Finally, I brought up the issue at the December 12, 1967, company safety meeting. I was concerned about the procedures being used to collect reactor water samples from the sampling station located in the reactor building at a location called "Minus-14." The Radiation Work Procedure (RWP) that was known as a "routine work permit" (which was used to distinguish it from a Special Work Permit - SWP) authorized the work of handling reactor water samples at the maximum radiation exposure limits for each one-liter sample at 50 mr. This RWP was written before the original start up of the plant in 1963 and was clearly outdated because the one-liter reactor water samples we were collecting in 1967 were reading between two to three roentgens per hour, a radiation dose rate over forty to sixty times the amount allowed in the original RWP!

Additionally, the reactor water sample collection point had become grossly contaminated with reactor water crud that had accumulated at the sampling station itself. The radiation dose rate at this location had increased more than 150 times in a little over twenty-four months. My discussions with the chemical engineer and later the radiation protection engineer before the company safety meeting on December 12, 1967, were fruitless, except for the unpleasant "counseling sessions" I received from Edgar Weeks for demanding that the company do something to correct the problem.

I remained steadfast in my position of demanding action and when I finally brought it up at the company safety meeting on December 12, 1967, plant management said it was an attempt on my part to embarrass my supervisors. One week following the December 12 safety meeting PG&E started construction on a biological shield wall that was placed in front of the reactor water sampling station to reduce exposure while collecting the reactor water samples.

The machine shop produced extension tools that were especially designed and made of stainless steel to collect the reactor water samples more safely. Plant management also had lead pigs constructed to carry the reactor water samples from the sampling station to the radiochemistry lab. I also brought up at the same company safety meeting other safety issues plant management had ignored (Chapters 3 and 4).

The company later denied that I had previously insisted on changes to the reactor water sampling station and the method of transporting the collected samples to the radiochemistry lab. Plant management claimed the company had taken it upon itself to reduce the radiation exposure and that I had nothing to do with the improvements that were made. Edgar Weeks simply and unjustifiably accused me of making unwarranted accusations against the company and harassing my supervisors at the December 12, 1967 company safety meeting.

Again, I used my Unemployment Insurance Appeals Board Hearing to establish the facts regarding the reactor water-sampling problem. PG&E had called Edgar Weeks and Raymond Skidmore to testify on behalf of the company.

The relevant portion of Mr. Weeks' testimony (pertaining to the reactor water sampling problem) obtained during my cross-examination of him follows:[59]

> **Mr. Rowen:** Isn't it true that in December 1967, I raised issues concerning radiation protection safety issues at a PG&E company safety meeting?
>
> **Mr. Weeks:** December '67. Yes, you did.
>
> **Mr. Rowen:** After that meeting, did you recall calling in all plant personnel that could leave the operating decks and discuss with them that safety meeting wasn't the place to bring these issues up?
>
> **Mr. Weeks:** I did not call the meeting. I remember the meeting but I did not call it.
>
> **Mr. Rowen:** Were you there at the meeting?
>
> **Mr. Weeks:** Yes. I was at the meeting.
>
> **Mr. Rowen:** Can you recall what was said then and by whom?
>
> **Mr. Weeks:** Yes. Mr. Warren Raymond, Assistant Plant Superintendent, talked to all maintenance personnel and operating personnel that could be free. And, the point he was trying to make, and he made it very clearly, I believe, was that if you have a problem that you think is or you see a problem when you see something that you think is unsafe, don't sit on it until the safety meeting, but take it to your supervisor right then and try to get an answer. Don't sit on it until the safety meeting if you really have a safety item. I believe that's the point that...that's the message I got from this discussion. I didn't talk to the group, he did.
>
> **Mr. Rowen:** I see. Fine. Do you recall that in the months before that safety meeting that there had been quite an effort by different persons in the bargaining unit discussing certain radiation protection safety problems. For instance, the reactor water sample station's high dose rate. At the time of the safety meeting, was this item clearly before management prior to the meeting?
>
> **Mr. Weeks:** I really don't know what question you're asking me. Are you taking about some specific incident before the safety meeting? Are you talking about just general discussion before the safety meeting?
>
> **Mr. Rowen:** I'll tie it down for you. The reactor water sample station with the high dose rates involved in collecting

samples. Hadn't myself, for one, discussed with the rad protection engineer and yourself on various occasions that there was a problem and we felt there should be something done about it?

THE REFEREE: I think you ought to identify the problem.

Mr. Rowen: The dose rate involved in collecting reactor water samples at the reactor water sampling station.

Mr. Weeks: I was aware that exposure rates were coming up when we began to pop fuel and that we were taking too much exposure at the reactor water sample station and our first line supervisors had been instructed to solve this problem and I am sure there must have been several discussions on it, yes. I am sure there must have been, but I don't recall any specific discussions. I just can't recall any specific time sitting down with you in discussing this problem.

There was an interruption in the recording of the proceedings and the Referee took a timeout. After getting the recorder back on line, the Referee continued the proceedings:[60]

THE REFEREE: All right, gentlemen, I think it's recording again. Proceed.

Mr. Rowen: I don't exactly recall where I was . . . (INTERRUPTED)

Mr. Weeks: Reactor water sample station. You were asking whether or not you had been discussing that.

Mr. Rowen: And, what was your response to that?

Mr. Weeks: Well, I gave you a response to that.

THE REFEREE: His response was to the effect that there certainly had been conversations on that point, that he remembered discussing it, but he didn't recall whether he specifically discussed it with you on any particular occasion.

Mr. Rowen: I see. Was it you that at the time were working under an RWP, that's a routine work permit that is required to work in the control area. Is it true that at the time we were working under a routine work permit that we were working with reactor water samples of only 50 mr hour dose rate?

Mr. Weeks: I couldn't answer that question. I don't — we could produce the RWP if necessary but, off hand, I don't know exactly what it said.

Mr. Rowen: I see. Do you ever recall the time that we were indeed working with reactor water samples under an RWP that said it was only up to 50 mr per hour dose rate when in fact the dose rate was over 2 R per hour.

Mr. Weeks: I can't testify that I know what exactly what they are to be said, so I really can't answer your question.

Mr. Rowen: I see.

THE REFEREE: Putting the question in another way perhaps you would be able to answer it. I think essentially what Mr. Rowen is getting at is, were you aware that at times you had permits to operate up to certain levels and, actually, the operation was at a very much higher level?

Mr. Weeks: No. I don't think I was aware of this but it could have happened because our operation, when you begin to experience fuel failure, our dose rate begins to come up. And, it's possible that the rad protection supervisor did not check the RWP. I really, I'm not sure whether he did or didn't.

THE REFEREE: Who would the RWP come from?

Mr. Weeks: It would come from…be signed by the radiation protection engineer and the plant superintendent and the various supervisors as well as a control technician. It's a … an RWP is a work permit that you could work under for long periods of time. We have special work permits that is good for only 8 hours that can be extended to a maximum of 24 hours, but the RWP is a long term work permit that spells out the conditions under which the operation can be done. He didn't really specify the conditions that actually were existing, and I can't honestly testify that I was aware of this.

Mr. Rowen: Well, let me … (INTERRUPTED)

Mr. Weeks: But, it may be very possible that this could have happened.

Mr. Rowen: Let me put the question this way. It is the rad protection engineer's responsibility to see that the conditions people will work under are properly stated on the RWP that there is…

Mr. Weeks: I think…I would say that he has the primary responsibility for this. Also, anyone that has an assignment made to it has a responsibility, so any supervisor really should be also responsible, but this is the rad protection engineer's work area and his primary responsibility, so he's the one that should keep up on this.

I was also able to cross-examined Ray Skidmore about the reactor water-sampling problem. Here's the relevant portion of Mr. Skidmore's testimony obtained during my cross-examination of him:[61]

Mr. Rowen: (Directed to Mr. Skdmore . . .) Do you recall a company safety meeting dating back to December 1967 at which I raised several radiation safety issues, I believe three, which included the reactor water sampling station, the off gas sampling station, and the contamination of personal clothing due to airborne radioactive conditions existing in the plant? Do you remember that meeting?

Mr. Skidmore: Yes, I was there.

Mr. Rowen: Can you recall what happened immediately following that meeting that afternoon?

Mr. Skidmore: Yes, I believe it was the same afternoon. We were called into the conference room and – everybody, in fact, was called into the conference room and we were told not to bring up matters such as you brought up at the safety meeting any more, that these matters should be brought up to our supervisors and not at a meeting. There was considerable talking on the subject.

Mr. Rowen: Generally speaking, that's what you remember?

Mr. Skidmore: Yes.

Mr. Rowen: Do you recall during the months preceding that safety meeting these various things being discussed rather at length with plant supervision?

Mr. Brown (PG&E Attorney): Which one, '67?

Mr. Rowen: Yes, '67.

Mr. Skidmore: Yes, these things were brought up by the CTs with negative results.

Mr. Rowen: Specifically, by which one of those control technicians?

Mr. Skidmore: You.

Mr. Rowen: Up until that meeting, had management really done anything about those problems? I'm referring to the high dose rates on the reactor water sampling — (INTERRUPTED)

Mr. Brown: Objection. There is no foundation that there was a high dosage rate.

THE REFEREE: I believe that Mr. Weeks testified that he had some knowledge of the fact that there was an increasing dosage rate. Does that satisfy your objection? Do you recall that?

Mr. Brown: I (PAUSE) – yes, I do recall that.

Mr. Rowen: Let me ask you that question in this way. When you first went to work in the plant –

Mr. Brown: Wait a minute. Let him answer that question –

Mr. Skidmore: Could he repeat the question?

Mr. Rowen: Mr. Skidmore, when you first went to work in the nuclear unit and started running reactor water samples, what was the dose rate involved?

Mr. Skidmore: You're talking about 50 mr. Real low.

Mr. Rowen: 50 mr?

Mr. Skidmore: Yes, real low.

Mr. Rowen: And that's what the RWP stipulated?

Mr. Skidmore: Yes. That was the maximum. We were not supposed to go over that.

Mr. Rowen: And presumably as low as what dose rate?

Mr. Skidmore: It read from 5 mr to 50 mr.

Mr. Rowen: And during the summer of '67, what was the dose rate on the reactor water samples we were collecting.

Mr. Skidmore: I'd say it was high as 2.5 R. It got up real high.

Mr. Rowen: Would you equate that in terms of mr? Would that be 2,500 mr?

Mr. Skidmore: That's correct.

Mr. Rowen: And had the RWP, which authorized us to do that work, been changed?

Mr. Skidmore: No

Mr. Rowen: Do you recall who was instrumental in getting RWPs changed?

Mr. Skidmore: You were.

Mr. Rowen: Was there anybody else involved to the best of your recollection?

Mr. Skidmore: I think Howard was in on it, but I'm not really sure, though I know you were.

No matter how much the PG&E attorney wanted to twist the facts and play obstructionist to my attempts to bring them out into the open, the Referee saw through what was taking place and didn't buy into it, and for that I shall be eternally grateful. Through the use of the transcripts of my two hearings before the California Unemployment Insurance Appeals Board, the transcription of the magnetic tape recording of the September 7, 1971 AEC meeting by Ms. Rowetta Miller, and the "findings" of the AEC's investigation of my "49 complaints," I was able not only to establish clearly the attitude of the Commission towards PG&E's lack of concern for unnecessary and senseless employee exposure to radiation but also to expose PG&E's many violations of the public trust.

Without these invaluable resources, the writing of *My Humboldt Diary* would not have been possible.

The author at 19-years of age in 1960

__III__

3. Off-Gas Samples & Management Prerogatives

Fall 1967

"PG&E's concern for employee radiation safety at the Humboldt Bay Nuclear Plant was best described as nothing more than lip service by PG&E management, which was simply PR stuff that provided PG&E an undeserved reputation for putting safety first in the nuclear workplace!"[62] [Bob Rowen]

Allegation #20: "Employee suggestion that longer cables be used on an off-gas detector, thereby permitting it to be moved and worked on out of a high radiation dose area, was not adopted by PG&E." AEC Finding: "This is a matter of management prerogative. No AEC regulation covers the matter in the absence of specific evidence of personnel overexposure occurring."[63] [AEC]

Reactor water sampling wasn't the only major radiation safety problem at Humboldt Bay. The off-gas sampling station became an ever-increasingly high-dose-rate work area for the nuclear control technicians who routinely collected and analyzed off-gas samples. These highly radioactive samples that presented huge radiological health hazards were collected from Unit 3's gaseous waste discharge by nuclear control techs every single day!

The radioactive gaseous waste was the result of the nuclear fission occurring in the reactor whenever the reactor was critical and online. The procedures that were used to collect, transport, and analyze the off-gas samples are explained later in this chapter. It was pointed out to the AEC investigators that PG&E plant management dug in its heels on refusing to address this serious radiation safety problem. I explained to AEC Chief Investigator, J. J. Ward, "Every time nuclear control technicians collected off-gas samples they were being unnecessarily exposed to very high levels of radiation, specifically to their hands, arms, and upper body including the face and head."

It was made clear to the AEC investigator how the dangerous exposure to the high levels of radiation at the off-gas sampling station could have been significantly reduced if the company would have been willing to invest in the necessary biological shielding at the sample station, coupled with a revamping of the sampling procedures. Because I remained adamant that the company address the problem of needless and senseless radiation exposure, PG&E chose to retaliate against me. I, therefore, made "management retaliation" part of my formal complaint to the Atomic Energy Commission.

After a "thorough" investigation that lasted several months, the AEC simply responded that as long as employees did not go over their exposure limits, it was management's prerogative if PG&E chose not to spend money to redesign the sampling station in order to reduce the radiation exposure involved with the work.[64]

This incredible response by the AEC is a perfect example of the regulatory agency not concerning itself with employee safety. Other examples included men working over an open reactor without wearing safety lines (Chapters 10 & 13) and employees receiving "unnecessary and senseless" amounts of radiation exposure as in the case of collecting and analyzing reactor water samples (review Chapter 2). This attitude and its underlying philosophy by both the AEC and PG&E was especially infuriating. The off-gas and reactor water sampling work performed by the nuclear control techs are a couple of excellent examples of PG&E's attitude and the company's underlying philosophy about employee radiation safety. PG&E's lousy attitude towards radiation safety wasn't limited to just its employees, however, it also reflected the company's attitude towards public safety, as well.

Interestingly enough, and after I had "paid the price" for pursuing a solution to the problem, PG&E eventually did modify the physical layout of the off-gas sampling station and revamped the procedures for collecting the highly radioactive off-gas samples.

As radiation monitors, nuclear control technicians subscribed to the principle of keeping radiation exposure to a minimum; we believed this was good radiation protection policy and it guided us in all of our decisions regarding personnel monitoring on a daily basis. In fact, our radiation protection training was based on keeping radiation exposure to the lowest possible level. PG&E's own Radiation Protection Training Manual stated:[65]

The basic purpose of a Radiological Protection Program
is to reduce to an absolute minimum the possibility of
adversely affecting an individual's health and welfare.

However, when PG&E had to spend some money to make things safer for atomic workers, as in the case of installing longer cables mentioned in "Allegation #20" (Chapter 13) that would have clearly reduced personnel radiation exposure, it was an entirely different story.

PG&E's concern for employee radiation safety at the Humboldt Bay Nuclear Plant was best described as nothing more than lip service by PG&E

plant management, which was simply PR rubbish that provided PG&E an undeserved reputation for putting safety first in the nuclear workplace!

Mr. Lawrence V. Brown, the PG&E attorney at my Unemployment Insurance Appeals Board Hearing, conducted a cross-examination of nuclear control technician Raymond Skidmore regarding the work associated with the daily collection and analysis of the reactor water samples. Mr. Brown's questions pertained to the time when the radiation dose rate levels at the reactor water sample station were extremely high and each of the 1 liter samples were ranging between 2-3 R/hr (review Chapter 2).

A similar situation existed with the collection and analysis of off-gas samples. Brown was driving home the point that it was okay for employees to be exposed to "unnecessary and senseless" radiation exposure as long as exposure limits were not exceeded. The relevant portion of Brown's direct examination of Skidmore follows:[66]

> **Brown (PG&E attorney):** So, that even though the company has a policy of not exposing you to any more radiation exposures than absolutely necessary, despite that, this work had to be done. Is that not true?
>
> **Skidmore (nuclear control technician):** That's true.
>
> **Brown:** And during the period of time that you were performing this work, isn't it also a fact that you carry a dosimeter that records the amount of exposure each day that you've incurred?
>
> **Skidmore:** That's true.
>
> **Brown:** And, assuming that you might have to work in the area of the reactor water for a considerable period of time, would not the dosimeter readings at some point in time indicate that you have reached the maximum amount of exposure under the AEC regulation?

After Skidmore set Brown straight on the difference between film badges and the use of pocket dosimeters, Brown continued his cross-examination further revealing his ignorance, this time regarding the occupational limits of radiation exposure (which is giving Brown the benefit of the doubt or else Brown knew exactly what he was doing in an attempt to mislead the Referee).

I personally believe Brown was briefed (coached) by plant management to make the point embodied in his previously mentioned cross-examination of Skidmore. Brown's little escapade with Skidmore, however, sidestepped the real issues. Brown totally and conveniently ignored plant management's refusal to correct the problem of unnecessary and senseless exposure along with several other radiation safety issues until they were brought up at the December 12, 1967, PG&E safety meeting, an action which opened up a huge can of worms for both Forrest Williams and Bob Rowen.

The AEC completely failed to address another element of the complaint that became known by the AEC as "Allegation #20" (which the AEC completely ignored when crafting this "allegation"). That other element of the complaint addressed plant management's adverse treatment of the employee who stood up and demanded at a PG&E safety meeting (December 12, 1967) that the company do something to reduce the "unnecessary and senseless" radiation exposure to employees at the off-gas sampling station as well as at the reactor water sampling station.

As a result of my "bold and brazen" action (as it was later referred to), two things happened: (1) Changes were made to the off-gas sampling station (as well as to the reactor water sampling station) thus reducing radiation exposure, and (2) I was raked over the coals by plant management for my actions at the safety meeting and told by Edgar Weeks, who accused me with having a poor attitude towards my supervisors and the company, that all this would be reflected in my employee performance evaluations.

The off-gas sampling station was indeed "beefed up" and "leaded-up" to reduce exposure to the control techs collecting the off-gas samples. Improvements were indeed made to the valving system to shorten the time it took to collect the samples, which also reduced exposure. Lead pigs (specially designed heavy containers constructed of lead and stainless steel) were indeed made to provide shielding to control techs transporting the off-gas samples from the sample collection point to the radiochemistry lab.

Immediately following the December 12, 1967, PG&E company safety meeting, a second "special" meeting of all available plant personnel was held. Plant management conducted the meeting with the acting plant manager, Warren Raymond, in charge of it.

Employees were told not to bring up the kinds of safety matters previously mentioned in future company safety meetings. Simply saying the employees were "told" doesn't state what actually took place at that meeting. Employees essentially were "ordered" not to bring up radiation safety issues at future safety meetings! Plant management later denied that such a meeting ever took place. However, I was able to use my Unemployment Insurance Appeals Board Hearing to establish that the "special meeting" did take place (review supporting testimonies in Chapter 2 on pages 69-73) albeit plant management then admitted it had taken place but claimed employees just needed to bring matters of radiation safety to the attention of their supervisors first.

Edgar Weeks claimed the issues that were raised at the December 12 safety meeting were never presented to plant management prior to the safety meeting and the purpose for raising the issues was simply to embarrass the company. The claim that the radiation safety issues had not been previously presented to plant management was pure hogwash and Weeks damn well knew it!

The sworn testimonies of Edgar Weeks and Raymond Skidmore established that the "special meeting" immediately following the December 12, 1969 safety meeting did occur. Their testimonies also established that employees were "told" not to bring up radiation safety issues at future safety meetings, that all such concerns needed to be presented to supervisors rather than brought up at company safety meetings. It was also established that every single radiation safety issue presented at the December 12 safety meeting had already been presented unsuccessfully to PG&E's HBPP nuclear management.

I attempted to pursue with Mr. Weeks that an effort had been made by several employees, and namely me, to address the radiation protection safety issues many times before the December 1967 safety meeting. I specifically asked Weeks, "At the time of the safety meeting, weren't these items clearly before management prior to the meeting?"[67]

Mr. Weeks responded, "I really don't know what question you're asking me. Are you talking about some specific incident before the safety meeting (or) are you talking about just general discussions before the safety meeting?"[68]

What Mr. Weeks said in conclusion was a blatant misrepresentation of what had taken place and he knew it! Weeks claimed under oath, "I just can't recall any specific time sitting down with you in discussing these problems."[69] Every time I bowed my neck with first line managers over my radiation protection safety concerns, I found myself in another "counseling session" talking with Weeks about them – he and I clearly had many heated discussions regarding them!

On Wednesday, December 13, 1967, the day following the safety meeting, I was called into the front office and given a severe tongue-lashing by Edgar Weeks for making accusations against plant management and the company. According to Mr. Weeks my conduct at the December 12 safety meeting was totally inappropriate and that it had better never happen again.

When all of this was later presented to the AEC as an official complaint about PG&E's treatment of an employee concerned about radiation safety and unsafe working conditions in the plant, the AEC responded, "This is a matter of management prerogative. No AEC regulation covers the matter without specific evidence of personnel overexposure occurring."[70] Again, the AEC's mindset was the same as that of PG&E; there was no desire to do what was reasonably necessary to keep radiation exposure to a minimum even though PG&E's own radiation protection program stated, and it's worth repeating again, "The basic purpose of a radiological protection program is to reduce to an absolute minimum the possibility of adversely affecting an individual's health and welfare."

When the union that PG&E's rank and file belonged to, the International Brotherhood of Electrical Workers (IBEW) Local Union 1245, had the opportunity to join with the Environmental Defense Fund and the Oil, Chemical and Atomic Workers International Union in 1972 to seek rule changes that would provide for occupational safety and health rights of employees of Atomic Energy Commission licensees (Chapter 14), the IBEW declined the offer to join the petition effort stating, "It would not be in the best interests of PG&E employees."[71] Even the employees' union was taken in by PG&E's "go nuclear" attitude and didn't want to do anything that would rock the company's "Go-Nuclear Boat!"

It's no wonder PG&E was so openly transparent about not giving a tinker's damn for the "unnecessary and senseless" radiation exposures suffered by plant workers, just so long as "overexposure" did not occur. As far as Forrest Williams and I were concerned PG&E viewed employees, and I am now also referring to permanent plant employees (and not just to transient employees brought in the plant from elsewhere for the same purpose), as "radiation sponges" to accommodate management's prerogative to keep costs down and view employees as tools of production without any regard to the long-term consequences of radiation exposure.

By mid-1967, the RWP (Radiation Work Procedure known as "Routine Work Permits") that authorized nuclear control technicians to collect and analyze daily reactor water samples was completely out of date and in violation of the company's Radiation Control Standards at the Humboldt Bay nuclear facility (review Chapter 2). These RWP's were always subject to review by AEC compliance inspectors.

It's worth repeating that every attempt to get plant management to address the problem before the PG&E company safety meeting held on December 12, 1967, had failed. When I forced the issue at the safety meeting, I caused a brouhaha that didn't turn out well for me. It's also important to point out that not once did the AEC compliance inspectors cite PG&E for violating this radiation control standard, which was part of the Humboldt Bay's operating license.

How serious was the reactor water RWP violation? The radiation dose rate to the control technicians from each of the 1-liter samples that were collected every day ranged from 50 to 500 times greater than what was allowed by the RWP, and the exposure to the technicians at the collection site approached 2,000 times what was allowed by the RWP. The control technician's radiation exposure rate at the reactor water sample collection site far exceeded the samples themselves.

The same type of violation occurred during the same period of time with the daily procedures of collecting and analyzing off-gas samples. The nuclear control technicians were receiving "unnecessary and senseless" radiation exposures and PG&E wasn't the least bit concerned about it; neither was the AEC! Therefore, I decided to present these items along with several others at the company safety meeting on December 12, 1967.

Another item of concern that I brought up at the December 12 safety meeting concerned an incident that occurred in the radiochemistry laboratory the day prior to the safety meeting. My work assignment the previous day was in the radiochemistry laboratory. As I began my shift, I was routinely checking around in the lab with a Beta Gamma survey instrument (called a "GM" - see Image 14) to ensure everything was in order. The workbenches, specific areas where chemical testing apparatuses were located, and the laboratory sinks were checked first. Then, as I started moving towards the two "*chem-lab*" hoods (used to exhaust toxic fumes from laboratory procedures) located at the far end of the laboratory, the GM started recording readings way above background, and when I arrived at the chem-lab hood area the GM went completely off scale.

This was strange because I had not yet brought any hot samples into the lab. I immediately went to access control to pick up a Beta-Gamma Dose Rate Instrument known as a "CP" (short for "Cutie Pie" — see Image 15) .I found dose rate readings in the range of 2-3 Roentgens per hour. The radiation was coming from radioactive materials that were in an unmarked plastic bag located in the cabinet beneath the right *chem-lab* hood. The area was unsigned; there were no radiation ropes or tape or any thing of that sort to indicate the existence of a high radiation dose rate area as required by the company's radiation protection standards and procedures.

If I had not discovered the radioactive materials, I would have been standing in front of the hood later in the morning analyzing samples receiving exposure mostly to my feet and lower legs from a very hot source without knowing it. My film badge and pocket dosimeters would not have picked up much of the exposure because they were being worn on my chest and not on my lower extremities.

I checked with the nuclear control techs who normally worked in the radiochemistry lab in an attempt to determine who was responsible for indiscriminately placing those hot radioactive materials in the cabinet under the *chem-lab* hood without any warning to other people. None of the CTs knew anything about those samples.

I raised hell about it, first with the chemical engineer and then the plant engineer stating these kinds of things should never happen, all to no avail. As it turned out, the guilty culprit was a student engineer who had put those radioactive materials in the cabinet while working on a special project with a member of plant management! The student obviously didn't know any better and the engineer with whom he was working apparently was not paying attention to what the student was doing – in other words, he was not properly supervised in the radiation controlled area!

When I pointed this out to the plant engineer, I was again told I was overstepping my authority; that I needed to learn the difference between management's prerogative and my "proper role at the plant as a CT." It was always all about management's prerogative and how I was overstepping my authority every time I raised safety issues. Management prerogatives prevailed even in matters of radiation safety. Edgar Weeks put it in writing in a disciplinary memo to Forrest Williams that clearly reflected PG&E HBPP management philosophy at the nuclear facility:[72]

> You are reminded that an employee must carryout an order given by his supervisor even if he believes this order is unreasonable. In cases involving safety the employee may object to performing an assignment, which he considers unsafe, in which case the objection, or question, would be given

consideration by his supervisor. If the supervisor determines that the assignment is safe and can be performed, the employee may not refuse to perform this assignment without facing the possibility that such refusal may incur disciplinary action.

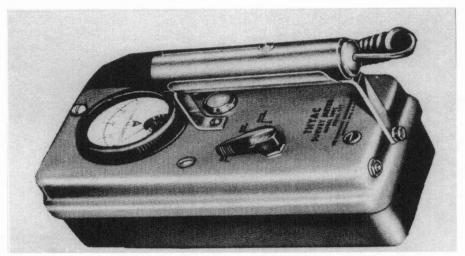

Image 15. "GM" Beta-Gamma Detection Instrument (From the author's files)

It is usually impossible to document how the company arbitrarily applies management prerogative in the nuclear workplace and the nonsensical reasoning that underlies it. However, a very good example of how it all works in the minds of PG&E management can be gleaned from the Forrest Williams disciplinary suspension and employment termination case.

Forrest Williams had been suspended from work without pay for refusing to do something he considered unsafe — and it was unquestionably unsafe! He was on suspension for four days "to think things over."[73] Forrest was told that if he did not agree to perform his work assignments without qualification upon his return to work, he would be terminated from the company. While Williams was on suspension he had a wart surgically removed from his hand.

When he returned to work, he asked not to be assigned work in the radiochemistry laboratory because of the open wound on his finger; he asked to stay out of the chemistry lab until his finger was completely healed. As a result of his request, Williams was assigned to radiation protection duties for one week.

On Monday of the following week, Bill Evans, one of the other nuclear control technicians, who had already been assigned to chemistry, went directly to the lab upon arriving at work. When Williams arrived, he first went into the change room to check the dressing on his finger. Edgar Weeks showed up and said, "Let's see that million dollar finger."[74] After looking at the wound on Williams' finger, Weeks said the wound had sufficiently healed to permit Williams to perform his assigned duties in radiochemistry laboratory.

Williams felt his finger had not yet sufficiently healed and wanted a few more days for his finger to completely heal before going into the lab.[75] Mr. Weeks said that he was not going to give Williams any more "healing time" and ordered him to immediately report to the Unit 3 radiochemistry laboratory. Williams refused to undertake what he felt to be an unacceptable risk by working in the lab before his wound had completely healed.

Williams was immediately sent home and subsequently discharged from PG&E the following day on May 26, 1970. The company doctor who examined Williams' finger on May 26 and Williams' doctor who examined the finger on May 27 both agreed that his finger had not yet healed. The company doctor, Dr. Dolfini, said that in his opinion the wound would not be healed until at least May 28;[76] Williams' doctor, Dr. Wittwer, said the wound would not be healed until May 29.[77]

PG&E's own HBPP Unit 3 Radiation Standards and Control Procedures stipulated:

> **The assignment of persons having skin breaks to work in radioactive materials areas should be avoided if possible.**

It was possible to avoid the assignment because other control technicians were clearly available to work in the lab. But even if other control technicians were not available, the nature and requirements of this particular assignment would have to be taken into consideration as to whether it was safe for Williams to perform the work assignment in the chemistry lab before his finger was completely healed.

The case in point included the part of the nuclear control technician's job that when assigned to radiochemistry was the collection, transport, and analysis of off-gas samples The off-gas sampling procedures required radioactive gas to be drawn into 14 cc vacuum vials at the off-gas sampling station. The vials were transported to the radiochemistry laboratory in lead pigs where they were placed by hand into a special container of water.

After the vials of off-gas were completely underwater and inverted, they were uncapped so that the trapped radioactive gas could be exposed to electrodes in the container. The gas was then ignited or "popped" by an electric arc across the electrodes. The gas literally exploded under water, leaving the container and the water in it highly radioactive. During this procedure, the technician's hands were completely immersed in the "hot" water (radioactively speaking). Sensitive feel was required for the procedure; therefore, the only hand protection worn was a pair of surgical gloves.

The surgical gloves could be potentially cut or torn without the technician knowing it during the collection of the samples or during the off-gas sampling procedure itself. If such a cut or tear occurred without the technician knowing it, and he subsequently immersed his gloved hands in

Image 15. "CP" Beta-Gamma Dose Rate Instrument
(From the author's file)

the "popping" container, small amounts of highly radioactive water could enter into the glove and remain there undetected by the nuclear control technician because he would not be able to distinguish it from the perspiration of his hands which normally collects inside the gloves.

Other mishaps could occur in the chemistry lab that might puncture or cut the surgical gloves, which would then provide the opportunity for highly radioactive liquids to enter the glove and contaminate the wound allowing the possibility of radioactive contaminants to enter the blood stream.

Why did Mr. Weeks force the chemistry issue on Williams? Plant management didn't need anybody in the radiochemistry lab; Bill Evans, one of the other control technicians, had already been assigned to work there. Plant management had already waited a week for Williams' finger to heal.

Why couldn't Mr. Weeks have waited a few more days before sending Williams into the radiochemistry lab? Was Williams' request for a few more days unreasonable? Two doctors didn't think so! The doctor who performed the surgery said Williams' wound had not yet healed. Even the company doctor agreed that Williams' wound had not yet healed.

In summary, Mr. Weeks was not interested in the risks he was asking Williams to take but was instead driven to exercise his management prerogative with an employee with whom he was personally at odds because of the employee's concern for radiation safety. Weeks put himself above both medical doctors when he determined on May 25 that Williams' wound was healed and ordered him "immediately" into the radiochemistry lab.

Attorney Frank Morgan, who represented Forrest Williams, reflected on PG&E's handling of the Williams matter with the following statement:[78]

> In light of Radiation Control Procedure Section II B 1, the company's position that they were even prepared to send Williams back to chemistry a week earlier on May 18 with an indisputable open wound is difficult to understand.[79] No wonder Mr. Williams and Mr. Rowen encountered disputes over safety matters.

The union attorney representing Williams in the arbitration case that eventually followed his termination advanced a "conspiracy theory" concocted by PG&E management and suggested this treatment of Williams provided what Mr. Weeks believed to be a convenient opportunity to get rid of one of the "conspirators."[80] *My Humboldt Diary: A True Story of Betrayal of the Public Trust* will address PG&E's incredible conspiracy, which will further expose PG&E's misguided strategy to defend a failed and dangerous technology.

Four Marine Pathfinders at Fort Benning June 1960 (author is on left)

__IV__

4. A Myriad of Betrayals

1967-68

"When I find out an AEC inspection is coming and we get a tentative date, I notify the supervisors and say in the message, be sure your house is in order, fellows."[81] [Edgar Weeks]

"...PG&E would receive advance notice of AEC compliance inspections. We would then be told to make sure the plant was ready for inspection and everyone was sent out to all areas of the facility to look for and correct problems. I reported this PG&E practice to Mr. J. J. Ward, AEC Investigator, and cited the contamination problems we had to clean up prior to the announced AEC inspections. I made it clear we were not allowed to talk to the AEC inspectors when they came into the plant and that plant management did not reveal the contamination problems to the AEC inspectors. What was the AEC investigator's response? 'Well, if they cleaned it up, what's your point?' I stated often that every AEC inspection should be unannounced just like those of the Strategic Air Command."[82] [Bob Rowen]

One would think it goes without saying that PG&E's nuclear house should always have been in order, 24-7! Well, it wasn't! But that really wasn't a problem for PG&E because the nuclear plant was given advance notice of inspections by the AEC compliance office, complete with a list of whom the inspectors would be and when they'd be *approximately* arriving at the plant.

The word would come down from the front office and we would go right to work putting "our house in order." After I complained publicly about the problem, both PG&E and the AEC used the power of the press to claim that some of the compliance inspections were unannounced. In the six years I worked at the nuclear plant, I never once saw an AEC compliance inspector in the plant that I did not know in advance that he was going to be there.

Advanced notice given to PG&E's nuclear plant management of impending compliance inspections by the AEC was a ridiculous and outrageous betrayal of the public trust. Why? Because this cozy relationship between the "regulators" and the "regulated" repeatedly provided PG&E opportunities to clean up citable conditions that were clear violations of the nuclear facility's operating license. This would enable the AEC to later proudly proclaim very publicly:[83]

> We believe that PG&E management personnel have fulfilled their responsibilities in a conscientious reliable manner. The Company has been cited only a few times for items of noncompliance and these items have been of a minor nature. There has been no evidence of irresponsible practices.

The AEC's legislative purpose of protecting atomic workers and the general public was unquestionably a shameful farce. (Chapter 13 of my *Diary* exposes the inadequacies of the Atomic Energy Commission's inept regulatory role)

Let us first consider some important general observations that have been made regarding radiation safety (some of which themselves are betrayals of the public trust) before delving into specific examples of PG&E's betrayals of the public trust at Humboldt Bay.

Of course PG&E would not have gotten away with the company's acts of betrayal of the public trust that my *Diary* will reveal and discuss, if the AEC had properly performed its regulatory function.

THE MOST AWESOME, THE MOST DEADLY, THE MOST DANGEROUS PROCESS . . .

We have yet to realize the full implications of "the most awesome, the most deadly, the most dangerous process that man has ever conceived," an observation made by Justice William O. Douglas on June 12, 1961.[84]

Justice William O. Douglas was addressing the "awesome ramifications" of nuclear power plant electrical generation when he issued his dissenting opinion in *Power Reactor Development Company v. Electricians.*

RADIATION FROM ATOMIC ENERGY IS A FAR, FAR MORE SERIOUS HAZARD TO HUMAN LIFE THAN ANYONE HAD EVER CONCEIVED IT TO BE . . .

Ten years after Justice Douglas wrote his June 12, 1961, observation previously mentioned, Drs. Gofman and Tamplin published their research findings that radiation from atomic energy is a far, far more serious hazard to human life that anyone had ever conceived it to be. Drs. Gofman and Tamplin also concluded that there is not a shred of evidence that AEC radiation standards for peaceful use of the atom are truly safe.

ESTABLISHING THE SAFETY OF ATOMIC PLANTS MUST COME FIRST . . .

When we look into the bowels of the historical development of nuclear power, we find another violation of the public trust in that it was perfectly okay for "safety findings" to be made after the construction of nuclear facilities.[85] And for that matter, it was also okay for the same illogical thinking to prevail regarding the long-term biological and genetic consequences of nuclear power plant operation.

LESSONS FROM HISTORY NOT HEEDED . . .

Not unlike the greedy, self-serving shenanigans of business tycoons during the Gilded Age buried in the annals of American history now generally ignored, we are again witnessing a disregard for employee and public safety, and for environmental protection. It's as if Americans are incapable of learning from the lessons of their own history. In today's caustic political environment we are constantly hearing a fervent outcry for the elimination of the Environmental Protection Agency and the fanatical demand for getting government "out-of-our-lives" altogether!

The antigovernment argument rages on claiming free-market mechanisms will take care of everything; that our liberties and freedoms are more important than our collective responsibilities to protect the workers, consumers, environment, and to provide for the public good.

The proponents of this line of thinking are currently spending tremendous sums of money in today's political arena to convince everyone else that we cannot trust our government. They equate government regulation to socialism or worse. They vehemently argue very loudly that government is eroding away our liberty and freedoms.

A couple of questions naturally emerge from the entire swirling hullabaloo about the government's overreach that's "eroding away our freedoms." Whose liberties and freedoms are we really talking about? Given the historical record regarding corporate responsibility, "Is it possible for an intelligent, well-informed American public to rely on corporations to protect workers, consumers, and the environment without meaningful and effective government regulation?

URANIUM MINES AND THEIR DEVASTATING IMPACTS ON PEOPLE . . .

We need to remember what happened in the uranium-mining region of the Colorado Plateau where the states of Colorado, Utah, New Mexico and Arizona share common borders. It was established during the fifties and sixties that miners in the Colorado Plateau "died simply because the government and the mining companies refused to apply well-established clinical data on the radiation hazards of uranium miners."[86] It was estimated 500 to 1,100 of the 6,000 who were uranium miners would die of lung cancer within the next 20 years because of excessive radiation exposure.[87] The Nuclear Juggernaut prevailed and the miners were not adequately protected.

The nuclear folks in America ignored the dangers the uranium miners of the Colorado Plateau had faced, dangers that incidentally had been documented by European scientists two decades earlier in a study that showed 65 percent of the uranium miners in the Erzgebirge Mountains of Germany and Czechoslovakia were dying during the 1930s of lung cancer.[88]

It wasn't only the uranium miners who were victimized by the nuclear establishment; there was also a huge problem with the radioactive waste from the mining operations known as "tailings." These tailings were used as landfill beneath schools, homes, stores, and other structures numbering in the thousands[89]

AEC CHAIRMAN GLENN SEABORG SAID, "ALL WE WANT IS THE TRUTH" . . .

In 1963 the Atomic Energy Commission asked Drs. John Gofman and Arthur Tamplin to undertake a series of long-range studies on potential dangers that might arise from the peaceful uses of the atom. Drs. Gofman and Tamplin were highly regarded research associates with impeccable credentials during the sixties at Lawrence Radiation Laboratory in Livermore, California. Arthur R. Tamplin was a group leader in the Biomedical Division at Lawrence Laboratory responsible for predicting the effects of radiation on man. John W. Gofman was Associate Director of the Lawrence Laboratory from 1963 to 1969 and a co-discoverer of several radioisotopes and had done extensive research in radiochemistry, macromolecules, chromosomes, cancer, and radiation hazards.

Nuclear generation of electrical power was the primary focus of these studies by Gofman and Tamplin. Chairman Glenn Seaborg of the U. S. Atomic Energy Commission assured the investigators that he wanted "favorable or unfavorable findings made available to the public"[90] stating, "All we want is the truth."[91]

Gofman and Tamplin succinctly summed up their research findings in the following two statements:[92]

Radiation, to be expected from several atomic energy programs burgeoning rapidly, is a far, far more serious hazard to humans than any of the so-called "experts" had previously thought possible.

The hazard to this generation of humans from cancer and leukemia as a result of atomic radiation is TWENTY TIMES as great as had been thought previously. The hazard to all future generations in the form of genetic damage and deaths, had been underestimated even more seriously.

Gofman and Tamplin learned to their great dismay that Seaborg's assurances were illusory. Their research findings proved to be quite unwelcome, and earned Gofman and Tamplin "a torrent of vitriol and personal condemnation from three major sources: (1) The U.S. Atomic Energy Commission; (2) The Joint Committee on Atomic Energy; and (3) The Electric Utility Industry."[93] Examing what these three groups had in common, Gofman and Tamplin concluded "these three groups act in concert as a powerful, promotional triumvirate for nuclear electricity generation."[94]

THIS UNIQUE PERSPECTIVE WAS ONLY MADE POSSIBLE THROUGH . . .

The writing of *My Humboldt Diary* from its unique perspective was only made possible through personal experience inside the nuclear juggernaut coupled with the following reflective conclusions of Gofman and Tamplin from which I grew much needed strength to survive the aftermath of my PG&E ordeal:[95]

> The entire nuclear electricity industry had been developing under a set of totally false illusions of safety and economy. Not only was there a total lack of appreciation of the hazards of radiation for man, but there was a total absence of candor concerning the hazard of serious accidents. The economics were being treated with rose-colored glasses. And the triumvirate knew all too well that the stampede to nuclear power, initiated by them, could not possibly tolerate the bright light of exposure to public scrutiny. The more deeply we probed, the more we realized how massive the deception truly was. It became quite clear that concealment of truth from the public was regarded as essential. And we realized very clearly why the violent reaction had greeted our presentation of the research findings concerning the radiation hazard to humans.

PG&E SURPRISINGLY AND PROFOUNDLY CHANGED ITS TUNE . . .

Edgar Weeks, PG&E's Humboldt Bay Plant Engineer, issued a prepared statement in response to one of my questions concerning the risk of chronic exposure to low-level ionizing radiation that I had raised very publicly at the May 20, 1970 PG&E safety meeting at Humboldt Bay (Chapter 10). His response appeared to be prepared by PG&E's legal department at corporate headquarters. This response by the company, which was two weeks after Forrest Williams and I were fired, came one month following the now infamous May 20 safety meeting in 1970.

Attached to the written summary of Edgar Weeks' presentation that was circulated throughout the plant and posted for several weeks in the Unit 3 Control Room of the nuclear facility, were the following statements couched in much doublespeak concerning the "acceptable risk" of occupational exposure to ionizing radiation. Weeks quoted from several sources including the International Commission on Radiation Protection, the National Committee on Radiation Protection, and the Federal Radiation Council.

The statements itemized below loomed out of the written summary of his presentation. Mr. Weeks and I had discussed and argued these points regarding radiation safety many times and I was more than surprised to see them in his presentation:

As a matter of principle it is sound to avoid all unnecessary exposure to ionizing radiation because it is desirable not to depart from the natural conditions under which man has developed by evolutionary processes.[96]

Exposure to ionizing radiation can result in injuries that manifest themselves in the exposed individual and in his descendants: these are called somatic and genetic injuries respectively.[97]

Late somatic injuries include leukemia and other malignant diseases, impaired fertility, cataracts and shorting of life. Genetic injuries manifest themselves in the offspring of irradiated individuals, and may not be apparent for many generations. Their detrimental effect can spread throughout a population by mating of exposed individuals with other members of the population.[98]

Any departure from the environmental conditions in which man has evolved may entail a risk of deleterious effect. It is therefore assumed that long continued exposure to ionizing radiation additional to that due to natural radiation involves some risk.[99]

Nearly two years earlier, I had tried to discuss my previously mentioned research findings (the ones that had caused me a lot of grief) with the nuclear plant's radiation protection engineer (ten of those findings are presented in Chapter 2 of my *Diary on* pages 60-62) and, after I brought up my "White Paper" (Appendix 1) on the related subject matter, I was immediately sent to Edgar Weeks to be raked over the coals.

After Mr. Weeks reviewed the material, he emphatically declared that my information was "one hundred percent wrong!" Weeks made it abundantly clear that he did not appreciate the "implied accusations" I was making against PG&E and its management personnel (review Chapter 2).

Nearly two years later Weeks made a complete turnabout after my May 20 *query declarare*: "I want to know if PG&E considers chronic exposure to low-level ionizing radiation carcinogenic?" Weeks announced at the June 23, 1970 PG&E safety meeting at Humboldt Bay that "the company's radiation protection standards are established on the basis of making radiation exposure an acceptable risk,"[100] and concluded his remarks with the following statement:

In the final analysis it remains for the individual to weigh the potential risks of working in this industry against the benefits he can expect to receive and judge by choice of occupations accordingly.[101]

This surprising declaration by Weeks (most likely prepared by PG&E's legal department) was presented to the HBPP employees shortly after Williams and I were fired from the company (see **Appendix III** for a comparison of my statements to those of Edgar Weeks).

PG&E's PATERNALISM REVEALED . . .

What did Mr. Weeks mean by "benefits?" He didn't expand on it in his remarks but I knew exactly what he was referring to because I had heard it many times in his private "counseling sessions" with me.

It's called a "paycheck" that employees should be thankful for because "it represents a very good livelihood that provides for the welfare of our families."

This paternalistic attitude by company officials was reflected even more clearly in the sworn testimony of Mr. Victor Novarino, PG&E Division Manager, during Forrest Williams' arbitration hearing. PG&E attorney, Lawrence V. "Bud" Brown wrote into PG&E's brief the following statement:[102]

His (Forrest Williams) refusal to do work he no longer considered safe or acceptable was discussed by the three levels of supervision at the plant: his immediate supervisor, Mr. Boots; the Power Plant Engineer, Mr. Weeks; and the acting Plant Superintendent, Mr. Raymond.

Later, after Mr. Williams was suspended, the matter was further discussed with him by the Division Personnel Manager, Mr. Taylor, and finally by the Division Manager, Mr. Novarino.

Mr. Novarino's testimony is indicative of the Company's concern for Mr. Williams and the effort put forth to dissuade him from a course of action inimical with his continued employment (Chapter 11).

Mr. Novarino's testimony included "He (Forrest Williams) was threatening, as I understood it, at the meeting to leave his employ, jeopardize his income and the fact that he had a family, which depended on that . . ." and " . . . as he still refused to accept the assignments, he was suspended for four days, rather than fired, to provide him a cooling-off period in which to consider the future effect of his action on his family as well as himself." . . .

Mr. Brown: Would you tell us very briefly, if you can, what took place at that meeting and any part of the discussion that you might have taken part in.

Mr. Navarino: Well, primarily I was interested in attending the meeting because this young man had appeared to be so adamant in his position that he couldn't continue doing work which he had been doing for several years as an employee. And having reached such a critical point, I wanted to let him know that there was a grievance procedure, which I'm sure he already knew. And yet he didn't follow the grievance procedure.

He was threatening, as I understood it, at the meeting to leave his employ, jeopardize his income and the fact that he had a family, which depended on that and act as a one-man committee in rebellion for something that he had been doing for quite a while. And I was interested in just what was making him do that.

What Navarino's testimony completely and shamefully ignored, and the PG&E attorney absolutely knew it, was the ever increasing levels of radiation throughout the plant thus making working conditions more dangerous and unacceptable to Williams.

ANOTHER EXERCISE OF ARBITRARY MANAGEMENT PREROGATIVES IN OUR NUCLEAR WORKPLACE . . .

On March 3, 1970, and again on March 6, 1970, there ensued a flap between Forrest Williams, a control technician assigned to nuclear instrumentation repair work, and his temporary supervisor, R. S. Chaffee. Mr. Chaffee was demanding that Williams work under a heat lamp while making repairs to a Log N amplifier.

Williams told Chaffee that he had done this work many times and the heat lamp was not necessary so long as all components were adequately cleaned at the conclusion of the repairs. Williams explained to Chaffee what was involved in the cleaning procedure and that it was an acceptable industry standard. Chafee left the nuclear instrument lab and when he returned to find Williams still working on the Log N amplifier without using the heat lamp, he charged Williams with insubordination. This insubordination resulted in time off without pay and a disciplinary entry into Williams' "black book" personnel file.

Mr. Chaffee was new and temporary to the Unit 3 nuclear instrumentation lab, having been reassigned as a temporary first-line supervisor from the instrument repair shop of Units 1 and 2. All the nuclear control technicians had done the kind of work that Forrest was doing and heat lamps were definitely not needed.

Chaffee knew a black book was being maintained by first-line supervision on both Williams and me, and it was clear to both of us that he wanted to make some points for himself with Edgar Weeks by writing Williams up; there was no other rational explanation for Chaffee's decision to force this ridiculous issue with Williams.

When John Kamberg was promoted from control technician to nuclear instrument foreman a few weeks following Chaffee's ridiculous escapade, he set the record straight stating heat lamps were not necessary for the kind of work Williams was doing so long as adequate cleaning of the components took place at the end of the repair work.

A POTENTIAL LETHAL EXPOSURE DUE TO LACK OF TRAINING . . .

Forrest Williams was the newest control technician added to the nuclear control technician group. Forrest had actually started work at the plant before I did. His first job at the plant was shift helper, which was at the very bottom of the Humboldt Bay Nuclear Plant food chain. Forrest was eventually promoted from shift helper to apprentice instrument repairman and was in the training cycles behind me by only a few months.

Forrest had served in the U.S. Navy and was involved in the atomic bomb testing program in the Pacific during his service time in the Navy as a crew member aboard a sea going rescue tug. Forrest was intelligent and highly motivated.

Forrest was selected into the nuclear control technician-training program from the apprentice instrument repairman-training program. Like me, Forrest had a strong desire to advance his education as evidenced by his commitment to attend college classes at night while completing PG&E's nuclear control technician apprenticeship training program and working full time during the day. Like me, he was willing to ask questions when he felt it necessary.

Forrest believed that when he first started working in the nuclear unit his training in radiation protection was sorely lacking, and he provided an example of what could have been a fatal exposure to radiation during his early tenure at the plant as an apprentice instrument repairman. He explained that on one occasion he had been assigned to work with Kenneth Sadoian, a student engineer who was investigating the spent fuel elements stored in the spent fuel pool.

They were using a borescope under water when Williams attempted to pull a fuel element up out of the water. The automatic stop on the hoist prevented him from completing the task.

Forrest later learned that if the stop had not been there, or had not functioned properly, and if the fuel element had been lifted out of the water he and the student engineer would have received a fatal dose of radiation.

Forrest had no idea at the time how catastrophic it would have been for him and the student engineer if he had pulled the spent fuel element out of the water. At the time of this incident, Forrest had worked in his new position for only three weeks. This incident was a major item of concern at the August 23, 1966, PG&E HBPP Safety Meeting that generated many questions that were embarrassing to plant management.

How could something like this have happened? Plant management was without question completely responsible for it! Essentially, the whole affair unfortunately just faded away and was forgotten about by PG&E management (at all levels).

TRANSIENT WORKERS USED AS RADIATION SPONGES SORELY LACKED RADIATION PROTECTION TRAINING . . .

Forrest Williams and I believed PG&E just maintained a facade of safety that personnel were being protected in the nuclear workplace; nuclear control technicians were under much pressure to maintain this appearance. Plant management often put temporary workers into hazardous areas with minimal training in radiation protection.

For example, PG&E management would bring in machinists from other non-nuclear plants to do repair and maintenance work during reactor refueling outages and plant overhauls. These temporary workers were lucky if they received even a minimal amount of instructions in the hazards they were being subjected to.

When these temporary employees (known as "radiation sponges") were assigned to do work in "hot" areas, they would sometimes "run off their dosimeter pencils" (i.e., go off scale on a 200 mr pocket dosimeter) because they were not closely watching their time. It was the job of the CTs to keep that from happening but we were often spread too thin to insure that all temporary workers throughout the plant were staying within the requirements of their SWPs.

For example, if an employee was wearing a 200 mr dosimeter, which was the range of the vast majority of the dosimeters in the plant, and the work location was in an exact 1-R field, the employee could only be in that work area for a maximum of 12 minutes before going off scale. If he were to continue working in that area, he would have to be given a newly charged dosimeter that would be good for another twelve minutes. The maximum amount of time the employee could work in the described area would be something less than 3 hours at which time he would be maxed out on his allowable occupational exposure (for a three month period) and therefore, he would have to be sent home.

The location directly under the reactor was one of the hottest radiation zones in the plant. The actual exposure rates immediately below the reactor vessel involved exposure rates far exceeding the example just provided. The incore flushing work at the bottom of the reactor vessel was extremely hazardous and will be covered later in my *Diary*.

Williams and I witnessed times when these employees would sometimes forget to wear their pocket dosimeters and film badges and the control technician in charge of monitoring the job and responsible for compliance with the special work permit (SWP) would then have to estimate the worker's exposure. I often wondered how many times this problem went undetected. As previously stated, the radiation protection personnel were all too busy to keep a close eye on everyone all the time and to carefully check each man as he reported for work and to check him out afterwards.

Contrary to plant management's claims, there were employees who were generally not skilled in checking themselves out of the controlled area and no one was assigned to ensure the workers were clean when they left Unit 3. It was the responsibility of each person to check himself for contamination with the frisker probe and the hand-and-foot counter (see Image 16).

Contamination could be imbedded in the soles of the shoes and detected by the foot counter. An employee (on his own) would then sometimes take his shoes off and wash them with water at the decon sink. While the soles were still wet, the employee would recheck himself to determine if everything was okay. A problem on occasion was the still wet shoe could moderate the radiation coming off the embedded particle thus allowing it to be taken off site without the employee knowing it.

We were constantly dealing with temporary workers who presented problems to themselves and to others. One specific example was a traveling mechanic who one day was working in the turbine enclosure area immediately after lunch. I personally discovered him running his finger around inside his mouth along his gums to clean out the remains of a peanut butter sandwich he had eaten. He did have his surgical gloves on but they were black with grime from the work he was doing on the open turbine. I immediately had him go to access control to rinse his mouth out and undergo a decon check.

After I explained why he should not have put his contaminated glove finger in his mouth that contained particulate matter from the radioactive steam driving the turbine, the transient employee said he didn't know that he was doing anything wrong.

I not only reported this incident to the radiation protection engineer (to no avail) but also later reported it to AEC investigator, Mr. J. J. Ward. Mr. Ward's response following his investigation: "PG&E has a training program for such employees, which appears to be satisfactory." (See "Allegation #17" and the related "AEC Finding" in Chapter 13)

PG&E's BETRAYALS OF THE PUBLIC TRUST MUST ALSO INCLUDE NOT ONLY THE . . .

PG&E's betrayals of the public trust must also include not only the radiologic insults to employees but to the general public as well. It is important to understand that the policies and practices inside a nuclear facility also reflect not only on the employees who work there but also on the environs of the facility and the general public at large for it is impossible to isolate one from the other.

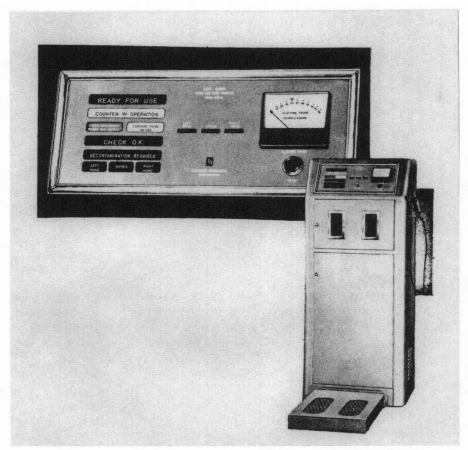

Image 16. Beta-Gamma Hand-and-Foot Counter (From the author's files)

PG&E's RABBIT PROJECT AKA PG&E'S RIDICULOUS RABBIT CAPER . . .

From the outset of nuclear operations at Humboldt Bay, PG&E operated an environmental monitoring program designed "to determine the effects the nuclear facility was having on the environs of the plant."

One incredible element of the program was the addition of the rabbit-testing program. This program began with the building of rabbit cages containing wire-screen floors and placing the cages on the ground with the idea that the caged rabbits would eat the grass poking up through the wire-screen bottoms. This "brainchild" was the product of the nuclear facility's radiation protection engineer who had a degree in air conditioning (although he may have had some help from PG&E's corporate headquarters).

The grass would absorb whatever amount of radioactive fallout was being released from the plant, which included the fission byproduct Iodine-131, from the 250 ft. gaseous radioactive waste discharge stack. Then after a time the rabbits would be taken to a local veterinarian for slaughter so the thyroid glands could be removed and sent to a special lab for analysis.

The goal of this project was to determine the amount of Iodine-131 being absorbed by the rabbits. When Iodine-131 is ingested into the body it seeks out the thyroid gland. I was made a reluctant *partner-in-crime* in this ridiculous radioactive environmental monitoring program described by a PG&E Senior Vice President in the following way: "...rabbit thyroids are forwarded to Hazelton Nuclear Science Corporation for iodine-131 analysis . . . Rabbit thyroids are mounted in a 3-inch by 3-inch diameter plastic container and counted on a 3-inch Na I (Te) crystal."[103]

While it is true that Iodine-131 is a radioisotope, which has medical and pharmaceutical uses, something PG&E was always quick to point out, it is also one of the major radiological hazards among the byproducts of nuclear fission.

Iodine-131 was a significant contributor to the ill health effects from open-air atomic bomb testing in the 1950s, and from the Chernobyl disaster. Due to its mode of beta decay, Iodine-131 is notable for causing mutation and death in cells, which it penetrates. For this reason, high doses of the radioisotope are paradoxically less dangerous than low doses, since they tend to kill tissues, which would otherwise become cancerous. Much smaller incidental doses of Iodine-131 than are used in medical treatment, are thought to be the major cause of increased thyroid cancers after accidental nuclear contamination.

While the PG&E rabbits were on the ground, they didn't eat very much grass. That was because, as anyone who has raised rabbits would have already guessed, the wire-screen floor of the cages became thick and matted down with rabbit droppings thereby eliminating grass as a food source.

PG&E plant management then modified its plan and put the cages on stands to raise the rabbits off the ground. That way most of their droppings could fall through the wire-screen floor of the cage, and the control techs were left with the responsibility of cutting the grass by hand and throwing the grass clippings into the cages.

The rabbits didn't do very well with this arrangement either so plant management decided to augment the rabbit "grass-food" supply with commercial rabbit food bought from a local feed store. The rabbits ended up eating mostly the commercial rabbit food bought from Nilsen Company, a local feed store in downtown Eureka and PG&E continued taking the rabbits to slaughter and sending the extracted thyroids to the lab for analysis.

The whole rabbit-testing program was one huge public relations scam that PG&E should have been ashamed of. I confronted plant management about it. I told Edgar Weeks that if the company really wanted to do something meaningful and more honest, we could put a couple of cows out there and let them graze on the grass; there was a lot of grass available for grazing. Mr. Weeks became irritated with me and said I was "overstepping my authority."

Image 17. Nilsen Company Feed Store, Eureka, California (Photo by author)

Edgar Weeks again expressed his unhappiness with my job performance, which was becoming routine for him. Of course my poor job performance was always couched in my "bad attitude" and personal desire to constantly criticize company policy and plant management. Law professor Bill Rodgers commented on PG&E's rabbit testing program, "The sophisticated thyroid analysis conducted at the Hazelton Nuclear Science Corporation might as well have been run on rabbits from Timbuctoo."[104]

AN IMMORAL AND ILLEGAL TRANSPORT OF SOGGY RADIATION WASTE BOXES . . .

The Humboldt Bay nuclear facility had experienced a series of unexpected reactor shutdowns. The fact that this happened in itself is another part of the Humboldt Bay story. What needs to be told here, however, is how the impact of these shutdowns resulted in the accumulation of excessive amounts of radioactive waste and how PG&E plant management chose to deal with that very serious problem.

A nuclear power plant produces waste materials not unlike fossil fuel plants, except the waste materials are radioactive. The HBPP Unit 3 waste materials ranged from old packing glands taken from valves that were serviced, to rags used in clean up operations following a variety of plant maintenance jobs; old electrical wire that been replaced; mop heads that were used to clean up radioactive liquid spills; waste paper, plastic, used pieces of welding rods, broken glass, chem-wipes, and various kinds of debris swept from the floor.

In summary, the waste materials consisted of all those throwaway materials following a routine refueling and maintenance outage to an emergency reactor shutdown when systems were opened up and work performed. All waste materials inside the radiation-controlled area of the plant were treated as radioactively contaminated materials and therefore designated as radiation waste.

In PG&E's Humboldt Bay nuclear facility the solid waste materials were identified as either "high-level" waste or "low-level" waste and treated accordingly. This part of my *Diary* only concerns the low-level radioactive waste materials that were accumulated during a series of unexpected outages. Low-level rad waste materials are still very much radioactive and consist of many different radioisotopes.

The regulations regarding the handling of low-level radioactive waste materials were very specific and quite demanding – at least in theory. These radioactive waste materials were placed in specially designed, heavily constructed cardboard boxes lined with thick acetate bags. These boxes were labeled with the hazardous radioactive material sign on all four sides of the box.

The content of each box could not exceed 80 pounds. When a radioactive materials box was full as determined by either volume or weight, it would be sealed, labeled, set aside, and replaced with a new box. Eventually the sealed boxes would be moved to the low-level radiation waste storage building located directly behind the refueling building. When the low level storage building approached full capacity, a freight truck would pick up the boxes of radioactive waste and transport them to the radioactive waste disposal site located in a desert area of eastern Washington.

A series of unexpected outages generated an exceptional amount of waste and the low-level storage building was filled to capacity. Boxes of radioactive waste started to stack up throughout the plant. Plant management decided to put wooden pallets on the asphalt pad located behind the low-level waste storage building in an area called Buhne Point.

This asphalt pad was on completely exposed higher ground with absolutely no protection from the elements. The radiation waste cardboard storage boxes were then stacked on top of one another four to six high. A large sheet of plastic was place over the stacked boxes, which was then covered by a large canvas tarp and tied down with rope.

Image 18. Radiation Hazard Sign (From the author's collection)

The entire pile of boxes continued to grow in size, as each time there was an outage more boxes were added to the pile. When boxes were added to the growing pile, all the protective coverings had to be removed and then replaced. The pile of radioactive waste storage boxes became huge.

I told plant management several times that those boxes needed to be shipped out because the developing situation on Buhne Point was becoming a dangerous problem. Then the nightmare happened!

A big storm hit the north coast with much rain and high winds. During the first night of the storm, the protective coverings became undone and the cardboard boxes soaked. The problem was discovered shortly after daybreak and we were sent to the area to try to secure the pile of soggy boxes. It was a total disaster. During the night, the gale force winds had caused an extremely hazardous condition and it was still raining extremely hard. Eventually, the pile of boxes was made secure with a lot more rope and new plastic but the damage had already been done – the integrity of the boxes had been lost.

PG&E finally had a truck come to the plant. It was parked outside the controlled area at the access gate closest to the pile of radiation waste boxes that were located inside the controlled area. I made the suggestion we replace all the soggy boxes, as there were a lot of them, by transferring their contents into new boxes. My idea was rejected.

With the aid of a forklift we started loading the truck. The weight of the upper boxes pushed down on the soggy cardboard boxes causing the sharp objects inside the boxes to puncture the acetate bags, which allowed rainwater to partially fill the bags.

Many of the boxes now weighed more that 80 pounds. As the boxes were being moved into the enclosed truck, I noticed water starting to drip from the belly of the truck. This was not a good situation to say the least! I complained and refused to put my name on the release papers, which really didn't matter because someone else ended up taking care of that.

The truck eventually pulled away from the plant with radioactively contaminated water dripping from the belly of it. The truck then travel north on US 101, turned east on Hwy 299 just north of Arcata, then turned north again on US I-5 at Redding, California and continued on all the way to Washington.

I was absolutely livid and expressed myself accordingly, which landed me in Edgar Weeks' office. Plant management had already raked me over the coals for my "always causing trouble" and for my "continued bad attitude." Mr. Weeks told me it was not my place to make the kinds of judgments that I was making and that it is my responsibility to promote harmony, not dissension.

According to Weeks, I was to follow orders and not question anything. Period! Well, I didn't buy it. The idea that I was to follow orders even if I believed they were unreasonable was totally unacceptable to me. I believed there was too much at stake.

AN EMPLOYEE GOES TO LUNCH RADIOACTIVELY CONTAMINATED . . .

PG&E employees in the Humboldt nuclear facility were continuously exposed to conditions during refueling and maintenance operations that frequently resulted in personal contamination of their bodies and clothing.

On April 29, 1970, during the morning hours, Raymond Skidmore, a nuclear control technician, was engaged in performing work in the first and second levels of the lower dry well. His work activities included removing switches on control rod drives, removing a dew cell, and replacing several solenoid valves located on the underside of the reactor vessel.

This particular work area in the plant, known as "Minus-66," was a miserable work environment because of the exceedingly high temperature, high humidity, extremely high radiation dose rates, large amounts of smearable radioactive contamination, and poor ventilation. Employees had to access this area under the reactor using a "man-lift," which was a 2-foot wide belt on rollers with a small platform just large enough for an employee to stand on and a corresponding handhold approximately chest high.

The man lift was accessed at the "Minus-14 elevation" and provided access to various areas along side of the reactor vessel all the way to the bottom of the access shaft. There was another secondary "step-off pad" and access control station to the area directly beneath the reactor at "Minus-66."

When the nuclear control technicians were assigned to flush incores and perform the related work directly under the reactor, they always felt they more than earned their pay that day. A major concern of mine about the work on the control rod drive switches was the amount of exposure to the head of the employee.

We had to get up close to the underside of the reactor vessel where the dose rate was in the several roentgens per hour range, which meant we could not be up in that area very long. The working quarters were tight, the air was stale, it was very hot and humid, and dripping wet everywhere. And again, it was an extremely high radiation area.

When Skidmore broke for lunch thus leaving the "Minus-66" area, he initially discovered at the "Plus-27" access control point that his coveralls, hood, and forearms were grossly contaminated.

After discarding his contaminated protective clothing and washing his forearms in the decon sink, he checked himself at the frisker station located just outside the access control dressing room and discovered his underclothing was also contaminated. He took those items of clothing off, put on his trousers and shirt and went to lunch. Upon returning from lunch, it was determined that a more thorough survey needed to be conducted.

According to a PG&E confidential memorandum signed by J. V. Boots, dated May 13, 1970, it was never clearly established who made the determination that a more thorough survey should have been conducted before Skidmore went to lunch; it was suggested in the memo that it was either Skidmore himself, or the Rad Protection Control Technician on duty, who was Don Woods.

In any event the subsequent survey, recorded in PG&E Special Radiation Survey Report No. 2214, revealed the following contamination levels of Skidmore's clothing: Undershirt 3,000 c/m; undershorts 3,000 c/m; socks 400 c/m; trousers 1,400 c/m; shirt 500 c/m; and shoe strings 200 c/m.

Skidmore had left Unit 3 to go to lunch radioactively contaminated. Upon returning from lunch, the rest of his clothing was confiscated and he had to take a shower at the decon station at access control.

Boots concluded his memo by stating the control technicians directly involved in this incident (naming Don Woods, Bill Evans, and Raymond Skidmore) were all "admonished for not following proper procedures." What those procedures were in this particular incident were never identified by Boots. It was just more convenient to engage in window dressing of the the real problem of the working conditions under the reactor.

GC EMPLOYEES LEFT THE NUCLEAR FACILITY RADIOACTIVELY CONTAMINATED AND THEIR CONDITION WAS DISCOVERED FOUR DAYS LATER . . .

One morning as I was heading out to the clean side of the railroad gate to do the routine job of surveying the painting equipment belonging to the General Construction ("GC") painters, I was thinking about what a great day it was. The painting crew was meeting me at the railroad access gate on the "clean side." I had my GM in hand, along with a large roll of plastic and the required unconditional release tags, ready to check their equipment and send the painters on their merry way, or so I thought.

Raymond Skidmore, one of the other control technicians, unlocked the gate from his side (inside the radiation controlled area), swung the gate open and between the two of us working together, we transferred the painting equipment from his side across the control line to a sheet of plastic I had laid down on my side believing everything was going to be a snap, since a preliminary survey by Skidmore had already indicated the equipment was ready for release. Skidmore did say he was having a bit of trouble with his background readings on his GM, which also added to the necessity for us to conduct this final survey. So what I was doing simply amounted to making a final check of the painting equipment to ensure it was okay for an unconditional release, which was standard procedure.

As I started to move the probe towards the equipment, the painters moved up closer to see what I was doing and the clicking in my earphones significantly increased.

"What the hell is going on here?" I asked.

The equipment was supposed to be clean, but initially nothing was making any sense as I moved the probe of the GM around the equipment. Then as I inadvertently moved the probe towards one of the painters, who had stepped up to see what I was doing, and the GM went crazy.

I immediately determined the painter was "crapped up" (a slang phrase used by atomic workers to indicate someone or something is radioactively contaminated)! I checked the other two painters; they were also "crapped up."

I asked them when they had last been in the radiation-controlled area and they all said, "We haven't been in there for several days."

I asked how they could have left the controlled area in this condition and they simply did not know.

I told all of them to go immediately through the gate and accompany Skidmore to access control.

They asked, "With our street clothes on?"

My response was, "Absolutely, do it right now! You're all crapped up anyway, so just go with Skidmore and I'll meet you guys at the step-off pad in a few."

I had to go around the outside of the plant, through the bottom part of

Unit #2, up a flight of stairs by Unit 2, then through the reactor control room to get to the change room and access control.

Skidmore had already confiscated all their clothing by the time I arrived and the two men were scrubbing down in the decon (decontamination) showers. I immediately notified the radiation protection engineer, Gail Allen, of the problem and he, in turn, immediately reported to access control.

While we were waiting for Allen, we checked the access control log to determine just when the painters were last in the radiation controlled area and sure enough, it had been four days since they had last been inside the radiation controlled area of Unit 3.

After explaining to Allen what had happened, I suggested we go to every place each of the painters had been during the past four days and check for contamination problems.

Allen quickly said, "No, we're not going to do that!"

He didn't even take a minute to think about it. It was obvious to me what was going down here, so I requested to meet with his supervisor, Plant Engineer Edgar Weeks. Again, I said we should backtrack to every place these men had been during the past four days. The answer from Weeks was the same. By this time I became enraged and expressed myself accordingly.

I told Mr. Weeks that the company was more concerned about its public image than about doing the right thing, and admittedly I wasn't very diplomatic about it; I mean, why should I have been? This was such a blatant disregard of public safety in exchange for maintaining the façade of how safe PG&E operated the nuclear facility and how far the company was willing to go to protect its public image.

The whole affair was covered up and the AEC, the California Department of Public Health, or any other regulatory body never had to address what had taken place. Let's be clear about this incident. If the public had been made aware of the incident at the time it happen, there would have been an outcry for action and an expectation that proper radiation surveys of the places these employees had been would have taken place.

This incident and its handling by PG&E was a flagrant and serious violation of radiation control, protection, and public safety policy and procedures.

PG&E later denied that this incident ever took place and the AEC concurred with the company stating, "No substantiation was found for this allegation." (See Allegation #49 in Chapter 13) The following is my direct examination of Raymond Skidmore at my California Unemployment Appeals Board Hearing:[105]

> **Mr. Rowen:** (Directed to Mr. Skidmore . . .) Referring to – and I can't remember the exact date – but in any event, do you recall surveying out some equipment for the GC painters?
>
> **Mr. Skidmore:** I have on many occasions.
>
> **Mr. Rowen:** Do you recall a particular occasion where you

found the GC painting crew contaminated?

Mr. Skidmore: Yes

Mr. Rowen: Can you explain what happened?

Mr. Skidmore: Jackson and – one of his crew members – wanted some material surveyed out. It was out at the fence.

Mr. Rowen: On the clean side or the controlled side of the fence?

Mr. Skidmore: No, it was on the crapped up side out back.

Mr. Brown (PG&E attorney): That means the controlled side.

Mr. Skidmore: The painters were on the clean side.

REFEREE: Where was this material, on the controlled side or the uncontrolled side?

Mr. Skidmore: I was trying to survey it out and I was getting my background, which wasn't normal, and so I took the GM . . . (INTERRUPTED)

I was on the clean side of the railroad gate along with the painters – Skidmore was on the radiation controlled area side of the railroad gate and pushed over the painting equipment onto the clean acetate I had laid down for my final check with the GM I had – the equipment was okay but the painters were not!

My direct examination of Skidmore continued:[106]

Mr. Rowen: (Directed to Mr. Skidmmore . . .) GM is a portable surveying instrument?

Mr. Skidmore: Right, and I found out that the painters were contaminated, and so I had to go up to the change room and check them out and I found out that all their clothing was contaminated and their bodies – I don't know the count, but several thousand and I had to have them take showers.

Mr. Rowen: Let me interject one question. Where was it that you suspected these painters received this contamination?

Mr. Brown (PG&E attorney): Objection. Calling for an opinion.

Mr. Rowen: He investigated this and it became known in company records.

REFEREE: Have you investigated the incident in question?

Mr. Skidmore: Yes, we did. We found out that the painters had been in the controlled area several days earlier.

Mr. Rowen: In the controlled area?

Mr. Skidmore: Yes, that this must have got them contaminated three or four days before and they hadn't checked out properly. All of their clothing was taken away from them and it went further.

Rowen got involved because he was CT II and he requested maybe they should be checked – check their homes, which Gail Allen refused to do. But he did have me go down and check the painter's cars, which I did do and I didn't find anything.

This line of questioning was interrupted, and then later revisited by the PG&E attorney a few minutes later.[107]

Mr. Brown (PG&E attorney): (Directed to Mr. Skidmore . . .) Now, calling your attention to your testimony with regard to surveying the GC crew, is it not a fact, Mr. Skidmore, that the very purpose of the control technician is to perform such surveys?

Mr. Skidmore: That's correct.

Mr. Brown And, the very reason for having you people there is to make sure that those persons who are contaminated don't get out of the area. Isn't that right?

Mr. Skidmore: That is not correct. The maddening part of it is that there is no way in the world we could, what you call police them, to keep these guys from . . .

Mr. Brown Go ahead. You started to say something.

Mr. Skidmore: Our job is to . . . we have three jobs. The "rad" protection job . . .

Mr. Brown I don't think you're answering my question and I . . . (INTERRUPTED)

Mr. Skidmore: No. That wasn't the answer to the question you asked, but . . .

Mr. Brown: Well, I'm saying at this point that it is because you apparently were performing your work when you picked up the fact that these men were contaminated and then . . . (INTERRUPTED)

Mr. Skidmore: Yes. That's it definitely.

Mr. Brown: And then, one of the control technicians examined the cars, isn't that correct, that these men rode in?

Mr. Skidmore: Yeah. I examined the cars.

Mr. Brown: The purpose of that would be to determine if they were carrying radioactive material out into the area beyond the plant. Isn't that true?

Mr. Skidmore: Uhmm.

Mr. Brown: And, if they were carrying out radioactive particles, they could be deposited at that place. That's your first point. Is it not true?

Mr. Skidmore: No.

Mr. Brown: Is it not the first place you would sit in after you walk out the plant . . . is not the place you would find radiation?

Mr. Skidmore: Can I explain why? You evidently don't understand. When you get contaminated, in particular this case, it's on your body; it's on the inside clothing.

So, now, your shorts and your T-shirt is contaminated . . .

It's all over you . . . Now, when the guy gets home, he takes off his clothes. It's on his body; it's on his T-shirt. It can get on his bedding. I don't know what all it can get on.

The guys don't take . . . in this case, the guy didn't even change his shirt, T-shirt. He wore it for several days and he was packing that stuff around with him.

Mr. Brown: And then, there are precautions that are taken when you determine that somebody had been carrying this stuff around with them?

Mr. Skidmore: The supervisor is in charge of it. All I did was . . .(PAUSE) I would say, you should have checked the homes . . . it wasn't done.

CONTAMINATED GROUND WATER FROM A LEAKY NUCLEAR SPENT FUEL STORAGE POOL . . .

PG&E installed several environmental test wells with most of them outside of the radiation-controlled area of the plant but all of them were inside the PG&E's HBPP security fence.

Nuclear control technicians would take samples from those environmental test wells and then analyze them in the 256-channel analyzer and print out the results using an "X-Y printer." The procedure for collecting a sample used a 1 inch stainless steel tube about 18 inches long, which we would lower into the well down a casing about 3 inches in diameter.

When the sample tube filled up with ground water, we would pull it out by an attached rope and pour it into a clean, one-gallon plastic jug. Each jug was marked with the appropriate well number.

When all the jugs were full, we would take the samples to the counting lab located inside Unit 3 and analyze them. After printing the results, we would compare what we came up with, with the graphs made of the spent fuel pool water, and then we would continue the process over time to look for any changes in the decaying characteristics and compare those result with a book of standards.

The conclusions were clear; the ground water samples produced the same graphs as the spent fuel pool water indicating the same radioisotopes were present, which established the spent fuel pool was leaking. This was suspected because the drop in the spent fuel pool level, which required adding more demineralized water to the pool on a regular basis, could not be explained simply due to evaporation alone.

Management personnel were involved in every step of the process except for the collection of the samples, and the results of the testing were closely guarded by the front office. I asked often what PG&E was going to do about this problem. Each time I was told the company was working on it. I was assured by plant management it wasn't as serious a problem as I was making it out to be.

It was my position that any radioactive contamination from the spent fuel pool that was getting into the ground water was totally unacceptable.

The spent fuel pool had fission byproducts from the leaking fuel elements that were dangerous to human health and none of it belonged in the ground water. I argued unsuccessfully that there were no safe levels for this stuff as plant management maintained.

A SERIOUS BREACH OF RADIATION PROTECTION SAFETY PROCEDURES IN EARLY MAY 1970 INVOLVING A WELDER . . .

On the morning of May 11, 1970, I was in Mr. Weeks' office attempting to discuss with him a serious radiation protection safety violation. I felt there had been a serious breach of radiation protection safety procedures and nothing was being done about it.

First line plant management personnel totally ignored the safety violation and Edgar Weeks went along with them. Why? Because at the time we were in the middle of an outage and workers were under the gun to get their work orders done as quickly as possible, which meant there was a wholesale cutting corners taking place throughout the nuclear facility. Whenever shortcuts could be taken to reduce the time on jobs everywhere in the plant, safety was often sacrificed along with employees receiving needless and senseless radiation exposure.

A welder came into an area where I was working, an area that had "the greatest source of contamination of this kind," referring to high levels of potential radioactive airborne contamination. There was no proper notification given, no air samples taken, no tailboard briefings, and no SWP for the job. The welder was just getting the job done as quickly as he could. Plant supervision ignored my complaint and did nothing. I later included this incident in my complaint to the AEC. The AEC "investigated" my complaint and issued the following finding: "There was no substantiation for this allegation" (see Allegation #12 in Chapter 13).

The following is part of my direct examination of Edgar Weeks at my Unemployment Insurance Appeals Board hearing:[108]

> **Mr. Rowen:** (Directed to Mr. Weeks) Are you aware of the incident in which a welder started cutting on packing which is probably the highest source, the greatest source of contamination of this kind in the pipe tunnel, when . . . (INTERRUPTED)
> **Mr. Weeks:** I don't remember discussing this with you on the morning of May 11 (INTERRUPTED)
> **Mr. Brown (PG& attorney):** I will object to the question on the basis there is no foundation laid to show that of Mr. Rowen, at all was affected by this particular incident.
> **Mr. Rowen:** I could rephrase my question.
> **THE REFEREE:** Just a minute. Just a minute. I think the

foundation is general. I think what we have here quite clearly is a stipulation in which Mr. Rowen had a very different idea of safety and what was necessary for safety in this radiation situation from his supervisors. And, I certainly feel it had a lot to do with his discharge. Therefore, I think it is material. I'd like to hear the answer to the question.

Mr. Weeks: Would you restate the question?

Mr. Rowen: I'll restate the question. During this discussion [on May 11] did I inform you that a welder had gone into pipe tunnel and worked just above our heads, mine and Terry Rapp's, a supervisor, cutting on or heating a packing line without any notification given to either Mr. Rapp or myself. Do you recall anything about that?

Mr. Weeks: I don't recall discussing it that morning, no.

Mr. Rowen: Do you recall the incident in general from any discussions?

Mr. Weeks: Yes. I think I heard about the incident. I surely can't remember the details of it.

How convenient for Mr. Weeks to say I can't remember the details of it after all the hullabaloo I had raised about the incident. I did manage to get Weeks to say, "I think I heard about the incident" but apparently the AEC couldn't even manage to accomplish that with him.

ANOTHER BREACH OF RADIATION PROTECTION PROCEDURES IN MARCH 1970 INVOLVING A VIP TOUR . . .

On March 30, 1970, PG&E provided a tour inside the refueling building to some dignitaries. Again plant management engaged in cutting corners, which resulted in violations of the company's radiation control standards. I insisted that the proper procedures be followed for the safety of the visitors coming into the nuclear facility. They had no idea of the dangers involved and relied on us to keep them safe. These people had every right to expect nothing less than our best efforts to ensure they would remain free of any radioactive contamination.

I suffered unpleasant consequences for insisting proper procedures be followed; the AEC failed to address those consequences. The only way I had to reveal what had taken place with this special VIP tour was to conduct the following direct examination of Raymond Skidmore:[109]

Mr. Rowen: (DIRECTED TO MR. SKIDMORE . . .) Mr. Skidmore, do you recall an occasion on or about March 30, 1970, that there was a tour in the refueling building of VIPs in which you were assigned to rope off and establish a clean control area within the radiation control areas for these people to make their tour? Do you recall this incident?

Mr. Skidmore: Yes.

Mr. Rowen: In you own words can you explain what was involved?

Mr. Skidmore: Jerry Boots was the engineer and he requested me to set up an area for them to come in the back gate and be able to tour around the head –

Mr. Rowen: The head of the reactor?

Mr. Skidmore: Yes, and they were supposed to go out again. He wanted me to do it to put down – I don't know what the name, but this is (INTERRUPTED)

Mr. Rowen: Seismograph paper?

Mr. Skidmore: Yes, that what we put down on the floor for the tourists to use. The only trouble, it was used paper and it was stored down in the refueling building.

Mr. Rowen: This is paper that had been used for possibly that purpose or some other purpose in that area?

Mr. Skidmore: This – (INTERRUPTED)

Mr. Rowen: Do you know what it was used for?

Mr. Skidmore: This paper was used for other tours, just for working, you know, it was stuff we used – we rolled it up and –

Mr. Brown (PG&E attorney): It was used more than once?

Mr. Skidmore: Right.

Mr. Rowen: For that same purpose? Well, let me clarify the question. What is the procedure that would normally be used to prepare a contaminated area for persons that were on a tour wearing their street clothes and no protective clothing at all?

Mr. Skidmore: Up until this time we have always used brand new paper, never used paper – this paper had been used.

Mr. Rowen: Why was that?

Mr. Skidmore: Because these guys are coming in their street shoes and the company didn't want them to get contamination on themselves and they didn't want to take a chance.

Mr. Rowen: Why do you figure that there was a departure from the general routine?

Mr. Brown (PG&E attorney): Objection.

Mr. Rowen: Mr. Skidmore, how long did it take to complete this job?

Mr. Skidmore: How long? It was a big rush job.

Mr. Rowen: How did you get involved with this job, to the best of your recollection?

Mr. Skidmore: They assigned me because they were shorthanded.

Mr. Rowen: Do you recall that I raised an issue with Jerry Boots concerning the fact that they needed a surveying instrument at the gate so that people could use it upon leaving the controlled area?

Mr. Skidmore: You brought the issue up because normally we are supposed to use new paper and barrier rope and we were not doing this. And you also brought up the issue that there should be some kind of checkout instrument so that when they left the area, and I believe they finally agreed with you, and put it at the gate for them to use.

COMMENT: It seemed to me that Skidmore's testimony was rather evasive in nature.

I knew Skidmore very well for we had worked together for several years. It was as if he was worried about losing his job.

Skidmore was not in the same situation as either Forrest Williams or Bob Rowen; He could ill afford to lose his PG&E paycheck.

A SERIOUS PROBLEM OF RADIOACTIVE AIRBORNE CONTAMINATION IN CONTROL ROOM OF UNIT 3 . . .

There were times when the airborne radioactivity became such a serious problem in the reactor control room, an area that was not even in the radiation controlled area of the plant, that employees needed to wear, and should have been required to wear, protective breathing masks as required by the radiation protection standards. Plant management did not require the employees to wear protective masks, nor were the employees required to wear protective clothing over their street clothes and protective booties over their shoes.

The problem was radioactive particulate matter that was spewing out of the 250-foot gaseous waste discharge stack that occurred whenever there was an outside temperature-inversion causing the sinking air to enter into the air intakes of the air conditioning system for Unit 3. During this condition employees were permitted to leave Unit 3 with radioactive contamination on their clothing and shoes.

It was my position that there shouldn't be any airborne radioactive contamination in the control room. If that was unavoidable, the employees should have been required to wear protective masks and clothing, the same as they were required to wear beyond the step-off pad inside the radiation controlled areas of the plant.

As far as I was concerned, the Unit 3 control room should have become an extension of the facility's radiation controlled area and treated accordingly, governed by the same radiation protection standards. When PG&E's radiation protection engineer disagreed with me, I voiced my *displeasure* with his position and things immediately went south for us!

Consequently, I found myself in Edgar Weeks' office discussing the matter; it turned into another "routine counseling session" in that I was reminded once again about my "bad" attitude, "poor" work performance, and the usual dictum that I needed to be "more cooperative" with plant management.

RADIOACTIVE CONTAMINATION ON VEHICLES IN THE EMPLOYEE PARKING AREA...

In addition to the radioactive airborne problem in the control room, we were also finding radioactive contamination on the vehicles in the employee parking area of the plant.

I caused an uproar over the radioactive contamination that was landing on employee cars. It was my uncompromising position that these conditions were totally unacceptable!

Most of the employees and all of plant management personnel disagreed with me because the radiation levels involved were considered "low-level." PG&E plant management claimed the amount of *smearable* radioactive contamination was under the 100 counts per minute threshold and therefore not in violation of the facility's radiation control standards. Nothing could have been further from the truth! And what about the school downwind from the plant! Those children did not deserve to be exposed to any amount of smearable radioactive contamination.

After making my own radiation surveys of the vehicles in the employee parking lot, I personally determined the amount of radioactive contamination on the vehicles exceeded what management had claimed.

I told Edgar Weeks that employees had a right to expect their automobiles to be free of any *smearable* radioactive contamination when they left the plant, adding that the general public also had an absolute right that our vehicles were completely free of any radioactive contamination. I demanded that PG&E install a decon station for all employee vehicles leaving the plant. My demand just resulted in more derogatory material placed into my personnel file.

MY PERSONAL RADIATION EXPOSURE HISTORY AT HUMBOLDT BAY, ANOTHER SHAMEFUL EXPLOITATION IN THE NUCLEAR WORLD OF PG&E AND THE AEC...

Following my termination from the company, I repeatedly asked PG&E for my complete radiation exposure record for the period of my employment at the nuclear facility (March 1964 to June 1970). PG&E did not respond to any of my requests. It was made clear to plant management that I was entitled to a complete record of my exposure to radiation as required by 10 CFR, Part 20 of the federal regulations. I continued to demand the exposure record that PG&E was required by law to provide within a specified time following my termination from the company but that didn't seem to matter to plant management.

When I complained to the AEC investigator, J. J. Ward, about this violation, he simply recorded my complaint as "Allegation #30: PG&E employee, whose employment was termination, was not furnished a report of his exposure within the required period specified in AEC regulations."

Ward then stated in his report, "AEC Finding: True. Included in October 28 notice to the licensee." That was the AEC's complete handling of the matter. There was no review by the AEC of what the exposure report revealed, consequently there was no evaluation of my exposure to radiation during my employment even though I expressed grave concern over the unnecessary and senseless exposures we were receiving.

When I asked Mr. Ward during our September 7, 1971, meeting if he had seen my radiation exposure record during his investigation, he said he hadn't. I also asked Ward if he made a request to see the report, he said he hadn't done that either.

Mr. Ward stated the AEC was not concerned with the work policies of PG&E in the nuclear facility regarding radiation exposure so long as employees did not receive exceed 3 rems of exposure per quarter, and no more that 5 rems of exposure per year. The work polices of PG&E was totally within the purview of PG&E's management prerogative. How would the AEC ever learn of any "overexposures" if the company did not volunteer to provide that information and the AEC made no inquiries on its own?

I eventually did receive a copy of my radiation exposure record from PG&E around the first part of October 1970 but unfortunately misplaced it. For years I have wondered about my actual radiation exposure at Humboldt Bay. Believing that I had lost those records, I asked the company that provided PG&E the film badge monitoring service and was told I would need to get that information directly from PG&E. I sent several letters to PG&E's corporate office in San Francisco requesting copies of those records and I never received a response to any of them!

However, as I was writing my *Diary* and pouring through my records I found the report that I thought I had lost. It is a five-page report with a cover letter, dated September 20, 1970, signed by Warren A. Raymond, Assistant Plant Superintendent, Humboldt Bay Power Plant. The report provides the "counting results of bioassay and whole body." Very honestly I do not know how to read or what to make of those data that are contained in this portion of the report.

However, the rest of the report provides startling information pertaining to my "Occupational External Radiation Exposure" to the "Whole Body"(Appendix IV of my *Diary*), to the "Skin of Whole Body" (Appendix V of my *Diary*), and to the "Hands and Forearms" (Appendix VI of my *Diary*).

According to the report on the "whole body exposure to gamma radiation," I exceeded the annual maximum exposure limit on October 14, 1969. The report on the "skin of whole body exposure to gamma and beta radiation," reveals that I exceeded the quarter maximum exposure limit on January 15, 1970, and the annual maximum exposure limit on June 15, 1970.

The most startling data in my radiation exposure record for my entire employment period, not to diminish in any way the significance of the aforementioned data, is the report on the "hands and forearms exposure to gamma radiation," which revealed exceeding the maximum annual limit of 5 rems seven times, and the maximum quarter limit of 3 rems twice during my employment period.

The high radiation exposure to my hands and forearms occurred during January 1967 to June 1970, which happened to coincide with the rising radiation dose rate levels associated with the collection and analysis of reactor water and off-gas samples during the same period of time. Plant management never once notified me that I had exceeded the maximum exposure limits.

ADVANCE NOTICE OF AEC COMPLIANCE INSPECTIONS . . .

Contrary to the claims of both PG&E and the AEC, PG&E would receive advance notice of AEC compliance inspections. We would then be told to make sure the plant was ready for inspection and everyone was sent out to all areas of the facility to look for and correct problems.[110] I reported this PG&E practice to J. J. Ward, AEC Investigator, and cited the contamination problems we had to clean up before the announced AEC inspections.

I made it clear we were not allowed to talk to the AEC inspectors when they came into the plant and that plant management did not reveal the contamination problems to the AEC inspectors. What was the AEC investigator's response? "Well, if they cleaned it up, what's your point?"[111] I stated time and again that every AEC inspection should be unannounced just like those of the Strategic Air Command.

I remember telling Edgar Weeks the AEC inspectors should be "looking at the plant in its normal state of operation" and not "in some phony prepared state just for the inspection." Again, my uncompromising position was a huge problem for Weeks and the rest of plant management and it made me very unpopular with them.

Unfortunately, most of the employees felt that I was in the wrong for suggesting that AEC inspections should always be unannounced and basically that all I was trying to do was cause trouble. They appreciated the advanced notices so they could correct problems and make the plant look good. I simply made it clear to everyone that the plant should always "look good," period, end of discussion! Speaking honestly, it was not a very popular stand for me to take with almost everyone at the plant; workers and management personnel alike. Plant workers thought this way because they didn't want anything to threaten their livelihoods, and plant management because it was their mission to make Humboldt Bay a successful nuclear venture for the company.

For several months before the company's safety meeting dated December 12, 1967, I raised a number of important safety issues with plant management. My numerous discussions at various times involved Jerry Boots, Chemical Engineer; Gail Allen, Radiation Protection Engineer;

Warren Raymond, Assistant Plant Manager; and Ed Weeks, Plant Engineer.

All of my discussions with the first-line supervisors were usually followed up with a second meeting with Ed Weeks for a "counseling session" addressing my poor attitude towards the company and for what he called my "troublemaking" ways. One of these safety issues concerned the previously mentioned airborne radioactive contamination levels found in the reactor control room that exceeded plant standards and required the use of protective masks, a problem that PG&E corrected after I brought it up at the December 12, 1967, safety meeting.

PG&E management did not want anyone who had radiation protection safety concerns about the nuclear unit talking with the AEC or any other regulatory agency. There was never any doubt in the minds of the employees regarding plant management's position. Of course, plant management never put it in writing and no one ever pressed the issue until I decided to do it.

I grew tired of being told that I could not talk with AEC compliance inspectors when they visited the plant. My reasons for wanting to present various radiation safety concerns to the compliance inspectors are explained throughout my *Diary*. Perhaps the best way to expose the company's attitude towards employees being "discouraged" from talking with the AEC and other outside regulatory agencies is the testimony of Edgar Weeks and the demeanor of PG&E attorney L. V. Brown during Weeks' testimony. The following is my direct examination of Mr. Weeks concerning my meeting with him on May 11, 1970:[112]

> **Mr. Rowen:** (Directed to Mr. Weeks . . .) Did you say to me that I would be placing myself in serious jeopardy if I went to the AEC?
>
> **Mr. Weeks:** I did not.
>
> **Mr. Rowen:** Did you state that is was inadvisable for me to go to outside agencies, including the Atomic Energy Commission — (INTERRUPTED)
>
> **Mr. Weeks:** Yes.
>
> **Mr. Rowen:** Concerning radiation safety violations?
>
> **Mr. Weeks:** I told you that I was not going to give you company time to see the compliance inspector on this visit. That, if on your own you wanted to go see him, it was obviously nothing I could do about it. But, my advice, I told you I felt that it was inadvisable. That's what I told you that it was inadvisable.
>
> **Mr. Rowen:** What does that mean?
>
> **Mr. Weeks:** It means I don't advise it.
>
> **Mr. Rowen:** Does it carry with it some force of -- (INTERRUPTED)
>
> **REFEREE:** He's already explained his answer.
>
> **Mr. Rowen:** I didn't have the chance at that time, and I do now.

REFEREE: You've already got . . . you asked the question and he answered it.

Mr. Rowen: I don't understand what he means by "inadvisable."

Mr. Brown (PG&E attorney): He indicated that he didn't wish to define it, I would say.

Mr. Weeks: No. I said I told him that I did not advise it. I could tell you. I don't have any objection to answering your questions. You say you didn't have an opportunity to ask me at that time I spoke to you, you had the opportunity to ask me anything you wanted to when you were in there. I didn't put any qualifications on what you could discuss.

Mr. Rowen: Then, let me ask you this way. Does inadvisable or ill-advisable statements that you made regarding my going to the AEC off the job as well as on the job?

Mr. Brown: Excuse me. He has already answered that question.

REFEREE: Agreed. He has answered the question. He said that it applied to off the job.

The next segment of Weeks' testimony pertaining to the California Administrative Code, Title 17 issue was provided in Chapter 1 but is included again here because it relates to the larger issue of being denied access to the AEC and the threat of retaliation by Weeks if I went to the AEC or made any public disclosure on my own. My direct examination of Mr. Weeks concerning my meeting with him on May 11, 1970, included the following testimony of Weeks:[113]

Mr. Rowen: (Directed to Mr. Weeks . . .) During the week preceding my suspension from work, did I ask to see a copy of the California Administrative Code, Title 17?

Mr. Weeks: Would you repeat the question, please?

Mr. Rowen: During the week preceding my suspension from work, did I ask to see a copy of the State of California Administrative Code, Title 17?

Mr. Weeks: Yes. You did.

Mr. Rowen: At the time of my original request, was there a copy in the plant?

Mr. Weeks: There is a copy in the "rad" protection chemical engineer's office, which happen to be in the trailer out the door just outside the plant, an auxiliary office.

Mr. Rowen: At the time of this request, were you under the impression that the State of California, Department of Public Health, still had jurisdiction as stated in the 1966 copy of the regulations?

Mr. Weeks: I wasn't sure because the company (PAUSE) —— I had been told that the law department had taken steps to put all of this under the AEC, and I had understood that this had been done, but I wasn't sure of it, so I got a clarification on that and I found out that the letter was still in the mill. It was essential for all intensive purposes; the in-plant radiation monitoring was not under the State of California jurisdiction anymore but was under the federal jurisdiction. As a matter of fact, it is under the federal jurisdiction and not the State of California. This has finally been completely resolved so that the state does not have jurisdiction on the in-plant monitoring program.

Mr. Rowen: But, at the time there was still a question?

Mr. Weeks: At the time, apparently, there were some questions. Somebody got fouled up on the mailing or something of this sort.

Mr. Rowen: Was I allowed time on the job to read these regulations?

Mr. Weeks: Oh, yes.

Mr. Rowen: While I was reading these regulations, did you have a discussion between yourself and Mr. Raymond, that I would not be given time on the job to write grievances referring to my note taking while I was reading these regulations?

Mr. Brown: I object to the question.

REFEREE: On what ground?

Mr. Brown: Oh, one, lack of material that obviously to begin with is irrelevant. And, second, you're asking about a discussion . . . Oh, I know, well, let me just simply state my objection. That is completely irrelevant in material to the issues.

REFEREE: What is the materiality of it?

Mr. Rowen: I intend to show that Mr. Weeks had reason to take action against me at the end of that week — (INTERRUPTED)

Mr. Brown: Mr. Rowen, if the point you're trying to make is that your supervisor tells you when you have to work or when you don't, well, the company will stipulate that our supervisors do that. They are paid to do that.

Mr. Rowen: That was my opinion.

Mr. Brown: Now, they better damn well do that.

Mr. Rowen: Yes, sir.

Mr. Brown: Now, is that the essence of your question?

Mr. Rowen: No. I will re-phase my question and see if you will accept it. Is it a matter of law that an employee has the right and his employer is obligated to allow an employee to — (INTERRUPTED)

Mr. Brown: Objection. This witness is not competent to

answer the question.

Mr. Rowen: It's stated on the notice of employees on the status board. Does it state that employer shall provide employees these regulations for the employee's inspection and review?

Mr. Weeks: The State, Title 17, we're talking about. Yes. They are supposed to be available for anyone that's working in radiation work to review.

Mr. Brown: Excuse me again, but it seems to me, Mr. Referee, that we're going around in circles. He's already testified that they gave him 40 minutes on company time to read it. What's the point of your question? They've bent over backwards in my opinion to allow you to read these damn things. Now, you question whether we have to do it or not. Apparently, whether we have to do it or we don't, in your case we did it.

REFEREE: What's the next part of your question, Mr. Rowen?

Mr. Rowen: I will conclude with this question. When you informed me that I was . . . that it was ill advisable for me to go to outside agencies with matters concerning radiation protection safety violations — (INTERRUPTED)

Mr. Weeks: Now, wait a minute. You're putting words in my mouth. I told you it was inadvisable to see the AEC inspector.

Mr. Rowen: Okay. When you informed me that it was inadvisable for me to see the AEC inspector, was that the company's position? Or was that your position?

Mr. Weeks: That was mine. I was speaking only for myself.

Mr. Rowen: That was based on your feelings concerning the matter?

Mr. Weeks: May I explain why I gave him that answer or is it — (INTERRUPTED)

Mr. Rowen: That's certainly relevant.

REFEREE: Go ahead.

Mr. Weeks: My feeling on this type of thing, I'm a great one for going through channels. Any employee in that plant, if he feels he has a problem; he should take it to his supervisors. If he doesn't get satisfaction there, he could bring the problem in to me or to Mr. Raymond, and if he doesn't get satisfaction there he could take it to the plant superintendent. We also have a grievance procedure. We also have a suggestion plan and the union, I assure you, is very interested in radiation safety. If the employee has anything of substance, he was going to get satisfaction by one of those routes. Now, if he goes around these normal channels and goes running to the compliance people saying these guys are all screwed up, it's going to cause a relationship between that employee, I don't care whether he's supervisory or bargaining unit, and other people in the plant. It's going to cause that relationship, in my opinion, to deteriorate. Now, they're going to develop a mistrustful attitude and they are going to think that, well, this guy is, you know, it's just a bad situation and that's why I did not, in my judgment, think it was advisable for him to see the AEC compliance inspector . . . . .

With Weeks still under oath, his testimony was moved into a new area that further exposed Weeks' attitude towards radiation safety and the desire of the company's attorney to avoid addressing serious radiation safety problems in public. My direct examination of Edgar Weeks continued addressing the previously mentioned welder incident involving radioactive airborne conditions in the pipe tunnel of Unit 3:[114]

Mr. Rowen: (Directed to Mr. Weeks . . .) What is the proper procedure for going into a work area where there is a potential airborne contamination?

Mr. Weeks: Potential airborne contamination?

Mr. Rowen: Because of cutting, welding or anything along those lines.**Mr. Weeks:** If you are going to be in breathing zone area of a welding job on contaminated material, you should wear a mask.

Mr. Rowen: Isn't it proper that first you run an air sample to establish the airborne concentrations?

Mr. Weeks: This is desirable to run an air sample first. If you're going to wear a fresh air mask, then it isn't necessary in my opinion to run the air sample.

Mr. Rowen: Do people normally wear fresh air masks when working in the — (INTERRUPTED)

Mr. Weeks: Well, the welder normally does, because he's the one working where the breathing zone is affected.

The following few lines of Weeks' testimony have already been presented but are included here to establish continuity:

Mr. Rowen: I see. Are you aware of the incident in which the welder started cutting on packing which is probably the highest source, the greatest source of contamination of this kind in the pipe tunnel, when — (INTERRUPTED)

Mr. Weeks: I don't remember discussing this with you on the morning of May 11.

Mr. Brown (PG&E attorney): I will object to the question on the basis there is no foundation laid to show that of Mr. Rowen was at all affected by this particular incident.

Mr. Rowen: I could rephrase my question.

REFEREE: Just a minute. Just a minute. I think the foundation is general. I think what we have here quite clearly is a stipulation in which Mr. Rowen had a very different idea of safety and what was necessary for radiation safety from that of his supervisors. And I certainly feel it had a lot to do with his discharge. Therefore, I think it is material. I would like to hear the answer to the question.

Mr. Weeks: Would you restate the question?

Mr. Rowen: I'll restate the question. During this discussion did I inform you of the fact that the welder had gone into the pipe tunnel and worked just above our heads, mine and Terry Rapp's, cutting on or heating a packing line without any notification given to either Mr. Rapp or myself. Do you recall anything about that?

Mr. Weeks: I don't recall discussing it that morning, no.

Mr. Rowen: Do you recall the incident in general from any discussions?

Mr. Weeks: Yes. I think I heard about the incident. I surely can't remember the details of it.

The rest of Mr. Weeks' testimony regarding the breach of radiation safety procedures involving the welder in the pipe tunnel:

Mr. Rowen: Do you remember enough details to note that a control technician took the air sample by smelling the air in the pipe tunnel with his nose?

Mr. Weeks: I never heard that before.

Mr. Rowen: Would that be proper procedure if it were done?

Mr. Weeks: Well, obviously not.

Mr. Rowen: How is it done? What is the proper procedure?

Mr. Weeks: Taking an air sample?

Mr. Rowen: Yes. To establish for the benefit of — (INTERRUPTED)

Mr. Weeks: There are two or three ways you can do it. You could take a Schmidt air sampler down to the area; you could put a filter paper on the suction of the Schmidt air sampler, run it for 45 minutes, if you're collecting a particulate sample, collect particulate on the filter paper for 45 minutes, turn the sampler off, take the filter paper upstairs and count it on the internal gas local portion of the counter (sic), and then, calculate the airborne activity.

Mr. Rowen: Isn't this a rather involved procedure?

Mr. Weeks: It's very simple. Anyone can do it.

Mr. Rowen: Relative to sniffing the air with your nose.

Mr. Brown: He already testified to it, didn't he?

Mr. Rowen: Okay. Fine. But, you would agree that it was improper for someone to take an air sample by — (INTERRUPTED)

REFEREE: He's has already indicated (INTERRUPTED) —

Mr. Brown: He's answered that question already.

REFEREE: I wonder if I could interject here and ask a couple of questions. You were about to go into another area, were you not?

Mr. Rowen: Well, I just wanted to submit one document in evidence concerning this and then go on to a new area.

REFEREE: All right. What is the document?

Mr. Rowen: This is a letter I received from the AEC, and I would like to ask Mr. Weeks if he is familiar with the . . . INTERRUPTED)

REFEREE: Just a moment before you ask the question.

Mr. Brown: I would object to the introduction or any line of questioning on the basis that the letter clearly and obviously points out that it occurred subsequent to your discharge and doesn't pertain to this hearing at all.

REFEREE: Objection overruled.

The document is marked as Exhibit 15.

However difficult it was for me to convey publicly what happened at the Humboldt Bay Nuclear Power Plant, I continued to press on using whatever means were available to me and was willing to accept whatever the consequences. Those consequences bore a heavy price for my family.

THE 1971 HUMBOLDT COUNTY GRAND JURY "FINDINGS AND RECOMMENDATIONS" . . .

The AEC was not the least bit interested in pursuing my complaints about PG&E reprisals against employees who were critical of the company's radiation protection safety program. The only action taken by the AEC was nothing more than a mere wrist slap for PG&E's implicit threat of retaliation for taking complaints to the AEC. Interestingly enough, the AEC just characterized PG&E's actions as simply "discouraging" an employee from talking with AEC inspectors.[115]

Essentially, the Environmental Protection Agency, the U.S. Department of Transportation, the California Department of Public Health, and the U.S. Attorney's Office in San Francisco were all powerless in dealing with the problems posed by PG&E and the U.S. Atomic Energy Commission. It turned out that the only alternatives available to me were the news media and the local grand jury. My experiences with the news media will be summarized in Chapter 15.

The Humboldt Grand Jury interviewed me on March 29, 1971, April 12, 1971, and April 26, 1971. The grand jury concerned itself with the "alleged violations of safety procedures and directives at the Pacific Gas and Electric Company Nuclear Plant, Humboldt Bay, County of Humboldt."[116] On May 5, 1971, the Humboldt County Grand Jury, acting through District Attorney William F. Ferroggiaro, Jr., approached the Atomic Energy Commission, Region V, Berkeley, California, and advised that Agency of complaints received concerning safety infractions at the Pacific Gas and Electric Company Plant, Humboldt Bay, in the County of Humboldt. On May 11, 1971, investigators from the Atomic Energy Commission arrived at the Office of the District Attorney, Courthouse, Eureka, California.

An official Atomic Energy Commission investigation ensured and continued through the summer months of 1971. "On September 8, 1971, the Office of District Attorney was advised the investigation was complete, and a verbal briefing was conducted by an investigator of the Atomic Energy Commission."[117] The AEC reported to the Humboldt Grand Jury "23 man-days were expended in field investigation, additional days were spent in the preparation and completion of reports."[118]

In its Interim Report, the Humboldt Grand Jury concluded:
Humboldt County Grand Jury suggests the following changes in procedure:

1. Atomic Energy Commission personnel make a concerted effort, as part of unannounced and periodic inspection tours, to contact different levels of employees, selected by random selection and include after-hour offsite conversations concerning conditions which effect overall radiation safety

2. The frequency of unannounced, random inspection tours by Atomic Energy Commission personnel be increased

3. Atomic Energy Commission give consideration to the location of Commission inspectors on a rotating or permanent onsite supervision and inspection. The Grand Jury is not unmindful of staffing deficiency and attendant difficulties but believes the constant supervision of value

4. The Humboldt County Grand Jury wishes to commend Bob Rowen for his continued and determined effort in bringing this situation to the attention of the public.

County grand juries are limited in what they can do. They can only investigate and make suggestions. Of course they can issue indictments but not when it comes to the policies and practices pertaining to the operation of a nuclear power plant.

The complex web of corruption and political chicanery by America's nuclear juggernaut is very much like the Gordian Knot that was tied by King Gordius of Phrygia. It's going to take more, a whole lot more, than a sword of a local grand jury to cut it.

__V__

5. Police Brutality

May 25, 1969

"In the course of testifying in this case, which raised questions of serious misconduct by Eureka City policemen, Mr. Rowen was unflinching despite the highly controversial nature of the case and the ominous presence of a number of Eureka policemen which would have intimidated many other people."[119] [George Duke]

Sometimes things happen that you could never have predicted, how they will come back to haunt you and become dreadful life-changing experiences! You do something you believe to be the right thing to do and it ultimately causes you and your family unimaginable grief.

This part of my *Diary* may at first appear to have nothing to do with Pacific Gas and Electric Company and the Humboldt Bay Nuclear Power Plant; but ultimately, and as difficult as it will be to believe, it played a major role in PG&E's conspiracy to discredit me and to make me a national security risk. (Chapters 11 & 12)

On the evening of Sunday, May 25, 1969, after returning home from a weekend family outing, my wife volunteered to make some oyster stew for dinner but said she needed a few things from the grocery store if I wanted it. Since homemade oyster stew was one of my favorites for a light dinner on a Sunday evening, I eagerly went to Harris & K Market in Eureka to pick up the things she needed.

When I arrived at Harris & K Market, I parked across the street from the corner neighborhood grocery store on the Harris Street side of the intersection and proceeded to walk across the street. As I was walking towards the entrance to the store, I noticed two individuals standing directly in front in the doorway of the store having what appeared to be a heated argument. I walked between them saying, "Excuse me, gentlemen" and entered the store.

While in the store the volume of the argument increased and the one individual, who appeared to be intoxicated, was by this time using profane and vulgar language.

I later learned that this individual was a 19-year-old boy named Donald Walters.

Walters looked to be a lot older than 19. The boy was tall and had a husky build. He had a dark complexion, long black unruly hair, a black, bushy mustache, and it was apparent that he hadn't shaved for several days. I remember Walters looking like a " rough customer," which I later related to his attorney. I also remember saying to myself while in the store shopping "that guy sure needs to be taught some manners," which I also related to his attorney. In my view the boy's behavior was totally inappropriate because there were women and children present as a large crowd of onlookers had gathered. Again, I later related this to his attorney, as well.

As I approached the checkout stand, which was inside and just to the left of the front entrance of the store, I heard Walters say to the other individual, while using very coarse language, "Go ahead, call your fucking, goddamned buddies."

Then the smaller, clean-cut fellow backed up a couple of steps and grabbed the phone that was hanging on the wall in the checkout area just inside the store. He dialed a number, said something rather quickly and hung up. It seemed within a minute or so, two police cars arrived on the scene, one traveling east on Harris Street and the other traveling north on K Street.

The front doorway of the grocery store was on the very corner of the building facing the intersection of Harris and K Streets. The two police cars came up onto the sidewalk and screeched to an abrupt stop almost in unison, essentially boxing Walters in. Both uniformed police officers jumped out of their respective cars. One of the officers came around the front of his car with his nightstick drawn. This police officer I later learned was Officer Jacobsen; the other one was Officer Hall.

Officer Hall quickly ran up to Walters and told him to turn around and step over to his car. Hall then asked Walters to place both hands on the roof of the car over the rear door. While Walters was being patted down, his wallet was removed and placed between the forefinger and thumb of his left hand. Then Officer Jacobsen, who had the nightstick in a ready position, took the wallet out of Walters' hand and put it into the left breast pocket of his own shirt.

Officer Jacobsen then told Walters to turn around and step away from the car. Officer Hall opened the rear door to his car. Walters then asked Officer Jacobsen for his wallet back. Officer Jacobsen told Walters he would give it back to him when he was "good and ready" (those are the words I remember Jacobsen had used although several statements contained in the DA investigators report all read "I will take care of it").

Officer Jacobsen then told Walters in a waspish manner to get into the car. Walters immediately responded, "Fuck you, you son of a bitch."

At that point Officer Jacobsen struck the boy with his nightstick delivering a tremendous blow to the left side of Walters' face. Walters was stunned and staggered forward. Jacobsen continued to savagely strike Walters on the head several more times. It sounded like Jacobsen was hitting a watermelon with his baton.

Officer Hall quickly moved in between Officer Jacobsen, who had clearly lost control of himself, and Walters, who was severely injured and going down. Officer Hall managed to quickly turn Walters around and push him by his hips and buttocks into the police car just as he collapsed onto the rear seat of the car. It looked ugly and it happened ever so quickly. I had the momentary urge to inject myself into the situation and would have had it lasted a few seconds longer. The two police cars quickly left the scene. I paid for my groceries and returned home.

After arriving home I informed my wife I had to immediately go to the police station and that I'd tell her why when I returned home.

At the police station, I encountered a problem. No one wanted to give me the names and badge numbers of the two officers that had made the arrest at the Harris & K Market about an hour earlier. They also refused to tell me if the fellow who was arrested was receiving proper medical care. The two employees at the front desk area just kept asking me many questions.

I repeated my request for the names and badge numbers several times and I also repeated my inquiry regarding the condition of the fellow who had been taken into custody. Eventually the two officers who arrested Walters appeared at the front counter and tried to engage me in a discussion.

It was apparent the police officers were not happy with me and that they obviously felt I was interfering in their police business. I did not appreciate the way they were interacting with me. They told me I didn't know all the facts about what had taken place. I simply responded, "None of that was of any concern to me," and I again repeated my request for their "names and badge numbers."

The other clean-cut fellow who was initially engaged with Walters showed up at the counter and chimed in with Officers Jacobsen and Hall. His name was Officer Millsap who was in civvies and apparently off duty. I didn't know he was a police officer until that very moment. I again said to all of them that I just wanted their names and badge numbers and that's all I wanted, and if they weren't going to provide that information I would just have to leave without it, stating again that I didn't wish to engage in any conversation with them. I waited for as long as I was going to and then started for the door.

As I was heading out of the office, they called me back, wrote down their names and badge numbers on a piece of paper, and then unceremoniously handed it to me. They kept asking me what I was going to do with the information they had given to me. I did not answer any of their questions nor did I engage in any further conversation with them.

I simply took the information and left the police station.

There was no question in my mind that those three police officers were very upset with me and I felt as though I had probably caused some problems for myself. Of course, I had no way of knowing what those problems might be. All of that became known during the next several months.

After I returned home that evening, my wife and I had a long chat about what had taken place. I remember her saying to me, "It wasn't a very good idea" for me to get involved. She also said, "I wish you wouldn't do any more." Her words still echo around in my head all these years later.

I also remember my response, "That's what's wrong with most people, they just don't want to get involved when they need to," explaining that when they see something that's wrong, they need to step up and be courageous enough to do something about it.

I made it clear to my wife that the police officer who beat the fellow with his baton was totally out-of-line and the incident needed to be reported; I said I was going to do just that! She shrugged her shoulders and said, "Oh well, you do whatever you feel you have to do but I still think it's not a good idea."

The next day I called the district attorney's office during my midmorning break at work and asked to talk to someone about an incident involving the use of excessive force by a police officer the evening before. After a long delay, a meeting was arranged for late that afternoon between Mr. William Ferroggiaro, District Attorney for Humboldt County, and myself.

When I arrived at the DA's office, I was escorted by a secretary into Mr. Ferroggiaro's office and was greeted by the DA and his Chief Investigator, Mr. Bob Hickok. I summarized what had happened at Harris & K Market, explaining that I did not know any of the people involved in the incident.

I told the District Attorney and his chief investigator that the one officer had clearly lost control and had used excessive force, making it abundantly clear to both of them that the officer's use of the baton was not warranted just because the boy being arrested used inappropriate language directed at the officer. I remember saying, however trite it may now sound, that it was totally improper for the officer to act as "judge, jury, and executioner."

There was absolutely no question in my mind that the indiscriminate blows delivered by Jacobsen were the result of him loosing control. He had become enraged which was evident in his facial expressions, tight lips, and the protruding veins in his neck. I had seen this kind behavior many times while serving in the Marines and I was totally familiar with it.

Any one of the blows delivered by Jacobsen, especially the ones that followed the first blow to the side of the face could have killed the boy. It turned out that the boy had to be taken to the hospital where he was treated for a fractured jaw and diagnosed with a concussion. He also received stitches to the top and to back of his head. The official written reports of all three police officers downplayed the severity of Walters' injuries. I never saw any of the medical reports. His attorney related to me the only knowledge I had of Walters' condition.

The District Attorney thanked me for bringing the incident to his attention and said he would look into the matter and get back to me with his findings. I never heard back from the DA regarding my complaint.

I eventually acquired a copy of the investigator's report that was done by the District Attorney's Office, which was made available to me through an unrelated discovery action (having to do with my litigation against the City of Eureka and PG&E to be explained later in my *Diary*). All three officers stated in their individual reports that Walters attempted to physically attack Officer Jacobsen. I will comment on what the police officers claimed in their individual reports following what all of them had to say in their official reports.

Officer Arnold Millsap wrote the following in his official Eureka Police Department (EPD) report, which was provided to the Humboldt County District Attorney:[120]

> WALTERS was being frisked and about to be placed in the other police car when the following happened: WALTERS turned on Officer JACOBSEN with clenched fists and yelled "FUCK YOU, YOU SON-OF-A-BITCH," and pulled back his right fist in a manner as to slug Officer JACOBSEN. Before WALTERS could finish the swing of his fist at Officer JACOBSEN, Officer JACOBSEN I (sic) his night stick (sic) to the suspect's head. This did not stop the suspect and at this time Officer HALL grabbed the suspects right arm to prevent him from hitting Officer JACOBSEN. This R/O was standing about 10 feet away and came to the Officer JACOBSEN aid when he saw the suspect'd (sic) doubled up left fist headed back for a swing at Officer JACOBSEN. As WALTERS again attempted to strike Officer JACOBSEN only this time with his left fist, Officer JACOBSEN applied (sic) the night stick (sic) twice more to the suspect's head. At this instant the R/O grabbed the suspect's left arm and the suspect was placed in the police car without further trouble. MACE was not used because Officer JACOBSEN did not have time to take it from his belt and Officer HALL was standing in the line of fire. The club was applied (sic) to the suspect's head because he was up against the police unit, officer Hall was in a position where he would have been hit had Officer JACOBSEN I (sic) to hit the suspect on the right arm, and this R/O was in a position where he would have been hit if Officer JACOBSEN had I (sic) to hit the suspect on the left arm. /s/ Officer Millsap #12

Officer Jacobsen provided the following statement in his separate official EPD report:

> Suspect WALTERS was told to come to the right rear door of Officer Hall's patrol Unit 38, and to place his hands on the

top of the vehicle. He did this. RO told Officer Hall to search him closely, while the Subject was watched by the RO. Officer Hall began to search the Subject. —

RO then reached out and took WALTERS' abele (sic) from his left had (sic) that was on the top of the vehicle. He had it between his thumb and index finger. On this action, WALTERS stood up and asked what RO was going to do with the wallet, and RO told him, "I will take care of it, don't worry about it." At this point WALTERS turned to his left and raised his right fist in a threatening manner and yelled at the top of his voice, "FUCK YOU." Officer immediately took action and hit the Subject across the side of his face with the baton which officer had been holding in the right hand. The Subject again raised his fist, yelling some ooscenity (sic), which Officer does not recall, and was pushed by Officer Hall as he swung his fist. RO again struck the Subject on the head with the baton. The Subject then ceased resisting and was placed in the rear of Unit 38.

Officer then followed Hall into the station. After the Booking procedure, the Subject was taken to HMC for treatment of a cut on the rear of his head. This cut was cleaned by personnel at the hospital and required three stitches. The damage to the side of the Subject's head did not require treatment. /s/ Jacobsen #27 EPD

Officer Hall's official EPD report provided the following account of what he claimed had taken place:

The Subject was instructed by R/O and Officer Jacobsen to go to R/O's police vehicle #38. Subject stood for a few/in (sic) a defying manner and finally went to the police vehicle and there was instructed to place his hands on top of the police vehicle while the R/O searched him. When the search was complete the R/O stepped back and was in the process of opening the rear door when Officer Jacobsen took a wallet from the Subject's left hand. The Subject turned toward Officer Jacobsen and ask him what he was going to do with the wallet. Officer Jacobsen replyed (sic) "I will take care of it, don't worry about it." At this time the Subject was facing directly at Officer Jacobsen and a short distance from him. The Subject yelled at the top of his voice "FUCK YOU, YOU SON-OF-A BITCH," and with his right fist doubled up raised his arm back in a threatening manner. At this time Officer Jacobsen I (sic) his baton to the left side of the Subject's jaw. The Subject started to raise his right arm again in a abeleding (sic) manner toward Officer Jacobsen and aginx (sic) Officer Jacobsen I (sic) the baton to the back of the Subject's head. At this time Officer Millsap secured the Subject's left hand and arm behind his back and the Subject was placed in the Police vehicle. During all of the above action the Subject was cussing in a very loud voice.

The subject was transported to the station by the R/O and the other to (sic) subjects were transported by Officer Jacobsen.

The Subject was taken to H.C.M.C. by R/O and Officer Jacobsen. There the doctor on duty treated the Subject. /s/ C.R. Hall #24 EPD

I knew what I knew based on what I personally and very clearly witnessed. Walters did not attack, or attempt to attack, Officer Jacobsen. It's apparent to me the police officers got together and agreed on what each of them were going to put into their individual reports. The only thing Walters was guilty of was verbally abusing Officer Jacobsen when he directed his statement to the police officer "Fuck you, you son of a bitch," which was totally improper and I testified to that.

I also testified that Walters had used inappropriate language and appeared to be drunk and was engaged in disorderly conduct in a public place in front of women and children. As distasteful as all of that was, I clearly stated for the Court that Officer Jacobsen was not justified in beating the boy, as he did – not even once!

On June 2, 1969, the investigator for the District Attorney's Office interviewed a witness (whose name I am withholding and will refer to him only as "the witness"). The entire investigator's interview follows verbatim except for replacing the name of the person being interviewed with "the witness." This document is contained in the official Investigator's Report at page 6:[121]

This investigator had a conversation with (the witness) at his home regarding the incident at Harris and K Streets Market Sunday night May 25, 1969. He stated that he had gone to the store to pick up a few needed items somewhere around 8:00 P.M. When he arrived at the store he observed two persons who appeared to be arguing. He didn't pay particular attention until the one subject became loud and profane / and then he observed the smaller of the two show something to the taller man and heard him tell him that he was a policeman. Shortly after this he observed a second man join the others and they appeared to be taunting the officer attempting to start a fight. (The witness) heard the officer at one point tell the individuals involved to leave and stop creating a disturbance or he would have to arrest them. This did not seem to impress either subject as they kept up their argueing (sic) with the officer, the taller dark haired individual using much profanity, which could be heard throughout the store.

Within a very short time (the witness) observed two Police cars arrive and two uniformed officers get out of the cars. They asked the Officer in plain clothes what the trouble was, and he stated that he placed the three individuals under arrest. (The third individual had been in the store buying a soda pop during most of the argument and had gone outside where the argument was happening just a moment or two before the uniform officers arrived. (The witness) observed the Officers put two of the individuals into a police car and the two of the officers placed the individual up against the police car and searched him. When they had completed the search they moved him back from the car and stood there for a minute talking about something. (The witness) stated that he thought he heard something about the subject's wallet, and the one officer said, "I'll take care of it." Then the subject stated something else and the officer said in a louder voice, "I told you that I'll take care of it." With that the individual in question turned to the officer and shouted at him in a voice that could be heard all over the area, "Fuck you." The officer then struck this individual on the head with his nightstick at least two times.

U/s asked (the witness) if he had observed any blows struck or attempted to be struck by the person in question, he stated, "No, they were just standing there talking to each other about something when this guy swore at the officer, and the officer hit him with the club." (The witness) further stated that everything would have been allright (sic) if the guy would have gotten into the car, but he didn't and he stood there and swore at the officer.

(The witness) stated that there were several people present in or around the store, that there was a woman standing directly in front of him during the entire course of this incident, and she heard and observed everything that he did. However, he did not know who she was, nor would he recognize her if he saw her again. He stated that the officers took a great deal of verbal abuse from the individual involved, but he did not see this person strike at the officers nor engage them in physical combat of any nature. /s/ Robert D. Hickok

Several days (may have been more like several weeks) after the arrest of Donald Walters, I received a telephone call from Mr. George Duke of the California Indian Legal Services headquartered in the San Francisco Bay Area. Mr. Duke introduced himself and said he was an attorney representing Donald Walters. He asked if I would be willing to talk with him about what had happened when Walters was arrested. I told him that I would and agreed to meet with him.

After describing what happened, Mr. Duke asked me many background questions and wanted to know what my view of Walters' behavior was leading up to his arrest. I told Mr. Duke that the boy's language was inappropriate and that he appeared to be intoxicated. Duke asked if I would be willing to testify in court about what I had shared with him. I said I would if I was subpoenaed, explaining I needed a subpoena in order to miss work.

During the ensuing months, Mr. Duke held several depositions and asked if I would sit in on some of them. I used personal necessity leave and took some time off from work without pay to attend the depositions. Plant management complained about the time I was taking off from work, especially for the purpose they had heard through the employee grapevine. Mr. Duke explained that he was not getting much cooperation from the police department and felt my presence would encourage more forthright responses from those he had subpoenaed for questioning.

I agreed to show up to some of the depositions that Mr. Duke wanted me to attend, if it would help him get to the truth of why the police officers behaved the way they did. My only role was just to be present during the depositions. Even though it was not my purpose for attending the depositions, I learned a lot more about Walters and about what had taken place between him and the Eureka Police Department before the Harris & K Market incident. Walters' mother was a Hoopa Indian and his father was white. There were police officers in the police department who believed Walters knew some people that were involved in some sort of illegal activities, and it seemed to me those activities may have had something to do with drug usage or perhaps with dealing drugs, although none of that that was ever clearly established from anything I heard.

Mr. Duke was able to establish during the depositions that the police wanted Walters to become an informant and that Walters didn't want any part of it. It appeared to me that Walters didn't even know what the police officers were talking about. Certain members of the police department were constantly harassing Walters by calling him "half-breed" and "squaw man" in public places.

I remember in particular one line of testimony regarding three police officers that went into an all night restaurant in downtown Eureka at about 3 am for a coffee break where they encountered Walters. I couldn't believe my ears when I heard the testimony regarding that chance encounter. Things like "How's our squaw man." "There's the squaw man, now," and talking loudly among themselves referring to Walters as a "half-breed."

All of these comments were aimed at one of two things or perhaps both: (1) Making Walters angry enough to goad him into a situation where the police officers would then need to respond and/or (2) causing Walters to cave in and give them the information "they believed he had on certain other individuals." Never once did Mr. Duke and I ever discuss any of the depositions, before or after the trial.

On December 29, 1969, one day following my 29th birthday, I received a subpoena to appear at the Humboldt County Superior Court in Eureka, California, on January 8, 1970, at 9 am. I informed PG&E plant management that I had received a subpoena to appear in a criminal trial.

Mr. Weeks wanted to know how long I was going to be off work. I had no idea. Mr. Weeks wanted to see the subpoena; he then wanted to make a copy of it. I asked him why he needed a copy of the subpoena. Mr. Weeks explained the company needed to have a copy of it. I objected because I saw no need for him to make a copy of the subpoena. He insisted upon making a copy of it and told me if I wanted to be paid for the time I'd be away from work I would have to agree to the company having a copy of it. I then reluctantly said it was okay for him to make a copy.

The word spread very rapidly throughout the plant that I was going to testify for the defense in a criminal trial. Both the prosecution as well as the defense had subpoenaed me, but the prosecution never called me to testify. The Walters case was published in the local newspaper with several of the witnesses to his arrest being interviewed by a reporter. Many of the employees at the nuclear plant held a dim view of my involvement in the Walters case and made derogatory comments about me, always behind my back but never to my face. Nevertheless, I did hear about some of them.

A good example of how people were generally viewing my involvement in this matter was reflected in an EPD document dated August 13, 1969, and signed by Chief Cedric Emahiser. This document pertained to a potential witness in the upcoming Donald Walters trial and it read in part: "... [potential witness] advises that on the night of the arrest and alleged incident, he was at the store with . . . and heard as well as observed what occurred that evening. In his opinion WALTERS asked for everything he received and more too, and he would be glad to testify in the Officer's behalf."[122] Chief Emahiser concluded his supplemental information memo: "A copy of this memorandum was handed to Officer MILLSAP with a suggestion that he make an effort to secure a signed statement from (the named potential witness) within the very near future."[123] Copies of this memo were sent to the Eureka City Attorney and to Officer Arnold Millsap, and it was marked as RECEIVED by the Humboldt County District Attorney's Office on August 14, 1969.[124]

Chief Emahiser also sent a separate memorandum report to the DA which read in part, "I was not at the scene, and although I am firmly against any instance of police brutality to any degree, I do not feel that I am in any position to second-guess the officers under my command" . . . "Again I say, I was not at the scene and I feel that any action taken by our officers was done by them in the personal belief that it was necessary and proper."[125]

I told both District Attorney William Ferroggiaro and his chief investigator, Bob Hickok, very clearly that Officer Jacobsen had used excessive force and that there absolutely was no doubt in my mind the police officer totally lost control and acted improperly.

The whole affair made me realize just how deep feelings of prejudice ran at the power plant. I remember some of the lunchtime conversations about affirmative action and one particular statement made by an employee who said he could always drop a pipe wrench down the access shaft if the company had to "hire one of them," adding that he had "a very good aim." What struck me was the lack of response by the others who heard that nitwitted statement, which made necessary my retaliatory commentary to all of them!

Donald Walters' trial started on January 8, 1970. It was necessary for me to show up for the very first day of the trial and remain at the Courthouse throughout the trial since I was subpoenaed by both the prosecution and defense. The prosecution never called me as a witness so I had to just wait outside the courtroom during which time I did some reading for one of the courses of study I was enrolled in at the university.

I was not allowed in the courtroom during the trial, except for when I gave my testimony. I don't remember how many days the trial took but I do remember being called as the last defense witness. After entering the courtroom early in the morning on the last day of the trial, I was sworn in and asked to enter the witness box. Mr. Duke immediately raised an objection to the several uniformed police officers sitting in the first row of the spectator's gallery, stating they were there to intimidate his witness. I remember turning to the judge at the same time he looked my way, and saying to him without really thinking about it, "They don't intimidate me at all, your Honor."

The judge, nevertheless, asked them to vacate the first row of seats. Mr. Duke asked me through a skillful line of questioning to explain what took place leading up to Walters' arrest. At one point, I was asked to leave the witness box and by using various people that were made available, reenact the details of the clubbing Officer Jacobsen gave Walters.

When I was cross examined by the prosecuting attorney, he specifically asked how I could remember the event in such great detail when tensions were running so high. It was as if he was accusing me of making things up as I was going along or that I had rehearsed my testimony, at least that's how he was making me feel with his approach.

I responded to the prosecutor by simply saying I served in a U. S. Marine Corps force reconnaissance unit. My marine pathfinder training instilled in me a high degree of discipline and excellent powers of observation in stressful situations. Another line of questioning by the prosecuting attorney focused on the use of the nightstick. He wanted to know what made me such an expert in the proper use of a nightstick. Again, I simply said I had been trained in hand-to-hand combat, which included the use of batons or nightsticks during my military service in connection with my guard duty assignment while stationed at Treasure Island. My testimony lasted for much of the day.

After I was dismissed, I left the Courthouse and went home because it was so close to quitting time. George Duke called later in the evening to say that the jury found Walters "not guilty" on all counts except one, and that was being drunk and disorderly in a public place. Mr. Duke also shared with me that the judge said to both attorneys after the trial was over that in his opinion the jury was most likely going to find Walters guilty on all counts until the last defense witness testified. Mr. Duke thanked me for my willingness to testify so courageously. He said most people would not have done so. I told Mr. Duke that I only did what I believe was the right thing for me to do and I felt that it was my civic duty.

I am confident that all three police officers were called by the prosecution to testify and were cross-examined by Mr. Duke. Their testimonies were probably based on their official reports. I also assume other witnesses were called to explain to the Court what they had witnessed; especially as related to whether Walter's attacked or threatened to physically attack Officer Jacobsen. Obviously the jury did not buy what the police officers had claimed in their reports. These are only assumptions because I was not in the courtroom when they testified.

Five months following the trial I found it necessary to ask Mr. Duke if he would write a letter on my behalf explaining my role in the Walters' trial. I explained to Mr. Duke the reasons for my request. Mr. Duke was empathetic and not at all surprised that I was having serious difficulties with the City of Eureka and with PG&E. I did not yet know just how serious these difficulties were going to be until another five or so months had passed after Duke wrote the following letter, dated July 2, 1970:[126]

> To whom it may concern:
> In defending Mr. Donald Walters in a criminal case in the early part of this year, I called Mr. Robert J. Rowen as a material witness to the incident, which was the subject matter of the case. I had interviewed Mr. Rowen several times before calling him as a witness but had no other personal acquaintance with him. Both in my interviews with him and in the course of his testimony, I found Mr. Rowen to have complete integrity and impartiality.
>
> Although the effect of his testimony was primarily to support the contentions of my client (who was in fact acquitted by the jury on two of the three charges against him, including the principal charge), Mr. Rowen also testified candidly when he did not have knowledge of the facts inquired into and in several instances even testified contrary to the interests of my client. I greatly respected his honesty for doing so and unquestionably his testimony was extremely persuasive with the jury. Indeed, the judge himself informed me after the trial that Mr. Rowen's testimony was highly persuasive to him.
>
> In the course of testifying in this case, which raised questions of serious misconduct by Eureka City policemen, Mr. Rowen was unflinching despite the highly controversial nature of the case and the ominous presence of a number of Eureka

policemen, which would have intimidated many other people.

I am please to write this letter on behalf of Mr. Rowen because of my respect for his honesty and courage. If I can provide any further information to vouch for his character, I shall be happy to do so.

/s/George Duke

I always thought it was a few weeks following his Humboldt County trial that Donald Walters' mother filed a $350,000 federal lawsuit on behalf of Donald Walters for the violation his her son's civil rights. However, after looking back over the documentation in my possession, it appears she may have filed the suit before his trial in the Humboldt County Court.

The total amount of the federal lawsuit was based on $100,000 from Officer Jacobsen, $100,000 from Police Chief Cedric Emahiser, $100,000 from the City of Eureka, and $50,000 from Officer Millsap. Officer Hall was not named in the federal suit.

Following the trial in the Humboldt County Court, the police department harassed my family in subtle ways at first and then in not so subtle ways as time wore on. A police car would follow my wife while she was going to and from work almost every day. No matter how many times she would turn the police car would remain behind her. The same thing was happening to me. I was pulled over often for nonsense stuff but never cited for anything.

The harassment intensified during the summer and continued into the fall of 1970. We were receiving phone calls at home during the middle of the night with no one on the phone; there was just obnoxious heavy breathing on the other end!

The Eureka gossip mill became extremely active with me as its focal point! My wife was hearing horrible things at her place of work and so were members of my extended family. Some of our closest friends were sharing with us what they were hearing.

I had a friend whose sister-in-law was a meter maid in the police department who would hear derogatory statements being made about me by police officers in the squad room at the police station, and that I was frequently a topic of discussion around the station. I heard from a good friend that my name came up at a private party that Officer Jacobsen attended. My friend said he knew the statements being made about me were untrue, malicious, and aimed at damaging my character. There were untrue things being said about me at the Rotary Club, the Lions Club, and other social organizations. It was as if there was some sort of concerted effort underfoot to smear my name.

Then one day as I was driving home from attending classes at Humboldt State I heard my wife's name on the car radio. At the time she was working in a temporary work assignment as a bank teller at the Humboldt National Bank's branch office located at Fifth and Myrtle Streets in Eureka. The news flash stated the bank had been robbed at gunpoint and the bank teller involved was Shirley Rowen. I panicked!

When I was able to get to a phone, I called the bank and was told my wife was okay and that she was at the police station being interviewed by the FBI.

When I arrived at the police station, I was told my wife was in a back office and that I could not see her. There was no way I was going to accept that and shortly thereafter I met with my wife. I found out from her that she had been escorted to the back room and was asked to wait there. A man then came into her room and interviewed her. She thought he was with the Eureka Police Department or with the FBI. It turned out he was a reporter from the Eureka KINS Radio Station, who had been allowed into the police facility. I was furious!

The reporter had to have been allowed into that portion of the police facility through a locked gate that required someone to buzz him in. No one in the police station could explain how that reporter was able to access the secured area of the police station my wife was in. The problem I was having with all of this is that the bank robber got away with an undisclosed amount of money and he knew my wife could identify him. The radio was putting out her name and we were in the phone book. I demanded police protection and the Eureka Police Department refused to provide it. I still remember the smirks on the faces of the EPD personnel I was dealing with when I requested police protection.

I couldn't figure out why all this was happening and I had no idea how best to deal with it. For the longest time I just tried to ignore it as best I could. But it just wouldn't go away! The worst part about it all was how it affected my wife and family, not to mention the affect it was having on my extended family and friends. There was one thing for certain. I definitely learned from this wretched experience who my real friends were!

Little did I know, however, that my real troubles were yet to be discovered; those discoveries were lurking just around the corner!

__VI__

6. Spent Fuel Shipping Cask

August 1969

"The fact that Mr. Gail Allen, PG&E's Radiation Protection Engineer, directed his nuclear control technicians to take samples in the areas of the cask previously determined to have the least amount of contamination (which were still above the DOT limits) and to specifically avoid those areas that had much higher levels of radioactive contamination (areas that represented much more than a third of the spent fuel shipping cask's outside surfaces) was dishonest and totally illegal. And clearly the support of his second-line supervisor was at the very least, unforgivable."[127] [Bob Rowen]

"Well, according to my understanding of Mr. Allen's own memorandum, he was precisely trying to do something dishonest."[128] [D.F.M. Hanley]

By the summer of 1969, I found myself immersed in an ever-expanding web of contentious debate with just about every member of PG&E's nuclear plant management team over how unsafe the Humboldt Bay Nuclear Power Plant had become for its employees and the general public.

My critical view of plant management's handling of radiation safety issues and a multitude of violations of radiation protection safety procedures at the nuclear facility had caused me to loose faith in this new technology and disenchanted with those responsible for ensuring employee and public safety. I did not agree at the time, nor do I accept the argument now, that the trials and tribulations of the Humboldt Bay nuclear facility were necessary for the development of nuclear power. There was and still is simply too much at stake!

By the latter part of 1967, I had already grown intolerant of PG&E's incontrovertible attitude toward nuclear safety and plant management's demonstrated willingness to expose employees to needless and senseless amounts of radiation in order to keep operational costs to a minimum. The company's treatment of employees as expendable tools of production was an unacceptable corporate mindset. Of course this is nothing new, as one would know from his or her study of American history, except now there was a brand new perilous element in the workplace – *radiation.*

PG&E's willingness to intentionally cover up mistakes to enable Humboldt Bay to maintain a façade of safety and efficiency was by any standard deceitful. Plant management's complicit enthusiasm to ignore the company's radiation control standards whenever it would either increase operational costs or prove embarrassing for PG&E to do otherwise was at the very least shameful.

Company management's behavior at every level to methodically and systematically misrepresent the impact of the real environmental radiation hazards posed by the nuclear facility was at the very least deplorable and unacceptable. PG&E's disregard for employee and public safety was unquestionably immoral.

In like fashion and for reasons that dovetailed with PG&E's malevolent behavior, I came to view the Atomic Energy Commission with contempt for being in bed with PG&E to promote Humboldt Bay and the future of nuclear power. For essentially these reasons the promise of what I once held and originally hoped would be a great career had slipped through my fingers like so many grains of sand as I approached the end of my tenure at Humboldt Bay.

I had come to realize that the lack of a genuine concern for public and employee radiation safety permeated the entire PG&E hierarchy from the very top all the way down to the local plant management level. It was difficult for me to understand why the vast majority of the workforce at Humboldt Bay agreed with plant management's handling of radiation protection safety issues.

Most of the employees chose to remain oblivious to the dangers of chronic exposure to low-level ionizing radiation in whatever form, and this was because they were immersed in a weird kind of *workplace emulation.*

Once realized, however, it was the norms of behavior within the nuclear facility that provided the insight for my understanding of why management was able to maintain this dysfunctional work environment. It was employee "ambition" or "endeavor" to impress their superiors to achieve "acceptance" and "security" within the nuclear workplace, and advancement for some employees within the nuclear employment hierarchy.

Never did even one member of plant management, and for that matter the vast majority of the peons, ever question the adequacy of PG&E's radiation protection safety program. They were unquestionably "good company men" who were undeniably gullible and willing to do whatever it would take to impress those above them in the company's hierarchy. For me it wasn't a matter of never having met such men as these but rather having been in a workplace culture so embedded with such people. The company's radiation protection safety program was a sham designed to provide only the appearance of a concern for safety – and, for the most part, the Humboldt Bay nuclear workforce bought into it hook, line, and sinker!

It is an indisputable fact that the company's official radiation protection safety program was in reality the product of PG&E's Nuclear Task Force that culminated in an effort clearly orchestrated by none other than two very close friends who became the nucleus of the company's nuclear program at Humboldt Bay.

These handpicked upstarts for PG&E's nuclear program were James C. Carroll, who remained in the company's corporate headquarters after their initial stints together at the Vallecitos Atomic Laboratory and later at the Dresden-1 nuclear facility, and his *collaborating abettor,* Edgar Weeks.

It was Weeks who emerged onsite as a "Nuclear Engineer" and later named the "Plant Engineer" in charge of all technical staff at Humboldt Bay thus making him the local, onsite nuclear point man for PG&E.

It was clearly the task of these two individuals to work collaboratively to make absolutely certain the Humboldt Bay nuclear facility would remain free of any controversy and to cover up anything that could later prove embarrassing to PG&E and detrimental to the future of nuclear power.

The vast majority of the non-management employees remained unconcerned about the radiation safety issues that were frequently raised because they simply relied on plant management to handle all those matters. They believed management personnel could be trusted to do the right thing. They accepted that all members of plant management responsible for PG&E's radiation protection safety program were well qualified to oversee not only all phases of the plant's radiation protection program but were also committed to rigorously enforcing all applicable laws, rules, regulations and PG&E's Radiation Control Standards and Procedures that were predicated on them.

The rank and file was convinced PG&E management was watching out for their safety and that the company was religiously following all the applicable radiation control standards that provided for employee and public safety. Nothing could have been further from the truth!

Forrest Williams and I were two employees who could see the company's approach to radiation safety for what it truly was. Both of us had military experiences that addressed radiation safety in a variety of different ways. We began discovering early on in our radiation protection training major discrepancies between our military experiences and our work at Humboldt Bay. Increasing radiation levels throughout the plant that rose well beyond design expectations accentuated those discrepancies in many different ways. As we assumed greater responsibilities in our radiochemistry and rad protection work assignments, it became a moral imperative for us to confront plant management on an expanding myriad of radiation safety problems. In retrospect I was unquestionably viewed as the most outspoken and PG&E's biggest critic aka "troublemaker."

Plant management always became extremely defensive whenever confronted with questions or expressions of concern regarding radiation safety thus making it virtually impossible to properly address radiation safety problems as they arose. This state of affairs put us on a collision course with plant management in general, and for me, with Edgar Weeks, in particular.

I could not abide cutting corners, breaking rules, and allowing needless and senseless radiation exposure to employees and to the general public in order to protect the company's bottom line. The collection and analysis of highly radioactive reactor water and off-gas samples (previously covered in chapters two and three) are just two examples of the problems we faced in dealing with PG&E management's attitude towards radiation safety.

Edgar Weeks constantly reminded me in his "counseling sessions" that I had a duty to be cooperative and to promote harmony. Weeks often made it clear that I should not criticize the company nor find fault with any of its managers. According to Weeks, it was in my best interests to promote Humboldt Bay and, if I was willing to do that, I could have a great career and be part of PG&E's expanding nuclear program.

PG&E constantly bombarded the employees at the nuclear plant with messages that impressed upon us how important we were to solving California's impending energy crisis. I remember passing a billboard sign on my way to work that had a woman wearing an apron and standing in her 50's-style kitchen with the words in huge lettering that read "DON'T BE A DISHWASHER, BUY ONE" – the billboard ad was signed "PGandE" in bold print, which seemed to get larger and larger each time I passed it on my way to work every morning.

We were frequently told at the plant that the company was dangerously close to facing brownouts and blackouts and, therefore, why it was imperative for PG&E to increase its energy production systemwide and nuclear power was going to be the way for the company to do it. The dishwasher ad was not the only way used by PG&E to promote a greater demand for electricity; the company's propaganda program was far-reaching and found in every nook and cranny of PG&E's electric service delivery system as well as in all of the company's spheres of influence - *everywhere*!

My work as a nuclear control technician caused me to become an unwilling participant to a multitude of *betrayals of the public trust*. These *betrayals* included not only the previously mentioned collection and analysis of extremely high dose rate reactor water and off-gas samples, but also the accidental discovery followed by the inappropriate handling of three employees who had four days earlier left the nuclear facility radioactively contaminated.

A review of PG&E's *betrayals* that directly involved me also included the environmental monitoring program of the ridiculous rabbit experiment testing for radioactive Iodine in the grasslands downwind from the plant, the improper release of soggy radiation waste boxes bound for the radiation waste disposal site in eastern Washington, employees receiving needless and senseless amounts of radioactive contamination as well as hideous amounts of radiation exposure while working directly under the reactor during refueling outages, collecting and analyzing samples of the ground water from environmental test wells that revealed the nuclear facility's spent fuel pool was leaking, radioactively contaminated vehicles in the employee parking lot, a transient worker recovering from cancer being improperly used by PG&E as a "radiation sponge," and PG&E receiving advanced notice of AEC compliance inspections enabling plant management to clean up citable violations of plant conditions.

There were still more PG&E *betrayals of the public trust* coming my way. My involvement with each of them continued to add to my already heavy burden of struggles with PG&E, which by the end of the sixties was growing exponentially. Each struggle resulted in an ever-increasing amount of turmoil for me personally and ultimately, and most regrettably, resulted in tremendous grief and hardship for my family.

The first of the more noteworthy of these *betrayals* occurred in August 1969 regarding the improper release of a nuclear spent fuel-shipping cask. Along with the nuclear spent fuel-shipping cask fiasco was the initial discovery of an extremely hot radioactive particle on the sole of an employee's shoe. The employee involved in this incident had not even been in the radiation-controlled area of Unit 3 during that particular workday (an extremely important fact to take special notice of)! More extremely hot radioactive particles were discovered on employee clothing and shoes during the ensuing months following that initial discovery of what became more generally known as the "mysterious particles."

PG&E sold radioactively contaminated scrap iron to an unsuspecting Eureka scrap iron dealer in February 1970 and then covered it up.

In March 1970 the Humboldt Bay Radiation Protection Engineer proclaimed the mysterious particles to be "fallout from the Chinese atomic bomb testing."

Perhaps the most grievous of all *betrayals* was the complete removal of the continuous air-sample monitoring system by PG&E at the South Bay Elementary School in April 1970.

The final PG&E *betrayal*, for me at least, was the aftermath that followed the company's May 20 safety meeting in 1970 that led to PG&E's infamous conspiracy resulting in a false police report that more than resembled the Machiavellian shenanigans of the McCarthy Era.

All of these *betrayals of the public trust* will be covered in the remaining portions of my *Diary* but first I want to briefly mention that I had invested heavily in my decision to become a nuclear control technician.

There were many hours of study late at night, night after night, and the countless weekends lost in my pursuit of the rigorous nuclear control technician-training program. As I approached the completion of the training program in 1968, I found myself questioning my decision to become a nuclear control tech. My whole nuclear control technician experience was by this time turning into an ugly, unimaginable nightmare and rapidly becoming the worst experience of my life. My wife was acutely aware of the turmoil swelling up inside of me, which left me feeling guilty about how all of my difficulties at work were affecting her and my family. However, the worst was yet to happen!

On August 6, 1969, another *betrayal of the public trust* occurred; this time it was the improper release of a nuclear spent fuel-shipping cask from PG&E's Humboldt Bay nuclear facility. As luck *or misfortune* would have it, I was the nuclear control technician assigned to the final decontamination effort and release of the 80-ton spent fuel-shipping cask. What ultimately proved to be a failed "decon effort" of the shipping cask had lasted for several days and nights, and now it rested squarely on my shoulders!

There had been many violations of the public trust but I became snarled in PG&E's handling of this one in a very big way! What was done was contrary to the public trust and covered up by lies, deception, and the old Potomac two-step in Washington. People with a whole lot more experience than I, orchestrated the cover up that took place. There was nothing in my background, education, or experience that would have enabled me to deal with it more effectively than I did. All I could do at the time was to stand my ground and do what I believed was the right thing for me to do.

Ultimately, the only follow up to what happened with PG&E's improper release of the nuclear spent fuel-shipping cask was for me to use the *forum* of my Unemployment Insurance Appeals Board Hearing that took place on October 3, 1970, and again on December 9, 1970.

My Unemployment Insurance Appeals Board Hearing was the only way for me to effectively expose what PG&E had done through the testimony of the Humboldt Bay Plant Engineer and two PG&E confidential memoranda, one by Edgar Weeks, Plant Engineer, and the other one by Gail Allen, Humboldt Bay Radiation Protection Engineer.

Of course, the "final" follow up to the spent fuel shipping cask incident of August 6, 1969, is the writing of my *Diary,* which will put this incident, along with the other PG&E *betrayals of the public trust* into the purview of the public for whatever impact it will have on PG&E's future credibility, and for that matter the credibility of the entire nuclear industry, as well.

At my Unemployment Insurance Appeals Board Hearing, L. V. Brown, an attorney from the company's corporate headquarters, represented PG&E and, out of necessity, I represented myself.

First a brief background is necessary to understand what nuclear spent fuel is, how it is handled, how it ultimately ends up in the nuclear spent fuel shipping cask, and then what is done with it after that.

Nuclear spent fuel elements are removed from the reactor core after they are no longer contributing to the desired power levels of the reactor. The nuclear spent fuel elements that are removed from the reactor are still extremely "hot," both radioactively and thermally, and therefore must be handled very carefully. Nuclear plant employees must always be shielded from the spent fuel elements because they are lethal if employees are directly exposed to them.

The nuclear spent fuel elements are transferred from the reactor core to the spent fuel pool for storage using a specially designed transfer cask. The 25-ton transfer cask is designed to do two very important things: (1) Keep the highly radioactive spent fuel elements relatively cool during the transfer from the core of the reactor to the spent fuel pool, and (2) protect the atomic workers from the intense radiation associated with the nuclear spent fuel elements.

The process of refueling the reactor starts with shutting down the reactor. After a time the huge biological shield is removed from the top of the reactor vessel, which is then followed by installing a stainless steel extension tank on top of the reactor vessel and filling it with demineralization water. After following the necessary procedures, the spent fuel elements previously selected for removal from the predetermined areas of the reactor core are prepared for transfer. Only a portion of the reactor core at any given point in time is removed and replaced with new nuclear fuel during a refueling outage.

Transferring the fuel elements had to take place under water by first lowering the refueling building's 25-ton transfer cask into the extension tank and down to the upper region of the reactor vessel. Once the transfer cask is in place, the selected spent fuel element is very carefully pulled out of the core of the reactor and into the transfer cask. The spent fuel element had to remain in water at all times for the purposes of cooling and moderating the radiation.

After the spent fuel element is secured inside the transfer cask, the bottom of the cask is sealed. Once the transfer cask is determined ready for the next step in the process, the huge overhead crane raises the transfer cask completely out of the extension tank.

As the transfer cask is coming out of the extension tank, the outside of the cask is hosed down with demineralized water to wash off as much surface contamination as possible. After it is completely out of the extension tank, it is then slowly moved by the refueling building's overhead crane towards the spent fuel storage pool, normally just referred to as the "spent fuel pool"

When the transfer cask arrives at the desired location over the spent fuel pool, the transfer cask is then lowered into the spent fuel pool and the underwater transfer of the spent nuclear fuel element into the designated storage rack location of the spent fuel pool takes place. The work involving spent fuel elements was performed by highly skilled control operators.

Image 19. Nuclear Fuel Transfer Cask over the reactor core
(From the author's files)

It was necessary to leave the nuclear spent fuel elements in the spent fuel storage pool for a long period of time to allow them to sufficiently decay so they could eventually be removed from the spent fuel pool and transported to a nuclear fuel reprocessing plant using a specially designed, 80-ton nuclear spent fuel shipping cask.

The spent fuel elements in the spent fuel pool were lethal if pulled directly out of the water, a point that again needs to be emphasized! To provide an example of just how radioactive the spent fuel elements were, nuclear control techs would place clear lead crystal items in "weighted" acetate bags (the same acetate bags used in the solid low-level radiation waste boxes), using several of them at a time and carefully sealing each one.

After the necessary preparations had been made, the control tech would lower the clear lead crystal items into the spent fuel pool down alongside the visible Cherenkov radiation glow of a relatively fresh spent fuel element. After a few seconds the bags of lead crystal items were pulled out of the spent fuel pool while the outside of them were decontaminated. The contents were then carefully retrieved from the acetate bags.

What was initially clear lead crystal wound up as either dark amber or a deep purple in color. (We always made sure the items themselves were not contaminated when we took them home) The intense radiation from the spent fuel elements simply changed the molecular structure of the lead crystal items. What would take many, many years of lying in the hot desert sun to make these changes in the lead crystal would take the spent fuel elements only a few seconds to accomplish.

The spent fuel pool water had become grossly contaminated because of the breakdown of the stainless steel cladding early in the operation of the nuclear facility. The failure of the stainless steel fuel cladding coupled with the single steam loop system design (page 54) of the nuclear power plant eventually made Humboldt Bay "the dirtiest atomic plant in the nation."

After the nuclear spent fuel elements had remained in the spent fuel pool sufficiently long enough to cool down to a level that would enable them to be transported to a nuclear fuel reprocessing facility, the spent fuel-shipping cask was scheduled. After the spent fuel-shipping cask arrived at Humboldt Bay, the control operators would break containment of the refueling building by opening the railroad doors. Containment of the building meant the entire refueling building was held under negative pressure so leaks in the building's structure for any reason would be inboard and not the other way around.

A Northwestern Pacific (NWP) locomotive would push the especially designed railroad flatbed car with the nuclear spent fuel-shipping cask resting on it into the refueling building. The locomotive would leave, the railroad doors would close, and containment of the refueling building would be reestablished. The 80-ton shipping cask was one of a kind and shared by all the nuclear facilities in the country.

Image 20. Nuclear Fuel Transfer Cask on its way to the spent fuel pool
(From the author's files)

After arriving inside the refueling building, the shipping cask was removed from its cradle by a large overhead crane and placed in an upright position in the staging area along side of the spent fuel pool.

The underwater transfer of the spent fuel took place by lowering the shipping cask into the spent fuel storage pool and placing the selected spent fuel elements into it. These fuel elements were still extremely radioactive, which required all of this work to be done under water. Once the nuclear spent fuel was loaded into the shipping cask, the cask was sealed and carefully pulled out of the spent fuel pool.

While the cask was slowly coming out of the pool, it was hosed down with demineralized water and allowed to hang above the pool for a more thorough hosing down to take place. The cask was then moved to a decon station along side of the storage pool where the arduous task of decontaminating the shipping cask began.

THE SPENT FUEL SHIPPING CASK INCIDENT (AUGUST 6, 1969)...

For several days and nights before August 6, 1969, plant personnel had worked around the clock attempting to decontaminate the spent fuel-shipping cask after it had been loaded with nuclear spent fuel and removed from the spent fuel pool.

The decon crews had tenaciously worked all night before the morning of August 6, 1969, using several decontamination strategies. They had very aggressively continued their use of soap and water to scrub down the shipping cask without much luck. Then they tried several other methods, including alcohol scrubs, during the wee hours of the morning but still without success. The cask remained very much contaminated.

By early morning on August 6, 1969, there were several maintenance workers and shift helpers trying to decontaminate the cask, and two nuclear control technicians had joined the effort, Raymond Skidmore and Bob Rowen. Gail Allen, Radiation Protection Engineer, was overseeing the work. We were still having problems removing the radioactive contamination from the cask.

Mr. Allen decided to have the cask washed with a strong solution of DC13, a powerful cleaning agent. After this special cleaning agent had been used several times, Raymond Skidmore and I started taking a series of smear samples. We were not getting even close to the desired results, especially in the midsection of the cooling fins on the outside of the cask.

The seal on the cask presented an even more ominous problem with contamination readings exceeding 20,000 dpm/100 cm^2.

Allen was visibly growing increasingly impatient and frustrated with the decon job. Everyone was doing their very best. Unfortunately, our efforts just weren't good enough!

By early afternoon, Allen realized that the shipping cask could not be further decontaminated using the decon solutions and techniques that were available to us by the deadline imposed on him by Edgar Weeks and I had every reason to believe Edgar Weeks was getting his marching orders from J. C. Carroll, PG&E's Nuclear Engineer at corporate headquarters in San Francisco.

The company wanted that cask out of the facility because of the high penalty late-fee the company had to pay for every day it kept the cask past the release contract date. According to law professor Bill Rodgers, "Allen was in a hurry to move the shipping cask to save the company $70,000."[129]

It became abundantly clear plant management wanted to "release the cask," regardless of its condition, by the end of the day on August 6, 1969. Arrangements had already been made for the NWP Railway to pick up the spent fuel-shipping cask. Meanwhile, the decon crew continued to work feverishly on the cask. Mr. Allen showed up at the job site in the refueling building mid-afternoon with his wipes in hand to take what he thought was going to be the final smears on the cask.

Skidmore and I watched Allen take those smears and we both agreed that he was not using proper technique for collecting those samples. He took his smear samples using a very noticeable "light" touch in various areas of the cask. Each smear sample was placed in a separate sample envelope and labeled with date, time, and specific location on the cask. Skidmore and I followed Allen to access control, we changed into our street clothes and I reported to the Rad Protection Desk.

I first analyzed Allen's samples in the IPC counter located in the reactor control room by the rad protection workstation. Mr. Allen was hovering over me the whole time I was doing my work. Then he decided to have the same samples counted again in the IPC counter located in the counting room where other kinds of radioactive samples were usually analyzed. The counting room IPC produced lower readings.

Meanwhile, Skidmore had returned to the refueling building to obtain still another set of smear samples. After Skidmore's last set of samples were counted and calculated, we found lower readings on the top and bottom areas of the cask, but the readings in the mid-areas of the cask were still extremely high.

Mr. Allen then gave me a direct order to go back down into the refueling building and take another set of smears, but this time only on the very "top and bottom four quadrants" of the cask, those areas that had just been previously determined to be the "coolest" areas on the cask. I looked at Skidmore in disbelief and shook my head. I could see the handwriting on the wall; this was not going to turn out well for me, but in spite of that I decided to do what I knew to be the right thing to do.

I objected to what he had ordered me to do but it was to no avail. Allen made certain that I took the smear samples exactly as he directed me to do. After returning to the counting room with the latest batch smear samples, I balked at following Mr. Allen's direct orders to count them. I told Allen we could not consider these samples to be the final samples. I made it clear to him that the smears he ordered me to take, and the manner in which he ordered me to take them, was not a true representation of the contamination on the outside surface of the cask, and that PG&E had an obligation to be honest and to do a better job of decontaminating the shipping cask even if that meant we had to keep the cask in the plant for a longer period of time.

Mr. Allen immediately became extremely upset with me and called the front office. He talked with Mr. Weeks about the problem I was creating for him and the scene that I was creating. I could hear Allen's side of the phone conversation and I knew this whole affair was going to get real ugly. I remember Skidmore quietly saying with a grin, "Bob, I think you've managed to step in it again — this time hugely."

After hanging up the phone, I was ordered by Allen to analyze the samples in the counting lab's IPC (the one that had previously produced the lowest readings) as he had originally directed me to do. He ordered me to do it immediately! What was taking place was so damned obvious and I knew that I was ultimately on a collision course with Edgar Weeks!

I ended up following the direct orders Mr. Allen had given to me but made it clear to him that I was strenuously protesting what he had asked me to do!

When the samples were counted and the calculations made, the results produced an average of 2,610 dpm/100 cm^2 of smearable radioactive contamination on Allen's selected areas of the cask. Mr. Allen then handed me pre-typed release forms to sign, which had me listed as the nuclear control technician responsible for releasing the cask. The form had my name pre-typed on it and my signature would have verified that the smearable radioactive contamination on the outside of the cask was in compliance with DOT regulations, that is, <2200 disintegrations per minute per 100 sq. cm^2 (2200 dpm/cm^2).

Following another unpleasant verbal exchange, Allen surprisingly changed the form by scratching out the " 2200 dpm/cm^2" and writing above it "2610 dpm/100 cm^2" then ordered me to sign the DOT release form. I objected to the whole damned situation saying again that we had not obtained honest results. The results simply were not a true representation of the actual radioactive contamination on the cask. He advised me that it was in my best interests to sign the release papers, which I finally did but only under protest!

Immediately after Mr. Allen left Unit 3 with the signed release forms in hand, I recorded what had taken place in the Control Technician Logbook (PG&E Logbook No. 62598-65):

> **G. Allen asked Rowen to sign the release papers for the spent fuel shipping cask stating the contamination levels of the cask to be less than 2200 d/m, when in fact they were greater than 2600 d/m. Further, G. Allen gave**

> **Rowen directions to take final smears for determination of release conditions on the top and bottom avoiding the middle area on all sides of the cask, when just previously, R. Skidmore took smears of the middle areas to find out of limit conditions. /s/ R. Rowen**

This entry into the control technician radiation logbook was made right at quitting time while I was still upset about what had taken place a short time earlier. Little did I realize at the time I made this entry into the official PG&E "Control Technician Log Book" just how much of a ruckus it was going to cause. Entries into the control technician logbook were routinely made throughout the day. The logbook was kept at the rad protection desk and maintained by the control technician assigned to radiation protection duty.

The next morning at one minute into the workday, I was called to the front office by Mr. Edgar Weeks. He had the control technician logbook in front of him and he was absolutely furious. Weeks held up the logbook and, while he was shaking it at me, wanted to know what the hell I thought I was doing, " . . . making an entry like this into this logbook?"

Mr. Weeks was red-faced and obviously very upset with me. His infuriating demeanor and aggressive behavior was extremely upsetting but I somehow managed to remain calm with the help of a little bit of insolent humor saying, "Calm down, please calm down before you have a stroke." Of course, that remark didn't help Weeks at all but it sure helped me by making me feel I was a little more in control.

I told Weeks my entry in the logbook was merely a brief and precise summary of what had taken regarding the spent fuel shipping cask; that my entry in the logbook simply represented what I felt was important regarding the incident. I also asked Weeks if he had any questions about the entry I had made. Of course, my question really didn't help matters much — And I knew that it wouldn't! It's just that I was now caught up in the swinging doors of a loosing situation.

Weeks responded saying this was another perfect example of my poor attitude towards the company and my supervisors. I responded by telling him that I totally disagreed with him and that I was just simply doing my job. My response caused Weeks to become absolutely enraged and out of control! I just got up and walked out of his office "without being dismissed."

Weeks followed up with another one of his notorious "counseling sessions" with me that afternoon. I was called back into his office after lunch for another one of his unwelcome assaults on my character, another tongue-lashing I had become so accustomed to receiving in his office. This one was put in writing, in a PG&E document entitled "Confidential Memorandum: Counseling of R. Rowen on 8/7/1969," which I eventually received through discovery proceedings.

The first three paragraphs of that memorandum read exactly as follows:

The Control Technician Log of 8/6/69 was, in my opinion, deliberately made out by Mr. Rowen in a manner intended to convey the impression that his supervisor, Mr. Gail Allen, was attempting to falsify radiation protection records. After discussing the events covered by the log entry with Mr. Allen, I decided to discuss the matter with Mr. Rowen.

I opened the discussion by asking Mr. Rowen to read the Log for 8/6/69 and then asking him if he believed that this was a proper entry. He was noncommittal. I asked if he understood the purpose of the Log. He said that he didn't because no supervisor had ever told him exactly what to put in the Log. I told him that his ignorance of the Log's purpose was a bit odd since he has had the responsibility of making it out since becoming a journeyman C.T. in 8/24/68. I spent several minutes explaining its use for recording significant radiation protection data and observations.

I emphasized that the report of facts and observations was to be objective. I told him that I believed that he had used the Log improperly on 8/6/69 to express his personal feelings about Mr. Allen's handling of a radiation protection problem. In addition, he had not even discussed his dissatisfaction with Mr. Allen. I told him that he had used poor judgment in this situation and strongly recommended he be objective in the future.

I responded to this follow-up counseling session in total amazement. The truth of the matter was that I did clearly understand the purpose of PG&E's Humboldt Bay Unit 3 "Control Technician Log Book," since it had been part of my apprentice control technician-training program. This is what I told Mr. Weeks that morning. In other words, Weeks simply lied in his cheap shot memo (one he thought I'd never see), and he lied not just once but several times in it!

It was made clear to Weeks that I had talked with Allen about my dissatisfaction with the way he was handling the release of the spent fuel-shipping cask. I reminded Weeks that Allen had called him from Unit 3 the previous afternoon about "the problem I was creating for the company." I sarcastically asked Weeks if he remembered that phone conversation.

Weeks was told that I overheard every word that Allen had said to him on the phone. I also told Mr. Weeks that he was already aware of my attempt to talk with Allen, and that I had the very clear impression Allen had received instructions from him to move forward with having me sign the release forms as I "was previously directed to do." Finally I told Mr. Weeks that I had expressed my thoughts about the shipping cask incident very objectively in the logbook. And yes, I also told Mr. Weeks that Allen was definitely attempting to falsify official PG&E "radiation protection safety records." It was for that very reason that I made the entry in PG&E's "Control Technician Log Book" in the first place.

Of course the nuclear spent fuel shipping cask incident raises another couple of questions. What was so blooming important for me to be the one to sign-off on the release of the nuclear spent fuel-shipping cask? If PG&E's Radiation Protection Engineer approved the violation, why then didn't he just sign the release forms? An even a better question, why didn't Edgar Weeks volunteer to take the responsibility with his signature on the DOT documentation? After all, the final in-house decision to release the cask came from his desk!

The only remaining recourse for me to address the nuclear spent fuel-shipping cask affair was to bring it up at my Unemployment Appeals Board Hearing with Mr. Weeks while he was under oath. After submitting Allen's confidential memorandum regarding his explanation of what had taken place and Weeks' counseling memo of me into the record and the ensuing discussions of both, the Referee took charge with his own examination of Weeks:[130]

> **REFEREE:** Mr. Weeks, you stated earlier with regard to the memorandum you prepared criticizing the log entries of Mr. Rowen of August 6th 1969; that you pointed out that the AEC inspector read those logs. How does that go along with your statement you conduct your operations in a goldfish bowl?
>
> **Mr. Weeks:** I think that goes along with it very well. I said that anyone can read the logs.
>
> **REFEREE:** Yes. And, therefore you don't want anything in the log that (INTERRUPTED)
>
> **Mr. Weeks:** No. Not at all.
>
> **REFEREE:** Well, what was wrong with what Mr. Rowen wrote in it? It was precisely a true recording according to the statement of the supervisor in question.
>
> **Mr. Weeks:** The way it was written … it was an attack against Mr. Allen, stating that Mr. Allen had tried to so something dishonest here, when in fact, as I understand Mr. Allen's memorandum and my discussion with him, he was perfectly sincere and correct in his actions. It was Mr. Rowen's opinion of what Mr. Allen did.
>
> **REFEREE:** Well, according to my understanding of Mr. Allen's own memorandum, he was precisely trying to do something dishonest.
>
> **Mr. Weeks:** Well, I disagree with you completely, then. He was not trying to do anything dishonest.
>
> **REFEREE:** I think Allen admitted he had. At any rate, the memorandum speaks for itself.

At the time of my two counseling sessions with Weeks on August 7, I could have asked Mr. Weeks to read the company's own memorandum about the proper use of the Control Technician Log Book, dated 8/29/1966, and signed by Gail E. Allen and Jerome Boots. After his reading of the memorandum I could have then asked Weeks to explain to me what it meant and how my use of the Log Book was improper. I would have done this except that I didn't have a copy of it with me at the time of those two miserable "counseling sessions" regarding the whole affair that day.

Looking back on it brings to mind just how difficult it was for me to deal with plant management in general, and with Edgar Weeks in particular.

In any event, the official PG&E Humboldt Bay Power Plant Unit 3 Memorandum reads exactly as follows:

> SUBJECT: Control Technician Log Book
> Effective January 3, 1966, the C.T. Log Book will be kept as a record of all important events* (which are defined on page 156 of my *Diary*) that occur during the day in Rad. Protection and Chemistry. It will be the duty of the R-2 man to maintain this log and sign the completed sheet each day.
> * "All important events" is defined as:
> 1. Unusual happenings such as Control Room contaminated, large spill, etc.
> 2. Unusual air sample data or chemistry data.
> 3. Brief rundown of day's activity.
> 4. Personnel contaminated.
> 5. Personnel clothing retained because of contamination.
> 6. Any violation of established standards.
> 7. Any other things felt important by the C.T. in this area.

All the journeyman technicians at that time were required to "READ, DATE, and INITIAL" this memorandum at the bottom of it, which in effect constituted a company directive. This document became part of the training materials for the apprentice nuclear control techs, which at the time included Bill Evans, Forrest Williams, and Bob Rowen.

The 8/8/69 Confidential Memorandum regarding the "counseling session" on 8/7/69 ended with Weeks writing the following:

> I also took this opportunity to counsel Mr. Rowen concerning several complaints I had received from first line supervision, concerning his continued "griping and complaining" about the Company and its poor treatment of employees. I reminded Rowen that he had a responsibility to promote harmony, not disrupt it. I reminded him that I was still not satisfied with his job performance and believed there was considerable room for improvement.

This was simply more of the same. My insistence on doing things right was bringing me much grief, especially from Edgar Weeks who had obviously embarked on a mission to break me down. He was not alone in this endeavor, however, because other members of plant management were engaging in the same effort with Weeks orchestrating it and assembling an ugly paper trail in my personnel file.

Many of the employees felt that I was just a troublemaker and said so in private conversations with their first line supervisors – it's *called "making points."* I heard about this stuff from a few of the employees who truly wanted to be helpful. However, it seemed as if most of the employees believed that I was personally attacking the very basis of their livelihoods and felt threatened by my confronting plant management the way I did.

In my attempt to address the spent fuel shipping cask incident dated August 6, 1969, and to address PG&E's cover-up of it, I wrote a lengthy letter to Mr. W. J. Burns, Director to the Department of Transportation (DOT) Office of Hazardous Materials dated February 13, 1972.

My letter to Mr. Burns was in response to a copy of a PG&E letter sent to the DOT dated October 6, 1971, that I had received from freelance writer Roger Rapoport.

My February 13, 1972, letter to Mr. Burns included the following salient points:

1. Acknowledgment of my receipt of a copy of PG&E's letter to the DOT dated October 6, 1971.
2. Notification of PG&E's deliberate misrepresentations of the facts concerning the spent fuel shipping cask incident dated August 6, 1969. (I provided a complete summary of what PG&E did with the details of exactly how PG&E did it)
3. PG&E should be challenged and held accountable. (I requested the DOT to thoroughly investigate the matter)
4. PG&E falsely represented the condition of the spent fuel-shipping cask. (I provided all the facts and the necessary supporting documentation)
5. PG&E claimed Mr. Warren Raymond contacted DOT when in fact Edgar Weeks claimed he made the call to the DOT. (I provided the testimony of Weeks regarding the call that was made to the DOT)
6. PG&E assailed my character in an attempt to discredit me. (I provided the findings of the Referee of my California Unemployment Appeals Board Hearing regarding PG&E's assertion that I was discharged with cause)
7. PG&E claimed Mr. Weeks did not imply that DOT "condoned" exceeding any limits specified in the regulations. (I provided Weeks' own testimony that proved otherwise)

8. PG&E claimed that I was directed to take final smears of the cask in accordance with established procedures. (I made it clear to Mr. Burns that this claim by PG&E was an outright fabrication by PG&E corporate officials and provided the evidence to prove it)

In my letter to Mr. Burns I explained that sometime during the morning of August 6 a decision was made by higher management of PG&E to release the cask to the Northwestern Pacific Railroad Company. Subsequently, orders were handed down to Mr. Allen to have the cask ready for release by 6 pm on August 6, 1969. By early afternoon it was apparent that the cask would not be ready for release because further attempts to decontaminate the cask were in vain.

I outlined my concerns and further stated that without any doubt the spent fuel-shipping cask was released by PG&E on August 6, 1969, with radioactive contamination levels far exceeding that which is allowed by the D.O.T. regulations and I provided documentation in support of my stated concerns. It was totally ignored because little did I realize the DOT really had very little clout when it came to dealing with the AEC.

In response to an item in my February 13, 1972 letter to Mr. Burns and in an attempt to clear up the problem the Referee was having with understanding PG&E's decision that it was okay to change the results of the pre-typed radiation survey form from 2200 dpm/100 cm^2 to 2600 dpm/100 cm^2, the Referee engaged Mr. Weeks in the following exchange during my second Unemployment Appeals Board Hearing held on December 9, 1970:[131]

REFEREE: (Directed to Mr. Weeks . . .) But, what I'm trying to find out, was at the time Mr. Allen asked Mr. Rowen to sign the papers and Mr. Rowen refused, was it known to Mr. Allen that the paper was not accurate, that it was an average of 2600 dpm, not less than 2200?

Mr. Weeks: I could only speculate that this was probably the first time this point was brought to his attention, was when Rowen refused to sign it. I could only speculate that.

REFEREE: I see.

Mr. Weeks: I do not believe Mr. Allen was attempting to be dishonest. It is his judgment that this was not a significant variation from 2200, about a 15 percent variation.

REFEREE: Well, if there is a rule that something can't exceed a certain figure, isn't anything over it significant?

Mr. Weeks: Well, this is why I checked with Mr. Guerilla, Department of Transportation, because I wanted to ask the same question you're asking. And, what he told us was that this was okay. This is not a significant change for an occasional shipment, but he didn't want us to get in the sloppy habit of doing this all the time and I assured him it had been the only time we'd ever done it to my knowledge and he seemed quite satisfied.

REFEREE: It's okay then if the rules are broken only occasionally.

Mr. Weeks: Well, those are your words, not mine.

REFEREE: They are my words.

This feisty exchange between the Referee and Weeks, although somewhat entertaining and revealing at the same time, actually begs the much larger and more significant question of what really took place! Mr. Allen's honesty as well as that of Mr. Weeks had to have been called into question for two very clear and convincing reasons.

First, Mr. Allen had previously determined the midsection of the cask (over 40 percent of the its surface area) to have much higher levels of smearable radioactive contamination, which he purposely avoided in his final evaluation of the cask. Edgar Weeks was fully aware of this. Second, both Allen and Weeks completely ignored the contamination levels on the major top-seal above the cooling fins of the cask. And what's most noteworthy here is the DOT and AEC both shamefully turned a blind's eye to what PG&E had done and the general public paid the price for it!

Mr. Roger Rapoport, author of the *Great American Bomb Machine*, submitted a list of 18 specific questions to the U.S. Atomic Energy Commission as part of his own research on the Humboldt Bay Nuclear Power Plant. Question #2 dealt with the spent fuel shipping cask incident dated August 6, 1969. The complete AEC responses to this item were as follows:

1. The average removable beta-gamma contamination observed on the cask prepared for shipment on August 8 (sic), 1969 was approximately 18% above Department of Transportation limit of 2200 disintegrations per minute for average removable beta-gamma activity. Since DOT is responsible for the safety of shipments of radioactive material in transit, the AEC does not have radiation limits applicable to the shipment of the cask.

2. The licensee reported that prior to shipment of the cask the above information was discussed with a Department of Transportation official who allegedly reported that he would not like it to be routine but that it was acceptable in this case.

3. A June 1971 AEC interview with the same DOT official revealed that the official could not recall the specific occasion but responded that he probably would have responded by saying that the excess was within the measurement statistical error limits of the measurements and would have approved the shipment

A careful and thoughtful reading of this AEC response reflects on the true nature of the regulatory function of the agency, and raises serious questions about reliability of the Atomic Energy Commission.

This AEC response further explains why I was having so much difficulty working in, what law professor William Rodgers called, "This den of self-satisfaction."[132] Rodgers was specifically responding to my difficulties with PG&E and the AEC by saying, "[The AEC] has praised the 'conscientious and reliable manner'[133] in which the business of safety is conducted at Humboldt Bay. It has found management to be extremely responsive to constructive criticisms."[134]

To summarize the nuclear spent fuel shipping cask incident of August 6, 1969, PG&E authorized its release in violation of DOT regulations. Company management personnel lied about the condition of the shipping cask; the shipping cask was clearly radioactively contaminated and totally out of compliance. The midsection of the cask representing approximately 40 percent of its surface area had radioactive contamination far exceeding the amounts allowed by law. The top-seal of the cask had over nine times the amount of contamination allowed by DOT regulations and this fact was totally ignored by PG&E, the AEC, and the DOT, yet that problem was clearly stated in a confidential memorandum written by the Radiation Protection Engineer, Mr. Gail Allen, and reviewed by the Plant Engineer, Mr. Edgar Weeks. This documentation was offered to the DOT and the AEC but was ignored by both.

If the excess contamination was "within the measurement statistical error limits of the measurements" and therefore would have been approved by the DOT as the AEC claimed, then why would the DOT official, who was supposedly contacted by PG&E and the AEC on different occasions, say that it was okay but that he would not like for it to be routine? In reality the measurements taken were not a true representation of the cask's condition. Having said that, one must ask, "What's the point of having stated release limits embedded in law for the purpose of protecting the public and then after the fact providing nuclear operators approval for violating the law and more specifically, doing it without any kind of a serious and rigorous investigation of what happened?"

The radiation protection engineer's decision to use the radiation IPC counter that produced the lowest readings reveals a greater concern for the company's bottom line than any concern for public safety. One of two things should have taken place. Time should have been spent to determine why there was a discrepancy between the two IPC counters, or at the very least the IPC counter located at the rad protection work station should have been the one that was used to determine the condition of the shipping cask. Why?

First, that particular IPC was generally considered more reliable and used for most of the CTs' rad protection work. Second, and in any event, to err on the side of caution by using the higher readings should have been considered the more desirable course of action.

The fact that Mr. Gail Allen, PG&E's Radiation Protection Engineer, directed his nuclear control technicians to take samples in the areas of the cask previously determined to have the least amount of contamination (which were still above the DOT limits) and to specifically avoid those areas that had much higher levels of radioactive contamination (areas that represented much more than a third of the spent fuel shipping cask's outside surfaces) was dishonest and totally illegal. And clearly the support of his second-line supervisor was at the very least, unforgivable.

There is another important observation that needs to be made concerning the use of the nuclear spent fuel shipping cask. The shipping cask weighing eighty tons that was used to carry radioactive spent fuel from Humboldt Bay to a reprocessing facility in New York [135] could only be shipped by rail. This cask was one of a kind especially designed for the purpose of transporting the highly radioactive spent fuel and the other nuclear power plants around the country were sharing it.

Transporting Humboldt Bay's nuclear spent fuel by rail began with the Northwestern Pacific Railroad (NWP) taking it south from Eureka to the San Francisco north-bay area for transfer to another rail carrier. About forty miles south of Eureka the NWP freight-train had to pass under the highly unstable Scotia Bluffs on a railroad trestle system that was more than a mile long that the NWP railway workers referred to as the "treacherous trestle."

Railroad bridge crews were specifically assigned to work exclusively on the Scotia Bluff trestles for more than forty years because the bluffs consisted of sandstone and were frequently damaged by massive blocks of falling sandstone.

Image 21. NWP Scotia Bluffs Trestle (Courtesy of the Fortuna Depot Museum)

My dad was a railroader all his adult life with the Santa Fe Railroad; Southern Pacific Railroad (SP), and the Northwestern Pacific Railroad (NWP), a subsidiary of SP. There was a history of numerous accidents on that section of rail due to frequent landslides from the Scotia Bluffs.

In 1953 the Scotia Bluffs had a massive landslide that swept NWP Engine 184 into the Eel River that took the lives of three trainmen. That particular accident was especially difficult for our family because my dad went into the water in an attempt to recover his friends. The recovery effort had to be completed by a hard hat diver from San Francisco.

I remember the discussions I had with my dad about the rail transport of the nuclear spent fuel across that section of track below the Scotia Bluffs. My dad said the trains had to slow down to 10 mph maximum to proceed across the Scotia Bluffs trestle system.

It's impossible to understand how the approval to transport the nuclear spent fuel-shipping cask by the NWP rail system became part of the approval process to build and operate the Humboldt Bay reactor facility. How serious would it have been had the 80-ton nuclear spent fuel-shipping cask landed in the Eel River?

Image 22. NWP Engine No. 184 Scotia Bluffs Trestle Salvage Project in 1953 (Courtesy of the Fortuna Depot Museum)

Was this another "tough" lesson for PG&E? Well, according to one PG&E official, there were numerous "tough" lessons that were learned at Humboldt Bay. In fact, on one occasion, Frederick "Fritz" Draeger, atomic information coordinator from PG&E's corporate headquarters in San Francisco, confidentially stated the company's first nuclear experience at the Vallecitos nuclear facility provided the technology gains used in the Humboldt Bay Nuclear Plant and likewise, the technological aka "tough" lessons learned at the Humboldt Bay nuclear facility would be applied at future PG&E nuclear plants.[136]

Fritz Draeger, nor anyone else from his office for that matter never, ever had anything to say about any of those "tough" lessons PG&E learned at Humboldt Bay that led to a slew of cover-ups! Quite to the contrary, the company spent millions on painting a rosy picture of the nuclear facility as being safe, efficient, and economical; and all the while having to frequently lie about what was taking place at the plant.

Draeger's only public admission that touched on the truth was simply, "Humboldt Bay was the oldest commercially operated reactor west of the Mississippi, and when it was built certain failures were expected to happen because the reactor was a first generation plant."[137] Draeger made this incredible statement and then immediately refused to debate or even publicly discuss what he meant by those "certain failures that were expected to happen" and how PG&E chose to address those failures.[138]

PG&E's claim that this "first generation plant" was safe amounted to nothing more than a house of cards, and company management would say or do anything to keep the public from learning the truth. The improper release of the spent fuel-shipping cask in August 1969 provides an excellent example of what PG&E management and the AEC were willing to do to maintain PG&E's house of cards. The AEC went along with this charade because it was the agency's foremost imperative to promote this failed and dangerous technology at the expense of employee and public safety.

__VII__

7. G&R Scrap Metals

February 1970

"Let there be no mistake about what happened, the company deliberately sold radioactively contaminated scrap metal to an unsuspecting local scrap metal dealer in Eureka and after it was discovered PG&E intentionally covered it up." [139] [Bob Rowen]

"That is one of the things that always gets you in trouble, Bob." [140] [Edgar Weeks]

On February 18, 1970, I was making a routine C survey when I discovered a piece of radioactively contaminated pipe on the workbench in Humboldt Bay's "cold" machine shop. "C surveys," as they were commonly called, were routinely conducted every week by nuclear control technicians, usually on Tuesday or Wednesday of each week, for the basic purpose of making certain no radioactive materials, tools, or equipment had accidentally or improperly left the radiation controlled area of Unit 3.

A portable Geiger-Muller "GM" beta-gamma detection survey instrument was used for C area surveys. Since "C" stood for "clean," C area surveys, "C surveys" for short, were conducted in certain areas of the plant outside of the radiation controlled area of Unit 3, and these C surveys always carried with them the expectation that no radioactive materials, tools, or equipment would be encountered during these routine radiation surveys.

This weekly routine was simply to serve as a "double-check" on maintaining a radiation free environment in the non-controlled areas of the Humboldt Bay Power Plant. These non-controlled areas included fossil fuel Units 1 and 2, the warehouse, the "cold" machine shop, the electrician's repair shop, the "cold" instrument shop, the CG painters' workshop, and all the administrative office areas of the plant.

The GM survey instrument had a probe attached by a cable approximately 3 feet long (review Chapter #3). The probe itself was essentially a gas filled chamber containing two electrodes, and the probe was equipped with a shield so that beta and gamma radiation could be identified. With the shield removed, both beta and gamma radiation could enter the probe, but with the shield in place only gamma radiation could be measured. This radiation survey instrument indicated the presence of beta and gamma radiation in three different ways: (1) The counting rate of the radiation entering the probe was indicated on a meter; (2) The individual counting events could be heard as a series of "clicking sounds" by the use of earphones, and (3) the counting events were indicated by a flashing neon light on the face of the GM.

There were certain areas of the plant outside the radiation-controlled area that were of special interest to the "C" Area Survey Program. They included the entire cold machine shop, the electrician's shop, the cold instrument shop, and the painters' workshop. These particular areas had tools and equipment that were often used in the radiation controlled areas of Unit 3. These tools and equipment were always very carefully surveyed out of the radiation-controlled area and put through a thorough decontamination process whenever it was deemed necessary.

As I was passing through the cold machine shop on the morning of February 18, 1970, I could hear the sporadic clicking of the GM in my earphones indicating normal background noise. Suddenly the clicking accelerated to an extremely loud and rapid count, indicating the presence of a radiation source. The probe did not completely saturate, so I knew it was not an extremely hot source requiring the use of a CP (review Chapter #3).

Nevertheless, there was definitely a radiation source present and one that should not have been where I had encountered it in the cold machine shop.

I had discovered a piece of 14-inch diameter iron pipe that was about 20 inches long near one end of the long fabrication workbench located in the center of the cold machine shop facility. Initially, I had no idea where this section of iron pipe had come from or who had put it there. I immediately marked off the area and went looking for some answers. After scurrying around the shop, I found a welder working in a corner of it behind a welding curtain at the far end of the machine shop. The welder informed me that he had found that particular piece of pipe in the scrap metal bin and was going to use it for a project he was working on. I then immediately checked the scrap metal bin and found it completely empty.

The section of pipe in question turned out to be one of 18-20 pieces of heavy iron pipe that had to be cut into roughly 20-inch sections in order to be removed from the suppression chamber of the reactor containment system. When the welder took the piece of pipe from the scrap metal bin that he was planning to use as part of his special project, he said the scrap metal bin was completely full.

The welder also told me there were a large number of similar pieces of pipe just like the one piece I had found on the workbench. He had no idea it was radioactively contaminated, and neither did any of the other workers in the maintenance department who spent a great deal of time working in the cold machine shop.

If the welder had started with his project using this piece of pipe, he would have applied heat to it, which would have caused the radioactive contamination to become airborne. The welder along with the other employees working in the cold machine shop would not have taken the necessary protective measures to protect themselves from airborne contamination. Protective measures would have been required if the work was being done in the radiation controlled areas of the plant under the authority of a Special Work Permit (SWP). Plant management pooh-poohed my publicly stated observation and chastised me for making it.

I learned from the maintenance foreman that arrangements had been made by "the front office" for G&R Scrap Metal Company of Eureka, a commercial scrap metal dealer, to buy and haul off all the scrap metal. I was also told the scrap metal company had already cleaned out the scrap metal bins a couple of days earlier. The way it was explained to me about what had taken place was totally out of the ordinary and sounded fishy.

The maintenance foreman had not seen the necessary paperwork on any sections of the pipe, which would have indicated that an unconditional release was given the material, nor did he see any release tags attached to any of it. It was the responsibility of the maintenance foremen to oversee the scrap metal bins and all waste containers in the plant.

I immediately reported the incident to the nuclear facility's acting radiation protection engineer, Jerome Boots, and requested we send a radiological survey team to the scrap metal company and retrieve the contaminated pipe so that it could be properly surveyed and disposed of.

After talking with his superiors, Mr. Boots flatly turned down my request. He dug in his heels and became very defensive and argumentative with me claiming that there was absolutely no need "to contact G&R Scrap Metal Company in order (in his own precise words), to call them simply to tell them they had no problem."[141] As we continued to discuss the matter, Mr. Boots became indignant with me and it was obvious I was again on a collision course with plant management.

I was not willing to accept the company's decision to refuse my request to retrieve the contaminated pipe from G&R Metals, nor did I agree with the company's claim that all the other sections of the suppression chamber pipe were free of contamination. If the pipe had been properly surveyed out of the radiation-controlled area of Unit 3, it would have been marked with an unconditional release tag. No one ever saw an unconditional release tag! There would have been a paper trail regarding the survey and release of those several sections of pipe. That paper trail was never found! The nuclear control technician who would have conducted the survey and completed the required paperwork would have remembered doing it — simply because it would have been a major job. However, none of the nuclear control technicians remembered ever making such a survey! And nothing concerning such a survey was found in the Radiation Control Logbook.

Plant management's position made absolutely no sense – it just didn't add up! In reality what had taken place was another *betrayal of the public trust* followed by an obvious effort to conceal it and then cover-up it up!

Mr. Boots wrote an internal company "confidential" memorandum, which read in part (all parenthetical statements were included by Boots' in his actual memo):[142]

> This section of pipe was one of two remaining on site; the other 18 pieces were sold to G&R Metals (Eureka) as scrap. It was explained to Rowen that this incident would be reported to the AEC, inasmuch as it was released from the controlled area with a higher count rate than the administrative limit of 100 cpm. Our evaluation was that this level of contamination constituted no hazard; furthermore, it was most likely that the pieces sold to G&R Metals were not contaminated because they were surveyed and the results indicated that they could be unconditionally released.
>
> Rowen was adamant, that G&R Metals be notified of this matter, but we maintained that it would serve no purpose to call them simply to tell them they had no problem. There ensued several discussions with Rowen, some with E. D. Weeks and some with myself. During one of these discussions between myself, Rowen and Woods (a CT), Rowen accused me of attempting to cover up the facts, misconstrue and misinterpret the applicable regulations, and loophole seeking tactics. He became angry and irrational; and when he likened me to Lt. Calley (who was implicated in the alleged massacre at My Lai in Vietnam) in my actions, I informed him that there was no point in discussing this matter further with him. Already, many hours had been consumed in discussing this matter with him.

When I eventually acquired (through discovery proceedings) and read this internal company "confidential" memorandum, I became as upset as I was the day of the incident – perhaps even more so!

This memo again clearly establishes plant management's disregard for public safety, desire to maintain a positive public image above all else, and exposes management's horrendous scheme to rid itself of radioactively contaminated pipe in the cheapest (and most inappropriate) way possible.

In my view Jerome Boots was merely the mouthpiece of those above him. Boots was at the bottom of the company's management hierarchy, and it was apparent to me that he was willing to say and do whatever the upper echelons of plant management wanted and expected from him.

The only three statements in Mr. Boots' memo that contained varying degrees of truth (except for "irrational" in statement #3) were the following:

1. "Rowen was adamant, that G&R Metals be notified of this matter," (absolutely true)

2. "Already, many hours had been consumed in discussing this matter with him," (somewhat true) and

3. "Rowen accused me of attempting to cover up the facts, misconstrue and misinterpret the applicable regulations, and loophole seeking tactics. He became angry and irrational; and when he likened me to Lt. Calley (who was implicated in the alleged massacre at My Lai in Vietnam) in my actions ..."

First, I freely admit that I definitely did compare Mr. Boots to Lt. Calley, who was in the news at the time for the reasons Boots mentioned in his memo.

However, there was absolutely no basis, and therefore no justification, for Boots to state in his memo, "...It was most likely the pieces sold to G&R Metals were not contaminated."

Boots also claimed in his memo that all the pieces of pipe "...were surveyed and the results indicated that they could be unconditionally released." I don't know for certain who was behind this statement; all I know is that it was in Boots' memo. In any event, this claim was a blatant fabrication because there was no unconditional release tag on any of the sections of pipe in the plant's scrap metal bin according to the welder who saw all of it before G&R cleaned out the scrap metal bin, and there was no paperwork ever produced (or even seen by the maintenance foreman, who was responsible for overseeing the handling and disposal of waste materials in the plant) indicating the pipe had been properly surveyed out of the radiation controlled area of Unit 3.

I eventually complained to the AEC about this incident and the way the entire matter was handled by PG&E. The AEC investigator, Mr. J. J. Ward, simply recorded my complaint in the official AEC investigativ report as follows: "Contaminated pipe was sold as scrap to a scrap dealer." Mr. Ward concluded in his findings:[143]

> No substantiation for the allegation was found. One piece of pipe from the same lot, which had not been taken off the premises was found to contain minimal amount of contamination inside the pipe and did not present a hazard from a public health and safety standpoint. It is not appropriate to infer that because one piece of pipe from a lot contained a minimal amount of contamination that therefore the rest of the lot was also contaminated.

Not only did PG&E cover up what plant management had done, the AEC willfully came to the aid of the company with its phony investigation

(Chapter 13, Allegation #11).

The Technical Specifications contained in Appendix A to the AEC Operating License No.DPR-7 (for the Humboldt Bay Nuclear Facility) states the following:[144]

> **All work involving radiation or radioactive materials shall be performed in accordance with policies set forth in the Company's Radiation Control Standards. The basis for these standards shall be the several AEC and State of California regulations pertaining to radiation safety.**

PG&E's Radiation Control Standards pertaining to unconditional release of materials from radiation controlled areas state the following:[145]

> **An 'unconditional release' may be given an item when . . .the direct survey (above background) shows less than 100 c/m beta-gamma . . .an "unconditional release" tag shall be properly filled out by Radiation Protection personnel and attached to the item prior to its removal from the Controlled Area.**

There was never a second piece of pipe found in the plant as Boots had claimed. The welder took one piece from the scrap metal bin and the rest of it was sold to G&R Metals of Eureka. I asked Mr. Boots for the paper trail on the pipe that was taken out of the radiation controlled area and he failed to produce it. Why? Because he couldn't; it didn't exist.

Later I found myself in Mr. Week's office again discussing the entire matter. Again, I asked to see the paperwork on the "unconditional release" of the pipe and he, too, refused to show it to me. If plant management had produced the paperwork, it would have immediately resolved the issue regarding the pieces of pipe that were sold to G&R Scrap Metals.

Certainly one of the other six nuclear control technicians would have been involved in surveying the pipe and releasing it from the radiation controlled area. After all, that was our job and no one; absolutely no one remembered doing it. No one even had a memory of how or when the pipe had left the controlled area of Unit 3.

The welder did not see an "unconditional release" tag on any of the sections of pipe. From my training and experience as a nuclear control technician, if one piece of something in a common lot is contaminated, then it's reasonable to assume the other pieces are also most likely contaminated.

This piece of pipe was just one section of a long suppression chamber pipe that was cut up and removed from the reactor containment system. If one piece, the only piece examined, was contaminated it was reasonable to assume —in fact, proper radiation monitoring required it—that the other pieces in the "same lot" were not only contaminated, but could have had more or perhaps less contamination than the only piece examined.

The AEC investigator's statement, "It is not appropriate to infer that because one piece of pipe from a lot contained a minimal amount of contamination that therefore the rest of the lot was also contaminated," is absolutely contrary to everything we subscribed to as nuclear control technicians responsible for radiation protection!

In any event, as part of an effective radiation protection safety program, every one of those pieces should have received a second survey, assuming a first one had already been made, which in my view at the time was extremely doubtful. There is every reason to believe that a survey was never made on any of the pipe – period!

Given the fact that the 18-20 pieces of pipe that were originally a long continuous section of pipe that had to be cut up so the pipe could be removed from the tight quarters of the suppression chamber of the reactor containment system clearly speaks for itself. After all, it was very heavy iron pipe that presented a disposal problem if treated as radioactive waste.

If the welder had not inadvertently picked up the one piece of pipe from the scrap metal bin the whole shipment of contaminated suppression chamber pipe would have ended up at the local scrap metal company and no one would have ever been the wiser. As far as I was concerned the AEC and the California Department of Public Health were worthless when it came to dealing with matters like this incident and PG&E had a lot to do with this regulatory "arrangement."

My only opportunity to expose this incident for what it truly was came to me after I had been fired from PG&E and denied unemployment benefits. Using the appeals process, I was able to subpoena plant management personnel and put direct questions to them regarding my difficulties at the PG&E nuclear facility and this included the G&R scrap metal incident.

It is noteworthy to point out once again that I had to represent myself while an attorney from the company's corporate headquarters in San Francisco represented PG&E. The PG&E attorney was thoroughly briefed by plant management before showing up to my California Unemployment Insurance Appeals Board Hearing.

During the Appeals Board Hearing, the Referee, D.F.M. Hanley, at one point during the proceedings conducted his own direct examination of PG&E's temporary Radiation Protection Engineer, Jerome V. Boots:[146]

> **THE REFEREE:** Mr. Boots, did I understand you to say that this piece of pipe upon which the tests were made was the last remaining piece of pipe, one of two remaining pieces of pipe out of a lot of 18?
>
> **Mr. Boots:** I think approximately 18 pieces were sold to G&R Metals as scrap and we had retained two on site. The one piece that was in the cold machine shop was being used to control (sic) a shield; it was a radiation shield to be used in the Unit 3 control area.
>
> **THE REFEREE:** And did you test both pipes that still remained?
>
> **Mr. Boots:** No, just the one.

THE REFEREE: Only the one was tested?

Mr. Boots: Well, let me back off on this. When a piece of pipe originally inside the cold area of Unit 3 is moved outside of the control area, it has to be surveyed. These pieces of pipe had been surveyed out several years prior to this time and they were outside the control area. These two pieces of pipe, which were kept outside were not sold to G&R Metals. We were using one of these to construct a shield to use in the control area.

COMMENT: Boots was making things up as he was testifying and he was blowing smoke at the Referee while doing it. First, there was no such thing as a cold area inside the controlled area of Unit 3 (the controlled area of Unit 3 was the controlled area of Unit 3 – Period)!

Second, he refereed to "two" pieces of pipe that "had been surveyed out for several years" and "kept outside" the controlled area of Unit 3, inferring they were in a separate location from all the other pieces of pipe. It was clearly established by the welder and his supervisor that the piece of pipe I found on the fabrication workbench in the cold machine shop came directly from the scrap metal bin that contained all the other pieces of pipe. All sections of pipe originally came from the same place, the suppression chamber of the reactor containment system.

I didn't want to interrupt the Referee while he was questioning Boots because he was pursuing his own train of thought, which I considered more important than the observation I just made. The Referee was interested in knowing why the second piece of pipe Boots had refereed to was not surveyed since it had also remained on site.[147]

THE REFEREE (CONTINUING): (Directed to Boots) And that was the one you performed the test on?

Mr. Boots: Yes.

THE REFEREE: Well, when you found out that there was at least something out of the ordinary with regard to this piece of pipe, why wasn't the other one tested to see what its state might be?

Mr. Boots: Well, based on the evaluation of the one, there was no problem.

THE REFEREE: Is it possible that the other piece of pipe might have shown either more or less of a count?

Mr. Boots: This would be unlikely because they were surveyed originally before they came out and this small but perceptible count above background was picked up by Mr. Rowen in the course of his survey.

THE REFEREE: If it had been detected before the survey, what would have been done?

Mr. Boots: It would not have been released from the yard unless such had been reevaluated and decided that it could be released.

THE REFEREE: Then, if there was some departure from the ordinary, it would not have been where it was in that condition, is that right?

Mr. Boots: Well, this is the reason that we run the clean area surveys to detect if anything did get out of the control area.

THE REFEREE: All right. Since it had been established by your own test that this particular piece of pipe should not have been allowed out of the control area and yet it had been, why couldn't the same thing have happened to the other piece of pipe?

Mr. Boots: It's possible.

THE REFEREE: But you were not interested enough to test it?

Mr. Boots: We evaluated the situation; we didn't see that – INTERRUPTED

THE REFEREE: As to the one piece of pipe?

Mr. Boots: Yes, but these were all the same types of pipe. It's all 14-foot pipe (sic) that came out of Unit 3.

COMMENT: It was eventually determined that there was more than 30 feet of pipe that was removed from the reactor suppression chamber. If Boots' statement in his testimony was correct, then there had to have been at least two 14-foot sections of pipe involved, which would have contributed to a greater need to retrieve the pipe that was sold to G&R Metals.

THE REFEREE (CONTINUING): (Directed to Boots) Are you saying that it would not have been possible for the radioactive count above background to have been different?

Mr. Boots: I'm not saying that. I'm saying it's unlikely that it would be any appreciable amount above that. Probably less than that.

THE REFEREE: What is the amount above background that is considered in these various standards you mentioned that would make a part considered to be radioactive to a dangerous degree?

Mr. Boots: Well, it's hard to answer that question specifically. It depends on – INTERRUPTED

THE REFEREE: In this case, it was established the cobalt was 60, did you say?

Mr. Boots: Yes.

THE REFEREE: What is the standard with regard to that?

Mr. Boots: I don't know the number offhand. These are in the records that we have on it.

THE REFEREE: Is it a great deal more than the 300 above background?

Mr. Boots: Yes.

THE REFEREE: In your judgment, there was no danger that

the piece(s) of pipe, which had been sold to G&R, might have been contaminated?

Mr. Boots: In my judgment there was no – I was not concerned in the least that it would have been contaminated.

THE REFEREE: Would you, in your judgment, concede, however that there was a possibility?

Mr. Boots: Remote, but possible.

THE REFEREE: When you are dealing with matters of radioactive danger, aren't even the remotest possibilities important?

Mr. Boots: Yes, yes.

THE REFEREE: And yet you objected to the claimant's (Rowen) wish to notify G&R so that some corrective action could be taken with regard to this material that had been sold that possibly might have been radioactive?

Mr. Boots: I did not feel it was necessary because these pipes had already been surveyed and if there was danger on these pipes, it would have been picked up in the survey.

THE REFEREE: You have already established that the survey hadn't been properly conducted. Otherwise, this piece of pipe you were testing wouldn't have been where it was.[148]

COMMENT: Boots' testimony ran full circle and reeked of a cover-up of what had taken place. In my judgment, Boots was caught in the proverbial swinging doors of having to keep his superiors happy with his testimony. After all, they were all sitting in the room listening to his very word!

Later testimony revealed the Radiation Protection Engineer had never even seen the survey forms pertaining to the contaminated pipe incident. I had asked the Referee for permission to question Jerome Boots on this very point, and was given an opportunity to do so. The following is Mr. Boots' testimony:[149]

Mr. Rowen: Mr. Boots, isn't it true that when these things are released from the controlled area there is a form that is made out by the – INTERRUPTED

Mr. Boots: Yes, a survey form.

Mr. Rowen: And isn't it true that I requested those at the time I found this particular piece of pipe?

Mr. Boots: Yes, I believe you did.

Mr. Rowen: And did you produce those forms to resolve as to whether or not they had been properly surveyed out?

Mr. Boots: No, I did not, because these files are kept–these files are kept in a nuclear unit building and it would take quite some length of time to dig these out.

Mr. Rowen: Isn't it true that the Local Investigation Committee subsequently held between the union and the company that this same issue was brought up for investigation and at that time it was requested that the forms be submitted?

Mr. Boots: When was this?

Mr. Rowen: July 1st or 2nd.

Mr. Boots: I don't recall that.

Mr. Rowen: Have you personally seen these forms, sir, since my request and have you found those forms?

Mr. Boots: No, I have not.

Mr. Rowen: I have no other questions.

The Local Investigation Committee (LIC) was made up of union and company representatives. The LIC convened a meeting around the first part of July (roughly three weeks after I was fired from PG&E) to investigate a number of items including the G&R Metals incident.

Since much of my involvement in this matter also involved Mr. Edgar Weeks, Jerome Boots' second-line supervisor, I recalled Mr. Weeks to testify and the following is his testimony regarding the contaminated pipe:[150]

Mr. Rowen: (Directed to Edgar Weeks) Concerning the contaminated pipe incident, you testified earlier that you had no criticism of the people making the survey. Do you know who those people were? Which control technicians made the survey?

Mr. Weeks: No. I never asked.

Mr. Rowen: Have you ever seen the release papers concerning the survey?

Mr. Weeks: I just asked to see them following this incident. I may have seen them when the survey was made. I don't recall having seen them, but I didn't specifically ask for them because 300 counts above background to me was essentially nothing. I didn't ask to check on the surveys.

This incredible wishy-washy testimony by Edgar Weeks reveals the arrogance displayed often by plant management, and it provides another excellent example of why PG&E management personnel could not be trusted to do the right thing. Weeks' testimony also reveals his total disregard for public and employee safety. G&R Scrap Metals did not deserve receiving radioactively contaminated materials and neither did the consuming public on down the distribution line.

Another sequence of testimony by Edgar Weeks regarding the G&R incident clearly revealed plant management's disdain for my general concern regarding PG&E's poor attitude towards the company's radiation protection program relating to both employees and the general public. With the permission of the Referee, I continued to press Mr. Weeks with my direct examination of him in an attempt to get to the bottom of his handling of the G&R incident and how he felt about my persistence in getting to the truth of it all, which I was able to accomplish in his following testimony:[151]

Mr. Rowen: (Directed to Edgar Weeks) Do you recall my asking you to see those surveys in our discussions concerning this contaminated pipe?

Mr. Weeks: I don't recall that you had asked. We had quite a lengthy discussion as I recall, about an hour.

Mr. Rowen: If I would have asked, would you have given me access to those release papers or dug them up and showed them to me?

Mr. Weeks: Probably not because, as you well know, these records are buried in these boxes out at our auxiliary warehouse out there and it would probably take hours to find them. These records are . . . we keep them, we keep all of these records, but they go back to 1963, when we went into operation, and they are in boxes and they are very difficult to get at, so I may have refused you if you asked for them.

Mr. Rowen: Isn't it true that as far as the control technician's duty is to comply with his first line supervisor's request to go out to those same boxes and dig up records for whatever the supervisor wants to use them for?

Mr. Weeks: If your supervisor asks you to go get . . . dig out records, yes, you should do it.

Mr. Rowen: Wouldn't you imagine I've done this on many occasions?

Mr. Weeks: If you were asked to I suspect you have, yes.

Mr. Rowen: Well, I went out to those boxes and looked for these release papers and I could not find them.

Mr. Weeks: At your supervisor's request?

Mr. Rowen: On my own . . . at my own request.

Mr. Weeks: Without your supervisor asking you to do it, you went out there on your own?

Mr. Rowen: That's right.

Mr. Weeks: Well, then, I'm afraid you were out of line.

Mr. Rowen: Okay. Fine. No further questions.

Mr. Weeks: That is one of the things that always gets you in trouble, Bob.

Let there be no mistake about what happened, the company deliberately sold radioactively contaminated scrap metal to an unsuspecting local scrap metal dealer in Eureka and after it was discovered PG&E intentionally covered it up.

Because my general distrust of plant management was increasing, I found myself looking into things more thoroughly and Edgar Weeks eventually became aware of it. One day I needed the calculations that I had made late the previous day and learned my work had been accidentally thrown into the trash, and that the trash had been emptied into the huge garbage bin outside along the edge of the employee parking area. Instead of redoing the calculations, and because some of the information I needed was in the work that was put into the garbage, I went out to the garbage bin to see if I could find it.

I not only found what I was looking for but many other things as well, including a few handwritten memos marked "confidential" that were obviously typed in the front office and then the handwritten versions thrown away, which were torn into several pieces. I could not believe some of the stuff that I had discovered digging through the garbage and I made it a practice of repeating the effort from time to time. I acquired some really interesting materials during my trips to the garbage bin. Of course, I was eventually caught going through the garbage and underwent more "counseling" by Weeks for doing it. Naturally I did not volunteer all my true reasons for rummaging through the garbage.

Returning to Weeks' continually referring to "300 cpm" as being "essentially nothing," which he testified to during my Appeals Hearing,[152] there was absolutely no legitimate basis for his claim in the G&R Metals case. Weeks simply was blowing smoke in an attempt to cover up what had taken place in this blatant disregard for public safety.

Weeks put himself at odds with PG&E's very own Radiation Control Standards. There was nothing in those Radiation Control Standards that could possibly justify the statement and/or claim Weeks had made during his testimony.

According to PG&E's Radiation Control Standards and the requirements of AEC Operating License No. DPR-7, which gave PG&E the legal authority to operate the nuclear facility, the 300 cpm above background could not justify under any circumstances an "unconditional release" of the pipe. PG&E Radiation Control Standard 6.1 was very clear: "An unconditional release may be given an item when the direct survey (above background) shows less than 100 c/m beta-gamma. An "unconditional release tag shall be properly filled out by Radiation Protection personnel and attached to the item before its removal from the Controlled Area."

Since Weeks would not authorize a trip to G&R Scrap Metals to check out the rest of those sections of pipe taken from the suppression chamber of the reactor containment system, no one will ever know whether those other pieces of pipe were even more radioactive than the one piece I found during a routine "C" survey in the cold machine shop.

What is truly disturbing (and alarming) about the G&R Scrap Metals incident is the obvious concern that the pipe was never surveyed for release to the public in the first place because the legally required documentation for such a survey was never produced nor did any of the nuclear control technicians remember conducting a survey of the suppression chamber pipe.

The real reason plant management did not want to check out the rest of the reactor suppression chamber pipe at G&R Scrap Metals had everything to do with public relations and PG&E's image in the community. Technicians dressed in white, wearing surgical gloves, and carrying around GM survey instruments in public places would not have made PG&E look very good and would have most assuredly generated many questions concerning PG&E's radiation safety program, and of course more pipe may have been found even more highly contaminated.

It was my view then and still is even now, that any amount of radioactive contamination released to the general public should have been totally unacceptable to PG&E, the AEC, the EPA, and to the California Department of Public Health. After all, the company's own radiation protection standards approved by the AEC and made part of the promise to the general public through the licensing process unequivocally said so, and there were no exceptions provided to these rules of behavior that PG&E was expected to follow and the AEC, etc., was expected to enforce.

The task of taking the contaminated pipe out of the controlled area and transporting it to the plant's scrap metal bin had to have happened under the cover of darkness most likely during a graveyard shift when there were few employees on the premises. Those responsible for having the contaminated pipe placed in the scrap metal bin never thought a welder would come along and grab one of the pieces of the pipe from the bin before G&R Metals showed up.

The G&R Scrap Metals incident was one of my many safety concerns of radioactive materials improperly leaving the plant. It was always extremely difficult to address those concerns in any meaningful way. Plant management would quickly close ranks around every attempt to address radiation safety problems and then translate each attempt as a reflection of a "lousy company attitude" and "poor job performance." That seemed to be the only way plant management personnel could operate. The methods used by plant management personnel in their attempts to keep employees in line were intimidation, coercion, and the threat of suspension without pay. Forrest Williams and Bob Rowen were willing to keep bucking the system because our concerns for radiation safety outweighed the company's desire to silence us, and neither of us was willing to kowtow to the injudicious motives of PG&E's nuclear plant management.

__VIII__

8. Chinese Fallout

March 1970

"Chinese Fallout, ahh, c'mon now"[153] [*The Sonoma Bugle*]

"Edith Kraus Stein was a student at South Bay Elementary School when the nuclear reactor first went online in 1963. Later in life, she developed a rare form of lung cancer, linked, she says, to radiation exposure."[154] [Japhet Weeks, *The North Coast Journal*]

By the late sixties we were frequently encountering extremely "hot" (radioactively speaking), shinny-black particles on the shoes and clothing of employees. I remember the first time one of these "mysterious particles," as they became known around the plant, was detected.

An employee was routinely checking himself out of the Unit 3 reactor control room when the hand-and-foot counter located by the primary exit point of Unit 3 became saturated, setting off the master alarm. I was on rad protection duty that day and was sitting at the control technician's rad protection control desk with my back to the hand-and-foot counter located just a few feet away. When the alarm sounded, I immediately jumped up and rushed over to the hand-and-foot counter to see what happened. I discovered that one of the employee's shoes was grossly contaminated.

After the shoe was removed, I checked it with a GM survey instrument, which immediately became saturated. I then quickly grabbed a CP dose rate instrument and found an extremely high dose rate reading of 2-3 R/hr on the sole of the employee's right shoe but I couldn't tell what was causing it.

It was later determined that the actual dose rate far exceeded the initial 2-3 R/hr reading because the CP instrument was attempting to read a "pinpoint" source, which it was incapable of doing.

177

The employee followed me into the instrument lab where I placed his shoe on a sheet of plastic at the nuclear instrumentation workbench. I first put on surgical gloves and goggles (to protect against high energy beta radiation) in preparation for working on the employee's shoe. Using a roll of masking tape, sticky side facing out, I rolled the tape back and forth across the sole of the shoe applying a fair amount of pressure. The shoe eventually came clean but the tape now had something very "hot" (again radioactively speaking) stuck to it. The employee's shoe was returned to him and he was cleared to leave Unit 3.

The employee claimed he had not been in the radiation-controlled area that day and wondered how he could have possibly gotten anything like that on his shoe. My check of the access control log validated the employee's claim.

After the employee left Unit 3, I took a closer look at the tape under a bright-light magnifying lens. There was a lot of stuff from the employee's shoe stuck to it. Using a pair of scissors I started cutting the tape into smaller and smaller pieces, checking each piece as I continued the process until I ended up with a small piece of tape, somewhat smaller than the size of a postage stamp, with a very conspicuous tiny shinny-black particle on it.

That tiny black particle was extremely radioactive, and due to the "geometry factor" involved, the CP could not determine just how "hot" it was because the CP dose rate instrument was not designed to accurately measure the actual dose rate of a pinpoint source, which is an important point worth repeating!

I called Gail Allen, the plant's radiation protection engineer at that time, and after explaining to him over the phone what had happened, I suggested he come up to the nuclear instrumentation lab and take a look at the particle I had found.

After Mr. Allen examined the particle, he stated he had no idea what the particle was or where it might have come from. I informed Allen the employee claimed he had not entered the radiation-controlled area at any time during the day, and that I had already confirmed the employee's claim.

Mr. Allen decided to throw the piece of tape with the particle still stuck to it into a low-level radiation waste box located on the other side of the main access control pad, which was an absolutely improper disposal of it. I emphatically objected to what he had done and I told him that we should have made a serious effort to determine what the particle was and just how "hot" it actually was since the CP instrument could not make that determination for us.

My suggestion was ignored and the particle remained in the low-level radiation waste box. Interestingly enough, there was no immediate conjecture to explain where the particle could have come from or how the employee might have picked it up on his shoe – and Mr. Allen definitely had no interest in pursuing it!

From the very outset of this confounded problem, it was my opinion that we needed to determine what radioisotopes were present in the particle, which would have provided some indication of its source. I demanded this be done!

My discussion of this incident with Mr. Allen turned into an argument that landed me in Mr. Weeks' office, which resulted in another one of his unwelcome "counseling sessions."

The discovery of that little "hot" black particle was the first of many more to follow, and they became known simply as the "mysterious particles." A strange kind of complacency settled in with the vast majority of the plant's nuclear workforce. For me, however, plant management's attitude regarding these mysterious particles was very troubling and I continued to complain about what I constantly referred to as "a very serious problem that was being ignored by PG&E."

It was impossible to estimate how many of these particles may have left the plant because many employees did a poor job of adequately surveying themselves out of Unit 3. Of course the foot-counter portion of the hand-and-foot counter would always pick up the contamination on the soles of the shoes (assuming the alarm settings were properly set) but the frisker probe had to be used for the clothing, and many of the employees would not take the time to use it properly and often wouldn't use it at all.

Another very real possibility is that some employees, who had never entered the Unit 3 control room, were picking up these mysterious particles outside of the restricted areas of Unit 3 and, therefore, were not required to use the hand-and-foot counter to check themselves. These employees would just leave the plant at the end of the day not knowing they were contaminated, the consequences of which would be unspeakable!

One day at quitting time, I found my own trousers contaminated. This wasn't the first time nor was it the last time this happened. This particular incident, however, provides a good example of the problem and makes it worth mentioning at this point. This is because I had a heated go-around with Edgar Weeks about the unresolved "mysterious particle" problem.

It was determined that there was one of these "mysterious" particles in the outside seam of the right leg of my trousers and PG&E confiscated them. I had to wear a clean pair of white coveralls home and change, which made me late to a night class I was taking at College of the Redwoods.

At every opportunity, and publicly as possible, I continued to press the "mysterious particle" issue with Gail Allen. My persistence was unwelcome and quite often landed me in Mr. Weeks' office for another one of his BS "we're working on it" *avowals* and that I "should zip it up, give it a rest." I never did heed his advice!

Mr. Allen finally issued an outrageous proclamation that our "mysterious particles" that were causing us so many problems were due to "Chinese Fallout" resulting from that country's atmospheric atomic bomb testing program. I asked Allen if this explanation was his personal opinion or if it was PG&E's official position. Allen's response was kind of vague but it sort of sounded like his statement was his own personal opinion. In any event, even if the statement was really his own personal opinion, Allen was making it as PG&E's Humboldt Bay Radiation Protection Engineer. My immediate response to Allen's nonsensical statement was simply that I could not accept the explanation unless or until the California Department of Public Health and/or some other environmental-health agency would verify it.

While it was true the Chinese had begun testing atomic bombs in 1964, I was convinced that Allen didn't know what he was talking about. In my view he was just making a ridiculously, wild assumption without any basis for it whatsoever. Looking back on it, I never saw anything that indicated the particles we were finding at our facility were also showing up at other places along the coastlines of California, Oregon, Washington, and Alaska. There may have been some increases to general backgrounds in certain areas along the Pacific coastlines but there were no discoveries of the particles like the ones we were experiencing at our facility.

Many of the employees accepted Allen's explanation and others didn't seem to care one-way or the other. Nevertheless, I continued to press on with the issue suggesting we collect a few of these particles and have them analyzed by whatever federal or state agency responsible for monitoring the possibility of "Chinese fallout" to see if these mysterious particles could actually be from Chinese bombs or if our plant was producing them. Plant management scoffed at the idea and refused to act on it. I can only speculate on why PG&E took that position.

Several years after I was fired from PG&E, I came across a PG&E document entitled "Report No. 15, Environmental Radiation Study In the Vicinity of Humboldt Bay Power Plant, Eureka, California." The PG&E document was identified as Report No. 4200.5-65. In the report I found the following statement: "The collection of air particulate samples, film packs and dosimeter readings was accomplished by personnel of the Humboldt Division under the direction of Mr. Gail Allen." (The nuclear facility's radiation protection engineer was Mr. Allen during that time). In that PG&E report was the phrase " . . . fallout resulting from atmospheric nuclear bomb testing of Communist China on October 16, 1964." J. V. Boots, the chemical engineer at Humboldt Bay, prepared this report. When Mr. Allen first made the claim that these extremely hot radioactive particles were from the Chinese atomic bomb testing, I did not believe him and reading this report by Boots a few years later did not change my mind.

Two years after Forrest Williams and I had been discharged by PG&E, the Atomic Energy Commission in a surprise inspection "discovered a highly radioactive, sand-grain-sized particle."[155] The AEC compliance inspectors, health physicist Harry S. North and reactor engineer Jess Crews, discovered the particle on April 4, 1972.[156] (Wow! Finally an AEC "surprise" visit to the plant! Perhaps our whistleblowing efforts did some good after all, especially after the 1971 Humboldt Grand Jury insisted upon it – review Chapter 4)

The very next day, the Eureka *Times-Standard* environmental reporter contacted Mr. North seeking "confirmation or denial of a report received by his newspaper that such a particle had been found."[157] Mr. North "refused to comment and referred the Eureka *Times-Standard* environmental reporter to a superior, George Spencer."[158] The Eureka *Times-Standard* news article that followed is most revealing to the discerning reader regarding the mysterious, extremely hot radioactive black particles that PG&E's Humboldt Bay radiation protection engineer, Gail Allen, had called "Chinese fallout."

I have interjected several comments throughout the portions of the April 6, 1972, Eureka *Times-Standard* article being quoted:[159]

> Spencer, a senior reactor engineer at Berkeley, said he was not aware of any such discovery, but indicated he had just returned from out of town and promised to contact North to determine the situation, and report back.
>
> Spencer failed to return the call, but Dale Cook, assistant to the manager for public information said a speck was found on the floor of the refueling building, a large building housing the reactor.

COMMENT: It's the common PR modus operandi in both government and the corporate world to turn potentially embarrassing questions or legal liabilities over to the PR experts who know how best to respond to minimize the damage by manipulating public opinion.

The April 6, 1972, Eureka *Times-Standard* article continued:[160]

> He said the speck's discovery was so insignificant that it was not reported by North to the home office. 'We're cleaning up specks like that all day long in our own plants,' Cook said, but indicated it would be analyzed to determine the isotopes and their intensity.

COMMENT: Mr. Cook didn't know what he was talking about or he was intentionally lying to the reporter about how dangerous such particles were if ingested. The AEC whitewashed its response to the reporter; see Chapter 13 regarding my letter to the AEC and the AEC response regarding this matter. The AEC never identified any of the other plants where the AEC was "cleaning up specks like that all day long" in their own plants.

The April 6, 1972, Eureka *Times-Standard* article continued:[161]

> We don't know where the hell it came from, Cook said during the interview, but reluctantly consented to report the results of the analysis to the Eureka *Times-Standard* newspaper.

COMMENT: The AEC eventually claimed the particle came from the "irradiated reactor fuel materials." How is that possible? The irradiated reactor fuel materials originate in the core of the reactor. *Right*? When it is removed from the core, it is transferred into a transfer cask under water and sealed, and then pulled out of the core while the outside of the cask is being completely and thoroughly washed down by demineralized water. *Right*? The transfer cask is then moved over to the spent fuel pool, lowered into it and transferred under water into the spent fuel storage racks. *Right*? The outside of the transfer cask is again completely and thoroughly washed down with demineralized water as it is pulled out of the spent fuel pool. *Right*? – Well, I'm just saying.

The April 6, 1972, Eureka *Times-Standard* article continued:[162]

> Cook said many such analyses are made during AEC inspection trips and indicated the information is not included in public files unless the company is cited. Cook said there are no staff reports on the inspections if the plant is found to comply with AEC rules, an apparent 'pass or fail' type of determination.

COMMENT: What does this mean when the rules are either inadequate or ignored? Moreover, the AEC is clearly admitting the inadequacies of its regulatory responsibilities in this PR statement, which further reveals another *betrayal* of the public trust.

The April 6, 1972, Eureka *Times-Standard* article continued:[163]

> Cook had promised the results of the analysis later in the week, but called back a few hours later with a report on the particle.

COMMENT: Because of the timing of Cook's actual response, the only "analysis" that could have been made had to be done in the nuclear facility by plant personnel overseen by PG&E management. The only lab equipment available for such an analysis was the 256-channel analyzer and a book of standards. To perform a complete analysis on the particle, it would have taken much more time than just a "few" hours within the normal working day following the actual discovery of the particle.

The April 6, 1972, Eureka *Times-Standard* article continued:[164]

> He said the particle was monitored with radiation detection equipment to have a reading of two roentgens per hour of Beta-Gamma radiation with the Beta window open, at a quarter of an inch distance from the particle. The Beta window is a shield, which blocks Beta radiation: a roentgen is a basic unit of radiation.

COMMENT: He was referring to a Cutie Pie (CP) dose rate instrument that could not have determined the actual dose rate because the particle represented a "pinpoint" source, which means the instrument was incapable of determining the real dose rate due to the "geometry-factor." And clearly the CP could not determine the radioactive isotopes in the particle.

The April 6, 1972, Eureka *Times-Standard* article continued:[165]

> With the Beta window closed, Cook said the reading was 200 milliroentgens Gamma per hour at one-quarter inch.

COMMENT: This would provide an indication that there was a strong source of beta radiation being emitted from the particle. Let there be no mistake, nearly two roentgens per hour of beta radiation along with "200 milliroentgens gamma per hour" from a pinpoint source is one hell of a lot or radiation if ingested into the body. All we know and what is reasonable to assume from this account is that the source of this radiation was the byproducts of nuclear fission, which encompasses some very dangerous radioisotopes if ingested into the human body.

The April 6, 1972, Eureka *Times-Standard* article continued:[166]

Persons knowledgeable about radiation, contacted Wednesday by the *Times-Standard*, said the radiation was considerable and would require lead shielding if taken outside the controlled radiation areas.

COMMENT: It would definitely require very careful and special handling.

The April 6, 1972, Eureka *Times-Standard* article continued:[167]

Cook said the particle, identified as Cesium 134 and Cesium 137, was a 'normal fission product seen in and around spent (reactor) fuel which is processed in that room' (the refueling building).

COMMENT: There is no way that determination could have been made, given the time element involved, and the fact that the particle was a "normal fission product." Also, what is Cook talking about here? Spent fuel is not processed in the plant's refueling building! That was an absurd claim by Cook. Humboldt Bay's spent fuel was processed in a New York facility.

The April 6, 1972, *Times-Standard* article continued:[168]

'It would not be abnormal in such a facility to see readings higher than that due to the nature of the products being worked on,' Cook continued, pointing out that the building is under negative pressure (the pressure inside is lower than outside the building) and the particles therefore could not blow out.

COMMENT: We did find particles from time to time, which had even higher readings. It's true the refueling building was under negative pressure while "containment" was in place. The primary purpose of this negative containment design was to keep airborne conditions contained within the refueling building (air would "leak" in rather than "leak" out).

However, there were times when containment would be broken, especially when the railroad doors were opened and when the airlock door at plus 12 elevation was intentionally left open to quickly move extremely hot radioactive wastes to the high level radiation waste storage vault using a team-relay system to reduce exposure to individual employees transferring the highly radioactive wastes to the high level vaults. With containment broken, these particles could be tracked or blown out of the building. Of course, these particles could be tracked out anyway because employees were constantly going in and out of the facility through the two refueling building airlocks all day long.

The April 6, 1972, Eureka *Times-Standard* article continued:[169]

> Cook said the intensity of the particle dropped in proportion to the distance. For example, at one-half inch, the 200 mr/hr reading would reduce to 100 mr/hr. And he emphasized that the refueling building was a controlled area in which the employees are normally required to wear special protective clothing including boots and cloth covers.

COMMENT: It's not clear what Cook's point is. Certainly, he's not trying to say that because of this finding with the CP that the particle doesn't represent much of a hazard, because if that's the case, then he's dead wrong! Of course, perhaps without intending to, he made the point that Forrest Williams and Bob Rowen had argued often with plant management. These particles are extremely difficult to detect because of their pinpoint nature from a radiation detection perspective.

Once found, however, it was impossible to determine how "hot" they were because of the "geometry factor" involved with the CP (the dose rate measuring instrument we used). We were finding them on employees who had not even been in the radiation controlled areas of the plant, which once again, is an extremely important fact to take special notice of!

Mr. Cook's reference to the requirement of wearing "special protective clothing including boots and cloth covers" means absolutely nothing. The "special protective clothing including boots and cloth covers" he was referring to did nothing to protect the face and most of the head, or prevent the possibility of in gestation of the particles through the mouth, nose, ears, and the eyes.

When employees prepared to enter the radiation controlled area under a "Routine Work Permit," which was the case the majority of the time, we took off all of our clothes in the change room on the "clean" side of the step-off pad except for our skivvies, socks, and shoes. Then we put on a clean pair of white coveralls, a surgical cap, cloth booties over our street shoes followed by rubber pull-on shoes, and a pair of surgical gloves. There is no way one of these particles could end up on the soles of the shoes or the street clothing of employees while being inside the radiation controlled area. Clearly those particles we were finding on employees at the hand-and-foot counter had to have been picked up on the soles or clothing outside the radiation controlled area because of the "special protective clothing" Cook referred to in his nonsensical PR statement.

The April 6, 1972, Eureka *Times-Standard* article continued:[170]

> If such a particle were by chance to have gotten into the 250-foot stack where off-gases from the reactor are released, 'the stack monitor would have detected it and the filter system screened it out,' Cook said.

COMMENT: How could that have happened? I'm confident Cook could not defend his entire statement if we would have had an opportunity to "cross-examine" him. We were picking up smearable radioactive contamination on employee vehicles in the "clean area" parking lot, which was clearly coming from the particulate matter falling out of the plume from the 250-foot radioactive gaseous waste discharge stack. Mr. Cook was clearly blowing smoke at the reporter, who didn't know enough to challenge Cook's ridiculous statements.

The April 6, 1972, Eureka *Times-Standard* article continued:[171]

> In conclusion, Cook said the discovery of the particle was 'just like going into a gas station and finding gasoline there.'

COMMENT: Well now, that's the dumbest statement Cook made in this interview: comparing this dangerous radioactive particle to gasoline. How does Cook's statement compare to Gail Allen's Chinese Fallout proclamation? Remember, Allen was PG&E Radiation Protection Engineer!

The April 6, 1972, Eureka *Times-Standard* article continued:[172]

> But two former nuclear control technicians, who say they were discharged for speaking out about safety matters, contend the discovery of the particle is significant.

COMMENT: PG&E officials never really denied the existence of these particles outside the radiation-controlled areas of the nuclear facility. How could they? PG&E was frequently confiscating personal clothing and reimbursing employees for the replacement of those articles of clothing taken by the company. PG&E's handling of the problem presented by these "hot" radioactive particles was tantamount to a cover-up by first blaming the Chinese, then by ignoring the problems posed by the high-level radiation waste storage vault and the radioactive gaseous waste discharge stack, and finally by "partnering up" with the AEC to pull it off.

The April 6, 1972, Eureka *Times-Standard* article continued:[173]

> Forrest Williams of Arcata and Robert Rowen, Jr. of Eureka, who left PG&E in mid-1970, said the danger with such particles is ingestion into the human body where the radiation seeks out vital organs.
>
> The machines used to calibrate the radiation dose, they say, are not designed to measure a pinpoint source and the actual strength of the particle, considerably higher than can be measured, must be determined through the use of math formulas.
>
> Rowen told the *Times-Standard* the very fact that the particle's intensity drops off so rapidly as distance from the speck increases is the reason why the particles are so deadly. He said the particles can be picked up on tools, shoes, or clothing and tracked from one place to another without detection.

One of Rowen's complaints to the Atomic Energy Commission concerned a VIP tour of the plant reactor room by visitors in street clothes. The only protection afforded the visitors, Rowen said, was paper placed on the floor. Rowen related that the visitors to the plant were not going to be given the usual radiation check required of plant employees, except that he insisted. Rowen said stray particles of the type discovered in the refueling building could have gotten on the street clothing of the visitors.

Williams said an airlock door at the back of the refueling building is sometimes used by employees, who could carry such specks to the outside.

The *Times-Standard* confirmed on a visit to the plant that the door is sometimes used. A reporter was escorted through the air lock to gain a better view of the reactor for picture taking purposes.

Rowen claims plant management has told him they don't know where the particles come from. He said management calls them 'Chinese fallout.' Rowen also reported he has found such particles on employees outside the plant, continuing: 'The likelihood is they got them from a clean area in the plant,' Rowen said in a recent interview. 'Normally people aren't allowed to wear their personal clothing in the plant.'

Rowen said such particles could also be blown across the flats toward the highway by prevailing winds passing over the high level storage vaults behind the plant, into which are tossed wrapped contaminated materials from the nuclear section.

COMMENT: J. J. Ward and his AEC investigation team intentionally failed to properly investigate this complaint; therefore, Ward's findings were clearly a cover-up (Chapter 13, Allegation #8).

The April 6, 1972, Eureka *Times-Standard* article continued:[174]

He said the contaminated materials are exposed to the open air when the vaults are opened and closed.

'I contend that if one of those particles is carried over the (South Bay) school and lands on a desk where a student is eating lunch on a rainy day, and he ingests one of those particles, who is going to know the difference? I don't mean to sound emotional about it, but this situation is not a far-fetched conjecture to my way of thinking,' Rowen stated.

Rowen said he discovered more particles than most of the control technicians. Actually, I was quite emotional about this problem and enraged, too, over PG&E's lack of concern for the hazards these "mysterious, hot black particles" subjected employees and the general public to, including the kids at the elementary school down wind from the plant. They do show up from time to time.' He related, adding, 'discovery depends on the conscientiousness of the employee.'

COMMENT: It's absolutely true that I had a passion for dealing with this problem, which put me in the cross hairs of plant management, generally, and Edgar Weeks specifically.

The April 6, 1972, Eureka *Times-Standard* article continued:[175]

Earlier this year, PG&E was specifically requested by this newspaper to respond to Rowen's comments.

Victor C. Novarino, Humboldt division manager for PG&E, refused by letter to answer these questions, especially specific queries: How is the high-level material handled? What procedures are there to prevent material from escaping when the lid is taken off these vaults? Have you ever had any experience with these unexplained particles?

Novarino's letter to the *Times-Standard* said the above questions related to 'allegations made by Mr. Rowen in the press and in public meetings. Our response to these allegations remains as stated in my statement to the press of January 28,1972: The numerous allegations concerning radiation safety raised by Mr. Rowen are clearly without merit as evidenced by the fact that the extensive investigation carried out by the AEC revealed no instances of unsafe practices which might affect either plant personnel or the general public. It is our view that the results of the AEC investigation show that the company has operated the Humboldt Bay Nuclear Unit in a responsible and conscientious manner and that the AEC inspection program has verified this fact over the years.'

COMMENT: Chapter 13 of my Diary, entitled "The AEC Whitewash – October 1970," responds to Mr. Novarino's response letter to the Eureka *Times-Standard* previously mentioned and to PG&E's press release dated January 28, 1972, which appeared as a lengthy editorial by the Eureka newspaper. I must admit that one of the pillars of my motivation for writing *My Humboldt Diary* is Novarino's letter to the Eureka *Times-Standard* and PG&E's press release dated January 28, 1972.

I became so inflamed by Cook's outrageous claims and ridiculous remarks quoted in the *Times-Standard* April 6, 1972, article that I immediately wrote a letter of my own to Mr. George Spencer, Senior Reactor Inspector for the Compliance Division of the AEC. The complete text of my letter, dated April 8, 1972, follows:[176]

Dear Mr. Spencer:

The Atomic Energy Commission recently made an inspection of PG&E's Humboldt Bay nuclear facility located at Eureka, California. On April 6, 1972, The Times-Standard featured a news story concerning an extremely "hot" radioactive particle, which was discovered during the recent AEC inspection. In this connection, I respectfully request answers to the following questions:

1. Can it be expected that a radioactive particle composed of only one element would be found loosely lying around in a boiling water reactor facility such as the Humboldt Bay Power Plant Unit No. 3?

2. What is the normal makeup of mixed fission products of the Humboldt nuclear facility?

3. Of a random sampling of sediment deposited in the spent fuel of the Humboldt plant, what percentage of the radioactive isotopes present would be Cesium? What other radioactive isotopes would be present?

4. What process is used to isolate Cesium from mixed spent fuel products?

5. Mr. Dale Cook of the AEC reported that the refueling building of the Humboldt Bay plant is under negative pressure so that the particle could not have blown out. Was the refueling building opened to the outside during the week preceding discovery of the particle? If so, how often and for how long?

6. Mr. Dale Cook of the AEC reported that if the particle were by chance to have gotten into the 250 ft. stack, the filter system would filter it out. Where in the plant's plumbing connecting the refueling building to the stack is this filter located?

7. What percent of the air that flows out through the stack also passes through the stack monitor?

8. What is the probability that a given particle in the air going out the stack (from whatever source) will go through the stack monitor? Will the control room readout reflect the existence of such a particle?

9. Would you please confirm or deny the following: The radioactive particle found on April 4, 1972, at

the Humboldt nuclear facility would be hazardous to the human body if ingested?

10. Was the particle discovered by design or by accident? What were the circumstances of its discovery?

11. What was the true dose rate of the particle?

12. When was the last time the area where the particle was found cleaned-up? Why didn't the cleaning process collect the particle?

13. Was the area surveyed after the last cleaning? If so, why wasn't the particle detected?

14. Since the particle was found have you surveyed for more? If so, did you find any more?

15. What were the precise location(s) of any and all particle(s) found? For example, how many feet from the railroad doors, etc.?

16. Would you agree that such a particle could be carried out of the refueling building and into the Unit No. 3 yard on the bottom of a 'rubber shoe sole' or on the 'tire of a fork lift?' If so, what precautions are taken to prevent this from happening? If not, why not?

17. And lastly, I would like to know which AEC plants find it necessary to cleanup these types of particles 'all day long.'

I would appreciate your answers to these questions at your earliest convenience.

Thank you for your cooperation. /s/ Bob Rowen

Mr. Spencer did not specifically answer any of my questions in his reply, dated May 5, 1972. However, his rely did state the following:[177]

The presence of such materials at AEC-licensed facilities has been taken into consideration in establishing AEC rules and regulations for the protection of both radiation workers and the general public.

COMMENT: Mr. Spencer's statement confirms that the AEC was not interested in protecting the public as much as it was in protecting the interests of PG&E and promoting nuclear power. These "mysterious particles" were unquestionably dangerous to human health and they were not absolutely contained within the nuclear facility, as they should have been.

The claim made by Mr. Spencer should have been rigorously challenged considering what had taken place at Humboldt Bay.

There is a sad footnote to all of this. Sometime during the early eighties, a young lady along with her husband came to the high school where I was teaching. The two of them wanted to talk privately with me about the Humboldt Bay Nuclear Power Plant. We all assembled in my classroom and talked for several hours after school that day. Her name was Edith Stein and she first explained to me that she was the daughter of my physical science teacher, Mr. Ralph Kraus, at Eureka Junior High School. She said her father had always talked highly of me and was proud of the public stance I took against the PG&E's nuclear plant. I told her that her father was one of my favorite teachers of all time. The conversation then turned to a much heavier topic.

Edith was a student at the South Bay Elementary School, and had later in life developed a rare form of lung cancer, and she wanted to know if I thought it could be connected to what happened at the Humboldt Bay Nuclear Power Plant. I remember how her question struck me.

My earlier fears were now coming around full circle. I didn't know how to adequately respond to her and I've regretted my lame response ever since. I had been working 12 to 15 hours a day in my teaching assignment at Trinity High School in Weaverville, California and I was tired. The demands of my new professional life and my heartfelt desire to heal my family's wounds from the PG&E debacle had caused me to put the Humboldt Bay Nuclear Power Plant experience as far behind me as possible. After we talked for a while, Edith wanted to know if I could write some letters, contact some people, or help her in some other ways. The bottom line response was simply that I didn't have enough time or energy to help her, and that is something I now have to live with.

Many years later, I received a phone call from Japhet Weeks (no relation to Edgar Weeks), someone I did not know from Adam. Japhet Weeks said he was doing some research on the Humboldt Bay Nuclear Power Plant; he wanted to talk with me about my experiences at Humboldt Bay. I had retired from the Trinity Union High School District, but was still working part-time for Shasta College and full-time in a temporary administrative position at Bishop Quinn High School in Palo Cedro, California, a few miles east of Redding.

I agreed to an interview with Japhet Weeks. During the interview, and in response to one of his probing questions, I briefly mentioned Edith's name and explained what had happened at Trinity High School. I told the reporter I had no idea how he could get in touch with her. He later published his article in The North Coast Journal in Arcata, California that received a California Newspaper Publishers Association Award. In his article, entitled *The Not-So-Peaceful Atom,* Japhet Weeks wrote:[178]

> Edith Kraus Stein was a student at South Bay Elementary School when the nuclear reactor first went online in 1963. Later in life, she developed a rare form of lung cancer, linked, she says, to radiation exposure.

Speaking to me from her home in Louisville, KY earlier this month, Stein, whose breathing was at times audibly labored because she only has one lung, said she still believes that the power plant was the reason for her cancer. 'We were in spitting distance of the plant and I think it did have something to do with it.'

She also cited the removal of the dosimeter from the school grounds as evidence that the utility has something to hide.

COMMENT: The final chapter of my *Diary* entitled "Humboldt Hill: An Untold Story" will address my heartfelt concerns for the victims who were downwind from PG&E's Humboldt Bay Unit 3 reactor.

The author at Camp Del Mar in October 1960

9. The Air Sample Monitor at the School

April 1970

"When I presented my theories to PG&E's radiation protection engineer, Mr. Gail Allen, he was adamant that these black particles were from the fallout of the atomic testing being done by the Chinese. His response, and the manner in which he gave it, left me with the unmistakable impression there had already been considerable discussion of all this in the front office of the plant."[179] [BobRowen]

"Both have made unproven accusations about conditions as being unsafe. For example, the high level radiation-waste storage vault and the fallout near the school and the recommendation for monitoring equipment there."[180] [John Kamberg]

It all sounded scientific and foolproof, so convincingly genuine that the concern for public safety was unquestionably of paramount importance to the operation of the Humboldt Bay reactor. All of this turned into hogwash when Humboldt Bay's nuclear fuel cladding failed.

PG&E along with the AEC had done a fantastic job selling the public on just how safe the nuclear facility would be and to prove it, an extremely "complex" environmental radiological monitoring program was developed, put in place, and highly publicized to convince the public nothing would escape from the facility that would endanger the public.

And if by chance something did develop, some kind of unexpected problem was to occur, it would be detected so corrective action could be taken – immediately!

But when it became necessary, both PG&E and the AEC closed ranks when problems did occur to maintain an all important façade of safety, and that's all it was!

The purpose of the "closing of the ranks" by PG&E and the AEC was to protect PG&E's failed and dangerous technology from any and all adverse public disclosures in order to continue promoting the future of nuclear energy.

There were a number of state and local agencies incorporated into the company's environmental monitoring program and emergency response plans, but the AEC was clearly in charge of it all and that was exactly the way PG&E and the AEC wanted it.

The Humboldt Bay Nuclear Power Plant's environmental monitoring program included 36 radiological monitoring stations with each having two environmental dosimeters and one film pack, also there were five continuous air-sample monitors included in PG&E's "elaborate" radiological monitoring program at Humboldt Bay.

These radiological monitoring stations were mostly located on Humboldt Hill, an area directly east and southeast of the Nuclear Power Plant encompassing an immediate area of approximately 25-30 square miles. There were additional stations located north of the nuclear plant in downtown Eureka (about 4-5 miles from the plant), still others further north as far as Fickle Hill behind Humboldt State University in the City of Arcata area (about 12-15 miles from the plant), and even more of them as far south as the City of Fortuna (about 18-20 miles from the plant).

The "stray radiation chambers" to which AEC Investigator J. J. Ward referred (Chapter 10) were special outside (weatherproof) environmental dosimeters. There were two environmental dosimeters located at each environmental monitoring station. They were used to provide an immediate indication of the amount of radiation energy in the environment at the location of each of the radiological monitoring stations since the last reading of them. A film pack was also located at each monitoring station and it was routinely collected and sent to a special laboratory for processing.

These film packs were used to establish the "official" record of the amount of radiation exposure at each environmental monitoring station during the scheduled monitoring period.

The environmental dosimeters and the film packs located at each of the PG&E's radiological monitoring stations were only able to measure radiation "energy." These particular-monitoring devices could not determine the type of radioisotopes in the radioactive particulate matter that was present at each of the environmental monitoring stations. Also important is to distinguish the difference between exposure to radiation "energy" and exposure to radioactive "particulate matter."

Simply stated, radioactive energy is like being in the presence of a light source. Turn on the light and you're in an "electromagnetic" energy field; turn off the light and you're no longer in the energy field. While in a radiation energy field, you are being "radiated."

With "radioactive particulate matter," however, it can be ingested into the body where it remains. (Think of particulate matter as dust particles in contrast to energy in the form of a ray of light).

Depending on the radioisotopes involved and their corresponding half-lives (the amount of time it takes a fixed amount of radiation energy to decay to one-half its original amount) continued *ingestion* of the radioactive particulate matter adds to the body burden of various organs, again depending on the radioisotopes that make up the particulate matter.

There are a number of very dangerous radioisotopes in the fission byproducts produced in a nuclear reactor. The various radioisotopes seek out certain organs in the body and remain there adding to the body burden. For example, Strontium-90 seeks out the bone and bone marrow, Iodine-131 seeks out the thyroid, and Cesium-137 is distributed throughout the whole body. Strontium-90 ends up in bone and bone marrow because it is chemically similar to calcium; Cesium-137 ends up throughout the whole body because it is water-soluble and biologically behaves like potassium.

The following is a simplified explanation of body burden using Strontium-90 as an example. Since Strontium-90 has a half-life of 28.8 years, if an amount of it emitting 4R was ingested; it would still be emitting 2R 28.8 years later and 1R 57.6 years after the original ingestion. If more Strontium-90 were continuously ingested following the initial ingestion, it would add to the body burden accordingly.

The only way to detect the actual radioactive particulate matter in the environment that could be ingested by either breathing it in or by oral intake was to rely on the five continuous air-sampling monitors in PG&E's Humboldt Bay radiological environmental monitoring program. Now I want to focus on my very specific concern for the "mysterious particles" that we were finding on the shoes and clothing of employees during the later part of the sixties and early seventies.

It is especially noteworthy to again point out that finding these extremely hot "mysterious particles" on the shoes and street clothing of employees at the hand-and-foot counter was almost never the result of the employee being in the radiation controlled areas of Unit 3. This is because of the required protective clothing that was worn by atomic workers and the meticulous procedures that were followed by the employees when crossing over the access control point (known as the "step-off pad") from the radiation controlled areas of the nuclear unit. So where were these "mysterious particles" coming from and how did they end up on employees?

There were three possible source(s) of these "mysterious particles." The most plausible explanation was the high-level radiation waste storage vault. However, it may have been possible for them to have blown out of the refueling building when containment was broken, they could have been tracked out of the refueling building on employees going through the two airlocks of the refueling building, or they could have fallen out of the plume of the radioactive gaseous waste discharge stack.

In my view these extremely "hot" particles most likely had to come from the high level radiation waste storage vault and were picked up by employees in any one of several places. These places could include the reactor control room, the change room on the clean side of access control, the reactor feed pump room, or the yard outside the controlled area. Employees then brought them into the Unit 3 control room.

Any one of these possibilities would mean only one thing: The "mysterious particles" were blowing around like particles of dust, which clearly meant they were not at all contained within the radiation-controlled area of Unit 3. If this postulation is true, and I wholeheartedly believe it is, then these "mysterious particles" could have ended up anywhere and probably did!

Ultimately, all of these possibilities may have contributed to the "mysterious particle" problem at Humboldt Bay. After all, the plant was extremely "dirty!"

It was my belief at the time (and still is), that the high-level radioactive waste storage vault produced the majority of these "mysterious particles." In any event, the "mysterious particles" were free to travel in the wind like so many particles of dust; and once out of the vault, the refueling building, or the radioactive gaseous plume, they could end up anywhere.

If employees outside the radiation controlled area picked up a "mysterious particle" and then entered the Unit 3 control room with it on them, the particle could be detected when the employee check himself out of Unit 3 at the hand-and-foot counter (which everyone had to do)! If the particle was on a shoe, there was no problem; it would be detected (assuming the alarm settings were properly set). If, on the other hand, it were on the employee's clothing, it would only be detected if the employee properly used the frisker probe at the hand-and-foot counter (which far too many employees failed to use properly)!

While I acknowledged the low probability of the event, these "mysterious particles" could only be picked up by PG&E on the filters at the five continuous air-sampling monitors. This was a serious, if not fatal, inadequacy of PG&E's environmental monitoring program given the discovery of these "mysterious particles" and the amount of them we were finding in the plant.

The filters in the five continuous air-sampling monitors were collected at the end of every monitoring period and sent to a special laboratory for processing. These high-tech air-sampling monitors were best described as "vacuum" machines that operated 24/7. A measured amount of air was pulled through the filter housings and deposited particulate matter from the air onto the filters. Each continuous air-sampling monitor was housed in a 27-cubic foot wooden structure with louvered sides to allow air to pass into the monitoring station. These stations were located at the base of a power pole in order to access an electrical power source to run the vacuum pump. A lock to prevent unauthorized entry into the monitoring station secured the unit.

I remember my discussion with the plant engineer during the fall of 1969 regarding my concern over the design adequacy of these continuous air-samplers as related to the collection of the "mysterious particles" we were experiencing at the nuclear facility. I agreed with the plant engineer that the design of the sampling station was probably adequate for monitoring "regular" radioactive airborne activity from the nuclear facility's radioactive gaseous waste stack; The amount the air samplers collected could be considered a reasonable representative sample of it but I questioned the air-sampling unit's ability to pick up these "mysterious particles" with any high degree of probability.

Because of the uniqueness of the "mysterious particles," I felt the company needed to install more air samplers in the downwind areas of the plant. Mr. Weeks summarily ended our discussion by telling me that I was "making a big deal over something that wasn't at all a problem." Mr. Weeks never convinced me that it was not a problem. He couldn't!

However remote the possibility might have been, I made it clear to Weeks there was still a fairly good chance these units could pick up some of these particles, especially at PG&E's Environmental Monitoring Station #14 located at the South Bay Elementary School. Without realizing it at the time I most likely planted seeds for thought that ended up at PG&E's corporate headquarters resulting in the decision to dismantle and completely remove the continuous air-sample monitoring station at the elementary school.

But wait! My discussion with Weeks not only covered the design of the air sample monitoring stations and my suggestion of installing more of them downwind from the plant, it also included my request to see the results of the lab work on the filters from each of the air sampling stations, especially the one at Station #14 located directly in front of the school. Weeks told me that information had nothing to do with my duties as a nuclear control technician and therefore it was of no concern to me.

PG&E's "extensive" environmental monitoring program was well established prior to the original start up of the plant and was touted by PG&E and the AEC as evidence of a genuine concern for public safety. The radiological monitoring program was up and running for many months before the initial start up of the nuclear facility to establish the normal background levels at the various locations of each specific monitoring station and for the Humboldt Hill area in general.

After the nuclear facility's initial start up, the nuclear control techs routinely made their rounds to all the environmental monitoring stations. During their environmental monitoring tour to each monitoring station, the nuclear control techs read the two environmental dosimeters, zeroed the chambers by recharging them, and collected the old and installed new film packs. The nuclear control techs also collected the old filters and replaced them with new ones at each of the five continuous air-sample monitoring stations. After the first year of reactor operations, the frequency of these monitoring tours by the nuclear control techs had to be increased a number of times because of off-scale readings of the environmental dosimeters.

The off-scale readings were due to the increasing radiation levels resulting from the breakdown of the fuel cladding in the reactor core. James C. Carroll, PG&E's nuclear engineer at corporate headquarters, later compared what I have called PG&E's "failed and dangerous" technology to the "criticisms of improper design and construction techniques in early color television sets that resulted in excessive radiation to people." [181] When he was asked to address the problem of Humboldt Bay's fuel cladding failure, Mr. Carroll responded, "I don't think we ought to answer that" [182] (Chapter 15).

The breakdown of the fuel cladding in the reactor core lead to increasingly higher levels of radioactive gaseous waste discharges from the nuclear plant's highly visible, red and white 250-foot radioactive gaseous waste discharge stack that loomed over the facility. If too much time had passed from the zeroing of the environmental dosimeters and the reading of them, they would go off scale and therefore could not be read. Humboldt Bay's radioactive gaseous waste discharge presented several fundamental problems.

The first of these problems was simply the location of the plant in relation to the South Bay Elementary School. The nuclear facility was located on the prevailing northwest wind line with the South Bay Elementary School; the elementary school was approximately 400 hundred yards directly downwind from the plant. The question has been raised many times regarding why the nuclear facility was built so close to the school in the first place. And if this wasn't baffling enough, why then wasn't the school relocated when radiation levels, with all the problems associated with them, began to rise way beyond what was originally expected from the approved design specifications of the plant? PG&E's decision to use stainless steel cladding rather than the more expensive zircaloy cladding had come back to haunt the company, and rightly so!

Moreover, PG&E's handling of "all the problems" associated with the Humboldt Bay nuclear fiasco has further haunted the company's grand design to "go nuclear," as it should have. It would be impossible for PG&E to defend its decision to build the Humboldt nuclear facility so close to and upwind from the elementary school; and then to continue to operate the plant after the breakdown of the fuel cladding had reared its ugly head – that was unconscionable.

There was the "sky-shine" from the radioactive plume that was directly over the school on typical days. The "sky-shine" refers to the radiation energy being emitted from the radioactive gaseous waste plume. Then there was the problem with a "sinking" radioactive gaseous waste plume when temperature inversions occurred.

Forrest Williams, one of the plant's nuclear control technicians, remembered one of his work assignments that involved a series of tests to determine the effects of temperature inversions on the radioactive gaseous waste plume. These tests were conducted to evaluate the behavior of the radioactive gaseous waste plume during temperature inversions.

Forrest described the testing program in the following way:[183]

> We ran a smoke test from the top of the "met tower" (PG&E's meteorological data collecting tower), which was the same height as the nuclear unit's radioactive gaseous waste discharge stack and located less than the length of a football field west-to-southwest from it. During the spring there is often a temperature inversion and a prevailing northwest wind. I have witnessed the smoke generated by a surplus U.S. Navy oil-fog generator located on the top of the tower, dive right down to the ground and blow across the freeway at ground level right into the schoolyard on the other side of the freeway.

Another problem was the potential radioactive fallout from the plume. This was one of the several reasons why PG&E conducted the "rabbit tests" (aka "The Rabbit Caper") to determine whether I-131 was leaving the plant (review Chapter 4).

Along with the radiological hazards posed by what was coming out of the 250-foot radioactive gaseous waste discharge stack, there was another ominous radiological hazard looming in the realm of possibilities for the students and staff at the elementary school, and the residents of the Humboldt Hill area, as well. These very real potential radiation hazards were the "mysterious particles."

When I presented my theories to PG&E's radiation protection engineer, Mr. Gail Allen, he was adamant that these "mysterious particles" were from the fallout of the atomic testing being done by the Chinese. His response, and the manner in which he gave it, left me with the unmistakable impression there had already been considerable discussion of all this in the front office of the plant.

After challenging Mr. Allen's explanation of placing the blame on the Chinese, I found myself in the front office and raked over the coals by Edgar Weeks and Warren Raymond. My suspicions were confirmed when Mr. Weeks and Mr. Raymond echoed Allen's claims. Their collective response did not pass the smell test. They made it clear that I was exceeding my authority and assuming things not authorized in my job description.

I told Mr. Weeks that if my theory regarding the high-level storage vault being the source of these extremely hot radioactive particles was correct, then the only thing protecting the school children downwind from the plant from these extremely hot radioactive particles was a chain-link fence and I became very emotional about it. I suggested to Weeks that PG&E needed to build an enclosure over the entire high-level radiation waste storage vault and maintain it under negative pressure, just like the design of the refueling building. We argued for a while about whether my idea was necessary. I knew that it was and I was absolutely certain of it. Weeks, on the other hand, said my idea was utter nonsense! There was absolutely no doubt in my mind that PG&E's high-level radiation waste storage vault presented an extremely serious environmental danger to the public, especially to the children at the South Bay Elementary School and to the residents of the Humboldt Hill community.

My suggestion to build the enclosure over the high-level storage vault became an uncompromising demand. Plant management remained totally unresponsive and adamant that I was making unwarranted accusations against the company and my supervisors.

When PG&E removed the continuous air-sample monitor from the front of the South Bay Elementary School, I became suspicious of PG&E's motives and demanded again to see the results of the analyses of the tests previously conducted on the filters collected from that particular sampling station known as Environmental Monitoring Station #14. Edgar Weeks refused my request and became very upset with me.

I didn't know what to do about all this. I talked to the union shop steward to no avail; he made it sound like PG&E wouldn't dare do something as stupid as what I was suggesting. To this day I don't know if anything was ever found on any of those filters at the elementary school, but what I do know is PG&E removed the air sampler so none of those "mysterious particles" could ever find their way to the air sample monitor in the schoolyard at anytime in the future! No air sampler; no future evidence of the "mysterious particles" blowing to the school.

The removal of the continuous air sample monitor from Environmental Monitoring Station #14 was an event that caused me much grief when I questioned why it was removed. I initially raised hell with all of my first-line supervisors about the air sampler being removed from PG&E's Environmental Monitoring Station #14. That particular air sample monitor was the single most important element in the company's entire environmental radiological mon[184]toring program and it made absolutely no sense for PG&E to remove it, unless the company was protecting itself against possible future legal problems with data that could be collected by the that monitor.

I repeatedly demanded an answer to why the continuous air-sampler unit was removed and PG&E would not provide one. What I got instead were threats of dire consequences from the company. Plant management began accusing me of making unwarranted accusations against the company, and I found myself in front of Edgar Weeks being warned about the trouble I was causing.

In summary, I was outraged when I discovered PG&E had removed the continuous air-sampler monitor from the front of South Bay Elementary School. When I returned to the plant from a routine environmental tour, I immediately asked the radiation protection engineer what happened to the air sampler at the school. The answer to my question was simply, "The company decided it was no longer necessary to have one at that location." I asked why not, pointing out that the air sampler at the school was the most critical element of our environmental monitoring program especially considering the "mysterious particles" we were finding at the plant.

After talking to my-first line supervisors, I found myself in the front office talking to Edgar Weeks. It was another one of those unpleasant sessions and again I was told that I was overstepping my authority, a phrase I was now constantly hearing from plant management. Weeks made it clear that my questioning the company's decision to remove the air sampler from the school was not part of my job description, that it was not my responsibility to question management, and I was told my complaining about the decision sounded like I was making accusations against plant management and the company. I told Weeks that PG&E's Chinese fallout claim was a bunch of crap and not a satisfactory explanation for the source of "mysterious particles" we were finding in the plant (review Chapter 8).

I also told Weeks the "mysterious particle" problem and PG&E's decision to remove the continuous air-sampler at the school was interconnected and transparent.

When I complained to the AEC about what PG&E had done, it was simply recorded by the AEC investigation team as "Allegation 39." The AEC "finding" was absolute nonsense (see my comments to AEC Allegation 39 and the related finding by the AEC investigation team in Chapter 13).

PG&E's Humboldt Bay Nuclear Power Plant management headed up by Edgar Weeks; the attorney from the PG&E's corporate headquarters, Lawrence V. Brown; and AEC investigator, J. J. Ward had all participated in conversations about the "mysterious particle" problem and the continuous air-sampler monitor at South Bay Elementary School and they all walked away with what to say.

Mr. Weeks confirmed on May 11, 1970, that the company had decided the air sampler at South Bay Elementary School was no longer needed.[185] Mr. Brown claimed on December 9, 1970, that the South Bay Elementary School conducted its own air-sampling program.[186] Ward claimed on September 7, 1971, that the AEC had its own continuous air monitor at the school[187] and that PG&E was not required to have one at the school nor was PG&E "required to maintain a specific number of offsite air samplers at all times for the the company's environmental monitoring program."[188]

Victor Dricks, NRC Public Affairs Officer in Arlington Texas, responding to a FOIA request I had made, informed me AEC did not have an air sample monitor at the school "because environmental monitoring programs were the responsibility of the licensee," and in the case of the Humboldt Bay Nuclear Power Plant, that would be the Pacific Gas and Electric Company.

The author overseas in 1961 preparing for a parachute drop.

_X_

10. The Infamous PG&E Safety Meeting

May 20, 1970

"PG&E complies with the AEC regulations with regard to personnel exposure. CAN IT BE SAID that compliance with the regulations guarantees that there will be no risk to the employee? The answer to this question is, 'NO.'"[189] [Edgar Weeks]

"This is the first I've heard about this, and I'm really pissed off about this. I've got a pregnant wife at home and I don't want to be bringing this stuff home. I want an answer about this. I want to know who can give me a definite answer."[190] [Virgil Teague]

Three extremely important radiation safety issues were raised with Edgar Weeks on May 11, 1970, putting me squarely in the crosshairs of PG&E's nuclear plant management. These radiation safety issues set the stage for my last battle over PG&E's lack of concern for public safety, and for the safety of employees in the nuclear workplace.

I made a request on May 11 to speak with Mr. Robert Dodds, the AEC compliance inspector who was in our facility at the time of my request. Edgar Weeks asked me why I wanted to speak to Mr. Dodds and I told him. Weeks immediately became enraged and, without mincing his words, he refused my request. I was told I needed to "first exhaust all of my in-house options" before going to the AEC or anyplace else for that matter.

Mr. Weeks was told I was through pursuing my "in-house options" because I had already done all that; I had talked to all of my immediate supervisors many times to no avail. I also told Weeks I had discussed ad nauseam my more recent radiation safety concerns with all of my second-line supervisors as well, included him, without an inkling of success.

I then told Weeks, "I now believe it's time for me to go directly to the AEC." At that point in time I still believed the AEC was interested in making sure PG&E was complying with the radiation control standards and procedures that were in place to protect employees and the general public. I eventually learned my belief was an illusion.

Mr. Weeks emphatically made it clear that he was not going to provide me access to the AEC inspector who was in the plant. Weeks told me it was "inadvisable" for me to go to the AEC on my own after hours. I clearly remember his demeanor, his facial expressions, his body language, and there was no way for me to take Edgar Weeks' statement as anything other than as a direct threat, which was very troubling and unsettling. However, Weeks' handling of the matter only deepened my resolve to do something about the company's attitude regarding employee and public radiation safety.

The three specific items I wanted to discuss with the AEC compliance inspector while he was in the plant were the following issues: (1) The unresolved "lifeline issue" involving employees while they were working over the open reactor core (introduced in Chapter 3 and covered later in this chapter), (2) the "flushing of incores" involving nuclear control techs working directly under the reactor in extremely hazardous working conditions during refueling outages (introduced in Chapter 4 and covered later in this chapter), and (3) the removal of the continuous air-sample monitor at the South Bay Elementary School (review Chapter 9).

It wasn't until my California Unemployment Insurance Appeals Board Hearing that I was able to clearly establish what had taken place during my May 11 meeting with Edgar Weeks.

L. V. "Bud" Brown, the company's attorney, had called Edgar Weeks as a witness for PG&E, but I also had subpoenaed him even though he is not listed as one of my witnesses on the index page of the official transcript. During my cross-examination of Edgar Weeks as a PG&E witness regarding certain events that had taken place at the May 20, 1970, company safety meeting, I asked the Referee for permission to question Weeks *as my witness* in order to clear up some confusion.

The Referee granted my request:[191]

> **Mr. Rowen:** (ADDRESSING THE REFEREE) I subpoenaed Mr. Weeks to appear as a witness for me, but I suppose I can just go ahead now and clear it up, so Mr. Weeks can be finished with this. Is that all right?
>
> **THE REFEREE:** Yes. Why don't you do that?"
>
> **Mr. Rowen:** Fine. Thank you. This is concerning a discussion . . . (INTERRUPTED)
>
> **THE REFEREE:** You are putting him on as your witness at this moment?
>
> **Mr. Rowen:** Yes, at lease for this one bit of testimony here. (Directed to Mr. Weeks . . .) This concerns a discussion that you and I had on May 11th 1970. Did I request to speak with

Mr. Dodds, an AEC Compliance Inspector, who was in the plant on a routine inspection?

Mr. Weeks: Yes, you did.

Mr. Rowen: Did you refuse that request?

Mr. Weeks: Yes, I did.

Mr. Rowen: And, as a result did we have a discussion regarding your denial of my request?

Mr. Weeks: Yes, sir. We took one hour.

Mr. Rowen: Did you ask me for my reasons for wanting to speak with Mr. Dodds?

Mr. Weeks: Yes, I did.

Mr. Rowen: And, did I give my reasons to you?

Mr. Weeks: Yes.

Mr. Rowen: Were these reasons in part based on certain radiation protection safety problems and violations that I had witnessed during the 1970 refueling outage?

COMMENT: The nuclear unit had just completed a reactor refueling outage that had taken place during March and April of that year.

Mr. Weeks (CONTINUING . . .): They were based on your allegations of what were unsafe radiation safety practices. I didn't necessarily agree with you.

Mr. Rowen: Did you admit to me that some of these were radiation protection problems and you would take appropriate steps to correct them?

Mr. Weeks: If you recall, I asked you first of all if you had discussed this with your supervisor, which is the normal procedure, and you said you had, so I called ... actually, you had said you discussed some of them with Mr. Boots and some of them with Mr. Parker. Well, Mr. Parker wasn't there, but I called Mr. Boots in and we discussed the items that you said you discussed with Mr. Boots. And, I told you what actions had been taken or whether action was contemplated on the items at the time. Some of the items you brought up, we had already taken steps to do something about. I had already issued instructions. One of them, I wasn't even sure whether we were going to do anything about it. To me it was, in the discussions I heard, some people thought it was a problem, some people didn't. And, I told you we could continue discussions on it and try to get it resolved, which we had tried to do.

Mr. Rowen: What particular item are you referring to?

Mr. Weeks: That's working over the reactor vessel before the extension tank is put on it after the head is removed.

COMMENT: The "head" to which Weeks referred was the huge biological shield covering the top of the reactor during normal operations. It was necessary to remove the biological shield in order to open up the reactor for refueling. Mr. Weeks, still under oath, continued his testimony:

> **Mr. Weeks** (CONTINUING . . .): I told you at that time that our maintenance foreman was against using a lifeline that you had suggested? He didn't like the idea. He thought it was more unsafe than doing it the way we have been doing it. Some of the supervisors agreed with the line of thinking you had at that time, that they should wear a safety line. I told you we would discuss it at our next meeting, which we did at our next supervisor's meeting and we didn't come to any real agreement on it.

> **Mr. Rowen:** Wasn't it true that our radiation protection engineer had laid it down as a rule that everybody must follow?

> **Mr. Brown (PG&E attorney):** Referring to what now?

COMMENT: The room was filling with tension! You could feel it! You could see it in the facial expressions of Edgar Weeks and the PG&E attorney. I was trying very hard to maintain my cool while at the same time, trying to get Weeks to reveal what had taken place at our May 11 meeting. Following Mr. Brown's asinine outburst, I staged a nonverbal *communiqué*. I momentary paused while glaring at the attorney, then looked away shaking my head in disgust, and finally I continued my questioning of Weeks after first pithily answering Brown's question![192]

> **Mr. Rowen:** (CONTINUING . . .) The fact that we were to use a safety line while working over the top of the open reactor so that no one could fall into it

COMMENT: A nuclear worker falling into the reactor unquestionably would be a catastrophic event! I pointed this out to the radiation protection engineer and stated that no one should be allowed on top of the open reactor without wearing a lifeline. He totally agreed with me but there were others who did not, including Edgar Weeks.

I did my best to confront Weeks and pin him down on this during my direct examination of him. Edgar Weeks was wishy-washy in his responses but I think Weeks' testimony revealed his attitude towards the radiation protection safety problem I was trying to get at and, therefore, his testimony speaks for itself.[193]

> **Mr. Weeks:** (CONTINUING . . .) You told me at the time that he had assured you before the outage that he was going to do that and I'm afraid I can't tell you ... I can't really say that this is the general rule. I don't remember seeing a written rule on this.

COMMENT: I have no idea what Weeks was talking about when he referred to "I don't remember seeing a written rule on this."

All "written directives" either originated at his desk or he signed off on them, because he was in charge of all technical staff and nuclear plant operations.

Mr. Boots had made his decision as the plant's radiation protection engineer to require the use of lifelines to be worn while working over the open reactor. Weeks did not enthusiastically embrace the idea because the maintenance foreman was opposed to it.

The simple truth of the matter was the maintenance foreman was not in the position to make decisions on behalf of the workers in his department regarding radiation protection safety policies and practices. That responsibility belonged to the radiation protection department. I continued my questioning of Mr. Weeks:[194]

> **Mr. Rowen** (CONTINUING . . .): Was Mr. Boots present at this discussion?
>
> **Mr. Weeks:** Yes, he was.
>
> **Mr. Rowen:** Did he admit to you that he had made that statement?
>
> **Mr. Weeks:** He admitted discussing it with you and telling you that he was going to look into it and take some action on it.
>
> **Mr. Rowen:** You don't recall him saying that yes, I told Mr. Rowen that the safety lines would be used?
>
> **Mr. Weeks:** I got the impression that he had agreed with you that they should be used, I don't remember his exact words but I got the distinct impression that he did agree with you before the outage, that we should use safety lines.
>
> **Mr. Rowen:** Isn't it true during the March-April outage Supervisors Andrew Kennedy and the instrument engineer (from the Bay Area) that came up to work with Kennedy during the outage along with control tech Les Gables and another employee went down onto the top of the reactor without a safety line and the rad protection engineer was notified and he said they had to come off the top of the reactor and put on a safety line before they could go back down and work?
>
> **Mr. Weeks:** I wasn't directly involved in these things. I can't testify that this happened the way you described it. I'm afraid I'd have to say I really can't answer your question.

Edgar Weeks knew damn well what I was talking about because he and I went round and around about it in his office on May 11 following the March-April refueling outage.

Kennedy and Gables had refused to comply with what the radiation protection engineer was requiring of everyone who went down onto the top of the open reactor to work, and Weeks was guilty of turning a blind eye to it and I told him so.

There was no way for him to have forgotten about the confrontation we had that was brought on by the position I had taken with him on this very issue!

Another radiation safety problem I had discussed with Mr. Weeks on May 11 had to do with the unresolved problem of routing out incores during refueling outages. This was dangerous work that was done directly underneath the reactor vessel in an area referred to as "Minus-66."

This area was in an extremely high radiation zone with temperatures in the work area exceeding 90 degrees and humidly approaching the 100 percent mark. The high radiation dose rates in the work area under the reactor limited the amount of time a nuclear control tech could spend down there to a matter of minutes. The part of our bodies most affected by the high radiation dose rate field was our heads!

During the procedures that were being used to flush incores, reactor water along with the highly radioactive "crud" from the bottom of the reactor would rain down on us with radioactive contamination that required us to go through a grueling decon process at access control.

The problem of routing out incores had existed for several years and it had gotten progressively worse; all attempts to get management to correct the problem were totally in vain!

Through my cross-examination of Edgar Weeks, I was able to establish for the Referee's benefit that I did continuously raise radiation safety issues that the company failed to address, and that I was refused permission to talk with the AEC inspectors about those issues. Also I clearly established for the Referee that I was told by Edgar Weeks it was "inadvisable" for me to go to the AEC or to any other any outside agencies on my own.

It is rare this kind of information from the inside of a "nuclear fish bowl" can be unequivocally established for public scrutiny. The following incredible testimony given by Edgar Weeks several months after I was fired by PG&E establishes the claims I have just made (Weeks had no idea what I might pull out of my briefcase which probably explains his somewhat candid responses to my questions): [195]

> **Mr. Rowen** (ADDRESSING MR. WEEKS): Did you admit that some of these problems had existed for several outages, for several years without being corrected?
>
> **Mr. Weeks:** Well, let's take it (PAUSE)...let's take it (PAUSE)...the first item (PAUSE)---I remember now exactly what was said. The first item concerned the problem of routing out incores. You were unhappy with the way we were doing that, and I told you I was unhappy with it too and, that I had already told Mr. Chaffee and Mr. Kamberg to come up with a better way of doing that for the next outage. And, in fact they were already working on it, and as a matter of fact, the problem has been solved now, I think, since we have redesigned this and we've contemplated doing it a different way on the next outage.
>
> **Mr. Rowen:** Why was everybody unhappy with it?

Mr. Weeks: Because the last time in 1970 when we used it in the April refueling outage, we had generally contaminated the area underneath the reactor when we routed out the incores and it caused a lot of confusion, a lot of problems, so that at that time ... (INTERRUPTED)

COMMENT: This refers to the March-April refueling outage that ended about four weeks before I was fired from PG&E and the one I wanted to talk to the AEC inspector about a week or so after the outage had ended.

Mr. Rowen: (CONTINUING . . .) Did it also contribute to large amounts of contamination to the personnel involved?

Mr. Weeks: Yes, it did.

Mr. Rowen: On their skin and faces?

Mr. Weeks: Not unsafe amounts but still in amounts that were a nuisance. We had to wash 'em off. There was contamination on some clothing, as I remember.

Mr. Rowen: I see. How long had this condition actually existed?

Mr. Weeks: This is the method we had used since 1966, along in there, when we first changed our incores. That was quite a number of years.

Mr. Rowen: It was indicated as early as that, that there was a problem, and that plant management was going to look into it, and try to correct the problem?

Mr. Weeks: I don't think anybody was completely satisfied with the way we were doing it, but it wasn't a really a big problem until the 1970 refueling outage. But, that's the only time that (PAUSE)---Well, I can't say for sure, maybe at one other time it was a mess, but I think that was the biggest mess. And, I know I resolved at that time to do something about it. And, before you ever came into that, steps have been taken to get it changed. It wasn't an item that was being ignored.

Weeks' testimony here really didn't make any sense. It was apparent that he was either grasping at straws in an attempt to confuse the Referee or perhaps he was trying to cover his own ass in front of the PG&E attorney (which actually may have not been necessary – I don't know).

In any event there remained a serious unresolved problem with the incore work being done under the reactor by the nuclear control technicians. Weeks' own testimony established that the incore problem had existed for more than four years during which time there were several outages involving incore work.

Although he tried to downplay the problem, Weeks admitted there were large amounts of radioactive contamination to the employees performing the work.

Edgar Weeks' testimony more than implied there is "safe amounts" of radioactive contamination to the "face and skin." Nothing could have been further from the truth, and this is especially true when the radiation is in either liquid and/or crud forms. Weeks' testimony clearly revealed his attitude towards radiation safety. It was precisely this kind of attitude that caused me to be constantly at odds over radiation safety with PG&E management, and especially with Edgar Weeks!

The third radiation safety issue I wanted to discuss with Mr. Robert Dodds, the AEC inspector who was in the plant when Edgar Weeks denied my request to meet with him, pertained to PG&E's removal of the continuous air-sample monitor at the school (review Chapter 9).

It is very possible that talking to the AEC compliance inspector at the time of my request would have produced a far different outcome regarding the issue of dismantling and the complete removal of the continuous air-sample monitor at the elementary school by PG&E.

I stewed for days over Weeks' treatment of me on May 11 and his inept handling of all the radiation safety issues I had discussed with him.

The morning of May 20, 1970, brought a series of life-changing events into our lives. Because Forrest Williams and I weren't getting anywhere with plant management concerning our radiation safety concerns, we impulsively decided to raise some of the more pressing issues very publicly at a company safety meeting scheduled for later that morning.

During our midmorning break on May 20, Forrest and I continued our discussions that had begun before the start of work that morning regarding our frustrations with Edgar Weeks and his arbitrary, unilateral and intimidating ways, and with plant management's total disregard for our safety concerns that we had raised often. Putting it bluntly, we were fed up!

My meeting with Edgar Weeks a few days earlier was still stuck in my craw! I had grown tired of the senseless "counseling sessions" with Weeks, which quite honestly was something I made clear to the employees we were talking with during our morning break.

There were a few employees who participated in our discussion that morning but Forrest and I were the most vocal and definitely more willing to do something about our concerns rather than just talk about them amongst ourselves.

Forrest and I decided to move forward with voicing our concerns at the upcoming company safety meeting. After all we reasoned, that was what these safety meetings were for – at least in theory – and a strategy I had successfully used in the past to get some much needed things changed albeit followed with grave repercussions every time.

In all honesty the idea to use the safety meeting this time was initially mine. I pointed out to the small group of employees that minutes were always taken at those meetings and supposedly reviewed by AEC compliance inspectors each time they made a visit to the plant.

I felt that if I couldn't talk to the AEC compliance inspectors while they were in the plant, I could at least bring our concerns up at a safety meeting and let the AEC inspectors read about them. Of course, plant management had already made it clear we were not to use safety meetings in this way;[196] that's because they wanted those minutes to always paint a rosy picture of plant operations.

Eventually I came to the realization that the real company concern for a "rosy picture" had more to do with the possibility of a public disclosure that the radiation safety problems existed in the first place.

Of course, at the very least it would prove embarrassing to the company if the problems existed and were never addressed but then there was also the possibility of future litigation on several fronts.

I pointed out to Forrest and the others that the minutes of the safety meetings became part of the plant's permanent record, and it appeared to be a good way to put our radiation safety concerns in front of the AEC and hopefully they would get into the public eye through normal external processes someday.

Little did we realize how PG&E management would respond this time to our use of the May 20 safety meeting. At this conjuncture I suppose it really didn't matter much to either of Forrest or me how management was going to respond because we were both totally disgusted with what was happening at PG&E's nuclear facility. However, neither of us could have ever imagined what would happen as a result of taking our radiation safety concerns to the company safety meeting that day; we had no idea what PG&E was capable of!

Forest and I quickly jotted down some notes before the meeting so we could stay focused on the concerns we had kicked around during our coffee break. I remember saying that we should keep our list to a few items because too many things would overwhelm the process. I also remember we had a good chuckle about that.

We each had our own ideas of what to bring up and central to mine was the "mysterious particles" along with the removal of the continuous air-sample monitor in front of the South Bay Elementary School. In my opinion the decision to remove the air sampler was one of the most grievous decisions made by PG&E management.

It remains my belief that the decision to dismantle and remove the continuous air-sample monitor from the school was made by PG&E's corporate headquarters in San Francisco, and that the "mysterious particles" and the removal of the air sampler were interconnected issues.

Also, I wanted to address my burning unanswered question about constant exposure to low-level ionizing radiation. We both decided to bring up the hand-and-foot counter problem.

As we spoke, a deadening silence initially fell over the PG&E's HBPP Assembly Building where the safety meetings were held.

The silence then exploded into several outbursts with people talking all at the same time. The chairman, Russ Peters, became angry and asked everyone to calm down, and then he asked us for our prepared statements. I responded that I didn't have a prepared statement, just some notes outlining what I wanted to cover. I asked my questions a second time.

Basically, I asked six questions at the safety meeting. First, I wanted to know if plant management considered chronic exposure to low level ionizing radiation as carcinogenic and, if so, to what extent. All previous attempts to get plant management to address that question had failed.

Second, I asked if plant management had any new thoughts about the nature and source of the "mysterious particles" we were finding on the soles of shoes and in the clothing of employees.

Third, we asked why the hand-and-foot counter had alarm settings that were set too high during the last outage.

Then I asked if PG&E was actually going to do something about the problem of flushing incores and if a decision had been made about the use of lifelines while working over the open reactor.

Finally, I asked if PG&E could tell us why the continuous air-sample monitor was removed from the front of the South Bay Elementary School, pointing out that I thought that monitor was strategically located and extremely important to our environmental radiological monitoring program, to the community, and especially to the elementary school.

Forrest addressed the problem of employees taking radioactive contamination off site, questioned the adequacy of the monitoring process when leaving the controlled area, and addressed the inadequacy of radiation protection training of some personnel. He also questioned the alarm settings on the hand-and-foot counter at the exit of Unit 3.

Every one of these concerns had already been brought up to plant management personnel several times, and each time the response was the same – nothing, absolutely nothing! Plant management had ignored our concerns and issued accusations that resulted in "counseling sessions," especially for me!

One employee at the safety meeting, Virgil Teague, an electrician who worked in Unit 3 from time to time, responded to the hand-and-foot counter issue with a dramatic outburst.

Teague's outburst probably contributed significantly to management's knee-jerk reaction that blossomed into a grandiose fabrication of a conspiracy that took on a life of its own (Chapter 11).

According to minutes taken by Ms. Cillay Risku, Virgil Teague made the following statement at the safety meeting:[197]

> This is the first I've heard about this, and I'm really pissed off about this. I've got a pregnant wife at home and I don't want to be bringing this stuff home. I want an answer about this. I want to know who can give me a definite answer.

In my view, Virgil may have gotten a little carried away with himself. He actually knew of our concerns before that meeting. I believe Virgil just wanted to support Forrest and me in our efforts to address our radiation safety concerns at the company's safety meeting.

It's possible a fair number of the employees did not know very much about what Forrest and I brought up at the meeting, but a few of them did. Most employees knew very little about how Forrest Williams and I were being treated and dealt with in "counseling sessions" behind closed doors in the front office.

It was not surprising that our questions raised at the safety meeting were never answered nor was it a big surprise that Forrest and I ended up in a lot of hot water for asking them. Forrest and I were never able to address what we "stirred up" following the meeting nor any of its consequences while we were still employed at the nuclear facility because we were out the door in short order.

I, however, was able to again address the questions Forrest and I had raised and management's reaction to them at my two Unemployment Insurance Appeals Board Hearings held on October 1 and again nine weeks later on December 9, 1970.

During my Appeals Hearings, Mr. John Kamberg, nuclear instrumentation foreman, addressed my first question raised at the company safety meeting concerning the biological effects of chronic exposure to ionizing radiation. The history behind the motivation to pursue this question includes an early, unresolved conflict, which arose in my radiation protection training provided by PG&E (review Chapter 2).

As I was exposed to more conflicting information on this subject, the more I wanted PG&E to address it. Private discussions with my supervisors, especially with the radiation protection engineers I had worked under (Gail Allen and Jerome Boots) and with Edgar Weeks, always ended up the same way. I was told the PG&E Radiation Protection Training Manual was based on the "latest and most reliable information available."

Most of the information contained in PG&E's training manual was taken from sources PG&E considered reliable including the training courses for the Dresden Nuclear Power Station and the Vallecitos Atomic Laboratory. As previously stated, my ABC Warfare training in the military led me to question some of PG&E's claims made in the company's rad protection training manual.

PG&E's training manual was prepared for use as a textbook for the Radiation Protection Training Course that was to be given all personnel assigned to the Humboldt Bay Power Plant whose work involved exposure to radiation. The Radiation Protection Training Manual was introduced in Chapter 2 of my *Diary* and is revisited here and expanded upon for emphasis.

Chapter IV of PG&E's Radiation Protection Training Manual Section B. entitled <u>Biological Damage</u> states, in part:[198]

> Cells are the building blocks of the human body. Each living cell consists of water and protein molecules. The protein molecules are complex arrangements of atoms held in pace by chemical bonds. Damage to the living cells by radiation is due either to the direct ionization of the atoms composing the protein molecules, or indirectly to the chemical action of oxidants formed when the water in the cells is ionized. Regardless of the process by which cells are damaged, the result is an alteration in cell structure or a reduction in cell reproduction and function. This is biological damage. Biological damage is not confined to that due to radiation. Cells are continually being damaged by the action of chemical, heat, and disease.

In the same Section B the following statement is made:[199]

> **The body has the ability to recover and repair damage parts. It is capable of replacing cells, which are damaged by radiation in the same manner as those damaged by mechanical, heat, or chemical injuries.**

By early 1970, I had accumulated a large volume of information that refuted much of the information in PG&E's radiation protection training materials. I wanted plant management to address the conflicting information; in fact, I demanded it!

PG&E was obviously ignoring all information pertaining to the biological effects of chronic exposure to low-level ionizing radiation coming from the scientific community that ran counter to the company's interests in advancing nuclear power.

Since plant management had consistently refused to respond to my persistent requests, and out of complete frustration, I decided to take the issue head-on and very publicly at the May 20 safety meeting.

I used my opportunity at my Unemployment Insurance Appeals Board Hearing to obtain through my cross-examination of PG&E's Nuclear Instrumentation Foreman John Kamberg the following testimony regarding my first question at the safety meeting:[200]

> **Mr. Rowen:** During the company safety meeting of May 20, 1970, do you remember me asking a question at the opening of new business where such matters are normally discussed: Does PG&E recognize ionizing radiation to the most general carcinogen known today?
>
> **Mr. Kamberg:** Yes, you did.
>
> **Mr. Rowen:** At that time did the chairman of the meeting ask what "carcinogen" meant?
>
> **Mr. Kamberg:** Yes. I believe the question was over everybody's head in the room.

Mr. Rowen: And I responded by saying, "carcinogen is a cancer-forming agent?"

Mr. Kamberg: Yes, you did.

COMMENT: What's interesting about Mr. Kamberg's response is the simple observation that every person in the room except the front office clerical staff were "graduates" of PG&E's Radiation Protection Training Program yet no one knew what carcinogen meant. Of course I should point out that I could not find the word "carcinogen" used anywhere in PG&E's Radiation Protection Training Manual.

All the issues I raised at the May 20 safety meeting had been previously presented to plant management without success. Plant management just "counseled" me for my "poor attitude," for my "poor job performance," and for my "troublemaking ways." I was constantly being accused of "overstepping my authority" every time I asked embarrassing questions or complained about violations of radiation control standards and procedures.

Nevertheless, I continued to complain about radiation safety problems. Nuclear control technicians were receiving unnecessary and senseless radiation exposure every time they collected and analyzed off-gas and reactor water samples. It took my very public "presentation" at a previous company safety meeting on December 12, 1967, for the company to address the problems that I had been complaining about for months.

Meanwhile Edgar Weeks had counseled me numerous times about the complaints he was receiving from the plant's radiation protection and chemical engineers concerning my "continual complaining."

It seemed to plant management that all I wanted to do was travel around the plant looking for something to complain about. Truth of the matter was simple. I did not want to receive any more radiation exposure than was necessary in order to do my job as a nuclear control technician.

Forrest Williams agreed with me and so did control techs Raymond Skidmore and Howard Darington. The others didn't seem to care that much; they preferred to maintain the peace and sometimes they'd advise me to do the same.

PG&E was turning the page behind the scenes on what the company considered a threat to its vital interests. The company was developing and "documenting" a complex conspiracy theory in voluminous files at the plant, at PG&E's Humboldt Division Personnel Office, and at PG&E's corporate headquarters in San Francisco.

After Forrest and I were fired from PG&E, we learned that PG&E management accused Forrest Williams and me of engaging in a concerted effort to install fear into "the rank and file" at the May 20 company safety meeting. We thereafter were accused of committing acts that were "tantamount to industrial sabotage" and a whole lot worse (Chapter 11).

John Kamberg, a former nuclear control tech, who had been promoted into the ranks of plant management as the Unit 3 nuclear instrumentation foreman, was called upon by the PG&E attorney, Lawrence V. Brown, to serve as a witness for the company at my first Unemployment Insurance Appeals Board Hearing on October 1, 1970.

The following testimony was initially in response to Mr. Brown's question regarding the proper use of company safety meetings and then shifted to our question regarding the hand-and-foot counter:[201]

Mr. Brown: ...Getting back to the safety meeting, safety meetings in general at your facility. If an individual feels that something is dangerous, he knows or thinks he knows of a condition that is dangerous, is it proper for him to state it at the safety meeting?

Mr. Kamberg: Definitely. In fact, I think one time or another I advised Bob if he felt he was not getting answers from individuals to use this as a method of getting answers, bring them up as something that is going to be in the minutes of the safety meeting, to get his answers in that way. But in no way did I advise him to make accusations against the company.

Mr. Brown: Well, in general, if you are talking about a work situation and you're saying the work situation is dangerous, by inference, you are, of course, accusing the company, are you not? The company is responsible for the conditions?

Mr. Kamberg: Well, yes. But in my opinion there is a slight difference. If you are asking a question, you're asking the person to explain why? You're not saying you're wrong. You're saying, show me why my idea is wrong. In my opinion there is a difference.

Mr. Brown: In your opinion, in what way did you regard Williams and Rowen?

Mr. Kamberg: In regard to Rowen's first statement, I'd take it as an inquiry. It's kind of hard to answer an inquiry. In case of the second statement he made about the hand-and-foot monitor, I think this was an out and out accusation of negligence on the part of management.

THE REFEREE: All right. Are you saying that an individual who thinks management is being negligent, and in a way he believes exposes persons to danger, should not say that at a safety meeting?

Mr. Kamberg: Well, here again, as it was pointed out once before, I don't believe Bob ever questioned me on this point. I am his supervisor in charge of that instrument. I don't believe he ever brought this question to me. I may be wrong. I don't recall it. So first off he didn't go through the right channels.

Mr. Brown: Is it your recollection, as it's stated there, that Mr. Rowen said the settings were deliberately set high.

Mr. Kamberg: Mr. Rowen had.

THE REFEREE: Not that he had.

Mr. Brown: Mr. Rowen accused management had deliberately set the setting too high. I underscore the word "deliberately."

Mr. Kamberg: I understand it that way.

Mr. Brown: Does that create any feeling on your part whether this was an accusation or a question?

Mr. Kamberg: Definitely. That management had deliberately set them high for a purpose.

Mr. Brown: Perhaps I misunderstood your testimony on that point earlier. But being a layman in this, perhaps I have had a very false impression in which case you certainly should clear it up. I got the impression from listening to you that you were saying that that's exactly what was done, that you had done it yourself.

Mr. Kamberg: Yes, I had done it myself, but I might add at this time I was a control technician. I was not management. I never consulted management whether I should or shouldn't. I did it as a labor saving device for myself. In other words, it saved me from having to serve 15 or 20 people, how many there were coming across, serving each one individually.

I could do the survey on one and find he was not contaminated and check and raise the alarm on the foot-and-hand counter and let the rest of them use it as that. I knew the hand-and-foot monitor was doing what it was supposed to be doing. It was, in fact, watching for 100 counts above background. I knew that because I checked it out. It was my responsibility.

Mr. Brown: Well, when you used that procedure, did it not have the effect of allowing subsequent men to pass through the device without setting off the alarm who might otherwise set it off before you raised it?

Mr. Kamberg: Definitely. Yes, but the point I am trying to make, in my check and analysis of the conditions, just the normal background of the area would set off the alarm.

Mr. Brown: I see. Your point was that you would raise it to a point, which would still furnish adequate protection and if there was an undue amount of radiation above the background the machine would – the alarm would go off?

Mr. Kamberg: Right.

Mr. Brown: Do I understand, Mr. Kamberg, you took this statement made by Mr. Rowen to be an accusation that the machine would – was deliberately set too high by management so it would be possible for people to go without setting the alarm off?

Mr. Kamberg: Right. That is the way I understand it.

COMMENT: It was obvious to me that the PG&E attorney and Kamberg had previously discussed what Kamberg's testimony was going to cover. I found it amusing that Kamberg would view my question regarding the hand-and-foot counter as an accusation; after all, he had been put in charge of it as the nuclear instrumentation foreman.

When it was my turn to conduct a cross-examination of Mr. Kamberg, I eventually turned my attention to the hand-and-foot counter issue and after some preliminary discussion about background levels, Mr. Kamberg gave the following testimony with some interruptions from the PG&E attorney):[202]

> **Mr. Rowen:** (Directed to Mr. Kamberg . . .) Let me ask you this. During the outage where this problem was at issue, would the background indeed have been the same, greater than, or less than the May 20th background?
>
> **Mr. Brown:** I am going to object to this line of questioning.
>
> **Mr. Rowen:** I am attempting to establish . . . (INTERRUPTED)
>
> **Mr. Brown:** You are limited to cross-examination on what I introduced into the record.
>
> **THE REFEREE:** You are mistaken about that, sir. We do not . . . (INTERRUPTED)
>
> **Mr. Brown:** I realize you don't follow the strict rules. As a matter of due process and fairness there has to be a certain limitation to cross-examination. The main essence of my objection is that the questioning doesn't at all seem to bear on what we are trying to get at here.
>
> **Mr. Rowen:** I will state for the referee the point I want to make. During the outage when the reactor was shut down the background at the hand-and-foot counter was much less than on May 20th, yielding a greater spread between the alarm settings, release limits and the background of the outage.
>
> **Mr. Brown:** My reason of objecting, our introduction of evidence related to your accusations we had deliberately set something too high.
>
> **Mr. Rowen:** This is what I wanted to get into. I have witnesses and documentary evidence to show . . . (INTERRUPTED)
>
> **Mr. Brown:** We realize this is a very liberal-type proceeding. It would appear we will (sic) be spending an endless amount of time that will prove nothing when we get through.
>
> **THE REFEREE:** Well, it seems to me that it's material. The claimant is attempting to show the claimant's statements he made at the safety meeting were essentially well-founded.
>
> **Mr. Brown:** His statement at the meeting was there was a deliberate setting.
>
> **THE REFEREE:** He is now attempting to prove that.

After considerably more wrangling, I was finally able to put my questions to Kamberg about the hand-and-foot counter and this was his testimony:[203]

> **Mr. Rowen:** You stated in your earlier testimony that you don't really remember whether I talked with you or not during the outage about the hand-and-foot counter, isn't that correct?
>
> **Mr. Kamberg:** I don't recall whether you did or not. If you can point out an incident where you did then maybe I can recall.
>
> **Mr. Rowen:** Do you have knowledge that I talked with Don Woods, who was the rad protection control technician on duty during the outage?
>
> **Mr. Kamberg:** About what, Bob?
>
> **Mr. Rowen:** About the hand-and-foot counter alarm settings were set too high.
>
> **Mr. Kamberg:** Yes, I think there were occasions when the point was brought up many times.
>
> **Mr. Rowen:** I am now asking if you have knowledge about me relating this to the control technician on rad protection during the outage?
>
> **Mr. Kamberg:** It may have been you. I can't swear to it.
>
> **Mr. Rowen:** Another question on the same subject. Do you have specific knowledge of Ray Skidmore, another control technician, approaching Jerry Boots during the outage about the hand-and-foot counter?
>
> **Mr. Kamberg:** No. If we're talking about specific knowledge, the answer is no. Anything along that order would be hearsay.
>
> **Mr. Rowen:** Then were you aware of some hearsay? (INTERRUPTED)
>
> **Mr. Brown:** I object. We are here to find out what he knows of his own direct personal knowledge. We are not interested in hearsay.
>
> **THE REFEREE:** Hearsay is admissible in these hearings as long as it appears to be material.
>
> **Mr. Brown:** Let's go on and finish expeditiously.
>
> **THE REFEREE:** We simply do not proceed in the manner as they do in court.
>
> **Mr. Brown:** Mr. Referee, I think I have been patient up to this point. The form of his question, to begin with, is not easily answerable. It's hearsay. It doesn't establish anything.
>
> **THE REFEREE:** Mr. Rowen, would you repeat the question if you are still interested in the answer?
>
> **Mr. Rowen:** Yes. Do you have any knowledge of Mr. Raymond Skidmore approaching Jerry Boots, the rad

protection engineer, concerning the hand-and-foot alarm settings being set too high?

Mr. Kamberg: Personal knowledge, no.

Mr. Rowen: Hearsay is admissible. Did you hear any talk about it?

Mr. Kamberg: Yes. I heard considerable talk about it in the lab prior to being a supervisor when (INTERRUPTED)

Mr. Rowen: I am talking about (INTERRUPTED)

Mr. Kamberg: There was a lot of talk. Since I have been a supervisor, that outlet of information has more or less ceased. I believe you're aware of that, Bob. Once you're a supervisor you're not part of the bull sessions any more. You don't get the feedback, hearsay, information you're asking for.

Mr. Rowen: Are you aware of any problems at access control?

Mr. Kamberg: As I stated before, Bob, I am aware questions have been brought, but you're asking me to state whether Ray said it or you said it or somebody else said it. I don't know who said it. Problems had been brought up.

Mr. Rowen: That's fine. Now I have just one final question. You discussed a labor saving device by turning the alarm setting up and down on the hand-and-foot counter as you desired to do without talking to management about it. Isn't that correct?

Mr. Kamberg: Yes.

Mr. Rowen: This was while you were a control technician?

Mr. Kamberg: Correct.

Mr. Rowen: Looking back on it, as a member of management now, would you say this is a poor-working-performance-type of thing, inadequate, failure to follow instructions, something along those lines?

Mr. Kamberg: Definitely.

Mr. Weeks responded to my question at a company safety meeting on June 23, 1970, which was an amazing two weeks after I was fired from PG&E. He first referred to a statement quoted from a January 20, 1970, letter from Secretary Finch of Health, Education, and Welfare to Senator Muskie, Chairman of the Subcommittee on Air and Water Pollution:[204]

> In view of our concern with the potential hazard of ionizing radiation in the environment, and as Chairman of the Federal Radiation Council, I am recommending that the Council institute a careful review and evaluation of the revelent (sic) scientific information that has become available in the past decade. I am recommending that this reevaluation provide, as definitively as possible, estimates of the risks associated with low levels of environmental radiation as applicable to projected radiation levels.

Mr. Weeks followed up this quote saying, "This reevaluation was directly spurred by statements of two scientists, Drs. Gofman and Tamplin."[205]

Weeks concluded his remarks saying:

> In the final analysis, however, it remains for the individual to weigh the potential risks of working in this industry against the benefits he can expect to receive and judge by choice of occupations accordingly.

The May 20, 1970, company safety meeting served as the launching pad for PG&E's development of a ridiculous conspiracy by several nuclear control technicians to do harm to the company with me as its primary focus. The minutes of the safety meeting initially was used to get the ball rolling and the PG&E attorney at my Unemployment Insurance Appeals Board Hearing tried to establish the validity of those minutes with the Referee. The following is the testimony of a front office secretary, Mrs. Cillay Risku, who took the minutes:

Mr. Brown: I'm now showing you Exhibit No. 4. I ask you if these are the verbatim notes that you referred to in your previous testimony?

Mrs. Risku: Yes, they are.

Mr. Brown: I have no further questions.

COMMENT: All I could do at the time was to shake my head. I looked at the Referee and shrugged my shoulders. I had already read Mrs. Risku's minutes and I was holding a copy of them in my hand and gestured them towards the Referee. The Referee responded,

THE REFEREE: (Directed to Mr. Brown . . .) May I see those documents?

COMMENT: While the Referee was reviewing the minutes, the PG&E attorney asked another question,

Mr. Brown: (Directed to Mrs. Risku . . .) May I ask one more question? Were these notes transcribed immediately after the meeting?

Mrs. Risku: The second page with the verbatim general discussion was transcribed directly after the meeting.

Mr. Brown: That's all I have.

COMMENT: I was chomping at the bit to ask one question of Mrs. Risku but I could see that the Referee had something he wanted ask first,

THE REFEREE: (Directed to Mrs. Risku . . .) Referring to Exhibit 4 where there are dots, as there are many times, what does that mean?

Mrs. Risku: That indicates areas in which I was not able to--- in other words, under the discussion, the men that were speaking fast or my shorthand was not rapid enough to keep up with the conversation and so that refers to lapses.

THE REFEREE: Then, you do not maintain that you actually did get a verbatim record?

Mrs. Risku: No, I did not.

THE REFEREE: Fine. Mr. Rowen, do you have some questions of Mrs. Risku?

Mr. Rowen: Yes. Referring to Exhibit 4, that's the notes supplemental to the minutes that you took, there's a notation at the top of the exhibit. Can you explain what that means?

Mrs. Risku: Yes. I would like to read it out loud. "The following notes are taken at the accident meeting at the Humboldt Bay Power Plant. These notes cannot be interpreted to be an accurate record of the proceedings. Participants of the discussion spoke in a rapid manner and there are many instances where more than one person was talking at the time." What I'm trying to say is that these notes could not be interpreted as being an actual, complete verbatim because of the fact that there were more than one person talking at the time. My shorthand is not rapid enough to have taken down the dialogue at the speeds in which it was given.

At the time of our employment terminations, Forrest Williams and I had not yet realized the full ramifications of the PG&E May 20, 1970, safety meeting. By the end of June 1970, as we were beginning to recover from the hullabaloo of being fired, it was for us like that old proverbial saying, "We could see the light at the end of the tunnel only to learn that it was an oncoming freight train."

__XI__

11. PG&E's Conspiracy

May-June 1970

"When PG&E's nuclear PLANT MANAGEMENT failed to effectively deal with us on its own terms, then the company's CORPORATE HEADQUARTERS took over and proceeded to equate our safety concerns with dissent, and dissent with conspiracy; a conspiracy to do harm to the company and its nuclear program and facilities."[206] [Rowen]

"I know that we will be the sufferers if we let great wrongs occur without exerting ourselves to correct them."[207] [Eleanor Roosevelt]

PG&E's incredible response to what had taken place at the May 20 safety meeting was swift and extremely reactionary. Berton F. Jones, PG&E's Senior Security Agent, was dispatched with great speed from corporate headquarters at 245 Market Street, San Francisco to Humboldt Bay.

His mission was to obtain written statements from certain hand-selected employees, review personnel files, interview top-level nuclear plant management personnel, meet with the local PG&E personnel manager, then collaborate with Police Chief Cedric Emahiser of the Eureka Police Department to fabricate a "confidential" law enforcement document that specifically named four of Humboldt Bay's seven nuclear control technicians: Forrest Williams, Raymond Skidmore, Howard Darington, and Bob Rowen as "threats" to PG&E.

After that police document was completed, it was then sent back to PG&E; an official copy of it was also forwarded on to the Federal Bureau of Investigation. It was never the intent of PG&E for any of the four nuclear control technicians named in it to ever become aware of it.

In the final analysis the true purpose of the "confidential" law enforcement document was to blacklist Forrest Williams and me from future employment in the nuclear industry because we would not be able to obtain the necessary security clearances in the future – *nuclear blacklisting* – a new kind of blacklisting of those inside the industry, who become critical of nuclear power and need to be *"neutralized,"* using "national security" as a means for pulling it off!

Berton F. Jones arrived at our nuclear facility the day after the company safety meeting and he first met with several senior plant management personnel including Edgar Weeks, Plant Engineer; Dale Nix, Plant Manager; and Warren Raymond, Assistance Plant Manager. Edgar Weeks was the mover and shaker in this group. Dale Nix was selected to serve as plant manager (as a figurehead only) because of his heroism as a crew member of a B-29 that flew numerous missions over Germany during WW II.

Edgar Weeks was clearly the "brains" of the nuclear triumvirate at Humboldt Bay and everyone kowtowed to him, including the two above him in the plant's management hierarchy. They all knew he was well connected at PG&E corporate headquarters through his alliance and close friendship with James C. Carroll, who coordinated all aspects of the *Humboldt Bay Project*. It was James C. Carroll who was named in a major lawsuit against PG&E involving the company's nuclear censorship and blacklisting shenanigans of an Emmy Award documentary producer (Chapter 15 – Nuclear Censorship and the Don Widener Story).

Working together at the direction of Edgar Weeks and Berton F. Jones, a list of employees was drawn up and handed over to Mr. Jones. This list was composed of six hand-selected "good company men" who were either already first line supervisors or aspiring to become one.

Mr. Jones started interviewing and taking written statements from the six employees late in the morning of May 21 and finished with them by the end of the day on May 22, 1970. His strategy was the same with all six men. He first engaged in a conversation with each man; he then wrote out a statement for each of them to sign.

In every instance, the statement began with "I, [the name of the employee], make this voluntary statement to Berton F. Jones concerning materials submitted at a safety meeting held May 20, 1970." Each statement ended with "I have read this statement, and everything is true to the best of my knowledge," and then the employee's signature followed. Every statement was in the handwriting of Mr. Jones and only the signature was in the handwriting of the employee.

Bert Jones was a smooth talker. He had the necessary skills to set the stage with the select group of employees that he had interviewed to extract from each of them exactly what he needed to execute the next part of his diabolical plan. A plan that once exposed was clearly a throwback to the McCarthy era.

Mr. Jones' plan came into focus after he was handed my personnel file.

There he found a copy of my subpoena to appear as a witness in the Donald Walters trial (review Chapter 5) and my original application for employment, where I had indicated my military service under previous employment experience.

A quick call to Eureka Police Chief Cedric Emahiser consummated the basis for what happened next. But first he needed to obtain "useful" statements from the special group of employees Edgar Weeks had handpicked for him.

The six carefully selected employees were John R. Kamberg, a nuclear control technician recently promoted to nuclear instrumentation foreman a few weeks prior to the May 20 safety meeting; Andrew Kennedy, Nuclear Instrumentation Engineer; George Tully, Electrical Plant Foreman; Russell D. Peter, Shift Foreman; Lloyd Barker, a machinist who was bucking for Plant Maintenance Foreman; and Russell Windlix, an electrician who was already being upgraded from time to time to Temporary Electrical Plant Foreman, when someone was needed to fill in for Mr. George Tully.

In the deposition of each employee it was established that Mr. Jones did not take any notes and there was no sort of recording device. Each employee testified that Mr. Jones wrote out the statement then asked the employee to sign it. Excerpts taken from the signed statements of the employees include the following:

> "At this meeting, attended by approximately 50 persons, the theme was accident prevention"[208] (John Kamberg)

> "Robert Rowen, control technician, and Forrest Williams, also a control technician, read prepared statements to the group"[209] (Russ Peter)

> "Although the remarks were phrased in the form of questions in a large degree, I believe there were other motives behind their questions"[210] (John Kamberg)

> "I believe Rowen is preparing some kind of publication which will compare present conditions here with research results concerning biological effects brought by radiation"[211] (John Kamberg)

> "I believe that both Rowen and Williams, in making these statements, wanted those present to know that unsafe conditions exist . . . This probably would create a unified drive toward increased protection and more stringent regulations"[212] (John Kamberg)

"Both have made unproven accusations about conditions as being unsafe. For example, the high level rad waste storage vault and the fallout near the school and the recommendation for monitoring equipment there"[213] (John Kamberg)

"There is a possibility that Robert Rowen has some vendetta he wishes to satisfy against the Company. This may have been building up over the past year. I believe this is possible through observing his general attitude through remarks he has made"[214] (John Kamberg)

"I construed their remarks as instrumentalities to embody fear in the minds of their listeners. Both created a feeling in me that we have to rise and force the Company to eliminate all radiation from personnel. That the Company should prevent all radiation from leaving the plant. Both Rowen and Williams tend to pick to pieces Company policy, including AEC regulations. I have noticed this from their remarks during the past few years"[215] (Andrew Kennedy)

"Rowen appears to be heading in the direction of becoming the Ralph Nader of the radiation field"[216] (Andrew Kennedy)

"Robert Rowen and Forrest Williams will do anything to embarrass supervision at the plant"[217] (Andrew Kennedy)

"I construed their remarks at this meeting to have been designed to discredit the Company. It appeared to me to be an attack on PG&E"[218] (George Tully)

"I believe they intended a plain move to disrupt and cause dissension among the physical forces"[219] (George Tully)

"I do not believe that their remarks were honestly meant to just try to bring up safety conditions for safety's sake"[220] (George Tully)

"In another vein, remarks were made about two years ago which gave me reason to doubt their intentions toward the Company or the community. Rowen and Williams were attending College of the Redwoods. The political aspects of communism were being discussed. Williams, in particular, but supported by Rowen, conveyed these thoughts: 'Well, I don't think communism is as bad as it sounds.' Each spoke about shutting down College of the Redwoods, implicitly by any force necessary"[221] (George Tully)

"Both Rowen and Williams seem to take pleasure in causing dissension. They have been troublemakers for at least two years at this plant. Williams has been an agitator since he finished his probation"[222] (Russ Peter)

"I believe the intent of both Rowen and Williams was to bring about a state of rabble rousing"[223] (Russ Peter)

"Both Rowen and Williams, in my opinion, intended to do some rabble rousing. I think they were trying to get back at the Company for grievances either fancied or factual"[224] (Lloyd Barker)

"Since these remarks, I have talked to some of the fellows in the shop; and they expressed fear of conditions if they were true"[225] (Lloyd Barker)

"I honestly do not know what either Rowen or Williams had in mind when they read those prepared statements concerning plant safety conditions"[226] (Russell Windlinx)

It needs to be pointed out that I am referred to as "Robert Rowen" in three different statements, by two different participants; twice by John Kamberg with whom I had worked for several years as a fellow nuclear control technician. John never once called me "Robert." I never went by Robert at work or any place else for that matter, all the employees without exception always called me Bob. The "Robert" thing was totally the handiwork of Mr. Jones and not that of any of the employees who supposedly gave those statements to Jones and signed their names to them. This was done without any coaching from Mr. Jones? It's also interesting that two of the statements, each made by an employee from entirely different departments within the plant, cited Forrest and me as engaging in "rabble rousing." Is this more evidence of Bert Jones' creative handiwork?

All of these statements became embedded in Mr. Jones' official company security report and it was never the intention of PG&E to allow us access to it. We came by the report through legal proceedings prompted by a discovery suit for a confidential law enforcement document that Mr. Jones had participated in fabricating (Chapter 12).

During a deposition conducted in litigation between myself as a plaintiff in Rowen vs. PG&E, Berton F. Jones, et al., defendants; Russell K. Windlinx gave the following testimony:[227]

Mr. Bruce Cogan (my attorney): Mr. Windlinx, I would like to show you a document labeled Exhibit A (referring to his written statement previously mentioned) and have you review it and read it through.

(Witness examining.)

Mr. Cogan: Are you familiar with this document?

Mr. Windlinx: Yes, I am.

Mr. Cogan: Were you contacted by any official of PG&E in the course of which this document was prepared?

Mr. Windlinx: How do you mean?

Mr. Cogan: Well, did you speak with Mr. Berton F. Jones in the Humboldt Bay Power Plant on or about May 20, 1970?

Mr. Windlinx: If that is the man who came up there, yes.

Mr. Cogan: All right. Were you requested by officials of PG&E to talk with Mr. Jones?

Mr. Windlinx: Yes.

Mr. Cogan: Did you before the meeting with Mr. Jones ever request any officials of PG&E to talk with an investigator or security individual from PG&E?

Mr. Windlinx: No.

Mr. Cogan: Do you recall having a conversation or interview with Mr. Berton F. Jones?

Mr. Windlinx: Yes.

Mr. Cogan: Do you know if anyone else was present during that conversation other than you and Mr. Jones?

Mr. Windlinx: There was no one else there.

Mr. Cogan: Did you take any notes or written memorandum concerning your conversation or discussion with Mr. Jones?

Mr. Windlinx: No.

Mr. Cogan: Do you know whether Mr. Jones made any written notes or memoranda concerning your discussion with him other than this document labeled Exhibit A?

Mr. Windlinx: I don't recall.

Mr. Cogan: Was there any tape recording apparatus present that you know of?

Mr. Windlinx: No.

Mr. Cogan: First of all, is this your signature?

Mr. Windlinx: Yes, it is.

Mr. Charles Denny (attorney representing Berton F. Jones): Referring to Exhibit A?

Mr. Windlinx: Exhibit A.

Mr. Cogan: Is the rest of the writing on Exhibit A your writing?

Mr. Windlinx: No.

Mr. Cogan: Do you know who wrote out the rest of the statement on Exhibit A?

Mr. Windlinx: On that sheet?

Mr. Cogan: Yes.

Mr. Windlinx: That would be the man I talked to.

Mr. Cogan: So Mr. Jones wrote it out for you – let me ask, did Mr. Jones write it out for you?

Mr. Windlinx: Yes.

Mr. Cogan: Did you have an opportunity to review what Mr.Jones wrote out on Exhibit A?

Mr. Windlinx: I read it before I signed it.

Mr. Cogan: And does this document, abeled Exhibit A, accurately reflect the recollections of events and occurrences that are mentioned in Exhibit A?

Mr. Denny: Just a second.

Mr. Windlinx: My memory is kind of vague about the whole thing. I don't know.

Mr. Cogan: Well, at the time that this statement was prepared, did you attempt to make sure that the statement was accurate, to the best of your knowledge at that time?

Mr. Windlinx: Yes.

Mr. Cogan: In this statement, does it state, "I, Russell K. Windlinx, make this voluntary statement to Berton F. Jones concerning incidents occurring at the Safety Meeting held May 20. 1970?" I am reading this over, and I want to make sure this is accurately stated on Exhibit A.

Mr. Windlinx: Yes.

Mr. Cogan: All right. Does it also state, "I honestly do not know what either Rowen or Williams had in mind when they read those prepared statements concerning plant safety conditions?"

Mr. Windlinx: Yes.

Mr. Cogan: Does it also state, "I have read this one-page statement, and everything is true, to the best of my knowledge?"

Mr. Windlinx: Yes.

Mr. Cogan: First of all, were you present personally at the Safety Meeting held on May 20, 1970?

Mr. Windlinx: Yes.

Mr. Cogan: Do you know who conducted that meeting?

Mr. Windlinx: No.

Mr. Cogan: Do you know approximately how many people were present at the meeting?

Mr. Windlinx: No.

Mr. Hillman (attorney for PG&E): I think the witness really means he doesn't recall, is that correct?

Mr. Windlinx: No.

Mr. Cogan: At this time you don't recall?

Mr. Windlinx: I don't recall.

Mr. Cogan: Can you make an estimate of the number of people at the meeting?

Mr. Windlinx: No, I can't.

Mr. Cogan: Where was the meeting conducted?

Mr. Windlinx: In the Assembly Building.

Mr. Cogan: Approximately what time of day was it conducted?

Mr. Windlinx: I don't recall.

Mr. Cogan: Do you recall if it was morning or afternoon?

Mr. Windlinx: No.

Mr. Cogan: Is it your recollections that Mr. Rowen and Mr. Williams made statements concerning plant safety conditions at that meeting?

Mr. Windlinx: I don't recall.

Mr. Cogan: Do you recall where you were seated, where you were in relation to the Assembly Building?

Mr. Windlinx: No.

Mr. Cogan: Do you recall where Mr. Rowen and Mr. Williams were seated in this meeting?

Mr. Windlinx: No.

Mr. Cogan: Can you recall whether or not you were in front of them or in back of them?

Mr. Windlinx: No.

Mr. Cogan: Do you recall ever seeing Mr. Rowen or Mr. Williams stand up at the meeting?

Mr. Windlinx: No.

Mr. Cogan: Do you recall whether Mr. Rowen or Mr. Williams ever had any documents or papers that were with them?

Mr. Windlinx: No.

Mr. Cogan: Is it basically your testimony at this time you can't recall why you have the opinion that they were reading from something, reading a prepared statement?

Mr. Windlinx: Would you say that again?

Mr. Cogan: Is it your testimony at this time in this deposition that you can't recall why you came to the conclusion that they had read prepared statements?

Mr. Windlinx: I don't know why.

Mr. Cogan: I am asking, do you recall at this time why you came to the conclusion that they were reading a prepared statement?

Mr. Windlinx: No.

Mr. Cogan: I believe you also in your statement have stated you honestly do not know what either Rowen or Williams had in mind. By that statement you were referring to what their purpose was in making these statements?

Mr. Windlinx: I don't recall.

Mr. Cogan: Do you recall at that particular time about how Mr. Rowen or Mr. Williams acted at the safety meeting that, in your opinion, would be disruptive in any way?

Mr. Windlinx: No, I don't recall.

Mr. Cogan: Do you recall whether there was any violence of any sort by Mr. Rowen and Mr. Williams at the meeting?

Mr. Windlinx: No.

Mr. Cogan: You don't recall or there wasn't any?

Mr. Windlinx: I don't recall any.

Mr. Cogan: All right. At the time that you wrote that–this statement was prepared in May of 1970–do you have any recollection at that time about the demeanor of Mr. Rowen or Mr. Williams at the safety meeting?

Mr. Windlinx: I don't recall.

Mr. Cogan: Do you recall at this time what Mr. Rowen or Mr. Williams said at that meeting?

Mr. Windlinx: No.

Mr. Cogan: Do you recall whether any official of PG&E made any reply to Mr. Rowen or Mr. Williams after they made these statements?

Mr. Windlinx: No.

Mr. Gogan: Thank you.

Mr. Denny: Thank you, sir.

I was at that deposition as an observer along with a few other people. There was no question how difficult it must have been for Russ to respond to the probing questions of my attorney, Mr. Cogan. It's very intimidating for an employee to answer questions truthfully with a high-powered PG&E attorney sitting across the table taking notes, especially if he's hoping for a promotion.

Mr. Jones used Russ, as he did with Lloyd Barker, in order to have a couple of "regular" employees in the group of six who would sign the statements prepared by Bert Jones. These statements were important to PG&E because they were instrumental in solidifying the conspiracy theory advanced by PG&E that culminated in the commissioning of a false police report. Mr. Jones was the point man in that effort (Chapter 12).

There was another discovery that surfaced during the preparation phase of the upcoming arbitration hearing. The IBEW Local Union 1245's Chief Shop Steward for the Humboldt Division wrote a confidential union memorandum. It chronologically summarized a string of events that led to the development of PG&E's conspiracy theory, which resulted in the commissioning of that false police report previously mentioned.   This internal union memorandum refers to the "LIC" (Local Investigation Committee) that was part of the grievance procedure that preceded my arbitration hearing held on December 1 and 2, 1970.

According to the union memo, Corbett Wheeler, Business Representative of IBEW Local Union 1245, "Indicated that some of the Supervisors' testimony during the LIC tended toward the charge that Rowen had 'communist' tendencies and was involved with the SDS, indicating a Company attitude that Rowen tended toward violence."[228]
Except for the SDS reference, I had already heard the other crap before but this "SDS" thing was brand new.

Later I found out that it was George Tully who had made that ridiculous statement. He claimed he had seen me at the College of the Redwoods (COR) Student Union talking with known members of the SDS. This floored me! First of all, I didn't even know there was an SDS group on the campus of COR. And how was it Tully knew such a group existed and who was in it? One thing for sure, his ridiculous statement made during the LIC fit perfectly with his written statement prepared by Bert Jones on May 22, 1970, that George Tully had signed.

The May 20, 1970, company safety meeting was not the first time we used a safety meeting as a forum to bring safety issues to plant management's attention in a very "public" way. For example, at the company safety meeting held on December 12, 1967, as previously stated in my *Diary*, I brought up several contentious radiation protection safety items for discussion. This bold venture of mine enraged plant management and earned me another tongue-lashing by Mr. Weeks because the problems I had raised were not "safety problems" but rather termed by plant management as simply "radiation protection operational problems."

I told Ed Weeks in his "counseling session" of me following the safety meeting that I completely failed to understand the difference between "safety problems" and "radiation protection operational problems" and made it clear to him that I would not be intimidated by him or any one else in plant management.

At a much later time, an attorney who reviewed the matter concluded that the issues I raised at the December 12, 1967, meeting "were anything but well-meaning and legitimate questions concerning safety . . . [the issues raised] were all serious, timely safety matters . . . as a result of Mr. Rowen's suggestions, substantial safety improvements in the off-gas sampling and radioactive materials storage procedures along with the collection procedures of extremely hot radioactive reactor water samples were made."[229]

Forrest Williams and I had often used safety meetings in the past as a means to address radiation safety issues when our previous attempts to address those issues with plant management had failed. Admittedly some of the items we brought up weren't as significant as the off-gas and reactor water sampling issues, but we still considered them important enough to bring up at the safety meetings. We believed that was the primary purpose of those safety meetings.

Forrest wrote a personal statement concerning the May 20, 1970, PG&E safety meeting and some of the developments that sprung from it, which follows in its entirety exactly as Forrest wrote it:[230]

> Concerning my alleged creating of a disturbance and engaging in disruptive conduct at the Humboldt Bay Power Plant safety meeting on May 20, 1970. It was not my intent to create a disturbance but only to correct deficiencies in our radiation protection safety program at the plant. Others whose duties included the monitoring of personnel and material shared my concerns. I read from no prepared statement. I did refer to some scribbled notes that I had made shortly before the meeting so I would include all the items of my concern.

> During the outage of the nuclear unit just concluded there had definitely been problems of high backgrounds in the locations where the monitoring of persons and material for release from controlled areas took place.

> My understanding of the purpose of a safety meeting and experiences in prior ones I had attended made me believe this was a proper forum to discuss these questions of radiation safety. Examples of these type of concerns being discussed at previous meetings were: the proper use of step-off pads, how to deal with the release from a controlled area of a person with serious injuries and possibly contaminated wounds, persons taking material out of controlled areas without proper monitoring, the proper use of radiation area barricade ropes. All these were subjects of discussion at previous safety meetings I had attended.

> The next day after the safety meeting of May 20, 1970, I was ordered to appear at the power plant conference room where I was introduced to a Mr. Bert Jones of PG&E security. He immediately began questioning me as to my motives in bringing up these questions of nuclear safety in a company safety meeting. I was surprised and shocked at this response to my concerns that were expressed in the safety meeting and it was apparent to me that anything I said was not going to help correct the problems of nuclear safety and from my past experiences with discussions with PG&E management, it was quite probable that what I said might be twisted and edited to my discredit and then represented to be the official record of what I had said.

Butunnecessarily high amounts of radiation was unacceptable and I thought my refusal to perform this work would initiate a review of the working conditions and cause modifications to methods of sampling and testing radioactive liquids and material that would drastically reduce this chronic exposure and remove unnecessary risks for all the technicians involved in this work.

During the week I was under suspension for my position on this issue, I was advised by the union shop steward that my returning to the job and having these problems worked on by the union could best resolve these problems. I returned to work and agreed to perform the assignments with this thought in mind.

While I was off on the one week suspension I had a growth removed from the end of the middle finger of my left hand and, as the doctor had to go quite deep in order to remove the growth, it was healing rather slowly and I requested to remain out of job assignments where I might be exposed to radioactive liquids while this wound was healing and for the first week after my return this request was honored. The policy of not working in radioactive materials with skin breaks was consistent with written company procedures and I was quite shocked when Mr. Weeks and Warren Raymond made an issue of forcing me into this type of work out of normal job assignment rotation after one week had been allowed me and the wound was still draining, although quite small. It appeared to me they had decided to push me until they could cause me to quit, as I had become an embarrassment to them. Their plan worked as I refused the job assignment while I still had the skin break and they terminated my employment with PG&E. /s/ Forrest Williams

In his personal statement, Forrest first addresses the May 20 safety-meeting flap, then he reflects on his suspension and ultimate termination of employment from PG&E. This will be completely summarized later in this chapter.

Referring to the issues I had raised at the May 20 safety meeting, every one of those "issues of concern" were discussed several times with plant management personnel prior to the safety meeting. Each time I was "counseled" for my "poor attitude" and for my "troublemaking." As an example of what typically followed any attempt I would make to address radiation protection safety issues, on August 8, 1969, the day following the release of the contaminated spent fuel-shipping cask (review Chapter 6), Mr. Weeks wrote the following in a Confidential Memorandum (repeated here from page 155 for emphasis):[231]

I also took this opportunity to counsel Mr. Rowen concerning several complaints I had received from first line supervision concerning his continual "griping and complaining" about the Company and its poor treatment of employees. I reminded him that he has a responsibility to promote harmony, not disrupt it. I reminded him that I was still not satisfied with his job performance and believed that there was considerable room for improvement.

It was always the same; I was to be cooperative and support plant management by "promoting harmony, not disrupt it" in spite of the serious radiation safety issues that were being ignored by the company.

By April of 1970 both Forrest Williams and I were fed up and finished with PG&E and the company damned well knew it. We were continuing our education at Humboldt State University. I had already decided to quit PG&E and attend HSU full-time in the fall of that year, and PG&E knew that as well. I believe PG&E considered both of us a threat to the company's plan to expand their nuclear program; therefore, decided to get rid of us by whatever means possible and "neutralize" us in the process.

Forest Williams made a decision on May 11, 1970, to refuse any future work assignments having to do with the handling of off-gas, reactor water, and radioactive laundry waste samples. Forrest was suspended for four days for what Victor Novarino, PG&E's Humboldt Division Manager, called a "cooling off period."[232] (PG&E's Humboldt Division encompassed all the company's operations in Humboldt County)

Novarino stated Williams "return to work at the end of the cooling off period was conditioned upon his performing all the work assignments of his classifications."[233]

Mr. Novarino took the position that Williams' refusal to do the work he had been doing for several years as an employee was "inimical with his continued employment"[234] with the company.

Williams made it clear that chronic exposure to unnecessarily high and excessive amounts of radiation exposure was no longer acceptable to him. He thought that by refusing to do the work it would initiate a review of the working conditions and thus bring about improvements in those working conditions.

After talking with the union shop steward, Williams was persuaded to return to work at the end of his suspension. Williams was told "it would be best to let the union endeavor to get the company to improve the working conditions concerning the unnecessary high levels of radiation exposure" involved with the work Williams was refusing to do. The following testimony by Mr. Novarino reveals his lack of understanding of the problem Williams was addressing with his refusal to do the work on May 11, 1970:[235]

Mr. Brown (PG&E attorney): (Directed to Mr. Navarino . . .)
Would you tell us very briefly, if you can, what took place at

that meeting and any part of the discussion that you might have taken part in.

Mr. Navarino (PG&E Humboldt Division Manager): Well, 1970critical point, I wanted to let him know that was a grievance procedure, which I'm sure he already knew. And yet he didn't follow the grievance procedure. He was threatening, as I understood it, at the meeting to leave his employ, jeopardize his income and the fact that he had a family, which depended on that and act as a one-man committee in rebellion for something that he had been doing for quite a while. And I was interested in just what was making him do that. But I really didn't find out at the meeting. He just took the position that it was a dangerous procedure that he was involved in. And knowing full well that the supervisors we have there felt that it wasn't, I think we reached an impasse at that point.

Mr. Brown: Did you personally point these things out to him that you have just been speaking of, Mr. Navarino?

Mr. Navarino: I believe I tried very hard to do that.

It's true that Forrest had been doing that work for several years. What Mr. Novarino was not able to get his head wrapped around was the simple fact that the radiation levels associated with that work had increased to a point where they were no longer acceptable to Forrest, or to any of us for that matter. I totally agreed with Forrest as we both had a huge problem with plant management's cavalier attitude towards our desire to reducee radiation exposure as much as possible.

During his time off, Williams had a growth removed from his left hand. When he returned to work on Monday, May 18, Williams requested that he not be assigned work in the radiochemistry lab because of his open wound. In keeping with the radiation protection standards regarding open wounds and the kind of work involved in the radiochemistry lab, Williams' request was granted.

One week later on Monday, May 25, Bill Evans was the control technician assigned to the radiochemistry lab, and Mr. Evans went ahead with the lab assignment upon reporting for work that morning.[236] When Williams reported for work that morning, he went first to the change room to attend the dressing on his hand. Mr. Weeks, Williams' second-line supervisor, found him in the change room and said, "Let's see that million dollar finger."[237] Mr. Weeks examined the wound on Williams' finger and said it had sufficiently healed.

Mr. Weeks then ordered Williams to go into the radiochemistry lab and perform the duties of that assignment. Williams felt that his wound was not yet sufficiently healed and asked for a few more days.[238] Mr. Weeks refused to give Williams any more time for his wound to heal, and Williams refused to undertake what he believed to be an unacceptable risk by returning to work in the lab on that day.

Edgar Weeks, Plant Engineer, took the position that Williams' wound was healed. Williams was immediately sent home that morning and officially discharged the very next day on May 26, 1970, for insubordination. Williams went to PG&E's doctor, Dr. Dolfini, sometime during the afternoon of May 25 to have his wound examined by him. Dr. Dolfini said his wound was not yet healed and in his opinion it would take until May 28 for it to completely heal.[239] Forrest then went to the doctor who performed the surgery on his finger, Dr. Wittwer, who also said Forrest's finger was not healed. It was the Dr. Wittwer's opinion that it would take until May 29 for it to be completely healed.[240]

The PG&E safety rule to which the company referred was introduced as Company Exhibit #9 in the Williams' Arbitration Hearing: Section II B 1 of PG&E's Radiation Control Procedure provides:

> The assignment of persons having skin breaks to work in radioactive materials areas should be avoided if possible.

Nuclear control techs were made aware of the "skin break rule" in our training. As nuclear control technicians responsible for the radiation safety monitoring of employees, we enforced that safety rule whenever it was necessary for the safety of employees for which we were responsible in the radiation-controlled areas of the plant.

At Forrest Williams' Arbitration Hearing, no company witness tried to explain the obvious conflict between the attempted chemistry assignment and Radiation Control Procedure Section II B 1. Rather, the company attempted to obscure the applicability of that Section of the Control Standards by suggesting that there was no applicable rule, which would have absolutely prohibited the assignment of an employee with a skin break to chemistry work (Tr. 68, 87).[241]

It was suggested by the company that the assignment of Williams to work in the radiochemistry lab was necessary and unavoidable. But on May 25 the assignment of someone other than Williams to chemistry was not only possible, such an assignment had actually been made before the order given to Forrest Williams by Edgar Weeks.[242]

Attorney Frank Morgan, representing IBEW 1245, made the following assertion in an explanatory notation marked #2 as a footnote in his brief:

> In light of Radiation Control Procedure Section II B 1, the company's position that they were even prepared to send Williams back to chemistry a week earlier on May 18 with an indisputable open wound is difficult to understand (Tr. 88).[243] It's no wonder Mr. Williams and Mr. Rowen encountered disputes over safety matters.[244]

To understand why Williams was so adamant about refusing the radiochemistry assignment until his wound was completely healed, it's necessary to briefly explain a portion of the lab procedure that was of most concern to Williams when Weeks gave him the direct order to go to the radiochemistry lab to perform the work that was assigned to him. The lab procedure in question was used in connection with analyzing off-gas samples.

After the radioactive gas samples were drawn into small vacuum bottles at the off-gas sampling station, the off-gas samples were transported to the radiochemistry lab where the sample bottles were placed by hand into a special bucket of water. The bottles were then inverted and uncapped under water so that the trapped radioactive gas could be exposed to electrodes in the bucket. The gas was then ignited or "popped" by an electric arc across the electrodes. The gas literally explodes under water, thus leaving the bucket and the water in it highly radioactive (Tr. 123).[245]

During this procedure, the technician's hands are completely immersed in the "hot" (radioactively speaking) water. Sensitive feel was required for this procedure, and the only hand protection that was worn was a pair of light, thermally sealed plastic gloves covered by a pair of light surgical gloves. Heavy outer gloves could not be worn (Tr.121-122).[246] The surgical gloves could have been cut or torn without the knowledge of the technician during another phase of the off-gas sampling procedure. If a cut occurred and the technician subsequently immersed his gloved hand into the "popping" bucket, quantities of highly radioactive water could have leaked into the glove. The radioactive water could remain there undetected because the technician could not distinguish it from the perspiration of his hands, which normally collected inside the gloves. Mr. Williams had also on occasion personally experienced leaks through cuts in his gloves, which had occurred without his knowledge (TR.123).[247]

I was incensed after learning what Weeks had done to Forrest Williams, and I considered it the final straw to all the crap plant management had been dishing out. After talking with Forrest on the phone that evening, as well as with a couple of other employees, and after talking at length with my wife about what went down with Forrest, I calmed down but felt I still needed to do something in protest of the company's action. As I was leaving home for work the next morning, I grabbed an empty detergent box with the fleeting thought of using it as a collection box for Williams.

When I arrived at work, I put it up on the bottom of the rad protection status board so everyone would see it. I wrote on it in very bold print, "Let's all support Forrest" or something to that effect. Things became very dicey shortly thereafter! Weeks ended up putting his finger in my face, within six inches of my nose and shaking it in an uncontrollable, threatening manner.

I asked him to get his finger out of my face and I probably used some inappropriate expletives while saying it! His response, "This is my finger and I can do whatever I want with it." I responded, "It's a good way to get the damned thing broken," again most likely using inappropriate expletives. I still had a lot of Marine in me and I came uncomfortably close to knocking him on his keister but I somehow maintained control of myself.

Plant management later denied this accounting of what happened in the reactor control room that morning between Weeks and myself but I was able to later establish what did happen through testimony of three key PG&E management personnel at my Unemployment Insurance Appeals Board Hearing. Warren Raymond, Acting Plant Manager, who was called as a Company witness, was the first of these management personnel called to testify.

The following is Mr. Raymond's testimony during my cross-examination of him:[248]

> **Mr. Rowen:** (Directed to Mr. Raymond . . .) Did he (Weeks) also state very clearly he had a perfect right to treat an employee that way?
>
> **Mr. Raymond (acting plant manager):** I couldn't say with any degree of certainty whether he did or didn't. He may have. I don't know.
>
> **Mr. Brown (PG&E attorney):** If you don't know, say you don't know.
>
> **Mr. Raymond:** I don't know.
>
> **Mr. Rowen:** Just to recap what the company alleges happened on May 29, and discussing it the following Monday morning on June first. Would you say Mr. Weeks was mad at me when we were talking at the rad protection desk when the finger-shaking incident took place?
>
> **Mr. Brown:** Just one minute. I don't believe he said he was standing at the desk within your observation or hearing when this finger-waving thing took place.
>
> **THE REFEREE:** The witness testified he didn't see any finger waving.
>
> **Mr. Rowen:** Okay.
>
> **Mr. Raymond:** I didn't see it.
>
> **Mr. Rowen:** At the grievance meeting Friday morning after the finger-shaking incident, did Weeks make the statement that that was as mad as he's ever gotten with any employee? At the meeting at which you were present.
>
> **Mr. Raymond:** Again I don't know.
>
> **Mr. Rowen:** Later that morning when I was in Mr. Weeks' and your office discussing my request for time off that afternoon, did Mr. Weeks admit that that was as mad as he had ever gotten at any employee and he "had temporarily lost his cool" I believe were the words he used?
>
> **Mr. Raymond:** During the meeting later on in the morning Mr. Weeks inferred maybe had had been wrong for shaking his finger. You had mentioned – (INTERRUPTED)
>
> **Mr. Rowen:** Just a minute. Did he say this to me or to you?
>
> **Mr. Raymond:** To you.

Mr. Rowen: He said it to me? He thought he was wrong in shaking his finder?

Mr. Raymond: He said maybe he shouldn't have shaken his finger.

Mr. Rowen: Did Mr. Weeks admit during the grievance meeting that I asked him not to shake his finger in my face? Did he admit I said that?

Mr. Raymond: I can't be sure.

Mr. Rowen: All right. Can you remember, even though you're not sure, did he then admit to the fact he said that that was his finger and he would shake it in my face if he wanted to?

Mr. Brown: Did you hear him making that statement?

Mr. Rowen: I am not asking if he heard the statement. He wasn't there. I am asking if he remembers Mr. Weeks admitting –(INTERRUPTED)

Mr. Brown: Did Mr. Weeks state that?

Mr. Rowen: I am not an attorney.

THE REFEREE: Perhaps it would be best now if you would restate the question.

Mr. Rowen: Okay. I will restate the question. During the grievance meeting on May 29 at 8:30, did Mr. Weeks admit to stating that he said that that was his finger and he would shake it in my face if he wanted to after I asked not to?

Mr. Brown: He already testified he didn't see it.

Mr. Rowen: I am asking – I will ask the question of Mr. Weeks. He was present at the meeting.

Mr. Raymond: I am at a loss right now to say what I exactly heard. Ed at one time during one of the meetings we had, said he may have said this. I was present at a meeting when he said he may have said this. He was not sure whether he said it. At one of the meetings during that day or the following Monday I was present at a meetings when Ed did say he may have said it. I am not sure which meeting it was.

After a few more minutes had passed dealing with the details of my suspension letter, the Referee suggested a 10-minute break was in order. The PG&E attorney said he had one more question:[249]

Mr. Brown: (Directed to Mr. Raymond . . .) Can I ask one question and then I am through? I am going to use the term Mr. Rowen has been using. On May 29 apparently certain incidents – and he referred to one as a grievance meeting. Do you recall Mr. Rowen at that time making a statement to Mr. Weeks, and I am quoting: "Rowen said to Weeks that 'shaking your finger in somebody's face like that would be a good way to get it broken'?" Do you remember that statement?

Mr. Raymond: May I answer this the same way. I heard Bob make the statement, whether it was at the specific meeting with the stewards in the morning or later on in the morning, I am not sure, I know he made the statement.

Mr. Brown: At least sometime on May 29?

Mr. Raymond: That is correct.

Mr. Brown: I have no further questions.

The next Company witness who testified during the direct examination by the PG&E attorney regarding the finger-shaking incident was John Kamberg, the plant's new Nuclear Instrumentation Foreman. Following Brown's direct examination of Kamberg, I followed with my cross-examination of him. I wanted Kamberg to describe in detail the events that occurred on the morning of May 29 regarding the finger-shaking incident; Kamberg's relevant testimony regarding the finger-shaking incident follows:[250]

> **Mr. Kamberg:** ... I was within four or five feet of them probably. They were talking in low voice. I wasn't paying too much attention to what was going on. Then I heard Bob say, "Would you mind not shaking your finger in my face?" I paid closer attention. I looked up and Ed Weeks was shaking his finger in Bob's face. I heard Ed Weeks reply to Bob's question: It was his finger and he could do what he wanted to with it.

COMMENT: John Kamberg definitely cleaned up the language that I had used.

This is Kamberg's testimony regarding the finger-shaking incident during my cross-examination of him:[251]

> **Mr. Rowen:** During the finger-shaking incident you testified that you saw at least the last half of it –
>
> **Mr. Kamberg:** From the time you requested that he cease shaking his finger in your face is when I started looking.
>
> **Mr. Rowen:** Did I make this statement: Would you please quit shaking your finger in my face?
>
> **Mr. Kamberg:** Yes.
>
> **THE REFEREE:** That is what he testified on direct.
>
> **Mr. Rowen:** If you will stand up for a minute, you are being myself and I being Mr. Weeks. When he was shaking his finger in that manner (indicating) and I made that request of him, did he then in terms of your memory, did you do this and say: "This is my finger and I'll shake it in your face?" He came closer. Do you recall him stated that: "This is my finger and I'll do what I want to with it?"
>
> **Mr. Kamberg:** Yes. Tempers were up. I observed your arms were down. Your arms were quivering. Tempers were high on both sides.

> **Mr. Rowen:** Did I make any moves in any way to threaten him?
>
> **Mr. Kamberg:** Bodily gestures, no, I don't believe so. Your hands were at your sides and very stiff.
>
> **Mr. Rowen:** Did I seem to have control of myself as far as you were concerned?
>
> **Mr. Kamberg:** I don't believe either party had control of himself if that is what you want to call it. You were, as I want to remember it – Ed was obviously shaking. He wouldn't be shaking his finger in your face. You were shaking to the point where your reply was with a quivering voice, your hands were shaking, and you were angry.
>
> **Mr. Rowen:** Okay. Then you admit Weeks was mad in your opinion?
>
> **Mr. Kamberg:** I think both parties were mad; yes.

The last witness I was able to question about the finger-shaking incident was Mr. Weeks himself. Weeks was called as a Company witness at my second Unemployment Insurance Appeals Hearing held on December 9, 1970, one week after my Arbitration Hearing.   The relevant testimony regarding the finger-shaking incident came during Mr. Brown's direct examination of him:[252]

> **Mr. Brown:** Mr. Weeks, I would like to now draw your attention to the day of May 29. If you will just relate the events that occurred the day that involved Mr. Rowen.
>
> **Mr. Weeks:** ... Bob said, "Please don't shake your finger in my face," I remember him saying that, and I was shaking my finger at him. I told Bob that he was going out of his way the past few days to make trouble and that he had better back off or he was going to find trouble. And I was still shaking my finger at him. And I could see he was getting mad and I was mad, . . .

Weeks also cleaned up the language I had used. In fact, it appears the two of them got together and rehearsed their testimony and agreed for whatever their reasons to make it look like I politely asked Weeks to get his finger out of my face.

In any event, I was finally able to establish through the testimony of three key company witnesses at my unemployment appeals hearing on December 9 what really happened in the control room on May 29 between Edgar Weeks and myself. I was not able to establish this at my arbitration hearing on December 2. Yes, I was upset with Weeks. I was probably the most upset with him as I had ever been. When he stated that I was going out of my way to make trouble and that I had better back off or I was going to find trouble, as he was all the while shaking his finger within six inches of my nose, I came very close to decking him. Yes, I was admittedly very pissed off at him and when I had a chance to collect myself, I felt it was in my best interest and the company's also, to just leave the plant. I did, even though Weeks refused to give me permission to do so.

When I arrived home I stewed all afternoon about what had happened that morning. It seemed to me that Weeks was clearly baiting me in the most aggressive way possible, and that he was really trying to get me to hit him, especially since there were a lot of witnesses if I had. That night I decided not to wait until Monday morning to talk to Weeks about what he did. I called him at home and told him that I would never allow him to do to me again what he did to me that morning or he'd find trouble. I later denied making the call and I wished I hadn't done that because PG&E turned it into something that it wasn't. I only used the verbiage that he had used with me that morning. Yes, it was a clear warning and I meant every word of it. I did not, at the time nor would I now, accept the notion employers can treat employees the way Mr. Weeks had treated me the morning of May 29 as a condition of employment.

PG&E has stated many times after I was fired from the company that the threatening of my supervisor during my phone call to him on the evening of May 29 occasioned my employment termination. The Referee of my Unemployment Insurance Board Appeals Hearing wrote the following in his Decision:[253]

> As to the incidents, which occurred on the claimant's last workday, the referee makes the following findings based upon a preponderance of evidence:
> - ➤ Mr. Weeks conceded that the manner of his reprimand of the claimant was improper. In the opinion of the referee it was also extremely provocative.
> - ➤ The claimant had opportunity and motive to make the telephone call referred to in the Statement of Facts, above.
> - ➤ Mr. Weeks was familiar with the claimant's voice and believed it was he who called. The referee concludes a preponderance of evidence indicated the claimant made this call.
>
> Considering the context out of which the telephone call arose, the contingent wording (the claimant's statement of what his course of action would be if in the future Mr. Weeks repeated his actions of that morning) plus the fact the supervisor did not interpret the remarks as a present threat of bodily harm. The referee believes the telephone call in question is more accurately described as a warning rather than as a threat.
>
> The referee concludes the claimant was discharged for reasons other than misconduct connected with his most

recent work, within the meaning of Section 1256 and 1030 of the code.

The Referee of the Unemployment Insurance Appeals Hearing also stated in this Decision:[254]

> In the opinion of the referee the principal cause of the claimant's discharge was his extreme safety consciousness. His efforts in this direction were to some extent a reproof of the more sanguinary attitude of certain of his supervisors. His attempts to bring these matters to the attention of the Atomic Energy Commission and to the attention of fellow employees were also greatly resented.

The company had many things to say about me after I left the company including that I was a "disgruntled ex-employee; my termination from the company was inevitable because of my continual unrelenting harassment of each of my supervisors; as well as my unfounded and irresponsible criticisms of the plant's operation." A disgruntled ex-employee meaning a former, angry and dissatisfied employee? Sure, I'll accept that!

If we truly understand what is meant by the phrase "disgruntled ex-employee," and if "continual, unrelenting harassment of each of my supervisors" meant I would not stand by and let them foster unsafe radiation safety practices, and that I was willing to step up and openly criticize the plant's operation, then I'll stand good for all of that, too!

As far as PG&E's specific references to the "unfounded and irresponsible criticism of the plant's operation" are concerned, I'll have *My Humboldt Diary* address those comments.

As PG&E was carrying out its plan to get rid of Forrest Williams and me, the company was also developing a "conspiracy theory" for the benefit of Chief Emahiser; the company needed to complete its plan to blacklist Forrest and me from future employment in the nuclear field.

PG&E Attorney L. V. Brown described Forrest Williams and myself as "Two employees who for reasons of their own have purposely set out to frustrate and demean their supervisors in the operation of the Humboldt Bay Nuclear Power Plant."[255] Mr. Brown also said:[256]

> The acts of Mr. Williams as well as those of Mr. Rowen were not just off-the-top-off-head, spur-of-the-moment acts. We believe that there was a common plan and common design on the part of these two people, and I might add one more who felt the company's safety program was not adequate; that it was unsafe.
>
> And they set themselves up to protest, sometimes openly and . . . sometimes in a more insidious manner to carry this protest not only to the supervisors but also at the same time degrade or cause the reputation of the supervisors to be downgraded in the eyes of the employees.

Mr. Brown accused Williams and Rowen of committing "acts tantamount to industrial sabotage."[257]

J. C. Carroll, an upper management executive from PG&E's corporate headquarters at 245 Market Street, San Francisco, stated in an internal PG&E memorandum:[258]

> Forrest Williams and Rowen were both great admirers of Gofman and Tamplin and had waged a campaign of harassment against the Company and the company's radiation safety program for several years.

This confidential memorandum was clearly intended for use only in PG&E's corporate headquarters at 245 Market Street, San Francisco. A copy of this informative memo was obtained through discovery proceedings in the Don Widener case against PG&E. Mr. Carroll was of course referring to the authors of *Poisoned Power: The Case Against Nuclear Power Plants* copyrighted and printed for the first time in 1971 nearly a year after Forrest Williams and I were fired from PG&E.

Neither Forrest nor I had seen the book while we were employed by PG&E because it first appeared well after we were separated from the company, nearly a year afterwards. Neither of us were acquainted with John W. Gofman and Arthur R. Tamplin in any way but we could have most assuredly contributed to their book by drawing upon our experiences as nuclear control technicians at the Humboldt Bay Nuclear Power Plant from the mid-sixties to June 1970. It's no wonder J. C. Carroll wanted to include Forrest and me in PG&E's "war" against the authors of *Poisoned Power: The Case Against Nuclear Power Plants*.

PG&E's J. C. Carroll put Forrest Williams and me in excellent company even though it was a bald faced lie when he did it! From PG&E's point of view, Forrest and I were undoubtedly troublesome employees. There is absolutely no doubt that we were *guilty* of criticizing PG&E for its radiation safety policies and practices, for plant management's lack of concern for employee and public safety, for continuous violations and subsequent cover-ups, and for perpetuating a culture of intimidation and fear designed to keep employees in line.

When PG&E nuclear plant management failed to deal with effectively us on its own terms, then the company's corporate headquarters took over and proceeded to equate our safety concerns with dissent, and dissent with conspiracy; a conspiracy to do harm to the company and its nuclear program and facilities.

PG&E officials decided to get rid of us and did so by manufacturing the conspiracy and generated employment records to support it. The emulation of the first-line supervisors along with the wannabes from within the rank and file enabled Edgar Weeks and his cohorts to pull it off.

In the effort to advance the Rowen-Williams conspiracy, it was ironically PG&E that engaged in a conspiracy of the very worst kind to destroy two "dissident" employees by assailing their character and defaming their reputations. The company sent PG&E security agent Bert Jones to the plant to do the bidding of PG&E corporate headquarters.

Mr. Jones took his marching orders like a good trooper from PG&E corporate headquarters and showed up at the Humboldt nuclear facility to collaborate with senior plant management, namely Edgar Weeks. Jones went through the personnel files in the nuclear facility and then visited Robert Taylor, the division personnel manager. Meanwhile, Jones' boss, James Neel, called Police Chief Cedric Emahiser of the Eureka Police Department, who happened to be a very good friend of Chief Emahiser.

Bert Jones received his orders from headquarters and began the process of weaving together a series of contrived, manufactured "facts" into an insidious plan. Once carried out, it resulted in a false police report, making Forrest Williams and Bob Rowen risks to national security. Attorney Frank Morgan said, "If there is any conspiracy involved, it is the conspiracy of certain company personnel to get rid of two and possibly four employees who ask embarrassing questions."[259]

__XII__

12. Police Report

June 3, 1970

"My understanding of the PG&E culture admittedly
came to me very slowly. My hellish PG&E experience
eventually led me to the conclusion that PG&E's
corporate culture, especially at the upper levels of
management, could more adequately be described as a
corporate cult."[260] [Bob Rowen]

"Eureka Police Chief Cedric Emahiser had taken the
PG&E report in good faith, later having the feeling he
had been used"[261] [William Rodgers]

In the naivety of my youth, it was difficult for me to understand the mean-
spirited, twisted motives of the company. My understanding of the PG&E
culture admittedly came to me very slowly. However long it took, my hellish
PG&E experience eventually led me to the conclusion that PG&E's
corporate culture, especially at the upper levels of management, could more
adequately be described as a corporate cult with nuclear plant management
wannabes feeding into it.

Why was PG&E calling me a communist and a subversive, accusing me
of engaging in acts of industrial sabotage and associating with the SDS
(Students for a Democratic Society – a radical leftist movement in the
1960s) when I did not even know a single SDS member, and claiming I was
involved in a plot to blow up the Humboldt Bay Nuclear Power Plant? And
how could all this garbage end up in a ridiculously false law enforcement
file that was sent to the Federal Bureau of Investigation? I wondered how on
earth intelligent, moral and ethical people who were supposedly loyal,
patriotic Americans could engage in making such perversely false
accusations.

It wasn't until several years later, and with the help of a law professor, that I began to develop an understanding of the company beyond that of my immediate employment experience. I learned PG&E had backed a John Birch Society film that was given wide distribution and had contributed to the Foundation for Economic Education (FEE). The "FEE is a group urging such 'reforms' as repeal of the income tax, United States withdrawal from the United Nations, and the abolition of public post offices, public education, public roads and public power."[262]

Who were these John Birch Society folks anyway? In finding the answer I came to realize what drove the inner workings of top-level PG&E management. It now appears to me it included the highest levels of management of privately owned utility companies all across America. Yes, as incredible as that may sound, I am now convinced the folks behind today's energy policies of the entire country are controlled by the philosophies of people like the Koch brothers. As far as I am concerned, they are the true enemies of the state! Actually, Fred Koch, the father of today's Koch brothers (who participated in the effort to buy the 2014 Election with hundreds of millions of dollars of their own money), founded the John Birch Society.

The John Birchers were ultraconservatives and considered "far right extremists" in every way. The Southern Poverty Law Center listed the John Birch Society as a "Patriot Group" that advocates or adheres to extreme antigovernment doctrines. Sound familiar? It should because it sounds very much like today's Tea Party! From my experience, anyone who disagrees with people like them is labeled a Marxist, a communist or worse.

Without question, the May 20 PG&E safety meeting landed nuclear control technician Forrest Williams and me in a lot of hot water; plant management went completely berserk! Of course it didn't take long for the PG&E folks at corporate headquarters to join the frenzy that followed. The safety meeting ended by lunchtime, and by the end of the day arrangements already had been made by PG&E's corporate bosses to send the company's senior security agent, Bert Jones, on his infamous mission to the Humboldt Bay Nuclear Power Plant; Jones arrived at Humboldt Bay the very next morning!

Within a week the die was cast, Bert Jones had completed his work, and a false police report was consummated on June 3, 1970. Law Professor Bill Rodgers summed up the police report fiasco in the following way:[263]

> However accustomed he was to serving the company, Eureka Police Chief C. E. Emahiser was more than a little surprised when contacted by PG&E about a plot among the power plant employees led by Bob Rowen.
>
> Emahiser met with Robert Taylor, PG&E local personnel manager, and talked to "someone" in the general office in San Francisco who told him the incredible details: Plans were afoot to blow up the Humboldt Bay nuclear power

plant.

No policeman in the country could refrain from acting upon such startling intelligence, and Emahiser did not. He conducted his investigation, and sent his findings back to PG&E and to the Federal Bureau of Investigation.

Professor Rodgers concluded:[264]

By the end of 1971, Emahiser's enthusiasm about the crime of the century had waned considerably. He told the Eureka *Times-Standard* environmental reporter 'he had taken the PG&E report in good faith, later having the feeling he had been used.'

That "someone" in PG&E's general office in San Francisco, who Professor Rodgers was referring to, was a "Mr. James Neel" who happened to be a good friend of Cedric Emahiser. James Neel was an ex-F.B.I. officer, an ex-Chief of Police, and the man in charge of PG&E's Security Department in San Francisco.[265]

Despite the feeling he had been used, the Eureka Chief of Police had his own underlying motivation to cooperate early on with PG&E in fabricating the police document. Cedric Emahiser was stewing about my testimony in the Donald Walters criminal trial and the federal civil suit that followed naming him as one of the defendants (review Chapter 5).

Of course, I had no control over any of that except that I was willing to report the use of excessive force used by Officer Jacobsen when it happened back in May 1969, which caused me to become involved in the whole affair. I have been asked many times if I would do it again, to get involved in the Walters police brutality case, knowing how it would eventually affect my family and me down the road. My answer has always been the same: Yes, I would, although I do regret how the whole affair affected my family. I did it because I believed it was the right thing to do!

This part of my *Diary* is perhaps the most telling part of the story about the Humboldt Bay Nuclear Power Plant and what happened there. It reveals how far PG&E management was willing to go to defend a failed and dangerous technology at Humboldt Bay, a nuclear facility that *Science Magazine* called in 1971 "one of the dirtiest" nuclear power plant in the nation – a point of fact that I shall often repeat for emphasis![266]

There is absolutely no doubt PG&E management at all levels knew exactly what the company's conspiracy was and further more that it was cleverly organized and carried out at the direction of top level PG&E corporate executives at 245 Market Street, San Francisco. Once the conspiracy was exposed, PG&E officials used a conservatively entrenched body of legal impediments to obtaining justice for those who were the victims of the conspiracy (Chapter 14).

Several months after my employment termination, a classmate and friend of my brother, Fred Rowen, and more than just a personal acquaintance of mine at Humboldt State University, approached me. He had something he wanted to share with me in private. We went to a building that usually had very few students in it during that particular time of day and found an empty study room for our private meeting.

As he reached into his brief case, he made it very clear to me that what he was about to show me was in the strictest confidence and when I finished reading it, he was going to destroy it because what he already had done and was about to do would cost him his job if it ever got out. The document was a confidential police report that he had made a copy of while he was on night duty at the Humboldt County Sheriff Office. (This individual's name is revealed in Chapter 14 of my *Diary* after explaining why it became necessary)

As I took the document from him that he was very slowly handing to me, he said that he knew me well enough to know this report was "something crazy." He said it made absolutely no sense to him at all and felt I should be made aware of it. As I started reading it, I remember him saying for me to read it as many times as I wanted but when I was finished with it he was going to take back it.

I also remember my immediate response to this document: Was this some kind of vicious, black-hearted joke; that initial response, however, quickly gave way to a chilly, numbing feeling that came over me and I could feel the blood draining from my face. I started shaking and I became momentarily speechless, as I couldn't say anything to the fellow who had handed this horrible thing to me. As I continued reading the document I became engulfed with a sick feeling that settled in the pit of my stomach. It felt like I was going to throw up. After a few more minutes had passed, I became wrapped with intense anger and a feeling of helplessness all at the same time.

A sudden urge to take off with the document struck me but I knew I had to honor the request to give it back. This document had appeared from out of the dark during the same time Forrest Williams and I were preparing for our arbitration hearings.

I explained to my friend that my attorney really needed to see it, and he agreed so long as it was in the strictest of confidence. Meanwhile, I collected my composure as best I could and decided to keep reading the document repeatedly so I could etch it in my memory, then write out a copy of it (that became my "simulation" of it) from memory when the fellow left.

My simulation of the report became the basis of a lawsuit that PG&E threw all of its resources at in order to keep me from obtaining a true copy of the police report. Not only did PG&E battle my attempts to obtain the document, so did the City of Eureka and the two private law firms that represented Bert Jones and Cedric Emahiser. All of these forces of opposition worked closely together and were largely supported by the unlimited resources of PG&E. PG&E did not want me to obtain a copy of it and went to great lengths to keep that from happening!

After a long protracted legal wrangle, I finally obtained a true copy of the police report only to run head-on into PG&E's army of attorneys who kept me from effectively pursuing PG&E's commissioning of it, an effort that was joined by the City of Eureka and the law firms of Mitchell, Dedekam, and Angell Attorneys at Law; Hill, Jansen, Corbett Roberts Attorneys at Law; and Crosby, Heafey, Roach and May Attorneys at Law.

The legal actions by PG&E, et al., are an ugly commentary on our system of civil justice. It made a mockery of what I had always admired with obvious naivety about our judicial system and its pursuit of truth and desire for achieving justice. My attorney and his small Eureka law firm, Mathews, Traverse and McKittrick Attorneys at Law, were up against unlimited resources in comparison. It was like David and Goliath, except my case did not have the same biblical ending (Chapter 14).

The two-page, single-spaced document was labeled "Original Information" and marked "Confidential (Police Only) Police Intelligence" Serial No.70-1795, dated 6/3/1970, and Cedric Emahiser, the Eureka Chief of Police, had signed it. Copies of it were cc'd to: Mr. Bert Jones, Pacific Gas and Electric Company, San Francisco; Mr. Robert H. Taylor, Pacific Gas and Electric Company, Eureka; Gene Cox, Humboldt County Sheriff; and Agent Miller, Federal Bureau of Investigation. The police document referred by name to four of PG&E's seven nuclear control technicians at the Humboldt Bay nuclear facility as a "Dissident Group."

The following is the entire report verbatim with each section of it shown in bold print, which then is followed by a personal comment or two.

The police report began:

The following information is received from Mr. Bert Jones, Pacific Gas and Electric Company, phone 415-781-4211 Ext. 4018, 245 Market Street, San Francisco, who offers the following information and would be very glad to receive any information on the subjects from this area.

COMMENT: This opening salvo in "Chief Cedric Emahiser's report" clearly establishes that the information contained therein came from PG&E, that is to say, "The following information is received from Mr. Bert Jones , Pacific Gas and Electric Company.

The police report continued:

Forrest E. Williams has been attending College of the Redwoods. Was discharged 4 days ago for being a dissenter, making threats against management, and being a constant troublemaker.

COMMENT: What is true in this section is that Forrest was attending College of the Redwoods at night as was I, and that he had been discharged from PG&E four days before the commissioning of this report; however, the rest of this statement is false and Bert Jones knew it! Forrest was terminated because he refused to comply with a direct order given to him by Edgar Weeks to perform an unsafe act (review Chapter 11).

The police report continued:

Robert J. Rowen was suspended from employment with the company, is a close partner of WILLIAMS, and has been bringing material into the plant by Rap Brown, Eldridge Cleaver and others who advocate force and violence. This man is also a radical, advocates burning, is a constant problem.

COMMENT: The only item with a degree of validity was the reference to the author of the book entitled *Soul On Ice*, written by Eldridge Clever. Forrest Williams and I were taking a political science class from Vernon Smith at College of the Redwoods, who assigned *Soul On Ice* as a required reading. This class was a general education requirement for the AA degree. The rest of this statement is false and absolutely utter nonsense (in fact, "utter nonsense" doesn't even begin to adequately characterize it)!

Forrest and I would study some of our assignments together during lunch and I do remember some comments made and eyebrows being raised by several of the employees regarding our discussions of the book, *Soul On Ice*.

We paid very little attention to the moronic comments they made about our commentaries on the book. Those employees really had no idea what the class was about and the assignments we were given (dealing with deep-rooted feelings of prejudice ingrained in the civil rights movement during the mid-sixties). The references to Rap Brown, advocating force and violence, being a radical, advocates burning, is a constant problem" were all made up by Bert Jones (and perhaps embellished by Cedric Emahiser).

Following the sections pertaining to Forrest Williams and me were the names of Howard Darington and Raymond Skidmore.

COMMENT: Both Darington and Skidmore were nuclear control technicians at the Humboldt Bay Nuclear Power Plant who were also critical of PG&E's radiation safety program. Howard Darington was very much involved with the union. Neither name, however, was followed by any personal information or description.

Next came the following paragraph quoted exactly as it appeared in the report:

These (4) young men were employed at the P. G. & E. Co. are a small gang of Militants, and the latter two appear to be followers of the first two in mention. They all reside at 1503 "O" Street, Eureka. If these (4) are as militant as they are presumed to be, and now that the two have been separated from the Company, it could be that they may become a menace to the local Company installations or cause problems in the area or journey to certain planned jobs elsewhere.

COMMENT: I'm absolutely convinced that Bert Jones provided this information as well as most of what's in the next section of the police report to Police Chief Cedric Emahiser. The information was totally made up to create the "law enforcement document" that PG&E wanted to lodge into the files of the Federal Bureau of Investigation to make us security risks so we would never again be able to obtain a security clearance to work in the sensitive security environment of a nuclear power plant.

During the legal wrangling that eventually addressed what PG&E and Cedric Emahiser had done, each blamed the other for what was contained in that police report. My proof to substantiate my claim that it was PG&E who provided the information is the specific citing of the "1503 'O' Street" address in the report.

On my original PG&E employment application, I specifically listed "1503" as my address where I was living when I applied for work with PG&E in 1962. But it wasn't "O" Street, where I was actually living at the time of the commissioning of the police report; it was 1503 "G" Street. My current address at the time the police report was commissioned was 2516 "O" Street, I only lived at 1503 "G" Street for a very short time during early 1962 following my discharge from the Marine Corps. Cedric Emahiser would not have known anything about that. As for the rest of it, PG&E knew we were all married with families and living in our separate residences; we certainly were not living in a "commune" as Bert Jones was suggesting!

The police report continued:

> **The writer contacted Personnel Officer Robert H. Taylor, local PG&E office and through Company telephone system Mr. Bert Jones was advised that there is no such address local of 1503 "O" Street. He will make a further check for the correct address and advise. Our Officer A. Millsap advises that on the trial of Donald Leonard Walters (arrested 5-25-69 for PC 148 and 647-F) ROWEN appeared as a witness for Walters, testified as to the proper use of Batons, is a confirmed "cop hater," was a U.S. Marine Pathfinder trained in demolitions, and considers Rowen as intelligent as well as a good organizer.**

COMMENT: It's probably true that there was no such address as 1503 "O" Street. When I originally applied for work with PG&E, I was living a 1503 "G" Street, which does exist (as I have previously stated)! It is true that I appeared as a witness in the trial of Donald Walters (review Chapter 5) but I was not then nor am I now a "confirmed cop hater." How ridiculous! I had at the time and still have now very good friends who were and are in law enforcement. In fact, my youngest son whom I am very proud of is a veteran police officer!

Interestingly enough, I was, in fact, "A U.S. Marine Pathfinder trained in demolitions." I guess that makes for good copy in a police report initiated by the outrageously preposterous charge that I was leading a dissident group involved in a plot to blow up the power plant.

The next section of the report read:

> The writer also contacted City Finance Director Paul McNeill about an altercation he had with ROWEN in August of 1967 over the refusal of Rowen to deposit 32.50 for water turn-on. He stated that ROWEN did not threaten him during a lengthy meeting, but his wife did shortly afterward received an obscene telephone call to the effect that her husband had better get off his back or he would splatter his guts all over the sidewalk. It is not known positively that ROWEN made that call but he was very strongly suspicioned then due to the time element and the nature of the conversation due to their verbal altercation on water deposits.

COMMENT: This entry in the police report by Emahiser was the result of Bert Jones collaborating with him on inserting fallacious information into the report. What is true about this matter is that I did have a discussion with the acting city finance director, Paul McNeill, about a required water deposit but I never threatened anyone. Jones is the one who came up with that outrageous accusation.

The conversation I had with McNeill had to do with my request to have the water service of a rental that I had switched to my name as the current tenants were moving and I had new renters wanting to move in right away. (I needed to have the water left on so I could clean the rental unit).

McNeill said the deposit was required to establish credit worthiness and it would be returned to the customer after six months, if there were no late payments and the customer requested it. I told McNeill that I had already established my credit worthiness several times over and that I had forgotten about the water deposits involved. Then I made an observation saying I wonder how many people forget about the deposit. I told McNeil that the deposit should be automatically returned to the customer after establishing eligibility for it.

McNeill disagreed and there ensued an argumentative discussion. I simply said automatically refunding the deposits to qualified customers would be a much better way of doing business and the city should reconsider its water deposit policy. And that was basically our conversation; however, that was not the end of the matter.

I later learned Paul McNeill and Robert Taylor, PG&E's personnel manager, were Rotarian buddies; that McNeill shared with Taylor the conversation I had with him "criticizing the city's water deposit policy."

At work several days later, I was called to the front office of the power plant and raked over the coals by Edgar Weeks for having had this conversation with the acting city finance director. I strongly objected and told Mr. Weeks that I wanted to have a meeting with the personnel manager. I made it clear that it was not any of PG&E management's business what I discussed with city officials on my own time regarding my own personal business. Edgar Weeks disagreed and became indignant with me.

Mr. Weeks said my disagreement with the city over water deposit fees was a bad reflection on PG&E. Weeks told me it's not proper or desirable to have employees of the company criticizing the policies of the city. My response to Weeks was, "That is pure bullshit!" Weeks wrote me up and put more derogatory material in my personnel file.

Burt Jones went to Robert Taylor, who gave Jones unfettered access to my personnel file that contained all the crap that plant management had inserted into it over the years. My employment file must have been a bonanza for Jones – a treasure trove of materials that he could use as a basis for fabricating the stories he gave Emahiser in order to complete his mission. Jones worked up the McNeill story just like he did with the rest of the fallacious material contained in the police report. How did he do it? Jones found copies of memos in my personnel file pertaining to my city water problem that involved Edgar Weeks, Dale Nix, and Robert Taylor.

Mr. Charles Denny knew that his client, Bert Jones, had lied when he denied making all those maliciously false statements to Chief Emahiser that ended up in the police report. Emahiser became a willing participant in PG&E's conspiracy because of my participation in the Walters trial albeit the Chief of Police said he "took the information in good faith but later felt that he had been used."

McNeill later admitted that he had talked to Taylor but said he was sorry for getting involved and that if he had it to do over again, he "would not touch the whole affair with a ten-foot pole." All I wanted and could have ever hoped for was to have my day in court as I was totally confident the truth of what happened would be revealed. The conspirators were doing everything possible to keep that from happening.

The second to the last paragraph in the report read:

> **Pete Mathieson, College of the Redwoods, states that he knows who WILLIAMS and ROWEN are and that they are from PG&E, but he knows nothing about them personally and only that they are constant bitchers over adult student fees and other matters of small import to others.**

COMMENT: First of all, I know how Mr. Mathieson was made aware that I "was from PG&E." Thomas Pugh (a member of management in PG&E's local gas distribution department), who served on the College of the Redwoods Board of Trustees, was made aware that I wrote a critical essay on the dangers of nuclear power plants as my English placement exam at the college. We were to select a controversial subject and write an essay on it. I passed the exam and was placed in English 1A. However, my essay found its way to PG&E, which I learned years later. Yes, Forrest and I did complain about the fees we had to pay for services we did not receive but nevertheless, we paid them anyway; Pete Matheson's "crap" did not belong in a police report with national security implications!

Finally, at the bottom of the second page, appeared the following statement:

12-30-70. Copies of contents of this report has been "Leaked" to two of the subjects in mention (Rowen – Williams?)

COMMENT: I approached Police Chief Emahiser and the Eureka City Attorney about the existence of the report around the time mentioned above but to no avail. Both of them just tried to make me feel that I was in a lot of trouble for even knowing about the report they claimed they knew nothing about.

All the contributors to Bert Jones compilation of statements became the basis for his official report to PG&E corporate headquarters and played into the development of PG&E's conspiracy (review Chapter 11). The company's conspiracy was most likely fashioned by PG&E's attorney Lawrence V. Brown in the company's industrial relations department. It was either James Neel, head of PG&E Security Department, or Lawrence L. Brown or both, who originally gave Berton Jones his marching orders to launch his investigation at Humboldt Bay commencing on May 21, 1970. However, Neel and Jones were not acting alone; there was direct involvement by the uppermost echelons of PG&E's corporate management.

When Mr. Jones completed his investigation, it is clear he gave his report with all of its supporting details, including a copy of the police report, to Lawrence V. Brown.[267] As an offer of proof that Bert Jones put together an official security report to aid Mr. Brown's effort, I'm providing George Tully's sworn testimony regarding his handwritten statement prepared by Bert Jones that contained the following verbiage at the very end of it, which is quoted verbatim as it appeared in the statement George Tully had signed (review Chapter 11 and repeated here for emphasis):[268]

> In another vein, remarks were made about two years ago which gave me reason to doubt their intentions toward the company or the community. Rowen and Williams at this time attended Redwood Junior College where I was taking some courses. The political aspects of communism were being discussed. Williams in particular, but supported by Rowen conveyed these thoughts (paraphrased): 'Well I don't think communism is as bad as it sounds.' Each spoke about shutting the school down – implicitly by any force necessary."

A deposition of George Tully was taken on May 29, 1975, in Eureka, California. Arthur J. Hillman, appeared as counsel on behalf of PG&E; Charles Denny of Crosby, Heafey, Roach and May from Oakland, California appeared as counsel on behalf of Bert Jones; and Bruce Cogan of Mathews, Traverse and McKittrick appeared on behalf of plaintiff, Robert Rowen. Tully's deposition provided a key line of testimony pertaining to the aforementioned statements made by George Tully in the written document prepared by Bert Jones and signed by Mr. Tully:[269]

Mr. Grogan (my attorney): (Directed to Mr. George Tully . . .) Well, let me ask you this: Did you obtain this information stated here that the political aspects of communism were being discussed; to the best of your knowledge, who were involved in discussing the political aspects of communism?

Mr. Tully: I can't recall that, sir.

Mr. Grogan: Did you participate in any conversation relating to the political aspects of communism?

Mr. Tully: I must have if I put it down there, sir.

Mr. Grogan: Do you recall if Mr. Williams was discussing the political aspects of communism?

Mr. Tully: That is what I have on my statement, must have been at the time.

Mr. Grogan: Now, how about Mr. Rowen?

Mr. Tully: I am not sure whether for certain, I don't remember or recall, I mean.

COMMENT: The PG&E attorney, Arthur J. Hillman, and the attorney representing George Tully, Charles Denny, both constantly interrupted the direct examination of Tully with one objection after another turning the whole deposition into a three-ring circus: Hillman-Denny-and Grogan. The examples are too numerous to recount here but they were absolutely ridiculous and both Hillman and Denny constantly jumped on my attorney like a couple of piranhas. After they finally settled the hash with several off the record discussion and after the threat of interposing more objections, Grogan's direct examination continued:[270]

Mr. Grogan: What did you base your opinion on that Mr. Williams in particular, but supported by Mr. Rowen, provided these thoughts, was that Rowen that made these statements or Mr. Williams?

Mr. Tully: No, Mr. Williams made the statements.

Mr. Grogan: When the statements were made, was Mr. Rowen present.

Mr. Tully: That I don't recall, sir. It says here and that is supported, by my memory, but I don't know, I can't remember.

Mr. Grogan: Do you recall whether anyone other that Mr. Williams and Mr. Rowen were present?

Mr. Tully: I don't recall, sir.

Mr. Grogan: On the second statement it says, "Each spoke about shutting the school down." What did you mean by that? Did both Mr. Williams and Mr. Rowen speak about shutting the school down?

Mr. Tully: I can't recall that, sir.

Mr. Grogan: Can you recall if the statement relating to shutting the school down occurred at the same time as the conversation or the statement about communism?

Mr. Tully: No, I can't.

Mr. Grogan: Who else was present when the statements about shutting the school down were made?

Mr. Tully: I don't recall that, sir.

Mr. Grogan: Now, after these statements were made did you make any complaints to any official about these statements?

Mr. Tully: No, sir.

Mr. Grogan: Did you consider them to be a serious matter?

Mr. Tully: I don't believe I did at that time.

Mr. Grogan: From the time say approximately 1968 until you discussed this with Mr. Jones, did you notify any official at PG&E relating to these statements?

Mr. Tully: No, sir.

Mr. Grogan: In your discussion with Mr. Jones, what prompted you to bring this matter up to Mr. Jones, did Mr. Jones ask you any specific questions that brought this out?

Mr. Tully: I can't recall that, sir.

Mr. Grogan: Do you recall whether you on your own brought this out, these statements, or were they in response to a question by Mr. Jones?

Mr. Tully: I can't recall that, sir.

Mr. Grogan: Did you on May 22, 1970, provide any other information to Mr. Jones other that what is reflected in this written statement, labeled Exhibit A?

Mr. Tully: I do not believe I did, sir.

Listening to the responses of George Tully to the questions Bruce Grogan put to him reminded me of the McCarthy hearings: "I can't recall that, sir" stated repeatedly! Tully never answered the question regarding how the subjects of communism and shutting down the school came up with Bert Jones. It was established by Tully that he was referring to a conversation that he claimed took place two years before he ever met with Jones but he couldn't remember anything about how any of it ended up in his signed statement.

PG&E management at every level knew the information Bert Jones gave to Chief Emahiser was false, completely and utterly false! The whole damned effort by Bert Jones was to make it appear that we were all involved in subversive activities.

Behind closed doors we were charged with plotting to blow up the power plant, that we subscribed to a communist ideology, and that we were involved with the SDS (Students for a Democratic Society, a "leftist" movement on college campuses during the sixties) on the College of the Redwoods campus.

PG&E's intentions were abundantly clear. PG&E's management personnel had conspired to put into the files of the Federal Bureau of Investigation false information that would make it impossible for any of us, especially Forrest Williams and me, to ever again obtain a security clearance for work in the sensitive employment areas of nuclear facilities.

It would become a modern day form of the old-fashion employment blacklisting made illegal decades earlier. PG&E believed we would never become aware of what was in the files of the FBI and that the company's dastardly deed on June 3, 1970, was considered by PG&E a done deal and we'd never be any the wiser. We would apply for a security clearance; it would not be granted; and there would be no specific reason given. That's the way the system worked and there would be nothing we could do about it!

Bert Jones was working for PG&E's security czar, James C. Neel, and enthusiastically doing the bidding of his PG&E bosses. They told him what they wanted and he worked hard to give it to them. James Neel worked with James Carroll, PG&E's Nuclear Engineer in charge of the company's Steam Generation Department at corporate headquarters, and Fritz Draeger, PG&E's Atomic Information Officer, and who knows who else in PG&E corporate headquarters to concoct this horrible plan and relied on Bert Jones to pull it all off.

At the very least Forrest Williams and Bob Rowen needed to be "neutralized" and rendered "future security risks" to the nuclear industry! And if somehow all of this got out into the public eye, all these PG&E folks would simply deny any involvement and pass the buck to their patsy, Chief Emahiser, who, with his own motivations, was dumb enough to allow himself to get sucked in to this insidious plot. Emahiser, on the other hand, felt protected because anything he produced could be claimed as a "privileged" document. Of course, if PG&E's plan ever saw the light of day and was exposed publicly, the reputations of Williams and Rowen would be ruined.

It was a fantastic, well-conceived plan. After Jones reviewed my personnel file at the plant and found my subpoena for Donald Walters' trial, Jones and Neel had a quick strategy session over the phone. Mr. Neel then sent Bert Jones to see an old friend, Police Chief Cedric Emahiser. The PG&E conspirators all believed that Emahiser would jump at the chance to get back at Rowen for his testimony in the Walters' trial and the Walters' federal civil rights violation suit that followed, and they were right!

It was easy for Chief Emahiser to do PG&E's bidding and to agree with the labeling of Rowen as a "confirmed cop hater." After all, the false police report the PG&E conspirators created with the help of Chief Emahiser would be considered "privileged" and no harm would ever come to any of them.

I began this chapter of my *Diary* stating the following:

In the naivety of my youth, it was difficult for me to

understand the mean-spirited, twisted motives of the company. My understanding of the PG&E culture admittedly came to me very slowly; my hard-founded experience eventually led me to the conclusion that it really wasn't just a corporate culture but rather something that could be more adequately described as a corporate cult.

Why was I being called a communist, a subversive, accused of industrial sabotage, associating with the SDS, involved in a plot to blow up the Humboldt Bay Nuclear Power Plant and ending up in a ridiculously false law enforcement file sent to the Federal Bureau of Investigation?

How could intelligent, moral and ethical people who are supposedly loyal, patriotic Americans engage in making such perverse accusations?

Now I'd like to revisit some of these very troubling questions and then expand upon the inquiry posed by them to reveal the only plausible explanation for what took place and Bert Jones' role in it.

I wondered for the longest time after my discovery of the police report why Bert Jones was so willing to report maliciously such false information to the Eureka chief of police.

It was easy for me to realize why Chief Emahiser was so willing to participate with Bert Jones in commissioning the report and inserting into the report that I was "a confirmed cop hater." I don't know to this day if that was his idea or if that, too, came from Bert Jones (albeit Officer Millsap supposedly said it), but where did those things that Bert Jones clearly contributed to the police report come from?

How could Jones have been so motivated to say and do such things? Why did he conduct the interviews of the very carefully selected employees the way he did?

Why did each employee contribute a brush stroke that led to his final product? While it was true that several of the nuclear control technicians were critical of the company's radiation safety protection program, and that Forrest William and myself were the most outspoken and consequently targeted by PG&E, why did our criticisms of the company translate to characterizations of us as dissidents, subversives, militants, and saboteurs?

Where did the wild accusations that we advocated violence, fire bombing and had communist leanings come from?

As I mulled over these questions, I came to the conclusion that Bert Jones had developed a framework for his investigatory report, a report that he could take back to his corporate bosses. However, I still was not able to fathom how he could have developed such an absurdly wild picture of us.

It wasn't until James McKittrick conducted a deposition of Bert Jones in late 1974 that I discovered Bert Jones' background, which revealed his formidable years. That discovery led me to hypothesize the only plausible explanation of why Jones did what he did.

While Jones was testifying, I was sitting at the end of the counsel table and scribbling some notes and doodling on a yellow tablet. I had written down the amount of time Jones said he had been with PG&E – 7 years.[271]

Before PG&E, Jones had his own private investigation company – for about 12 years.[272] McKittrick wanted to know what he did before going into business for himself. Jones responded, "I was in the FBI."

A couple of questions later McKittrick asked Jones what position he had with the FBI. "Special agent," was his reply.

Then Jones stated he was with the FBI for "a little over six years."[273] I sketched a timeline, which indicated he went to work for the FBI around 1949, maybe as early as 1947. Considering how old I thought he was at the time he was being deposed, I estimated his age to be around 24 to 27 years of age when he started with the FBI. Then it struck me that he was professionally reared smack-dab in the era of McCarthyism and trained by the J. Edgar Hoover regime.

Senior Security Representative Berton F. Jones had developed an impressive resume that was perfect for the corporate culture dominated by the ideals of the John Birch Society, an opinion based on PG&E's sponsorship of John Birch "educational" materials and the corporate management's right-wing orientation.

All of this has spun around in my head for years, and what I'm left with is the only explanation that makes any sense to me. My search for answers to the PG&E conspiracy has connected management at corporate headquarters, to an ultraconservative mindset reflective in many ways to the ideals espoused by the John Birch Society.

Thanks to the revelation made possible by law professor Bill Rodgers, this connection came to light when I discovered that PG&E had backed a John Birch Society film with very wide distribution,[274] a film with sections of which were taken verbatim from the John Birch Society *Blue Book*, "[which] presents an impression of the United States lying helplessly in the closing jaws of a world Communist conspiracy," according to Cabell Phillips of the *New York Times*.[275]

PG&E contributed to the Foundation for Economic Education (FEE), a Far-Right reactionary group. One primary cornerstone of this ideology is limited government. This belief holds "that government is best which governs least, or perhaps not at all."

The proponents of this notion believe in laissez-faire capitalism, private property, the profit motive, and the ability to pursue one's self-interest regulated only by Adam Smith's "invisible hand" in a free-market, and not at all by the government.

Of course, Adam Smith assumed that people were basically good; that self-interest was not tantamount to uncontrollable greed because the "invisible hand" would take care of that.

Perhaps Smith was correct as long as single proprietorships prevailed in the marketplace; however, Smith could not have envisioned in 1776 the arrival of huge, powerful corporations that arrived on the American scene during the latter part of the nineteenth century. Smith pointed to the need for government, but that need was designed only to provide the framework within which Smith's "invisible hand" would work the way he had envisioned in markets consisting of many buyers and many sellers.

Today's corporate mindset is opposed to government regulation, economic interventionism of any kind, and to all forms of socialism. Our cherished American freedoms and individual liberties are translated by this corporate mindset as a corporate right to pursue its own corporate interests with its vast financial resources and the manipulation of elected officials at all levels of government. Anyone who disagrees with them or opposes their conduct is branded a socialist, communist, or worse.

We have seen throughout America's history that corporate conduct has all too often been rooted in a convoluted view of the proper role of government and the failings of the general populous to understand the incessant need for government intervention.

All any of us need to do is take a long hard look at our history and learn the lessons from it. For just a few examples ranging from the nineteenth century throughout the twentieth century and on into the twenty first century, look at the problems the American people have had with the oil and railroad industries, the meat packing industry, the underlying reasons for the 1929 stock market crash, the aluminum industry, ATT, and the more recent failures of Wall Street, BP in the Gulf, and even the production of eggs in the Midwest, and one unmistakably finds greed at the root of all of it.

If we add the nuclear option with its dire consequences to corporate America's history of running amok, then we are unmistakably making the gravest mistake of all not only for our present but future generations, as well.

I eventually chose to believe the renowned experts of my time, and reject the claims by the nuclear juggernaut. I reached my conclusions based on what I learned from my personal research and professional experience working in a nuclear facility.

I grew tired of and extremely frustrated with all the nonsense occurring inside the nuclear workplace. The attitudes of the managers, and the philosophies that underlie those attitudes, is absolutely scary. This is a pleading for something that must not happen because of the reasons that are revealed in my *Diary*.

We cannot rely on corporate America to do the right thing nor can we rely on government to do the right thing when government is bought and paid for by corporate money (e.g., Koch money), which is exactly what is happening in America today.

__XIII__

13. The AEC Whitewash

October 1971

"We believe that PG&E management personnel have fulfilled their responsibilities in a conscientious reliable manner. The Company has been cited only a few times for items of noncompliance and these items have been of a minor nature. There has been no evidence of irresponsible practices."[276] [AEC]

"The safety record of the nuclear industry is such that it can withstand close scrutiny. In fact, there can be little doubt that it has withstood the most careful scrutiny ever given to a major enterprise in the history of mankind."[277] [Edgar Weeks]

"The AEC has found PG&E management to be 'extremely responsive' to 'constructive criticisms.'"[278] [James Carroll]

The true story of America's nuclear juggernaut's *betrayal of the public trust* can best be told by revealing the PG&E-AEC complicit cover-up of a multitude of radiation safety violations by the Pacific Gas and Electric Company at its Humboldt Bay Nuclear Power Plant; Then PG&E's use of the AEC's "handiwork" tells the rest of this incredible story.

This well-orchestrated cover-up by PG&E and the AEC had one very specific goal: To promote the future proliferation of nuclear power plants by protecting a failed and dangerous technology at Humboldt Bay. PG&E used whatever means was necessary to silence or "neutralize" anyone who got in the way by using lies, deception, character assassination and worse!

263

After I was fired from PG&E, I received welcome advice from several really fine people for whom I have great admiration and respect. I will always be grateful for the invaluable assistance and support they provided my family and me. After it was realized just how much danger I had placed myself in, it was strongly suggested that I go public as quickly and in as many different ways as possible. Thank god I took that advice to heart!

Following my Unemployment Insurance Appeals Board Hearing, my Arbitration Hearing, and heeding the advice that I was given, I decided to force the hand of the AEC.

I had realized by this time the AEC probably wasn't going to be of any real help for reasons that will become clearer in the following accounting of the AEC's whitewash of PG&E's Machiavellian shenanigans and the company's shameful disregard for radiation safety.

However, I felt that if I could somehow get the AEC to "go on record" with the way it went about doing its regulatory business, it would prove helpful in revealing just how self-serving the nuclear juggernaut actually was. I ended up with a whole lot more than I had thought possible; thus proving how inadequate and untrustworthy the AEC truly was (with the NRC now determined to follow suit). Moreover, my whistleblowing effort abled me to expose an AEC-PG&E conspiracy that clearly establishes PG&E as a corporate criminal – and I cannot express that strongly enough!

On April 30, 1971, I wrote a five page letter to the Director of the Division of Licensing and Regulation of the United States Atomic Energy Commission in Washington D.C. In my letter I stated:

> During my employment with the Pacific Gas and Electric Company, and while I was employed as a nuclear control technician, I experienced the inadequacies of the law and procedures pertaining to the control and regulation of nuclear power plants.

I also stated in my letter to the Director, "This letter may be considered the initial groundwork of my going on public record concerning these inadequacies." I quoted the following from the Decision of the Referee of the California Unemployment Insurance Appeals Board:[279]

> STATEMENTS OF FACTS
>
> A preponderance of evidence indicate that during the last year or two of Mr. Rowen's employment he was involved in many disputes with higher management over his reports of safety violations. The following are cited as examples:
>
> 1. The routine work permit under which a group of employees were working in the summer of 1967 permitted exposure of only five to 50 mr's but frequently the exposure was in the area of 2500 mr's.
>
> 2. A supervisor ordered a technician to take smears of materials to be shipped from the nuclear plant at

the top and bottom of the container but not in the center. This would have the effect of minimizing the radiation count. After the supervisor had been informed the count exceeded the level permitted for such shipments, he asked the claimant to sign a previously prepared shipping document, which indicated the radiation level was within tolerable limits. When the claimant refused, he (the supervisor) corrected the shipping document to show the correct figure and then ordered the shipment processed, contrary to the governmental regulation involved. The claimant accurately reported the entire incident in the daily log he was required to keep as part of his duties. He was severely reprimanded by Mr. Weeks for having done so on the ground this was not a "proper" use of the log, pointing out that the Atomic Energy Commission inspectors had access to the log.

3. On one occasion VIP's were to be conducted through part of the facility where they might be exposed to radiation, and the plans of the claimant's supervisor did not call for monitoring these persons as they left the danger area to determine the rate of exposure, if any. At the claimant's insistence this was corrected.

4. Men were permitted to work over the open core of the nuclear reactor without wearing a safety harness to prevent their falling down into the core. Mr. Weeks confirmed this danger involved in working over an open "Core" without a safety harness but indicated the company was working on the problem, and, in addition, some of the workers believed the harness itself would be a safety hazard.

A short time prior to the claimant's discharge, he asked Mr. Weeks for permission to speak to the Atomic Energy Commission inspector concerning the violation noted immediately above, and other conditions the claimant believed unsafe. He was refused permission to make his report to the inspector.

In this letter to the Director of Licensing and Regulation of the Atomic Energy Commission, I also quoted from a letter sent to the California Department of Human Resources Development by the Pacific Gas and Electric Company:[280]

As a Control Technician, Mr. Rowen was required to

carry out specific assignments following well-defined procedures, in which he had been instructed, under the supervision of an engineer who is an expert in the field of radiation safety.

It was not the claimant's responsibility to check on the safety procedures of the Company. He did on numerous occasions make allegations and protest that the Company's actions were unsafe and did not meet Federal requirements. However, he was never able to show how the "unsafe" Company actions failed to meet Federal requirements.

The operation of the Humboldt Bay Power Plant, where the claimant was employed, has been inspected by the Atomic Energy Commission at least three to four times a year since the nuclear unit went into operation in 1963, and as a result of these thorough inspections, the Commission has been favorably impressed with our radiation safety program.

The stage was now set for my whistleblowing with the AEC. Following my April 30, 1971, letter to the U.S. Atomic Energy Commission, I received a phone call from Mr. J. J. Ward, who identified himself as an investigator for the AEC. Ward acknowledged my letter to the AEC in Washington D. C. and explained he was assigned to follow up with me.

After we talked on the phone for a while, Ward said he wanted to meet with me in person to discuss more fully my concerns about the Humboldt Bay Nuclear Power Plant. We agreed to meet on May 11, 1971. Ward told me that he would get back to me with a time and place for our meeting.

I was surprised by Ward's selection of the location for our meeting. It was a sleazy motel on Highway 101, not far from the nuclear site. Ward gave me a room number and the time for our meeting and asked me to bring all of my documentation to the meeting.

The arrangement didn't feel right to me. I suspected I was being set up for something.

I previously had decided to outline my concerns and present them orally to Ward, and I also decided to take a tape recorder with me.

Ward answered the door and introduced himself and invited me into his room. As I walked into the room, I immediately noticed two other gentlemen sitting in the room out of my view when I was first standing outside the door. I stiffened, and asked Ward who these gentlemen were? Ward quickly introduced them and explained they were part of his team.

I selected a location in the room that kept me between Ward, his two assistants and the outside door to his room.

After introductions I set up my tape recorder. Ward quickly objected, saying, "The AEC does not approve of the use of tape recorders in situations like this," and that he was "personally opposed to my use of the recorder."

I explained to Mr. Ward that my understanding of the purpose of our meeting was for me to present my concerns about the Humboldt Bay nuclear facility, and since I'd be doing all the talking, I'd simply be recording what I had to say. I asked him how the AEC could possibly object to that.

After some argumentative discussion (and I was determined to have it my way!), Ward finally agreed to the recorder as long as he received a transcription of the recording, if one was made.

I met with Ward on three occasions, May 11, May 19, and September 7, 1971, and I taped every one of those meetings but I only had a transcription made of the third and final meeting held on September 7, 1971. Rowetta Miller, a professional transcriber who worked for the Humboldt County Superior Court handled the transcription. I invited a reporter for the Eureka *Times-Standard* newspaper (whose name is being withheld at his request), to accompany me to this third meeting between J. J. Ward and myself.

At first, Ward objected to the reporter being present at this meeting expressing his concern, "This meeting would be reported on in the newspaper."[281] Ward stated he hadn't cleared someone else being present at this meeting and chastised me for not being more candid with him about bringing someone with me to this meeting. The reporter then interjected a couple of points saying:[282]

> **Reporter:** If I can be of any assistance here – our discussions have so far been confidential. PG&E knows nothing of our discussions. The only thing I have done is a feature on the refueling outage.
>
> **Ward:** Do you have some competence in the nuclear field?
>
> **Reporter:** No, I don't. I wish I did. But this is something I've been trying to learn something about. You could talk in confidence to Bob and he could tell me the same things later on.
>
> **Ward:** That's his prerogative.
>
> **Reporter:** As far as my quoting you as a source, I can consider this conversation off the record and take what I can get from Bob. He can release to me whatever he desires. I don't mean to be here to hamper you.

Ward also made a point of telling me that the AEC had made every effort to maintain my anonymity during his investigation that he and his team had conducted; however, he had learned that PG&E was already aware that I had made several complaints to the AEC concerning PG&E's nuclear facility.

In this vein, Ward stated:[283]

> The company does now know that you have made these allegations but I want to assure you that this hasn't been through our mischance or through our efforts whatsoever. Specifically, the Environmental Protection Agency apparently went to them and a copy of their correspondence apparently has been received by the company so this we learned just by chance from discussions with the company.

In setting the stage for the report of his investigative findings he was about to present to me, Ward stated he came up with "forty-nine various statements or allegations" that I had made to him during our first two meetings, and he added "some of which seemed to be more observations than allegations."[284] What the hell was he trying to say to me, I thought – some were "observations" rather than allegations?

It was immediately obvious that Ward's linguistic double-entendre was leading to a whitewash that was going to cover up PG&E's misdeeds, and as it turned out my suspicions were well founded!

A 15-page document was provided to me by the AEC. It is presented here exactly as written by the AEC investigator with a personal *"COMMENT"* following each "AEC Finding." Many of these items (notice that all forty-nine items are listed as "allegations") are also commented on elsewhere in my *Diary* in much greater detail and will sometimes be referenced again in several of my personal "comment sections." I also repeat some testimony already presented in earlier chapters of my *Diary* to provide emphasis or clarification. The following is the AEC document with my "comments" added:

> Pursuant to a complaint alleging certain radiation safety deficiencies in the operation of the Humboldt Bay Nuclear Plant by Pacific and Electric Company (PG&E), AEC instituted an investigation of the matter during May, July, and August 1971. During the course of the investigation, 49 allegations were identified and reviewed by the AEC investigation team. There follows a listing of each allegation and a summary of the AEC's finding:[285]
>
> **Allegation #1:** Routine Work Permits used by PG&E did not reflect the levels of radiation exposure currently experienced in particular areas of the plant, particularly those for taking reactor water and off-gas samples.
> **AEC Finding:** The reference in the allegation to Routine Work Permits should be to a form maintained by PG&E called Radiation Work Procedures (RWP's), which provides, among other things, a space for setting forth current radiation levels. A review of current RWP's revealed that the radiation levels were either omitted from the RWP or incomplete. This matter was included in the Notice of Violation, which was sent by AEC to PG&E on October 28, 1971.

COMMENT: This allegation specifically addressed the reactor water and off-gas sampling stations during the summer of 1967. In my April 30, 1971, letter to the AEC, I quoted the Referee's "findings" in his "Statement of Facts" in his Decision re: Case Number SF – 1319, which read:[286]

A preponderance of evidence indicated that during the

last year or two of the claimant's employment he was involved in many disputes with higher management over his reports of safety violations. The following (is) cited as (an example): The routine work permit under which a group of employees were working in the summer of 1967 permitted exposure of only five to 50 mr's but frequently the exposure was in the area of 2500 mr's.

FUTHER COMMENT: Why did Ward refer to "A review of current RWP's" and point out "the radiation levels were either omitted from the RWP or incomplete" in his "AEC Finding" and completely ignore my complaint. This had absolutely nothing to do with my complaint. My complaint was made clear to the AEC investigator as well as in my April 30, 1971, letter to the to the Director of the Division of Licensing and Regulation of the United States Atomic Energy Commission that I was specifically referring to PG&E conduct during the summer of 1967.

The exposure the control technicians were receiving was five hundred times what the RWP had authorized in the official records of the company. The RWP covering this radiation work during this time was complete, every word of it as well as every section of it; it just incorrectly stated the amount of radiation exposure of the working conditions and to what the CTs were being subjected. The Referee gleaned this in his "Statement of Facts" from the testimony of company officials.

Following the company safety meeting held on December 12, 1967, management began the process of constructing biological shielding around both the reactor water and off-gas sampling stations, which finally acknowledged the problems I had been complaining about for months. Weeks' own testimony addressed the problem in response to a direct question regarding it:[287]

> **Mr. Weeks:** I was aware that exposure rates were coming up when we began to pop fuel and that we were taking too much exposure at the reactor water sample station and our first line supervisor had been instructed to solve this problem and I am sure there must have been several discussions on it, "Yes."

FURTHER COMMENT: There was plenty of history regarding this problem. The RWPs for both the reactor water and off-gas sampling were written at the plant's startup and were never updated. The RWP for the reactor water sampling station clearly established exposure limits of 5 to 50 mr, which made sense when it was written. However, as the plant became increasingly contaminated because of the breakdown of the original stainless steel fuel cladding, conditions changed and plant management did not adequately respond in a timely fashion to those changing conditions. In fact, those changing conditions involved exposures at times in excess of 3R per hour on the 1 liter sample bottles and a whole lot more than that at the reactor water sampling station.

I can state unequivocally that plant management didn't care! And I am clearly in the best position to know that because of all the "counseling" sessions I had with Mr. Edgar Weeks because of my continual and relentless complaining about it! The snide remark made by the AEC investigators referring to my allegation referencing Routine Work Permits should be to a form maintained by PG&E called Radiation Work Procedures (RWP's) was simply intended to contribute to their overall effort to make me look as "out of whack" as possible. The truth of the matter is that the in-house staff called the RWP's "Routine Work Permits" to distinguish them from Special Work Permits (SWP's) and Mr. Ward and his AEC investigators knew that!

Finally, the minutes of the December 12, 1967, PG&E safety meeting would have clearly established the violation that I presented to Chief AEC investigator J. J. Ward.

After all, it was for that very reason that I brought up my unresolved radiation safety problems at the company safety meetings, so they could be reviewed by the AEC. Ward either chose to ignore those minutes or collaborated with PG&E not to bring them into his investigation.

No one could have claimed that those records were not available because Weeks had testified under oath that PG&E had all the records that dated clear back to the start up of Unit 3 in 1963. What Ward did was to simply review "current RWPs" that supposedly revealed only "minor" infractions; he purposely did an end run around my complaint. How convenient for PG&E!

> **Allegation #2:** On August 6, 1969, PG&E shipped a spent fuel cask having contamination levels above those permitted by Department of Transportation (DOT) regulations.
>
> **AEC Finding:** DOT regulations establish a removable contamination level of less than 2200 disintegrations per minute (dpm). The cask was shipped at 2600 dpm. PG&E advised that clearance was obtained from DOT before shipment by phone. The cognizant employee at DOT did not recall the conversation, but stated that approval would have been given by him because the levels of contamination in question were within the statistical error limits of measurement of the instrument used for measuring contamination.

COMMENT: Why did the AEC improperly state the DOT regulations? The applicable DOT regulation states less than 2200 dpm/100 cm^2, which means the amount of smearable radioactive contamination on the outside surface of the cask cannot be more than 2200 dpm "for every 100 sq. centimeters!" As previously pointed out in Chapter 6, just how much over the DOT limit was the "stated" contamination level?

The 20,000 dpm around the seal of the cask was a gross contamination problem that was totally ignored by PG&E, the AEC, and the DOT, yet that problem was clearly stated in a confidential memorandum written by

PG&E's Radiation Protection Engineer, Mr. Gail Allen, and thereafter reviewed by the Plant Engineer, Edgar Weeks.

The aforementioned company memorandum was available to the AEC. Why did the AEC choose to ignore it? If the excess was within the "measurement statistical error limits of the measurements" (which was the first time I've ever heard that statement in the context of radiation protection compliance!) and, therefore, would have been approved, why then would the DOT official who was supposedly contacted say that he would not like for it to become routine? After all, if it were "within the measurement statistical error limits of the measurements," wouldn't it be okay at anytime?

What about PG&E's Radiation Protection Engineer's choice of using the radiation IPC counter that produced the lowest readings? What about PG&E's Radiation Protection Engineer ordering the control tech to take samples in the areas of the cask he previously determined to have the least amount of contamination (which were still above the DOT limits) and specifically and purposefully avoiding those areas that had a much higher amount of radioactive contamination, a combined total area that represented about forty percent of the spent fuel shipping cask's outside surfaces (review Chapter 6)? The AEC clearly partnered up with PG&E to cover up what had taken place with the improper release of the radioactively contaminated spent fuel-shipping cask on August 6, 1969.

> **Allegation #3:** But for the insistence of one employee, PG&E would have permitted a visitors' tour of the refueling building without following established radiation safety procedures (review Chapter 4 – "Another serious breach of radiation protection procedures in March 1970 involving a VIP tour")
>
> **AEC Finding:** As indicated by the allegation itself, no violation of any kind occurred.

COMMENT: In my August 30, 1971 letter to the AEC, I quoted the Referee's "findings" in his "Statement of Facts" in his Decision re: Case Number SF – 1319, which read (repeated here for emphasis):

> A preponderance of evidence indicates that during the last year or two of the claimant's employment he was involved in many disputes with higher management over his reports of safety violations. The following (is) cited as (an example): On one occasion VIP's were conducted through part of the facility where they might be exposed to radiation, and the plans of the claimant's supervisor did not call for monitoring these persons as they left the danger area to determine the rate of exposure, if any. At the claimant's insistence this was corrected.

FURTHER COMMENT: What the AEC failed to recognize was that it would have been a clear violation if I had not confronted management and in doing so brought reprisals, which is something the AEC chose to ignore because the Commission made it clear that it did not want to concern itself with "labor-management issues." It's definitely a "cozy" arrangement when the regulators don't protect employees who insist on following the regulations when the company chooses not to. Even worse is when the company causes an employee to become guilty of complicit conduct in violating the law in order to keep his job.

Allegation #4: PG&E permitted employees to perform work over the reactor core without wearing a safety harness and rope as required by company practice.

AEC Finding: True; however, the condition was corrected at the time. An employee advised his supervisor of the situation and harnesses were then used. There are no AEC requirements relative to the use of safety harnesses.

COMMENT: First, there was no "required company practice." That was the whole point of my complaint to the AEC and criticism of PG&E nuclear plant management! The condition absolutely was not "corrected at the time" nor was it ever corrected! The best way to ascertain the real truth of this matter is to provide the testimony of Edgar Weeks at my California Unemployment Appeals Board Hearing held on October 1, 1970, which raised serious questions about the integrity of the AEC investigators (review Chapter 10 – Weeks' testimony repeated here for emphasis):

Mr. Rowen: I have a new area that . . . I subpoenaed Mr. Weeks to appear as a witness for me, but I suppose I can just go ahead and clear it up, so Mr. Weeks can be finished with this. Is that all right?

THE REFERREE: Yes. Why don't you do that?

Mr. Rowen: Fine. Thank you. This is concerning a discussion . . .

REFEREE: You are putting him on as your witness at this moment?

Mr. Rowen: Yes. At least for this one bit of testimony here. This concerns a discussion that you and I had on May 11, 1970. Did I make a request on May 11 or on May 10 to speak with Mr. Dodds, an AEC compliance inspector, who was in the plant on a routine inspection?

Mr. Weeks: Yes, you did.

Mr. Rowen: Did you refuse that request?

Mr. Weeks: Yes, I did.

Mr. Rowen: And, as a result did we have a discussion regarding your denial of my request?

Mr. Weeks: Yes, sir. We took one hour.

Mr. Rowen: Did you ask me for my reasons for wanting to

speak with Mr. Dodds?

Mr. Weeks: Yes, I did.

Mr. Rowen: And did I give those reasons to you?

Mr. Weeks: Yes.

Mr. Rowen: Were the reasons based, in part, on certain radiation protection safety problems, and violations that I had witnessed during the 1970 refueling outage?

Mr. Weeks: They were based on your allegations of what were unsafe radiation safety practices. I didn't necessarily agree with you.

Mr. Rowen: Did you admit to me that some of these were radiation protection problems and you would take appropriate steps to correct them?

Mr. Weeks: If you recall, I asked you first of all if you had discussed this with your supervisor, which is the normal procedure, and you said you had, so I called . . . actually, you had said you discussed some of them with Mr. Boots and some of them with Mr. Parker. Well, Mr. Parker wasn't there, but I called Mr. Boots in and we discussed the items that you said you discussed with him. And, I told you what actions had been taken or whether action was contemplated on the items at the time. Some of the items you brought up, we had already taken steps to do something about. I had already issued instructions. One of them, I wasn't even sure whether we were going to do anything on it. To me it was, in the discussions I heard, some people thought it was a problem, some people didn't. And, I told you we would continue discussion on it and try to get it resolved, which we had tried to do.

Mr. Rowen: What particular item are you referring to?

Mr. Weeks: That's working over the reactor vessel before the extension tank is put on after the head of the reactor is removed. I told you at that time that our maintenance foreman was against using a lifeline that you had suggested. He didn't like the idea. He thought it was more unsafe than doing it the way we have been doing it. Some of the supervisors agreed with the line of thinking you had at that time, that they should wear a safety line. I told you we would discuss it at our next meeting, which we did at our next supervisor's meeting and we didn't come to any real agreement on it.

Mr. Rowen: Wasn't it true that our rad protection engineer had laid it down as a rule that everybody must follow?

Mr. Brown (PG&E attorney): Referring to what now?

Mr. Rowen: The fact that we were to use safety lines working over the top of the open reactor, so that no one could fall into it.

Mr. Weeks: You told me at the time that he had assured you before the outage that he was going to do that and I'm afraid I can't tell you . . . I can't really say that this is the general rule. I don't remember seeing a written rule on this.

Mr. Rowen: Was Mr. Boots present at this discussion?

Mr. Weeks: Yes. He was.

Mr. Rowen: What did he admit to you when you asked him that statement?

Mr. Weeks: He admitted discussing it with you and telling you that he was going to look into it and take some action on it.

Mr. Rowen: You don't recall him saying that, "Yes, I told Mr. Rowen that the safety lines would be used?"

Mr. Weeks: I got the impression that he had agreed with you that they should be used. I don't remember his exact words but I got the distinct impression that he did agree with you before the outage, that we should use safety lines.

FUTHER COMMENT: The truth of the matter was that there were employees who continued to refuse to use the safety harness and safety line, and no written rule was ever implemented. The AEC inspection team lied and PG&E again pounded me in the press with the "groundless allegation" I had made. The AEC inspectors may have claimed that they didn't have all the information when the AEC "finding" was written, however, it's a huge leap to say, "The situation was corrected at the time and the harnesses were then used."

Allegation #5: PG&E management refused to permit one of its employees to talk to an AEC inspector during a plant inspection.

AEC Finding: True. AEC Form 3 encourages each employee to communicate with the AEC concerning any matters relating to public health and safety. This matter was included in the October 28 notice to the licensee.

COMMENT: When a company can demand with impunity that employees shall not go "public" or report to regulatory agencies problems in the nuclear workplace, then the public will remain ignorant of those problems. From my experience, employees need to be protected from employer abuse when employees refuse to "toe the company line" when the company is acting against the public interest. There should be harsh penalties for companies that retaliate against whistleblowers rather than receive the occasional wrist slap, and the same goes for regulatory agencies that are in bed with the companies they regulate.

Allegation #6: PG&E gave its employees directions; both implied and expressed, not to talk with AEC inspectors.

AEC Finding: Except for the employee referred to in #5 above, no other employee interviewed reported the existence of any such express direction. There was some belief of an unwritten understanding that employees should not talk to AEC inspectors, but this was not widely held.

COMMENT: Top-level management in the plant made it abundantly clear that all employee concerns about radiation safety needed to be processed within the company management structure and never taken outside the company. When asked a direct question about my going to the AEC, Weeks testified, "I told you that I was not going to give you company time to see the compliance inspector on this visit. That, if on your own you wanted to go see him, there was obviously nothing I could do about it. But, my advice, I told you, it was inadvisable. That's what I told you that it was inadvisable."

I attempted several times to have Weeks address just what he meant by "it was inadvisable." Weeks never explained what he meant by "inadvisable," and the company attorney interjected on Weeks behalf and said the witness "did not wish to define or explain it."

What this unsatisfactory exchange left me with was the fundamental question: How did Weeks intend for me to interpret his statement that it was "inadvisable" for me to talk to the AEC compliance inspector? If the State Department issued a statement that it is inadvisable for the President to visit the village at this time that tells me that something bad could happen to the President if he went to that place. That's how I interpreted Weeks' statement. It was an ominous warning, and was no doubt meant to be just that!

One last point, in order for me to "go see the AEC inspector on my own time," I would have had to travel to the AEC Regional Office in Berkeley, which was over five hours away from Eureka one way. Just how did Weeks think that I would be able to pull that off?

> **Allegation #7:** In August 1969, off-scale stray radiation chamber dosimeter readings occurred in three stations of the plant's environmental monitoring program.
>
> **AEC Finding:** True; however, the stray chambers are set to go off scale at a low 10 milliroentgens. They have gone off scale at other times, sometimes because of vandalism, etc., but are still recorded as off scale. Each stray chamber is backed up by a thermoluminescent dosimeter (TLD) and a film badge at the same location. Comparison of the TLD, film badge, and stray chamber readings for this period showed correlation and all readings were within an acceptable range.

COMMENT: Those environmental monitoring stations around the plant were there for a very good reason. The AEC finding that referenced vandalism as a possible cause for the off-scale readings, was in this case, utter nonsense. It's true that vandalism can cause erratic or off-scale readings. These particular environmental dosimeters were two per station, which makes for a total of six, not three, and they were all down the prevailing wind-line from the plant during the monitoring period in question. I asked to see the results of the film badge readings for the same period and PG&E plant management refused my request.

Besides all the foregoing, the overriding reasons for the bulk of the off-scale readings over time was due to the increasing levels of radiation releases from the 250-foot radioactive gaseous waste discharge stack caused by the breakdown of the original stainless steel fuel cladding that was loaded in the reactor. This general problem made necessary a more frequent reading of those environmental dosimeters from what was originally planned for in the initial start up of the plant. Let there be no mistake, the ACE investigators definitely knew this when they conducted their investigation. This finding makes a mockery of the AEC's role for thorough and responsible regulatory conduct!

> **Allegation #8:** The high-level waste storage vault used by PG&E at the plant presents a radiation safety problem due to airborne radioactive material.
>
> **AEC Finding:** No substantiation for the allegation was found. Radioactive materials placed in the vault were either placed in drums or wrapped in plastic prior to deposit in the vault. There was no indication that the integrity of the drums or plastic bags had been penetrated.

COMMENT: Did the AEC investigators actually remove the biological top shield and look into the vault? I think not! For the AEC investigators to say, "There was no indication that the integrity of the . . . plastic bags had been penetrated" had to result from one of two things. The AEC investigators either accepted the word of plant management or they outright lied about it. The fact is that the plastics bags that were put into the vault often had sharp objects in them and when other things were thrown on top of them, punctures to the bags would occur.

It was important to get the new waste materials into the vault as quickly as possible because they were extremely "hot" (radioactively speaking).

Removing the lid of the vault was not an easy task because a chain hoist was used to raise the heavy reinforced concrete lid weighing several tons. Once the lid was in the air; it had to be pushed off the vault using an overhead track system. The process had to be reversed and the lid realigned over the vault to reinstall it. PG&E approved a suggestion (#19-1000) on May 16, 1966, to install an electric hoist over the high-level waste storage vault in order to reduce the amount of time employees would be working in and around the vault with the lid removed. This would have significantly reduced radiation exposure to personnel. The company never installed the electric hoist! I did, however, receive a monetary award of $15 and accolades from the suggestion committee for making the suggestion.[288]

> **Allegation #9:** Accidental spill of aged reactor water in the low-level storage area of the plant.
>
> **AEC Finding:** True; however, PG&E conducted a survey and cleanup of the area. The Control Technician's Log for August 28, 1969, indicates that contamination levels in the area did not exceed 100 counts per minute, a negligible

amount.

COMMENT: The Humboldt Bay Power Plant reactor water was extremely "hot" (radioactively speaking) and had the full range of fission byproducts in it. The spill was not dealt with for an unknown amount of time. When radioactive liquid is spilled on a surface like the floor, it evaporates leaving particulate matter that can blow around like dust, which becomes an airborne problem. This radioactive "dust" can then be inhaled if an employee is not wearing a protective breathing mask. Employees should not breathe in any amount of radioactive particulate matter for obvious reasons. Again the AEC downplayed the seriousness of the concern and the measurement expressed in the AEC "finding" doesn't make any sense. Was it 100 counts per minute per square foot of smearable radioactive contamination or was it a GM reading held in various locations. I have to assume the survey, if one was actually conducted, refers to smearable radioactive contamination for the reasons previously cited but then the measurement stated in the AEC finding is not properly quantified, which makes the statement totally meaningless.

There is no indication in the finding of whether an isotope study was performed on the radioactive samples collected, again, if indeed a survey of the area was actually made.

> **Allegation #10:** The settings on the hand-and-foot counter alarms used by PG&E during plant shutdown periods were higher than the usual release limits in effect at the plant.
>
> **AEC Finding:** The calibration of these alarms is very difficult due to the low levels of radiation over background being measured. The varying calibration settings for the alarms resulted from PG&E attempts to arrive at a setting, which would permit the alarms to function properly. AEC has no regulation requirement with respect to the calibration or alarm points of hand-and-foot counters.

COMMENT: This "allegation" was one of the more contentious issues that caused PG&E management to close ranks and initiate the company inspired Bert Jones investigation into what PG&E eventually called "acts tantamount to industrial sabotage." Forrest Williams and I raised it at the May 20 safety meeting because the hand-and-foot counter was allowing employees to leave the plant with contamination on them during a recent major refueling outage. Williams discovered one employee who had returned to the plant with radioactive contamination on him, which was subsequently covered up. There are pages of testimony in the transcript of my Unemployment Insurance Appeals Board Hearing regarding this issue. Since it is too voluminous to quote the entire testimony regarding this incident, a few pertinent portions of it are provided here to reveal PG&E's way of doing business and the company's attitude towards radiation safety. After PG&E's attorney, Mr. Brown, stated he had "no further questions" for PG&E supervisor, John Kamberg, the Referee took over:[289]

THE REFEREE: Mr. Kamberg, at a safety meeting, is one of the purposes of the safety meeting for persons in attendance to call to management's attention conditions that they regard unsafe?

Mr. Kamberg: Yes.

THE REFEREE: Assuming then for the moment that Mr. Rowen believed he had some factual basis for the matters he brought up, bringing them up would not have been improper, would it?

Mr. Kamberg: If he was sincere about it; if he believed there was this danger, I believe your statement is correct . . .

THE REFEREE: Would the making of accusations rather than asking questions, would that also be proper at the safety meeting if the individual believes his accusations are factual and that they do relate to a dangerous condition?

Mr. Kamberg: Well, I don't know if that would be for me to decide. I don't think I would go out to a meeting and make an accusation. I think I would inform them in a way by a question rather than by accusation. Whether it's proper, I don't know.

Mr. Brown (PG&E attorney): . . . Getting back to the safety meeting, safety meetings in general at your facility. If an individual feels that something is dangerous, he knows or thinks he knows of a condition that is dangerous, is it proper for him to state it at the safety meeting?

Mr. Kamberg: Definitely. In fact I think one time or another I advised Bob if he felt he was not getting answers from individuals to use this as a method of getting answers, bring them up as something that is going to be in the minutes of the safety meeting, to get his answers in that way. But in no way did I advise him to make accusations against the company.

Mr. Brown (PG&E attorney): Well, in general, if you are talking about a work situation and you're saying the work situation is dangerous, by inference, you are, of course, accusing the company, are you not? The company is responsible for the conditions?

Mr. Kamberg: Well, yes. But in my opinion there is a slight difference. If you are asking a question, you're asking the person, asking him to explain why. You're not saying you're wrong. You're saying, show me why my idea is wrong. In my opinion there is a difference.

Mr. Brown: In your opinion, in what way did you regard Williams and Rowen?

Mr. Kamberg: In regard to Rowen's first statement I'd take it as an inquiry. It's kind of hard to answer an inquiry. In the case of the second statement he made there, about the hand and foot monitor, I think this was an out-and-out accusation of negligence on the part of management.

COMMENT: It needs be pointed out that John Kamberg was by this time a member of management, having been recently promoted to the newly created position of nuclear instrumentation foreman from within the ranks of the nuclear control technician group.

THE REFEREE: All right. Are you saying that an individual who thinks management is being negligent, and in a way he believes exposes persons to danger, should not say that at a safety meeting?

Mr. Kamberg: Well, here again, as it was pointed out once before, I don't believe Bob ever questioned me on this point. I am his supervisor, in charge of that instrument. I don't believe he ever brought this question to me. I may be wrong. I don't recall it. So first off he didn't go through the right channels.

Mr. Brown: Is it your recollection, as it's states there, that Mr. Rowen said the settings were deliberately set?

Mr. Kamberg: Mr. Rowen had.

THE REFEREE: Not that he had.

Mr. Brown: Mr. Rowen had accused management of deliberately setting the settings on the hand-and-foot-monitor too high. I underscore the word "deliberately."

Mr. Kamberg: I understand it that way.

Mr. Brown: Does that create any feeling on your part whether this was an accusation or question?

Mr. Kamberg: Definitely. That management had deliberately set them high for a purpose.

Mr. Brown: Perhaps I misunderstood your testimony on that point earlier. But being a layman in this, perhaps I have had a very false impression in which case you certainly should clear it up. I got the impression from listening to you that you were saying that that was exactly what was done, that you had done it yourself.

Mr. Kamberg: Yes I had done it myself, but I might add at this time I was a control technician. I was not management. [Kamberg was promoted to management in early May 1970 and the major refueling outage took place during the previous several weeks] I never consulted management whether I should or shouldn't. I did it as a labor saving device for myself. In other words, it saved me from having to survey 15 to 20 people, however many were coming across, surveying each one individually. I could do the survey on one and find he was not contaminated and check and raise the alarm setting on the hand and foot monitor and let the rest of them use it as that. I knew the hand-and-foot-monitor was not doing what it was supposed to be doing. It was, in fact watching for 100 counts above background. I knew that because I checked it out. It was my responsibility.

The company attorney summed up with the following final question:[290]

Mr. Brown: Do I understand, Mr. Kamberg, you took this statement made by Mr. Rowen (at the May 20th safety meeting) to be an accusation that the machine was deliberately set too high by management so it would be possible for people to go without setting the alarm off?

Mr. Kamberg: That is the way I understand it.

FURTHER COMMENT: I was sure the Referee saw through Kamberg's testimony, the motivation behind it, the obvious coaching and prepping that had previously taken place, the inconsistencies, and Kamberg's obvious high level of discomfort with the whole affair, but I did not want to take a chance that the Referee adequately understood the complexities of Kamberg's testimony. After all, I knew Kamberg. We had worked together for years and his body language and facial expression were easy for me to read, and at the same time I could see the Referee struggling with the subject matter. So I decided to zero in on Kamberg's testimony, which meant on Kamberg himself, totally for the benefit of the Referee. Clearly, I was not comfortable with doing this but I decided it needed to be done. I opened my cross-examination of Kamberg with the following:[291]

Mr. Rowen: I would like to ask you now, do you recall specifically, do you recall how long ago it was when the alarm settings were set prior to May 20 and who set them?

Mr. Kamberg: You mean officially by management?

Mr. Rowen: Officially by management.

Mr. Kamberg: I would think in the neighborhood of 1964, '65. Mr. Kennedy set up the alarm settings and had a note on the front of the instrument where they were set and they were not to be changed.

Mr. Rowen: Was that note on there May 20, 1970?

Mr. Kamberg: I couldn't swear to it. I don't believe it was.

Mr. Rowen: Were, in fact, the alarm settings above the release limits when you and I investigated this in the afternoon of May 20, 1970?

Mr. Kamberg: This one instance, yes; the two other instances – Well, now, just a moment. I would have to review the yellow record on it. I don't remember what the background was. They were set at 600 counts per line.

Mr. Rowen: Mr. Referee, as a matter of record, I subpoenaed the yellow card as one of the documents.

THE REFEREE: Will the attorney for the company undertake to present that card at the next hearing?

Mr. Brown: Yes.

THE REFEREE: Fine.

Mr. Rowen: I have a number of questions I would like to ask relating to your job knowledge about the hand-and-foot counter. When we investigated it that afternoon, who initiated the investigation?

Mr. Kamberg: You did.

Mr. Rowen: And you and I worked together, my being under your supervision?

Mr. Kamberg: Right.

Mr. Rowen: We found the background to be at a certain level. I won't specify the level at this point. We do have it on the record, on the yellow card.

Mr. Kamberg: Okay.

Mr. Rowen: Did we find the release limits – alarm setting to be above the release, above this stated background by 40counts?

Mr. Kamberg: Purely by memory. It could be official if those yellow cards were present. You cannot set the thing at exactly 100 counts.

Mr. Rowen: This is true. This is not my question. My question – On direct you testified that the setting was instead 40 counts above the release.

Mr. Kamberg: Forty counts?

Mr. Rowen: Forty counts. That is what you testified to.

Mr. Kamberg: I don't recall that.

Mr. Rowen: I think the record will bear it out.

Mr. Kamberg: I don't recall making that statement.

Mr. Rowen: My case in point being on May 20 was the reactor fired off and under full load?

Mr. Kamberg: I don't know. I am not aware what the load actually was. It was under way.

Mr. Rowen: At critical?

Mr. Kamberg: Yes.

Mr. Rowen: Let me ask you this. During the outage where this problem was at issue, would the background indeed have been the same, greater than, or less than the May 20th background?

Mr. Brown: I am going to object to this line of questioning.

Mr. Rowen: I am establishing – INTERRUPTED

Mr. Brown: You are limited to cross-examination on what I introduced into the record.

THE REFEREE: You are mistaken about that, sir. We do not – (INTERRUPTED)

Mr. Brown: I realize you don't follow the strict rules. As a matter of due process and fairness there has to be a certain limitation to cross-examination. The main essence of my objection is that the questioning doesn't at all seem to bear on what we are trying to get at here.

Mr. Rowen: I will state for the referee the point I want to make. During the outage when the reactor was shut down the background on the hand-and-foot counter was much less than on May 20th, yielding a greater spread between the alarm settings, release limits, and the background during the outage.

Mr. Brown: My reason for objecting, our introduction of evidence related to your accusations we had deliberately set something too high.

Mr. Rowen: This is exactly what I want to get to. I have witnesses and documentary evidence to show — (INTERRUPTED)

Mr. Brown: We realize this is a very liberal-type proceeding. It would appear we would be spending an endless amount of time that will prove nothing when we get through.

THE REFEREE: Well, it seems to me that it is material. The claimant is attempting to show the statements he made at the safety meeting were essentially well founded.

Mr. Brown: His statement at the meeting was there was a deliberate setting.

THE REFEREE: He is now attempting to prove that.

Mr. Brown: All right. Ask the question.

Mr. Rowen: The question was: Based on his job knowledge and experience, would the background have been lower during the outage than during the afternoon of May 20, 1970?

Mr. Kamberg: Are you asking me?

Mr. Brown: He is asking you.

Mr. Kamberg: I would say that the background would be lower during the outage than it would be while you're on line.

Mr. Rowen: At a later date, making reference to the yellow card and the information contained thereon –

THE REFEREE: Incidentally, the referee will appreciate it if the parties, during the recess of this hearing, if you care to do so, I would appreciate it if you each submit some material explaining these matters in more detail, these technical matters.

Mr. Brown: It was prepared with response to these questions. If you would like, I will be happy to give you a copy.

THE REFEREE: Will you give a copy to Mr. Rowen if you have a copy?

Mr. Brown: I have only one copy but I will get one for him.

THE REFEREE; Mr. Rowen, you can express your agreement or disagreement with the – to the relevant parts of that document. If you need to supplement it, you may do so.

Mr. Brown: At the next meeting?

THE REFEREE: In writing so I will know more about the technical matters, which apparently have some pertinence. Off the record.

(Discussion off the record.)

Back on the record.

Mr. Rowen: You stated in your testimony that you don't really remember whether I talked to you or not during the outage about the hand-and-foot counter, is that correct?

Mr. Kamberg: I don't recall whether you did or not. If you can point out an incident where you did and then maybe I can recall.

Mr. Rowen: Do you have knowledge of the fact that I talked with Don Woods, who was the rad protection control technician on duty during the outage?

Mr. Kamberg: About what, Bob?

Mr. Rowen: About the hand-and-foot counter alarm settings were set too high

Mr. Kamberg: Yes, I think there were occasions when the point was brought up many times.

Mr. Rowen: During the outage, whether you brought it up or someone else, you, Don, or me, whatever the point had been brought up. I am asking if you have specific knowledge about me relating this to the control technician on rad protection during the outage. Do you have any knowledge of that?

Mr. Kamberg: It may have been you. I can't swear to it.

Mr. Rowen: Another question on the same subject. Do you have specific knowledge of Ray Skidmore, another control technician, approaching Jerry Boots during the outage on the same subject about the hand-and-foot counter?

Mr. Kamberg: No; if specific knowledge, no. Anything along that order would be hearsay.

Mr. Rowen: There was some hearsay?

Mr. Brown: I object. We are here to find out what he knows of his own direct personal knowledge. We are not interested in hearsay.

THE REFEREE: Hearsay is admissible in these hearings as long as it appears to be material.

Mr. Brown: Let's go on and finish expeditiously.

THE REFEREE: We simply do not proceed in the manner they precede in court.

Mr. Brown: Mr. Referee, I think I have been patient up to this point. The form of his question, to begin with, is not easily answerable. It's hearsay. It doesn't establish anything if he found out.

THE REFEREE: Would you repeat the question if you are

still interested in the answer?

Mr. Rowen: Yes. Do you have knowledge of Mr. Raymond Skidmore approaching Jerry Boots, the rad protection engineer, concerning the hand-and-foot counter alarm settings being set too high?

Mr. Kamberg: Personal knowledge, no.

Mr. Rowen: Hearsay is admissible. Did you hear any talk about it?

Mr. Kamberg: Yes. I heard considerable talk about it in the lab prior to being supervisor when –

Mr. Rowen: I am talking about –

Mr. Kamberg: There was a lot of talk of this nature. Since I have been a supervisor, that outlet of information has more or less ceased. I believe you're aware of that, Bob. Once you're a supervisor you're not part of the bull sessions any more. You don't get the feedback, hearsay, information you're looking for.

Mr. Rowen: My final question. You discussed a labor saving device by turning the alarm settings up and down on the hand-and-foot counter as you desired to without talking to management about it?

Mr. Kamberg: Yes.

Mr. Rowen: This is while you were a control technician?

Mr. Kamberg: Right, I believe.

Mr. Rowen: Looking back on it, as a member of management now, would you say this is a poor-working-performance type of thing, inadequate, failure to follow instructions, something along those lines?

Mr. Kamberg: Definitely. I would hate to have my crew doing that.

Mr. Rowen: What would you do?

Mr. Kamberg: I would ask them not to.

Mr. Rowen: As simple as that?

Mr. Kamberg: Yes.

Mr. Rowen: Would you document it?

Mr. Kamberg: I don't think so.

Mr. Rowen: In the type of log you were keeping on me?

Mr. Kamberg: As I already testified to I was instructed by my boss to keep that log, Bob. You're asking me if I would to it personally.

Mr. Rowen: Okay, I am finished.

Mr. Brown: Nothing further.

THE REFEREE: Thank you all very much.

FUTHER COMMENT: Going back over the testimony of Kamberg and the arguments of the company attorney in the form of objections and his unwillingness to accept the Referee's procedures of the Hearing for getting to the truth, it reveals how difficult it would be for anyone to get "inside" information about unsafe practices and how easy it is for PG&E to conceal them from the public.

> **Allegation #11:** Contaminated pipe was sold as scrap to a scrap dealer.
>
> **AEC Finding:** No substantiation for the allegation was found. One piece of pipe from the same lot, which had not been taken off the premises was found to contain minimal amount of contamination inside the pipe and did not present a hazard from a public health and safety standpoint. It is not appropriate to infer that because one piece of pipe from a lot contained a minimal amount of contamination that therefore the rest of the lot was also contaminated.

COMMENT: Who wrote this finding? Sounds like the creative thinking of PG&E's very own Jerome Boots and Edgar Weeks. Did the AEC investigators ask for the paper trail on the unconditional release of the pipe? Did the AEC investigators review the Radiation Control Standards and the requirements contained in the AEC's very own Operating License No. DPR-7 issued to PG&E? (review Chapter #7 for a complete accounting of what actually took place)

> **Allegation #12:** PG&E permitted employees to weld and cut contaminated pipe without using protective masks.
>
> **AEC Finding:** No substantiation for this allegation was found.

COMMENT: Mr. Ward and his investigation team did not state this "allegation" properly. One can only wonder why! I explained to Ward in detail a situation in which a welder had entered the pipe tunnel and engaged in his work directly over two other employees, one of whom was myself and the other Mr. Rapp, in the same area without a proper notification being given and the necessary safety precautions followed. The following testimony from the California Unemployment Appeals Board Hearing reveals that the incident did in fact occur!

> **Mr. Rowen:** (Directed to Edgar Weeks) Are you aware of the incident in which a welder started cutting on packing which is probably the highest source, the greatest source of contamination of this kind in the pipe tunnel, when . . . (INTERRUPTED)
>
> **Mr. Weeks:** I don't remember discussing this with you on the morning of May 11th,
>
> **Mr. Brown (PG&E attorney):** I will object to the question on the basis there is no foundation laid to show that of Mr. Rowen was at all affected by this particular incident.
>
> **Mr. Rowen:** I could rephrase my question.
>
> **THE REFEREE:** Just a minute! Just a minute! I think the foundation is general. I think what we have here quite clearly is

a stipulation in which Mr. Rowen had a very different idea of safety and what was necessary for safety in this radiation situation from his supervisors. And, I certainly feel it had a lot to do with his discharge. Therefore, I think it is material. I'd like to hear the answer to the question.

Mr. Weeks: Would you restate the question?

Mr. Rowen: I'll restate the question. During this discussion (on May 11th) did I inform you of the fact that the welder had gone into pipe tunnel and worked just above our heads, mine and Terry Rapp's, a supervisor, cutting on or heating a packing line without any notification given to either Mr. Rapp or myself. Do you recall anything about that?

Mr. Weeks: I don't recall discussing it that morning, no.

Mr. Rowen: Do you recall the incident in general from any discussions?

Mr. Weeks: Yes. I think I heard about the incident. I surely can't remember the details of it.[292]

FUTHER COMMENT: It should be pointed out that I was able to get some answers to questions that PG&E would have preferred not to answer because plant management did not know just what evidence I had in my possession and what I could have, therefore, pulled out of my brief case to prove them lying. This would have been extremely embarrassing to the huge egos I was dealing with. I believe the AEC could have done a much better job of investigating my allegations had the regulatory effort been more legitimately concerned with the regulatory responsibilities entrusted to it by the American public! It would have been much more meaningful for the AEC to have had PG&E officials testify under oath rather than the "cozy informal manner" used in the facility's front office over a cup of coffee.

Allegation #13: PG&E permitted "crud" to build up at the primary reactor water sample station that resulted in high-level radiation exposures which were greatly reduced by the addition of shielding and remote tools approximately six months after the matter was brought to the attention of management.

AEC Finding: As indicated in the allegation, the matter was corrected by PG&E. The matter was not investigated further.

COMMENT: Another example of the AEC letting PG&E off the hook. The reactor water sampling station had become a huge problem for technicians who had to collect reactor water samples daily for analysis in the radiochemistry lab. There was high-level radiation exposure at the sampling station for the reasons stated. While it's true plant management eventually had a biological shielding wall installed and remote extension handling tools made, it took an incredible six months and my constant complaining about the problem to get it solved. This did not endear me with Edgar Weeks, Jerome Boots, and the rest of plant management (review Chapter 2). The AEC simply concluded that the problem had been corrected and that was the end of it!

One would think the AEC would have been concerned about how long it took PG&E to correct the problem, the unnecessary exposure of employees to a high level radiation field, and the treatment of an employee who persisted on having plant management correct the problem (all of these issues were clearly presented and explained to the AEC, obviously to no avail).

> **Allegation #14:** PG&E permitted "crud" to build up at the off-gas sampling station that resulted in high-level radiation exposures which were reduced by the addition of shielding and extension handles.

> **AEC Finding:** As indicated by the allegation, the matter was corrected by PG&E. The matter was not investigated further.

COMMENT: As was the case with the reactor water radiation safety issue, the AEC did not address what it took to get PG&E to "correct" the problem. Employees were unnecessarily receiving high radiation exposures and I constantly raised this issue with plant management with no success until I took it to the December 12, 1967, company safety meeting, which brought me much grief! Again, the PG&E retaliatory response directed at me was of no concern to the AEC. This was a hard lesson for me to learn regarding the regulatory function or, should I say, the lack thereof!

> **Allegation #15:** Even though the ring finger of an employee was purposely exposed to a radiation source, the film was reported by the personnel monitoring company as zero.

> **AEC Finding:** No date of the incident was reported. No record of any such exposure was found. The personnel monitoring company has a reputation for reliability.

COMMENT: I wonder if the AEC actually checked on the reliability of the personnel monitoring company. How did the AEC determine whether this "reputation" was actually deserved? Or did the AEC just stand behind the PR shield of claims made by this private company? I also learned that this company would not provide exposure records directly to a former employee who requested them because PG&E controlled the release of such information.

One employee had a film badge reading returned from the radiation monitoring company PG&E was using with exactly 5,000 mr on it. If it had gone over, it would have been a serous violation. The employee knew that he had received more than the allowable 5,000 mr for that reporting period but PG&E covered it up and nothing was done about it!

> **Allegation #16:** A chemist (non-PG&E employee) stored radioactive samples without the knowledge of PG&E in an unshielded cabinet, which samples were later discovered and disposed of.

> **AEC Finding:** As indicated in the allegation, the matter was corrected by PG&E. The matter was not further investigated.

COMMENT: Why not? The ACE glossed over this problem. The handling of this matter by the AEC was tantamount to a cover-up of a potentially embarrassing plant practice of improper training of transient (temporary) workers in the nuclear unit. Again, I underwent "counseling sessions" because of my troublemaking ways, and again the AEC just ignored the efforts of plant management to keep employees in line.

> **Allegation #17:** Offsite PG&E employees (traveling maintenance crews) were not sufficiently trained in radiation (protection) matters.

> **AEC Finding:** PG&E has a training program for such employees, which appears to be satisfactory.

COMMENT: Nothing could have been further from the truth. One might ask just how the AEC arrived at that conclusion. We were constantly dealing with travelers who presented problems to themselves and others.

One specific example concerned a traveling mechanic who was working in the turbine enclosure area immediately after lunch. I found him running his finger around inside his mouth along his gums to clean out the remains of a peanut butter sandwich he had eaten (review Chapter 4 - Transient employees as radiation sponges). He did have his surgeon gloves on but they were black with grime from the work he was doing on the open turbine. The turbine was powered by highly radioactive steam that was coming directly from the reactor. I immediately had him go to the decon station to rinse his mouth out and start the decon process. After I explained why he should not have put his contaminated glove finger in his mouth because it had radioactive particulate matter on it as grime from the turbine blades that he had been working on, he said he no idea that he was doing anything wrong.

> **Allegation #18:** But for the objections of one employee, during the early part of 1970, electricians would have been permitted to calibrate an instrument transmitter in an area where dose rates were 3 to 4 roentgens per hour at the work location.

> **AEC Finding:** As indicated in the allegation, PG&E corrected the matter. A review of film badge records for the first three quarters of 1970 showed no excessive exposure to PG&E employees.

COMMENT: Again, the AEC failed to address the real problem. To begin with, those employees should have never been allowed to perform that work in that particular location without proper biological shielding. As seen throughout the AEC findings, the agency's regulatory function was void of any effort to address needless and senseless radiation exposure and to protect employees from retaliation who raised safety concerns. This incident provides another peephole into the ugly inner workings of the "regulated" and the "regulators," and exposes the attitudes and philosophies of both.

> **Allegation #19:** Although a PG&E employee exposure record for 1967 showed 5 rads (the annual exposure limit), he believed his actual exposure exceeded 5 rads.

AEC Finding: A review of dosimeter record weekly cards for the employee indicated that the 5 rad limitation was not exceeded. The employee was assigned non-radiation work for the last two or three months of 1967.

COMMENT: Pocket dosimeters are never used to provide an official record of radiation exposure. They are used to estimate the amount of exposure the employee is receiving each day and on each "hot" job. The dosimeters were always used in tandem with the film badge, which were always placed together in a location on the employee closest to the "hottest" source of radiation (if that was known, which unfortunately wasn't always the case).

For example, if the greatest radiation source was overhead, the dosimeters and film badge would be worn on the cap covering the head of the employee. However, the real issue with this "allegation" was the "exact" exposure of 5 rads reported by the film badge company. What are the odds of ending up with exactly 5 rads of exposure? The odds are much better with the state lottery! The employee in question knew that he had exceeded the 5R limit proving the film badge company PG&E was using was not reliable (review Comment to AEC Allegation #15).

Allegation #20: Employee suggestion that longer cables be used on an off-gas detector, thereby permitting it to be moved and worked on out of a high radiation dose area, was not adopted by PG&E.

AEC Finding: This is a matter of management prerogative. No AEC regulation covers the matter in the absence of specific evidence of personnel overexposure occurring.

COMMENT: This is a perfect example of the AEC not concerning itself with employees receiving needless and senseless amounts of radiation exposure. This attitude, this philosophy was especially maddening to me. As radiation monitors, nuclear control technicians subscribed to the principle of keeping radiation exposure to a minimum; we believed this was good radiation protection policy and it guided all of our decision making on a daily basis. Our radiation protection training was ostensibly based on keeping radiation exposure to the lowest possible level.

PG&E's own Radiation Protection Training Manual states "The basic purpose of a Radiological Protection Program is to reduce to an absolute minimum the possibility of adversely affecting an individual's health and welfare."[293] However, when PG&E had to spend some money to make things safer for atomic workers, as in the case of installing longer cables mentioned in this "allegation" that would have clearly reduced personnel radiation exposure, it was a different story best described as pure lip service by PG&E management. This was simply PR stuff that provided PG&E a reputation for safety that was not deserved!

Allegation #21: Employees were permitted to work without protective masks in the Reactor Control Room at times when the airborne radioactive contamination levels exceeded plant standards and required such masks. Employees under the foregoing circumstances were permitted to go home with contaminated clothing.

AEC Finding: True; however, PG&E took corrective action by modifying its air intake for the air conditioning system. The allegation that employees were permitted to go home with contaminated clothing was not substantiated.

COMMENT: The "allegation" that employees were permitted to go home with contaminated clothing was not substantiated. I wonder why? However, it was true, as noted by the AEC investigators, that employees should have been wearing protective masks in the Reactor Control Room so they wouldn't breathe in radioactive particulate matter but somehow the AEC investigators concluded that the radioactive contamination would not end up on employee clothing. In the Reactor Control Room employees did not wear protective clothing over their street clothes or the protective booties over their shoes. They just wore their normal clothing. Another AEC "finding" that makes absolutely no sense! This again points to the regulators being in bed with the regulated, a recurring theme throughout my *Diary*.

Allegation #22: In the spring of 1970, stack effluent from the plant contaminated the cars in the parking lot and no corrective action was taken by PG&E, and the employees were permitted to drive their cars home.

AEC Finding: Contamination did occur, but PG&E made a prompt survey of the cars and determined that the contamination levels were below the Department of Transportation smearable radioactive contamination release limits of 100 counts per minute per square foot (cpm/sq. ft).

COMMENT: With the exception "contamination did occur," this finding is untrue! Where did the AEC investigators get the information they used to reach this conclusion?

Those cars were contaminated and the contamination levels exceeded what was stated in the finding. Not only that, DOT regulations had noting to do with the contamination levels on our vehicles in the PG&E parking lot of the nuclear facility. All of this was under the jurisdiction of the Atomic Energy Commission. Ward was simply passing the buck for the ignorant and gullible public!

I remember what happened to me when I went to the parking lot on my own to check my car; I was absolutely furious with what I found. Unfortunately I had no place to turn but to express my feelings to plant management, which I did with extremely spiteful results.

Imagine for a moment that the company would have admitted to the actual radioactive contamination on the employee's vehicles that they were going to drive home after work that day. What would that have looked like for PG&E?

The vehicles were in direct line with the South Bay Elementary School that was just 400 yards downwind from the nuclear facility. What would that have looked like if the problem had been made public? We're talking about smearable radioactive contamination coming out of the 250 foot radioactive gaseous waste discharge stack of the nuclear plant; that's particulate matter that can be compared to dust that's blowing in the wind, except this dust is radioactive with radioactive isotopes resulting from the fission process in the reactor.

Where in the hell was the AEC in all of this?

Allegation #23: PG&E cleaned up plant in anticipation of AEC inspection.

AEC Finding: No substantiation for this allegation was found. AEC has and is conducting unannounced inspections at the PG&E plant.

COMMENT: The AEC finding is utter nonsense, which I cannot state emphatically enough! I worked in the nuclear facility from 1964 to 1970, and never once did I witness an unannounced AEC inspection. On the other hand, I can remember many times when we were told to clean up citable conditions because the AEC compliance inspectors from the AEC Regional Office in Berkeley were planning a trip to the plant.

PG&E knew ahead of time of all AEC compliance inspections. It was clearly my position that the AEC should inspect the plant in its normal operating condition rather than in some "prepared state" just for an inspection. I could not have made this point any clearer to the AEC Chief Investigator, J. J. Ward, at our September 7, 1971, meeting.

After providing Ward some examples of PG&E cleaning up citable violations before the AEC inspectors arrived at the plant, Ward responded. "Well, if they cleaned it up, what's your point?"[294]

I dug in my heels and emphatically stated, "Well, my point is that these inspections were not representative of the plant in its normal operating condition."[295]

Ward's quick and clearly argumentative response was simply, "Well, could you ever expect it to be?"[296]

Weeks testified in the California Unemployment Appeals Board Hearing in response to a question by the Referee that the AEC was "required by legislation to make one unexpected visit per year."[297] This tidbit of testimony by Weeks was never challenged during the Hearing but I am confident that plant management did in fact receive advance notice of every single AEC compliance inspection.

In response to the Referee's very next question, Weeks gave the following testimony:[298]

> When I find out an inspection is coming and we get a tentative date, I notify the supervisors and I say in the message, be sure your house is in order, fellows. And, I'm sure they get the word out. Just like, if you're driving along and somebody

says, there's a black and white car, and you glance down at the speedometer, I mean it's . . . quite frankly, yes, I get the word out to my supervisors to make sure everything is in order. We're going to have an inspection.

FURTHER COMMENT: A careful review of and a thoughtful reflection on Weeks' testimony reveals an attitude and philosophy that, when coupled with the attitude of the AEC Chief Investigator, J. J. Ward, again clearly paints the unmistakeable cozy relationship between the regulated and the regulators.

Allegation #24: Radiation waste material was improperly packed and stored prior to shipment for disposal.

AEC Finding: True; however, PG&E repacked the leaking containers and a survey of the containers and the area indicated that the contamination levels were below DOT smearable radioactive contamination release limits of 100 cpm/sq. ft.

COMMENT: J. J. Ward did not properly state the allegation. The first part of Ward's statement is true in that, "Radiation waste materials was improperly packed and stored," however, it was not repacked and the materials were loaded on a truck and shipped with radioactive liquids dripping from the belly of the truck (review Chapter 4 – An Immoral and Illegal Transport of Soggy Radiation Waste Boxes).

Who did J. J. Ward and his investigation team talk to and what records did they review? I was the control technician on duty assigned to that job and what the AEC "finding" is laying claim to is patently false! Another cover up of a totally unacceptable violation and it's abundantly clear that both the AEC and PG&E must share in the culpability of this corporate misdeed and the unsuspecting public must once again suffer the consequences of it!

Allegation #25: PG&E permitted off-gas samples to be analyzed in an unsafe manner.

AEC Finding: Not True.

COMMENT: This "allegation" was not stated correctly. Mr. Ward knew that my complaint pertained to the problem Forrest had with Edgar Weeks. It referred to the Forrest Williams incident when Ed Weeks required him to work in the radiochemistry lab, which involved analyzing off-gas samples. Williams refused to do it because of an open wound, which had not completely healed. Edgar Weeks sent him home and the company subsequently fired him the next day. Williams was reinstated nine months later because the Arbitrator found that Williams was justified in refusing to do the work while his wound had not yet completely healed (review Chapter 11). The AEC investigators chose to word this allegation the way it reads so they could conclude "Not True," which again made a mockery of the AEC's regulatory role.

It's obvious the AEC wanted to avoid getting involved in the labor-management dispute so the investigators simply decided to lie about the whole affair and quite frankly they got away with it. No employee should be required to do unsafe work in the nuclear workplace, especially when the applicable radiation control standards prohibit it!

Allegation #26: Possible inadequate sampling and measurement for radioactive contamination levels of the discharge from the laundry waste tank.

AEC Finding: Not true.

COMMENT: Here again the AEC investigators lied. What is untrue is the AEC statement that there was "Possible inadequate sampling and measurement for radioactive contamination, etc." There was, in fact, inadequate sampling and measurement for radioactive contamination levels of the discharge from the laundry waste tank. The AEC investigators did not state the basis for their finding because they did not have one!

Who did they interview? What records did they review? Did the AEC investigators have those responsible for handling the discharge from the laundry waste tank demonstrate and explain how that work was done? For example, there were extremely "hot" coveralls, booties, caps, and hoods that were worn during the incore flushing work under the reactor that had to be "washed." That protective clothing was grossly contaminated and the laundry waste system was totally inadequate to handle the contamination levels that were involved.

Allegation #27: PG&E employee inadequately trained to work with radioactive materials, e.g., examining fuel elements.

AEC Finding: The investigation indicated that there was some substance to this allegation. This matter was included in the October 28 notice to the licensee.

COMMENT: Just what does "there was 'some substance' to this allegation" mean? It was clearly a downplay of the seriousness of what could have happened – watered down response to a complaint about a very serious problem by the regulators for the benefit of the regulated (review Chapter 4 – "A potential lethal exposure due to lack of training").

Allegation #28: The current radiation protection personnel employed by PG&E at the plant are inadequately trained.

AEC Finding: The investigation indicated that there was some substance to this allegation. This matter was included in the October 28 notice to the licensee.

COMMENT: Again, just what does "there was 'some substance' to this allegation" mean? What exactly was the AEC referring to? The allegation as stated is a classic red herring by the AEC investigators. My complaint didn't even refer to radiation protection personnel but rather to employees (mechanics, machinists, electricians, welders, and the like) who were put into the radiation controlled areas of the plant to perform work, and specifically identified transient workers brought into the facility as radiation sponges. Another downplay of the seriousness of the matter, this time a twisting of the facts by the regulators, to fit a scenario that begged the real question – all for the benefit of the regulated (review Chapter 4 – "Transient workers used as radiation sponges sorely lacked radiation protection training").

Allegation #29: PG&E permitted the use of a blower to blow away radioactive contamination in work areas without sampling for airborne contamination.

AEC Finding: No substantiation for this allegation was found.

COMMENT: Where did the AEC inspectors look for their "substantiation" of this allegation? Who did they talk to? What records did they review? What would it have taken for the AEC investigators to have substantiated this allegation? Is it reasonable to assume that anyone would admit to violating the radiation control standards and procedures?

Allegation #30: PG&E employee, whose employment was terminated, was not furnished a report of his exposure record within the required period specified in AEC regulations.

AEC Finding: True. Included in October 28 Notice to the licensee.

COMMENT: That employee was none other than Bob Rowen! According to Forrest Williams, he did receive his exposure record in a timely fashion. However, I did not and I eventually discovered why.

Following my termination from the company, I repeatedly asked PG&E for my complete radiation exposure record for the period of my employment at the nuclear facility from March 1964 to June 1970. PG&E would not respond to my request. It was made clear to plant management that I was entitled to a complete record of my exposure to radiation as required by 10 CFR, Part 20 of the federal regulations. I continued to demand the exposure record that PG&E was required by law to provide within a specified time following my termination from the company but that didn't seem to matter to plant management.

When I complained to the AEC investigator, J. J. Ward, about this violation, he simply recorded the matter as "Allegation #30: PG&E employee, whose employment was terminated, was not furnished a report of his exposure within the required period specified in AEC regulation." Ward then stated in his report, "AEC Finding: True. Included in October 28 notice to the licensee."

That was the AEC's complete handling of the matter. There was no review by the AEC of what the exposure report revealed, consequently there was no evaluation of my exposure to radiation during my employment even though I expressed grave concern over the senseless and needless exposures we were receiving. I asked Mr. Ward if he had seen my exposure record at anytime during his investigation. He said he hadn't. I asked Ward if he had even requested to see my exposure record and he said he hadn't done that either.

Mr. Ward stated the AEC was not concerned with the work policies of PG&E in the nuclear plant regarding radiation exposure as long as employees did not exceed 3 rems of exposure per quarter, and no more that 5 rems of exposure per year. The work polices of PG&E was totally within the purview of management prerogative, Ward said. How would the AEC have learned of an overexposure unless PG&E either reported it to the Commission or the AEC took it upon itself to review the exposure records of employees?

I eventually did receive a copy of my radiation exposure record from PG&E around the first part of October 1970 but unfortunately misplaced it before I met with Mr. Ward and his AEC investigation team. For years I have wondered about my actual radiation exposure at Humboldt Bay and believing that I had lost those records, asked the company who provided PG&E the film badge monitoring service for duplicate records. I was told I would need to get that information from PG&E. I sent letters to PG&E's corporate office in San Francisco requesting copies of those records and never received a response to any of them.

However, as I was writing my *Diary* and pouring through my records I found the report that I thought I had lost. It is a five-page report with a cover letter, dated September 20, 1970, signed by Warren A. Raymond, Assistant Plant Superintendent, Humboldt Bay Power Plant. The report provides the "counting results of bioassay and whole body." Very honestly I do not know how to read or what to make of the results that are contained in this portion of the report. However, the rest of the report provides startling information pertaining to "Occupational External Radiation Exposure" to the "Whole Body" (Appendix IV), to the "Skin of Whole Body" (Appendix V), and to the "Hands and Forearms" (Appendix VI).

According to the report on the "whole body exposure to gamma radiation," I exceeded the annual maximum exposure limit on October 14, 1969. The report on the "skin of whole body exposure to gamma and beta radiation," reveals that I exceeded the quarter maximum exposure limit on January 15, 1970, and the annual maximum exposure limit on June 15, 1970.

The most startling data in my radiation exposure record for my entire employment period, not to diminish in any way the significance of the aforementioned data, is the report on the "hands and forearms exposure to gamma radiation." It revealed exceeding the maximum annual limit of 5 rems seven times, and the maximum quarter limit of 3 rems twice during my employment period. The high radiation exposure to my hands and forearms occurred during January 1967 to June 1970, which happened to coincide with the rising radiation dose rate levels associated with the collection and analysis of reactor water and off-gas samples.

> **Allegation #31:** Inadequate training of certain PG&E employees led to said employees handling plutonium-beryllium neutron sources with their hands instead of with remote handling tools.
>
> **AEC Finding:** Because of conflicting information, unable to

substantiate allegation.

COMMENT: What was conflicting about the information? I personally witnessed what happened along with several other employees. Did the AEC find some employee who admitted to what had taken place and others who denied it? Why did the AEC not get to the bottom of what took place? A greater effort should have been made to get to the truth, and PG&E should have been, at the very least, reprimanded for the lack of proper training.

Allegation #32: A cobalt 60 source was dropped to the floor while being handled by certain PG&E employees.

AEC Finding: True. The source was accidentally dropped to the floor; however, proper handling, sampling and cleanup procedures employed by PG&E resulted in no overexposures to employees.

COMMENT: The AEC finding is simply not true! Again, another cover-up!

Allegation #33: PG&E employees were briefed in a (high) radiation (dose-rate) area (2 roentgens per hour field) as to their duties rather than in a radiation-free area.

AEC Finding: No substantiation for this allegation was found.

COMMENT: Utter nonsense! This did take place and more than once to say the least. These kinds of events are hard to prove after they happen. The only way to effectively deal with them is right when they happen but PG&E's established working conditions did not allow for it. Besides, from the AEC's point of view, this kind of thing was the prerogative of company management as long as there were no "over exposures involved," which was stated by Ward often during our September 7 meeting.

Allegation #34: But for the action of one employee, certain PG&E employees would fail to wear their film badges.

AEC Finding: As indicated by the allegation itself, no violation occurred. The matter was not investigated further.

COMMENT: This kind of response by the AEC has already been addressed in previous comments to similar AEC findings. When employees became "troublemakers" by insisting proper radiation procedures be followed, plant management retaliated! Again the AEC considered these kinds of things as internal company affairs and not subject to the purview of the AEC. As a result the AEC looked entirely past the retaliatory conduct of the company.

Allegation #35: A spill of radioactive liquid materials occurred outside the southwest airlock of the refueling building.

Finding: No substantiation for this allegation was found.

COMMENT: Could that be because the spill was covered up? What would it have taken for the AEC to substantiate it? Did company management have to come clean and fess up? If there were some employees willing to admit to it and others who chose to deny it, would the AEC investigators have found "Because of conflicting information, unable to substantiate allegation" as the AEC finding was stated to allegation #31?

Allegation #36: Animals used to test grass near plant for I-131 level were fed mostly commercial feed rather than grass surrounding the plant, thereby making negative test results invalid.

Finding: No substantiation for this allegation was found.

COMMENT: Did the AEC inspectors go to Nilsen's Feed Supply at the corner of Fourth and Broadway Streets in Eureka to check the invoices addressing the amount of commercial rabbit food PG&E purchased? Why did the AEC inspectors choose to say, "Animals" rather than "rabbits" because I gave Mr. Ward a full accounting of what took place and specifically zeroed in on the testing of rabbit thyroids for I-131? Why didn't PG&E keep a log of just how much commercial rabbit food was being given to the rabbits on a daily basis, and why didn't the AEC ask for such a log? Finally, I clearly suggested to Mr. Ward that he and his team should check with the feed store on the amount of commercial rabbit food PG&E had purchased (review Chapter 4 – "PG&E's rabbit project AKA PG&E's ridiculous rabbit caper" for the details).

Allegation #37: Certain PG&E employees showed exposures based on dosimeter results greater by a factor of 50 above that shown on their film badges for the same period of exposures.

AEC Finding: Not true. Personnel monitoring records indicated that there was satisfactory correlation between film badges and dosimeters.

COMMENT: Not true? Did the AEC inspectors inspect records on each individual employee or did they aggregate the data to reach their conclusion? The only way this "allegation" could have been properly investigated was for the inspectors to look at the dosimeter and film badge records for each employee individually from 1965 to 1970 in search of major discrepancies. Would this have been a monumental task? Yes, but it would have been well worth the investigative effort. If they had done that, they would have found the "allegation" to be absolutely true!

Allegation #38: One employee was discouraged by PG&E management from raising specific matters concerning radiation safety during a union safety meeting.

AEC Finding: The matter was not investigated because a PG&E union-sponsored safety meetings is a labor-management matter.

COMMENT: How convenient for the AEC investigators to misstate my complaint letting PG&E once again "off the hook." We were not talking about "union safety meetings." We were talking about "company safety meetings." There's a huge difference! The company did not want radiation safety problems brought up at those company safety meetings because the AEC supposedly reviewed the minutes of those safety meetings and hopefully some action would be taken by the AEC to require PG&E to address the radiation safety issues we were facing.

Some of the employees ended up using the company safety meetings anyway to expose radiation safety problems in the plant, albeit this course of action had its adverse consequences for those who did, and this was especially true for me. My *Diary* addresses two very good examples of what happened to those who used the company safety meetings to express radiation safety problems; the one example was the company safety meeting dated December 12, 1967, and the other was the May 20, 1970, company safety meeting. The AEC investigators chose to ignore the complaint altogether by using a dishonest tactic of misstating the complaint and then standing behind the "labor-management relations shield" argument. Refer to Raymond Skidmore's testimony and Edgar Weeks' testimony regarding the second meeting by Warren Raymond after the December 12, 1967, meeting.

> **Allegation #39:** The number of offsite air samplers was reduced by PG&E from 5 to 1. One air sampler should be located at the nearby school.
>
> **AEC Finding:** True; however, PG&E is not required to maintain a specific number of offsite air samplers at all times for their environmental monitoring program. At the time of the inspection, AEC maintained a number of offsite air samplers including one at the school.

COMMENT: What in the world was the AEC investigator talking about? It's so damned obvious the AEC partnered with PG&E to respond to my complaint.

I made absolutely clear in my complaint to J. J. Ward that PG&E had removed the air sampler from the front of South Bay Elementary School sometime in early 1970. I did not mention anything in my complaint about the removal of any of the other air samplers in PG&E's environmental monitoring program. In fact, at the May 20, 1970, PG&E safety meeting, when I raised hell about the removal of the air sampler in question at the South Bay Elementary School, there were no other air monitors that had been taken out of service at the time. To be clear, the only air sampler that was removed from service was the one at the elementary school (The reasons for PG&E's decision were obvious and are discussed in Chapter 9).

Ward stated in his finding, "At the time of the inspection, AEC maintained a number of offsite air samplers including one at the school." What inspection was he talking about? Did he mean the "investigation" that he conducted a year after I was fired from PG&E? Who knows? Well, one thing was known with absolute certainty, the AEC did not have an air sampler at the elementary school during the entire time I was employed at the Humboldt Bay Nuclear Plant. I know this because I routinely made radiological survey rounds as one of my duties as a nuclear control technician during that entire period.

I contacted the Nuclear Regulatory Commission in August 2010 seeking the answer to the following question: "Did the AEC have a continuous air-sample monitor at the South Bay Elementary School at any time before December 31, 1970?" Victor Dricks, NRC Public Affairs Officer in Arlington Texas, responded telling me the AEC did not have an air sample monitor at the school because, and I quote, "Environmental monitoring programs were the responsibility of the licensee," and in the case of Humboldt Bay, PG&E.

This AEC finding is a revelation that further proves the AEC investigation was a farce. I knew there was no continuous air-sampler maintained by the AEC at the South Bay Elementary School but I needed an independent verification of it for the purpose of writing my *Diary*. The AEC finding clearly stated that the "AEC maintained a number of offsite air samplers, including one at the school."

During my September 7 meeting with Mr. Ward, we had an intense discussion about the off-scale readings of the environmental dosimeters in PG&E's environmental monitoring program. Ward had stated there were three off-scale readings. I corrected him by saying that there were three stations with two chambers per station, which meant there were six off-scale readings, all of which were directly down wind from the plant.

I was dispelling his claim the chambers can give "false readings" which can be caused by any number of things. Again, I said it was not plausible that all six of these chambers would go off scale all at the same time for any of the reasons he mentioned.

Then Ward said that's why we have a backup and he suggested an air sample monitor at the school. We had already talked about PG&E's removal of the continuous air-sample monitor at the school and the hullabaloo that created at the May 20, 1970, safety meeting.

Following my tirade about the "schoolhouse full of kids" and the urgent need to find out why the chambers had off-scale readings because "at least for the moment you don't know what they've been exposed to and for what reasons," the following discussion appeared on the transcription of the tape recording of the September 7, 1971, meeting:[299]

> **Mr. Ward:** (Int'g) When you have a continuous air monitor.
> **Mr. Rowen:** Well, that's – where?
> **Mr. Ward:** At the school.
> **Mr. Rowen:** A continuous air monitor at the school?
> **Mr. Ward:** Yeah.
> **Mr. Rowen:** Not to the best of my knowledge.
> **Mr. Ward:** No. Not to your knowledge but the AEC has one there.

FUTHER COMMENT: Again, this meeting with Ward to discuss the "findings" of his investigation was held on September 7, 1971. The fact that a reporter was present may have elicited the unfounded comment from Ward concerning the AEC air sampler at the school, which did not exist – it never existed!

Connecting the dots reveals a thickening of the PG&E-AEC plot. The

PG&E attorney, Mr. L. V. Brown, had already made a similar statement at my Unemployment Insurance Appeals Board Hearing inferring that the school had its own air sampling program during his cross examination of Raymond Skidmore. The purpose of Brown's statement was to influence the Referee to reach an erroneous conclusion in favor of PG&E.

Brown attempted to accomplish this "planting of the seed" by asking Skidmore, "Well, isn't it a fact that the school conducted its own air sampling program sometime before this meeting (referring to the May 20, 1970, safety meeting)?"[300]

There ensued a very confusing exchange between the attorney and Raymond Skidmore about the differing roles of dosimeters and air samplers in the monitoring program at the school. The PG&E attorney wasn't as dumb as he was letting on; He knew the difference between dosimeters and the air samplers.

Brown even went so far in this ridiculous charade as to ask Skidmore, totally for the benefit of the Referee, "Well, isn't it a fact that the school conducted its own air sampling program, sometime before this meeting?"[301]

I remember that the Eureka *Times-Standard* environmental reporter fell prey to this nonsense advanced by both the company and the AEC when he told me that PG&E's removal of its air sampler was not a major problem because there were others on the school property during the period in question.

I stated unequivocally to the reporter that he had been lied to by both the AEC and PG&E. I made it abundantly clear to the reporter that there was no additional air sampler at the school. I asked the reporter, "Why would PG&E even want to remove the air sampler at the school in 1970 that had been in service since before the startup of the reactor in August 1863? That particular air sampler was the most critical monitoring device in PG&E's entire radiological monitoring system at Humboldt Bay. Then I told the reporter that some time down the road the kids and staff at that school as well as the residents of the Humboldt Hill community during the mid-sixties to early seventies may very well have legitimate legal claims against PG&E and the government for what happened at Humboldt Bay.

> **Allegation #40:** Radioactive material leaking from the spent fuel pool is finding its way into the water table.
> **AEC Finding:** Not true.

COMMENT: This finding is unequivocally false! PG&E had installed five environmental test wells; all of them were inside the plant's security fence. Nuclear control technicians would take samples from those test wells and then analyze them in the 256-channel analyzer and print out the results on an X-Y printer. The procedure used for collecting the samples used a 1" stainless steel tube about 18" long, which we would lower into the well down a casing about 3" in diameter.

After the sample tube filled up with ground water, we would pull it up by the attached rope and pour the water sample into a one gallon plastic jug.

Each jug was marked with the appropriate well number. When all the jugs were full, we would take the samples to the counting lab where they would then be analyzed. After printing the results, we would compare what we came up with to the graphs of the spent fuel pool water. We would continue the counting process over time to look for any changes in the decaying characteristics and compare those results with a book of standards.

The conclusions were clear; some of the ground water samples produced the same graph-characteristics as those of the spent fuel pool water samples, which established that the spent fuel pool was leaking. This was suspected because the drop in the spent fuel pool level, which required adding more demineralized water to the pool on a regular basis, could not be explained simply due to evaporation alone.

Management personnel were involved in every step of the process except for the collection of the samples. This whole process was very well known with a lot of plant personnel involved. How could the AEC investigators come up with the conclusions they did? In fact, a Humboldt Bay Nuclear Power Plant Historical Site Assessment was performed by Enercon Services, Inc., and completed in September 2006. This Site Assessment was part of the decommissioning of the nuclear plant. The following is quoting verbatim the section of the Site Assessment pertaining to the spent fuel pool:[302]

In March 1966, it was discovered that a leak in the spent fuel storage pool liner had developed. Operating procedures were developed to minimize leakage and investigations were conducted to determine the magnitude of any groundwater contamination that could have occurred.

Samples of groundwater from the plant wells, the reactor caisson sump, and two of three test wells did not reveal signs of contamination. One test well drilled north of the spent fuel storage pool (between the pool and the bay) revealed evidence of contamination, but the levels were a factor of 100 below allowable drinking water limits.

The test wells have been monitored regularly since that time and results of the surveillance have indicated no increase in activity.

The methodology used for the Site Assessment involved a review of company documents, property inspections, and personal interviews.

The company documents included: environmental reports, environmental monitoring reports, licensee event reports, plant safety, analyses, radiological surveys, and plant operating logs.

The personal interviews included current and former nuclear plant personnel who were selected based on their employment history at the facility.

These interviews were held during the site inspection

and via telephone during the Historical Site Assessment process. "Interview efforts were focused on personnel who were employed during the time that Unit 3 was in operation. Personnel were interviewed that held positions in maintenance, qualified reactor operators and radiation protection.

FURTHER COMMENT: " . . . Undocumented events were not discovered during this process, but the interviews did prove helpful in assessing the historical operations."[303]

I am compelled to point out a few of things about this report by first asking a couple of questions. To begin with: (1) How reliable were the "company documents," and (2) Who were the company employees with whom the "personal interviews" were conducted? My *Diary* reveals the problem with the company's "environmental reports, environmental monitoring reports, licensee event reports, plant safety, analyses, radiological surveys, and plant operating logs."

PG&E made every effort to ensure these types of "company documents" were void of anything that would cast the nuclear facility in a negative light. Then of course the selection of employees to be interviewed should also be held in suspect. Neither Forrest Williams nor I, two former employees who were willing to tell the truth about the nuclear facility and who had nothing further to lose with PG&E, were ever contacted. I trust my *Diary* will fill in what's missing in the Historical Self Assessment. There is one final note on the Historical Site Assessment (I). Section 5.1 of the report reads:[304]

> This Historical Site Assessment documents those events and circumstances occurring during the history of the facility that contributed to the contamination of portions of the site environs above background levels. Information relevant to changes in the radiological status of the site following publication of the Historical Site Assessment (I) will be considered a part of the ongoing characterization evaluations and decommissioning activities.
>
> These ongoing activities include the expansion of the site groundwater investigation and evaluation of subsurface contamination will drive continuing remediation and/or mitigation efforts as appropriate.

FURTHER COMMENT: This small amount of verbiage in the report appears to be slipping in an admission of "contamination to portions of the site environs" without creating a stir. It's not clear what the intent or motivation is but I can unequivocally state without fear of contradiction that the ground water samples that we collected had the same radioisotopes in them that we found in the nuclear spent fuel storage pool, which proved without question that the spent fuel storage pool was leaking.

Allegation #41: PG&E permitted contaminated tools to be used in the clean machine shop.

AEC Finding: No substantiation was found for this allegation.

COMMENT: I have no idea where this allegation came from. It certainly was not anything I presented to Mr. Ward.

Allegation #42: PG&E permitted contaminated tools to be used in the hot machine shop.

AEC Finding: No substantiation was found for this allegation.

COMMENT: Again, where did this allegation come from? Besides, tools and equipment were often contaminated in the controlled area. We would clean such things as best we could by removing the smearable radioactive contamination but as long as these things remained in the radiation-controlled area, it wasn't "considered" a problem if the employees took the necessary rad protection precautions and followed the required radiation safety procedures.

Allegation #43: PG&E approved employee's safety suggestion (award given) but it was not implemented.

AEC Finding: The use of employee suggestions is within the management prerogative of PG&E. The matter was not investigated.

COMMENT: This allegation had to do with the suggestion of installing an electric hoist over the high-level waste storage vault for the purpose of reducing radiation exposure to personnel. The electric hoist would have replaced an old chain hoist that required a lot more time to operate, thereby exposing personnel to more radiation than was necessary. The company safety committee approved this suggestion and provided a financial award to the employee (which was me) who made the suggestion, but the electric hoist was never installed. This is worthy of mention because PG&E made a big deal out of all the avenues available to employees to seek safety improvements in the plant as a means of trying to prove that I didn't follow them because I simply desired to make trouble for my supervisors and embarrass the company.

Allegation #44: PG&E permits the spent fuel pool to remain uncovered approximately 80% of the time.

AEC Finding: True. There is no requirement that the spent fuel pool be covered.

COMMENT: The spent fuel was designed to be covered up when personnel had no need to access it. Covering up the pool would virtually eliminate the evaporation of extremely contaminated spent fuel pool water and provide another layer of protection to workers who might otherwise accidentally fall into the pool. If the AEC would have been concerned with minimizing radiation exposure to employees as much as it is practical, the ACE would have jumped all over this ongoing practice by the company. After all, how much trouble (especially in terms of cost) would it have been to pull the cover over the entire pool when the pool was not being accessed for whatever reason?

Allegation #45: The seat of the forklift was contaminated.

AEC Finding: True. PG&E records show that forklift was frequently surveyed and decontaminated.

COMMENT: The forklift went in and out of the radiation-controlled area all the time. The seat was contaminated. The contamination was in the seat as well as often on the seat. When the fork lift was surveyed out of the controlled area, I have no doubt that the smearable radioactive contamination was removed each time, what the AEC investigators identified as being "decontaminated." However, what was left was the contamination that could not be "wiped or scrubbed off."

The problem was when the fork lift was in the clean areas of the plant and being used outside in the rain, the seat would become wet and the embedded contamination would then surface and come into contact with workers in their normal street clothes. At the end of the day these workers would then go home without having to survey out because they were never in the controlled area that day; they were just sitting on a radioactively contaminated seat that had become wet due to inclement weather. All this was explained to Mr. Ward so I have to ask, what was he thinking when he and his team conducted their investigation and wrote the AEC finding?

Allegation #46: One PG&E employee has a radiation-related injury to his fingers and fingernails.

AEC Finding: Not True.

COMMENT: The only discussion I had with AEC investigator, J. J. Ward that this "allegation" could possibly relate to was the definite problem Forrest Williams had with the unhealed wound on his finger and how Weeks had handled it. It was in total violation of our radiation protection standards (review Chapter 11). The AEC just didn't want to get crossways with PG&E on this matter.

Allegation #47: Two PG&E employees were contaminated in the head region during refueling outage in April 1970.

AEC Finding: No substantiation was found for this allegation.

COMMENT: Amazingly lousy investigatory work! Refer to Weeks' testimony in Chapter 4.

Allegation #48: It is possible for the plant's domestic water system to become radioactively contaminated due to an improper piping design, and that such contamination had occurred.

AEC Finding: No contamination of the domestic water supply has occurred. Since is appeared possible that the contamination could occur, however, this matter was included in the October 28 notice to the licensee. The resolution of this matter is stated in the licensee's reply dated November 19, 1971, to the notice and the AEC acknowledgment letter dated December 22, 1971.

COMMENT: If I had been permitted to talk to the AEC inspector about this radiation safety concern, the AEC discovery would have been made in a much more timely fashion, not a year and a half later (review Chapter 10)!

Allegation #49: Offsite, non-PG&E personnel became contaminated at the plant and they were permitted to leave without proper decontamination being effected.

AEC Finding: No substantiation was found for this allegation.

COMMENT: This allegation doesn't read properly and I'm confident it was by plan and design. It was referring to the CG painters who became contaminated in the nuclear facility and the problem was discovered four days after they had worked in the radiation controlled area of Unit 3. The CG painters were not "permitted to leave" the nuclear facility; they just left without anyone knowing it.

The problem was accidently discovered several days later and there was plenty of documentation of the incident. There was an incident report filed that detailed exactly what happened! There was the access control log that clearly established the GC painters being in the radiation-controlled area. Their personal clothing was confiscated, which produced a paper trail on the reimbursement to the employees for new clothing. Of course, there was the memorandum by Edgar Weeks chastising me for insisting we visit every place these employees had traveled during the time they were away from the plant in the radioactively contaminated condition we found them in, which was again, quite by accident.

The AEC investigators obviously did not talk to Edgar Weeks and Gail Allen about this incident or else they both lied about it. It's also obvious they did not talk with nuclear control technician Raymond Skidmore because I know he would not have lied about what happened (review Chapter 4 – "CG employees left the nuclear facility radioactively contaminated and their condition was discovered four days later")!

SUMMARY AND CONCLUSIONS . . .

The AEC watered down everything I presented to them and worked with plant management personnel to cover up the problems that I had complained about.

In fact, the AEC investigators selected only a few items, and twisted those around in order to issue PG&E some inconsequential "wrist-slaps."

This monumentally corrupt investigation by Ward and his AEC investigation team allowed PG&E, not only to save face, but also to protect the company's failed and dangerous technology at Humboldt Bay. It was nothing but a whitewash that would be used by PG&E to further discredit me.

Although it didn't appear to me that he intended for it to happen, during a heated conversation he and I were having at the September 7, 1971, meeting, Ward admitted he and his AEC investigation team "saw the black book" that PG&E management had maintained on me. Wow! That speaks volumes about how low PG&E management will stoop and the willingness of the AEC to work with PG&E to protect the failed and dangerous technology at Humboldt Bay to promote the future proliferation of nuclear power plants.

As I waded my way through all this swamp water, I begin to realize through personal hard experience that the AEC could not be relied on to do the right thing because the Commission was responsible for both regulating and promoting nuclear power, an inherent conflict of interest.

The environmental writer for the Eureka *Times-Standard* in Eureka, California, covered a public meeting held in Arcata, California, on Tuesday, February 1, 1972, featuring Frederick R. "Fritz" Draeger, the atomic information coordinator for PG&E's corporate office in San Francisco. Draeger refused to debate me in public regarding the nuclear plant issues I had previously raised earlier in a local public meeting sponsored by the Northcoast Environmental Center. Two months before this public meeting, the Eureka *Times-Standard* had submitted 70 questions to PG&E that were based on the charges I had previously made and the environmental writer for the Eureka *Times-Standard* pointed out his newspaper had not yet received a response from PG&E.

Draeger would not debate me because "The AEC has already debated the issues," he said, adding "all serious allegations had been proven wrong by the AEC."

__XIV__

14. Convoluted Litigation

1971-1977

"When a publication is absolutely privileged, there is no liability, even though it is made with actual malice."[305] [PG&E]

"The cause of action ordinarily accrues when, under the substantive law, the wrongful act is done . . . And the general rule is that the statute will begin to run though the plaintiff is ignorant of his cause of action or the identity of the wrongdoer."[306] [PG&E]

"I have learned through personal experience that our system of justice is more illusionary than real"[307] – My *Diary*, and especially this chapter of it, reveals why this is true. [Bob Rowen]

Silencing and neutralizing the critics of nuclear power is covered in Chapter 16 of my *Diary*. This chapter of my *Diary* examines our "system of justice" relating to those who come forward with radiation safety violations occurring inside the nuclear industry. The underlying premise of this chapter is that we cannot trust those whose primary concern is the bottom line nor can we rely on our institutions of government that are controlled by them to protect us from their abuses – an examination of our system of justice reveals why.

In writing this portion of my *Diary*, I feel it is important for me to point out my prejudices and to reveal the core values of my belief system. Also important is to be candid about my personal feelings regarding American jurisprudence and the vagaries of the system and its bureaucratic ineptitude caused by the flagitious influences of the rich and powerful, conservative forces of our society. My *Diary*, and especially this chapter, explains why I feel this way.

Throughout our history we find an endless number of politicians who were bought and paid for by the wealthy — and nothing much has changed. With few exceptions, these are the folks with their influential backers who in reality "write and interpret" our laws. We want to believe truth ultimately prevails in our beloved country; that the sacrifices of countless Americans on the battlefield were worth the price of preserving our American values of justice, equality, fairness, tolerance, and the pursuit of truth that we hold most dear.

We want to believe these values that make up our endearing American ideology will trump greed, corruption, and corporate abuse. Well, they don't! I have learned through hard personal experience that our system of justice is more illusory than real.

My first working title for this chapter of my *Diary* was "Seeking Justice" but decided to rename it "Convoluted Litigation" instead; but this part of my *Diary* is clearly all about the difficulties of achieving justice in our "system of jurisprudence," and I am using the phrase broadly. It is a system controlled by the powerful, wealthy conservative interests in our country with corporate America smack dab in the middle of it.

I am not an attorney but found myself having to swim around in the pond of America's system of jurisprudence, filled with alligators, piranhas and sludge. It was once a strongly held personal belief that truth prevails, that our system of justice was designed to cause that to happen – based on the simple notion that in America the "cream of truth" would always rise to the top. I have learned our system of justice isn't at all designed for that to happen!

I once believed it didn't really matter how much money one had, the system itself would respond to the basic human need to get to the truth, and justice would ultimately prevail – I sincerely believed that one could count on that happening in America. I was young and naïve. I discovered, through my experiences in dealing with what PG&E, et al., had done, that the legal system responds to the corporate power brokers with little regard for truth, for the principles of fair play, or for how people are affected by the unscrupulous, immoral and unethical behavior of corporations and the agencies of government controlled by them.

When I first learned of the police report and the role PG&E played in the commissioning of it, I believed I could get the whole affair straightened out and those responsible for it would be held accountable. I also believed the City of Eureka and its Chief of Police would face the consequences of their actions.

Why did I believe these things? I thought people who were subpoenaed to testify in a court of law would be protected from any form of retaliation. I also thought the malicious use of law enforcement agencies, by those with self-serving, ulterior motives with intent to harm others for their own gain, would be held accountable. I was totally unaware of the applicability of how statutes of limitation serve as impediments to justice. When I was made aware of the role of the statutes of limitation and how they are applied, it made no sense to me that if an act of wrongdoing is discovered after the statute of limitation time-period has transpired, an action against the wrongdoer is barred. While in some cases the idea that when the injured party first becomes aware, when he or she "first knew or should have known" of the wrongful act, establishes the actual start of the statute of limitations' clock, but even that notion is submersed in very murky waters.

SEEKING JUSTICE WITH THE UNITED STATES ATTORNEY – "it's not a right protected by federal law" . . .

My letter to the United States Attorney for the Northern District of California, Mr. James L. Browning, Jr., dated May 13, 1972, sums up my feelings about the police report matter in a response to Mr. Browning's handling of my complaint:[308]

Dear Mr. Browning:
Thank you for your letter of November 10, 1971. In your letter you stated the following about my police report problem:
"Even assuming that it could be proved beyond a reasonable doubt that the exercise of your right to testify in the Walters trial was sought to be derogated, the fact remains that you did in fact testify, and, in any event, the right to testify in a state court prosecution is not a right protected by a Federal law."
The fact is, Mr. Browning, that I was once again subpoenaed to testify in the Walters case, this time in a Federal court on January 5, 1972. What I am about to say is to relieve me of certain burdens thus placing these burdens on the judicial system wherever they belong – State or Federal.
The effect of the police report intimidated me on the witness stand in the Federal trial. This was compounded by the presence of the Eureka police officers in the federal courtroom during my testimony regarding the particulars of the Walters case in the state trial proceeding. I was constantly fearful of saying something in the federal trial proceeding that might result in further injury to my wellbeing and to that of my family. The impression of hesitancy on my part to answer many of the questions put to me resulting from my inability to keep a clear mind due to the fear of saying something that would result in antagonizing the Eureka Police Department was surely conveyed to the jury.

That Walters lost his case is not on my conscience; I tried very hard to fulfill my responsibilities as a citizen. On the other hand, I know in my own mind that I was Walters' key witness and due to the undue constraints placed on me, the expression of my credibility was not what it should have been.

False claims of a serious nature made with malice in a police department record stemming from a citizen's testimony in a court of law is a severe form of intimidation, which ultimately deters citizen involvement in the judicial processes of this country. This is especially true when such records are sent to the Federal Bureau of Investigation.

As you already know, I tried every approach available to me to correct this problem before my appearance as a witness in the United States District Court on January 5, 1972. All my efforts were in vain.

The cold calculated moves paid off for the City of Eureka, its Police Chief, and certain of his men. As for people like me, there is a price, which must be paid for the exercise of supposed rights. As for people like Walters, they pay the highest price of all.

My letter to the United States Attorney produced nothing, absolutely nothing, other than an opportunity to get some of it off my chest.

SEEKING JUSTICE WITH THE FEDERAL GRAND JURY – "find your own attorney" . . .

The Federal Grand Jury later advised me that what happened to me as a result of my participation as a witness in the Walters' trial was a civil matter and not a criminal one, which meant I could either find a good attorney and pay for the litigation costs or an attorney who would be willing to take my case on a contingency basis.

The first San Francisco attorney I contacted wanted $5,000 up front, which I could not afford to pay. The second attorney wanted $15,000 up front.

Needless to say, I continued my search for an attorney and found more of the same. Most of the attorneys felt an action against those responsible for what was done would involve PG&E, which would be very expensive because of the company's unlimited resources and, therefore, could drag the case out forever – in the name (or pursuit) of justice? If I were able to come up with the money to take on such an undertaking, I would have had no problem finding an attorney but it would have required a very large sum of money that I did not have.

My continued search for an attorney produced a strong recommendation by Ray Towbis of California Citizens for Clean Energy. Towbis suggested I call David E. Pesonen, a San Francisco attorney, who had already taken on PG&E successfully regarding the proposed Bodega Bay Nuclear Plant. Towbis believed Pesonen would jump at the opportunity to represent me and said he'd probably take the case on a contingency basis.

Considering what I had heard about him, there was no question Pesonen knew what PG&E was capable of, and I firmly believed he understood what PG&E had put me through. But when I learned he was associated with a law firm that also represented the Black Panthers, I steered away from the idea of going with Pesonen because I had been accused by PG&E of engaging in the same sort of things the Black Panthers were known for during those years.

WITH THE HINDSIGHT OF 20/20 VISION – "it was the biggest mistake of my life!" . . .

I contacted James R. McKittrick, a Eureka attorney, and briefly explained my situation to him. After talking with his law partners, McKittrick told me he was willing to take my case on a contingency basis. Choosing this option was the only way I could go because I didn't have the financial resources to do otherwise. All the other attorneys I contacted in Eureka either seemed to be in the hip pocket of PG&E or afraid to take on the company.

When I made the appointment to meet with McKittrick for the first time, he asked me to bring the documents that I had referred to and we would go over them together. McKittrick sounded confident that I had a strong case based on what I had told him over the phone but he wanted to see the documents for himself so he could further evaluate the case and develop a strategy for moving forward with it. I was elated. It all sounded quite good to me.

Looking back on that decision with the hindsight of 20/20 vision, I wished I had decided in favor of David Pesonen. Choosing McKittrick over Pesonen was the biggest mistake of my life! The result of what took place with McKittrick added to my education, an education I could never have gotten in any of my studies at the university.

MY "REAL" EDUCATION BEGAN ON THE MORNING OF MAY 29, 1970 — "If you're looking for trouble, you're going to find it" . . .

My "real" education began the day Edgar Weeks, my second-line supervisor at PG&E's nuclear facility, teed off on me with his finger ending up within six inches of my nose. With a red-face and the veins protruding in his neck, while his check and jaw muscles were flexing and visibly tight, Weeks was telling me through his clenched teeth, "If you're looking for trouble, you're going to find it!"

It was all over a soapbox that I had hung up on the bottom of the radiation status board in the control room of Unit 3. The purpose of the soapbox was to collect contributions for Forrest Williams who had been fired a couple of days earlier for refusing to follow a "direct order" to perform an unsafe job-related task in the radiochemistry laboratory (review Chapter 3).

My soapbox had a sign on it, which read, "Let's all contribute to Forrest Williams for the bold stand he made for all of us." Did I think at the time plant management might get a little upset with me for doing this? Probably, but by this time I had had it with plant management and really didn't care anymore what those people thought!

The best way to summarize what happened is to provide a portion of the testimony given by Edgar Weeks in a direct examination of him conducted by PG&E attorney L. V. Brown at my California Unemployment Insurance Appeals Board Hearing:[309]

> **Mr. Brown (PG&E Attorney):** Mr. Weeks, I would like to now draw your attention to the day of May 29. If you will, just relate the events that occurred on that day that involved Mr. Rowen.
>
> **Mr. Weeks:** On the morning of May 29, I went to Unit No. 3 area which is the nuclear unit, the area behind the reactor board, or the radiation status board, and there was a box hanging under the radiation status board, and people were standing around talking about the sign on it that read, "Let's support Forrest for the bold stand he made for all of us."
>
> **Mr. Brown:** For the record, the witness is referring to Forrest Williams who had been discharged just a few days prior to this.
>
> **Mr. Weeks:** Mr. Raymond, who was the Acting Superintendent that day, said that the box would have to come down and he knew that Bob Rowen had put the box up.
>
> I offered to take the box down but Mr. Raymond said that I should get Bob to do it. So – so I did not know where Bob was, but I walked around the front of the reactor board and Bob was there. I asked him to come with me.
>
> We went together around to the back of the reactor board in front of the radiation status board where the box was. Mr. Raymond told Bob that the box would have to come down, that it wasn't proper. Bob questioned him as to his right to take up a collection for Mr. Williams. Mr. Raymond informed him that he could take up a collection from his own group but that the box would have to come down.
>
> Bob, as I said, made no move to take the box down, so at that time I said, 'You have been told by the acting plant superintendent to take the box down, so take it down.' Bob replied with a very emphatic 'Yes, sir,' very loud and I believe,

insolent, but he did take the box down.

I said, 'Thank you, Bob' and I said, I believe, 'I appreciate that,' and Bob started toward the instrument shop which was very close by with the box.

He got almost to the instrument shop door and turned around and said in the same tone of voice that, 'Yes, sir, you're welcome, sir' and then I, at that time, I said, 'Bob, come back, I want to talk to you' but he turned around and went in to the instrument shop with his box.

But he came out almost right away without the box and at that time, I confronted Bob and I told him that I thought he was being insolent in the way he responded to my question to take the box down and I didn't appreciate it at all, that I had received reports from other supervisors about this type of behavior on his part when they told him to do things and I didn't appreciate that either.

Now, Bob's supervisor that day was John Kamberg and he came up about just almost, as I remember, right after I started talking to Bob, and he was standing very close to Bob, and to my left. No one else was in the area close by.

There could have been someone behind me, but I was talking very low to Bob, so low that even Kamberg could not hear me. Bob said, 'Please don't shake your finger in my face.' I remember him saying that, and I was shaking my finger at him.

I told Bob that he was going out of his way the past few days to make trouble and that he had better back off or he was going to find trouble.

And I was still shaking my finger at him. And I could see he was getting mad and I was mad, so I stopped and was ready to drop it with that.

Actually, Weeks did a pretty good job of summarizing what took place that morning with a couple of notable exceptions. He left out his response to me when I asked him to quit shaking his finger in my face, "This is my finger and I'll do what I want with it!" at which time he moved it within about six inches of my nose, still shaking it (review Kamberg's testimony in Chapter 11). He also left out my response with all of its expletives to the continued finger shaking that what he was doing was, " . . . a good way to get your finger broken (and I probably referred to more than just his finger)," and I meant every word of it! And to be sure, Edgar Weeks knew that I meant it! Weeks was correct on almost everything else.

From his point of view, I was going out of my way to make trouble and that I "had better back off" or I "was going to find trouble." I have often wondered, "Just what did Weeks mean by that statement?"

Quite honestly, I had had enough of Weeks and that place for one day. I tried to handle my request "properly" but finally said to hell with it and left the plant. I was extremely upset and totally disgusted with that place and the management people who ran it. It was best for all concerned that I just leave, even though Weeks didn't want me to!

I did make a phone call to Weeks at his home that night, not to threaten to do bodily harm to him as he had claimed but to tell him that I absolutely did not appreciate the way he had treated me at work that morning and that it had better never happen again – and that's the truth of it.

No one deserves being treated that way and PG&E supervisors have absolutely no right to interact with employees in the manner in which Edgar Weeks did with me that morning – PG&E, all the way up and down the corporate ladder, totally disagreed with me!

When I arrived at work the following Monday morning, I was immediately confronted about my phone call to Weeks so, on the spur of the moment, I decided to deny making the call altogether – a decision that if I could do it over, I would handle differently.

For whatever Weeks' reason, and for the reasons of the others who became involved in my employment termination, things were made up and done so with a blatant disregard for the truth and for how their unscrupulous, unethical, malicious and illegal actions would affect the lives of so many truly good people.

Through my experience with the Pacific Gas and Electric Company, I learned the corporate machine has no feelings, no conscience, and thus no remorse for destroying people when the corporation believes it is in its own best interests for doing so.

PG&E knew I was leaving the company in a few months to continue my education at Humboldt State University, and the company knew I was going to remain a critic of the Humboldt Bay Nuclear Power Plant. The company also knew that I believed with an abiding conviction that PG&E was covering up a technology failure. I eventually learned, and learned it the hard way, that PG&E management would go to any length, using the most unimaginable means, to protect the company's future interests in nuclear power.

PG&E was also aware that I was keeping a diary of my experiences at that place, and the company knew I was gathering files and paperwork that would document my various criticisms of the plant. I can say this with absolute certainty and support my claim with the written statements of John Kamberg and Andrew Kennedy made on May 22, 1970 (review Chapter 11): "I believe Rowen is preparing some kind of publication which will compare present conditions here with research results concerning biological effects brought by radiation" by John Kamberg (PG&E's Nuclear Instrumentation Foreman); and "Rowen appears to be heading in the direction of becoming the Ralph Nader of the radiation field" by Andrew Kennedy (PG&E's Nuclear Instrumentation Engineer). Notwithstanding who actually made these statements, Bert Jones or Kamberg and Kennedy, the statements speak for themselves.

SEEKING JUSTICE – "using an unemployment insurance hearing" . . .

I had filed for unemployment benefits and was denied. PG&E claimed my employment termination was "due to misconduct connected with [my] most recent work." I disagreed and appealed the decision. What followed turned into a trial of sorts where I was able to subpoena witnesses and documents, etc. The "trial" was in reality two "hearings" before a Referee of the California Unemployment Insurance Appeals Board.

It was necessary for me to represent myself because I could not afford an attorney but PG&E sent an attorney from the company's corporate headquarters in San Francisco.

Much of the testimony quoted in *My Humboldt Diary* came from those proceedings. During those two hearings, I addressed several radiation safety issues in an attempt to show the Referee the real reasons why PG&E wanted to get rid of me. I focused on the events of May 29 in an attempt to address the "misconduct charge in connection with [my] most recent work," and I addressed the phone call issue. I did not overtly admit to making the phone call to Edgar Weeks but rather focused on whether Weeks actually felt threatened by the alleged phone call asking if the alleged incident was reported to the police department. Although I had previously denied making the phone call, I decided I was not going to do that in these proceedings. The Referee wrote a nine-page decision, which read in part (repeated here from Chapter 11 for emphasis and clarification:[310]

> In the opinion of the referee the principal cause of the claimant's discharge was his extreme safety consciousness. His efforts in this direction were to some extent a reproof of the more sanguinary attitude of certain of his supervisors. His attempts to bring these matters to the attention of the Atomic Energy Commission and to the attention of fellow employees were also greatly resented.
>
> As to the incidents, which occurred on the claimant's last workday, the referee makes the following findings based upon a preponderance of evidence:
> 1. Mr. Weeks conceded that the manner of his reprimand of the claimant was improper. In the opinion of the referee it was also extremely provocative.
> 2. The claimant had opportunity and motive to make the telephone call referred to in the Statement of Facts.
> 3. Mr. Weeks was familiar with the claimant's

voice and believed it was he who called. The referee concludes a preponderance of evidence indicates the claimant made this call.

Considering the context out of which the telephone call arose, the contingent wording (the claimant stated what his course of action would be if in the future Mr. Weeks repeated his actions of that morning) plus the fact the supervisor did not interpret the remarks as a present threat of bodily harm, the referee believes the telephone call in question is more accurately described as a warning rather than a threat.

The referee concluded that I was discharged from PG&E for reasons other than misconduct. The truth of the matter is that I did make a call to Edgar Weeks but not for the reasons PG&E later claimed.

Weeks collaborated with someone between the Friday evening phone call and the following Monday morning that turned the whole affair into something that it wasn't. It's even possible that Weeks and whoever had already developed a contingency plan Friday afternoon in the event of a phone call. In any event, there was a diabolical plan — a conspiracy — that was underway during all of this (that I was completely unaware of at that point in time but eventually became complete aware of it) that resulted in the false police report and the well executed hatchet job by PG&E.

From my vantage point, it appears that it was Bert Jones who functioned as the architect of PG&E's diabolical plan but he obviously took his marching orders from corporate headquarters. The goal was to protect the failed and dangerous technology at Humboldt Bay and PG&E's aspirations of "going nuclear" in the future. I truly believe J. C. Carroll and L. V. Brown from PG&E corporate headquarters along with Edgar Weeks at Humboldt Bay worked closely with Jones to carry out his fiendish plan for reasons explained throughout my *Diary*.

PG&E's LETTER TO THE EDITOR – "written in PG&E's Machiavellian style" . . .

On April 29, 1972, *The National Observer*, a publication of Dow Jones Company, published an article on the front page entitled "Fire Me?" written by Michael T. Malloy. The reporter had called me earlier in the month and conducted a telephone interview regarding my difficulties with PG&E. I answered all of his questions and agreed to send him copies of the documents he specifically requested.

Michael Malloy's article made two references to me, one indirectly and the other was a direct reference. PG&E's extremely quick response to this article again provides an excellent peek into the twisted, inner thinking of the company. The first reference to me in Michael Malloy's article read:[311]

> A nuclear-power technician who says he was fired from a California atomic-energy plant for reporting unsafe conditions has inspired a legal effort to make the Atomic Energy Commission (AEC) protect other workers from being similarly fired. This effort spearheaded by the Environmental Defense Fund, but not supported by the International Brotherhood of Electrical Workers Local Union 1245 or PG&E, was successful.

The second direct reference to me in Malloy's article was under the subheading "Being Right Isn't Enough," which read (the complete text of it):[312]

> Robert J. Rowen, Jr., was a technician at a Pacific Gas and Electric Company atomic power plant near Eureka, California. He says he was fired for complaining about unsafe practices; the company says it fired him for threatening a supervisor. A labor-management arbitrator upheld the company, but a California Unemployment Insurance Appeals Board Referee upheld Rowen. The AEC confirmed some of Rowen's complaints and formally criticized his employer for preventing him from talking with AEC inspectors. Rowen now drives a school bus.

PG&E's letter to the Editor of *The National Observer*, dated May 2, 1972, was a quick and repugnant response to Malloy's April 29 article. PG&E laid out the company's criticisms of the reporter Michael T. Malloy in the typical PG&E Machiavellian style (an observation I'm very comfortable with and confident in making):[313]

> Dear Sir:
> A review of the record clearly shows that Mr. Michael T. Malloy misrepresented the facts in his April 29 *National Observer* article, "Fire Me?"
> First, the article states that "a California Unemployment Insurance Appeals Board referee upheld Rowen" in his denial of threatening his supervisor with bodily harm, which led to his dismissal. That statement is patently false.
> The discharge of Robert Rowen, Jr. was not the specific issue at the Appeals Board hearing. The hearing was to determine whether he was entitled to unemployment benefits. Concerning the circumstance of his discharge, however, the appeals board referee stated that the preponderance of evidence showed that Mr. Rowen made the threatening phone call to his supervisor.

It is important to point out that the Appeals Boards' findings paralleled those of veteran arbitrator Sam Kagel in the arbitration hearing requested by Rowen's union, International Brotherhood of Electrical Workers, Local #1245. Kagel's findings concerning Rowen's sworn testimony stated that 'Insofar as Rowen's specific denial is concerned, serious doubts were raised concerning his credibility.'

Contrary to the implications of the article, the U.S. Atomic Energy Commission sustained only one of Rowen's 49 allegations concerning the safety of the Humboldt plant. That allegation centered around Pacific Gas and Electric Company's failure to provide Rowen with radiation exposure records 90 days after his discharge. This situation resulted from the company's misinterpretation of an AEC regulation, which had been changed.

Further, the article implies that Rowen was prevented from talking to AEC inspectors. Again, the record does not bear this out. In fact, the AEC asked the company to comment on this allegation. PG&E responded by pointing out that (1) Rowen was not prevented from conferring with an AEC inspector on his own time, and (2) our handling of his request was fully consistent with AEC requirements. The AEC termed the company's response 'satisfactory.'

It is true that Rowen now has a part-time job as a bus driver. It is also true that, despite his allegations about the plant's safety, Rowen has driven elementary school children out to tour the Humboldt plant.

One of the curious aspects of Mr. Malloy's article is that the section pertaining to Rowen was sub-headed "Being Right Isn't Enough." Being wrong is scarcely an improvement."

This incredible piece of literary work was composed by Christopher C. Newton, probably with the help of PG&E attorney L. V. Brown and others in corporate headquarters, was sent to the reporter's boss, and bcc'd to a Who's Who Registry of PG&E executives including some familiar names: J. C. Carroll, I. W. Bonbright, B. Bunnin, H. J. LaPlante, V. C. Novarino, W. Raymond, and LRM/ADM/RRG (whoever those PG&E people were).

My family, at the time of Malloy's article and PG&E's response to it, was living on my wife's limited income as a bank teller, my veteran's monthly benefits, a part-time job driving a school bus for Arcata Union High School District, a part-time reader of calculus papers for the math department at Humboldt State University, a few small scholarship awards, and a few stipends for speaking in the Cluster Program at HSU.

The PG&E snide remark, "It is true that Rowen now has a part-time job as a bus driver. It is also true that, despite his allegations about the plant's safety, Rowen has driven elementary school children out to tour the Humboldt plant" was truly a low blow and speaks volumes about PG&E's corporate culture.

SEEKING JUSTICE THROUGH ARBITRATION – "it was a stacked deck" . . .

Attorney Frank Morgan, representing IBEW Local 1245, wrote what some described as a persuasive 21-page brief for the arbitration cases Nos. 35 (Williams) and 36 (Rowen).[314]

Mr. Morgan's brief began:
> In his opening statement on these discharge cases, counsel for PG&E made a remarkable and revealing statement concerning a "conspiracy" afoot in the Humboldt Bay Nuclear Power Plant, an insidious plot involving Mr. Williams and Mr. Rowen and others to raise questions about the efficacy of the company's safety program in this nuclear power station.

Mr. Brown's (PG&E attorney) statement continued:
> We believe that the evidence will show that there was a common plan and a common design on the part of these two people and that probably the thrust, if we get down to the bare bones, of what all of this means is simply that these two men – and I might add one more.
>
> In fact, there were three dissenters in the plant, three people who dissented, who felt that the company's safety program was not adequate, that it was unsafe. And they set themselves up to protest, sometimes openly and, I believe the record will demonstrate, sometimes in a more insidious manner to also at the same time degrade or cause the reputation of the supervisors to be downgraded in the eyes of the employees.

Mr. Morgan's brief continued:
> Now, we are prompted at the outset to ask, what is so surprising – so "insidious" – about Nuclear Control Technicians raising questions about the company's safety program.
>
> After all radiation safety is their job. So we have read the transcript of these proceedings carefully searching the record for the evidence which company counsel promised would fill out the conspiracy theory.
>
> We urge the arbitrator to do the same, to read through the

transcript searching for evidence of the "conspiracy" which the company depicts as the central theme of these cases. And we suggest that the arbitrator will find, as we have, that the search is in vain, that no such evidence is to be found.

For all this record reveals, the company's conspiracy theory is an empty spook, perhaps a defensive reflex resulting from a couple of conscientious employees touching the Humboldt Bay facility in a soft spot.

The very hollowness of the company's conspiracy theory, however, does serve to point out what these cases are really all about, and they have little to do with Mr. Williams' refusal to perform a job assignment or Mr. Rowen's alleged telephone call.

Rather the cases deal with what happens to an employee who does his job too well, who raises too many embarrassing questions about the safety program and procedures, which he is charged with carrying out.

Mr. Williams and Mr. Rowen did raise questions – and as this record shows, sound and important questions – concerning safety at Humboldt Bay.

But the company has equated questioning with dissent, and dissent with conspiracy; and it is clear on the basis of the entire record of both these that the discharges were the result of the company's belief in the existence of this "conspiracy" – rather than the specific events of May 25 and May 29 which triggered the discharges.

So again we urge the arbitrator to review this record in light of the company's conspiracy theory and specifically to search for evidence indicating either improper motivation on the parts of Williams and Rowen in raising the safety questions they did throughout their tenure as control technicians or that the questions themselves were in any way improper.

That evidence will not be found; and if there is any conspiracy involved in this case, it is the conspiracy of certain company personnel to get rid of employees who ask embarrassing questions.

The arbitration hearings were held in Eureka before Arbitrator Sam Kagel of San Francisco. PG&E management personnel from the company's corporate headquarters in San Francisco who were present at the arbitration hearings included PG&E Attorney L. V. Brown; I. Wayland Bonbright, Manager of PG&E's Industrial Relations Department; and of course, James C. Carroll, PG&E's General Office Nuclear and Supervising Steam Generation Engineer, who later maliciously made false statements about

NBC News Producer, Don Widener, in connection with Widener's production of "Powers That Be" (Chapter 15).

One of the many reasons I felt the arbitration hearing was a stacked deck right from the very beginning of the hearing was because of the familiarity demonstrated between the Arbitrator and the PG&E attorney. It struck me as odd for the Arbitrator to call the PG&E attorney "Bud" early in the proceedings before the first company witness was called.

The Arbitrator's familiarity with Mr. Brown was unsettling, which made me very uncomfortable. Within a minute or so into my hearing, there was the following exchange between the Arbitrator and the attorneys regarding a company witness:[315]

> **Mr. Brown:** And if I may, before I call my first witness, I think I owe counsel an answer to a question that he raised earlier and which I did not answer. With relation to the first two exhibits, Mr. Morgan, that were submitted at that time in order that we might have Mrs. Risku here to lay the proper foundation. We don't like to keep young ladies away from their homes at night if we can possible avoid it.
> **Mr. Morgan:** You are so kind!
> **The Arbitrator:** Since you didn't know we were going to meet tonight!
> **[Laughter]**

I didn't see any of it as a laughing matter. We were in a PG&E facility with company materials, photos, and numerous PG&E items all over the place. It was not a neutral site at all. It was the PG&E downtown office on Sixth Street in Eureka. Every place I looked, every place anyone looked, was unmistakably PG&E's turf. Then there was another exchange involving the Arbitrator that made me feel even more uncomfortable:[316]

> **The Arbitrator:** Let me ask a question about Dr. Wittwer. Is he here in town?
> **Mr. Morgan:** He is here in town. His nurse---who is a difficult woman to deal with! --- (INTERRUPTED)
> **The Arbitrator:** Wait a minute. I will be dealing with nurses now for every hospital in San Francisco for the next three months!

It was not only what the arbitrator said but also the way he said it. He would "be dealing with nurses . . ." made me suspicious of his attitude towards those nurses. I realize I was tense and feeling rather defensive at the time but I believe for very good reason. I felt the whole affair was a stacked-deck favoring the company because it didn't seem to me that the union's attorney was very well prepared; however, I do believe he was well intentioned.

Mr. Morgan became very sympathetic to my situation and volunteered to help me. His later *pro bono* efforts definitely proved to be very beneficial to me as I traveled down my very long and bumpy litigation road.

On the other hand, the PG&E attorney without question was "totally prepared." The PG&E attorney, L. V. Brown, had unlimited resources supporting him and that was glaringly obvious.

In contrast, Frank B. Morgan was representing the union – IBEW Local 1245. Mr. Morgan was with the San Francisco law firm of Brundage, Neyhart, Grodin and Beeson, Attorneys at Law, on retainer by IBEW 1245.

It was apparent Morgan's budget was limited in contrast to that of the PG&E attorney. Morgan was inadequately prepared for our arbitration cases because he lacked not only the resources of time and staff but also sufficient access to both of his clients, Forrest Williams and Bob Rowen. The union had nearly 20,000 members but only seven of them were nuclear control technicians and the union recognized how important the proliferation of nuclear power plants was to PG&E and future jobs for the rank and file.

I wanted to participate in the proceedings of my own arbitration case but the union would not allow it. It was my contention the PG&E witnesses needed to be cross-examined by me because I knew them. I felt the radiation safety issues needed to be clearly presented and explained to the Arbitrator.

The union's attorney would not allow it because the Arbitrator and apparently the union, too, was only interested in one thing – the company's charge of my "threatening one of my supervisors with bodily harm." It was my feeling that the Executive Board of IBEW 1245 was more in tune with the company, and the attorney representing the union essentially had his hands tied by the internal politics of the union.

The following example very clearly reveals what I am referring to regarding the "internal politics of the union." I participated with the Environmental Defense Fund in a petition effort to change the AEC rules and regulations to provide better protection for nuclear control technicians and workers in nuclear facilities.

The Chief Shop Steward for the Eureka Unit of the IBEW 1245 in PG&E's Humboldt Division, Howard Darington, who was also named in the police report, wrote the following resolution known as Motion No. 3111-72-2 (which was MSC by the IBEW LU 1245 Eureka Unit), in an attempt to enlist the support and cooperation of the International Brotherhood of Electrical Workers, Local Union 1245, to join in with the national effort of the Environmental Defense Fund (EDF) and the Oil, Chemical and Atomic Workers International Union to provide better protections for workers in nuclear facilities:[317]

> **WHEREAS** the PG&E has been licensed by the Atomic Energy Commission (AEC) to construct, operate and maintain a nuclear utilization facility in accordance with

rules and regulations stated in their License, Technical Specifications and Radiation Control Standards, and

WHEREAS members of IBEW LU 1245 are employed in PG&E's nuclear utilization facilities, and

WHEREAS members of LU 1245 specifically trained as radiation monitoring technicians to raise serious questions concerning the adequacy and efficacy of the Company's radiation safety program, and

WHEREAS the company attempted, by various methods, to stifle questioning by its radiation monitoring technicians, and

WHEREAS the officials of LU 1245 were unable to protect its members against harassment by PG&E for raising sensitive questions concerning radiation safety issues, and

WHEREAS The Environmental Defense Fund, Incorporated (EDF) is petitioning the AEC requesting promulgation of rules protecting the occupational safety and health rights of employees of AEC Licenses,

THEREFORE BE IT RESOLVED that IBEW LU 1245 shall join with the Environmental Defense Fund, the Oil, Chemical and Atomic Workers International Union and Robert J. Rowen as a petitioner in support of the petition requesting promulgation of rules protecting the occupational safety and health rights of employees of AEC licenses, and

BE IT FURTHER RESOLVED that LU 1245, in addition to joining as a petitioner, attempt to persuade the IBEW International to also join as petitioner in support of the petition."

The Executive Board of IBEW 1245 issued a "Non-concur" stating that this resolution was "seeking changes that would not be in the best interest of the overall membership of the union," referring to PG&E employees in general, and specifically to the aggressive "Go Nuclear" program of the Pacific Gas and Electric Company during the early 1970s.

The national petition effort by EDF was successful without the support of the International Brotherhood of Electrical Workers Local 1245. I was commended by the EDF for my role in the petition effort with no thanks to my own union!

The following provides an example of how I was represented at my arbitration hearing. When PG&E's attorney, Mr. Brown, conducted his direct-examination of Jerome Boots, PG&E's acting radiation protection engineer, during my arbitration case regarding the G&R radioactively contaminated pipe incident, which consumed six pages of transcript space, Boots misrepresented the facts of the incident and outright lied about the applicable rules regarding the unconditional release of radioactively contaminated materials. It was obvious the PG&E attorney and Jerome Boots had rehearsed his testimony.

Mr. Boots also made the same nonsensical argument regarding the rest of the 18 pieces of the reactor suppression chamber pipe that he offered the Unemployment Insurance Appeals Board Referee, but his testimony was not challenged at my Arbitration Hearing.

The Arbitrator, who could have injected himself into Boots' testimony, chose to remain silent. While I was sitting there witnessing the proceedings, it took everything I could muster up to remain civil (which meant silent)! The union's attorney consumed less than half a page of transcript space in his cross-examination of Jerome Boots regarding the G&R incident:[318]

> **Mr. Morgan:** (Directed to Mr. Boots . . .) With regard to the pipe incident, Mr. Boots, and these other 18 pieces: Are there company records that indicate the other pieces of pipe were in fact surveyed out?
>
> **Mr. Boots:** I haven't personally seen them. But I assume there are because I remember Gail Allen was supervising the radiation protection crew at the time.
>
> **Mr. Morgan:** Did you make any attempt to check whether there are such records?
>
> **Mr. Boots:** No, I did not.
>
> **Mr. Morgan:** You in fact don't know that they were surveyed out.
>
> **Mr. Boots:** I was told by Gail Allen that they were surveyed out.
>
> **Mr. Morgan:** What was the disposition of these other pieces of pipe?
>
> **Mr. Boots:** They were sold to G&R Metals.
>
> **Mr. Morgan:** What kind of an organization is that?
>
> **Mr. Boots:** I really don't know for sure. I know that they were sold to them as scrap. That's all I know.

And that was the end of the "G&R" matter at my arbitration hearing! (review Chapter 7, keeping in mind that my cross-examination of Boots at my Unemployment Appeals Board Hearing was one week after the Arbitration hearing had taken place).

It was obvious the Arbitrator wasn't the least bit interested in the G&R incident, which was made clear by his facial expressions and body language.

The company attorney didn't even bring up the subject during his direct-examination of Edgar Weeks.

The rest of my radiation protection safety concerns were handled in this PG&E-IBEW Arbitration *farce* in a similar fashion. The union attorney did his best to sum up my case in his final brief to the Arbitrator. The following are a few excerpts from his brief:[319]

Whatever view the arbitrator may take (sic) of the events of May 29, it is the union's position that the primary reason for Mr. Rowen's discharge was that the company had long before tagged him as the leader of the "dissenters" (from what is never made clear) and chief among the phantom conspirators. Following the safety meeting of May 20, total war was declared on "dissent." As the chemistry lab incident of May 25 provided a handy excuse for removing Williams from the "conspirators" ranks, the events of May 29 provided an opportunity for getting rid of Rowen.

It is clear from this record that the company considered Rowen the "leader" of the great safety "dissent," head goblin of the phantom conspiracy. Indeed, the record does reveal that Rowen was involved in many disputes with his supervisors over his reports of safety violations. What the record does not indicate is that with regard to any of these conflicts Rowen was improperly motivated.

The minutes of a plant safety meeting held on December 12, 1967, indicate that Rowen brought up several items for discussion. This upset Rowen's supervisors because the problems he raised were not 'safety problems' but were 'radiation protection operational problems.'

Apart from this linguistic *tour de force*, there is nothing in this record to indicate that the questions Rowen raised at this meeting were anything but well-meaning and legitimate questions concerning safety. A review of Rowen's testimony regarding the specific items he discussed at the December 1967 meeting shows they were all serious, timely safety matters. In fact, as a result of Rowen's suggestions at this meeting, substantial safety improvements in the off-gas sampling and materials storage procedures were made."

It was obvious that the Arbitrator was not the lease bit concerned with the problems I was having with the company because of my willingness to openly challenge PG&E's "management's prerogative" whenever plant management chose to ignore sound radiation safety practices and the company's own Radiation Control Standards that were part of the AEC's license given to PG&E to operate the nuclear facility. I guess the Arbitrator, as well as the union, was willing to simply leave those issues to the Atomic Energy Commission.

I can unequivocally and in good conscience state that the Arbitrator refused to acknowledge the real reasons why PG&E wanted to get rid of me. As far as the company's charge that I threatened my supervisor over the phone with bodily harm, nothing could have been more ridiculous.

Unfortunately, I denied making the phone call in question and I couldn't change that – and that gave the Arbitrator all he needed to issue his decision in favor of the company.

If the company had wanted to fire me for what I actually said to Edgar Weeks in the reactor control room on the morning of May 29, while he was shaking his finger in my face, then fine. But Weeks knew that would not have accomplished what I believe was the company's ultimate goal – and that was not only to get rid of me, but also to "neutralize" me in the process.

I don't know with whom Edgar Weeks collaborated between Friday night and Monday morning. I do know there was a monumental distortion of what my phone call to him was truly about, which was somehow part of PG&E's conspiracy that was occurring during the same time to produce the false police report.

The Arbitrator allowed Forrest Williams to return to work without back pay, which Williams did for just one day. The fact that the Arbitrator allowed Williams to return to work because he was terminated without just cause but then said PG&E would not have to pay him his lost wages from the termination date (more than nine months) made absolutely no sense but the Arbitrator's decision did kept PG&E happy and I think the union, too.

Howard Darington later told me that, in his opinion, "the arbitration cases needed to end the way they did," *(because it was somehow necessary for a split decision)*, adding, "and besides the company was really after you."

When Williams returned to work for just the one day, he did so to tell plant management that he could no longer work for a company like PG&E. Following his announcement to PG&E nuclear plant management Williams walked away from his PG&E ordeal leaving all of it behind him – forever.

I would have left the company within a few months anyway not only to continue my education at Humboldt State University but also because I had had enough of PG&E.

I had reached the conclusion that it was not safe to work at PG&E's Humboldt Bay Nuclear Power Plant. And like Forrest, I could not see myself working until retirement for a company like PG&E.

Bill Evans, another nuclear control technician, had left the company and the Humboldt area. I had heard later that Bill had returned to Eureka and was offered to what amounted to a "promotion" at the nuclear facility but he declined PG&E's offer. (That's what I heard but was never to verify it because I had moved from the area and was busy getting on with my life)

Darrell Porter was discharged from the company because he was no longer willing to subject himself to radiation exposure and requested another assignment within PG&E.[320] The company was not willing to offer him something else, even though there were plenty of alternatives in the Humboldt division, but instead ordered him to return to the nuclear facility and resume his regular duties there by a certain deadline or he would be terminated.[321] Mr. Porter chose to accept the termination.[322]

SEEKING JUSTICE FROM THE NATIONAL LABOR RELATIONS BOARD – "but it was to no avail because" . . .

In their continuing pursuit of justice, the four nuclear control techs named in the police report turned to the National Labor Relations Board (NLRB) for help. With the help of the union's chief shop steward for PG&E's Humboldt Division, Howard Darington filed a charge of an unfair labor practice against PG&E with the NLRB on September 27, 1971. I am citing this document because it provides an excellent summary of what happened at PG&E from Howard Darington's point of view; Darington left no stones unturned for the benefit of the NLRB. The entire text of the charge read as follows: [323]

BASIS OF THE CHARGE

Introduction
The information contained herein outlines the factual background pertinent in this matter, describes the nature of the charges, and provides evidence in support of the charges, all of which serves as adequate grounds for charging the Pacific Gas and Electric Company with an unfair labor practice.

Background
The Pacific Gas and Electric Company (PG&E) owns and operates the Humboldt Bay Power Plant at Eureka, California, which includes PG&E's first nuclear facility. The plant operates under license issued by the U.S. Atomic Energy Commission (AEC) pursuant to regulations adopted by the Commission.

The regulations are designed to safeguard employees working in the plant and the public in the vicinity of the plant from possible radiation hazards. The plant construction permits and operating license were granted by the AEC only after submission of detailed design specifications and operational and administrative procedures that PG&E will use to assure the safeguarding of the employees working in the plant and the public in the vicinity of the plant from possible radiation hazards.

The PG&E has committed itself to the use of nuclear energy in the expansion of its electric generating facilities over the next few decades. The PG&E, especially after a failure to convince the public of the safety of its proposed Bodega Bay Nuclear Plant, has engaged in an intensive public relations program designed to alleviate the fears and concern of the general public concerning the radiation safety and pollution of a nuclear-fueled electric generating facility.

This public relations program could be seriously impaired if the general public were to become convinced that the PG&E does not conduct its operation of the nuclear fueled generating facilities in the manner in which it has claimed in the various documents submitted to various agencies in support of PG&E obtaining an operating license for PG&E proposed nuclear facilities.

A major element in the plant operating procedures to assure the safeguarding from possible radiation hazards is the establishment of a special classification for the purpose of monitoring the radiation working conditions and radiation work procedures of the plant personnel to ascertain that they are performing their duties in the nuclear plant in accordance with the regulations applicable to the nuclear plant operation.

In 1962, the PG&E by agreement with the International Brotherhood of Electrical Workers, Local Union 1245 (IBEW 1245), established and conducted comprehensive on-the-job training program to assure the Control Technician is well acquainted with his specific duties and responsibilities. The Control Technician job classification required a 42 month formal apprenticeship training program – the longest period of training for any job classification within the IBEW 1245 bargaining unit at PG&E.

A significant portion of the duties performed by the Control Technician fell within the radiation protection duties in which the Control Technician was formally charged in the job description with the responsibility in the Company's radiation program to perform contamination and radiation level surveys to assure nonhazardous conditions, to maintain records of survey results, to instruct shift personnel in proper radiation protection, and to assist and advise other employees in the decontamination of equipment and the handling, packaging, and storing of solid radioactive waste.

By virtue of his training, his experience, his job responsibilities, and his intimate knowledge of actual on-the-job radiation practice and procedures, the Control Technician shares a legitimate concern for the proper application of the administrative procedures designed to safeguard the employee working in the plant and the public in the vicinity of the plant from possible radiation hazards.

At times, while pursuing this legitimate concern, most of the Control Technicians found themselves in conflict with decisions of their supervisors, when the supervisors would transgress an administrative procedure for economic reasons.

The Control Technicians found that discussion with plant supervision was ineffective to gain satisfactory resolution of the issue and attempted to carry their protest to a more effective forum.

To combat the raising of sensitive issues related to radiation safety, the Humboldt Bay Power Plant supervision has engaged in and is engaged in a continuing practice of admonishing, reprimanding, disciplining and otherwise coercing employees who attempt to raise questions concerning the adequacy and efficacy of the Company's radiation protection safety program.

The Humboldt Bay Power Plant supervision mainly involved were: Dale Nix, Raymond Ramsey, Warren Raymond, Edgar Weeks, Jerome Boots, Andrew Kennedy, Robert Chaffee, and Gail Allen.

While all of the Control Technicians privately criticized the plant Supervision's suspension or bending of administrative safeguards, only those whose sense of duty overcame their reticence due to the Company's coercive practices would pursue the various issues to various forums in an attempt to have their concern adequately answered.

Several, less reticent, Control Technicians were attempting to clarify and change what they felt were either transgressions of or poor safeguards from possible radiation hazards. During May and June of 1970 the PG&E intensified its practices designed to stifle questioning by the Company's radiation protection employees by attacking, through various means, the Company's most active critics.

False Allegations by the PG&E

On or about May 22, 1970, agents of the Pacific Gas and Electric Company maliciously and knowingly made false accusatory statements charging four of its seven nuclear Control Technicians of being members of a group who was participating in, or had the propensity to participate in, various unlawful acts directed at damaging and disrupting the Company's property and services.

The PG&E claimed to Chief Emahiser of the Eureka Police Department that Howard J. Darington IV, Robert J. Rowen Jr., Raymond R. Skidmore, and Forrest E. Williams,

Jr. are known dissenters, are members of a group and hold group meetings, read Ray Brown, Eldridge Cleaver, and others, advocate fire bombing and violence, live in common at 1503 "G" Street, Eureka, California, and are involved in a plot to blow up the Humboldt Bay Power Plant.

These claims resulted in the circulation of a June 3, 1970 police report containing false information.

Two copies of this report were circulated to the Pacific Gas and Electric Company, one to Robert Taylor, PG&E Humboldt Division Personnel Manager and one to Bert Jones of PG&E's Security Department; several copies were circulated to various local law enforcement agencies; and one copy was sent to the Federal Bureau of Investigation.

Those agents of the Pacific Gas and Electric Company who are known to have had a direct involvement in this police report are Messrs. Robert Taylor, Burt Jones, and Lawrence Brown.

Employment Discharge of Robert Rowen and Forest Williams

On May 25, 1970, the PG&E discharged Forrest Williams, and on June 1, 1970, the PG&E suspended Robert J. Rowen and on June 5, 1970, discharged him.

Both of these actions were submitted to arbitration by the IBEW 1245.

The arbitration cases were heard on December 1 and 2, 1970, with the Arbitrator issuing his decision on March 30, 1971, sustaining Robert Rowen's discharge and reinstating Forrest Williams without back pay.

While the Arbitrator found that the PG&E had terminated Robert Rowen for cause, a State of California Unemployment Appeals Referee, stated, "In the opinion of the Referee the principal cause of the claimant's discharge (Robert Rowen) was his extreme safety consciousness. His efforts in this direction were to some extent a reproof of the sanguinary attitude of certain of his supervisors. His attempts to bring these matters to the attention of the Atomic Energy Commission and to the attention of fellow employees were also greatly resented."

The Referee concluded that Robert Rowen was discharged for reasons other than misconduct.

The Company had the right to appeal the Referee's decision and elected not to do so.

Real Basis for PG&E's Allegations

The employees accused by the PG&E of being members of a group and hold group meetings, of participating in acts tantamount to industrial sabotage, and of being involved in a plot to blow up the Humboldt Bay Power Plant are all members of the IBEW 1245 and participate in the functions of the IBEW 1245.

They have been present at several "group" meetings related to their conditions of employment with the PG&E. These meetings constituted the following:

(1) Robert Rowen, Howard Darington, and three other Humboldt Bay Power Plant employees were members of the Union sanctioned committee representing the employees at the Humboldt Bay Power Plant to evaluate job problems related to the nuclear unit. Howard Darington served as the employee's spokesman when the Union arranged a meeting between members of this committee and plant management.

(2) Howard Darington, Raymond Skidmore, Robert Rowen, and Forrest Williams attended and participated in meetings of the Control Technicians employed at Humboldt Bay Power Plant to consider, formulate and submit proposals to the IBEW 1245 concerning a PG&E proposed amend to the job definition, duty assignments, and lines of progression of the Control Technician job classification.

(3) Howard Darington and Raymond Skidmore were selected by the Control Technician group as employee members of the IBEW 1245 committee that met with PG&E management at the headquarters of the IBEW 1245 with Ronald T. Weekly, Business Manager, L. L. Mitchell, Senior Assistant Business Manager, and Lawrence Foss, Business Representative, all of IBEW 1245, to discuss the impact of the PG&E proposed amendment on the Control Technician job definition on the PG&E's radiation safety program.

(4) On numerous occasions, Howard Darington, Raymond Skidmore, Robert Rowen, and Forrest Williams attended the monthly Union meetings in Eureka.

In every case where the four accused employees met in a group it was in a Union function generally related to the conditions of employment of employees in the PG&E's nuclear plant.

Further, the other three named employees met

individually with Howard Darington at his residence on numerous occasions to discuss their conditions of employment since Howard Darington was the Chief Shop Steward of the PG&E's Humboldt Division, in addition to several other official appointive and elective position in the Union.

All of the meetings of the four accused employees were concerned with activities protected under the Labor Management Relations Act.

Conclusion

Contrary to the provisions of the National Labor Relations Act, the PG&E willfully conspired to construct and continue a coercive element in the employment of Forrest Williams, Howard Darington, Robert Rowen, Raymond Skidmore, and others in direct violation of their rights "to engage in concerted activities for the purpose of collective bargaining or other mutual aid or protection." On April 14, 1971, the PG&E reinforced their practice by allowing this coercive element to stand. On April 23, 1971, the PG&E, in correspondence with Frank Morgan, Attorney representing IBEW and Forrest Williams, acknowledge they had received copies of the June 3, 1970 police report, and after determining that the information in the report was of no value to the Company and extraneous to the employment of the persons named, claims they destroyed all Company records of the "letter." (It was verified by the Humboldt County District Attorney's office that this document is a police report and not a letter.)

Such destruction of valueless information does not exonerate the Company from conspiring to make the unfounded charges that their "dissenting" employees are participating in, or have the propensity to participate in, various unlawful acts directed at damaging and disrupting the Company's property and services.

The National Labor Relations Board responded to these charges through its Regional Director, Mr. Roy O. Hoffman, on October 26, 1971. Mr. Hoffman wrote the following in his official Notice of Decision:[324]

As the allegations of the charge pertain to matters occurring more than six months prior to the filing of the charge and inasmuch as Section 10(b) of the Act precludes issuance of a complaint based upon unfair labor practices occurring more than six months prior to the filling of the charge, I am, therefore, refusing to issue complaint in this matter.

A copy of this official notice was sent by certified registered mail, return receipt requested, to PG&E corporate headquarters in San Francisco. PG&E officials must have been elated but chose not to respond, not yet anyway, because the control technicians named in the NRLB charge were provided an opportunity to appeal the Regional Director's Decision to the NLRB's General Counsel in Washington, D.C.

The appeal was also written by the Union's Chief Shop Stewart in PG&E Humboldt Division, Howard Darington, and was dated November 5, 1971. The full text of the appeal read as follows:[325]

> The Charging party hereby appeals the refusal by the Regional Director of Region 20 to issue complaint in the above captioned case (Case No. 20-CA-7013).
>
> The Regional Director refused to issue complaint in the matter on the basis that allegations of the charge pertain to matters occurring more than six months prior to the filing of the charge.
>
> The Charging Party submits the gravamen of the charge is that Pacific Gas and Electric Company is in violation of Section 8(a)(1) of the Act by permitting to stand, uncorrected, its knowingly false information or charges submitted to the local police department that some of its nuclear power plant employees (those who are most active in exercising their Section 7 rights in pursuit of clarification and modification of Pacific Gas and Electric Company's radiation safety practices) are members of a group who are participating in, or have the propensity to participate in, various unlawful acts directed at damaging and disrupting Pacific Gas and Electric Company's property and services.
>
> The Charging Party further submits that the charge is timely under Section 10(b) of the Act since Pacific Gas and Electric Company's most recent action affirming its intent to maintain the restraint or coercion of its employees in their Section 7 rights occurred in Pacific Gas and Electric Company's act of omission committed on and after April 14, 1971 when it refused to honor the request of one of the injured parties to grant relief from the Pacific Gas and Electric Company's damaging prevarications.
>
> The Charging Party holds that the knowledge that Pacific Gas and Electric Company will, and apparently can with impunity, make malicious and known false accusatory charges against its dissenting employees to police agencies

tends to restrain and coerce Pacific Gas and Electric Company employees from exercising their rights to engage in concerted activities for the purpose of collective bargaining or other mutual aid or protection.

Having successfully retaliated against four employees who had exercised their Section 7 rights, Pacific Gas and Electric Company's April 14,1971 refusal to exercise its capability to afford relief from the continuing effect of the official law enforcement records initiated solely by Pacific Gas and Electric Company's knowingly false information is in effect an act of omission which reinforces Pacific Gas and Electric Company's unfair labor practice by allowing a restraining or coercive element to continue to existence against its injured employees.

Pacific Gas and Electric Company employees are cognizant that the effect of a Pacific Gas and Electric Company's undisputed claim reported as the result of a police investigation and retained in the files of official law enforcement agencies is to: (1) Subject the injured employees to possible future harassment by police agencies in the event that some disgruntled member of the general public attempts to, by unlawful means, disrupt Pacific Gas and Electric Company's property or service, and (2) diminish the injured employee's opportunity for other employment, especially in the area of nuclear energy since employment in the area of nuclear energy very often requires a security clearance.

The Charging Party holds that since this act of omission, occurring less than six months prior to the filing the charge, is reasonably calculated to restrain or coerce employees in their Section 7 rights the Regional Director should issue a complaint in this matter and proceed to eliminate Pacific Gas and Electric Company's unfair labor practice and to undo the effects of the violation of the Act as much as possible.

The NLRB General Counsel issued its decision on November 24, 1971. The Official Notice of the Decision simply read:

Your appeal in the above matter has been duly considered. The appeal is denied. For substantially the reasons set forth in the Regional Director's letter of October 26, 1971, further proceedings herein are deemed unwarranted.

Now PG&E management was able to act with jubilation, and it did! The company published in the December 24, 1971, issue of *PGandE WEEK* that went out to every PG&E customer in its monthly billing statement: " . . . the National Labor Relations Board dismissed the charge against the company in favor of PG&E and a later appeal was also dismissed."[326]

There was no mention by PG&E that the charge was dismissed solely because the charge was not filed within 6 months of the actions upon which it was based. Of course, one should first question the validity of the six-month rule and second, how such a rule would even apply to a case like this one. I had basically struck out on every attempt to deal with what PG&E had done.

MY LAST HOPE FOR ACHIEVING JUSTICE – James R. McKittrick . . .

My last hope for achieving justice rested with James R. McKittrick. I remember the first day I met him. His secretary escorted me into his office and I found him talking on the phone. He motioned for me to sit down in a chair across from his desk. I put my briefcase and box of materials down at my feet and picked up a newspaper and pretended to read it. McKittrick's was using very course language, which turned out to be his usual way of talking. I was surprised by not only the coarse language he was using but by what he was saying as well.

What I heard was rather shocking. McKittrick said something to the effect that he "had already gotten him off once," and "this time it's going to take $50,000 up front" before he'd take this case. Whatever he was talking about and with who was none of my business, but I thought it strange for him to engage in that kind of conversation with me in the room; McKittrick didn't even yet know me.

On the very first day that I met with McKittrick, I gave him a copy of my simulation of the police report (see Appendix VII) and explained to him how I had developed it. I provided McKittrick an outline of my difficulties with PG&E and with the City of Eureka. McKittrick reviewed enough of my document file to conclude that my situation was something he was willing take on, and he sounded excited, seemed extremely optimistic, and he convinced me that he was confident he could "hit those bastards where it mattered" – in their deep pockets.

After I showed McKittrick my simulation of the police report, he said we'd have to sue for the document first before he would be able to file a defamation suit against PG&E. I believed McKittrick in that we had to have "a certified true copy" of the police report before filing a "major complaint" against PG&E. After we talked bout it, McKittrick suggested that my simulation of the police report might have been an exaggeration of the actual document because of my emotional involvement with PG&E. I assured McKittrick that I didn't think so but he insisted we needed to get a true copy of the police report before he could file the "kind of lawsuit my simulation and additional description of it would suggest."

However, I later learned that McKittrick believed my simulation and further description of it was probably an over reaction to whatever I had read in the copy of the report that was shown to me. McKittrick decided to initially file a suit for access to the police report. I remember him saying that we needed to gain access to the actual police report before we filed a slander and or defamation suit, and he also said, "Just as soon as we get the police report in our hands, we will immediately file the suit which will be based on what the report actually says."

McKittrick's position sounded logical but it didn't feel quite right to me. It eventually turned out to be a flawed plan that played into the hands of PG&E, Burt Jones, Chief Emahiser, and the City of Eureka.

I saw a copy of an official police document on December 1, 1970, that was signed by Cedric E. Emahiser, Chief of Police. Immediately after seeing the document, I constructed a simulation of it from memory. A few days later I went to Emahiser and requested permission to see the police report, making it known to him that I was certain of its existence. Permission was denied. Chief Emahiser seem surprised and upset that I even knew about the report.

ATTORNEY FRANK MORGAN – "now working pro bono" . . .

During the first week of January 1971, I contacted William Ferroggiaro, Humboldt County District Attorney, and during the second week of January 1971, the Chief Investigator of the DA's Office advised me that such a report did in fact exist. Attorney Frank Morgan, now working pro bono, wrote a letter on my behalf to Ferroggiaro dated January 18, 1971, which read in part:[327]

> When the existence of the report became known, Mr. Rowen requested the police department to permit him to read the report. The request was denied by the Chief of Police.
>
> At this point Mr. Rowen sought the aid of your office in gaining access to the report and spoke with Mr. Hickok regarding the matter. I understand that Mr. Hickok did read the report in question in the police department offices and is now familiar with its contents. Still, however, the police department apparently refuses to permit Mr. Rowen to see a copy of the report, and I understand that your office now has under consideration the question whether Mr. Rowen should voluntarily be permitted to see the report.
>
> The purpose of this letter is to urge you, in your capacity as District Attorney, to advise the Chief of Police that he can and should permit Mr. Rowen access to the report. It is our

opinion (albeit formed without specific knowledge of the report's contents) that refusal to permit Mr. Rowen to read the report, as well as whatever communications from PG&E prompted its preparation, raises serious constitutional questions.

This is particularly so insofar as the report appears to have been prepared in response to the private inquiry and interests of one citizen of this state (PG&E) and was not instigated or motivated by an overriding governmental interest.

If Mr. Rowen's legitimate interest in access to the report is denied, I foresee a protracted legal wrangle. I urge you to do what you can at this point to avoid this.

Mr. Ferroggiaro wrote back on January 27, 1971, acknowledging Morgan's January 18 letter and confirming my visit to his office and Mr. Hickok's visit to the Eureka Police Department. Ferroggiaro explained he had talked about Morgan's request with Melvin Johnson, Eureka City Attorney, and with Mr. Walter Birkelo, Eureka City Manager, and suggested Morgan should "make direct contact with those gentlemen, both of whom are superior to the Chief of Police."[328]

Mr. Ferroggiaro further explained to Morgan that the District Attorney's office "retains no statutory control or direction of a police agency within the county and the matter appears to be one 'civil in nature.'"[329]

Mr. Morgan followed up with Ferroggiaro's suggestions and sent identical letters to Mr. Birkelo and Mr. Johnson summarizing his reason for writing the letters, and pleaded the case for releasing the police report.

The City Attorney, Melvin Johnson, responded in a letter dated April 16, 1971, to District Attorney William Ferroggiaro that read in part:[330]

> The Robert Rowen matter is now the subject of inquiry by the Grand Jury . . . it is the position of the City that Police Chief Cedric Emahiser's report was made within the course and scope of his employment and is a police department record . . . such records are exempt from public records disclosure requirements . . . based on the facts of this particular case, the public interest in preserving the confidentiality and integrity of police department records of complaints and investigation of these complaints is served by not making the record public and clearly outweighs the public interest served by disclosure of the record. . . .the privilege to refuse to disclose official information and identity of informers is claimed . . .
>
> We believe that disclosure of the information and the identity of the informer is against the public interest because

there is a necessity for preserving the confidentiality of the information and identity of the informer that outweighs the necessity for disclosure in the interests of justice."

MORGAN'S PERSUASIVE ARGUMENT – "by far the best effort by any attorney working on my behalf" . . .

Mr. Morgan wrote a letter in response to the Eureka City Attorney, dated April 27, 1971, which was by far the best effort by any attorney acting on my behalf. Mr. Morgan nailed the issues involved for what they were and the arguments therein eventually became the basis for McKittrick's success in persuading the Court to release the police report to me eight months later. Morgan's letter read:[331]

Dear Mr. Johnson:

I have received your letter of April 20, 1971, enclosing a copy of your letter of April 16, 1971, to Mr Ferroggiaro outlining the City's reasons for refusing to make available to Robert Rowen the police report, which is now the subject of Grand Jury inquiry.

I understand the principles underlying Section 6255 of the Government Code upon which you rely in denying access to the report in question to Mr. Rowen and the other persons names therein.

To be sure, the public does have an interest in preserving the confidentiality and integrity of certain police department records, and this interest is properly recognized in the Code provisions to which you refer.

The public interest is not served, however, when these principles are selectively applied and the laws of this state are relied upon to deny access to such records to some citizens legitimately concerned about the truth of their contents while the same records are freely made available to other citizens whose interests therein are no greater.

It cannot be denied that the records which you now contend must be protected from scrutiny by Mr. Rowen have <u>already</u> been made available – voluntarily – by Chief C. Emahiser to other private citizens of your community, namely Pacific Gas and Electric Company and certain of its employees.

In those circumstances, it seems clear that whatever legitimate interest the Eureka Police Department might otherwise have had in the confidentiality of the records in question has already been waived by the actions of Chief Emahiser in disclosing these records to a select portion of the public it serves.

1. In your letter of April 16, 1971, you express concern that "improper precedents are not established." Consider, however, the propriety of the precedent, which you are in the instant situation creating:

2. A private citizen lodges a complaint relating to alleged criminal activity and in conjunction therewith requests your police department to investigate certain other citizens of your community

3. Your police department makes such an investigation and concludes that no further public action is warranted, no arrest is made; no indictment issued.

4. Nevertheless, the resulting police report is made available to the complaining citizen for whatever private purposes it might serve the complaining citizen. At the same time, access to the report is denied the persons most directly concerned – namely, those named in the complaint.

5. In this action forwarding "the public interest in preserving the confidentiality and integrity of police records of complaints and investigation of those complaints . . ."

Are the citizens of your community now to understand that they might request investigation of alleged criminal activities of their fellow citizens and then be provided copies of police reports relating thereto, even where the report concludes that no further public action is warranted?

One way or the other you cannot help but set a precedent in this case.

We suggest that, far from avoiding an improper precedent, your present position sanctions one.

In the long run the public interest, which your position in this matter purports to protect, can be served only by equal application of the laws.

Insofar as it has apparently been determined by the police investigation in question that no further public action is warranted, and the report has been voluntarily made available by the police chief to one interested party (the complainant), the public interest in evenhanded administration of the laws will now be served only by making the report equally accessible to the other legitimately interested persons.

The laws of this state, which you cite either prohibit disclosure of the police report to both the employees of Pacific Gas and Electric Company to which it was given and to Mr. Rowen, or they permit both to see the report.

Basic constitutional principles as well as the state laws upon you rely prohibit you from granting to the company the privilege you would now deny Bob Rowen, and in the name of the public interest you would serve, we ask you to reconsider your position in this matter."

THE JUDGE EXAMINES THE POLICE REPORT FOR HIMSELF . . .

The City Attorney never responded to Frank Morgan's letter. Nevertheless, this argument by Morgan ultimately prevailed after much legal wrangling had taken place. I had to ultimately insist that my attorney present Morgan's argument to the Court and have the Judge obtain a copy of the police report and examine it for himself.

I remember the day I laid into my attorney. Using the kind of language McKittrick was accustomed to using, I said, "Why don't you quit fucking around with my case and use the argument Frank Morgan has suggested." I was referring to Morgan's argument that the privilege had been waived when Chief Emihiser gave copies of it to PG&E personnel.

I demanded McKittrick go into the courtroom and present Morgan's argument to Judge Watson and ask the Judge to examine the police report for himself. I told McKittrick the police report clearly establishes that a copy of it was given to PG&E. McKittrick asked if I was absolutely certain of that and said it would be disastrous to the case if I were wrong.

I told McKittrick I was certain of it, and I reminded him that he was informed of that the first day I met with him. We went over my simulation of the police report in finite detail. I couldn't help but feel McKittrick was for some reason purposely dropping the ball; that he was sabotaging my case. I told McKittrick that if he didn't present my request to the Court, then I was going to Judge Watson myself. McKittrick complied with my request.

The Judge obtained a copy of the police report and examined it *in camera*, then subsequently ordered the City to provide me a true copy of it. When McKittrick saw the report, he said, "This damned thing is everything you said it was and more." Well, one thing was for sure, in McKittrick's own words, my simulation was in no way an exaggeration.

I don't know if McKittrick was patronizing me or if he was honestly surprised by the content of the report. McKittrick filed the "big lawsuit." But all that had transpired up to that point was just the tip of the iceberg. McKittrick filed my lawsuit on December 14, 1972.

THE PLOT HAD ALREADY THICKENED – long before receiving the police report and "in preparation for the legal battles" ...

The conspiratorial plot had already thickened in preparation for the legal battles looming on the horizon. Eureka City Attorney, Melvin Johnson, called upon PG&E to help defend the City's position. An effort to collaborate on the strategy to battle my attempt to gain access to the report developed into an underhanded fishing expedition, and if I were to be successful in obtaining a copy of the police report, they "would be ready."

Strategy amongst attorneys to manipulate the Court is the honorable thing to do in Johnson's way of thinking and PG&E agreed. Their actions were not based on truth and had nothing to do with the pursuit of justice.

The Eureka City Attorney called PG&E's legal department and talked with Mr. Henry LaPlante. After what appears to have been an inspirational private confab within PG&E's legal department, and very possibly involving amongst others, Henry LaPlante, L. V. Brown, and Arthur L. Hillman, a PG&E letter, dated January 10, 1972, and signed by Henry J. LaPlante, was sent to Eureka City Attorney Melvin Johnson that revealed the incredible machination:[332]

> Dear Mr. Johnson:
>
> This will confirm our telephone conversion of last week in which I assured you that this company would cooperate with your office in resisting Mr. Rowen's Superior Court petition to obtain a copy of the Police Department's report concerning him.
>
> Enclosed per your request is a list of damages to PG&E facilities caused by sabotage and another list reflecting attempted acts of sabotage. This information is supplied to you on a confidential basis and solely for your use in connection with the petition filed by Mr. Rowen. I am not sure exactly how you intend to use this information, but we would appreciate advance notice of any release of this information.
>
> The information contained in both lists has been published by various news media. It therefore occurs to me that perhaps it would be desirable to request a stipulation that the sabotage and attempts occurred prior to the report. This would eliminate the need to present any testimony.
>
> Failing this, you might ask the court to take judicial notice that acts of sabotage and attempted sabotage had taken place prior to the making of the report. If the court goes along with this, there again would be no need to present any testimony. If neither approach succeeds, perhaps you might make an offer of proof.

If the court agrees that the police report involves legitimate police concern in view of this sabotage, perhaps it would not be necessary to present testimony on this unless Rowen insists upon it. Finally, if testimony is required we should have advance notice so that we can make sure we can produce a witness for whichever item or items of testimony is desired.

At your request, I contacted Attorney Dick Zigfried of the PTT Company, telephone (415) 399-2562. I told him that you would probably be in touch with him today to make a similar request of his company. He seemed favorably disposed and is expecting your call.

Please let me know if I can be of any other assistance to you in connection with this matter.

Thank you for sending me a copy of Rowen's petition, which I have just now received.

The attachments to LaPlante's letter provided dates of 23 incidents ranging from February 1968 through June 1971 involving "pipe bombs, sticks of dynamite, fire bombs, Molotov cocktails, and various other kinds of explosives."

The IBEW Local Union 1245's Chief Shop Stewart for the Humboldt Division, Howard Darington, wrote an internal confidential union memorandum chronologically summarizing the police report matter (which was marked "Deposition Exhibit #92" during my deposition that was conducted by legal counsel for Pacific Gas and Electric Company on May 28, 1975).

HOWARD DARINGTON'S SUMMARY – regarding what had taken place between PG&E, the IBEW 1245, and the City of Eureka . . .

Although Howard Darington's memorandum unfortunately was not acted upon by the IBEW 1245 in any way, it provides an excellent summary of what took place regarding the involvement of PG&E, the union, and local governmental officials and I shall be eternally grateful to Howard Darington for putting this summary together:[333]

About July 2, 1970, Corbett Wheeler (Business Representative, IBEW Local Union 1245) indicated to Bob Rowen that some of the Supervisor's testimony during Rowen's LIC (Local Investigation Committee – part of the grievance procedure which led to the arbitration hearing on December 1 and 2, 1970) tended toward the charge that Rowen had "communist" tendencies, that he is involved with the SDS, indicating a Company attitude that Rowen tended toward violence.

Around November 9, 1970, Fred Rowen, Bob's brother, was told by a friend (who wishes to remain anonymous due to a sensitive job) that there was a lot of mud slinging by the PG&E Company against Bob Rowen in the community in official police circles.

Around November 22, 1970. Bob Rowen was told by Virgil Teague that Virgil's sister-in-law, Gail Freeman, a meter maid for the City of Eureka, overhead a discussion between some police officers concerning Bob Rowen. The general gist of the overheard conversation was that there is an official report that Bob Rowen has explosives in his possession and intended to use them against the PG&E Company.

About November 22, 1970 Rowen had a discussion with Fred's friend and asked him what the mud slinging was about. The friend said it is a police report that it reported about conspiring to blow up the power plant or firebombing, that there are four names involved in it.

He asked who is Bert Jones (PG&E Security Department investigator) and Robert Taylor (PG&E Humboldt Division Personal Manager) and said they each received a copy of the report.

He stated the report indicated the four accused people read Rap Brown, Eldridge Cleaver and others, that they advocate fire-bombing and the report claims they are known dissenters and members of a group. He said he had seen a copy and it was circulated around among the law enforcement agencies in the area and had been laying around on a counter for quite some time.

On November 23, 1970 I reported in general the above to J. J. Wilder (Assistant Business Manager, IBEW, Local 1245) by phone and made a request to find out if any action could be taken to give Bob Rowen the opportunity to defend himself against these charges.

On December 1, 1970 (the day of the Williams and Rowen arbitration hearings) the friend showed a copy of the police report to Bob Rowen but would not let Bob have a copy of the report, but he did agree to show it to Rowen's lawyer that night (Frank Morgan).

That evening Bob Rowen told Foss, Wilder and Morgan about the report and said he felt they needed to get the report into the arbitration hearing as a defense concerning the Company's attempts to discredit him. F. Morgan and Rowen went to the friend's house but the friend had changed his mind about showing the report to Morgan due to pressure from his wife who feared for his job: he did discuss the report with Morgan.

On December 9, 1970 during Rowen's Unemployment Insurance Appeals Hearing Rowen attempted to get the report introduced into the hearing but the Company refused: Brown objected on the basis that Rowen had to first lay the foundation on how he came to have knowledge of the report. Since Rowen respected his source's confidence he couldn't get the report introduced into evidence (through the power of subpoena from company files).

Around December 28, 1970 Rowen described the report to Mr. Hickok, Chief Investigator of the Humboldt County District Attorney's office. About a week later Mr. Hickok and District Attorney Ferroggiaro discussed the report. The DA expressed concern and said such a report would be irregular, but he did not have authority to take from the Eureka Police Department files, however he would put his chief investigator Mr. Hickok on it to see what could be found out about the report and report that to Rowen. The DA told Rowen that the report could be subpoenaed through his arbitration process.

Within a couple of weeks Mr.Hickok told Rowen that the report is everything Rowen claimed and more; that it is irregular, that a copy had been sent to the FBI, and, in his own personal opinion, is a violation of Rowen's constitutional rights.

Around December 29, 1970, Rowen also talked to Police Chief Emahiser about the report. Chief Emahiser told Rowen that PG&E had come to him with a charge that Rowen, Williams, Darington and Skidmore were planning to bomb the Humboldt Bay Power Plant. (Rowen asked Chief Emahiser if the plant wasn't out of the City Police jurisdiction; the Chief replied that the PG&E office was in Eureka and that most of Rowen's "cohorts" lived in Eureka.)

Chief Emahiser said he went to the local PG&E office at Sixth Street and that he and Robert Taylor talked to PG&E's San Francisco office and he received PG&E's accusations on which he based his investigation. The Chief wouldn't give Rowen a copy of or access to the report unless someone of higher authority ordered him in writing, to do so.

Around December 30, 1970, Rowen also talked to Eureka's City Manager Birkelo explaining the situation of the report and asked for the opportunity to defend himself and clear his record. Birkelo subsequently met with the DA, Police Chief, and City Attorney Johnson and later told Rowen that he could not have a copy or access to the report, that Rowen's attorney could take care of the situation and the City had nothing further to discuss with him.

The City Manager told Rowen he had read the report and affirmed that the report was essentially as Rowen claimed it to be. The City Attorney had advised that the City could be subject to liability for libel and recommended that the City not cooperate with Rowen concerning the report.

About March 30, 1971, Rowen and Williams inquired of Mr. Hickok the method of presenting the Humboldt County Grand Jury with his concern over this police report. (He accuses the Police Chief and PG&E of conspiring to falsify a police report.) Without prior warning, District Attorney Ferroggiaro took Rowen and Williams into a meeting with the Grand Jury's screening committee. The Grand Jury will consider and let Rowen and Williams know of their preliminary findings. (One of the Grand Jury members asked why Rowen's Union didn't do something about this police report.)

April 26, 1971 – the Humboldt County Grand Jury screening committee met with Rowen and confirmed Rowen's statements concerning the contents of the police report.

The committee acknowledged that the circumstances of the report was improper and further that the Grand Jury will take the matter up further in their deliberations concerning the City Police Department's involvement in this matter.

However, they said the Grand Jury does not have the authority to give Rowen a copy of the report since this matter is a civil matter between the four people involved and the PG&E. They told Rowen that DA Ferroggiaro would inform him how to obtain a certified copy of the report.

DA Ferroggiaro told Rowen that since the Chief had given a copy of the report to PG&E was a violation of the law in favor of PG&E and that, based on this misdeed, Rowen should have private counsel present a petition to a judge requesting a copy of this report (sue for the document).

The DA feels that Rowen would then receive the report through the courts. NOTE: One of the Grand Jury members (Leonard Cahill) is a local union official. He claims that when Rowen gets a copy of that report, Rowen's union and its lawyer should present the report to the arbitrator for reconsideration of Rowen's case – that this report would shed new light on the case.

JUDGE WATSON's FIRST DECISION, THE CITY OF EUREKA's RESPONSE, THEN FINALLY JUDGE WATSON's OCTOBER 25, 1972 DECISION . . .

On August 23, Superior Court Judge, W. G. Watson, Jr., issued his opinion, "The report should be disclosed to petitioner as prayed for – any privilege having been waived when it was given to Pacific Gas and Electric Company."

The Court ordered disclosure of the document on September 15, 1972. The City of Eureka immediately filed a motion to have the Court set aside and vacate its Order made on September 15, 1972, and to permit the filing of a request for findings of fact and conclusions of law.

The City of Eureka stated "this motion is made on the grounds that the Order filed herein on September 19, 1972, is not in conformity with the requirements of law and that findings of fact and conclusions of law are necessary for a proper and final determination in this matter."

Finally, the Court acted on October 25, 1972, and issued a Judgment, which read:

> This matter having come on regularly to be heard before Judge William G. Watson, Jr., in Department 1 of the Superior Court in and for the County of Humboldt, State of California on the 13th day of October 1972 and James R. McKittrick having appeared for petitioner Robert Rowen, and Melvin Johnson for respondent City of Eureka, and the court having rendered it Memorandum of Opinion in the above-entitled proceeding and good cause appearing therefore; IT IS HEREBY ORDERED, ADJUDGED AND DECREED that the City of Eureka, and particularly the Chief of Police thereof shall afford petitioner an opportunity to examine and copy that certain Police Report which is the subject of the above entitled proceeding forthwith.

In response to the Court order, the City of Eureka delivered a certified true copy of the police report (see Appendix VIII) to my attorney, James McKittrick, on November 7, 1972.

McKittrick called me with the news. He said, "This damned thing is everything you said it was and more," and he filed the defamation suit. I remember telling my wife that we finally have an official copy of the police report, thanks to Judge Watson. I also remember my wife starting to cry when my 7-year-old son, Robbie, asked, "Is it over daddy?" I looked at his mother and the expression on her face said it all, and I said to Robbie, "No, not yet but don't worry because the hard part is over." Little did I realize how wrong I was!

MY FIRST DEPOSITION ON APRIL 11, 1973 . . .

The attorneys representing the conspirators engaged me in two all day depositions; the first on April 11, 1973; and the second on May 28, 1973. In support of the conspiracy within PG&E and between PG&E and the City of Eureka, Hillman moved into my military service very early during my April 11 deposition. His line of questioning regarding my military service was the most daunting, loathsome, and contemptuous experience I have ever had in my entire life!

One would have to understand the value I placed on my military service, the pride I felt having served in a Marine force reconnaissance unit, and the personal sense of accomplishment with which I had left the Marine Corps. Mr. Hillman used all of that against me for reasons of his own while he was doing the bidding of the conspirators.

My attorney, Steven Rosenberg, who was for some reason sitting in for my regular attorney, James McKittrick, just sat there without objecting to Hillman's line of questioning. It was a line of questioning that had absolutely nothing to do with my case against PG&E, the City of Eureka, Cedric Emahiser, and Bert Jones.

McKittrick later explained that Hillman was developing an argument PG&E could use to support the conspiracy between all of them regarding the content of the police report. McKittrick said PG&E was obviously going to use as their defense that I was capable of doing the kinds of things PG&E's Bert Jones had accused me of in the police report.

Hillman had asked me a total of 94 questions concerning my four years in the Marine Corps. After establishing that I had entered the Marine Corps after leaving school at sixteen, his first question regarding my military service was, "Did you receive any special training in the Marine Corps?" Then Hillman asked, "Would you describe for me the special training you received in the Marine Corps?" His line of questioning entered into an extensive exploration of my training in jump school, pathfinder school, guerrilla warfare, demolitions, ABC (atomic, biological, and chemical warfare), noncommissioned officers school, amphibious assaults, the use and types of various small arms, and the machine gun.

Hillman asked about the basic mission of Marine pathfinders. He wanted to know if pathfinders perform any intelligence activities, engaged in "attack patrols, operated as teams or individually, and if there was any specialization of skills within a pathfinder unit." When he asked me what kind of training I had with small arms and I responded, in part, the "M3A1." He then asked if that was the "grease gun," which surprised me – the fact that he knew the M3A1 was known as the "grease gun." Hillman knew a lot about my unit in the Corps and that was very troublesome to me.

Mr. Hillman wanted to know the caliber of every weapon I had been trained to use. He wanted to know the leadership structure within a pathfinder team and what rank I held. It appeared he already knew the answers to the questions he was asking me.

(Special note: I discovered quite my accident at a Marine reunion a couple of years ago of how Hillman probably knew the answers to the questions he was asking me but my wife insisted that I not include any of it in my *Diary* and even though I was sorely attempted not to pay any attention to her, I decided to honor her wishes)

Mr. Hillman wanted to know if members of pathfinder teams specialized in just one area or if pathfinders received training in all areas. He wanted to know if each team member had a specialty assignment, and if so, what was mine. At first, Mr. Hillman made it appear he knew my specialty might be in demolitions but he learned that I was the machine gunner on my team. However, Hillman continued to pursue a line of questioning regarding my training in demolitions.

He wanted to know what types of demolitions we used and seemed pleased to hear that we used plastic explosives. Hillman then pursued this whole line of questioning further with, "What type of demolition work were you trained in?" and "Did it include training in demolition of enemy installations of various types, buildings, and that sort of thing?"

His questioning then addressed the types of detonators and the mechanics of using them. Then he asked questions about my ABC training including the detonation of nuclear devices, and the effects of wind and radiological hazards?

Hillman also wanted to know about the "bacteriological portion" of my ABC training and connected that portion of his questioning to sabotage activities. He wanted to know if I served in Vietnam or Cambodia and for how long I had served overseas.

This outrageous line of questioning was completely out of line and without any justification. It had nothing to do with my lawsuit. Hillman knew that because he was basing all of his questions on the contents of the police report. The police chief said he received the information from PG&E's Bert Jones and Robert Taylor (the police chief told the Eureka-*Times Standard* environmental reporter, that he took the information in good faith, later feeling he had been used by PG&E). Bert Jones denied making any of the statements recorded in the police report. All of PG&E's actions, now through the unscrupulous actions of Arthur Hillman, became the mother of all red herrings.

MY SECOND DEPOSITION ON MAY 28, 1973 . . .

The conspiracy within PG&E, and between PG&E and the City of Eureka is further revealed by the deposition of me that was conducted on

April 11, 1973, by Arthur L. Hillman and Victor M. Corbett, attorneys for the Pacific Gas and Electric Company, both of whom were joined by Herman Koelewyn, attorney for the City of Eureka. After the usual introductory remarks, Mr. Hillman immediately confronted me about my files that I was supposed to bring with me to the deposition:[334]

> **Mr. Hillman (PG&E attorney):** (Directed to Mr. Rowen . . .) Were you informed by your attorneys that your deposition had been noticed for 9:00 A. M. on April 11th?
> **Mr. Rowen:** That's correct.
> **Mr. Hillman** Were you informed by your attorney that the notice of deposition directed that you bring certain documents and other things with you to the deposition?
> **Mr. Rowen:** No, I didn't receive that notice.
> **Mr. Hillman:** (Directed to Mr. Rosenberg . . .) Did you inform him of the listing of the documents listed on the notice of the taking of deposition?
> **Mr. Rosenberg (my attorney filling in for McKittrick):** I didn't, but I see he has a file with him.
> **Mr. Hillman:** Perhaps the problem will be alleviated if we can go through the notice and ascertain whether you've brought these documents with you. If you like you can show Mr. Rowen a copy of the notice of deposition and it may aid him in answering the questions we have.
>
> In the notice the term "Document" refers to all memoranda, reports, correspondence, communications, letters, notes, handwritten or otherwise, drafts, agenda and minutes of meetings, sketches, diagrams, drawing, books, papers or other printed matter or copies of such memoranda, reports, correspondence, communications, letters, notes handwritten or otherwise, drafts, agenda and minutes of meetings, sketches, diagrams, drawing, books, papers or other printed matter.

Shortly afterwards we went off the record and I went to my attorney's office with him to get the file he had of the documents I had provided McKittrick (which admittedly was only a portion of my inventory). I became very upset with what was happening, first because I did not know all of this was going to happen and especially in this manner; and second, I expressed that if PG&E and the City of Eureka had "legal access" to all of my records then I should have the same access to all of theirs!

I had copies of very private letters between myself and others, people that I did not want PG&E to go after. My only reason for having those documents with me was to refresh my memory concerning certain facts that were contained in those documents so I could truthfully answer questions put to me during my deposition.

I did not realize I was going to have to turn over everything, except any "private communications" between my attorney and myself. Unfortunately, any communications between myself and other attorneys became fair game for PG&E, including attorney David Pesonen, who had litigation proceedings in progress with PG&E. Pesonen had agreed to assist McKittrick but was not an attorney of record. I became frustrated with the whole damned situation during the day. I found Hillman to be arrogant, pompous, condescending, and without any sense of morality. Of course, that was how PG&E wanted him and the reason he was on the company payroll.

PG&E was on a fishing expedition, which became abundantly clear during my two depositions conducted by PG&E attorneys when they started poring over my files that I was court-ordered to bring to them.

I carefully watched their behaviors as they were discovering this document and that and I kept fielding their repeated question, "Is this all of it?" Then I would time and again slowly shove more stuff across the table, and each time I observed their behaviors with some amusement. The process continued for much of the day. I really didn't give them everything they would have most likely wanted to receive.

Again, "Is this all of it?"

I responded, "This is most of what I have, there may still be some things in boxes that I wasn't able to get to before coming here today." Actually, I had more, much more, but that was all I was able to give them because my attorney had failed to provide me the request; I didn't want to embarrass him in front of the PG&E attorneys.

During my April 11, 1973, deposition, I had refused to provide the name of the person in the Humboldt Sheriff Department that gave me a copy of the police document to read; my refusal created quite a stir with Hillman and Corbett. Nonetheless, my position remained clear which I had to state several times. After a couple more rounds of utter nonsense, my attorney finally said, "I'm going to stop this inquisition!"[335] He then found it necessary to say to me, "Forget about it, don't answer anymore."[336]

The PG&E attorneys were not yet finished with their insinuations. At my second deposition and after hours of interrogation by Arthur Hillman and Charles Denny, Mr. Denny laid the following question on me:[337]

> **Mr. Denny:** (Directed to Mr. Rowen) Have you at any point in time, whether during the time you were in the Army or the Marines or at the same time received any type of psychological or psychiatric care?

I had a very difficult time with PG&E's attack on me for a very long time and this deposition conducted by PG&E's Arthur Hillman and Charles Denny that ended on May 28, 1975, was devastating. It has weighed heavily for all these years that PG&E would stoop so low as to protect a failed and dangerous technology and those responsible for defaming me. Neither

Hillman or Denny had any desire to pursue the truth; their only goal, their only purpose was to protect their guilty clients!

On December 14, 1972, my initial complaint for slander had been filed in the Superior Court of the State of California in and for the County of Humboldt and named Pacific Gas and Electric Company, Bert Jones, and several Does, as defendants. The initial complaint was amended on March 21, 1973, which was now a nine-page complaint that read in part:

> On or about the 3rd day of June 1970, defendants Bert Jones and Doe 1, orally uttered statements to C. Emahiser, then Chief of Police for the City of Eureka, State of California, in which said defendants falsely and maliciously stated that (all pertinent portions of the police report) . . .
>
> Said statements and utterances were false and defamatory and known to be such by defendants, and were made by defendants through ill will and malice towards plaintiff and with the intent, design and purpose on the part of said defendants to injure plaintiff in his professional standing and reputation, and to discredit and defame plaintiff and bring plaintiff into public discredit in his profession, and to bring him into public contempt and ridicule . . .

Pacific Gas and Electric Company answered the complaint on May 7, 1973. In the answer to the complaint, PG&E admitted to the company name and that it provided electric service to the public in California for "light, heat and power."

PG&E admitted that Berton F. Jones was an employee of PG&E as an investigator in PG&E's Security Department. PG&E admitted that I was an employee of the company from April 10, 1962, to June 5, 1970, and that I was employed at PG&E's Humboldt Bay Power Plant as a nuclear control technician until my termination from the company on June 5, 1970.

PG&E then summarized the reasons for my termination. PG&E admitted that Berton F. Jones spoke with Cedric Emahiser on or about June 3, 1970, "Concerning matters of interest to PG&E, the Police Department of the City of Eureka, and other law enforcement agencies, including matters related to the security and safety of the PG&E power plant located at Humboldt Bay, California."

A portion of said conversation concerned plaintiff. PG&E admitted Cedric Emahiser "prepared a confidential police intelligence report . . . and therein admits that portions of said report were based, in part, upon information obtained by Emahiser from Jones."

PG&E also admitted that copies of the report were distributed to the Federal Bureau of Investigation, to the Sheriff's Department of the County of Humboldt, State of California and to Berton F. Jones and Robert H.

Taylor of PG&E.

Finally, PG&E stated in the answer to the complaint that I knew of the existence of the report as early as October 1970, and on or about December 1, 1970, I "learned the contents of said report and was aware of the names of all persons, individual, corporate or otherwise, who in any way supplied or were represented as having supplied any information to Chief Emahiser for the preparation of said report."

PG&E then denied "each and every allegation of paragraphs I, II, III, IV, V, VI, VII, VIII, IX, X, XI, XII, and XIII" of the amended complaint not expressly admitted to.

PG&E's incredible grand finale in the company's answer to the amended complaint was the following:[338]

1. The cause of action by Rowen was barred by the Statute of Limitations,
2. The communications in question, and each of them, complained by Rowen in the amended complaint herein, were made in good faith and without malice towards Rowen, and
3. The statements referred to in the complaint were privileged under the guarantees of the First and Fourteenth Amendments to the United States in that they constitute fair comment and criticism of Rowen, a public figure, and said statements concerned subject matter of public concern and public issues and were made without actual malice.
4.

How does our system of justice, that pursues the truth and is interested addressing the wrongful acts of "persons, individual, corporate or otherwise," handle such hogwash as contained in PG&E's response to the amended complaint?

PG&E filed a Notice of Motion and Motion for Summary Judgment July 21, 1975. The Court scheduled the matter for August 4, 1975, at which time PG&E would move the Court for an order dismissing the complaint. PG&E's request was based on the following:

1. The alleged statements attributed to defendant were absolutely privileged and made in an official proceeding authorized by law –to wit, the reporting of possible criminal activity to a police officer.
2. The alleged statements attributed to defendant were privileged in that they were made without malice to a person interested therein by one who was also

interested.

3. The alleged causes of action by plaintiffs, and each of them, are barred by the statute of limitations.

4. The alleged statements, insofar as they refer to plaintiffs Raymond Skidmore and Howard Darington, are not defamatory as a matter of law.

PG&E cited a provision in California law in support of its position that the alleged statements were absolutely privileged:[339]

When a publication is absolutely privileged, there is no liability, even though it is made with actual malice.

PG&E also cited another provision of California law in support of its position that the cause of action is barred by the Statute of Limitations:[340]

The cause of action ordinarily accrues when, under the substantive law, the wrongful act is done . . . And the general rule is that the statute will begin to run though the plaintiff is ignorant of his cause of action or the identity of the wrongdoer.

A memorandum of points and authorities in opposition to PG&E's motion to dismiss the case was filed with the Court on August 25, 1975. This thirteen-page memorandum contained five main "points and authorities" supported by legal arguments establishing that triable issues of fact do exist.

On October 3, 1975, Judge Watson issued his ruling on PG&E's motion to dismiss the case, which read, "Having read and considered the memorandums filed by the parties, together with the exhibits thereto, there are, in the opinion of the Court, triable issues remaining. The motion for summary judgment to dismiss the case is denied."

This was great news for my family; we're finally going to get our day in court! Whoops, not so fast. The conspirators panicked and immediately regrouped.

The Legal Fray Began . . .

➢ "Notice of motion for reconsideration or clarification of ruling on motion for summary judgment" was filed on October 10, 1975;

➢ "Notice of motion and motion for an order bifurcating the defense of the statute of limitations, and memorandum of points and authorities in support thereof" was filed on October 16, 1975;

➤ "Declaration in support of application for an order shortening time and order" filed on October 16, 1975;

➤ "Ruling on motion to reconsider" issued on October 23, 1975;

➤ "Notice of motion for reconsideration of ruling on motion to reconsider" filed on October 23, 1975;

➤ "Supplemental memorandum of point and authorities in opposition to motion for summary judgment" filed on November 17, 1975;

➤ "Memorandum in opposition to request for reconsideration" filed on December 9, 1975;

➤ "Notice of motion to file amendments to complaints" filed on December 12, 1975.

The fray continued on into the new year with names of attorneys apearing out of nowhere that I hadn't heard of before; these attorneys were obviously working together representing PG&E, Bert Jones, and the City of Eureka. These new names included Charles T. Van Deusen, Christine Helwidk, and F. Ronald Laupheimer along with the more familiar names of Charles W. Denny, Victor M.Corbett, and Arthur L. Hillman all of whom were affiliated with law offices in the California cities of San Francisco, Oakland, and Eureka:

➤ Memorandum of points and authorities in opposition to motion to file amendments to complaints" filed on January 9, 1976;

➤ Memorandum in opposition to motion to amend" filed on February 13, 1976;

➤ Reply memorandum of Bert Jones in support of motion for summary judgment" filed on February 13, 1976.

The fray finally ended on February 13, 1976, with the Court ruling in favor of all defendants and against Rowen. The Court succumbed to an overwhelming force of opposition by the conspirators who were clearly armed with Machiavellian motives and a self-serving selection of legal arguments void of any desire to seek justice by doing the right and honorable thing. It was truly another stacked deck!

At this point, it's only fair for me to provide the complete text of Judge W. G. Watson's ruling on the motion to reconsider and the motion to amend issued on February 13, 1976, and his order for entry of summary judgment in favor of PG&E, Bert Jones, et al., also issued on February 13, 1976:

RULING ON MOTION TO RECONSIDER AND MOTION TO AMEND

The Court heretofore had granted a motion for summary judgment in this matter. Prior to its entry, plaintiff filed what is termed a motion for reconsideration of a ruling.

Since the initial motion for summary judgment was made by defendants, the motion to reconsider on the granting of the motion would not be proper. However, since the motion to reconsider was filed prior to the formal entry of an order granting the summary judgment, the Court has reviewed the matter in question and is of the opinion that its initial Memorandum of Opinion states the view of the Court; and the motion to reconsider is denied.

Plaintiffs have also filed a motion to amend to state a cause of action allegedly for conspiracy in this matter – the stated object being, of course, to avoid the statute of limitations defense heretofore raised.

The amendment comes some 2-1/2 years after the filing of the initial complaint and much beyond that offices the actions alleged, and for that reason should be denied. In addition, the matters alleged are matters raised and considered by the Court in connections with the motion for summary judgment.

On both bases, then, the motion to amend is denied. The motion for summary judgment having been granted, the summary judgment will be entered.

ORDER FOR ENTRY OF SUMMARY JUDGMENT IN FAVOR OF DEFENDANTS AND AGAINST PLAINTIFF

Plaintiff's motion for reconsideration of the Court's Ruling dated October 22, 1975 on defendants' motion for reconsideration or clarification of ruling on motion for summary judgment came on regularly for hearing before me on November 10, 1975. James McKittrick appeared as counsel for plaintiff Robert Rowen. Victor Corbett appeared as counsel for defendant Pacific Gas and Electric Company, and Jack B. McCowanJr., as counsel for defendant Bert Jones.

> After full consideration of all papers filed by the moving and responding parties hereto, and oral arguments of counsel, it appears and the Court finds that defendants have shown by admissible evidence and reasonable inferences from that evidence that the action has no merit and that plaintiff has presented no triable issues of fact.
>
> It is ordered that plaintiff's motion herein be, and it hereby is, denied. It is further ordered, adjudged and decreed that judgment be, and hereby is, entered in accordance with this order in favor of defendants Pacific Gas and Electric Company and Bert Jones and against plaintiff Robert Rowen and that Robert Rowen's complaint be, and hereby is, dismissed with costs to said defendants.

Now it's time to vent. This decision by Judge Watson was the most unjust application of the law by a legal system – an American legal system – against an American citizen who was just trying to do the right and honorable thing. This judge handled all the proceedings regarding PG&E's misconduct that was clearly embodied in a conspiracy between Bert Jones, Robert Taylor and Cedric Emahiser that involved the most malicious motivations to destroy those who were willing to speak out against a company that was breaking the law and thereby subjecting employees of the company and the public to radiation hazards.

Again, I'm not an attorney and although I've learned a lot about how our legal system works, I'm afraid I have to say that Judge Watson took the course of least resistance to maintain whatever it was that kept him in good stead with the politics of the community – not the community of the general public as a whole but with those who are influential within that community.

The summary of PG&E's argument before the California Court of Appeal read exactly as follows:[341]

> The evidence reveals and appellants' own pleadings admit that their claims are based on those statements alleged to have been made by Jones during his conversation with Chief Emahiser on June 3, 1970. The first of the appellants' complaints was not filed until December 14, 1972.
>
> The evidence furthers shows, knowledge of that conversation more than one year before any of their complaints were filed. The causes of action stated in appellants' complaints are absolutely barred by the statute of limitations. Finally, the evidence shows that the various legal arguments posed by appellants as a means to get by the bar of the statute of limitations are inapplicable.

˜ PG&E argued that the proper course of action for Rowen and Williams, et al, "Would have been to file their complaints within the statutory period and then to have sought, through discovery, a copy of the police report, if they deemed it necessary to prove their claims."

Contrary to claims by PG&E and Bert Jones, it was not immediately obvious that a provable conspiracy had taken place. According to PG&E through the efforts of the City of Eureka (and maintained up to but not included in PG&E's appeal court argument) the communication between officials of PG&E and the Chief of Police for the City of Eureka was privileged and protected from disclosure.

PG&E argued that this complaint had nothing to do with the PG&E's radiation safety protection program at the Humboldt Bay Nuclear Power Plant. On the contrary, it had everything to do with it along with the company's desire and actions to permanently silence the critics of it.

It was a useless argument since the governmental privilege had already been claimed and had to be overcome. There was nothing inherently automatic about achieving this in current law. The effort thereby amounted to breaking new legal ground, which was accomplished by the written argument put forward by attorney Frank Morgan, working *pro bono*, based on a suggestion made by Humboldt County District Attorney William F. Ferroggiaro, and reinforced by the 1971 Humboldt County Grand Jury and its foreman, Sara Parsons.

PG&E proudly quoted a U.S. Supreme Court decision in its brief sent to the California Court of Appeals:[342]

> **Statutes of limitations are vital to the welfare of society, and are favored in the law. They are found and approved in all systems of enlightened jurisprudence; they promote repose by giving security and stability to human affairs; important public policy lies at their foundation; they stimulate to activity and punish negligence.**

If one was unaware of the source of this statement, it would naturally be assumed that the attorneys for PG&E, Bert Jones, Police Chief Cedric Emahiser, and the City of Eureka all got together and wrote it themselves, with PG&E orchestrating the effort for it certainly sounded like the inner thinking of PG&E's *corporate* America.

The simple truth is this quote appeared in a Supreme Court case dated 1894,[343] just a mere two years before another infamous decision of the U.S. Supreme Court known as Plessy vs. Ferguson. It argued in favor of the "separate but equal" doctrine in American jurisprudence – An infamous decision that carried forth in American history for a little more than half a century.

One might argue that the one decision had nothing to do with the other, and the observation might be right – sort of. However, when viewed through the progressive prism in the historical search for truth, justice, and equality focused on and defined by *the right thing to do*, they were both wrong!

PG&E threw unlimited resources at the Rowen case, which resulted in a long protracted legal wrangle, which is exactly the way PG&E wanted it! PG&E successfully argued that the statute of limitation, which was upheld by the California Appellate Court, barred my complaint.

Why did McKittrick fail to file the slander/libel/defamation suit when I first met with him? There has been some wild speculation about that because McKittrick was too good of an attorney not to recognize the procedural need to do that. What was McKittrick's connection to PG&E, either directly or indirectly? I will never know.

It was suggested by David Pesonen that I might want to consider an action against McKittrick. I did not immediately respond to Pesonen's suggestion. However, my difficulties with PG&E came up in a conversation with Al Wilkins, a parent of one of my students and an attorney in Weaverville, California where I was working and living at the time. He suggested I contact Bill Coshow, an attorney in Redding, California, and share with him what had happened in my PG&E case. I followed up with Mr. Wilkins' suggestion to contacted Mr. Coshow.

After summarizing my case and explaining what had happened, Mr. Coshow said a "a first year law student would have known better."

I told Coshow that I thought McKittrick may have been bought off by PG&E but of course I had no proof of it.

Coshow just grinned and said, "I'm surprised you're still alive and that you haven't met the same fate as Karen Silkwood."

My response, "Actually, Mr. Coshow, I've been told that before."

Mr. Coshow agreed to handle a legal malpractice action against McKittrick. Coshow told me this was going to be one of the easiest cases he has ever handled and it turned out to be true. I agreed to an out of court settlement of $50,000.

McKittrick ended up involved in some questionable behaviors and associating with some shady people. As I was writing this portion of my Diary, I decided not to repeat the things that I had heard about James McKittrick that may have led to his suicide.

After McKittrick committed suicide under what appeared to be some alleged questionable circumstances, I was notified that the Court was supervising an effort to dispose of his files. I petitioned the Court for McKittrick's "work product" files pertaining to my PG&E case but was unsuccessful. My purpose was to see if there was anything in McKittrick's "work product" files, e.g., phone notes, memos, correspondence, etc., that indicated any kind of collusion between McKittrick and PG&E, and to expose it publicly if that were the case.

The Court ruled on August 26, 1996, that McKittrick's "work product documents are the property of the Estate of James R. McKittrick and not the property of Mr. McKittrick's clients." According to Gena Rae Eichenberg, Attorney for Petitioner (Humboldt County Bar Association), in her reply brief in support of the protective order that had been issued, I was not entitled to McKittrick's "work product" relating to my case against PG&E.

Ms. Gena Rae Eichenberg's concluding remark in her reply brief read: "Those materials, constituting the attorney work product, belong to the attorney and this Court properly issued its Protective Order. Consequently, Mr. Rowen's remedy is to negotiate with Mr. McKittrick's heir, his son, James O. McKittrick, for Mr. McKittrick's work product."

My attempts to obtain my attorney's so-called "work product" files pertaining to my case against PG&E failed. And to this day I am left to wonder what was in those files that I wasn't supposed to see.

Author in the boonies overseas with his A-6 machine gun (1961)

"R&R Marine Pathfinder Team (Sub Unit 1) - Okinawa 1961 (author at lower right)

__XV__

15. Nuclear Censorship & the Don Widener Story

1971-1979

> **Jack Lemon (Narrator):** This reactor in northern California has been operating since the 1950's but not without criticism. Such as faulty fuel rods, a problem since corrected. We asked PG&E's James C. Carroll about such criticisms.
>
> **Don Widener (Producer):** Mr. Carroll, as you know, there has been published criticisms of the plant here for using improper construction materials in the beginning. Can you describe what that's all about?
>
> **James C. Carroll (PG&E):** Well, this is analogous to a problem you have in your industry. There were criticisms of improper design and 21 construction techniques in early color television sets that resulted in excessive radiation to people.[344] [James Real, *Mother Jones Magazine*]

The Don Widener story is also part of my story, therefore, I am including it in my *Diary*, which focuses on silencing and neutralizing the critics through nuclear censorship, blacklisting, and character assassination.

Don Widener called me during the latter part of December 1970. Mr. Widener introduced himself as a producer of news documentaries for NBC TV and told me he was aware of my difficulties with PG&E. Widener wanted to know if I would be willing to meet with him and talk about the Humboldt Bay Nuclear Power Plant. I said I would be happy to, explaining that I had been talking to anyone and everyone who wanted to hear about that place and the people who worked there.

We met and I suggested we go together up on the hill overlooking the plant, which we did. We stopped at one of the environmental monitoring stations and talked for a long while.

I summarized my history at the nuclear facility, and provided Mr. Widener examples of a wide variety of radiation safety problems at the plant. Widener wanted to know why the radiation levels were skyrocketing at Humboldt Bay. I remember my response just like it was yesterday, "That's simple to explain, Mr. Widener. It's because of the breakdown of the stainless steel nuclear fuel cladding PG&E initially used at start up."

Widener told me that he had read about the fuel-cladding problem in *Look Magazine* and asked if I had seen the article; I told him that I hadn't.

Following my interview with Widener, I got ahold of a copy of the magazine to see what Widener was talking about. Jack Shepherd, Senior Editor for *Look Magazine,* wrote the article Widener had read; its title was *"The Nuclear Threat Inside America."*

When I started reading Shepherd's article, I couldn't put it down because I found a modicum of solace in its content that validated many of my PG&E-AEC issues of concern.

Shepherd wrote, "AEC sees its mission as a crusade, Howard B. Brown, Jr., assistant general manager, says: 'We have circumnavigated the globe many times over, spreading the gospel about the peaceful atom.' Opponents are heretics."[345]

Shepherd's next paragraph introduced me to Drs. Gofman and Tamplin:[346]

> Drs. John Gofman and Arthur Tamplin of AEC's Lawrence Radiation Laboratory (Livermore, California), argue that AEC's 'safe radiation dose' is unsafe. If everyone got AEC's safe dose, they claim, there would be 16,000 to 24,000 more cancer and leukemia deaths a year in the U.S. They demand an immediate reduction to a tenth of the AEC level.
>
> AEC fumes. 'Gofman, Tamplin and their allies are . . . trying their case in the press and other public forums,' said James T. Ramey, an AEC commissioner. We used to call such characters 'Opera Stars.'
>
> Dr. Gofman has rebutted: 'there is no morality . . . not a shred of honesty in any one of them – none. I can assure you, from every bit of dealing I've had . . . there is absolute duplicity, guaranteed duplicity, lies at every turn, falsehood in every way, about you personally and about your motives.'

The latter part of this passage in Jack Shepherd's *"The Nuclear Threat Inside America"* struck a cord! I could have written that passage to describe what was happening to me.

So I decided to become familiar with the work of Drs. Gofman and Tamplin and when their book, *Poisoned Power: The Case Against Nuclear Power Plants*, came out later that year, I read it from cover to cover with immense interest.

Mr. Widener and I discussed the stainless steel fuel cladding problem at length and how that problem caused the plant to become grossly contaminated throughout, which led to the many confrontations I had with management over radiation safety issues at the plant. Mr. Widener explained that he wanted to go into the plant to do some filming and was hoping to conduct some on-camera interviews. He asked me for some ideas regarding topics he might consider and suggestions regarding who would be best for him to interview.

I told Mr. Widener I thought the number one topic would be the company's decision to use stainless steel cladding over zircaloy in the first loading of the reactor core. As far as Mr. Widener's question concerning who would be the best candidates for on-camera interviews, I remember telling Widener I would really be surprised if PG&E would allow any of the regular plant employees, including members of local plant management for that matter, to be interviewed on-camera. If the company did allow plant employees to be interviewed, however, I said PG&E corporate headquarters would most certainly handpick them.

I did say to Widener that if he could manage to interview any members of plant management, I recommended he try to get Edgar Weeks on camera and one of PG&E's radiation protection engineers, either Gail Allen or Jerome Boots. In addition to the fuel cladding issue, I suggested he bring up the higher releases of radioactive gases and the "mysterious particle" problem as they affect the folks downwind from the plant.

If he had time for it, I suggested he consider asking questions about the release of the spent feul shipping cask in August 1969, the employees who had left the nuclear facility contaminated for several days, the spent fuel pool that was leaking into the ground water, and about the selling of contaminated pipe to G&R Scrap Metals. I explained to that if he could manage to talk about these things, he would end up with a startling view of the Humboldt Bay nuclear facility and plant management's philosophy regarding employee and public safety.

I also told Mr. Widener he shouldn't mention my name or he would probably get the door slammed in his face. I wished him the best of luck with his trip into the plant and asked if he would let me know how it turned out for him.

Don Widener was an award-winning producer of news documentaries for KNBC-Los Angeles. Widener had already produced three highly acclaimed documentaries: The environmental blockbuster *"The Slow Guillotine,"* followed by *"Timetable for Disaster,"* and *"A Sea of Troubles."* *"The Slow Guillotine,"* Widener's first news documentary, which dealt with air pollution, was acclaimed as "a best news documentary" and won Widener the Emmy and the Alfred I. DuPont awards. Widener was looking to add another production, *"Powers That Be,"* to his resume when I met him.

"Powers That Be" turned out to be a harsh, frightening look at the activities of the AEC and the dangers inherent in the nuclear industry. The

program was narrated by Jack Lemon and was initially shown on May 17, 1971, by KNBC-TV in Los Angeles – in fact, that initial showing turned out to be its one and only public showing. Following the broadcast of *Powers That Be*, Mr. Jerry Haynes of Southern California Edison contacted PG&E's James C. Carroll. The following is Mr. Carroll's testimony regarding their conversation:[347]

> **Mr. Pesonen (attorney for Don Widener):** (Directed to Mr. Carroll) Southern California Edison Company is another utility in California?
>
> **Mr. Carroll:** Yes. In the southern – INTERRUPTED
>
> **Mr. Pesonen:** They also operated a nuclear power plant that we saw in the film, don't they?
>
> **Mr. Carroll:** Yes, they did.
>
> **Mr. Pesonen:** Was it Mr. Haynes that told you about this?
>
> **Mr. Carroll:** Jerry Haynes.
>
> **Mr. Pesonen:** And he's an engineer with Southern California Edison?
>
> **Mr. Carroll:** That's correct.
>
> **Mr. Pesonen:** Had he seen the film?
>
> **Mr. Carroll:** Yes. He told me he had seen it.
>
> **Mr. Pesonen:** And what did he tell you about the film?
>
> **Mr. Carroll:** I believe he mentioned that it was a very strongly antinuclear film, and that it was the one that I appeared in. I was surprised to hear that that I had appeared in it. And he indicated that I looked very bad in the film, that it appeared that I was unable or not willing to answer a question that had been given to me. Words to that effect.
>
> **Mr. Pesonen:** Did he specify to you specifically any words that he recalled having been said in the film with respect to you?
>
> **Mr. Carroll:** No, he hadn't.
>
> **Mr. Pesonen:** Was Mr. Haynes, by the way, a nuclear engineer or involved in nuclear operations for Southern California Edison?
>
> **Mr. Carroll:** I believe that at that time he was the plant engineer at the San Onofre Power Plant.

PG&E used its incredible corporate-might to put the kibosh to *Powers That Be*. PG&E's behind the scenes, underhanded maneuvering ultimately resulted in the blacklisting of Widener in the film industry – and silencing his *Powers That Be* film forever!

After the initial showing of *Powers That Be*, PG&E immediately responded with a letter writing campaign against the film and its producer, bombarding network and government officials alike with accusations of distortions and unethical conduct by Widener. The Emmy award-winning producer was accused by PG&E of doing things that were technologically impossible in the early 1970s, and the initial accuser was PG&E's very own

James C. Carroll. And PG&E's corporate headquarters fully supported Carroll in his effort to "crucify" Widener.

After arriving at the Humboldt Bay Nuclear Power Plant on February 10, 1971, Widener and his filming crew were escorted around the outside of the facility by PG&E's Fritz Draeger, Atomic Information Coordinator. A few filming shots were made mainly of the effluent canal area. Widener and his crew were then taken to the admin building and into the power plant's conference room where he was introduced to James Adams, PG&E's Marine Biologist, and to James C. Carroll, PG&E's Nuclear and Supervising Steam Generation Engineer from corporate headquarters in San Francisco.

It was decided that on-camera interviews would take place in the reactor control room of Unit 3; however, there were preliminary discussions held in the conference room of the anticipated subject matter regarding the ensuing on-camera interviews to be conducted in the reactor control room.

Widener's first question in the conference room concerned the problem with the faulty first generation stainless steel fuel cladding. J. C. Carroll responded by saying a proper explanation to this "situation that occurred several years ago would take five to ten minutes." Carroll would later write in an internal company memorandum, "We offered the opinion (to Widener) that we did not see how fuel cladding problems were really of much public interest."[348] Carroll also stated in his memorandum that Widener didn't know very much about the power industry and seemed to be more interested in controversy.[349]

Carroll later recalled that he walked out of the conference room believing Widener had decided not to bring up the fuel cladding problem during the formal on-camera interview because of the lengthy response the question would require. Again, Carroll had told Widener that explaining the fuel cladding problem would take too much time during an on-camera interview.

Once in the reactor control room, however, and to Carroll's shocking surprise, Widener's first substantive question addressed PG&E's faulty nuclear fuel rods in the early sixties. After all, that's why Widener went to Humboldt Bay in the first place – to ask probing questions! Why? Because that was his job.

On July 13, 1971, two months after the documentary was shown to a large Los Angeles viewing audience, J. C. Carroll sent an angry letter to Station Manager Robert Howard of KNBC-TV in Los Angeles. In his letter, Carroll attacked Widener's production of *Powers That Be* claiming "this 'so-called' documentary is the most irresponsible piece of journalism purporting to present a technical subject to a lay audience which I have ever encountered,"[350] then added, "It is replete with half truths, innuendos, and worse."[351] Carroll's letter was worked over by a number of key people in PG&E's corporate headquarters. Mr. Carroll accused Widener of a gross breach of journalistic ethics by secretly taping a pre-interview discussion about the fuel rods and then splicing the recording into the formal interview. Here's the piece of the film that was so upsetting to Carroll:[352]

Jack Lemon (Narrator): This reactor in northern California has been operating since the 1950s. But not without criticism. Such as faulty fuel rods, a problem since corrected. We asked PG&E's James C. Carroll about such criticisms.

Don Widener (Producer and on-camera interviewer): Mr. Carroll, as you know, there have been published criticisms of the plant here for using improper construction materials in the beginning. Can you describe what that's all about?

James C. Carroll (PG&E's nuclear engineer): Well this is analogous to a problem you have in your industry. There were criticisms of improper design and construction techniques in early color television sets that resulted in excessive radiation to people.

Don Widener: What was it exactly that the critics were talking about in your case?

James C. Carroll: I don't think we ought to answer that it's too lengthy a question.

Jack Lemon: Long questions. Sometimes short answers. It's tough to get a matched set.

Mr. Carroll's response would have been too lengthy an answer for a taped interview? Carroll summarized in his letter of complaint to Station Manager Robert Howard of KNBC-TV what he would have said in response to Widener's question regarding the faulty fuel rods. Interestingly enough, Carroll's written explanation in his letter to Mr. Howard takes less than a minute to read aloud!

Don Widener filed a lawsuit against PG&E, J. C. Carroll, and several others involved in the company's attempt to discredit him and his professional work. The suit was initially handled by a Los Angeles law firm that had been worn down by PG&E's vast legal resources, the lead attorney became a judge, and the suit was virtually on the rocks going no place.

Widener called me and we talked about the problem he was having with his lawsuit. I suggested he call David Pesonen in San Francisco. I told Mr. Widener that Pesonen had represented the Sierra Club in a number of actions against PG&E and has a reputation of being an outstanding San Francisco attorney with fire in his gut.

Mr. Widener wanted to know why I wasn't using David Pesonen to handle my difficulties with PG&E, and I explained my situation. I told Widener I thought his situation was different than mine and stressed that Pesonen is willing and very capable of taking on PG&E. Widener checked around then called David Pesonen who agreed to take his case and the rest is history!

In order to lay completely bare Carroll's ridiculous position, it was brought up again during Mr. Widener's suit against the Pacific Gas and Electric Company, James C. Carroll, et al. The attorney of record for PG&E was Arthur Hillman, with whom I was very familiar (review Chapter 14), F.

Ronald Laupheimer and Charles Denny, with whom I also was very familiar. Laupheimer and Denny accompanied Arthur Hillman in representing PG&E.

David E. Pesonen of the San Francisco law firm Garry, Dreyfus, McTernan, Brotsky, Herndon Pesonen, Inc represented Don Widener.

At one point during the trial Mr. Pesonen attempted to have Mr. Carroll address the fuel-cladding problem:[353]

> **Mr. Pesonen:** And one reason you were changing the cladding was because these little cracks had developed which was causing the leak – causing radioactive gasses to leak out of the fuel?
>
> **Mr. Carroll:** That's the basic reason. But there's some history here that we're not talking about.
>
> **Mr. Pesonen:** I'm sure it's a very complicated subject.
>
> **THE COURT:** If you'd like to explain the answer, you may do so.
>
> **Mr. Carroll:** Well, I'd like to explain the Valecitos boiling water reactor was originally built as a prototype by GE principally for developing fuel and fuel cladding. And it went into operation in 1957.
>
> Now, at that time there were two candidate-cladding materials available. One was Type 304 stainless steel, which had been used extensively in earlier boiling water reactors that had been developed by the government. The other was a material called zircaloy, which is an alloy of the element zirconium, which had been developed for the Navy's submarine program, which had never operated in a commercial boiling water reactor.
>
> Both types of fuel were tested in the late Fifties at Valecitos. The stainless as expected worked quite well at Valecitos, although it takes several years to get substantial amount of radiation exposure on the fuel.
>
> The zircaloy had many early-life problems. And at that time General Electric was designing our Humboldt Plant, had intended to put zircaloy in the first core. But because of the problems that had been found at Valecitos with these prototype zircaloy assemblies, recommended to us and we accepted their recommendation that for at least the first core the conservative thing to do was to put the stainless steel fuel in the first core, even though stainless steel fuel was more expensive fuel to use.
>
> And that's how we ended up with stainless in the initial core.
>
> **Mr. Pesonen:** Mr. Carroll, I've timed that answer to his Honor's question, and it took exactly one minute and 45 seconds.

COMMENT: I would love to have been in Mr. Pesonsen's shoes. First

Pesonen did a masterful job bringing out the absurdity of Carroll's statement that any explanation regarding Mr. Widener's fuel cladding question, "would have been too lengthy an answer for a taped interview." Beyond that, however, and realizing that it really wasn't the subject matter of the Widener's trial, I would have challenged Mr. Carroll's misstatements about stainless steel fuel when in fact there is no such thing; he should have been talking instead about the stainless steel cladding.

But more importantly, I would have challenged Carroll's claim that stainless steel cladding was more expensive than zircaloy. Carroll's statement was absolutely false! His statement was made to give the jury the impression that PG&E was truly concerned for safety and therefore willing to spend more money for the supposed reliability of the stainless steel option selected by PG&E. Carroll's response was pure legalistic hogwash!

My reading of Mr. Carroll's testimony left me with the clear impression that this segment of Carroll's testimony was prepared by PG&E's legal department and was sitting in the ole proverbial can should Carroll have an opportunity to use it during his testimony at the trial.

This scheme by PG&E was developed because of the company's apparent concern over the adverse public impact of an article critical of nuclear power that appeared in *Look Magazine*. While the title of the *Look Magazine* article was never mentioned during the Widener's trial, there were numerous references made to it.

The article actually provided an important strand that ran throughout the trial and Carroll's testimony. Mr. Pesonen had his reasons for wanting to know why J. C. Carroll was selected for the on-camera interview. Pesonen very cleverly led into the exploration of how Mr. Carroll became involved in the handling of Mr. Widener with the following testimony:[354]

> **Mr. Pesonen:** Mr. Carroll, you know that this case is about a film that was made in 1971 called "Power That Be." There's no dispute in this case about that. Now, in 1971, it's true, isn't, that the subject of nuclear power was a matter of considerable public controversy?
>
> **Mr. Carroll:** I don't know really that I can agree with that statement. Certainty there was some controversy. But meaning the general public – I think today even I would have a hard time characterizing the fact that nuclear power is a very controversial subject. I think my evidence for that statement is the recent Harris Poll, which showed that the public really has very few concerns about nuclear power.
>
> **Mr. Pesonen:** Did you read the retraction of that poll by Mr. Harris?
>
> **Mr. Carroll:** No, I didn't.
>
> **THE COURT:** Let's get on to the preliminaries relating to the production of this documentary.
>
> **Mr. Pesonen:** Most of this was preliminary, Your Honor. The

witness has just opened up the subject that we'll drop for now. I do want to just ask you this, Mr. Carroll. Are you saying that there was a small group of people who viewed nuclear power as controversial, but that the man on the street, the average person – INTERRRUPTED

THE COURT: Whether it's small or large is immaterial right now. Let's get on to the matters and things leading up to the interview of this man and the production of the documentary that's the subject of this trial.

Mr. Pesonen: Well, let's do what His Honor has just suggested. Let's get down to brass tacks on this. How did you first learn that there would be an NBC crew interested in doing some filming at the Humboldt Bay Nuclear Power Plant?

Mr. Carroll: I received a phone call from the then assistant plant superintendent, Mr. Warren A. Raymond.

Mr. Pesonen: What did Mr. Raymond tell you?

Mr. Carroll: That Mr. Draeger from our Public Information Department had contacted him, and that Mr. Draeger had told him about arrangements that he had made for Mr. Widener and his crew to come to Humboldt for purposes of filming and interviewing people.

Mr. Pesonen: You did not first learn about it from Mr. Draeger, then?

Mr. Carroll: No, I did not.

Mr. Pesonen: What steps did you take when you heard from Mr. Raymond that there was – Mr. Widener and his crew were going to go to the Humboldt Plant?

Mr. Carroll: I called Mr. Draeger to get more information on it.

Mr. Pesonen: Did Mr. Raymond tell you anything in that first conversation that made it seem particularly important for you to call Mr. Draeger?

Mr. Carroll: Yes. As I recall – and I may have things mixed up between what Mr. Raymond told me and what Mr. Draeger subsequently told me – but that he did indicate that Mr. Draeger had said some things that suggested Mr. Widener was somewhat antagonistic toward nuclear power and he was somewhat alarmed by some of the places that Mr. Widener had filmed in the course of preparing this documentary

Mr. Pesonen: Mr. Raymond tell you that or Mr. Draeger?

Mr. Carroll: I can't really say. Mr. Draeger certainly told me that in a subsequent conversation. I know Mr. Raymond was somewhat concerned, and that was why I called Mr. Draeger about it.

Mr. Pesonen: Did Mr. Raymond seem apprehensive that some representatives from the news media were going to come and ask questions about your nuclear plant?

Mr. Carrol: I guess probably – or as I recall, Raymond also had heard from Mr. Draeger about the LOOK article which had appeared a couple of months earlier with some very erroneous allegations made about our plant.

COMMENT: The *Look Magazine* article the PG&E officials were so concerned about was entitled "The Nuclear Threat Inside America" by Jack Shepherd, senior editor of *Look Magazine*. The article appeared in the December 15, 1970 edition of the magazine, over six months after Forrest Williams and I were fired from PG&E. The only reference in Shepherd's article pertaining to the Humboldt Bay Nuclear Power Plant was the following (this is the reference *in toto* to Humboldt Bay):[355]

> **At Humboldt Bay in California, fuel tubes cracked because cheaper stainless steel had been used instead of a more reliable alloy. Workers repaired the cracks, and the plant broke down again.**

COMMENT: That was it! – The totality of Shepherds' reference to Humboldt! — I knew Shepherd was correct in what he said about the "fuel tubes cracked because cheaper stainless steel had been used instead of a more reliable alloy." After all, I had worked in that plant and lived on a daily basis with the results of what happened to the nuclear fuel cladding breakdown. That's why the radiation levels of the off-gas and reactor water samples we collected and analyzed on a daily basis skyrocketed. It was precisely because of the fuel cladding failure that *Science Magazine* dubbed Humboldt the dirtiest nuclear plant in the nation.[356] Mr. Pesonen's direct examination of J. C. Carroll continued:[357]

Mr. Pesonen: It's your interpretation that they were erroneous, but in any event, there was an article that appeared about a month or so before in LOOK magazine that suggested that there was some serious safety problems at the nuclear power plant unit at Humboldt Bay; isn't that correct?

Mr. Carroll: I don't think I'd say safety problems. They talked about improper materials of construction and things of that nature.

Mr. Pesonen: Release of radiation into the environment?

Mr. Carroll: I'm not sure the article talked about that.

Mr. Pesonen: In any event, that article came up in one or the other of these discussions with Mr. Raymond or with Mr. Draeger?

Mr. Carroll: Yes.

Mr. Pesonen: You also said that Mr. Raymond expressed either his or Mr. Draeger's concern over some of the places that Mr. Widener had filmed. Mr. Widener doesn't work for PG&E, does he?

Mr. Denny (PG&E attorney): Your Honor, I'm going to object to that question.

Mr. Pesonen: I'll withdraw that question.

Mr. Pesonen: Mr. Carroll, what places did Mr. Widener's film that gave Mr. Draeger or Mr. Raymond concern?

THE COURT: That's if you know or if they so informed you.

Mr. Carroll: Yes. I was informed that Mr. Widener's itinerary prior to coming to Humboldt included the Nevada Test Site where nuclear weapons have been tested over the years, the Rocky Flats Arsenal, I guess it's called, in Colorado where nuclear weapons are assembled, and the Hanford Facility, which is a military reactor, plutonium production complex.

Mr. Pesonen: Did you have concern that Mr. Widener had gone to these places and filmed?

Mr. Carroll: Well, I guess I should go back a bit. The understanding I derived from Mr. Draeger and I believe from Mr. Raymond was that Widener was doing a documentary on power generation in general, including nuclear power. And it seemed very peculiar to me that such a documentary would include facilities that are totally unrelated to power generation.

Mr. Pesonen: Mr. Carroll, you know, do you not, that there is a reactor at the Hanford Facility called the N Reactor, right?

Mr. Carroll: Incidentally.

Mr. Pesonen: It does produce electricity?

THE COURT: Let him answer the question.

Mr. Carroll: Incidentally. The N Reactor is a reactor operated for the Atomic Energy Commission. Its principal purpose is the production of plutonium for weapons. In fact, when it was first built, there was no power generation facility. It was added incidentally.

Mr. Pesonen: And the Humboldt Bay reactor produces plutonium, does it not?

Mr. Carroll: Not weapon-grade plutonium.

Mr. Pesonen: Plutonium is produced, as a by-product in the fuel after it's operated, is it not? That's a yes or no question, Mr. Carroll.

Mr. Denny (PG&E attorney): Excuse me, Counsel. I'm going to object. I think he's arguing with the witness.

Mr. Pesonen: I think the witness is evading the question.

Mr. Carroll: I'm trying to clarify a point.

Mr. Pesonen: No. You're trying to make an argument.

THE COURT: Let him answer the question. This isn't going to be a debate between you. Go ahead.

Mr. Carroll: Well, the point I was trying to make –
INTERRUPTED

THE COURT: Is there a difference between plutonium for the development of war material and plutonium for use in the development of electric power?

Mr. Carroll: Well, the plutonium produced from a power reactor is unsuitable for weapons purposes.

Mr. Pesonen: That's the same element, is it not?

Mr. Carroll: Yes.

COMMENT: Plutonium is a very dangerous alpha emitter if ingested and it has a very long half-life. Plutonium is extremely harmful to human health even if only very small amounts of it are ingested into the human body.

Management personnel at the Humboldt Bay Nuclear Plant maintained the Humboldt reactor did not produce any plutonium and the employees had nothing to worry about regarding the biological hazards of plutonium. I never had the opportunity to discuss the subject with Mr. Carroll, but I wished I had!

I was given the impression the Donald Widener Trial was all about how PG&E had treated Mr. Widener, which had everything to do with the way the company had treated the critics of its nuclear plant. However, I came across the following testimony, which I found peculiar:[358]

THE COURT: (Directed to Mr. Pesonen . . .) And I instructed you at the beginning of the trial that we're not going to try the pros and cons of nuclear power. We were going to confine ourselves if we possibly could to whether or not a liable was committed, and if so, whether or not it was a privileged communication, whether or not anything was said or done with malice, and whether or not there was any damage sustained.

I fully realize the trial was the result of a complaint filled by Widener for what PG&E and Mr. Carroll had done to him, but it would seem the Court would have been interested in what PG&E's *modus operandi* was for dealing with those who were critical of the company's nuclear program at Humboldt Bay. This outburst by the Court followed an attempt by Mr. Pesonen to address a document marked Plaintiff's Exhibit No. 14 pertaining to an internal PG&E memorandum written by Mr. Carroll. This document clearly revealed what PG&E had done and Mr. Carroll's involvement in the underhanded affair. The last portion of Mr. Pesonen's treatment of the document was what precipitated the Court's outburst:[359]

Mr. Pesonen: (Directed to Mr. Carroll . . .) Now, let's take a look at the last, the next to the last paragraph. Do you have a copy before you, Mr. Carroll?

Mr. Carroll: Yes.

Mr. Pesonen: The first sentence says: "Upon arriving at the airport, Adam, Carroll and Draeger found Widener and his crew talking with Forrest Williams and Bob Rowen." What was the significance of Mr. Widener and his crew talking with Forrest Williams and Bob Rowen?

Mr. Carroll: What was the significance of it?

Mr. Pesonen: Yes. You went to the pains of putting it in your memorandum. Why did you put it in there?

Mr. Carroll: I think I explained it in the remainder of the paragraph.

THE COURT: Read the rest of the sentence.

Mr. Carroll: (Reading) "These two individuals are former Control Technicians at Humboldt Bay Power Plant who were discharged by the Company in May 1970. Both individuals had a long history of insubordinate conduct.. They were great admirers of Gofman and Tamplin and had waged a campaign of harassment against the Company on its radiation safety program for several years. Williams was finally discharged for refusing to do routine radiochemistry work on the grounds that it was 'unsafe' from the standpoint of radiation exposure. Rowen was ultimately discharged for a telephone threat of bodily harm to one of his supervisors."

Mr. Pesonen: Did you consider that it was improper for Mr. Williams to refuse to do work that he thought was unsafe to his own health?

THE COURT: Don't answer the question.

Mr. Denny (PG&E attorney): Again, your Honor –

THE COURT: Objection sustained.

Mr. Pesonen: And it's true, isn't it, that at this very time this interview was going on, Mr. Rowen had been discharged because he had gone to the Atomic Energy Commission and complained about serious safety violations at the Humboldt Bay Nuclear Power Plant? That's true, isn't it?

Mr. Denny: I'm going to object, your Honor, on the ground of relevancy.

THE COURT: Objection is sustained.

Mr. Pesonen: At the time you wrote this memorandum, Mr. Carroll, you knew, did you not, that the Humboldt County Grand Jury was investigating the charges raised by Mr. Rowen about the operation of this plant and hazards to public safety?

Mr. Denny: Same objection.

THE COURT: Objection is sustained. The jury is instructed to disregard the question.

Mr. Pesonen: Do I understand that your Honor does not want to permit me to go into the Grand Jury investigation of this claim at all?

THE COURT: You certainly do.

COMMENT: Mr. Pesonen asked the Judge if he could just briefly state his purpose for asking the question. The PG&E attorney once again objected saying, "I object to speeches." The Judge responded, "You may at a time other than this. During a recess." And that was the end of it!

Mr. Carroll had written blatant lies in his memorandum about Forrest Williams and Bob Rowen, and he was never held accountable for them; not that the Widener trial was the proper place for that to happen. It's just galling that Carroll's dishonesty could not have been exposed in support of what was actually before the Court in the Widener trial!

However, the pretrial deposition of Mr. Carroll was more revealing than what the Judge allowed to come out during Widener's actual trial. Two PG&E attorneys, Arthur Hillman and Charles Denny, both of whom were very much involved in my case, represented Mr. Carroll. The following testimony was given in the pretrial deposition of Mr. Carroll:[360]

> **Mr. Pesonen:** Now, in Exhibit 5, you also mentioned in the next-to-the-last paragraph, a person named Robert or Bob Rowen. Do you know Bob Rowen?
>
> **Mr. Carroll:** Yes, I do.
>
> **Mr. Pesonen:** Was there a controversy between PG&E and Bob Rowen at the time this film took place?
>
> **Mr. Carroll:** Yes.
>
> **Mr. Pesonen:** Mr. Rowen, in fact, had made some allegations about the operation of the plant, which the company disputed?
>
> **Mr. Denny:** Again, we are getting far afield. I am going to object to this particular question. I can see no relevance to this particular –
>
> **Mr. Pesonen:** Well, the witness considered it relevant in his memorandum: (Reading) "Upon arriving at the airport, Adam, Carroll and Draeger found Widener and his crew talking with Forrest Williams and Bob Rowen.These two individuals are former Control Technicians at Humboldt Bay Power Plant who were discharged by the Company in May 1970.
>
> Both individuals had a long history of insubordinate conduct. They were great admirers of Gofman and Tamplin and had waged a campaign of harassment against the Company on its radiation safety program for several years. Williams was finally discharged for refusing to do routine radiochemistry work on the grounds that it was 'unsafe' from the standpoint of radiation exposure. Rowen was ultimately discharged for a telephone threat of bodily harm to one of his supervisors."
>
> The last paragraph, closing paragraph, writing in the memoranda is: "All indications are that Williams and Rowen came to the airport and contacted Widener. It did not appear that Widener had video-taped their discussion, but this does not mean he might not come back for an interview."

COMMENT: When Mr. Widener was finished with his filming at the plant, he called me to arrange a meeting at the airport. I then called Forrest and together we went to the airport. I don't recall seeing Carroll or any of the PG&E people there, but in any event Carroll jumped to the conclusion I had contacted Widener, which was not the case.

Mr. Carroll's deposition continued:

Mr. Denny: Now, you have a further question in that area?

Mr. Pesonen: Yes, I do.

Mr. Denny: Okay. State your question. If I have an objection, I will make it.

Mr. Pesonen: I can ask from the witness: What was the nature of the controversy in existence between Mr. Rowen and Pacific Gas and Electric?

Mr. Denny: Again, I think that is a bit broad. I think what you have read apparently describes the situation. You want to know any other information?

Mr. Pesonen: I may.

Mr. Pesonen: Have you ever contacted, with respect to the Rowen case, an investigator working on behalf of PG&E, named Bert Jones?

Mr. Hillman: Can I see what you are referring to? You are referring to something.

Mr. Pesonen: This is my document. I am refreshing my recollection of the name. I don't have to show it to you.

Mr. Denny: Again, Counsel, I think the memorandum in question gives a description of what apparently was known at that time about the contact between Mr. Widener and the two individuals. I don't think the subject really has any relevancy insofar as this particular lawsuit is concerned, because, as I understand it, I have seen the film, and I don't think either of the two gentlemen were in the film that Mr. Widener did. I don't see how it can be relevant.

Mr. Pesonen: I think it is very relevant if Widener has had a discussion with Rowen before he went to the plant.

Mr. Hillman: You are saying, "If"?

Mr. Pesonen: If he did.

Mr. Hillman: This is afterwards. What the memo says is "Upon arriving at the airport." That is after the interview, I believe, is my understanding, that Mr. Carroll and Mr. Draeger were on their way back home, and the Widener crew is out there, the filming has been completed, and that they have – INTERRUPTED

Mr. Pesonen: They may very well have discussed with Rowen the quote "Hatchet job" that he did on Mr. Carroll.

Mr. Denney: I have no objection to your asking this witness if he either overheard or had any information about the actual discussions that took place between Mr. Widener and these two gentlemen. Certainly that might be relevant.

Mr. Pesonen: Well, this is part – INTERRUPTED

Mr. Denny: But to go into the whole background – INTERRUPTED

Mr. Pesonen: But if the company has an investigator who had had some contact or some interest in a person who the witness says is relevant to the subject matter, I want to know what kind of investigations you have got. I could ask it interrogatories, and I can ask the witness if he has participated in any investigation.

Mr. Denny: There again, I don't agree with that. If he has knowledge of any contacts between these people and Mr. Widener, I think that might be relevant, but – INTERRUPTED

Mr. Pesonen: Well, I can get at that indirectly. I won't ask any questions about the contents. Let me just ask this, and I won't pursue that further.

Mr. Pesonen: Have you discussed the Rowen controversy with Mr. Bert Jones? He can answer that yes or no.

Mr. Denny: I can appreciate he can answer yes or no, but again, I still think that the question is entirely irrelevant and I can't see how it can lead to discoverable evidence, until you can first tie up that these two gentleman had anything to do with Mr. Widener.

Mr. Hillman: What controversy?

Mr. Pesonen: The witness says there was a controversy.

Mr. Hillman: He describes it in the memorandum.

Mr. Pesonen: That is part of the controversy. That is a characterization of Mr. Rowen, not of the controversy.

Mr. Denny: I'm a little bit lost. Could you explain to me how it might be – how any controversy, which led to the discharge of these two gentleman, how any information beyond that can have any relevance to this lawsuit?

Mr. Pesonen: Tremendous. If there are ulterior purposes in the letter that is the subject matter of Mr. Widener's claim against the Company, that is clear evidence of malice.

Mr. Denny: As far as Mr. Widener is concerned.

Mr. Pesonen: No, as far as Mr. Carroll is concerned.
If he has a purpose other than writing out the facts, other than that are in the film – INTERRUPTED

Mr. Denny: Ask him that question, whether or not his letters had any relationship. Certainly they are not mentioned in his letters. The two gentlemen – wait a second – INTERRUPTED

Mr. Hillman: Off the record.

Mr. Denny: Williams and Rowen are not in the film.

Mr. Pesonen: Nor is Adams, nor is Draeger.

Mr. Denny: And they are not mentioned in the letters that Mr.

Carroll wrote to KNBC. So, I still don't see how that's relevant.

Mr. Pesonen: Well are you saying that the only thing that is relevant are the things that the witness himself put in his letters to KNBC; are you narrowing this case down to that kind of dimension?

Mr. Denny: Off the record.

Mr. Pesonen: I think this ought to be on the record. I am paying for it.

Mr. Denny: I made an objection. I will object to this inquiry as not being relevant, unless you can show some relevancy to this particular lawsuit.

Mr. Pesonen: The relevancy is the witness' state of mind at the time the libel was uttered, and that's as far as I have to go.

Mr. Denny: Well, again, I will object to your characterization as being the fact that there is any libelous material in either one of those letters.

Mr. Hillman: I will object to the question and instruct the witness not to answer. He read from his memorandum. I think the contents in the memorandum show why he reported it.

And I think any inquiry as to further background about the investigations that were done in regard to Williams and Rowen of which this witness may have knowledge is irrelevant to this particular case, and irrelevant to the subject matter of this case, and I instruct him not to answer.

Mr. Pesonen: Certify that, please.

In addition to the revealing "disclosures" of this testimony that were attached to a letter, dated May 8, 1974, from David Pesonen to James McKittrick, was the enclosure of James C. Carroll's memorandum entitled <u>Summary of Visit by Don Widener of NBC TV on February 10, 1971 to Humboldt Bay Power Plant</u>, dated February 14, 1971. In Mr. Pesonen's letter to McKittrick, he stated, "Enclosed is a copy of part of Carroll's deposition and an exhibit touching upon Bob Rowen's troubles with PG&E that may be useful to you."

Although I did not receive McKittrick's "work product" for which I had petitioned the Court, I did receive the aforementioned correspondence buried the materials that was finally handed over to me after McKittrick's suicide. I have since wondered why McKittrick never shared this information with me all the while he was representing me? (In response to my request in 2010, David Pesonen provided transcripts of the depositions of James C. Carroll and Frederick R. Draeger, along with the transcript of proceedings on appeal in the Don Widener vs. PG&E trial.)

Mr. Carroll's angry letter was worked over by a number of PG&E executives and then took on a life of its own. PG&E's Washington lobbyist, Ralph B. Dewey, wrote three almost identical letters, dated July 28, 1971, addressing ". . . this insidious kind of news gathering." Dewey's letters were clearly a condemnation of Widener's *Powers That Be*. These letters were sent to FCC chief Dean Burch, to Senator John Pastore, Chairman of the Senate Communications Subcommittee, and Senator Warren Magnuson, chairman of the Senate Commerce Committee.

On behalf of PG&E, Dewey zeroed in on Widener by submitting a copy of Carroll's letter to NBC along with his own charges:[361]

> The attached letter to NBC from one of our executives complains bitterly about an NBC reporter's chicanerous (if not illegal) use of interview material . . . This case involves the use, over the air, of parts of a tape-recording of pre-interview discussions between an NBC reporter and one of our senior engineers, Mr. J. C. Carroll . . . This represents a new low in news management and biased reporting and was a clear attempt to discredit an individual and an entire industry (nuclear power); the facts take the hindmost.

After a careful review of the film was made, KNBC-TV Station Manager Robert Howard, replied to J. C. Carroll on August 13, 1971:

> We believe that your (Carroll's) interview was conducted in a professional manner, that there was no recording of any kind done without your knowledge, and that your interview was not in any way distorted, used out of context, or altered.

Nicholas Zapple, counsel to Senator Pastore's subcommittee, told lobbyist Dewey that J. C. Carroll's accusations were "off base." William R. Ray, chief of the FCC's Complaints and Compliance Division, reported that PG&E never followed up its original complaint, and that no evidence was ever presented to warrant action by the FCC.

Regarding Robert Howard's August 13th letter, Mr. Pesonen attempted several times to get it before the jury in Widener's trial. The PG&E attorney strenuously objected every time on the grounds that what Mr. Howard had stated in his August 13th letter was hearsay and had nothing to do with Widener's case. Each time the PG&E attorney made his objection the Court sustained it.   There ensued the following Court dialogue concerning the admissibility of Howard's letter:[362]

> **Mr. Pesonen:** Your Honor, may I say something?
>
> **THE COURT:** Well, I have you at a disadvantage and I don't want to debate it with you. I've ruled. If you want to discuss it at length, we can at the 3:00 o'clock recess.
>
> **Mr. Pesonen:** My reason in asking the Court's leave to say something at this point, your Honor, is that the Plaintiff's view of the importance of Mr. Carroll's – of the contents of the reply to Mr. Carroll by the station in response to the letter we've talked so much about in this case is very crucial for the jury's understanding any of the next matter that I plan to get into.
>
> **THE COURT:** The jury will understand more about it from

the witnesses whose testimony as adduced in this trial and not from somebody who wrote a letter with his own conclusions and opinions that is absolute hearsay so far as this case is concerned. And in my judgment it would be prejudicial and it will not be permitted.

Mr. Pesonen: It's not offered for the truth of the –

THE COURT: I know it isn't, and it's not offered for the truth of the truth of the contents, but rather that a letter was in fact received. It's stipulated. If it isn't, I find it was.

Mr. Denny: Yes, your Honor –

THE COURT: And it's hearsay that would be prejudicial, and I won't permit it. I'd like to debate it with you at 3:00 o'clock, but not now.

Mr. Pesonen: What I'd suggest is it's so important to us, I'd like special leave to discuss it with the Court in Chambers at this point.

THE COURT: At this point? Then we'll have a ten-minute recess at this time, Ladies and Gentlemen.

(Brief recess taken.)

COMMENT: I don't know what was discussed in Chambers but somehow Mr. Pesonen was able to convince the Judge to allow him to pursue Howard's letter to simply lay foundation for a critical juncture in Widener's case. Mr. Carroll's testimony continued:[363]

Mr. Pesonen: Continuing with Mr. Carroll, your Honor.

Mr. Pesonen: Now, Mr. Carroll, you received a reply from Mr. Howard to your letter of July 13 we've talked about earlier?

Mr. Carroll: Yes, I did.

Mr. Pesonen: And in that letter Mr. Howard told you that KNBC had conducted an investigation of the assertion in your letter that there had been off camera taping dubbed into the film, did he not?

Mr. Denny: Again, your Honor, I think I'll object on the grounds of hearsay again.

THE COURT: Objection overruled.

Mr. Carroll: Had conducted an investigation? I don't really recall those words precisely.

Mr. Pesonen: Well, would looking at the documents refresh your recollection?

THE COURT: Let me bring it to a conclusion this way. You did get a letter dated August the 13th?

Mr. Carroll: Right.

THE COURT: From Mr. Howard of KNBC?

Mr. Carroll: Yes.

THE COURT: And in that letter did he not deny all of the material allegations that have been contained in your earlier letter?

Mr. Carroll: Yes, he did.

THE COURT: And denied them item, by item, by item?

Mr. Carroll: Yes.

THE COURT: All right. And in the concluding paragraph of the letter, he did invite you if you felt that you had been – well, I'm not going to interpret it. Reading it once more:

"The controversy over the development of nuclear power still continues to be a live issue. Since you appeared once before as a spokesman for P.G. E. on this subject, we invite you to appear as a guest on one of our interview programs.

We believe that it would be particularly worthwhile for you to do so if you believe that you were not given an adequate opportunity to present your views in the documentary.

Sincerely, Robert T. Howard, Vice President, NBC, General Manager, KNBC."

Did you receive that letter?

Mr. Carroll: I did.

THE COURT: All right.

Mr. Pesonen: Mr. Carroll, after receiving that letter, you wrote back again to Mr. Howard, did you not?

Mr. Carroll: I did.

Mr. Pesonen: May I see Plaintiff's 10 in evidence, please?

Mr. Pesonen: Let me show you a document marked Plaintiff's 10 in evidence, Mr. Carroll, and ask you if that is not a copy of your reply to Mr. Howard?

Mr. Carroll: Yes, it is.

Mr. Pesonen: And that letter was a reply to the one we've just been talking about that his Honor just asked you some questions about that was dated –

THE COURT: August 13.

Mr. Pesonen: August 13th, 1971?

Mr. Carroll: That's correct.

Mr. Pesonen: Now in your letter which is Plaintiff's 10, your letter of August 24, you set out – strike that. In Mr. Howard's letter to you of August 13th, he requested that you set forth some specific complaints about bias and distortion in the film, did he not?

Mr. Denny: Same objection, your Honor.

THE COURT: Well, let me see the letter. May I just see that letter? At least he had denied all of the charges that you made. Did he invite your comments?

Mr. Carroll: I don't think in so many words he invited them.

THE COURT: In any event, you did see fit to write another communication to Mr. Howard?

Mr. Carroll: That's correct.

Mr. Pesonen: And in that communication, which is Plaintiff's 10, you attempted to set forth some of your specific objections to the content of the film called "Powers that Be," did you not?

Mr. Carroll: Yes. Among other things in that letter.

Mr. Pesonen: Among other things. Now, Mr. Carroll, you have occasion, do you not, in the ordinary course of your work to see numerous technical publications come in and go across you desk?

Mr. Carroll: Yes, I do.

Mr. Pesonen: And among those technical publications that you see is the magazine *Science* published by the American Association for the Advancement of Science, do you not?

Mr. Carroll: I don't regularly see the magazine *Science*, no.

Mr. Pesonen: Before you wrote your letter of August 24, 1971 to Mr. Howard, your reply to his letter to you, you had seen, had you not, the issue of *Science* magazine dated June 18th, 1971?

Mr. Carroll: I don't know whether I had or had not. That description doesn't mean anything to me.

Mr. Pesonen: Let me show you a document that was marked Plaintiff's 20 to your deposition, Mr. Carroll. Mr. Carroll, let me show you first your deposition, Volume Two, Page 110, beginning at Line 12 through Page 111, Line 7.

Mr. Denny: Is there a pending question?

Mr. Pesonen: Yes. I asked of the witness if he had seen before his letter to Mr. Howard of August 24th the June 18th issue of *Science* magazine. And I now ask him if looking at that section of his deposition from Page 110, Line 12 to page 111, Line 7, refreshes his recollection whether he had seen that issue of *Science* magazine before writing this letter to Mr. Howard.

Mr. Carroll: Does it refresh my recollection? Yes, it does. I recall the article that is discussed in here.

Mr. Pesonen: You recall the article that appeared in the issue of *Science* that was headlined "Reactor Emissions: AEC Guideline Move Toward Critics' Position"?

Mr. Denny: Again, I'm going to object, your Honor. We're going into a matter that is irrelevant. I'm going to object on the grounds of irrelevancy, again, your Honor. It has nothing to do with the lawsuit.

Mr. Pesonen: This is preliminary, your Honor.

THE COURT: If it's preliminary, go ahead.

Mr. Pesonen: Let me show you a copy of that article, Mr. Carroll, and ask you if you had seen that article before you wrote your letter to Mr. Howard?

Mr. Carroll: I can't be certain. I suspect that since this is the June issue, I would have seen it before I wrote my July letter.

Mr. Pesonen: One purpose of your letter of August 24th you supplied to Mr. Howard was to set the record straight on some matters concerning the subject of nuclear power set forth in the film produced by Mr. Widener that you had complained about in your July 13th letter; isn't that correct?

Mr. Carroll: I gave a few examples of where I felt that the documentary was inaccurate, yes.

Mr. Pesonen: Now did you consider it important to tell Mr. Howard when you wrote him on August 24th that in the magazine published by the American Association for the Advancement of Science the Humboldt Bay nuclear power plant had been described as one of the dirtiest reactors in the United States with respect to the release of radioactive gases into the environment?

Mr. Denny: Again, your Honor, I will object on the grounds of relevancy. It has absolutely no relevancy to this lawsuit.

Mr. Pesonen: May I respond?

THE COURT: Yes.

Mr. Pesonen: The witness has testified that he set out to tell Mr. Howard – to set the record straight on nuclear power in light of Mr. Widener's film. Now, he knows that this prestigious publication has described the very reactor that is the subject of this film as one of the dirtiest in the country for spilling radioactive gases into the environment, and he didn't tell Mr. Howard about that.

THE COURT: Well, it's not an issue in this case. The issue whether this man was mistreated or not in that documentary, and whether or not he has committed a liable on Mr. Widener, and any resultant claim of damage that might result. Now, I said at the outset we're not going to try the pros and cons of nuclear power. Whether or not the plant at Humboldt is the dirtiest one in the country or the cleanest one in the country is not an issue here. Whether or not there was an article in a particular science magazine that dealt with the subject is wholly immaterial.

COMMENT: As I read through the transcript of Widener's trial, it was obvious the judge had a bias favoring PG&E and nuclear power. One observation described what had taken place in the following way:[364]

> As the trial got under way it became apparent that Judge Arnold was not going to rain favors on Widener. At one point, the PG&E lawyers strongly objected to the admission of its compromising memo-and-letter file into evidence.
>
> Pesonen pointed out 'the monumental irony of this

corporation that set out to suppress a film, talking about the protection of its letters.'

'They have the right to suppress the film, so far as this case is concerned,' commented the judge.

The rest is an interesting history with Widener ultimately prevailing – sort of, as far as his lawsuit was concerned; however, NBC succumbed to the pressures brought by PG&E. NBC decided to lock up Widener's news documentary film putting the kibosh to future showings *of Powers That Be* to the American public. Thanks to PG&E, Don Widener's reputation was ruined and his career as a TV documentary producer was over. All because of J. C. Carroll's answer to Widener's question concerning PG&E's decision to use "improper construction materials in the beginning," referring to the cheaper stainless steel cladding:

> Well, this is analogous to a problem you have in your industry. There were criticisms of improper design and construction techniques in early color television sets that resulted in excessive radiation to people.

The simple truth is PG&E did not want James C. Carroll's statement in front of the American viewing audience! After all, Mr. Carroll was PG&E's Nuclear and Steam Generation Engineer in charge of the company's nuclear program at the company's corporate headquarters. The failure of the stainless steel nuclear fuel cladding was a huge problem for the employees in the plant and to the general public beyond the nuclear facility. PG&E's problem of the nuclear stainless fuel-cladding failure that resulted in excessive amounts of radiation to employees and to the public had absolutely nothing to do with "early color television sets."

After a month long trial a San Francisco jury unanimously returned a verdict against PG&E and awarded Don Widener the biggest libel award to an individual in the history of English common law in the amount of $7.75 million; $7 million in punitive damages and $750,000 in compensatory damages.

Judge Byron Arnold reversed the jury award, thereby rendering the month-long jury effort meaningless. The case slowly wound its way through the appellate courts, one of which ultimately ordered a new trial.

Widener's attorney, David Pesonen, said that after a week of pretrial motions, and an eight-year ordeal for Widener, PG&E agreed to a settlement of $475,000 in January 1979. Widener died of lung cancer on April 22, 2003, at a hospice in Henderson, Nevada. Are we now left to believe that Carroll's nonsensical argument coupled with the final outcome of Widener's lawsuit excuses PG&E's horrendous corporate behavior and represents true justice achieved? I think not!

The Don Widener story needs to be told because it reveals very clearly what PG&E is capable of and how the company goes about doing its business.

One footnote to the Don Widener story is an observation made by James

Real in his article entitled "#1 On The Nuclear Blacklist:"[365]

> Don Widener's vindication has met with restrained enthusiasm by the people who produce commercial television.
>
> 'Don is a very competent guy,' explained a defensive network production executive, 'but he's on this First Amendment jag. Christ, you can't go around suing *advertisers*!'

Advertisers? Well now, that strikes another cord! PG&E is a huge advertiser and wields tremendous influence over the media. Advertising dollars provide important revenue streams to the media and advertising accounts often dominate editorial policies.

There is another part of PG&E's way of doing business that needs to be told. In my view most people are not all that much aware of the impact the media has on public opinion and the role the advertising dollar plays. My hypothesis simply stated: PG&E will dictate editorial policies to the media or the company will withdraw its advertising business. It's just that simple!

As I was writing my *Diary* I was reflecting back on the two following Eureka *Times-Standard* editorials. They were immediately published upon completion of the 20-part Eureka *Times-Standard* series covering my complaints about the Humboldt nuclear facility, I remembered a meeting that took place between PG&E corporate officials from San Francisco and the publisher along with his managing editor of the newspaper at the luxurious Ingomar Club in Eureka. Corporate executives from Thompson's Newspapers also attended the meeting. The Ingomar Club is housed in the world famous Carson Mansion and serves as a private club with exclusive membership requirements.

The 20-part Eureka *Times-Standard* series ended on July 11, 1972. The very next day, Dan Walters, the newspaper's managing editor wrote a lengthy less than favorable editorial bringing my credibility into question. Walters raised the following two questions:

> 1. Is Rowen a sincere advocate of safer nuclear power or a disgruntled former employee with a grudge?
> 2. Is PG&E "covering up" and persecuting him or is it conscientiously following safe operating procedures and merely defending itself against a malcontent?

Mr. Walters' answers to the two questions he posed in his editorial were the same as those PG&E offered up time and again in other forums in a variety of other places. Walters clearly revealed his bias in his editorial entitled *"Motive, Credibility Issues at A-Plant"* when he wrote the following:

> Nuclear power is still somewhat new and a great many persons are nervous about it.

The argument is not, as some persons may think, about the concept of nuclear power itself. Rowen has not questioned the validity of nuclear power as the power source of the future.

We firmly believe that declining fossil fuel (oil, gas, coal) reserves make the development of nuclear power essential. Environmentalists talk about limiting power demands but no fair and reasonable plan for doing so has been offered.

So long as demands continue to rise, the utilities must respond to it and nuclear power appears to be the most efficient means of doing so.

One week later the Eureka *Times-Standard* published a lengthy editorial, this time in the name of Victor Novarino, Manager of PG&E's Humboldt Division. The article was most likely prepared by PG&E's Public Information Office at the company's corporate headquarters in San Francisco. This "editorial," dated July 19, 1972, entitled *"PG&E Atom Plant Safe, Efficient"* provides an excellent example of exposing PG&E's, PR program and the role of the advertising dollar in PG&E's relationship with the media for what it truly is. The "editorial" was preceded with the following editor's note:

Victor C. Novarino has been manager of PG&E's Humboldt Division since 1962 and was division power engineer here from 1946 to 1953. He is president of the Eureka Rotary Club and past president of the Eureka Chamber of Commerce and of the Humboldt County Council Chambers of Commerce. He has been a director of the Salvation Army Board and of the Redwood Region Conservation Council. He has been a member of the Advisory Board of St. Joseph Hospital and a member of the Executive Committee of the Boy Scouts[366]

The entire text of Novarino's article follows without comment (although my *Diary* addresses every aspect of it):

When our Humboldt Bay Power Plant's nuclear unit began commercial operation in August 1963; it attracted more attention than the two units already there. It was powered by nuclear energy and was the eighth nuclear power plant in the United States.

Like all electric power plants, it was built to serve a need. Northern California needed its electricity. Severe winter storms often damaged transmission lines connecting the Humboldt region with other sources of power and this area needed its own independent source of electricity. The nuclear unit was also a symbol of a step forward. Even in 1963 it was evident that nuclear energy would be a valuable asset to California and the nation as other fuel supplies were decreasing. Humboldt Bay nuclear unit could show the way for other nuclear power plants in providing safe, clean power.

Thanks to a group of dedicated employees, Humboldt Bay nuclear power unit has fulfilled its promise.

The people at this plant have accomplished their main objective – supply reliable power. Humboldt Bay Nuclear Power Plant leads all 23 operating nuclear power plants in the nation in its record of availability for service, and its fuel cost is the lowest in the entire PG&E system.

The people at Humboldt Bay have proved that nuclear fission is a clean, reliable source of energy. They have demonstrated the soundness of the plant's basic design so well that it has become the pattern for others across the nation. Problems were expected, and they occurred. None were serious, but solving them gave added assurance that the generating unit would be available when needed.

Twenty-four of the 78 people now working at Humboldt nuclear unit were on the job when it was started. Warren Raymond, plant superintendent, was one of them. He earned one of the first Atomic Energy Commission operator's licenses in the nation 15 years ago, while at the Vallecitos plant, near Livermore. That plant, jointly operated by PG&E and the General Electric Co., was the first nuclear power plant licensed by the AEC. It generated electricity commercially from 1957 until it was retired from service in 1967.

In the years since Raymond obtained his license, about 80 PG&E employees, trained by the company, have taken the tough AEC reactor operator's examination. Not one has ever failed to pass the examination and obtain his license, a record unique in the industry.

Ed Weeks, power plant engineer, was on the original Humboldt nuclear staff. So was Russell Peter, supervisor of operations. Whether they were present the first day or joined the staff later, all the people at Humboldt Bay nuclear unit have earned my sincere respect.

The AEC has conducted inspections at Humboldt Bay approximately four times a year, announced and unannounced.

The inspections include checking records, inspecting the plant and its equipment, and examining the way jobs are done. The inspectors are thorough and their detailed reports sometimes indicate "discrepancies" – items that should be corrected or changed.

But in all the years of inspections at Humboldt Bay there have been only a few AEC citations for noncompliance and these have been of a minor nature. This record would be impossible without people who know their jobs, know their plant, and are willing to go beyond the requirements of their positions.

Just meeting those requirements calls for a high degree of skill and knowledge, plus personal integrity. If an employee can't meet them, he just can't work at a nuclear installation. The people at Humboldt Bay do things right, and continually prove that they are doing things right.

Just a few of their routine daily nuclear safety procedures are impressive. All radioactivity is carefully monitored. Sensitive instruments help do the job, but instruments are only valuable tools for trained men who understand them and can use them and can interpret what they say. All radioactive emissions from the stack are checked. One instrument could do the job, but two are used. The second is an 'operating spare,' ready to take over the important monitoring job instantly if the first one fails.

These men also analyze gases and liquids in their laboratory. Their analyses double-check the accuracy of the instruments and determine exactly what radioactivity leaves the plant. It has never exceeded AEC limits.

Humboldt nuclear unit people check all the liquids in the nuclear power process inside the plant, then do a final radiation check on the discharge canal leaving the facility.

The workers at Humboldt Bay also keep a close watch on the surrounding area for any evidence of radioactivity. They use 36 monitoring points outside the plant, and four different radiation detectors at each one. Independent organizations, including the AEC, confirm their findings that Humboldt Bay nuclear unit is operating safely.

More than 77 people work here, and have full knowledge of what goes on in a nuclear power plant. They find nothing to fear. They go quietly and efficiently about their job, providing a needed service for all of us.

Largely on the basis of their record of safety and efficiency, PG&E is building a $660,000,000 nuclear power plant near San Luis Obispo and plans to build another, to cost $742,000,000, near Point Arena."[367]

Something happened at the Ingomar Club meeting between "PG&E's top brass and the *Times-Standard's* top brass," which included corporate executive from Thompson's Newspapers, Inc.

Image 23. I can only speculate what on what took place during early July 1972 at the Ingomar Club located at the Carson Mansion in Eureka, California (Photo by Fred and Virginia Rowen)

I couldn't remember enough of the details to properly address the incident in my *Diary* although I don't believe I ever really knew the details of what had taken place. However, I felt I needed to include this incident in the telling of the Humboldt Bay story so I tracked down the Eureka *Times-Standard* environmental reporter who wrote the series. It took some doing to find him because he had moved around a lot since he had left the Eureka *Times-Standard*.

When I finally connected with him, it was by email made possible by a former associate of his that I finally stumbled across. She said she knew where he was and would get the word to him that I was trying to contact him. It all seemed very mysterious, almost cloak and dagger like, and all I could do was to wait for him to contact me. After what seemed to be a very long time, I received the following email from the reporter:

> Bob, I understand you've been looking for me. What's up?

I immediately responded with the following reply:

> It's really good to hear from you. I hope everything is going well for you. I'm finally writing my book now that I'm retired. There is considerable interest in it and new revelations regarding what happened at 245 Market Street back in the day regarding Forrest Williams and me. I'd love to chat with you about some things and I presented the following questions to him:

1. What is your view of what happened at the Ingomar Club towards the end of your series?
2. Were you invited to it?
3. Why did you leave The Times-Standard?
4. Are you familiar with the Don Widener case?
5. Did you ever talk with David Pesonen while you were writing the series?
6. Are the photos you used during the series still available?
7. If so, how could I get copies of them?
8. Did you know I was successful in a legal malpractice suit against McKittrick?
9. Are you aware that McKittrick became involved with the Mafia?
10. Did you know that McKittrick committed suicide on December 28, 1994?

I am now in touch with David Pesonen, and he has provided me copies of transcripts and internal company memoranda obtained through his discovery proceedings during the Widener case. Widener won his case against PG&E and the folks who testified in his case were the same players at corporate headquarters that were involved with the four nuclear control technicians at Humboldt Bay.

Looking forward to hearing from you. /s/ Bob

I anxiously waited for the longest time for the reporter's response not knowing if he would even reply. His reply finally came on October 21, 2010. When I received it, I was both surprised and disappointed. Surprised by the tone of it and disappointed by its dismal content.

His reply was not like that of the reporter I had come to know when he was writing the series. Neither was he like the one I had heard when we talked by phone a few years later after I had started teaching in Trinity County. At that time he still sounded upbeat and positive, and as for the series he had written for the Eureka *Times-Standard*, he referred to it as, "I think it's still a good read after all these years."

However, the reporter's response to my email had a very different tone and I chose not to respond to it; his email read:

Boy, you're talking about stuff I have long forgotten. Seems like it happened to somebody else.

I remember the series being a thankless story for all the effort I put into it. I'm not particularly interested in dredging up old stuff and would prefer not to be in your book. Not sure what you stand to gain from writing it.

The name Don Widener rings a bell. I know he did a series titled something like, 'The Powers That Be.' Was he a reporter for the S.F. newspaper? If it's the same guy, the last I heard of him he was walking the coast of California and writing about it each week. The columns got spacier and spacier and finally disappeared.

David Pesonen also rings a bell, but exactly why escapes me.

The meeting at the Ingomar Mansion was a meeting of the PG&E brass with our newspaper brass. We had presented written questions to them for answering. The newspaper changed publishers during the writing of the story after that meeting.

Interesting about McKittrick. My understanding from those in law enforcement is that there is no actual group defined by the name 'Mafia.' It's a loose term, kind of like the nebulous 'they.'

Good luck with the book. I hope over the years you found something more that PG&E to fill up your life. Are you still living in Humboldt County? /s/ (reporter's first name)

Since the reporter expressed a desire not to be mentioned in my *Diary*, I will therefore, not use his name. However, this part of the story will be told without his name since what happened at the Ingomar Club is a part of what happened at Humboldt Bay. What I do remember about the mysterious meeting at the Ingomar Club was the impression it left me with. Top-level management from both Thompson Newspapers and PG&E met at the Ingomar Club to discuss 70 questions regarding the Humboldt Bay Nuclear Power Plant arising out of the reporter's coverage of the plant; PG&E answered only seven of those questions for public comment. When the newspaper reporter presented those questions to PG&E, it created quit a stir. After that meeting at the Ingomar Club, things changed considerably making life for my family and me even more difficult.

1961 SEATO Inspection of Marine Pathfinder Sub Unit 1 (author is on the left)

__XVI__

16. *Silencing* the Critics of Nuclear Power

1970 – Present

"It's like a Soviet mock-examination. You're mentally ill because you have a difference of opinion about important affairs."[368] [Bob Seldon]

"Have you at any point in time, whether during the time you were in the Army or the Marines or at the same time received any type of psychological or psychiatric care?"[369] [Charles Denny]

"One company doctor described Mr. Aiken, who went into the nuclear industry after learning electronics in the Marine Corps, as suffering from a 'delusional disorder, persecutory type.' The psychiatrists declared Mr. Aiken a threat to security, and the company revoked his security clearance."[370] [Matthew Wald]

"Silencing and neutralizing" its critics is an essential goal —a vital necessity for the very survival— of America's nuclear juggernaut. This is especially true when the critics come from within the nuclear establishment because they know best what goes on inside of it. These critics are considered the "most dangerous" and must be gotten rid of, sometimes in the most mind-boggling, inconceivable ways. Once accomplished, and if still alive, they are labeled "whistleblowers," or worse, and forever branded "disgruntled ex-employees."

We cannot trust America's power brokers nor can we rely on our institutions of government that are controlled by them to protect us from their abuses. When these power brokers argue for less government in our lives, they are in reality trying to make life simpler for themselves.

Within America's nuclear juggernaut and without question, the best source of information about radiation safety violations, corruption, cost cutting, waste, fraud, design failures, cover-ups, and abuse of institutional authority – in both the private and government sectors – has been the employee from within the ranks who is willing to speak out.

These acts of courage should have been encouraged rather than stifled or worse. We needed to have nuclear employees empowered as watchdogs of wrongdoing but such has not been the case. We needed to ensure that nuclear whistleblowers had full access to the courts and due process, but the undue influences of the nuclear juggernaut, for the most part, have prevented it.

In order to understand, and hopefully accept, the role of *nuclear* whistleblowing in our society, one needs to recognize the motivations that underlie it. To paraphrase Brian Martin, author of "Whistleblowing and Nonviolence," *nuclear* whistleblowing is speaking out in the public interest, to expose corruption or dangers to nuclear employees, the public or to the environment.[371] Nuclear employees are in the very best position to serve as watchdogs of wrongdoing in nuclear facilities because the operators of those facilities cannot be trusted and the regulators of them cannot be relied upon.

Because they usually act individually, *nuclear* whistleblowers are extremely vulnerable and need to be protected from retaliation and suppression. The lengths to which organizational elites will go to suppress whistleblowers are amazing and hard to appreciate without hearing, first-hand, stories of reprisals.[372]

My *Diary* has revealed what happened at Humboldt Bay; it will also provide a few summaries of other first-hand stories of reprisals. First however, a thoughtful examination of the tremendous power and influence the new power brokers have over our mass media, the marketplace, and our political system reveals a further degradation of the values that once made America strong. My *Diary* shall confine itself to the nuclear juggernaut, which is merely a reflection of what could be a much larger commentary on the emergence of America's new power brokers. Janine Wedel called the emerging new power brokers the "shadow elite," – the "main players in a vexing new system of power and influence" – which, in the context of *My Humboldt Diary*, puts American society on a collision course with nuclear disaster. The stakes are simply too high to allow this to happen!

PG&E and those, whose PG&E's influence has touched, have claimed that I "have not questioned the validity of nuclear power as the power source of the future" (e.g., review Dan Walters' editorial in Chapter 15). Nothing could be further from the truth!

The ramifications of the misuse of nuclear energy; the irresponsible operations of nuclear facilities resulting in the poisoning of our air, soil, and water; the lack of meaningful government control over nuclear plant operators; the unresolved problem of nuclear waste disposal; the devastating biological effects of radiation; and the horrendous unimaginable ramifications of natural disasters that can befall nuclear plants are far, far too great to allow even one more nuke to be built.

America's nuclear juggernaut's shameful treatment of those who have stepped up to expose what all too often a takes place inside America's nuclear industry, and the related regulatory functions of government, is the most effective way to expose why the general public cannot trust the *nuclear-industrial complex*. Without doubt, the defenders of the technology will push back from their own history of crucifying nuclear control technicians, reactor operators, nuclear engineers, nuclear consultants, research scientists, nuclear management personnel, and even people in the news media who, through their research, have developed a critical view of nuclear power.

My *Diary* will reveal in a very personal way what has happened and is still happening (*and why*) to the so-called "most dangerous critics" of the nuclear industry, those on the inside of America's nuclear *community* – past and present. I mention, "Revealing in a very personal way" because I am going to reflect on what has happened to *"nuclear whistleblowers"* based on my own experience of being one.

As I have previously mentioned in my *Diary*, I know of no one who set out to become a whistleblower in America's *nuclear-industrial complex*. However, I do know from firsthand experience the consequences of whistleblowing and the stigma that goes with being labeled a *"nuclear whistleblower."* And I am fully aware of the public ridicule the defenders of the technology will unmercifully throw your way.

The investment that is required to become a "nuclear insider" is far too great to just end up whimsically throwing it all away. It would absolutely make no sense for a highly skilled and educated professional to become a "mindless whistleblower" engaged in mere senseless "acts of stupidity." Far from it, nuclear whistleblowers answer to a higher calling: A genuine concern for employee and public safety. Without a doubt, the legacy of past *nuclear whistleblowers* will be etched into the annals of history, which will hopefully be added onto by responsible nuclear insiders of the future. My *Diary* shall first broach the subject of *nuclear whistleblowing* with that which I am most familiar.

PG&E's Neil Aiken and Bob Rowen have a lot in common . . .

Neil Aiken and Bob Rowen certainly have a lot in common. They are both former Marines, former employees of PG&E, former nuclear plant workers, critical of PG&E's approach to safety, and were willing to speak up about safety problems at PG&E's nuclear power plants and fired from PG&E for doing so albeit the company cited other reasons for their terminations.

Also there were differences between Aiken and Rowen. Neil Aiken was a shift foreman at PG&E's newest Nuke at Diablo Canyon in San Luis Obispo and had more than 20 years of service with the company; Bob Rowen was a nuclear control technician at PG&E's oldest Nuke at Humboldt Bay in Eureka with 9 years of service with the company.

Both Aiken and Rowen were in the excellent company of other PG&E employees who were also critical of PG&E's way of doing business in the utility's *nuclear world*. These other PG&E employees were nuclear control technicians Raymond Skidmore, Forrest Williams, and Howard Darington.

Because Neil Aiken, a longtime PG&E employee, had "complained publicly about safety problems and management inaction at the Diablo Canyon Nuclear Power Plant," the company *arranged* to have Aiken diagnosed with "paranoid delusions." PG&E later claimed it had only public safety in mind when it sent Mr. Aiken to company selected psychiatrists for "evaluation."[373]

Savannah Blackwell, wrote an article for the *San Francisco Bay Guardian* entitled "PG&E, Corporate Criminal: The utility likes to pretend it's a good corporate citizen – but the record shows otherwise."[374]

Blackwell reported, "Although PG&E likes to insist it is a tolerant and responsible company, it has a long history of retaliating against any employee who blows the whistle on its irresponsible practices."[375]

My *Diary* is replete with examples of PG&E retaliation against employees at Humboldt Bay. Blackwell cited a more recent example at Diablo Canyon:[376]

> At PG&E's April 1998 shareholders meeting, Neil Aiken, a shift foreman at the Diablo Canyon Nuclear Power Plant, stood up and told shareholders about safety problems that came from cost cutting at the plant.
>
> Aiken told the audience he came forward only in desperation, because he had exhausted all possible routes of solving the problem within the company. He also released a report detailing the safety issues called 'Going Critical' at the same time.

As the nuclear industry was moving into the Twenty-first Century, the Diablo Canyon Nuclear Power Plant became PG&E's newest nuclear flagship for the entire country. The company would do anything to defend the technology and the "reputation of the plant" as well as that of the company, which amounted to more of the same that occurred at PG&E's first nuke at Humboldt Bay.

According to Blackwell, "PG&E executives forced Aiken to undergo psychiatric evaluation. He was locked out of the plant and forced off his job after 24 years." As a footnote to the Aiken case, Blackwell added, "The Project on Liberty and the Workplace took up his case, and the U.S. Department of Labor found PG&E guilty of retaliation."[377]

Retaliation by PG&E was nothing new and it took on many different forms. For Bob Rowen, it was PG&E's charge that he had communist leanings, advocated fire bombing and violence, and was a ringleader of a group involved in a plot to blow up the Humboldt Bay Power Plant. PG&E knowingly and maliciously provided this false information to the Chief of Police for the City of Eureka. He in turn provided a false police report to the Federal Bureau of Investigation for the purpose to make Rowen a security risk – a new form of blacklisting – *nuclear blacklisting*. Making things worse, PG&E then raised the question of whether Rowen had ever received any psychological or psychiatric care. Sound familiar?

Lawrence Radiation Laboratory research scientists John W. Gofman and Arthur R. Tamplin (1963-1969) . . .

Drs. John Gofman and Arthur Tamplin were asked by the Atomic Energy Commission (AEC) in 1963 to undertake a series of long-range studies on the potential dangers that might arise from the "peaceful uses of the atom." These two scientists were internationally known for their research on the effects of radioactivity on the environment, and particularly on man. AEC Chairman Glenn Seaborg assured Gofman and Tamplin that the AEC wanted favorable or unfavorable findings made available to the public. "All we want is the truth," Chairman Seaborg said in 1963.[378]

Gofman and Tamplin concluded in 1970 (repeated from Chapter 2 for emphasis):[379]

> The entire nuclear electricity industry had been developing under a set of totally false illusions of safety and economy. Not only was there a total lack of appreciation of the hazards of radiation for man, but also there was a total absence of candor concerning the hazard of serious accidents. The economics were being treated with rose-colored glasses. And the triumvirate knew all too well that the stampede to nuclear power, initiated by them, could not possibly tolerate the bright light of exposure to public scrutiny. The more we probed, the more we realized how massive the deception truly was. It became quite clear that concealment of truth from the public was regarded as essential.

In presenting their extensive research findings Drs. Gofman and Tamplin honestly believed that, "In a rational society, where the health and welfare of citizens would be considered paramount, such research findings would have been warnings welcomed." Instead they received a torrent of vitriol and personal condemnation from the nuclear power brokers, and especially from the electric industry.[380] Dr. John Gofman responded to the personal attacks, including one made by AEC Commissioner James T. Ramey:[381]

> There is no morality . . . not a shred of honesty in any one of them – none. I can assure you, from every bit of dealing I've had . . . there is absolute duplicity, guaranteed duplicity, lies at every turn, falsehood in every way, about

you personally and about your motives.

PG&E's Forrest Williams (1970) . . .

Nuclear control technician Forrest Williams was considered insubordinate because he refused to comply with a direct order given by a PG&E manager to perform an unsafe act in Humboldt Bay's radiological laboratory. The direct order that was given to Forrest Williams was a clear violation of PG&E's Radiation Control Standards and Procedures yet the company unsuccessfully tried to frame it otherwise (review Chapter 3).

Beyond his refusal to comply with the direct order previously mentioned, Williams decided he was no longer willing to work for a company that was willing to expose employees to "needless and senseless" amounts of radiation because it was more economical for the company to treat employees as "expendable tools of production."[382]

Williams said in a 2008 interview by a *North Coast Journal* reporter:[383]

> They knew they were cutting corners. They knew they were doing it. I don't think they considered the safety as far as exposure . . . it was their attitude. As long as the law allows it we can do it, and fudge on it a little.

PG&E's Raymond Skidmore and Howard Darington (1971) . . .

Nuclear control technicians Raymond Skidmore and Howard Darington were nuclear plant workers engaged in union activities related to radiation protection and nuclear plant safety conditions of employment at PG&E's Humboldt Bay Nuclear Power Plant.[384]

They were accused by PG&E of being members of a group and holding group meetings, and of participating in acts tantamount to industrial sabotage. Skidmore and Darington were identified in a police report that was sent to the FBI as members of a dissident group involved in a plot to blow up the Humboldt Bay Nuclear Power Plant.[385]

I had lost contact with Raymond Skidmore after leaving the Humboldt area in 1972, but during a 2008 interview, I gave a *North Coast Journal* reporter Raymond Skidmore's name and said he probably still lives somewhere in the Eureka area. The reporter found Skidmore, interviewed him, and reported the following in a *North Coast Journal* article entitled "The Not-So-Peaceful Atom" dated March 20, 2008:[386]

> Raymond Skidmore still lives in the area. The 74-year-old has suffered from a stroke and pancreatic cancer since retiring from PG&E . . .
>
> He was there that summer in 1969 when Allen intentionally took light swabs off of the spent fuel cask.
>
> As for why he was never fired, 'PG&E probably figured Rowen was the leader, causing all the trouble,' Skidmore

said, then his voice trailed off and he looked away. He didn't seem too keen on remembering the past.

However, he did mention that even after Rowen and Williams left, unsafe practices continued at the plant. He kept a logbook where he recorded safety complaints, which, coincidentally, went missing the day he was scheduled to talk to a representative from the AEC.

'There were just a few of us who tried to do the job right,' he said.

Kerr-McGee's Karen Silkwood (1974) . . .

Karen Silkwood was a nuclear power plant technician at the Kerr-McGee Cimarron River nuclear facility in Crescent, Oklahoma. The Cimarron facility manufactured fuel rods that were used in nuclear reactors. After Silkwood had uncovered safety problems at her facility, she became a union activist as a member of the Oil, Chemical and Atomic Workers International Union.

Because company management had ignored the health and safety problems at her facility, Silkwood along with a couple of union officials went to Washington, D.C., to confer with national union leaders and the AEC. Their complaints about the Kerr-McGee facility included the lack of training given employees, failure to minimize contamination, poor radiation monitoring practices, and uranium dust in the lunchroom.

After compiling evidence of the plant's safety violations, she arranged to deliver it to a *New York Times* reporter and a national union representative. On her way to the meeting with the newspaper reporter, she was killed in a suspicious car accident and the evidence she had with her was never found.

Attorney Gerry Spence represented Karen Silkwood's father and children, who charged that Kerr-McGee was responsible for exposing Silkwood to dangerous levels of radiation. Spence won a $10.5 million verdict for the family. In 1984, the Supreme Court of the United States upheld the family's right to sue under state law for punitive damages from a federally regulated industry.

Silkwood's story was made into the 1983 film *Silkwood* staring Meryl Streep as Karen Silkwood, with Kurt Russell and Cher in supporting roles.

General Electric's nuclear engineers Dale Bridenbaugh, Richard Hubbard, and Gregory Minor (1976) . . .

Known as the "GE Three" at San Jose, Dale Bridenbaugh, Richard Hubbard, and Greg Minor were nuclear engineers who "blew the whistle" on safety problems at nuclear powers plants in 1976. The three nuclear engineers questioned the design adequacy of GE's Mark 1 reactor that was being used throughout America. It accounted for five of the six reactors at the Fukushima Daiichi Nuclear Power Plant in Japan.

The nuclear engineers claimed the design of the Mark 1 reactor did not take into account the dynamic loads that could be experienced with a lost of coolant. Bridenbaugh told ABC News in an interview, "The impact loads of the containment could tear the containment apart and create an uncontrolled release."[387]

The former Japanese Ambassador to Switzerland, Mitsuhei Marata, wrote a letter in October 2013 to President Barack Obama warning him of what he called "the most pressing global security issue" of our time about the Fukushima nuclear disaster. The full text of Ambassador Mitsuhei Murata's letter reads:[388]

> Dear Mr. President,
> Much reported contaminated water problem at Fukushima Daiichi is overshadowing the Unit 4 crisis, which is the most pressing global security issue. A mega earthquake surpassing intensity 6 plus will make collapse the already wrecked building and the cooling pool containing ten times more cesium137 than Chernobyl. There are in total 15,093 fuel rods assemblies at the site. Frequent earthquakes continue to rattle the building. If the worst happens, the total evacuation will be imposed and it will be, as top scientists of the world warn, the beginning of a major global catastrophe.
> It is urgently needed to set up an international task force to assist Japan by deploying all possible means to reduce the risks of the imminent first unloading of spent fuel from the Unit 4 conditions of unprecedented complexity. This requires the establishment of a new system based on the full assumption of responsibilities by the Government of Japan. The enormous amount of funding needed must be totally supervised by the Government, not by TEPCO (Tokyo Electric Power Company). This is the crisis of Japan as a nation, not the crisis of the management of TEPCO. One of the lessons of Fukushima should be the shift of the priority; from economy to life.
> The task force to be created under the new system, consisting of best experts, American and other, would provide, based on neutral assessment, adequate strategies for the stabilization of the Fukushima Daiichi.The world is pinning hopes on your historic role, symbolized by your vision "the world without nuclear weapons."
> With highest and warmest regards,
> Mitsuhei Marata
> Former Japanese Ambassador to Switzerland

All three engineers had simply quit in 1976 in protest of General Electric's Mark 1 nuclear reactor design and gained the attention of the antinuclear movement for doing so.

After leaving their responsible positions in General Electric's nuclear energy division, the three nuclear engineers established themselves as consultants on the nuclear power industry for state governments, federal agencies, and overseas governments. The consulting firm they formed, MHB Technical Associates, was the technical advisor for the 1979 movie "The China Syndrome" which won several Academy Awards.

NBC's new documentary producer Don Widener (1979) . . .

Emmy Award winning producer, Don Widener, lost his contract with NBC because PG&E put the squeeze on his documentary film that was "critical" of Humboldt Bay's improper nuclear fuel cladding materials used in the first loading of the reactor core in 1963. PG&E ruined Widener's reputation, ended his career as a producer of news documentaries, and outrageously engaged in "nuclear censorship" (review Chapter 15).

Nuclear quality assurance inspector Chuck Atkinson (1982) . . .

In his treatise on whistleblowing, Brian Martin provided the following example of the lengths to which organizational elites will go to suppress whistleblowers:[389]

> Chuck Atkinson was a quality assurance inspector at a nuclear power plant being constructed in Texas. Initially committed to nuclear power, in 1980 he became an anonymous whistleblower concerning safety violations. He was suddenly dismissed in 1982 after reporting problems to his employer, Brown and Root that would have required redoing work. On the day he was fired, an inspector at the Nuclear Regulatory Commission revealed his identity as a whistleblower to plant officials; since he was no longer employed, the NRC would not maintain his anonymity. After testifying publicly against the industry, he was blacklisted. For example, after obtaining a job at another power station, he was fired a few days later after his new employers found out about his whistleblowing. Atchison lost his job, his home, his credit rating, his sense of personal safety, and his self-esteem as a breadwinner.

I wished I had read Brian Martin's treatise on whistleblowing before embarking on my effort to address what was happening at PG&E's Humboldt Bay Nuclear Power Plant. I also wished I would have realized from the very outset that I should not have relied on the IBEW Local 1245 for any meaningful help from my union. One part of Brian Martin's treatise on whistleblowing that truly resonated with me was the following:

Many individuals who speak out did not intend to be a whistleblower . . . and do not think of themselves as whistleblowers.

They simply speak out in the expectation that the issues they think important will be addressed honestly and effectively. They are terribly shocked when; instead, they become the target.

One reason why these "unintentional whistleblowers" have so little chance of success or even survival is that they have not mobilized support beforehand.

They are lone dissidents typically up against the full power of an organizational hierarchy.

It took a long time for me to realize and accept that I was indeed a "whistleblower." This personal reflection reminds me of one of my favorite all-time, one-liners from the movie, "The Natural" staring Robert Redford when he says, "We have two lives ... the life we learn with and the life we live after that. Suffering is what brings us towards happiness." This indeed has brought me solace during the aftermath of my PG&E experience.

Nuclear Energy Services' Arnold Gundersen (1990) . . .

Gundersen has more than 40 years of nuclear power engineering experience. Mr. Gunderson was a senior vice president with Nuclear Energy Services (NES) and coordinated projects at over 60 nuclear power plants in the United States during his career. Gundersen has B.A. and M.S. degrees in nuclear engineering, had an Atomic Energy Commission Fellowship in 1972, was a licensed reactor operator, and holds a nuclear safety patent.

Gunderson's nuclear career spanned employment services with Northeast Utilities Services Corporation as a nuclear engineer, New York State Electric Gas as an engineering supervisor, and Nuclear Energy Services (NES) as a senior vice president of the Connecticut-based consulting firm.

In 1990 Gundersen discovered radioactive material in an accounting safe while he was employed at NES. Three weeks after he reported safety violations to the NES company president, he was fired.

Katherine Boughton briefly chronicled part of the Gundersen story in *The Litchield County Times* in her article entitled "The Whistleblower":[390]

Since then (after Gundersen was fired from NES), he has become a dedicated whistleblower, taking on the industry that once supplied him and his family with a comfortable lifestyle and a bright future. Mr. Gundersen made the transition between these two worlds after he uncovered what he felt were safety violations at NES and reported the problem to management. Soon after making this report he was dismissed from this job and began a five-year effort to prove his case. He asserts he was blacklisted by the industry for discussing the alleged violations with state and federal regulators and was eventually sued by NES $1.5 million for defamation. The suit was settled out-of-court.

A report prepared by the U.S. Nuclear Regulatory Commission eventually concluded that there had been irregularities at NES, and a second document, prepared by the Office of the Inspector General, noted that the NRC had violated its own regulations by improperly steering business to NES. But that vindication was small solace to the Gunderson family, who had by then lost their home.

'Without the intervention of Sen. Joseph Lieberman and Sen. John Glenn, we would have been dog meat,' Mr. Gundersen said. 'We would have been selling apples on the street. My bitterness is not toward my former employer, but toward the government agencies that did nothing to rectify it. I had believed in the government, but now I know that it is an organism and when you attack it, it reacts like an organism.'

Now a physics and mathematics teacher at Marvelwood School in Kent and director of the school's summer program, Mr. Gundersen has come to grips with the ruination of his previous career. 'I took a fourfold pay cut when I came to Marvelwood, he said, 'but I really feel alive everyday. I don't spend a lot of time prepping for class, but I spend hours figuring out how to present the materials. Marvelwood is a school for kids who need second chances. We have them for four years, and when you see one go off to a good school – that feels wonderful.'

Day by day Mr. Gundersen enjoys his teaching position, but he has yet to forget the safety violations he reported while still employed in the nuclear industry, or the duplicity he says brought him to financial ruin.

After reading this article I realized how much Mr. Gundersen and I have in common, although I was finished with my nuclear career in 1970 before he started his in 1972. As a nuclear control technician, I was further down the nuclear food chain than that of a nuclear engineer; and I certainly was not in management like Mr. Gundersen. However, we both witnessed radiation safety violations in our respective realms of nuclear experience, we publicly addressed those violations, and we both suffered the consequences of doing so. Mr. Gundersen and I both ended up teaching with part of my teaching assignments also including mathematics.

Mr. Gundersen's and my whistleblowing experiences, although more than 20 years apart, had much in common. We both experience many of the same things. For three years following blowing the whistle on his employer, harassing phone calls in the middle of the night awakened Gundersen and his family.[391] Gundersen became concerned about his family's safety; said he was blacklisted, citing an April 22, 1991, letter concerning him that the company sent to 78 people; and he was harassed, then fired for doing what he thought was right.[392]

According to a report in The New York Times:[393]

> Mr. Gundersen's case, according to a number of whistleblowers and others interviewed, is not uncommon, especially in the nuclear industry. Even though nuclear workers are encouraged to report potential safety hazards, those who do say that they risk demotion and dismissal. Instead of correcting the problems, whistleblowers and their supporters say, industry management and government attack them as the cause of the problem.
>
> Driven out of their jobs and shunned by neighbors and coworkers, whistleblowers turn to each other for support.

COMMENT: It's not worthwhile for nuclear employees to be encouraged to report potential safety hazards, etc., when they believe they'd be placing themselves in jeopardy for doing so.

I don't believe the same way as Gundersen, when he said, "My bitterness is not toward my former employer." What Gundersen had to say about the government being an organism, is exactly how I feel about the corporation.

Northeast Utilities' Paul Blanch (1990) . . .

Nuclear engineer Paul Blanch became a whistleblower after he discovered safety problems in the late 1980s and early 1990s and was brushed aside by both Northeast Utilities and the Nuclear Regulatory Commission. Eric Pooley summarized Paul Blanch's fall from grace in his *Time Magazine* article entitled "Nuclear Warriors," dated March 4, 1996:[394]

> In 1990 Northeast engineer Paul Blanch discovered the instruments that measured the coolant levels inside the reactor at Millstone 3 were failing. Blanch was force out, and the problem went uncorrected. In 1993 the NRC's William Russell told the inspector general that the agency had exercised "enforcement discretion," a policy that allows it to waive regulations. Later Russell said the remark had been taken out of context.

Paul Blanch said he was only doing what the law required when, between 1988 and 1993, he brought four safety issues to the attention of Northeast Utilities and the Nuclear Regulatory Commission. After coming forward, Blanch said that Northeast supervisors harassed him and that the NRC did little to protect him, despite federal and state laws designed to prevent such treatment.[395]

Joseph Fouchard, chief spokesman for the Nuclear Regulatory Commission, said, "We take whistleblowers seriously, and we expect our licensees to take them seriously also." The commission had found, "Among other things, that managers at the utility, in retaliation, improperly sought to give the engineer, Paul M. Blanch, bad performance evaluations . . ."[396]

The NRC's handling of Blanch's complaint sounded pretty good until he responded, "I feel very vindicated."[397] But then he added, "They agreed with me, but in the meantime I (was) unemployed. The action against Northeast and to protect me should have occurred within three months: Why (did) it take four years?"[398]

Anthony Castagno, a Northeast Utilities spokesman said in response to the NRC's action, "Our position is that no employees or supervisors or managers did anything that violated regulations at all. We don't believe there was any harassment or intimidation."[399]

Mr. Castagno said that the NRC had investigated the company in 1990 after other workers complained of harassment, and that it had found the majority of employees felt comfortable raising safety concerns.[400] But the follow-on to Mr. Castagno's statement was contained in the report the NRC had issued regarding Mr. Blanch's complaint, "Various workers at Northeast Utilities said they would not raise safety issues with management, because of the way Mr. Blanch had been treated."[401] Northeast Utilities responded to the NRC report on Blanch's complaint saying they were working on a detailed rebuttal and would file it within the 30 days allowed under the commission's rules.[402]

In 2013, Mr. Blanch wrote a treatise entitled "Safety Culture is not Possible Without Regulatory Compliance"[403] that thoroughly explains the importance of rigorous regulation by the NRC in establishing a genuine nuclear "Safety Culture." After providing summaries of comparison between various nuclear safety cultures, and citing some observations made in documents from the International Atomic Energy Agency (IAEA), Blanch provided eight recommendations.

Blanch said, "The nuclear industry must recognize it will never solve the Safety Culture problem until the NRC takes the following actions (citing his eight recommendations at the conclusion of his "Safety Culture" treatise)."[404] All eight of Blanch's recommendations are well thought out but the following two caught my eye:

1. The NRC must strictly enforce, in a timely manner, all of the regulations applicable to each plant's CLB (Current Licensing Basis), especially those that allege retaliation. This is an absolute requirement to assure adequate protecting for the public and the environment.

2. The NRC must be clear and consistent in its expectations and consequences for regulatory non-compliance. The only way to compel

compliance is through enforcement. Utilities
only comply with regulations when the cost of
compliance is less that the cost of noncompliance. A strong enforcement policy is
the key.

COMMENT: The AEC didn't provide rigorous regulation of the nuclear
industry and the NRC hasn't fared much better. Is it even possible to achieve
meaningful government regulation when, especially in today's political area,
we have the "best" government corporate and special interest money can
buy?

Joseph Wampler, his career destroyed a second time (1991) . . .

In the early 1980s, when Northesat Utilities' Seabrook Station in New
Hampshire was under construction, Joseph Wampler warned the Nuclear
Regulatory Commission (NRC) that many welds were faulty. His
complaints went unanswered, and he was eventually fired and blacklisted.

Wampler moved to California and revived his career. But in 1991 the
NRC sent a letter summarizing Wampler's allegations – and providing his
full name and new address – to several dozen nuclear companies. His career
was destroyed a second time and Wampler ended up working as a carpenter.
The NRC fined Northeast $100,000 for problems with the welds.[405]

Northeast Utilities' George Galatis (1996) . . .

George Galatis was a senior nuclear engineer at Northeast Utilities,
which operated five nuclear plants in New England during the early 1990s.
Mr. Galatis discovered unsafe procedures being routinely used at the
Millstone 1 Nuclear Power Plant in Waterford, Connecticut.

Galatis eventually took his concerns to the Nuclear Regulatory
Commission only to learn that the NRC had "known about the unsafe
procedures for years."

Millstone was using the unsafe procedures to save about two weeks of
downtime for each refueling – during which Northeast Utilities had to pay
$500,000 a day for replacement power.[406]

The unsafe procedures involved the full off-loading of the reactor core in
violation of the radiation control standards and procedures contained in the
company's operating license. It was eventually determined that the full-core
off-loads had been conducted by Northeast for 20 years.

Not long after going to the NRC, Galatis experienced harassment,
retaliation, and intimidation and believed his "nuclear career was over."[407]
"I believe in nuclear power," Galatis once stated, "but after seeing the NRC
in action, I'm convinced a serious accident is not just likely but inevitable.
This is a dangerous road. They're asleep at the wheel. And I'm road-kill."[408]

Northeast Utilities' George Betancourt (1996) . . .

George Betancourt was also a senior nuclear engineer at Northeast Utilities. Mr. Betancourt remembered the day he met George Galatis up close and personal. When Galatis approached Betancourt about the problem of routinely performing "full-core off-loads," dumping all the hot fuel during refueling outages into the spent-fuel pool, the following discussion took place between them:[409]

Galatis: How long has this been going on?

Betancourt: We've been moving full cores since before I got here, since the early '70s.

Galatis: But it's an emergency procedure.

Betancourt: I know. And we do it all the time.

The two nuclear engineers discussed the full range of the dangerous possibilities that were involved with the full-core off-loads at Millstone. They concluded their discussion:[410]

"If Millstone lost its primary cooling system," Galatis told Betancourt, "the pool could boil. We'd better report this to the NRC."

"Do that," Betancourt said, "and you're dogmeat."

Both nuclear engineers knew Northeast Utilities had earned a reputation of harassing and firing employees who raised safety concerns. But if Galatis wanted to take on this issue, Betancourt told him, "I'll back you."[411]

In January 1996, Northeast Utilities laid off 100 employees. To qualify for their severance money, the workers had to sign elaborate release forms pledging not to sue the utility for harassment.[412]

URS Corporation's Walter Tamosaitis (2013) . . .

Walter Tamosaitis, a senior scientist with the URS Corporation, was fired because he warned about fundamental design flaws at the nation's largest facility to treat radioactive waste in Hanford, Washington. Ralph Vartabedian of *The Los Angeles Times* reported:[413]

When senior scientist Walter Tamosaitis warned in 2011 about fundamental design flaws at the nation's largest facility to treat radioactive wastes in Hanford, Washington, he was assigned to work in a basement room without office furniture or a telephone.

The Los Angeles Times also reported:[414]

The Hanford site is the nation's most contaminated property, holding 56 million gallons of highly radioactive sludge in underground tanks, some of which are leaking.

The complex sits on a plateau above the Columbia River, which could be threatened if the cleanup fails to contain the tank waste.

Two years following his 2011 warning about the problem at the Hanford site, "Tamosaitis, a systems engineer with a doctoral degree who had directed a staff of 100 scientists until he began expressing concerns about safety, said URS officials showed up and ordered him to box up his personal belongings, then escorted him out."[415]

After Tamosaitis was fired from the job that he had held for 44 years, he lamented, "I enjoyed working and trying to do something for the country. They killed my career. It sends a message to everybody else that they shouldn't raise issues. Forty-four years of service, a PhD, a recognized expert in nuclear engineering – none of that mattered." [416]

NRC's Larry Criscione and Richard Perkins (2012) . . .

Lawrence S. Criscione and Richard H. Perkins were employed in the Nuclear Regulatory Commission and became reluctant whistleblowers when they found it necessary to accuse the NRC of being both disconcertingly sluggish and inappropriately secretive about severe – and in one case, potentially catastrophic – flood risks at nuclear power plants that sit downstream from large dams.[417]

According to engineers and nuclear safety advocates, an un-redacted version of the report by the NRC that highlighted the threat flooding poses to nuclear power plants located near large dams – suggested that the NRC misled the public for years about the severity of the threat.[418]

David Lochbaum, nuclear engineer with the Union of Concerned Scientists (USC), said, "The redacted information shows that the NRC [was] lying to the American public about the safety of U.S. reactors."[419]

The Huffington Post reported:[420]

> Evidence in the report indicated that the NRC knew for more than a decade that failure of the dam upriver from the Oconee Nuclear Station in South Carolina would cause floodwater to overwhelm the plant's three reactors and their cooling equipment – not unlike what befell Japan's Fukushima Dai-chi facility after an earthquake and tsunami struck in 2011.

> Three reactors at Fukushima experienced a full meltdown, which contaminated surrounding farmland and exiled hundreds of thousands of residents.

According to the leaked report, the NRC stated unequivocally in a 2009 letter to Duke Energy that it believed "a Jacassee Dam failure is a credible event." Lawrence Criscione quoted Admiral Rickover in his September 18, 2012, letter to NRC Chairman Allison Macfarlane:

> A major flaw in our system of government, and even in industry, is the latitude to do less than is necessary. Too often officials are willing to accept and adapt to situations they know to be wrong. The tendency is to downplay

problems instead of actively trying to correct them.

Criscione wrote, "Admiral Rickover served 63 years as an officer in the United States navy – longer than any other naval officer in U.S. history. He spent the last half of his career developing the nuclear powered submarine force and commercial nuclear power."[421] His letter to the NRC Chairman pointed out the following:[422]

> On March 11, 2011, an earthquake and tsunami struck the Japanese nuclear facilities at Fukushima Dai-ichi. The floodwalls built to protect the reactor plants were too short and the 49-foot wave that hit the plants took out the emergency electric power.
>
> With no way to remove decay heat, over the next several days heat built up in the reactor cores until it melted the fuel, breached the steel reactor vessels, and eventually breached the containment building.
>
> The utility owner – TEPCO – was aware of analyses that showed their tsunami walls were not adequately sized. But in the spirit of Admiral Rickover's quote, they were willing to accept and downplay situations they knew to be wrong instead of actively trying to correct them.
>
> Why did the utility behave so irresponsibly? Because it is human nature to focus on immediate problems and to delay addressing "what ifs."
>
> And a 49-foot tsunami was a very low probability "what if."

Lawrence Criscione, along with Paul Blanch, together wrote a letter to Senator Joseph Lieberman dated December 18, 2012.[423] The two nuclear engineers addressed what they referred to as their "grave concern" regarding the failure of the NRC to protect the public from a potential catastrophic impact of a dam or natural gas transmission pipeline failure.

Blanch referred to the potential energy release in a gas line rupture at the Indian Point Nuclear Power Plant as being equivalent to that of the 2010 explosion and fire in San Bruno, California. He pointed out that the gas lines passing through the Indian Point facility are the same vintage, however they are much larger in capacity.[424]

Lawrence Criscione referred to his concern resulting from a failure of Jocassee Dam and the catastrophic impact that would have on the Oconee Nuclear Station.

Criscione said such an event would be similar to that experienced at Fukushima following the tsunami.[425]

Regarding the potential for a catastrophic flooding event at dozens of U.S. nuclear power plants downstream from dams around the country, Larry Criscione and Richard Perkins have charged the NRC with deliberately withholding information from the public to cover up for the agency's own failure in addressing these serious safety concerns.[426]

Whistleblowers don't always agree . . .

Even whistleblowers don't always agree. Richard Perkins wrote in his letter to the NRC's Office of the Inspector General, "The Nuclear Regulatory Commission staff may be motivated to prevent the disclosure of this safety information to the public because it will embarrass the agency."[427]

Perkins added, "The redacted information includes discussion of, and excerpts from, NCR official agency records that show the NRC has been in possession of relevant, notable and derogatory safety information for an extended period but has failed to properly act on it."[428] Although Criscione is critical of the NRC'S inaction and secrecy, he does not suspect they are concealing a more nefarious agenda.

"It's just general incompetence," Criscione said. "The NRC is an agency of [about] 3,000 people and there is a fair amount of turnover. I think we just dropped the ball at peak times and critical stages throughout the last couple of years and the issue didn't get addressed to the level it should (have been)."[429] According to AFP reporter Keith Johnson, Arnold Gundersen, a former nuclear power executive who served as an expert in the investigation of the Three Mile Island accident, had a different take on why the NRC is failing to enforce strict safety regulations:[430]

'We've got a pronuclear commission and employees at the NRC who are painfully aware that if they do any major modification to these facilities the industry will shut plants down rather than fix them because they become too expensive to operate,' said Gundersen.

'The NRC guys get paid by the number of reactors that are out there. So if 20 reactors shut down, NRC funds dry up by about 20%. That leaves them with more people to do less work. My guess is there would be layoffs. So it's in their best interest to regulate up to the point of modification.

Summary . . .

Considering my nuclear experience and what I've learned since, there really isn't a whole lot of difference between the *old* AEC and the *new* NRC. It's the underlying philosophy and motivation that drives the operational regulatory function.

Gundersen probably comes closer to hitting on the problem, at least to some degree. However, I would argue that it's a whole lot more complicated than that; I believe the real problem of achieving meaningful regulation stems from the enormous control and influence of the power brokers of America's nuclear juggernaut.

From my vantage point of having been in the trenches, the following observation best describes the root of the problem. It's a *paraphrase* of what one nuclear "whistleblower" once said, that describes my PG&E employment experience perfectly; which reflects on the larger problem that is addressed throughout my *Diary*:

> The Humboldt Bay Nuclear Power Plant management personnel conveyed the following: The three simple rules here are: (1) If it's legal, it's ethical; (2) If we get away with it it's legal; (3) And the only right you have as an employee is the right to seek employment elsewhere.

The Humboldt Bay nuclear plant management personnel did not convey this message in a vacuum. Plant management personnel would not have conveyed this message unless they knew they could get away with it.

Why did they get away with it? Because it wasn't just at Humboldt Bay, it was top to bottom throughout PG&E's nuclear management hierarchy. But it wasn't just the PG&E management hierarchy that embraced this philosophy; it permeated America's entire nuclear juggernaut – and without a doubt, still does!

Forrest "Bud" Williams & Bob Rowen
2010

__XVII__

17. Humboldt Hill: An Untold Story

"We were within spitting distance of that plant and I think it did have something to do with it . . ."[431]
[Edith Kraus Stein]

As I was continuing the research for my *Diary*, something happened that caused me to add another chapter – eventually this chapter. In October 2010, I made a trek to Eureka to conduct a couple of interviews an acquire some photos. My Eureka itinerary included stops at the *Times-Standard* newspaper office, Humboldt County Historical Society, Clarke Historical Museum, Humboldt State University Library, Humboldt County Library, North Coast Journal office, and the South Bay Elementary School to meet with the school district's superintendent.

I was interested in obtaining some photos of the 1971 refueling outage at the Humboldt Bay Nuclear Power Plant. These photos were used in published articles that appeared in the Eureka *Times-Standard* newspaper during the summer of 1972. The particular photos I was interested in included the biological shield on top of the reactor vessel, the transfer cask used for moving spent fuel from the core of the reactor to the facility's spent fuel pool, and employees working over the top of the open reactor without wearing lifelines.

The Eureka *Times-Standard* environmental reporter that covered the 1971 refueling outage had mentioned in his coverage the newspaper photographer who was allowed access into the reactor refueling building through the west airlock doors to take these photos. I wanted to get my hands on these photos because I felt they would be helpful in telling the Humboldt Bay story.

In addition to my trip to the *Times-Standard* newspaper office in the high hopes of acquiring the photos, I also wanted to talk with Paul Meyers, the new superintendent of South Bay Elementary School District in order to determine whether the school had any archived records pertaining to memorandums of understanding, agreements, or contracts between the school district and PG&E, the AEC, and/or the California Department of Public Health regarding the environmental radiological monitoring program at the school site. I struck out on both on both visits.

The first couple of employees at the Eureka *Times-Standard* with whom I spoke said a key staff member at the newspaper had left the newspaper under a set of "mysterious circumstances" that I didn't really understand (and it appeared they didn't intend for me to). The "PG&E" photos I was interested in were in a file that apparently disappeared with him – at least that is what the employees speculated. Nevertheless, I continued my search for them. Every attempt I made with different people at the newspaper office resulted in a dead end. Even my pursuit of these photos in the Record Archives Department of the Humboldt State University Library resulted in failure.

Upon arriving at the South Bay Elementary School, I first showed my wife what was left of the infamous Environmental Monitoring Station 14 located in front of the school. I shared with my wife what that radiological monitoring station represented in the overall history of the Humboldt Bay Nuclear Power Plant. She was amazed and asked why the plant was allowed to continue operating after it started to fail. A short time later, we left Station 14 and entered the front office of the school. There we met Superintendent Paul Meyers with whom I had scheduled an appointment.

After introducing myself to Mr. Meyers, I showed him the photo that I had brought with me of the South Bay Elementary schoolyard with the PG&E nuclear facility in the background. The photo was from my personal collection. It was on the front of a PG&E public relations brochure that was published around 1968. Its purpose was to promote nuclear power.

This photo was designed to convey how safe the Humboldt Bay Nuclear Power Plant was by showing children playing in a schoolyard downwind from the 250-foot radioactive gaseous waste discharge stack looming in the background. I explained to the school superintendent why I found the photo so disgusting. There wasn't much of a reaction from him; I could tell he wasn't impressed with my critique of it, and for the moment, I didn't understand why.

I also mentioned the *North Coast Journal* article mentioning Edith Kraus Stein, a former student at his school during the sixties. Meyers remembered, "Seeing the article," but he didn't have anything to say about it. Even after some prodding, he remained noncommittal. Meyers appeared to have a more positive view of PG&E than I. Following our meeting; I learned that Meyers that was a member of PG&E's Humboldt Bay Power Plant Advisory Board. This probably explained why he didn't have much to say about the nuclear plant or PG&E. It seemed as though he may have talked to someone at PG&E about me after I made the appointment to meet with him and before our meeting, but that is speculation on my part.

My wife and I both felt after we left the school that he was more of a politician than anything else. Nevertheless, it really didn't make any difference how he viewed PG&E or nuclear power because I was only interested in getting certain historical information about the nuclear plant. In retrospect, however, my only real concern that I was left with had to do with whether he had contacted PG&E officials about my meeting with him and if he shared what I had said about the schoolyard photo.

My meeting with Mr. Meyers quite shockingly revealed that the kinds of records I was interested in "that the school may have had at one time were probably lost in a fire." Interesting enough, there apparently "was a fire in the storage room where those records would have been kept" – at least that was what I was told.

Mr. Meyers was a pleasant enough fellow who shared with my wife and me that he was fairly new at the school, that he didn't know very much about what had happened in the past regarding the nuclear plant but that he had lived in Humboldt County for several years. Meyers had previously worked at an elementary school in Ferndale, a small community about 30 miles southwest of Eureka.

He took us to a room that was currently being used for the storage of records at the school to double check what was in there but nothing pertaining to the Humboldt Bay nuclear facility was found. After Meyers had looked into various boxes I remember him saying, "There's nothing here dating further back than the eighties." This meant there were no records pertaining to PG&E's radiological monitoring program during any of the time the plant was in operation.

However, as we left the record storage area and were returning to the school office, I asked Meyers if he knew of any former employees with whom I could talk that might have some institutional memories of the sixties and early seventies at the school. I struck gold!

A current office employee overheard my question and volunteered the name of the school secretary, Mrs. Betty Tatka, who had worked at the school from the mid-fifties to the mid-seventies. Even more surprising was that she still lived in the same house she had lived in during her employment at the school.

Mrs. Tatka's home bordered the school property on the northeast side, just a stone's throw from the school's playground. It was an exciting discovery.

After we left the school, my wife and I immediately went to Mrs. Tatka's home. I introduced myself and explained that I was doing some research for a book that I was writing about the nuclear plant and would very much appreciate talking with her, that I had some questions perhaps she could answer. She said she would be willing to talk with me but indicated she had an appointment coming up in about an hour or so. It was 9:30 in the morning so we agreed I should come back at 2 pm that afternoon.

When my wife and I returned to Mrs. Tatka's home, we found three ladies there. Janet Smith, who was Mrs. Tatka's daughter, Mrs. Tatka, and a lady who lived next door. I again explained my purpose for being there and how I discovered Mrs. Tatka.

Almost immediately we started talking about the history of the nuclear plant and the article in the *North Coast Journal* mentioning Edith Kraus Stein. I briefly related to them the history of the stainless steel cladding problem and how that problem earned PG&E's nuclear plant the reputation of being the dirtiest atomic plant in the country. I also identified and briefly discussed some of the serious problems we experienced at the nuclear facility during the time I worked there and how PG&E management responded to them.

I explained the problem of the "mysterious particles" we were finding in the plant and PG&E plant management's explanation that those "mysterious particles were from Chinese fallout." I also told them about the problem with the high-level radiation waste storage vault and the very real potential of radioactive particles flying out of the vault and traveling downwind from the plant. My concern over PG&E's decision to remove the continuous air-sampler from the front of the school was explained to them. I summarized what happened to those of us who criticized the company's decision to remove it.

Before very long, my wife and I were hearing the names of people in the Humboldt Hill neighborhood who were suffering from a multitude of health problems.

Mrs. Tatka opened up and said she "always wondered about that plant." Her husband had died of lung cancer. Her daughter, Janet, who grew up in the Humboldt Hill neighborhood next to the school and attended South Bay Elementary School, had a rare form of MS.

When I looked at the list of names of people in the Humboldt Hill area with health problems that Janet Smith had drawn up while we were sitting around Mrs. Tatka's dinning table talking, I found the number of their friends and neighbors who had MS startling. There were also a large number of cancer victims on Janet's list, as well. There were several kinds of cancer mentioned but lung cancer appeared to top the list. I was not only struck by the number of people they had identified with health problems but also by the emotion with which they were sharing the information.

Coincidently, the lady at the Humboldt County Historical Society I had talked with the day before shared with me that her very good friend who lived on Humboldt Hill had died of lung and liver cancer at the age of 58; saying, "She had never smoked a day in her life."

Mrs. Tatka asked, "Why was PG&E allowed to put that plant there?" She added, "We were here first and the school was there first."

Also she said, "The school was so close to the plant and downwind, too."

Mrs. Tatka said a couple of times that it just didn't make any sense to her for PG&E to put that plant there. After she had asked her question a couple of more times of why PG&E was allowed to put that plant there, I responded without first giving my response much thought. Admittedly, my response was more of a knee-jerk reaction that came from my heart rather than my head. I told her that she could thank her friends and neighbors for believing everything PG&E had to say about how safe the plant would be and how much the plant would benefit the local economy. In regard to the claims the AEC had made, I explained why I felt people should not have believed those claims either.

My response included reference to PG&E's proposed nuclear facility at Bodega Bay and the public outcry there causing that proposal to fail after PG&E had spent more than a million dollars in site preparation. I also mentioned PG&E's proposed Pt. Arena nuclear project involving two much larger units than the Humboldt Bay nuclear facility and how that project went down in flames because of the public's opposition to it.

Then I thoughtlessly added that I felt the level of sophistication in those communities was much greater than in the Humboldt community. Janet nodded her head in agreement but said nothing.

Quite honestly, I felt terribly bad for what I had said to the ladies after we left Mrs. Tatka's home. My wife suggested that I should have responded differently. After thinking about it, I knew she was right. I ended up feeling as though I had put my foot in my mouth, and that I should have been much more sensitive, more compassionate and understanding. Tentative arrangements were politely made for a follow-up visit, which never happened.

It felt to my wife and me as though the folks we had talked with that day, and the others they had mentioned, would be interested in hearing more about the plant and sharing with us a more detailed accounting of health problems in the Humboldt Hill community. That is what I was hoping for. However, for whatever their reasons it appeared they later decided to close ranks and not become involved in any more conversations with me about the plant.

Maybe it was because of what I had said in response to Mrs. Tatka's question. Or perhaps, after they talked further with each other, it was because of the bad press I had received in the past. Maybe they had received some advice, either directly or indirectly, from PG&E sources, not to have any further conversations with me. I don't know. All I do know is that I did unsuccessfully reach out again a few times to meet with them.

In any event, I suppose I can't blame them because all they knew about me was what they had read in the local newspaper and all the horrible things PG&E had said about me.

The reason I wanted to talk with anyone who was willing to talk with me, from the Humboldt Hill area and from the school, in particular, was because of the interview Japhet Weeks had with Edit Kraus Stein. In connection with that interview, Japhet Weeks wrote the following in his article entitled, "The Not-So-Peaceful Atom" (repeated here from Chapter 8 for emphasis):[432]

In 1986, Stein asked the Humboldt County Board of Supervisors to investigate whether or not there was a causal link between the nuclear power plant and what she said, based on anecdotal data collected from former classmates and school employees, were numerous incidents of rare forms of radiation induced cancers. A study focusing on the incidents of cancer in downwind communities has never been conducted even though the Redwood Alliance, a local renewable energy advocacy group, applied for a grant to conduct one in the late '80s. They based their grant application in part on an analysis of a National Cancer Institute (NCI) data by Humboldt State University professor Charles Chamberlain. It was Chamberlin's contention that the NCI data warranted a more in-depth, local study.

I was hoping to connect in some way with what Ms. Edith Stein had referred to as "anecdotal data collected from former classmates and school employees" but was unsuccessful in doing so. There was no doubt in my mind that it would be extremely difficult if not downright impossible for me to pry open that can of worms and lay bare the details of what Edith had alluded to. I know in my heart of hearts that PG&E's Humboldt Bay Nuclear Plant has harmed people – both inside the plant and outside of it, especially those innocents who were downwind from the reactor.

Why is it that follow-up long term studies were never conducted on the populations that passed through the South Bay Elementary School during the 1960s and early 1970s? This question deserves serious consideration by all concerned.

An even better question is: Why weren't such studies required from the very onset of PG&E's going online with the nuclear power plant. After all, the South Bay Elementary School was downwind for the plant's radioactive gaseous waste discharge stack as well as from the high-level radiation waste storage vault when its lid was removed and its contents exposed to the open air.

Both of these questions deserve an honest debate by all sides willing to put everything on the line for complete and total public scrutiny! Available to the AEC and PG&E was a mobile whole body counting unit that could have been used annually to verify whether the children and school employees at the South Bay Elementary School were free from in gestation of any radioisotopes that could very well have escaped from the plant.

There were plenty of reasons to support the notion that such inquiries would be necessary based on the empirical data known to the scientific community at the time PG&E applied for an AEC license to operate the plant.

I finally reached Edith in October 2010 and talked with her by phone for over two hours. She had a lot to say! She had moved to Texas, was doing fairly well all things considered. I explained to Edith that I had talked with Betty Tatka, who was the South Bay Elementary School Secretary during the time Edith was in attendance at the school. I summarized what Mrs. Tatka and her daughter had shared with me. Edith remembered Mrs. Tatka and had very nice things to say about her.

Edith also remembered the "box" at South Bay Elementary on the highway side of the school's front parking lot with the humming sound that constantly came from it. Edith was referring to the constant air sampler at Station #14. She talked about a family trip made to Oregon one summer while she was still of elementary school age. She remembered PG&E's Atomic Exhibit at the Lane County Fair showing South Bay Elementary School students wearing film badges, and students sitting in outside classrooms directly under the 250-foot radioactive gaseous waste discharge stack at PG&E's Humboldt Bay nuclear plant.

Edith said she never once saw a student wearing a film badge at her school the whole time she was in attendance. That is where she attended elementary school during the sixties.

I remember when Edith and her husband came to the high school where I was teaching in Trinity County and we reminisced for a while about that visit. Edith shared with me her experience with asking the Humboldt County Board of Supervisors to investigate whether or not there was a causal link between the nuclear power plant and the incidents of cancer in the staff and student populations at South Bay Elementary. In this connection, she shared her concern with the "conflict of interest" involving the pronuclear "expert" witness that the Board of Supervisors had called upon provided by PG&E.

Edith ended our phone conversation with a heartfelt dire warning to me, saying, "Be careful, please be careful, Bob. These are ruthless people who are capable of doing pretty awful things." Her words touched me in a soft spot.

As I finish writing *My Humboldt Diary*, I can only hope that it will generate a motivation to take up the task Edith Kraus Stein once suggested: For an independent research group to conduct comprehensive follow-up longitudinal studies on the South Bay Elementary School student and staff populations during 1963-1976, on the residents of the Humboldt Hill community in like fashion, as well as on the employees who worked at the plant during the same period of time.

The author
2014

Epilogue

"Never doubt that a small group of thoughtful, committed people can change the world, it's the only thing that ever has."[433] [Margaret Mead]

To paraphrase Lois Gibbs, founder of Citizens Clearinghouse for Hazardous Waste, the truth won't stop the abuses of the nuclear establishment, but organization and information exchange within, and between, concerned communities will.

It is my sincere hope that *My Humboldt Diary: A true story of betrayal of the public trust* will provide the spark necessary to ignite a call to action. The nuclear power brokers could not be trusted to do the right thing in the past, and there is no reason to believe they will act any differently in the future. Although my *Diary* primarily focuses on the Pacific Gas and Electric Company's Humboldt Bay Nuclear Power Plant and what happened there, it also exposes what typically happens throughout the nuclear establishment.

The nuclear regulators got a new face-lift in January 1975, when the NRC *replaced* the AEC. However, the *new* regulators wearing different hats were still the same people with the same attitudes and philosophies and not much has really changed since!

On the flip-side, the *regulated* have spent millions on developing new public images but things haven't much changed with them either. These public relations campaigns were designed to convince the public that they had put their ugly histories behind them and are now "new companies" concerned about the environment, now committed to protect employees and provide for public safety, and now responsible for complying with the law and the regulatory requirements of their operations – all of which would require the *power of greed* to be subjugated.

The "new" PG&E, for example, reaffirmed its corporate "employee code of conduct" for all of its employees, including "all officers of the company."

Peter Darbee, Chairman, CEO, and President of the PG&E Corporation, along with Chris Johns, President of the Pacific Gas and Electric Company, issued a joint statement after Johns became president of PG&E in 2009 stating the purpose of this code of conduct "is to outline our values and to describe our standards for conduct, compliance, and avoiding conflicts of interest."[434]

Darbee and Johns stated, "This employee code supports our continuing commitment to honest and ethical conduct and compliance with laws, rules, and regulations, and our company policies, standards, and procedures."

The following is shown verbatim from one section of PG&E's Code:[435]

RAISING CONCERNS

We are all expected to communicate honestly and openly with supervisors and others in leadership positions and, in good faith, raise concerns, including those about safety; possible misconduct; and violations of laws, regulations, or internal requirements.

1. When concerns are raised, employees in supervisory and other leadership positions are expected to:
2. Listen to understand,
3. Take concerns seriously,
4. When appropriate, contact internal resources to investigate, and
5. Take any appropriate action in response to investigative findings.

Adversely changing an employee's condition of employment for a nonbusiness reason (i.e., "Retaliation") is not acceptable. Employees in supervisory and other leadership positions may not retaliate, tolerate retaliation by others, or threaten retaliation.

In October 2002, Savannah Blackwell referred to PG&E as a "corporate criminal" and candidly wrote, "The utility likes to pretend it's a good corporate citizen – but the record shows otherwise."[436] Blackwell explained, "Although PG&E likes to insist it is a tolerant and responsible company, it has a long history of retaliating against any employee who blows the whistle on its irresponsible practices." What PG&E did to Neil Aiken was one of Blackwell's examples (review Chapter 16).[437]

Another example of a PG&E employee suffering retaliation by the company was engineer Jim Sprecher, who had served as one of the prosecution's star witnesses in the 1997 Nevada County fire case. Sprecher had written a report that concluded the company was letting trees go untrimmed for too long and jeopardizing public safety. Sprecher testified that instead of heeding his concerns, PG&E demoted him, relegating him to an unimportant job and ostracizing him socially.[438] Sprecher also testified that his report mysteriously disappeared at work after Nevada County prosecutors contacted him.[439]

PG&E also has a history of coming down hard on reporters who are critical of the utility. Don Widener, NBC news documentary producer, who was attacked by PG&E officials at the company's corporate headquarters for his production, "*Powers that Be,*" eventually received an out-of-court settlement of nearly a half million dollars from PG&E after a seven year legal battle (review Chapter 15).

According to Savannah Blackwell, the company retaliated against another reporter who was critical of nuclear power. Blackwell reported, "Energy writer J. A. Savage sued PG&E in 1988, charging that the company had gotten her fired from two jobs because she had once worked for an antinuclear group and had written for the *San Francisco Bay Guardian*. She settled the suit for an undisclosed sum in 1995 after the state Court of Appeals found that her allegations had enough merit to go to trial."[440]

"PG&E wields considerable power over the press covering its activities," Judge Williams Newsom wrote in a 1993 appeals court opinion dealing with the question of whether PG&E should be able to blacklist reporters who work for the *Bay Guardian*:[441]

> In the case of a public utility enjoying such extensive monopolistic authority . . . there is an important public interest in assuring the freedom of the press in reporting on matters lying within the exercise of its franchise.

Blackwell concluded, "PG&E has used its formidable power to undermine that constitutionally protected freedom. The haze of P.R. the company generates regarding its operations has proved effective in protecting the utility's empire – at the direct expense of the public's financial interests, safety, and health."[442]

The Pacific Gas and Electric Company has never admitted to any wrongdoing at Humboldt Bay and most likely never will. It's not the PG&E way – even insofar as the *new* PG&E is concerned! Furthermore, it's not the American corporate way either to admit to any "sins of the past." The idea of "confession," the idea of needing to own up to wrongdoing to move forward in a more positive way, is embedded in the American culture for personal misconduct but that's not at all true for corporate misconduct.

Blackwell also reported, "In 1997, PG&E was tried and convicted in criminal court for endangering the lives and property of gold country residents by failing to trim tree branches near electrical wires frequently enough to prevent major fires. Evidence showed that PG&E had diverted tree trimming money to fatten profits and salaries of top corporate executives." This again is another example of a recurring theme in American corporate behavior.

PG&E's release of the radioactively contaminated spent fuel-shipping cask at Humboldt Bay in August 1969 was wrong, dead wrong! It wasn't just PG&E that had culpability in this blatant act of wrongdoing; it also involved several other "partners in crime" including the U.S. Department of Transportation and the United States Atomic Energy Commission (review Chapter 6).

The utility's handling of the discovery of three contaminated GC painters was wrong, so wrong that it should have been considered a criminal act. It certainly was nothing less than a violation of the public trust (review Chapter 4)!

Selling contaminated scrap metal to the unsuspecting G&R Scrap Metal Company of Eureka, and PG&E's subsequent refusal to address what PG&E had done, was morally wrong and a betrayal of the public trust (review Chapter 7).

The unacceptably high settings on the hand-and-foot counter used as a final check to assure that employees were not leaving the plant with radioactive contamination on them and plant management's response to efforts to address the problem was wrong (review Chapter 10).

What PG&E did to NBC news producer Don Widener was wrong (review Chapter 15).

The Local Union 1245 of the International Brotherhood of Electrical Workers refusal to participate in the rule making effort to provide employee safeguards in the nuclear workplace was wrong (review Chapter 3).

The arbitrator's reinstatement of Forrest Williams without any back pay nine months following his "discharge for cause" was wrong as was the union's willingness to accept the arbitrator's decision (review Chapter 14).

PG&E's corporate officers responsible for the commissioning of a false police report to make security risks out of employees who were critical of the company's nuclear operations, then using the vast legal resources of the company to avoid facing the consequences of that horrendous corporate misdeed was wrong (review Chapter 12)!

The AEC's "findings" of the Commission's investigation of a multitude of radiation safety violations at Humboldt Bay were wrong (review Chapter 13).

The way in which PG&E used those AEC "findings" in the press and elsewhere to discredit the effort to expose the radiation protection safety problems at the company's atomic plant in Eureka was wrong (review Chapter 13).

PG&E's removal of the continuous air-sampler at the South Bay Elementary School was not only wrong but also grossly immoral and a betrayal of the public trust of the very worse kind (review Chapter 9)!

PG&E's Radiation Protection Engineer at Humboldt Bay passing off the "mysterious" extremely radioactive black particles that were found on employee clothing as "Chinese fallout" was not only ludicrous but morally wrong; it was a serious breach of employee and public safety and another betrayal of the public trust (review Chapter 8).

The Eureka *Times-Standard* initially took seriously its effort of covering the Humboldt Bay story, thanks to the tenacious effort of the newspaper's environmental reporter who worked tirelessly on covering it. The reporter initially had the support of his boss. On January 20, 1972. Dan Walters, Managing Editor of the Eureka *Times-Standard*, wrote the following letter to Dale Cook, Public Information Officer, U. S. Atomic Energy Commission:[443]

This is a formal request to the Atomic Energy Commission for a copy of the complete staff report on an investigation of the Humboldt Bay Power Plant Unit No. 3 operated by Pacific Gas and Electric Company near Eureka, which resulted in an October 28, 1971, letter to the company notifying it of two citations and 'certain other matters.'

The investigation, which according to the letter was conducted on May 11-12, 19-20, July 20-21 and August 2, 1971, concerned 49 instances wherein radiation protection procedures or practices were alleged by a complainant to be deficient or radiation incidents were alleged to have occurred.

Although the letter does not state the name of the complainant, there is ample proof available to this newspaper that he is Robert J. Rowen, Jr., 2504 "O" Street, Eureka. On December 23, 1971, the Humboldt County Grand Jury announced it had been carrying on an investigation based on allegations made by Rowen. The Grand Jury's announcement contains statements quoted verbatim from your October 28 letter.

Mr. Rowen is well aware of our interest in this matter, and has no objection to the release of information on his case. If necessary, we can provide you with written permission on release of the material from the individual involved, who himself has apparently been denied access to the report.

We have been investigating Rowen's complaints ourselves, and find his complaints to you are very similar to those he has expressed to us. We would, therefore, find your reasons for dismissing a majority of Rowen's charges invaluable information.

For reason known primarily to Rowen, he feels the investigation was incomplete and has expressed the opinion that there are discrepancies between the material developed by your office and his personal knowledge of the situation in the power plant at the time. For this reason, we believe we must have the data supporting your conclusions to determine for ourselves that the AEC's conclusions are justified.

We are of the opinion that the release of this information is vital to the safety of the public in the Humboldt Bay area and is of significant interest to a large segment of the population.

Refusal of your agency to release the information, we feel, would be a violation of the spirit, if not the letter of the Freedom of Information Act. We hope no further action is necessary on our part.

On the same day, January 20, 1972, the Eureka *Times-Standard* environmental reporter sent the following letter to Representative John Moss, Jr.:[444] (It may be helpful to review Chapter 13: Re: September 7, 1971, my third and final meeting with AEC Chief Investigator, J. J. Ward; the Eureka *Times-Standard* environmental reporter attended and witnessed that meeting firsthand.)

> Attached you will find a carbon copy of a letter we have sent to the Atomic Energy Commission. It concerns an investigation prompted by the complaints of a longtime former employee of the company on radiation procedures and practices at the Humboldt Bay Power Plant Unit No. 3.
>
> We have conducted an investigation for the past several months into the employee's complaints and have received information from other sources corroborating his story.
>
> The Atomic Energy Commission has, on at least two occasions denied us access to a staff report which contains the justification for the fact that all but about six of Rowen's allegations were dismissed entirely by the AEC, and only two citations issued.
>
> We feel you should be aware of the AEC's recalcitrance in releasing the report, in view of your recent concern with disclosure of public documents to the public. We would like to be able to call on your office for assistance in obtaining the report, should it become necessary.
>
> If there is other information that you need at this time, please contact me at the above address or get in touch with Thompson Newspapers Washington Bureau at 1135 National Press Building. Ken Dalecki in that office has knowledge of the situation.

The Eureka *Times-Standard* environmental reporter wrote PG&E corporate a letter asking the following 70 questions. These questions were alluded to in Chapter 15. I am providing the entire list of questions because these questions caused PG&E to react in a very powerful and influential way and they provide insight into the reasons why PG&E responded the way the company did:[445]

> 1. What were the specific conclusions reached during the recent environmental monitoring program involving dye tests and sampling of Humboldt Bay? How did they compare with earlier testing?
> 2. I have heard the tests were halted suddenly. Is this true? Why were they stopped, if true?
> 3. During your interview November 3, the statement was made that established limits don't assume a threshold. If this is so, why do you make such a

point of saying that the plant output is less than half of those established limits?

4. In your comment on the "Sierra Club takes on PG&E" article in the San Francisco Chronicle, you refer to a study of possible modifications to further reduce effluents from the Humboldt Bay plant and comment that "no action is planned in implementing this study until the AEC finalizes their numerical guidelines.' Since the AEC has said plant effluents should be as low as practicable, why not modify the plant to produce the lowest possible emissions and install the necessary equipment as soon as possible? Are you hoping the AEC will not be as strict as the proposed tenfold reduction, therefore making your modifications less expensive?"

5. What are your major sources of information of public health aspects of radiation, especially concerning the dangers of radioactivity? What textbooks are used and what are their dates of publication? When was the last time the information was updated? Who is responsible for the preparation of training manuals on radiation safety? What are their qualifications for this?"

6. I have already requested the stack gas reading for the period March 15 until the refueling outage in June 1971. Daily averages are sufficient for most of the period, but I would like the continuous monitoring record (a copy of it) for April 7 and May 14, from 12:01 a.m. to 5 p.m. on those days.

7. What are the exact duties in the job classification(s) held by Bob Rowen?

8. How long and during what dates was he employed with your company?

9. What was the stated reason for his termination of employment?

10. Would you consider Bob Rowen overly concerned with radiation protection safety during his employment? Did this concern have any bearing on his dismissal? How?

11. Rowen states he was prevented from talking to Atomic Energy Commission inspectors while they were on tour of the plant. Is this true? How could he carry on his job as a radiation process monitor without discussing details with the AEC?

12. Your vice-president and general counsel, R. H. Peterson, received a letter from the Dept. of Transportation concerning surface contamination limits on the spent fuel-shipping cask. The letter was prompted by a letter from Rowen in which he quotes testimony by Ed Weeks implying DOT approval of the activities referred to. The DOT asked for comment from PG&E. Has an answer gone to the DOT? If so, what was your reply?

13. Rowen tried several times to obtain from your San Francisco office the name of the firm, which reprocesses the spent fuel. He couldn't get an answer. Isn't this information that you, as a public utility should volunteer? What is the firm's name?

14. On June 26, a radiation process monitor is alleged to have accidentally dumped ten gallons of highly radioactive wastewater in the nuclear unit caisson sump, which automatically discharges into the effluent canal to Humboldt Bay. Rowen claims the accident resulted in part from the monitor's inadequate training. He also maintains the determinations of radiation liquid were not accurate because samples were taken the next day from a mop that had been rinsed. Did this take place? What were the radiation levels recorded? What are you doing to prevent such an occurrence from happening again?

15. Rowen said he found the outside yard area in the proximity of the nuclear unit control fence radioactively contaminated with about 1,000 counts per minute per square foot of smearable radioactive contamination. Has this occurred? How often? Why did this happen, if true, and what steps are being taken to prevent its reoccurrence?

16. How many times did Atomic Energy Commission inspectors visit the plant in 1971? How many times did you know in advance they were coming?

17. Was a police report ever filed with local agencies on Bob Rowen and others at the plant? What did this report say?

18. Who supplied the police with the information? Which officer took the report?"

19. Attempts by this newspaper to obtain a copy of the report from the City of Eureka, which apparently

took the report, have failed. Why are these public agencies afraid to let the report be seen?

20. Would you provide me with a copy of the report? If not, why not?

21. Rowen claims routine work permits and special work permits are violated regularly. He cites one instance, which took place during the refueling outage in 1970 in which a welding job was done during the refueling outage in the vicinity of radioactive gases, a condition apparently not permitted under the terms of the special work permit for the job. Is this true?

22. Are safety lines required when working over the open reactor core? Why not, if they are not required?

23. How do you react to the statement that 'a lot of the training that they (plant management) give the employees looks pretty good on paper, but the actual quality of the training isn't all that good'?

24. What kind of training is given employees brought in from nonnuclear installations? How often is this done? (Non-nuclear employees working in the nuclear plant.) Is it true they are brought in and given large does of radiation to keep the exposure of the nuclear employees at a minimum?

25. What is the procedure for setting the hand-and-foot counter? Who determines how high they are set?

26. What kind of an attitude do your lower level employees have toward the job? When they get a little more knowledgeable about the job, do they become lax in the observance of safety procedures?

27. Rowen claims contamination comes from high-level storage vaults, even though the containers are wrapped. He says the wrappings get torn, allowing radioactive particles to escape. He further claims the contamination can escape beyond the confines of the plant because a building does not enclose the vault. How is this high-level material handled? What procedures are there to prevent material from escaping when the lid is taken off this vault?

28. Rowen cites problems with radioactive particles, which he says management refers to as 'Chinese fallout.' The particles, it is said, come from an unknown source. Have you ever had any experience with these unexplained particles?

29. Rowen claimed that the children at South Bay Elementary School are not monitored. According to the Atomic Energy Commission, the children wear film badges. How many are wearing badges and at what interval are they checked? Has any of the "Chinese fallout" been found at South Bay School?

30. Rowen alleges that on several occasions, the dosimeters located at three or more of the monitoring stations in line with the stack gas plume went off scale. According to statements made to me earlier, the majority of the radiation recorded is background. How can you make calculations when the dosimeters go off scale?

31. How often do those devices go off scale? What did the film pack for the period show when they went off scale on August 12, 1969?

32. What is your procedure for monitoring the dosimeter stations at the present time? How often are they checked, and by whom? Is this any different from when Rowen was performing the job?

33. In what direction is the prevailing wind over the plant?

34. What is average background radiation at station 14?

35. Is it not possible for you to arrange your program so that the dosimeters don't go off scale? How would this be done?

36. What would be your procedure if a number of dosimeters were found to be off-scale?

37. Rowen describes an incident in which some painters became contaminated in late 1967 or early 1968 in a clean area of the plant. Rowen said he requested management to allow him to go to the painters homes and make a radiation check, and was turned down. Why the refusal? What would be the harm in the extra check

38. I understand you hold safety meetings. What is their purpose? Is there anything which management does not allow to be discussed?

39. Did plant management keep a 'black book' or any kind of a record on Rowen of a subjective nature, other than normal employee records? If so, where is that book now and what does it contain?

40. Rowen claims the company's safety records are not valid, that the 'company has come along and asked the guys to reverse their decision or modify their

decision.' He claims that Warren Raymond specifically issued a directive that employees were not to raise nuclear safety issues at safety meetings. Was such a memo issued? If so, when?

41. Are the minutes of the safety meeting open to AEC inspection? Does the AEC generally review the minutes as part of their inspections?

42. Was Rowen often criticized at the management level for raising questions about radiation safety?

43. What kind of issues did Rowen raise at safety meetings? (Possibly in December 1967.)

44. Rowen says he was fired for threatening a supervisor. He indicates he would swear under oath that he did not make the threat on the evening as alleged. He concedes that some comments made earlier in the day might be construed as a threat, but insists he did not make that call. Were there any witnesses to the call to Ed Weeks? If so, who?

45. Rowen claims Raymond accused him of trying to push him off the highway on the way to work. Was such an accusation made? If so, when did the incident occur and what happened?

46. On May 21,1970 Rowen is alleged to have been the object of an investigation by PG&E security officials. What was the purpose of the investigation and its conclusion? To what use was the information made? Any connection with the police report?

47. Rowen alleges a major discrepancy between employee estimated exposures and reported exposures of film badge reports by Radiation Detection Company in January and February 1970.True? How do you account for the discrepancy at this particular point in time? How often do such discrepancies occur?

48. Rowen claims a PG&E employee was brought into the nuclear unit without sufficient screening and later discovered to have a history of skin cancer. Did this actually happen? What were the circumstances?

49. Rowen says the employees from the other plants are not given any choice as to whether they want the exposure from the nuclear plant. Is this true?

50. Rowen's exposure charts indicate he received progressively greater rates of exposure each year he was at the plant. How do you explain this?

51. Rowen said the greater exposure each year is because the plant is becoming progressively 'dirtier' each year of operation. Is the plant 'dirtiness' increasing yearly because the plant is an old plant and problems have been encountered with it?

52. Have you a training manual for nuclear employees (each grade) with the radiation dangers listed therein?

53. What are the qualifications of plant supervisorial personnel? What educational background is required, in terms of nuclear power? Is the majority of the education in nuclear power obtained in cram-courses type classes?

54. Have employee cars ever been contaminated with radioactivity? At what levels? If so, how did this occur, and how is it being prevented from happening again?

55. Please comment on Rowen's statement that, 'There isn't anything in the main systems in the plant that you cannot get into without running into serious contamination problems.'

56. One of Rowen's criticisms centers on the environmental monitoring reports. He said that as an employee he was involved in a monitoring program using rabbits. The rabbits were apparently to have eaten fresh grass, I gather, to determine if any radioactivity was in the grass and making its way into the animal's diet. Rowen said most of the rabbits' feed came from Nilsen Feed Supply, negating any valid testing attempts. He also said intake amounts were not measured scientifically. Comment on this testing program and others. Are your programs like this in other areas, if true?

57. List your environmental monitoring programs in total.

58. Sometime before February 18, 1970, a metal pipe was cut in sections and sold to GR Metals, apparently without proper survey. Rowen claims the pipe he found (one section of it) to be contaminated and that the company refused to contact GR for survey of other sections. What is your version of this story?

59. Rowen said he was prevented from writing incidents at the plant in the log, such as a time in late 1968 or 1969 when the AEC announced an inspection and

the reactor pump room was found extremely contaminated. Is this company practice, or was Rowen an isolated incident? How often are bad situations cleaned up just before the AEC arrives?

60. Rowen describes an incident in which radiation waste boxes had accumulated around the plant and stored outside where they were rained on. The boxes filled with water, which was undiscovered until they were loaded on a truck. The incident is said to have taken place in late winter or early spring of 1970. Did this take place? What is the company's version of what happened, if it did?

61. Rowen claims that the cutie pies could only be calibrated for 50 per cent of the scale in the last half of 1969. Is this true? How can accurate measurements be made if this condition exists?

62. Rowen says the ground water in the dip well samples has been found to be radioactive. He claims the spent fuel pool has leaked and that some of it has seeped into ground water, although it apparently did not reach beyond the plant fence. Is this true? The AEC apparently feels a possible problem exists on this. What is being done to improve the chances of this not happening?

63. Has radioactivity ever been found in the well samples? If so, what is being done to prevent a reoccurrence?

64. During an interview with the AEC, I was told PG&E would be contacted on the morning of September 8 to discuss the results of the investigation by investigator John Ward. Did Ward discuss the investigation that day? Did he mention items of noncompliance?

65. How much of the AEC's regulatory activity with respect to Humboldt Bay done verbally, and not put into AEC's public files?

66. Have you responded to the written citations by AEC? What was your response?

67. How often are adverse comments made about the plant operation in the logbook? Is there any kind of implied sanction against such comments?

68. Would you have any objections to my questioning in private some of your nuclear control technicians?

69. Rowen claims briefings are often done in a high-radiation area. True? Why prolong exposure, if so?

70. What do the employees do during reactor incore flushing maneuvers? Has the procedure changed since Rowen was employed at the plant?

These were excellent questions (with only a couple not stated correctly) that PG&E needed to answer – truthfully! There were no honest, forthright responses from PG&E corporate officials. PG&E choose instead to launch an underhanded, malicious campaign using its vast public relations and legal resources to discredit the critics of their failed and dangerous technology.

This campaign was guided by an ultraconservative mindset rooted in the trappings of McCarthyism and the John Birch Society, part of which was executed by a J. Edgar Hoover "trained" PG&E security agent as was his boss, Mr. Neel. The meeting at the Ingomar Club to which the Eureka *Times-Standard* environmental reporter referred raises serious questions about what took place there.

In the reporter's strange e-mail to me dated October 8, 2010, that was in response to my inquiry dated October 1, 2010, he lamented, "The meeting at the Ingomar Mansion was a meeting of the PG&E brass with our newspaper brass. We presented written questions to them for answering. The newspaper changed publishers during the writing of the story after that meeting" (review Chapter 15: Re: Dan Walter's editorial).

The Pacific Gas and Electric Company only vaguely responded to seven questions, held a meeting with the "newspaper brass" at the Ingomar Club, had Dan Walters write a scathing editorial discrediting Bob Rowen the very next day, then corporate headquarters provided a "press release" that was published in the name of PG&E's Humboldt Division Manager, Victor Novarino. The Eureka *Times-Standard* newspaper, owned by Thompson Newspapers Inc with corporate offices in Washington D.C., experienced a reorganization of its staff in Eureka (the details of which I was never privy to).

In turning the final pages of *My Humboldt Diary*, I will mention again the totality of my six-year experience at the Humboldt Bay Nuclear Power Plant and what happened there followed by many more years that can only be described as an unimaginable hellish ordeal, a horrendous nightmare that took its toll on everything I loved and held most dear – the unfortunate cost of whistleblowing, I suppose. It is more than that, much more! It is living with the personal knowledge of what PG&E did at Humboldt Bay and the inept public response to it all. – which has provided to a large degree the motivation for finishing my *Diary*.

The Humboldt Bay Unit 3 reactor that originally cost approximately $33 million to build was permanently shut down after only 13 years of operation because it was sitting on top of an earthquake fault. Humboldt Bay's decommissioning costs is currently running more than a billion dollars with no real end in sight. And unbelievably, it's the ratepayers that are picking up the tab rather than the stockholders of the company.

The nuclear spent fuel is permanently housed in Holtec dry storage casks on the Humboldt Bay site because there is no other place else to put it. Commonwealth Edison/Exelon quality control engineer Oscar Shirani called the safety of the Holtec storage cask into question.[446] Shirani became another reluctant whistleblower in the nuclear industry because of the shoddy construction of the casks. According to Kevin Kamps, "Oscar Shirani was made to pay dearly for his integrity, and outspoken refusal to simply shut up about the [many] Holtec QA violations," and Kamps further explained:[447]

> [Oscar Shirani] endeavored to get Exelon to place a Stop Work Order on the manufacture of Holtecs. Instead, Exelon subjected him to harassment by his own supervisors, and eventually ran him out of the company.
>
> Exelon and the U.S. nuclear power industry blacklisted him for the rest of his life. Oscar Shirani alleged that he never signed off on the audit form granting Holtecs a clean bill of health. Shirani alleged that his signature on that audit report was forged.
>
> Neither the NRC nor the Department of Labor provided any support, relief, or assistance to Shirani, thus abandoning his to his fate, to both agencies' eternal shame.

The following is a portion of Kevin Kamps summary of Oscar Shirani's concerns about the Holtec Storage Casks:[448]

> Exelon, the largest nuclear utility in the United States, uses Holtec casks for irradiated fuel storage at its reactor sites. In 1999 and 2000, Oscar Shirani, as a lead quality assurance (QA) auditor for Exelon, identified numerous "major design and fabrication issues" during a QA inspection of Holtec International (the cask designer), and Omni Fabrication and U.S. Tool and Die (the subcontractors responsible for manufacturing the casks).
>
> In fact, he identified a "major breakdown" in the QA program itself. The problems were so severe that Shirani sought a Stop Work Order against the manufacturer of the casks until the problems were addressed. Instead, he was run out of Exelon.
>
> According to Shirani, these design and manufacturing flaws mean that the structural integrity of the Holtec casks is indeterminate and unreliable. Although NRC has dismissed Shirani's concerns, NRC Region III (Chicago office) dry cask inspector Ross Landsman refused to sign and approve the NRC's resolution of Shirani's concerns, concluding that this kind of thinking let to NASA's Space Shuttle disasters. He stated in September 2003, 'Holtec, as far as I'm concerned, has a non-effective QA program, and U.S. Tool and Die has no QA program whatsoever.'

Landsman added that NRC's Nuclear Reactor Regulation division did a poor follow-up on the significant issue identified, and prematurely closed them.

Shirani alleges that all existing Holtec casks, some of which are already loaded with highly radioactive waste, as well as the casks under construction now, still flagrantly violate engineering codes such as those of the American Society of Mechanical Engineers (ASME) and American national Standards Institute (ANSI), as well as NRC regulations. He concludes that the Holtec casks are 'nothing but garbage cans' if they are not made in accordance with government specifications.

Besides the problem with the onsite storage of nuclear spent fuel, there is the problem of what to do with the highly radioactively contaminated reactor vessel that still remains on the Humboldt Bay site.

My *Diary*'s Final Reflections:

PG&E's refusal to check the public places where three contaminated nuclear plant workers had been during a period four days after leaving the nuclear plant contaminated, the company's refusal to retrieve radioactively contaminated materials that had been improperly released and sold to an unsuspecting scrap metal company, and the removal of the constant air sample monitor at the school speaks volumes about the company's lack of concern for public safety.

A fire destroyed all the school district's permanent records pertaining to the radiological monitoring program at the South Bay Elementary School adds to the mystique of what really happened at Humboldt Bay.

The U.S. Atomic Energy Commission was abolished in 1974 and replaced with the U.S. Nuclear Regulatory Commission that continues to be plagued to this very day with the same dysfunctional regulatory behavior that made the AEC unacceptable to the American public.

Arnie Millsap, the police officer who participated in the commissioning of the false police report calling me "a confirmed cop hater," became the Chief of Police for the City of Eureka after Chief Cedric Emahiser retired from the Eureka Police Department.

Humboldt County District Attorney William Ferroggiaro became a superior court judge.

The attorney James McKittrick who "represented" me committed suicide.

The Eureka *Times-Standard* managing editor Dan Walters who wrote the scathing editorial discrediting me after the meeting at the Ingomar Club, now writes for the Sacramento Bee.

The next time you see a shameful PR spin like a photo of children playing in a schoolyard downwind from a nuclear facility belching out radioactive gaseous waste, remember what you have read in my *Diary*. Also remember what you've read in my *Diary* about the dangerous and uncontrolled, extremely "hot" radioactive particles blowing downwind from a nuclear facility (and tracked to who knows where else); also remember not only the government's role but PG&E's nuclear management's response to those abominations.

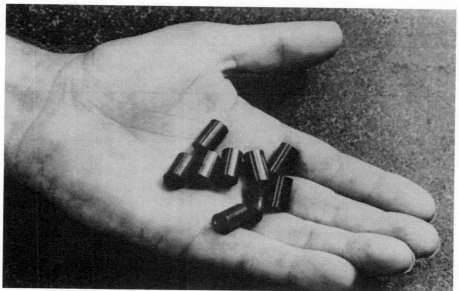

Image 24. Pellets of Uranium Dioxide Fuel (From the author's file)

Finally, please . . . please don't get taken in by photos of outdoor classrooms located directly under a 250-foot radioactive gaseous waste stack with elementary school children learning that "A" stands for "atom" directly under it depicting how safe nuclear power is, or a photo previously mentioned of children playing in a schoolyard downwind from a nuclear power plant, again depicting how safe nuclear power is. (All of these disgusting PR photos promoting nuclear power are shown on page 69 of PG&E's *public relations* book entitled, "From Sawdust to Uranium: The History of Electrical Power Generation in Humboldt County and Pacific Gas and Electric Company's Humboldt Bay Power Plant." (Copyright 2013 by Pacific Gas and Electric Company and available from the Humboldt County Historical Society, 703 Eighth Street, Eureka, California 95501; and from the Clarke Historical Museum, 240 "E" Street, Eureka, California 95501)

The nuclear fuel pictured in the palm of a hand before it is radiated is far, far different from what it is after it has been subjected to neutron bombardment in the reactor during the fission process.

These PR photos are shameful attempts to convince the public that nuclear energy is safe. I trust my *Diary* has proved helpful in understanding why we cannot trust the owners of nuclear power plants, cannot rely on the regulators of them to do the right thing; and, therefore, why we must not build any more nuclear plants!

Sometimes I reminisce about my life in the Corps as a young Marine and how I could have avoided my horrendous PG&E experience had I shipped over when I returned home from overseas. But then I would not have had my wonderful family, nor would I have had my teaching career where I felt I made a real difference in the lives of many.

My first career as a nuclear control technician, which ended early in my civilian adult life, provided me invaluable lessons that made me a better educator in my second and longer career than anything I could have ever learned in my university studies and the credentialing program at HSU. Moreover, however, my Humboldt Bay experience put me in a unique place in time that left me with an even greater responsibility: Sharing *My Humboldt Diary* with those who are concerned about our future and wanting to make the world a better place than the way we found it. We must never "go nuclear." There is far too much at stake!

List of Appendices

Appendix 1
PG&E's Nuclear Task Force
(Chapter 2)

Gail Allen
Edgar Weeks
James Carroll
Robert Patterson

Name, Title, Education, and Formal Nuclear Training
of each member

Member: Gail Allen
Title: Radiation Protection Engineer
Education: B.S. Degree in Air Conditioning Engineering from California State Polytechnic College in June 1950
Formal Nuclear Training:
>   USPHS Courses at the Taft Sanitary Engineering Center:
>>   1) Radionuclides in air - 1 week, February 1961
>>   2) Radionuclides in water - 1 week, February 1961
>>   3) Radioactive Pollutants in water - 1 week, March 1961
>>   4) Reactor Safety and Hazards Evaluation - 2 weeks, September, 1961
>   Topics in Nuclear Power Engineering, U.C. Extension, Fall Semester 1961

Member: Edgar Weeks
Title: Nuclear Engineer
Education: B.S. Degree in Electrical Engineering from University of California in February 1953.
Formal Nuclear Training:
>   Dresden Technology Course, APED, 6 weeks, May-June in 1957;
>   Radiation Monitors Course, VAL, 60 hours, 1958;
>   Nuclear Instrumentation, U. C. Extension, Fall Semester 1957;
>   Radiological Health, USPH & California Public Health Depart., 3 weeks, spring 1958;
>   Reactor Survey Course, APED, Spring Semester 1961 (sections on instrumentation, core and fuel design);
>   Basic Nuclear Instrumentation, APED, Fall and Spring Semester 1960-61.

PG&E's Nuclear Task Force
(continued)

Member: James C. Carroll

Title: Senior Steam Generation Engineer in PG&E's Corporate General
Office
Education: B.S. Degree in Chemical Engineering from University of
California in June 1952. Formal Nuclear Training:
> Dresden Technology Course, APED, 6 weeks, May-June in 1957;
> Radiation Monitors Course, VAL, 60 hours, 1958;
> Nuclear Instrumentation, U. C. Extension, Fall Semester 1957;
> Radiological Health, USPH & California Public Health Depart.,
> 3 weeks, spring 1958;
> Nuclear Engineering Mathematics, APED, Fall and Spring
>   Semesters
> 1958-1959.

Member: Robert Patterson

Title: Nuclear Engineer
Education: B.S. Degree in Mechanical Engineering from Cooper Union School of
Engineering in June 1953.
Formal Nuclear Training:
- Introduction to Nuclear Physics, U, C, Extension, Fall Semester 1956;
- Nuclear Reactor Engineering, U. C. Extension, Spring Semester 1957;
- Radiological Health, USPH & California Public Health,
  3 weeks, spring 1958;
- Nuclear Physics, U. C. Extension, Fall Semester, 1958;
- Nuclear Radiation Detection, U, C, Extension, Spring Semester, 1959;
- Radiation Biology, U. C. Extension, Spring Semester, 1961;
- Reactor Survey Course, APED, Spring Semester 1961 (instrumentation,
  core design, and operation).

Appendix II
(Chapter 2)

"My White Paper"

What follows is the "white paper" to which I referred in Chapter 2, the one that got me into a lot of hot water with PG&E plant management, and with the folks at PG&E corporate headquarters.

As you read this, keep in mind that I wrote it during my twenties while taking heavy academic loads at College of the Redwoods and at Humboldt State University, while at the same time finishing up my nuclear control technician-training program.

(Note: I borrowed heavily from a basic radiation biology textbook used at the Bowman Gray School of Medicine to write this paper, which was only intended for the employees involved in radiation protection work at the Humboldt Reactor in 1968)

The Physiological and Biological Effects of Ionizing Radiation

The biologic effects of ionizing radiation represent the efforts of living things to deal with energy left in them after an interaction of one of their atoms with an ionizing ray or particle. For any living system, this energy will be in excess of the system's requirements for normal function; it will be a deviation from the proper energy relationships within that system.

Since all matter (whether living or not) is made up of atoms, and since radiation interactions with matter occur at the atomic level, the understanding of atomic structure itself is fundamental to the understanding of radiation interactions in general and, in particular, for the understanding of the development of radiation damage in living things.

An atom (any atom) may be compared to the solar system; there is a central, massive portion (the nucleus) and a number of small bodies (orbital electrons), which rotate about it in discrete orbits. The distance between the sun and planets and between the planets themselves are very great, so that most of the solar system is empty space. The atom also is mainly empty space. Because of the 'emptiness' of matter, ionizing radiations may pass through the space of many atoms before they chance to interact with a portion-nuclei or electrons-of any one of them.

The massive central portion of the atom consists of two major components-positively charged protons and uncharged neutron. The mass of the protons and that of the neutrons is nearly the same. Both protons and protons in the nucleus are in constant motion. The protons repel each other, exerting a force against each other, which would tend to make them fly apart. But the repulsive force between protons is held in check by an opposite, cohesive force, one that binds the mutually repellent protons together. The energy required to do this is known as the binding energy of the nucleus.

In atoms there is, practically speaking, a segregation of mass and charge; most of the mass and all of the positive charge reside in the nucleus. All the negative charge is in extra-nuclear, orbital electrons. Furthermore, the charges are balanced. In the atom the number of protons in the nucleus and the number of electrons in the orbits are equal. The number of positive and negative charges is equal, and atoms, as a whole, are electrically neutral. The force, which binds electrons in their shells (does not permit them to drift away from the nucleus), is called the binding energy of the orbit.

The principal means by which ionizing radiations dissipate their energy in matter is by the ejection of orbital electron from atoms. The removal of one or more of these orbital electrons is called ionization. Atoms are electrically neutral, but when they are ionized the loss of an orbital electron leaves them positively charged. The ionized atom and the dislodged electron constitute an ion pair.

It is the process of ionization that is chiefly responsible for the biologic damage produced by ionizing radiation.

Ionizing radiations maybe classified according to their physical properties. They fall into two general categories: those, which have mass (corpuscular or particulate) and those, which are energy only (non-particulate or electromagnetic). Those with mass may be charged or uncharged, but non-particulate radiations are never charged.

The primary types of ionizing radiation found in a nuclear power plant are alpha, beta, neutrons, and gamma rays.

Detectable injury or damage to living things as a result of exposure to ionizing radiation is the result of a long, complex chain of events. The first of these is the transfer of energy from an ionizing radiation into the matter of which living things are composed. The mode of energy transfer characteristic of ionizing radiation is the production in matter of excited and ionized atoms or molecules.

Gamma photons (rays) have no mass or charge. In their interactions with matter the energy of the photons is transferred by collision usually with an orbital electron in an atom of the absorbing medium. Following such a collision an electron will have been ejected from the atom (ionization) with high energy and at a high speed. The energy given to the electron will be dissipated from it as it moves through the medium; it will ionize and excite atoms, which it interacts.

Nearly all radiation effects are dependent upon the amount of energy absorbed (the dose), and this is often most difficult to determine. The most important physical technique for measuring radiation is the determination of the amount of ionization produced by radiation within a specified air volume. Air is readily available; its ionization is rather easily measured; and the techniques are generally reproducible.

Ionization produced by radiation is a random process; ordinarily, an ionizing particle will have sufficient energy to remove an orbital electron from any atom with which in chances to interact. Any atom, without preference, may lose an electron in this way and is itself, ionized.

Now, there are two quite different mechanisms by which chemical changes in molecules may be brought about by ionizing radiation. One is direct action, i.e., a molecule is ionized by the passage through it of either an electron (secondary to electromagnetic radiation) or another ionizing particle. The other is indirect action. The changed molecule has not itself been ionized or excited by a particle; no ionizing radiation passes through it. It is changed, however, because it received the energy of an ionizing particle by transfer from another molecule, which has been ionized through the direct action of radiation.

Cells (and, therefore, living things which are composed of cells) are extremely complex mixtures or solutions. Water is the solvent, and the chemical reactions, which make up the process called 'metabolism' take place in it. There is, of course, some variation, depending upon the tissue, but, on the average, cells consist of about 70 to 80 percent water. The cell molecules (proteins, carbohydrates, nucleic acids, inorganic substances) are myriad, but they are either dissolved in or suspended in a watery medium. When cells or tissues are irradiated, most of the energy transfer goes on in water, because the water present the largest number of 'targets' for the radiation.

Chemical changes can be brought about in cells if the energy of the ionizing particles is transferred to them from the ionized water. It is obvious then, with respect to changes brought about in the molecules of which cellular constituents are composed, that the interaction of ionizing radiation and water, and the chemistry (the reactions possible) of irradiated water, will be very important. The degree of change, brought about by radiation, in the constituents of the cell depends upon that brought about in the molecules of which the cells is composed. The number of alterations, for example, in the structure or function of chromosomes, of mitochondria, or of any organelle, depends upon how many molecules within the organelle have been changed. The changes in these molecules following irradiation are dependent primarily upon their interaction with the products of irradiated water, and, to a lesser but by no means insignificant extent, upon the direct interaction of the molecules with radiation.

When water is irradiated, it has been shown that the final products include H, OH, H2O2 and HO2, none of which is formed as in immediate result of the passage of an ionizing particle through a water molecule. They must in some way have been formed from the two ions, which are produced by irradiation (H2O+ and H2O-). The ions H2O+ and H2O- are not stable; they are not believed to persist in this form for more than a small fraction of a second before undergoing some change. They are said to dissociate almost immediately (10^{-16} seconds) into entities, which are called free radicals. The free radicals, then, will diffuse through the irradiated system, reacting with and producing the chemical changes in anything with which they interact. In this way the energy of an ionizing particle is exchanged into water and from water, to another, possibly in tact, molecule. The reactions of free radicals are reasonably indiscriminate; a free radical may interact with another free radical, with a molecule already damaged by radiation, or most important, with an intact molecule, possible a solute molecule - one previously unchanged by radiation. Finally, and very important, free radicals may interact with organic molecules - the molecules of which cells and tissues are built - and change them. When this takes place the indirect action of radiation has occurred. The first step in the process is the exchange of energy in water (the solvent) from an ionizing particle. But the last step is a change in one of the molecules of solute, one of the molecules of which the cell is built.

Not all the products of free-radical interactions are harmful to living systems. Water is a product, so is molecular hydrogen. And, after a free radical has interacted, it is, itself, extinguished; it no longer exists. But this does not mean that all danger is past for the remaining cellular constituents. Some of products of such reactions are poisons; still others are free radicals themselves, capable of further reactions and, consequently, further transfer of the energy of the ionizing particle. Organic free radicals may represent not only changed molecular constituents of the cell, but also substances that are free to attack other such constituents and spread molecular change still further.

The various molecular species of which cells are composed (water, proteins, amino acids, fats, the nucleic acids, to name a few general categories) have specific functions. This is not to say that each of them has only one function, or that all the functions of every molecular species are known. It is to say that the labors of the cell as a whole are divided among its various components, and that the components function, in cellular activity, in harmony with each other. Every component of the cell - each of its molecular species - is important, perhaps even indispensable, for the maintenance of normal metabolism and for viability, because each has its special role to play in formal metabolism.

All these events have occurred at the molecular levels - a most basic level of organization in the cell. They are the initiating events leading to damage - the transfer of energy from ionizing radiation to the substance of the cell (ionization) and the subsequent transfer of this energy among the molecules of the substance (free radicals, oxygen effect). The oxygen effect has not been discussed, but nevertheless, is an important consideration of the radiation effect.

But these events are not the events that are seen; they are not results of irradiation that are ultimately detected and called "radiation effects." There can be no doubt that events such as those previously described do occur, but, at present, they fall at the very limits of, and often beyond, our ability to detect them.

What is detected are the further consequences - developments in cells that follow these initiating events, alternations in structure and function at much high levels of organization, for example, changes in cellular organelles, or in their functions. Curiously, such detectable changes are never seen directly after irradiation of a living system but at some later time. Immediately after irradiation, the irradiated system appears generally unaffected, unchanged by its experience. But the 'normalness' of it all is apparent, for later (the time varies; it is related to the magnitude and rate of administration of the dose) changes will appear which can only have been the result of exposure to radiation.

The time lapse between irradiation and the appearance of changes is called the 'latent period.' It should not, however, be regarded as a time in which nothing related to the radiation exposure is going on. Rather, it is a very important time, the time in which the changes brought about in the instant of radiation exposure are somehow developed into major detectable defects in structure or function. It should, perhaps, better be called a 'period of hidden changes,' for, in it, the almost infinitesimal amounts of energy put into living things by ionizing radiation, the alterations produced in a few molecules, are multiplied over and over, until structures involving literally hundreds of thousands of molecules and forming major subdivisions of the cell are changed, almost always for the worst.

Appendix III
A Comparison of Statements
(Chapter 4)

The following is the comparison of my earlier statements regarding the biological effects of radiation exposure (presented in Chapter 2) to those made almost two years later by PG&E's Plant Engineer, Edgar Weeks (presented in Chapter 4).

My following "10 statements" represented some highlights of my research on the physiological and biological effects of ionizing radiation. When I presented this information to plant management seeking answers to my questions regarding PG&E's radiation protection training manual, I ended up in a lot of hot water with Edgar Weeks, PG&E's Plant Engineer, and with PG&E's corporate headquarters.

A couple of years later, and a couple of weeks after I was fired from the company, Edgar Weeks made a presentation to the HBPP employees at a company safety meeting that contained "4 remarkable and very surprising statements."

Rowen's 10 Statements
(from Chapter 2 with sources)

1. "Fortunately the cells have a remarkable capacity for self-repair, but if they are subjected to injury for a long enough time they will finally die and give rise to cancer-producing cells. Small doses of radiation below the permissible levels produce a significant though small depression of the white-cell numbers. This was shown, for example, at Los Alamos in 1948 by Dr. N. P. Knowlton, Jr., in a group of ten workers who received on the average 200 mr a week of gamma radiation for 77 weeks. But still smaller doses of irradiation will produce detectable abnormalities in the lymphocytes even when the white-cell count is unchanged, as was shown first at the University of Rochester by Dr. M. Ingraham II in 1952. Although the very small changes in the blood-cell

numbers do not seem to produce any immediate ill effects, they may be the forerunners of anemia, leukemia, and other serious and fatal blood diseases." [Radiation: What it is and how it affects you, by J. Schubert, Ph.D., Biologist, chemist, world-renowned authority on radiation poisoning, & by Re. E. Lapp, Ph.D., Nuclear physicist., p.79 & p.110, 1957.]

2. "With genetic damage: the numbers of mutations induced is simply proportional to the amount of the radiation administered, and there is no minimal or "safe" dose of radiation below which no injury occurs (my emphasis added)." [Heredity and The Nature of Man, by Dr. Theodosius Dobzhansky, Professor at the Rockefeller Institute; Professor of Genetics at the California Institute of Technology; Professor of Zoology at Columbia University, p.135, 1964.]

3. "Exposure to radiation over the total body shortens the life span. This is true whether the exposures to radiation are given over short or long periods of time (within limits, the effects seem independent of dose-rate level). Life shortening is not restricted to the aftermath of total-body radiation; if only parts of the body are exposed, this effect can be elicited as well. The life shortening effect is dependent on dose-rate as well as total dose." [Basic Radiation Biology, by D.J. Pizzarello, Ph.D. Associate Professor of Radiology (Radiation Biology) and by R.L. Witcofski, Ph.D. Assistant Professor of Radiology (Medical Physics), The Bowman Gray School of Medicine, p.251, 1967.]

4. "It is known that chronic exposure to radiation dose levels two or three times the orders of magnitude higher than natural sources (amounting, on the average, to 125 mr per year) could result in any number of various categories of pathological injury, including leucopenia, anemia and leukemia or other forms of cancer." [Ionizing Radiation by American Public Health Association, p.16, 1966.]

5. "Each exposure to ionizing radiation adds to the body's burden of insults or stresses. Chronic effects of radiation are cumulative and irreversible. Avoid or prevent unnecessary exposure." [Public Exposure to Ionizing

Radiation, American Public Health Association, p.43, 1958.]

6. "Each person chronically exposed to small doses of radiation may develop grave physical disturbance years after the exposure." [Radiation, Genes, and Man, by Wallace, Cornell University, p.98, 1959.]

7. "For mankind any increase in mutation frequency remains highly undesirable." [The Science of Genetics, by C. Aierbach, p.233, 1961.]

8. "Certain technological inventions have inadvertently increased the mutability . . . ionizing radiations are mutagenic, that is, they increase the frequency of mutation in the progeny of exposed individuals." [Heredity and The Nature of Man, by Dr. Dobzhansky, p.135, 1964.]

9. "Genetic damage includes the mutations induced in the reproductive tissues and transmitted to the progeny. The physiological damage, no matter how grievous, is confined to the exposed generation; the injury dies with the injured persons. The genetic damage may inflict harm on the descendants of the exposed persons, and for many generations after the exposure." [Ibid.]

10. "One of the strangest and most perplexing aspects of radiation is its ability to leave its imprint on tissue in such a way that injury may become manifest after a long period of time (known as the *latent period*). One case has been recorded in which forty-nine years elapsed between irradiation and appearance of injury. Radiologists and dentists who have worked with radiation for many years without apparent injury have retired only to have delayed injuries - skin ulcers and cancer - show up many years afterwards. The very fact that cause and effect are so widely separated in time makes it difficult to enforce strict rules about radiation safety. Frequently men who overexpose themselves develop a cavalier 'I can take it' attitude, based upon the lack of immediate ill effects, only to learn years later that they were not immune to damage." [Radiation: What it is and how it affects you, by J. Schubert, Ph.D. and by R. Lapp, Ph.D., p.46, 1957.]

Edgar Week's Statements
(from Chapter 4 with sources)

1. As a matter of principle it is sound to avoid all unnecessary exposure to ionizing radiation because it is desirable not to depart from the natural conditions under which man has developed by evolutionary processes. [Quoted from Edgar Weeks' written summary of remarks made at PG&E June 23, 1970 Safety Meeting at Humboldt Bay Nuclear Power Plant, p.2.

2. Exposure to ionizing radiation can result in injuries that manifest themselves in the exposed individual and in his descendants: these are called somatic and genetic injuries respectively. [Taken from Attachment #3 to Edgar Weeks' written summary of remarks entitled "Considerations on the Potential Risks to Individuals Employed in Radiation Work" presented at PG&E Safety Meeting at Humboldt Bay Nuclear Power Plant, identified as Item #23.

3. Late somatic injuries include leukemia and other malignant diseases, impaired fertility, cataracts and shorting of life. Genetic injuries manifest themselves in the offspring of irradiated individuals, and may not be apparent for many generations. Their detrimental effect can spread throughout a population by mating of exposed individuals with other members of the population. [Ibid. Item No.24.]

4. Any departure from the environmental conditions in which man has evolved may entail a risk of deleterious effect. It is therefore assumed that long continued exposure to ionizing radiation additional to that due to natural radiation involves some risk. [Ibid. Item No.29.]

Appendix IV
(Chapter 13)
Whole Body Exposure
for the employment period
March 1964 to June 1970

Whole Body Exposure	(REM)	Gama	Comments
3/9/64 - 7/15/64	0.030		
7/15/64 - 10/15/64	0.150		
2 quarters ending 10/15/1964		0.180	
10/15/64 - 1/15/65	0.020		
1/15/65 - 4/15/65	0.120		
4/15/65 - 7/15/65	0.520		
7/15/65 - 10/15/65	0.730		
4 quarters ending 10/15/65		1.390	
10/15/65 - 1/14/66	0.670		
1/15/66 - 4/15/66	0.180		
4/15/66 - 7/15/66	0.230		
7/15/66 - 10/15/66	0.270		
4 quarters ending 10/15/66		1.350	
10/15/66 - 1/14/67	1.220		
1/14/76 - 4/14/67	0.820		
4/15/67 - 7/14/67	0.340		
7/15/67 - 10/15/67	1.200		
4 quarters ending 10/15/67		3.580	
10/15-67 - 1/14/68	1.360		
1/15/68 - 4/15/68	0.820		
4/15/68 - 7/14/68	0.190		
7/14/68 - 10/14/68	0.260		
4 quarters ending 10/14/68		2.630	
10/15/68 - 1/14/69	2.510		
1/15/69 - 4/14/69	0.730		
4/15/69 - 7/14/69	1.350		
7/15/69 - 10/14/69	2.010		
4 quarters ending 10/14/69		6.600	**EXCEEDED ANNUAL LIMIT**
10/15/69 - 1/15/70	1.100		
1/15/70 - 4/14/70	0.220		
4/15/70 - 6/15/70	2.130		
3 quarters ending 6/15/70		3.450	

Appendix V
(Chapter 13)
Skin of Whole Body Exposure
for the employment period
March 1964 to June 1970

Skin of Whole Body Exposure	(REM)	Gama	Beta	Combined Total	Comments
3/9/64 - 7/15/64	0.03			0.03	
7/15/64 - 10/15/64	0.15			0.15	
2 quarters ending 10/15/1964		0.18			
10/15/64 - 1/15/65	0.02			0.02	
1/15/65 - 4/15/65	0.12			0.12	
4/15/65 - 7/15/65	0.52			0.52	
7/15/65 - 10/15/65	0.73			0.73	
4 quarters ending 10/15/65		1.39			
10/15/65 - 1/14/66	0.67			0.67	
1/15/66 - 4/15/66	0.18			0.18	
4/15/66 - 7/15/66	0.23			0.23	
7/15/66 - 10/15/66	0.27			0.27	
4 quarters ending 10/15/66		1.35			
10/15/66 - 1/14/67	1.22			1.22	
1/14/76 - 4/14/67	0.82			0.82	
4/15/67 - 7/14/67	0.34			0.34	
7/15/67 - 10/15/67	1.20			1.20	
4 quarters ending 10/15/67		3.58		3.58	
10/15-67 - 1/14/68	1.36		1.40	2.76	
1/15/68 - 4/15/68	0.55			0.55	
4/15/68 - 7/14/68	0.19			0.19	
7/14/68 - 10/14/68	0.26			0.26	
4 quarters ending 10/14/68		2.36		2.36	
10/15/68 - 1/14/69	2.51			2.51	
1/15/69 - 4/14/69	0.73			0.73	
4/15/69 - 7/14/69	1.35			1.35	
7/15/69 - 10/14/69	2.01			2.01	
4 quarters ending 10/14/69		6.60		6.60	**Exceeded Ann Limit**
10/15/69 - 1/15/70	1.10		3.20	4.30	**Exceeded Qtr Limit**
1/15/70 - 4/14/70	0.22			0.22	
4/15/70 - 6/15/70	2.13			2.13	**Exceeded Ann Limit**
3 quarters ending 6/15/70		3.45		3.45	

Appendix VI
(Chapter 13)
Hands and Forearms Exposure
for the employment period
March 1964 to June 1970

Hands & Forearms Exposure	(REM)	Gama	Comments
3/9/64 - 7/15/64	0.030		
7/15/64 - 10/15/64	0.150		
2 quarters ending 10/15/1964		0.180	
10/15/64 - 1/15/65	0.020		
1/15/65 - 4/15/65	0.120		
4/15/65 - 7/15/65	0.520		
7/15/65 - 10/15/65	0.810		
4 quarters ending 10/15/65		1.470	
10/15/65 - 1/14/66	0.800		
1/15/66 - 4/15/66	0.180		
4/15/66 - 7/15/66	0.230		
7/15/66 - 10/15/66	0.680		
4 quarters ending 10/15/66		1.890	
10/15/66 - 1/14/67	1.390		
1/14/76 - 4/14/67	1.080		
4/15/67 - 7/14/67	0.870		
7/15/67 - 10/15/67	2.530		
4 quarters ending 10/15/67		5.870	**Exceeded Annual Limit**
10/15-67 - 1/14/68	3.360		**Exceeded Qtr Limit**
1/15/68 - 4/15/68	1.290		
4/15/68 - 7/14/68	0.480		**Exceeded Annual Limit**
7/14/68 - 10/14/68	0.260		
4 quarters ending 10/14/68		5.390	**Exceeded Annual Limit**
10/15/68 - 1/14/69	2.510		
1/15/69 - 4/14/69	0.920		**Exceeded Annual Limit**
4/15/69 - 7/14/69	2.280		
7/15/69 - 10/14/69	2.010		**Exceeded Annual Limit**
4 quarters ending 10/14/69		7.720	**Exceeded Annual Limit**
10/15/69 - 1/15/70	1.100		
1/15/70 - 4/14/70	0.220		
4/15/70 - 6/15/70	2.130		**Exceeded Annual Limit**
3 quarters ending 6/15/70		3.450	**Exceeded Qtr Limit**

Appendix VII
(Chapter 14)
My Simulation of Police Report

Simulation

EUREKA POLICE DEPARTMENT
EUREKA, CALIFORNIA

Original Information   X

Serial

Supplemental

Date   June 3, 1970

Offense
Officer(s) O, Faehiser, Chief

Forrest E. Williams Jr. 551 42 3444 (a personal description)....
attended College of the Redwoods. . . .

Robert J. Rowen, Jr. 552 52 9526 (a personal description) ....
he has read Rap Brown, Eldridge Cleaver, and others, He advocates
fire bombing, violence, ...

Howard J. Darington IV, 552 40 6467 (nothing else)

Raymond R. Skidmore, 558 42 1907 - (nothing else)

These persons are known dissenters, members of a group and hold
group meetings, ... they live at 1503 O Street ....

Please report to PG&E any findings of these charges ....

Rowen was a Marine Pathfinder trained in demolitions .. Rowen
appeared as a witness in the Walter's Case .... Rowen is a
confirmed, "cop hater" ....

Rowen possibly made a phone call to Mr. McNeils wife but there
is no way to pin that on Rowen but there is the question about
whether he made the phone call or not ....

Generally nothing to report from Sacramento .... Rowen had a traffic
accident in 1958 while he was home on leave from the 1st Force
Recon, Co. ,...

Rowen and Williams were complainers and protesters at the Jr. College
about adult fees.

There is no such address as 1503 O Street.

cc Bert Jones, PG&E San Francisco.
   Robert Taylor, Personnel Manager, PG&E Eureka.

Appendix VIII (a)
(Chapter 14)
Actual Police Report (page 1)

"Confidential" (Police ...) "Police Intelligence"

Original Information ☒
Supplemental ☐

EUREKA POLICE DEPARTMENT
Eureka, California.

Serial 70-17954

Date 6-3-70.

Offense: Information, Possible Disident Group, Eureka.
Officer(s) C. Emahiser, Chief.

The following information is received from Mr. Bert Jones, P.G. & E. Co., phone 415-781-4211 Ext. 4018, 245-Market Street, Security Division, San Francisco, who offers the following information and would be very glad to receive any information on the subjects from this area.

FORREST E. WILLIAMS, JR., WMA, 5-7, 160, Brn, Brn, Dob 12-27-33, SS #551-42-3444, has been attending College of the Redwoods. Was discharged 4 days ago for being a dissentor, making threats against management, and being a constant trouble maker.
ROWEN J. ROWEN, JR., WMA, 6-4, 210, Brn, Blue, SS #552-52-9526, was suspended from employment with the Company, is a close partner of WILLIAMS, and has been bringing material into the plant by Rap Brown, Cleaver and others who advocate force and violence. This man is also a radical, advocates burning, is a constant problem.
HOWARD DARINGTON the 4th, WMA.
RAYMOND SKIDMORE, WMA.   (no personal description at this time)

These (4) young men were employed at the P.G. & E. Co. power-plant, one of small gang of Militants, and the latter two appear to be followers of the first two in mention. They all reside at 1505-"O" Street, Eureka. If these (4) are as militant as they are presumed to be, and now that the two have been separated from the Company, it could be that they may become a menace to the local Company installations or cause problems in the area or journey to certain planned jobs elsewhere.

The writer contacted Personnel Officer Robert H. Taylor, local P.G. & E. offices and through Company telephone system Mr. Bert Jones was advised that there is no such address local of 1505-"O" Street. He will make a further check for the correct address and advise. Our Officer A. Milligan advises that on the trial of Donald Leonard Walters (arrested 5-25-69 for 20 148 and 647-F) ROWEN appeared as a witness for Walters, testified as to proper use of Batons, is a confirmed "cop hater", was a U.S. Marine Pathfinder trained in demolitions, and considers Rowen as intelligent as well as a good organiser. The writer has also contacted City Finance Director Paul McNeill about an altercation he had with ROWEN in Mount of 1967 over the refusal of ROWEN to deposit $2.50 for water turn-on. He stated that ROWEN did not threaten him during a lengthy meeting, but his Wife did shortly afterward receive an obscene telephone call to the effect that her husband had better get off his back or he would smatter his guts all over the sidewalk. It is not known positively that ROWEN made that call but he was very strongly suspicioned then due to the time element and the nature of the conversation due to their verbal altercation on water

In checking the local current City Directory we find the above names and addresses listed as follows:

495.

EXHIBIT A

Appendix VIII (b)

(Chapter 14)
Actual Police Report (page 2)

Original Information ☐
Supplemental ☐ (Page #2)

EUREKA POLICE DEPARTMENT
Eureka, California

Serial 78-179
Date 6-3-70

Offense   Information, Possible Dissident Group, Eureka.

Officer(s) C. Emahiser, Chief.   (continued from page #1)

FORREST E. (La Reida) WILLIAMS, Appr. Tech. P.G. & E Company,
1635-29th St., Arcata.
ROBERT J. ROWEN, JR., Tech. P.G. & E., 2515-"O" St., Eureka.
RAYMOND P. (Joyce) SKINNER, Control Tech. P.G? & E, 3342-"X" St, Eurek
HOWARD J. (Joanne) _____, Control Tech. P.G. & E, 2423-"D" St, Eure

The current Telephone Directory lists the following:
ROBERT ROWEN,   2504-"O" St., Eureka,   443-5737
RAY SKINNER,   3342-"X" St., Eureka,   443-0736
HOWARD DIXXXXXTON,   2423-"D" St, Eureka, /   442-2610.
Forrest WILLIAMS,   No telephone currently listed.

The local Sheriff's Office was checked and they have no adverse reports
on file on any of the above mentioned subjects. This Department has onl
____ 1958, ROWEN, minor traffic accident, then of 1st Marine Division,
F.M.F. Camp Pendleton, Oceanside, Calif. Minor traffic
violations 1955-52, Armed Services driver AB-745423
and Calif. driver E-654647.
1957 to 64, RAYMOND SKINNER, Job 6-25-33, minor traffic, driver
license Calif. D-279257.

"Pete" Mathieson, College of the Redwoods, states that he knows who
WILLIAMS and ROWEN are and that they are from P.G. & E., but he knows
nothing about them personally and only what they are constant bitchers
over adult student fees and others matters of small import to others.

In our original telephone conversation Mr. Bert Jones indicated that
he had checked with the Bureau-CII, Sacramento, but had not obtained
much information on these four subjects. We have been unable to
ascertain very much either but the report will be cross-indexed and
any information of mutual interest will be relayed to P.G. & E. Company
authorities.

Cc/To Mr. Bert Jones, San Francisco.
To Mr. Robert H. Taylor, Eureka.
To Sheriff Gene Cox, Eureka.

C. Emahiser, Chief.

To F.B.I. Agent Miller —

12-30-70. Copies or Contents of this report has been "Leaked"
To Two of the subjects in question (Rowen - Williams ?)

(2) cc To City Manager 1-26-71
(2) cc To City Attorney 1-11-71

Glossary
(abbreviations, acronyms, phrases, and terms)

AEC – U.S. Atomic Energy Commission. Created by an Act of Congress in 1946 to promote and regulate the peacetime development and use of atomic science and energy.

alpha particle (radiation) – Alpha particle radiation is one of three basic types of radiation found in a nuclear power plant. (For the other two see beta particle and gamma radiation) Alpha particles consist of two protons and two neutrons bound together into a particle identical to a helium nucleus. An alpha particle is a fast moving helium nucleus. Alpha particles carry a charge of +2 and strongly interact with matter. They are generally produced in the process of alpha decay, but may also be produced in other ways. Alpha decay is a radioactive process in which a particle with two neutrons and two protons is ejected from the nucleus of a radioactive atom. They travel only a few inches through air and can easily be stopped with a sheet of paper; however, alpha particles are extremely hazardous when an alpha-emitting isotope is inside the body.

beta particle (radiation) – Beta particle radiation is one of three basic types of radiation found in a nuclear power plant. (For the other two see alpha particle and gamma radiation) Beta particles are high-energy, high-speed electrons or positrons emitted by certain types of radioactive nuclei. The beta particles emitted are a form of ionizing radiation also known as beta rays. The production of beta particles is termed beta decay. Beta decay is a type of radioactive decay in which a beta particle (an electron or positron) is emitted from an atomic nucleus. Beta decay is a process, which allows the atom to obtain the optimal ratio of protons or neutrons. Beta particles are subatomic particles ejected from the nucleus of some radioactive atoms. They are equivalent to electrons. The difference is that beta particles originate in the nucleus and electrons originate outside the nucleus of an atom.

boiling water reactor – Simply stated, a boiling water reactor is like a giant tea pot that uses nuclear energy (in a reactor) to boil water to make steam. The steam is pressurized to power a turbine in a single-loop system that in turns drives a generator to make electricity. In a single-loop system, the turbine is powered by radioactive steam.

borescope – (Sometimes referred to as a boroscope) An optical device consisting of a rigid or flexible tube with an eyepiece on one end, an objective lens on the other linked together by a relay optical system in between. The optical system in some instances is surrounded by optical fibers used for illumination of the remote object. An internal image of the illuminated object is formed by the objective lens and magnified by the eyepiece, which presents it to the viewer's eye.

boroscope – see borescope.

Chernobyl – On April 26, 1986, Reactor #4 at the Chernobyl Nuclear Power Plant near the town of Pripyat, Ukraine, exploded. The explosion took place at 1:23am while the neighboring town of Pripyat slept. Two workers were killed instantly. 40 hours later, the residents of Pripyat were ordered to evacuate, and most never returned; by that time, many of the residents had suffered varying degrees of radiation poisoning (and later birth defects).

DOT – U.S. Department of Transportation

EPA – Environmental Protection Agency

EPD – Eureka Police Department

film badge – Worn by nuclear workers to record exposure to radiation.

fission – A nuclear process of splitting the atom into smaller parts (lighter nuclei). The fission process produces free neutrons and photons (in the form of gamma rays), and releases a very large amount of energy. Some of the free neutrons then collide with other atoms thus splitting them, resulting in a chain reaction. When the atom is split, the binding energy (the energy holding the atom together) creates the release of energy "heat" that contributes to the boiling of the water in the reactor. The reactor control operator using the reactor's control rod drives controls the amount of fission that is occurring in the reactor (see incores).

Fukushima – The nuclear power plant facility in Japan that experienced a catastrophic failure at the Fukushima I Nuclear Power Plant on 11 March 2011, resulting in a meltdown of three of the plant's six nuclear reactors. The failure occurred when the plant was hit by a tsunami triggered by the Tohoku earthquake; the plant began releasing substantial amounts of radioactive materials beginning on 12 March, becoming the largest nuclear incident since the Chernobyl disaster in April 1986.

fusion – A nuclear reaction in which two or more atomic nuclei collide at a very high speed and join to form a new type of atomic nucleus. During this process, matter is not conserved because some of the matter of the fusing nuclei is converted to photons (energy). Fusion is the process that powers active or "main sequence" stars. The fusion of two nuclei with lower masses than iron (which, along with nickel, has the largest binding energy per nucleon) generally releases energy, while the fusion of nuclei heavier than iron *absorbs* energy. The opposite is true for the reverse process, nuclear fission. This means that fusion generally occurs for lighter elements only, and likewise, that fission normally occurs only for heavier elements. For what was used in the Humboldt Bay reactor, see fission.

gamma radiation – Gamma radiation is one of three basic types of radiation found in a nuclear power plant. (For the other two see alpha particle and beta particle radiation) Gamma radiation is high-energy photons that are emitted by radioactive nuclei. Gamma radiation is very high-energy ionizing radiation. Gamma rays originate in the nucleus, while X-rays originate in the electron cloud around the nucleus.

half-life – The decay rate of a radionuclide is given in terms of its half-life. The half-life of a radionuclide is defined, as the time required for one half of the atoms originally present to decay. For example, the half-life of Plutonium-239 is 24,110 years; the half-life of Cesium-137 is about 30 years; and the half-life of Iodine-131 is about 8 days. Half-life is denoted by the symbol $T\frac{1}{2}$.

HBPP – Humboldt Bay Power Plant. An electric producing power facility near Eureka, California on Humboldt Bay during the period of 1963 to 1976 consisting of two fossil-fuel units (Units 1 and 2) and one nuclear unit (Unit 3).

high-level radiation waste storage – At Humboldt Bay, this was an outdoor vault for the storage of high-level radiation waste and it was exposed to the open environment when the lid was removed, which meant loose radioactive particulate matter was subject to blowing out of the vault, especially on windy days, when the lid was removed.

incores (Incore instrumentation) – Incore instrumentation measures neutron flux distribution in the reactor core. The "incores" refer to the movable incore neutron detectors from selected core locations that send signals to the reactor control room proportional to the neutron flux and provides the reactor control operators necessary "core burn" information.

Latent period – The period of time it takes for the exposure to ionizing radiation to manifest the resulting injury, which often takes a period of time making it difficult to connect the effect with the cause. This is true for both somatic and genetic injuries and explains why many proponents of nuclear power including many nuclear workers develop a cavalier attitude towards radiation exposure.

low-level radiation waste storage – At Humboldt Bay specially designed cardboard boxes with plastic bag liners were used for low-level radiation waste disposal and stored in an outside building behind Unit 3 until it was picked up and transported by truck to a radiation waste disposal site in eastern Washington State.

Millstone – Millstone originally consisted of three reactors owned and operated by Northeast Utilities. The facility is located near Waterford, Connecticut.

mr – milliroentgen. A unit of radiation equal to one thousandth of a roentgen.

NLRB – National Labor Relations Board.

NRC – Nuclear Regulatory Commission. Replaced the AEC in 1974 because an increasing number of critics during the 1960s charged that the AEC's regulations were insufficiently rigorous in several important areas, including radiation protection, reactor safety, and environmental protection.

nuclear blacklisting – A phrase coined by the author to indicate locking nuclear employees out of the industry using a variety of methods including the use of revoking or otherwise causing employees to loose their security clearances needed for employment in nuclear facilities.

nuclear control tech – Job title used by PG&E's control technicians at the Humboldt Bay Nuclear Power Plant during the sixties and early seventies.

Nuclear Juggernaut – Author's reference (a phrase taken from Drs. Goffman and Tamplin in *Poisoned Power*) to the "nuclear power brokers" – America's nuclear- industrial complex – made up of all the special interests that stand to gain by the proliferation of nuclear power.

Nuclear-Industrial Complex – A phrase coined by the author to represent the "nuclear" equivalent to the military-industrial complex. Also called the "nuclear juggernaut." Refers to the power brokers in industry and government that promote the proliferation of nuclear power and stand to reap fantastic profit from nuclear power plant construction, manufacture of nuclear components, and kickbacks from government subsidies.

Nuclear fuel – Nuclear fuel is made of uranium dioxide, consisting of uranium-235 and uranium-238. The uranium dioxide is made into dense, black cylindrical pellets with a diameter of about the size of a pencil and less than an inch long.

NWP – Northwestern Pacific Railroad Company. A subsidiary of Southern Pacific Railway (SP) and had track system that ran from Eureka to the San Francisco North Bay area.

Pandora's Promise – A pronuclear production aimed at turning public opinion towards an acceptance of nuclear power. It "appears" to be a documentary film that is aimed at discrediting the antinuclear movement. It totally misrepresents the real facts of the dangers of nuclear power.

PG&E – Pacific Gas and Electric Company.

pocket dosimeter – A radiation measuring device that provided an estimate of exposure.   Usually two pocket dosimeters were used at a time and enabled nuclear workers to monitor their exposure while they were working in the radiation controlled areas of the nuclear facility.

privileged document – In reference to my Diary, a police document that was considered essential to police business and not made available to members of the public, including the subject(s) named in the document.

radiation control log – An official log maintained by nuclear control technicians of all events in the radiation controlled areas of the nuclear plant that the control technician considered important.

Radiation Control Standards – PG&E's official policy covering every aspect of the Humboldt Bay Nuclear Power Plant's radiation protection program.

Radiation Protection Procedures – Specific radiation protection safety policies and procedures that were designed to protect personnel whose work involved exposure to radiation and were included in PG&E's Radiation Control Standards.

Rem – A unit of effective absorbed dose of ionizing radiation in human tissue equivalent to one roentgen.

Roentgen – A unit of ionizing radiation, the amount producing one electrostatic unit of positive or negative ionic charge in one cubic centimeter or air under standard conditions.

RWP – Radiation Work Permit, also more commonly called "Routine Work Permit." A nuclear plant license requirement that specifies in a written document the routine working conditions of an ongoing nature in a radiation controlled area. RWPs are in contrast to SWPs (see SWP).

SP – Southern Pacific Railroad

spent fuel shipping cask – an especially designed 80-ton shipping container use to transport spent fuel elements by rail from a nuclear plant to a reprocessing facility in New York State.

spent fuel storage pool – a stainless steel pool containing demineralized water with special storage racks designed to hold nuclear spent fuel elements for a period of time sufficient to allow the radiation levels to decay.

statute of limitations – A specified period of time within which legal actions must be filed in order to be considered by the courts.

SWP – Special Work Permit. A nuclear plant license requirement that specifies in a written document the special working conditions of a unique and temporary nature in a radiation controlled area (usually in effect for no more than a maximum of 8 hours). Special Work Permits are in contrast to RWPs ("Routine or Radiation Work Permits") that covered work in a radiation controlled area of a routine or ongoing nature.

Three Mile Island – The Three Mile Island accident was a partial nuclear meltdown that occurred on March 28, 1979 in one of the two Three Mile Island nuclear reactors in Dauphin County, Pennsylvania.

transfer cask – A 25-ton cask inside the refueling building used to transfer nuclear spent fuel from the reactor core to the spent fuel storage pool via an overhead double-track crane.

Workplace Emulation – A phrase used by the author to describe the norms of behavior in the nuclear facility workplace involving employee ambition or endeavor to impress superiors in order to first achieve "acceptance" and "security," and then hopefully advancement in the nuclear employee hierarchy.

Chapter Notes

Preface & Chapter One

[1] Quote taken from "The not-so-peaceful atom" by Japhet Weeks, The North Coast Journal, March 20, 2008.

[2] Science Magazine, June 18, 1971, Vol. 172 no. 3989, pp. 1215-1216.

[3] **The Hon. John Pastore, a *paraphrase* from PG&E Life, November 1963, p.3.**

This epigraph sets a satirical tone for my *Diary* of what happened at Humboldt Bay. Pastore's name appears again in Chapter Fifteen — The Don Widener Story.

[4] PG&E Atomic Information Officer, Frederick R. "Fritz" Draeger, quoted in "A-Plant Spokesman Backs Firm's Record, Avoids Debating During Session," Eureka *Times-Standard*, February 2, 1972, p. 12.

[5] PG&E Atomic Information Officer, Frederick R. "Fritz" Draeger, quoted in "A-Plant Spokesman Backs Firm's Record, Avoids Debating During Session," Eureka *Times-Standard*, February 2, 1972, p. 12.

[6] AEC Facility Operating License No. DPR-7 (Docket No. 50-133; re: PG&E's license application dated April 27, 1959, as amended, p. 1).

[7] Root, Garret and Herbert, Rand, *From Sawdust to Uranium*, Pacific Gas and Electric Company, 2013), p. 69.

[8] John W. Gofman and Arthur R. Tamplin, *Poisoned Power: The Case Against Nuclear Power Plants*, (Emmaus, PA: Rodale Press, 1971), p. 32.

[9] United States Geological Survey Information Center.

[10] United States Geological Survey Information Center.

[11] Root, Garret and Herbert, Rand, *From Sawdust to Uranium*, Pacific Gas and Electric Company, 2013, p.82.

[12] U.S. Nuclear Regulatory Commission, History, Atomic Energy Commission.

[13] Edgar Weeks' counseling memorandum dated 8/7/69.

[14] State of California Unemployment Insurance Appeals Board, In the matter of Robert J. Rowen, Claimant/Appellant vs. Pacific Gas Electric Company, Employer/Respondent: Case No. SF-1319, December 9, 1970 (2nd Hearing), transcript p. 76, lines 4-28, p. 77, lines.

[15] Arbitration Cases Nos. 35 and 36, IBEW, Local 1245 vs. PG&E, Brief of Respondent PG&E, p. 25.

[16] Deposition of Robert Rowen, April 11, 1973; line 14 on p.19 through line 4 on p. 30; (PG&E asked nearly 100 questions on direct); Robert Rowen, et al. vs. Pacific Gas and Electric Company, Exhibit A, p. 382.

[17] The Eureka *Times-Standard* dated December 22, 1971, p. 1.

[18] Confidential PG&E Memorandum by James C. Carroll, February 10, 1971, p. 2.

[19] Quoted from a written statement by Bert Jones, PG&E security agent from corporate headquarters, signed by Andrew Kennedy, Nuclear Instrumentation Engineer, May 21, 1970.

[20] Quoted from a written statement by Bert Jones, PG&E security agent from corporate headquarters, signed by John Kamberg, Nuclear Instrumentation Foreman, May 21, 1970.

[21] Quoted from a written statement by Bert Jones, PG&E security agent from corporate headquarters, signed by George Tully, Plant Electrical Foreman, May 22, 1970.

"Then it struck me that [Bert Jones] was professionally reared smack dab in the era of McCarthyism and trained by the J. Edgar Hoover regime." (*Diary*, **page 258**).

[22] William Rodgers, Corporate Country, *Rodale Press*, 1973, pp.193-194.

[23] Ibid. p.194.

In *Corporate County*, Law Professor William H. Rodgers, a distinguished legal authority, " . . . exposes the influence peddling and propaganda campaigns of corporations, which extend into the realm of coercion, fraud and criminality. The bullying, bribery and conflicts of interest are exposed. America's mammoth companies run roughshod over the wants and needs of the people to maintain their obsolete, hazardous or destructive, but invariably profitable, technologies."

[24] TheEureka *Times-Standard*, December 23, 1971, p.1.

Chapter Two

[25] Bob Rowen, *My Humboldt Diary.* (page 53)

These two epigraphs (Notes 25 & 26) set forth a theme for Chapter Two.

[26] Drs. John W. Gofman and Arthur R. Tamplin, 1971 (page 56).

[27] Wah Chang, Allegheny Technologies, Technical Data Sheet, *Zirconium Alloys*, 2003.

[28] Gofman, John W. and Tamplin, Arthur R.,*Poisoned Power*: *The Case Against Nuclear Power Plants Before and After Three Mile Island*, Rodale Press, 1971 and 1979, p. 74.

[29] Ibid., pp. 74-75.

[30] Ibid., p. 75.

[31] Pacific Gas and Electric Company, Radiation Protection Training Manual, Humboldt Bay Power Plant, prepared by the PG&E Nuclear Task Force.

[32] Ibid. Cover page.

[33] Ibid. p. 2.

[34] Ibid. Title page and Preface.

[35] Ibid.

[36] PG&E document entitled Appendix II-10, dated January 1962.

[37] Edgar Weeks' sworn testimony before the California Unemployment Insurance Appeals Board Hearing: Case No. SF-1319; 2nd hearing dated December 9, 1970, p. 24, lines 6-9.

[38] PG&E document entitled Appendix II-10, dated January 1962.

[39] Ibid.

[40] Ibid.

[41] Ibid.

[42] PG&E document entitled Appendix II-8, dated January 1962.

[43] Telephone interview dated October 25, 2010.

[44] Pacific Gas and Electric Company, Radiation Protection Training Manual, Humboldt Bay Power Plant, Prepared by the PG&E Nuclear Task Force, p. 26.

[45] Ibid. p. 24.

[46] Ibid. p. 25.

[47] *Radiation: What it is and how it affects you*, by J. Schubert, Ph.D., Biologist, chemist, world-renowned authority on radiation poisoning, by Re. E. Lapp, Ph.D., Nuclear physicist, p. 79 p. 110. (1957)

[48] *Heredity and The Nature of Man*, by Dr. Theodosius Dobzhansky, Professor at the Rockefeller Institute; Professor of Genetics at the California Institute of Technology; Professor of Zoology at Columbia University, p.135. (1964)

[49] B*asic Radiation Biology*, by D.J. Pizzarello, Ph.D. Associate Professor of Radiology (Radiation Biology) and by R.L. Witcofski, Ph.D. Assistant Professor of Radiology (Medical Physics), The Bowman Gray School of Medicine, p. 251. (1967)

[50] *Ionizing Radiation,* by American Public Health Association, p. 16. (1966)

[51] *Public Exposure to Ionizing Radiation*, American Public Health Association, p. 43. 1958.

[52] *Radiation, Genes, and Man*, by Wallace, Cornell University, p. 98. (1959)

[53] *The Science of Genetics*, by C. Aierbach, p.233. (1961)

[54] *Heredity and The Nature of Man*, by Dr. Dobzhansky, p. 135. (1964)

[55] Ibid.

[56] *Radiation: What it is and how it affects you*, by J. Schubert, Ph.D. and by R. Lapp, Ph.D., p.46. (1957)

[57] Personal diary.

[58] The Eureka *Times-Standard*, "A-Plant Spokesman Backs Firm's Record, Avoids Debating During Session, February 2, 1972, p.12.

[59] Edgar Weeks' testimony, California Unemployment Insurance Appeals Board Hearing, In the Matter of Robert J. Rowen vs. Pacific Gas and Electric Company Case No. SF-1319. 2nd hearing dated December 9, 1970, pp. 65-67.

[60] Ibid. pp. 67-69.

[61] Ibid. pp. 102-104.

Chapter Three

[62] Bob Rowen, *My Humboldt Diary.* (pages 76-77)

These two epigraphs (Notes 62 & 63) set forth a theme for Chapter Three.

[63] AEC 15-page document dated September 7, 1971, provided to the author listing "49 allegations" and the AEC's "finding" to each of them. (page 287)

[64] Taken from the AEC 15-page document dated September 7, 1971. Provided to the author listing "49 allegations" and the AEC's "finding" to each of them.

[65] Radiation Protection Training Manual, Humboldt Bay Power Plant, Pacific Gas and Electric Company, Radiation Control Standard 1.4, Rev. September 1, 1961, first paragraph.

[66] California Unemployment Insurance Appeals Board Hearing, In the Matter of Robert J. Rowen vs. Pacific Gas and Electric Company, Case Number: SF 1319, (2nd Hearing) dated December 9, 1970, Transcript, p. 115.

[67] Ibid. p. 66.

[68] Ibid.

[69] Ibid. p. 67.

[70] AEC Findings, J. J. Ward, Investigator, dated September 7, 1971.

[71] Internal IBEW, Local 1245 document referring to "Motion No. 3111-72-2 (which was MSC by the LU 1245 Eureka Unit) and reported on by the Chief Shop Stewart of the Eureka Unit, Howard Darington, dated spring 1972.

[72] *PG&E Official Humboldt-Electric Generation Memorandum*, "Subject: Employee Discipline for Insubordination," by E. D. Weeks, dated March 9, 1970, p. 2, 5th paragraph.

[73] PG&E Letter from Dale Nix, Humboldt Nuclear Power Plant Superintendent, to Forrest Williams, dated May 13, 1970.

[74] Arbitration Hearing, IBEW Local Union 1245 vs. Pacific Gas and Electric Company, Case No. 35, dated December 1, 1970.

[75] Ibid. Tr. 113 and Brief for the Complainant, pp. 3-4.

[76] Ibid. PG&E, Exhibit #3.

[77] Ibid. IBEW, Exhibit #1.

[78] Ibid. Brief for the Complainant, p. 6, re: Note #2.

[79] Ibid. Tr. 88.

[80] Ibid. p. 10, lines 29-30.

Chapter Four

[81] **Edgar Weeks, Nuclear Plant Engineer; State of California Unemployment Insurance Appeals Board; Rowen vs. PG&E: Case No. SF-1319. Transcript p. 92. December 9, 1970.**

These two epigraphs (Notes 80 & 81) set forth a theme for Chapter Four.

[82] **Bob Rowen,** *My Humboldt Diary.* **(page 116)**

[83] Report of the Atomic Energy Commission: Safety Evaluation By the Division of Reactor Licensing, Dkt. No. 50-133, Humboldt Bay Plant unit No. 3, July 22, 1968.

[84] William O. Douglas, Dissenting Opinion, U.S. Supreme Court: Power Reactor Development Co. v. Electricians – 367 U.S. 396. (1961)

[85] U.S. Supreme Court: Power Reactor Development Co. v. Electricians – 367 U.S. 396. (1961)

[86] R. Rapoport, *The Great American Bomb Machine* (E. P. Dutton Co., Inc., 1971), p. 117.

[87] Ibid.

[88] Ibid.

[89] Ibid. p. 121.

[90] Gofman, John W. and Tamplin, Arthur R., *Poisoned Power: The Case Against Nuclear Power Plants* (Emmaus, PA: Rodale Press, 1971) p. 25.

[91] Ibid.

[92] Ibid.

[93] Ibid. pp. 25-26.

[94] Ibid.

[95] Ibid. pp. 26-27.

[96] Quoted from Edgar Weeks' written summary of remarks made at PG&E June 23, 1970 Safety Meeting at Humboldt Bay Nuclear Power Plant, p. 2.

[97] Taken from Attachment #3 to Edgar Weeks' written summary of remarks entitled "Considerations on the Potential Risks to Individuals Employed in Radiation Work" presented at PG&E Safety Meeting at Humboldt Bay Nuclear Power Plant, identified as Item #23.

[98] Ibid. Item No.24.

[99] Ibid. Item No.29.

[100] Quoted from Edgar Weeks' written summary of remarks made at PG&E June 23, 1970 Safety Meeting at Humboldt Bay Nuclear Power Plant.

[101] Ibid. p.4.

[102] Quoted from Arbitration Hearing Cases Nos. 35 and 36; IBEW, Local 1245 vs. PG&E, held December 1 and December 2, 1970, Brief of the Respondent, pp. 45.

[103] Letter from PG&E Senior Vice President and General Counsel, to R.L. Doan, AEC's Division of Reactor Licensing, August 22, 1966.

[104] William Rodgers, *Corporate Country*, Rodale Press, 1973, p. 205.

[105] Taken from Raymond Skidmore's testimony, California Unemployment Insurance Appeals Board Hearing, Case No.SF-1319, 2nd hearing dated December 9, 1970, Transcript. p.106.

[106] Ibid.

[107] Ibid. pp. 120-122.

[108] Taken from Weeks' testimony, California Unemployment Insurance Appeals Board Hearing, In the Matter of Robert J. Rowen vs. Pacific Gas and Electric Company Case No.SF-1319, 2nd hearing dated December 9, 1970, Transcript. pp. 109-110.

[109] Taken from Raymond Skidmore's testimony, California Unemployment Insurance Appeals Board Hearing, Case No.SF-1319, 2nd hearing dated December 9, 1970, Transcript. p.109-111.

[110] Taken from Weeks' testimony, California Unemployment Insurance Appeals Board Hearing, Case No.SF-1319, 2nd hearing dated December 9, 1970, p. 94, lines Nos.3-17.

[111] Transcription of Magnetic Tape Recording of Meeting between J. J. Ward R. J. Rowen, dated September 7, 1971, (Transcriber: Rowetta Miller), p. 36, lines Nos.26 & 27.

[112] Taken from Weeks' testimony, California Unemployment Insurance Appeals Board Hearing, Case No.SF-1319, 2nd hearing dated December 9, 1970, Transcript. pp. 78-80.

[113] Taken from Weeks' testimony, California Unemployment Insurance Appeals Board Hearing, Case No.SF-1319, 2nd hearing dated December 9, 1970, Transcript. pp. 76-78.

[114] Taken from Weeks' testimony, California Unemployment Insurance Appeals Board Hearing, Case No.SF-1319, 2nd hearing dated December 9, 1970, Transcript. pp. 80-83.

[115] Taken from an "Interim Report" of the 1971-72 Humboldt County Grand Jury, p. 3, item 6.

[116] Ibid. p.1.

[117] Ibid.

[118] Ibid.

Chapter Five

[119] **George F. Duke, Director, California Indian Legal Services, July 2, 1970.**

This epigraph provides a window into the understanding of my involvement with an injustice of police brutality and its connection to my difficulties with PG&E.

[120] Humboldt County District Attorney Office, Investigator's Report, dated June 1969, Arrest of Donald Lenard Walters – 647(f) – 148 P. C. p. 9 (Report signed by Officer Arnold Millsap #12 EPD).

[121] Humboldt County District Attorney Office, Investigator's Report, dated June 1969, Arrest of Donald Lenard Walters – 647(f) – 148 P. C. p. 6.

122 Humboldt County District Attorney Office, Investigator's Report, dated June 1969; Arrest of Donald Lenard Walters – 647(f) – 148 P. C. p.14. (Attachment marked "Supplemental Information" and signed by Chief C. Emahiser EPD).

123 Ibid.

124 Humboldt County District Attorney Office, Investigator's Report, dated June 1969, Arrest of Donald Lenard Walters – 647(f) – 148 P. C. p.14 (attached).

125 Ibid. p. 13 (attached).

126 Letter from George F. Duke, Director, California Indian Legal Services, 2327 Dwight Way, Berkeley, California 94704, dated July 2, 1970.

Chapter Six

127 Bob Rowen, *My Humboldt Diary.* (page 160)

These epigraphs set the theme for Chapter Six. (Note 126 is found on page 160 and Note 127 is found on page 155) of my *Diary*.

128 D.F.M. Hanley, Referee. State of California Unemployment Insurance Appeals Board: Rowen vs. PG&E, Case No. SF-1319 dated December 9 1970. Transcript p.92.

129 William Rodgers, *Corporate Country*. (Rodale Press, Inc. 1972), p. 192.

130 D.F.M. Hanley, Referee. State of California Unemployment Insurance Appeals Board; Rowen vs. PG&E: Case No. SF-1319 dated December 9, 1970. Transcript p. 92.

The Referee sees through the claim that PG&E's nuclear operation isn't really a "fishbowl" as claimed by PG&E's HBPP Nuclear Engineer. (Found in my *Diary* on pages 154 & 155)

131 Ibid. p. 52-53.

132 Rodgers, op. cit., p. 204.

133 Safety Evaluation by the Division of Reactor Licensing, DKT No. 50-133, Humboldt Bay Power Plant unit No. 3, July 22, 1968.

134 "PG&E Annual Meeting with AEC Region V Compliance Personnel," prepared by J. C. Carroll, PG&E, September 14, 1970, quoting AEC personnel.

135 Rodgers, op. cit., p. 191.

136 "A-Plant Spokesman Backs Firm's Records, Avoids Debating During Session," Eureka *Times-Standard*, February 2, 1972, p. 12.

137 Ibid.

138 Ibid.

Chapter Seven

[139] Bob Rowen, *My Humboldt Diary.* (page 174)

These epigraphs set the theme for Chapter Seven. (Notes 138 & 139 are found in my *Diary* on page 174)

[140] Edgar Weeks testimony on December 9, 1970

[141] PG&E Internal Confidential Company Memorandum /s/J. Boots: Subject: Robert Rowen – Control Technician: February 18, 19, 1970.

[142] Ibid.

[143] AEC 15-page document provided to Bob Rowen listing "49 allegations" and the AEC's "findings," re: Allegation #11.

[144] Chapter IX, Administrative and Procedural Safeguards and Operating Procedures, Basic Operation Principles, item 5.

[145] PG&E HBPP Unit 3 Radiation Control Standard: 6-1.

[146] California Unemployment Insurance Appeals Hearing, Robert Rowen vs. PG&E; Case No. SF-1319. 2nd Hearing on December 9, 1970; Robert Rowen vs. PG&E. Tr. pp. 11-12.

[147] Ibid. pp. 12-13.

[148] Ibid. p. 14-15

[149] Ibid. p. 15.

[150] Ibid. p. 59.

[151] Ibid. pp. 59-60.

[152] Ibid. p. 59.

Chapter Eight

[153] Sonoma County's *The Bugle*, March 13, 1972.

These epigraphs set the theme for Chapter Eight. (Note 153 is found in my *Dairy* on page 190)

[154] Japhet Weeks, "The Not-So-Peaceful Atom," *The North Coast Journal*, March 20, 2008, p.14.

[155] "Radioactive Particle Found Here," Eureka *Times-Standard*, April 6, 1972, pp. 12.

[156] Ibid.

[157] Ibid.

[158] Ibid.

[159] Quoted from the Eureka *Times-Standard*, "Radioactive Particle Found Here," April 6, 1972, pp. 12.

[160] Ibid.

[161] Ibid.

[162] Ibid.

[163] Ibid.

[164] Ibid.

[165] Ibid.

[166] Ibid.

[167] Ibid.

[168] Ibid.

[169] Ibid.

[170] Ibid.

[171] Ibid.

[172] Ibid.

[173] Ibid.

[174] Ibid.

[175] Ibid.

[176] Author's letter to George Spencer, Senior Reactor Inspector for the Compliance Division of the AEC dated April 8, 1972.

[177] George Spencer's reply letter to author dated May 5, 1972.

[178] Japhet Weeks, "The Not-So-Peaceful Atom," *The North Coast Journal*, March 20, 2008, p.14.

Chapter Nine

[179] Bob Rowen, *My Humboldt Diary.* (page 199)

These epigraphs set the theme for Chapter Nine. (Note 178 is found in my *Diary* on page 199, and Note 179 is found on page 225 of my *Diary*)

[180] John Kamberg, PG&E Nuclear Instrumentation Foreman, May 21, 1970.

[181] Real, James, "*#1 On the Nuclear Blacklist: The Purge of Filmmaker Don Widener,*" Mother Jones, December 1978, Volume III.NO.X, p. 24.

[182] Ibid.

[183] Personal interview of Forrest Williams.

[184] Author's personal diary: Entry regarding meeting with Edgar Weeks on May 11, 1970.

[185] Ibid.

[186] California Unemployment Insurance Appeals Board Hearing, In the Matter of Robert J. Rowen vs. Pacific Gas and Electric Company, Case Number: SF 1319, (2nd Hearing) dated December 9, 1970, Transcript, p. 124.

[187] Atomic Energy Commission, Report of Investigative Findings, dated September 7, 1971, Transcription of Magnetic Tape Recording (Transcriber: Rowetta Miller), p. 30

[188] Quoted from the AEC "Finding" to Allegation #39.

Chapter Ten

[189] Remarks made by Edgar Weeks on June 23, 1970 at PG&E's Safety Meeting at HBPP.

These two epigraphs set the theme for Chapter Ten. (Note 189 refers to a quote found on page 212 of my *Diary*)

[190] A statement by PG&E employee, Virgil Teague, an electrician at HBPP recorded in the "official" minutes of PG&E's May 20, 1970 HBPP Safety Meeting by Mrs. Cillay Risku.

[191] Edgar Weeks' testimony: California Unemployment Insurance Appeals Board Hearing. Robert Rowen vs. PG&E: Case No. SF-1319, 2nd Hearing dated December 9, 1970. Tr. pp. 70-72.

[192] Ibid. p. 72

[193] Ibid.

[194] Ibid. pp. 72-73.

Edgar Weeks' incredible testimony regarding the issue of using safety-lines by employees working over the open reactor is found on pages 205-207.

[195] Ibid. pp. 73-75.

[196] Weeks' testimony, California Unemployment Insurance Appeals Board Hearing: Case No. SF-1319; 2nd hearing dated December 9, 1970, pp. 65-67.

[197] Minutes of PG&E's May 20th 1970 Safety Meeting, taken by Mrs. Cillay Risku.

198 PG&E's Humboldt Bay Power Plant Radiation Protection Training Manual, available to employees before the actual initial startup of the facility in August 1963, Chapter IV, p. 24.

199 Ibid.

200 John Kamberg's testimony: California Unemployment Insurance Appeals Board Hearing, Case No. SF-1319; 1st Hearing dated October 1, 1970, p. 57.

201 John Kamberg's testimony: California Unemployment Insurance Appeals Board Hearing, Case No. SF-1319; 1st Hearing dated October 1, 1970, pp. 49-52.

202 Ibid. pp. 60-61.

203 Ibid. pp. 66-68.

204 PG&E document entitled "Considerations on the Potential Risks to Individuals Employed in Radiation Work" identified on page 4 as "Gist of remarks presented by E. Weeks at the June.

205 Ibid.

Chapter Eleven

206 Bob Rowen, *My Humboldt Diary.* (page 245)

This epigraph (Note 206) addresses the role of PG&E corporate headquarters and refers to page 245 of my *Diary.*

207 Eleanor Roosevelt. 1943.

This epigraph (Note 207) sets forth the theme for Chapter Eleven . . .

. . . and it explains why we must address acts of wrongdoing.

208 Quoted from a wrItten statement by Bert Jones, PG&E security agent from corporate headquarters, signed by **John Kamberg**, Nuclear Instrumentation Foreman dated May 21, 197

209 Quoted from a written statement by Bert Jones, PG&E security agent from corporate headquarters, signed by **Russ Peter**, Nuclear Unit Shift Foreman dated May 21, 197

210 Quoted from a written statement by Bert Jones, PG&E security agent from corporate headquarters, signed by **John Kamberg**, Nuclear Instrumentation Foreman dated May 21, 197

211 Ibid.

212 Ibid.

213 Ibid.

214 Ibid.

[215] Quoted from a written statement by Bert Jones, PG&E security agent from corporate headquarters, signed by **Andrew Kennedy**, Nuclear Instrumentation Engineer dated May 21, 1970.

[216] Ibid.

[217] Ibid.

[218] Quoted from a written statement by Bert Jones, PG&E security agent from corporate headquarters, signed by **George Tully**, Plant Electrical Foreman dated May 22, 1970.

[219] Ibid.

[220] Ibid.

[221] Ibid.

[222] Quoted from a written statement by Bert Jones, PG&E security agent from corporate headquarters, signed by **Russ Peter**, Shift Foreman dated May 22, 1970.

[223] Ibid.

[224] Quoted from a written statement by Bert Jones, PG&E security agent from corporate headquarters, signed by **Lloyd Barker**, Plant Machinist dated May 22, 1970.

[225] Ibid.

[226] Quoted from a written statement by Bert Jones, PG&E security agent from corporate headquarters, signed by **Russell Windlinx**, Electrician dated May 21, 1970.

[227] Robert Rowen, Plaintiff vs. PG&E, Bert Jones, et al., Defendants; Deposition of Russell K. Windlinx taken on May 29, 1975, No. 53310., pp. 8-13.

[228] Rowen vs. PG&E; Deposition of Robert J. Rowen, Jr., Deposition Exhibit #92: Confidential Union Memorandum, May 28, 1975.

[229] Arbitration Hearing; IBEW, Local 1245 vs. PG&E, held December 1 and December 2, 1970, Brief for the Complainant, p. 15.

[230] A personal written statement by Forrest Williams dated October 28, 2010.

[231] PG&E document entitled "Confidential Memorandum: Counseling of R. Rowen on 8-7/69," dated 8/8/69, signed by E. D. Weeks

[232] Arbitration Hearing dated December 1 2, 1970. PG&E Brief, p. 5.

[233] Ibid.

[234] Ibid.

[235] Arbitration Hearing, December 1, 1970, Nos.35 and 36, IBEW Local Union 1245 vs. PG&E Tr., pp. 91 - 92.

[236] Arbitration Hearing, December 12, 1970, Nos. 35 and 36: IBEW, Local Union 1245 vs. PG&E, Quoted from the Complainant's Brief, p. 3.

[237] Ibid. p. 3.

[238] Ibid. p. 4.

[239] Ibid. (Re: Company Exhibit. #3)

[240] Ibid. p.4. (Re: Union Exhibit #1)

[241] Arbitration Hearing; IBEW, Local 1245 vs. PG&E, held December 1 and December 2, 1970.

[242] Ibid. p. 6.

[243] Ibid.

[244] Ibid.

[245] Ibid.

[246] Ibid.

[247] Ibid.

[248] Unemployment Insurance Appeals Hearing, Rowen vs. PG&E, 1st hearing on October 1, 1970, Case No. SF-1319, Tr. pp. 25-27.

[249] Ibid. p. 33.

[250] Ibid. p. 36.

[251] Ibid. pp. 53-54

[252] Unemployment Insurance Appeals Hearing, Rowen vs. PG&E; 2nd Hearing on December 9, 1970; Case No. SF-1319. Tr. p. 36.

[253] Unemployment Insurance Appeals Hearing, Rowen vs. PG&E, Case No. SF-1319, Decision of the Referee, February 2, 1971, p. 8.

[254] Ibid. p.7.

[255] L. V. Brown, Arbitration Proceedings in the Matter of IBEW 1245 vs. PG&E, Case NOS. 35 36, Brief of the Respondent, December 1, 1970, p. 25.

[256] L. V. Brown, Arbitration Proceedings in the Matter of IBEW 1245 vs. PG&E, Case NOS. 35 36, December 1, 1970, TR. p. 144.

[257] L. V. Brown, Arbitration Proceedings in the Matter of IBEW 1245 vs. PG&E, Case NOS. 35 36, December 1, 1970, TR. p. 144.

[258] PG&E internal memorandum entitled SUMMARY OF VISIT BY DON WIDENER OF NBC TV ON FEBRUARY10, 1971 TO HUMBOLDT BAY POWER PLANT dated February 14, 1971. (See Chapter 15 for Don Widener's difficulties with PG&E)

[259] Frank Morgan, Arbitration Proceedings in the Matter of IBEW 1245 vs. PG&E, Case NOS. 35 36, Brief of the Complainant, December 1, 1970, p. 2.

Chapter Twelve

[260] Bob Rowen, *My Humboldt Diary*. (p.256)

[261] William H. Rodgers, Jr., *Corporate Country*, Rodale Press, Inc., 1973, p. 209

[262] L. Metcalf V. Reinemer, *Overcharge* (New York: David McKay, 1967), p. 191.

[263] Rodgers, *Corporate Country*, op cit.

[264] Ibid.

[265] Rowen vs. City of Eureka and Cedric Emahiser, Superior Court of the State of California, County of Humboldt, No. 51768, Testimony of Cedric Emahiser, May 25, 1972.

[266] *Science Magazine*, Published by the American Association for the Advance of Science, June 18, 1971,

[267] Robert Rowen, et al, plaintiffs vs. PG&E, et al, defendants; Case Nos. 53310, 53414, 54094, and 54095. Deposition of Berton F. Jones, dated November 8, 1974, pp. 2526.

[268] Robert Rowen vs. PG&E, No. 53310, Deposition of George Tully, May 29, 1975, Exhibit A, p. 2.

[269] Robert Rowen vs. PG&E, No. 53310, Deposition of George Tully, May 29, 1975, Tr. pp.34-35.

[270] Ibid. pp. 35-36.

[271] Robert Rowen, et al, plaintiffs vs. PG&E, et al, defendants; Nos. 53310, 53414, 54094, and 54095. Deposition of Berton F. Jones dated November 8, 1974, p. 5.

[272] Ibid.

[273] Ibid.

[274] L. Metcalf R. Reinemer, Overcharge (New York: David KcKay, 1967, p. 199.

[275] Cabell Phillips, New York times, May 18, 1926, p. 26.

Chapter 13

[276] Report of the Atomic Energy Commission, Safety Evaluation By the Division of Reactor Licensing, Dkt. No. 50-133, Humboldt Bay Plant Unit No. 3, July 22, 1968.

The epigraph supported by Note 275 provides a clear and evident motivation for why I wrote my *Diary*.

[277] Quoted from the written summary of the "gist of remarks" presented by Edgar Weeks at the June 23, 1970 Safety Meeting at the Humboldt Bay Nuclear Power Plant, p.4.

When examined by the contents of my *Diary*, the epigraph supported by Note 276 exposes these PR claims constantly made by PG&E for how dishonest and misleading they were.

[278] PG&E Annual Meeting with AEC Region V Compliance Personnel," prepared by J. C. Carroll, PG&E, September 14, 1970, quoting AEC personnel.

The epigraph supported by Note 277 reveals how PG&E used the AEC to provide the general public a completely false view of PG&E's corporate responsibility.

[279] California Unemployment Insurance Appeals Board, Decision of the Referee, In the Matter of Robert J. Rowen vs. Pacific Gas and Electric Company, Case Number: SF 1319, January 28, 1971, pp. 4-6.

[280] PG&E letter to the California Department of Human Resources Development dated June 26, 1970.

[281] Atomic Energy Commission, Report of Investigative Findings, dated September 7, 1971, Transcription of Magnetic Tape Recording (Transcriber: Rowetta Miller), p. 6.

[282] Ibid. p. 3.

[283] Ibid.

[284] Ibid. p. 5.

[285] AEC 15-page document provided to Bob Rowen listing "49 allegations" and the AEC's finding to each of them.

[286] California Unemployment Insurance Appeals Board, Decision of the Referee, In the Matter of Robert J. Rowen vs. Pacific Gas and Electric Company, Case Number: SF 1319, January 28, 1971, p. 4.

[287] California Unemployment Insurance Appeals Board Hearing, In the Matter of Robert J. Rowen vs. Pacific Gas and Electric Company, Case Number: SF 1319, (2nd Hearing) dated December 9, 1970, Transcript, p. 67.

[288] PG&E Employee Suggestion No. 19-1000, Electric Hoist #3 – H.B.P.P., dated May 16, 1966, and approved November 29, 1966 by Victor C. Novarino, Humboldt Division Manager.

[289] California Unemployment Insurance Appeals Board Hearing, In the Matter of Robert J. Rowen vs. Pacific Gas and Electric Company, Case Number: SF 1319, (1st Hearing) dated October 1, 1970, Transcript, p. 48.

[290] Ibid. pp. 49-52.

[291] California Unemployment Insurance Appeals Board Hearing, In the Matter of Robert J. Rowen vs. Pacific Gas and Electric Company, Case Number: SF 1319, (1st Hearing) dated October 1, 1970, Transcript, pp.58-68.

[292] California Unemployment Insurance Appeals Board Hearing, In the Matter of Robert J. Rowen vs. Pacific Gas and Electric Company, Case Number: SF 1319, (2nd Hearing) dated December 9, 1970, Transcript, p. 82.

[293] Radiation Protection Training Manual, Humboldt Bay Power Plant, Pacific Gas and Electric Company, 4-1, Rev. September 1, 1961

[294] Atomic Energy Commission, Report of Investigative Findings, dated September 7, 1971, Transcription of Magnetic Tape Recording (Transcriber: Rowetta Miller), p. 36.

[295] Ibid. pp. 36-37.

[296] Ibid. p. 37.

[297] California Unemployment Insurance Appeals Board Hearing, In the Matter of Robert J. Rowen vs. Pacific Gas and Electric Company, Case Number: SF 1319, (2nd Hearing) dated December 9, 1970, Transcript, pp.93-94.

[298] Ibid. Transcript, p. 94.

[299] Atomic Energy Commission, Report of Investigative Findings, dated September 7, 1971, Transcription of Magnetic Tape Recording (Transcriber: Rowetta Miller), p.30.

[300] California Unemployment Insurance Appeals Board Hearing, In the Matter of Robert J. Rowen vs. Pacific Gas and Electric Company, Case Number: SF 1319, (2nd Hearing) dated December 9, 1970, Transcript, p.124.

[301] Ibid.

[302] Historical Site Assessment prepared by Enercon Services, Inc., Murrysville, Pennsylvania, September 2006, Section 6.4.1.

[303] Ibid. Section 5.5.

[304] Ibid. Section 5.4.

Chapter Fourteen

[305] **PG&E: Defendant Notice of Motion and Motion for Summary Judgment, Rowen vs. PG&E, No. 53310, July 17, 1975, p.7.**

These epigraphs set the theme for Chapter Fourteen.

[306] **Ibid. p.15.**

[307] **Bob Rowen, *My Humboldt Diary.* (page 305)**

This epigraph further sets the theme for Chapter Fourteen by expressing that America's system of justice is not at all what I had always thought it was.

[308] Personal correspondence to James L. Browning, Jr., dated May 13, 1972.

[309] California Unemployment Insurance Appeals Board Hearing, In the Matter of Robert J. Rowen vs. Pacific Gas and Electric Company, Case Number: SF 1319, (2nd Hearing) dated December 9, 1970, Transcript, pp. 35-36.

[310] DECISION OF THE REFEREE, State of California, In the Matter of Robert J. Rowen, Jr. vs. Pacific Gas Electric Company, Case. No. SF-1319 dated January 28, 1971, pp. 7-8.

[311] Quoted from an article entitled "Fire Me" published in *The National Observer*, dated April 29, 1972, p. 1.

[312] bid.

[313] PG&E letter sent to the Editor of *The National Observer*, dated May 2, 1972.

[314] Frank B. Morgan, Arbitration Proceedings in the Matter of IBEW 1245 vs. PG&E, Case NOS. 35 36, Brief of the Complainant, February 11, 1971, pp. 1-2.

[315] Arbitration Proceedings in the Matter of IBEW 1245 vs. PG&E, Case NOS. 36, December 2, 1970, Transcript p. 142.

[316] Ibid. p. 234.

[317] Resolution by the Eureka Unit of the IBEW 1245, Motion No. 3111-72-2.

[318] Arbitration Proceedings in the Matter of IBEW 1245 vs. PG&E, Case NOS. 36, December 2, 1970, Transcript p. 192.

[319] Frank B. Morgan, Arbitration Proceedings in the Matter of IBEW 1245 vs. PG&E, Case NOS. 35 36, Brief of the Complainant, February 11, 1971, starting on p.10.

[320] Letter from Warren A. Raymond, Power Plant Superintendent, to Darrell Porter, dated August 11, 1972.

[321] Ibid.

[322] Letter from Darrell Porter to Robert Taylor, PG&E Personnel Manager Humboldt Division dated August 18, 1972.

[323] NLRB Charge Against Employer (PG&E), Case No. 20-CA-7031 dated September 27, 1971.

[324] Letter from Roy O. Hoffman, NLRB Regional director, to Robert Jr. Rowen, Jr., Case no. 20-CA07013, dated October 26, 1971.

[325] Letter send t NLRB's General Counsel in Washington, D.C. dated November 5, 1971.

[326] Taken from *PGandE WEEK*, December 24, 1971.

[327] Letter from attorney Frank Morgan to Humboldt County Attorney William Ferroggiaro, dated January 18, 1971.

[328] Letter from Humboldt County District Attorney William Ferroggiaro to attorney Frank Morgan dated January 27, 1971.

[329] Ibid.

[330] Letter from Eureka City Attorney Melvin Johnson to Humboldt County District Attorney dated April 16, 1971.

[331] Letter from attorney Frank Morgan to Eureka City Attorney Melvin Johnson, dated April 27, 1971.

[332] Letter from Henry LaPlante, PG&E, to Eureka City Attorney Melvin Johnson, dated January 10, 1972.

[333] Confidential IBEW 1245 internal memorandum; written by PG&E Humboldt Division Chief Shop Steward, Howard Darington.

[334] Deposition of Robert Rowen, Rowen vs. PG&E, April 11, 1973. TR. pp. 4-5.

[335] Ibid. p.158.

[336] Ibid. p.159.

[337] Ibid. p. 232.

[338] Defendant PG&E Answer to first Amended Complaint for Slander, Rowen vs. PG&E, No. 53310, dated May 7, 1973, pp.4-5.

[339] Defendant Notice of Motion and Motion for Summary Judgment, Rowen vs. PG&E, No. 53310, July 17, 1975, p. 7.

[340] Ibid. p. 15.

[341] Taken from Robert Rowen, Plaintiff and Appellant vs. PG&E, Defendants and Respondents, In the Court of Appeal of the State of California, 1 Civil No. 39,847, Respondent's Brief, dated March 28, 1977, p. 2.

[342] Quoted from Robert Rowen, Plaintiff and Appellant vs. PG&E, Defendants and Respondents, In the Court of Appeal of the State of California, 1 Civil No. 39,847, Respondent's Brief dated March 28, 1977, p. 11.

[343] Shaim v. Sresovich, 104 Cal. 402, 406 (1894).

Chapter Fifteen

[344] **In the script of Don Widener's nuclear documentary film, *"Powers That Be"* and taken from an article entitled *"#1 On the Nuclear Blacklist"* by James Real, Mother Jones Magazine, December 1978, p.24.**

[345] Jack Shepherd, Senior Editor, *LOOK Magazine*, December 15, 1970, p. 21.

[346] Ibid. pp. 21-22.

[347] Donald Widener vs. PG&E, Court of Appeal of the State of California, Reporter's Transcript of Proceedings, re: Testimony of James C. Carroll dated October 15, 1975, pp. 426-427.

[348] PG&E Internal Company Memorandum entitled "Summary of Visit by Don Widener of NBC-TV on February 10, 1971 to Humboldt Bay Power Plant by J. C. Carroll, dated February 14, 1971, p. 1.

[349] Ibid. p. 2.

[350] Donald Widener vs. PG&E, Court of Appeal of the State of California, Reporter's Transcript of Proceedings, re: Testimony of James C. Carroll dated October 15, 1975, p. 537.

[351] Ibid. p. 538

[352] "#1On The Nuclear Blacklist," James Real, *Mother Jones Magazine*, December 1978, p. 4.

[353] Donald Widener vs. PG&E, Court of Appeal of the State of California, Reporter's Transcript of Proceedings, re: Testimony of James C. Carroll dated October 15, 1975, pp. 357-358.

[354] Ibid. pp. 342-444.

[355] Jack Shepherd, Senior Editor, *LOOK Magazine*, December 15, 1970, p. 24.

[356] "AEC Guidelines Move Toward Critics' Position," *Science Magazine*, June 18, 1971.

[357] Donald Widener vs. PG&E, Court of Appeal of the State of California, Reporter's Transcript of Proceedings, re: Testimony of James C. Carroll dated October 15, 1975, pp. 344-346.

[358] Ibid. p. 425.

[359] Ibid. pp. 423-425.

[360] Taken from James C. Carroll's deposition at p.37, Donald Widener, Plaintiff vs. PG&E, provided to James R. McKittrick by David Pesonen, covered by letter dated May 8, 1974.

[361] Donald Widener vs. PG&E, Court of Appeal of the State of California, Reporter's Transcript of Proceedings, re: Testimony of James C. Carroll dated October 15, 1975, p. 490.

[362] Ibid. p. 498.

[363] Ibid. p. 500.

[364] Taken from "#1 On The Nuclear Blacklist," James Real, *Mother Jones Magazine*, December 1978, p. 30.

[365] #1 On The Nuclear Blacklist," James Real, *Mother Jones Magazine*, December 1978, p. 32.

[366] The Eureka *Times-Standard*, Eureka, California, July 19, 1972, p. 4.

[367] Ibid.

Chapter Sixteen

[368] Attorney Bob Seldon, Project on Liberty and the Workplace, taken from "U.S. Probe Backs Nuclear Worker in PG&E Dispute" by Carrie Peyton, Sacramento Bee Staff Writer, November 23, 1999.

This epigraph sets the initial theme for this chapter.

[369] Attorney Charles Denny, PG&E. et al., taken from the Deposition of Rowen, May 28, 1975.

These epigraphs further set the theme for Chapter Sixteen by exposing the sinister means PG&E will use to destroy the reputation of employees who are critical of the company.

[370] Matthew Wald, "Questioning Whistle-Blower's 'Delusions'"— *The New York Times*, April 11, 2000.

[371] Brian Martin, "Whistleblowing and Nonviolence," *Peace Change*, Vol.24, No. 1 January 1999, Peace History Society and Consortium on Peace Research, Education, and Development, p. 15.

[372] Ibid. p. 19.

[373] "Questioning Whistle-Blower's 'Delusions'" by Matthew Wald, *The New York Times*, April 11, 2000.

[374] Savannah Blackwell, "PG&E Corporate Criminal," *San Francisco Bay Guardian,* October 16, 2002.

[375] Ibid.

[376] Ibid. (See also *San Francisco Bay Guardian*, "Nuclear Leak," April 22, 1998)

[377] Ibid. (See also *San Francisco Bay Guardian*, "PG&E Fires Whistleblower," April 5, 2000)

[378] Gofman, John W. and Tamplin, Arthur R. *Poisoned Power*, Rodale Press, 1971, p.25.

[379] Ibid. pp. 26-27.

[380] Ibid. pp. 25-26.

[381] Jack Shepherd, Senior Editor, *LOOK Magazine*, December 15, 1970. p. 21-22.

382 Taken from a personal interview by the author.

383 Japhet Weeks, "The Not-So-Peaceful Atom," *The North Coast Journal*, March 20, 2008, p.12.

384 NLRB Charge Against Employer (PG&E); Case No. 20-CA-7031 dated September 27, 1971.

385 National Labor Relations Board; Case No. 20-CA-7031. September 27, 1971, p. 6

386 Japhet Weeks, *The North Coast Journal*, "The Not-So-Peaceful Atom," March 20, 2008, p. 15.

387 ABC News interview by Mathew Mosk dated March 15, 2011.

388 Letter from former Japanese Ambassador to Switzerland, Mitsuhei Murata to U.S. President Barack Obama published October 28, 2013.

389 Brian Martin, "Whistleblowing and Nonviolence," *Peace Change*, Vol. 24, No. 1 January 1999, Peace History Society and Consortium on Peace Research, Education, and Development, p. 19.

390 Katherine Boughton, *The Litchield County Times*, "The Whistleblower" " (partial text reprinted with permission); December 10, 1999.

391 Julie Miller, "Paying The Price For Blowing The Whistle," *The New York Times*; February 12, 1995.

392 Ibid.

393 Ibid.

394 Eric Pooley, "Nuclear Warriors," *Time Magazine*: Blowing the Whistle on Nuclear Safety, March 4, 1996, p. 53.

395 Susan E. Kinsman, "Northeast Utilities Whistleblower Leaves Job After Telling of Safety Flaws," *The Courant*, March 29, 1993.

396 Wald Matthew, "Regulator Says Connecticut's Largest Power Company Harassed Worker," *The New York Times*; May 5, 1993.

397 Ibid.

398 Ibid.

399 Ibid.

400 Ibid.

401 Ibid.

402 Ibid.

403 http://www.cectoxic.org/Safety_Culture_Report_by_Blanch_9_13.pdf

[404] Ibid., pp.20-21.

[405] Eric Pooley, "Nuclear Warriors," *Time Magazine*: Blowing the Whistle on Nuclear Safety, March 4, 1996, pp. 52-53.

[406] Ibid. p. 48.

[407] Ibid.

[408] Ibid.

[409] Ibid. pp. 47-48.

[410] Ibid. p. 48.

[411] Ibid.

[412] Eric Pooley, "Nuclear Warriors," *Time Magazine*: Blowing the Whistle on Nuclear Safety, March 4, 1996, p54.

[413] Ralph Vartabedian, "Company fires scientist who warned of Hanford waste site problems," *Los Angeles Times*, October 3, 2003.

[414] Ibid.

[415] Ibid.

[416] Ibid.

[417] Tom Zeller Jr., "Nuclear Power Whistleblower Charge Federal Regulators With Favoring Secrecy Over Safety, *The Huffington Post*, December 4, 2012.

[418] Tom Zeller Jr., "Leaked Report Suggest Long-Known Flood Threat To Nuclear Plants, Safety Advocates Say, *The Huffington Post*, October 19, 2012.

[419] Ibid.

[420] Ibid.

[421] Lawrence S. Criscione, Letter to NRC Chairman Allison Macfarlane, dated September 18, 2012.

[422] Ibid.

[423] Lawrence S. Criscione and Paul M. Blanch, Letter to Senator Joseph Lieberman, dated December 18. 2012.

[424] Ibid., and Enclosure 1.

[425] Ibid., and Enclosure 2.

[426] Keith Johnson, "American Whistleblowers Go Public; Reveal Threat to Nation from Reactors," *American Free Press*, December 19, 2012.

[427] Ibid.

[428] Ibid.

[429] Ibid.

[430] Ibid.

Chapter Seventeen

[431] Edith Kraus Stein, taken from *The North Coast Journal*, March 20, 2008, p. 14.

[432] Quoted from the North Coast Journal article, "The Not-So-Peaceful Atom," March 20, 2008, p. 14.

Epilogue

[433] Margaret Mead, 1962.

The epigraph supported by Note 432 will hopefully cause the reader of my *Diary* to consider the consequences of nuclear power and become involved in an effort to address the issues giving rise to those consequences.

[434] PG&E Corporate Code of Conduct. (2010)

[435] Ibid.

[436] Savannah Blackwell, "PG&E Corporate Criminal," S*an Francisco Bay guardian*, October 16, 2002.

[437] Ibid.

[438] Ibid.

[439] Ibid. (See also "Vanishing Report," *San Francisco Bay Guardian*, May 21, 1997.)

[440] Ibid. (See also "Reporter Beats PG&E," *San Francisco Bay Guardia*n, November 8, 1995.)

[441] Ibid.

[442] Ibid.

[443] Letter from Dan Walters, Managing Editor of the Eureka *Times-Standard*, to Dale Cook, Public Information Officer, U. S. Atomic Energy Commission, January 20, 1972.

[444] Letter from the Eureka *Times-Standard* environmental reporter (whose name is being withheld at his request) to Congressman John E. Moss Jr., dated January 20, 1972.

445 Seventy questions on Humboldt Bay Power Plant by the Eureka *Times-Standard* environmental reporter (whose name is being withheld by request), undated correspondence, pp. 3-9.

446 J.A. Savage, "Whistleblower Alleges PG&E Proposed Dry Casks Slipshod," *California Energy Circuit*, Vol. 1, No. 1, Berkeley, California, September 5, 2003.

447 Docket ID No. NRC-2012-0246. Public comments on NRC WC DGEIS by Kevin Kamps, December 20, 2013.

448 Taken from a summary prepared by Kevin Kamps, Nuclear Waste Specialist at Nuclear Information and Resource Service in Washington, D.C. July 22, 2004.